Augustin Louis Josse

Grammar of the Spanish language

With practical exercises

Augustin Louis Josse

Grammar of the Spanish language
With practical exercises

ISBN/EAN: 9783337085674

Printed in Europe, USA, Canada, Australia, Japan

Cover: Foto ©Paul-Georg Meister /pixelio.de

More available books at **www.hansebooks.com**

A

GRAMMAR

OF THE

SPANISH LANGUAGE,

WITH

PRACTICAL EXERCISES.

THE FIRST PART

Containing *essential Observations and Directions* with respect to Ancient and Modern Orthography; A List of the Abbreviations which are frequently found in writing and books; A Treatise on Pronunciation and Alterations in Orthography, founded upon the latest Rules established by the Academy of Madrid; Comparative Rules of the Spanish and English Languages; A general Scheme of the Terminations of Regular Verbs; An alphabetical List of the Irregular Verbs, conjugated in their order; A Table, illustrating the use of Prepositions in Spanish; Lists of the Names of different Countries, Islands, Capes, Seas, Rivers, Cities, and Christian Names.

THE SECOND PART

Containing a Collection of Exercises interlined; A Vocabulary; Familiar Phrases and Dialogues; Spanish Extracts; Literary and Mercantile Correspondence and Documents; A Treatise on Spanish Versification; and an Appendix upon SER and ESTAR. *The whole* carefully accented, to facilitate the pronunciation.

BY M. JOSSE.

REVISED, AMENDED, IMPROVED, AND ENLARGED

BY F. SALES, A. M.,

Instructer of French and Spanish at Harvard University, Cambridge.

SIXTEENTH AMERICAN EDITION.

"PEU DE PRÉCEPTES, ET BEAUCOUP DE PRATIQUE."

FIRST PART.

BOSTON AND CAMBRIDGE:

JAMES MUNROE AND COMPANY.

1860.

NOTA BENE.—The ELEVENTH EDITION of this Grammar has been carefully revised, corrected, and improved with a few additions and alterations.

Cambridge, 1843.

At the Bookstore of the publishers of this Grammar may be found the following *Elementary and Classical Works* prepared for students of all classes and ages, by F. SALES, corrected according to the latest rules on Orthography by the SPANISH ACADEMY, the only legitimate standard on this subject, with necessary English notes at the bottom of the pages, and the pronunciation made very easy with a few rules and prosodial accents.

CARTÍLLA ó SILABÁRIO y MÉTODO PRÁCTICO de enseñar á leér, pára los Estádos de la América Setentrionál y Meridionál. (Spanish Alphabet and Spelling Book.) 16th edition.

RUDIMENTS of the SPANISH LANGUAGE. 1 small vol. 18mo.

COLMÉNA ESPAÑOLA, or SPANISH EXTRACTS, with English notes at the bottom of every page. 1 vol. 18mo. 8th edition.

CÁRTAS MARRUÉCAS, or DESCRIPTION of SPANISH CUSTOMS, MANNERS, INSTITUTIONS, &c., followed by a SELECTION of POEMS, by CADÁLSO. 1 vol. 12mo.

FÁBULAS LITERÁRIAS de DON TOMÁS DE IRIÁRTE, with English notes.

EL SÍ DE LAS NÍÑAS, Comédia de DON LEÁNDRO FERNÁNDEZ DE MORATÍN, with English notes added to this 4th edition.
(These two last works in 1 vol. large 18mo.)

EL INGENIOSO HIDALGO DON QUIJOTE DE LA MANCHA, compuesto por MIGUEL DE CERVANTES SAAVEDRA. Nueva edicion clásica, ilustrada con notas históricas, gramaticales y críticas, por LA ACADEMIA ESPAÑOLA, sus Individuos de número Pellicer, Arrieta y Clemencin. Retrato de Cervantes, diez ilustraciones de las principales aventuras de Don Quijote, y un Mapa geográfico que representa los parages por donde anduvo ; 4a. edicion Americana, en 2 tomos 12mo.

SELECCIÓN DE OBRAS MAÉSTRAS DRAMÁTICAS, con notas, conteniendo LA ESTRELLA DE SEVILLA por Fr. Lope Felix de la Vega Carpio; EL PRÍNCIPE CONSTANTE, y EL MÁGICO PRODIGIOSO por Don Pedro Calderon de la Barca; 3a. edicion mejorada.

TO THE

PATRONS AND LOVERS OF THE SPANISH LANGUAGE

IN THE

UNITED STATES OF NORTH-AMERICA,

THIS SIXTEENTH EDITION,

amended, improved and enlarged,

OF

Josse's Grammar,

IS

RESPECTFULLY DEDICATED,

BY

THEIR OBEDIENT SERVANT,

THE EDITOR.

NOTICE.

THIS Grammar is now so well known and its utility so generally acknowledged, that we deem it unnecessary to set forth its peculiar merits by comparisons derogatory to other similar publications. We will just assure the public that this edition has been carefully revised and corrected, and that such additional improvements have been made as a due regard to the arrangement of the former editions of this work would comport.

Boston, February, 1832.

ADVERTISEMENT TO THE THIRD AND FOURTH EDITIONS.

WE have the satisfaction of announcing to the liberal and enlightened patrons and lovers of the Spanish Language in these United States, that a Third Edition of Josse's Grammar is about to be issued from the press. We will not aver that it is exactly the same in all its parts as the last Edition, though this had been honoured by flattering commendations; but we will confidently assert that if the previous Editions merited the approbation of the most competent and respectable judges of similar productions, the present will be found still more deserving of general acceptance.

Every part of the work has been carefully and minutely examined, and such parts as were susceptible of melioration have been assiduously amended.

We will not detail the particulars in which this Edition is superior to the preceding, as it would be a tedious enumeration of corrections and improvements; but Instructers and Students will perceive it in almost every page; especially in the rules and illustrations regarding the use of the Future and Conditional tenses; in the degree of perfection to which the Alphabetical List of the Irregular Verbs has been brought; in the new lights introduced upon the right use of the Verbs HABÉR and TENÉR, SER and ESTAR and other verbs occasionally used as Auxiliaries; in short, upon every other point which is singular and peculiar to the Castilian tongue.

For the relief of those who may learn by this METHODICAL and PRACTICAL SYSTEM, we have thought proper to mark with an acute accent the vowel of every word in the Grammar on which the stress in pronouncing is laid; so that, after a few lessons, no uncertainty can remain respecting this important subject.

Boston, 18th August, 1827. — Fourth Edit. 1829.

ADVERTISEMENT TO THE SECOND EDITION.

GRATEFUL for the approbation that our labours have met with in the rapid diffusion of a large edition of this Grammar, and encouraged by the favourable judgment passed on the theoretical and practical method observed in this elementary work, by the most distinguished philologists and eminent scholars in our country; we now present to the American nation a second edition carefully revised, considerably altered, and improved throughout; particularly in the arrangement of the Conjugation of the Irregular Verbs; in giving the English signification of the Table of Prepositions published by the Royal Academy; in prefixing an Article to every word in the Vocabulary to denote its gender; and in assimilating as far as possible the English phraseology to the Spanish, in the Familiar Phrases and Dialogues.

We have enlarged this new edition by the addition of interesting Extracts from some of the best Spanish Writers; with specimens of critical, familiar, and commercial Letters; Mercantile Documents; a Treatise on Spanish Versification, translated from the latest Paris edition of Josse's Grammar, and a copious Table of Contents; the whole corrected in conformity to the most recent decisions on orthography of the Spanish Academy.

Our earnest purpose having been to render this publication extensively useful and acceptable to all classes and ages of learners, the public may rest assured that no pains have been spared to attain so desirable an object.

Boston, May, 1825.

ADVERTISEMENT TO THE FIRST EDITION.

FROM the first appearance in this metropolis of Josse's Grammar, a desire has been entertained of adapting it to the English language; but the little encouragement hitherto promised, in the United States, to an undertaking of this kind, has delayed its execution.

1*

This system however has been used, and recommended to such learners of the Spanish Language as were well acquainted with the French, and we have always had the satisfaction to find them well pleased with it, commonly expressing their regret, that it had not yet been adapted to the English language.

The recognition of the North and South American Sovereignties by our Government, has determined us to make the attempt. This glorious act on the part of our nation opens such a boundless field for scientific, political and commercial advantages to the rising generation, that we could not deny ourselves the gratification of aiding the generous purpose by presenting a *key*, which will, it is hoped, open an easy way to the attainment of knowledge, honours, and wealth.

The English and Spanish Grammars, which we have hitherto used, are so irregular and incorrect, that it has required the utmost patience and perseverance of both teacher and pupil to wade through them. To this should be added the enormous price at which they are imported and sold, tending to prevent many a studious youth from acquiring a language, not only noble and beautiful, but spoken in so many regions of the earth, that the benign rays of the star of day are perennially smiling upon and fertilizing some one of them.

This work of adaptation and improvement has been commenced and finished, at different intervals, in the course of the last season, as our regular occupations would permit. We have endeavoured to perform our task faithfully; should our labour meet with approbation, we shall be rewarded; should a contrary fate await it, we shall console ourselves with the reflection that our motive was good. In the meantime it is requested that all defects which shall be discovered be made known, and any improvements suggested which may occur; so that this grammar in future editions may be rendered as perfect as possible.

We have thought proper, in order to render this work complete, and save an additional expense, to insert the Vocabulary and Dialogues of Fernandez at the end of the second part, altering the orthography according to the latest rules of the Spanish Academy. The object of collections of this kind is to teach the most necessary and usual words and phrases in civil and familiar conversations; a sure method, after passing carefully through the Grammar and Exercises, of learning to speak a foreign language with propriety.

Boston, October, 1822.

ESSENTIAL OBSERVATIONS AND DIRECTIONS.

As we have adopted in our publications the modern system of Orthography of the Spanish Academy, and this may occasion some perplexity to the Students who use Neuman and Baretti's Dictionary, which is printed according to the ancient orthography, the following rules must be remembered and attended to.

1st. The words that may not be found in the combinations JA, JE, JI, JO, JU, GE, GI, should be looked for in the combinations XA, XE, XI, XO, XU, and *vice versâ.*

2d. The words that may not be found in the combinations CE, CI, may be looked for in the combinations ZE, ZI, and *vice versâ.*

3d. The words that may not be found in the combinations CUA, CUE, CUI, CUO, will be looked for in the combinations QUA', QÜE, QÜI, QUO.

4th. Those that may not be found in the combinations CA, QUE, QUI, will be looked for in the combinations CHÂ, CHÊ, CHÎ.

5th. Those that may not be found in the combinations OS, US, will be found in the combinations OBS, UBS.

6th. Those that may not be found in the combinations ESC, EST, will be found in the combinations EXC, EXT.

7th. Those that may not be found in the combination ET, will be found in the combination EPT.

8th. Those that may not be found in the combination TRAS, will be found in the combination TRANS.

9th. Those that may not be found with the suppression of the syllable HA, HE, in the middle of words done for the sake of euphony, as in *Azár,* for Azahár ; *Comprendér* for comprehendér, &c. they must look into the Dictionary according to the last manner.

10th. Those that may not be found with the letter i, may be looked for with the letter Y.

11th. Those that may not be found with one N, will be found with double N.

12th. Those that may not be found with the letter B, will be found with the letter V, and *vice versâ.*

N. B. In looking for words in the Dictionary, the student should bear in mind that *ch, ll,* and *ñ* are distinct characters from *c, l,* and *n,* and that the words with these simple letters must be looked thoroughly through, before finding the words commencing with the above compound characters.

COMMON SPANISH ABBREVIATIONS.

A. C.	Áño Cristiáno,	*in the year of Christ.*
A a.ᵃ	Arróba, *or* arróbas,	*twenty-five pounds.*
A.ˢ	Áños,	*years.*
A. A.	Autóres,	*authors.*
A. V. E.	Á. V.ʳᵃ Es.ᶜⁱᵃ,	*to Y. E.*
Adm.ᵒʳ	Administradór,	*administrator.*
Ag.ᵗᵒ	Agósto,	*August.*
Am.ᵒ	Amigo,	*friend.*
Ant.ᵒ	António,	*Anthony.*
Ang.ᵒ	Angósto,	*narrow.*
App.ᶜᵒApp.ᶜᵃ	Apostólico, ca,	*apostolical.*
Art.	Artículo,	*article,*
Arzbpo.	Arzobíspo,	*archbishop.*
At.ᵒ	Aténto,	*respectful.*
B.	Beáto	*blessed.*
B.	Vuélta,	*turn over.*
Barr.	Barríl,	*barrel.*
B.ʳ	Bachillér,	*bachelor.*
B. L. M.	Béso ó bésa las mános,	*I kiss, or he kisses the hands.*
B. L. P.	Béso ó bésa los piés,	*I kiss or he kisses the feet.*
B.ᵐᵘ P.ᵉ	Beatísimo Pádre,	*most blessed father.*
C. A. R.	Cat.ᵒ Ap.ᶜᵒ Rom.ᵒ	*Cath. Apost. Rom.*
C. M. B.	Cúyas mános béso,	*whose hands I kiss.*
C. P. B.	Cúyos piés béso,	*whose feet I kiss.*
Cam.ᵃ	Cámara,	*chamber.*
Cap.	Capítulo,	*chapter.*
Cap.ⁿ	Capitán,	*captain.*
Capp.ⁿ	Capellán,	*chaplain.*
Col.	Colúmna,	*column.*
Comis.	Comisário,	*commissary.*
Comp.ᵃ	Compañía,	*company.*
Cons.ᵒ	Conséjo,	*council.*
Conv.ᵗᵉ	Conveniénte,	*convenient.*
C—v.	Cuénta de vénta,	*Account of sale.*
C—C.	Cuénta Corriénte	*Account current.*

Corr.te	Corriénte,	*current.*
C.do	Cuándo,	*when.*
C.to C.ta	Cuánto, ta,	*how much.*
D.or D.n D.n	Don, Dóña,	*mister, mistress.*
D. D.*	Doctóres,	*doctors.*
D.r or D.or	Doctór,	*doctor.*
D.s	Diós,	*God.*
D.ho dha.	Dícho, dícha,	*said, ditto.*
Dro.	Derécho,	*right or duty.*
Dic.re, 10.re	Diciémbre,	*December.*
Doz.	Docéna,	*dozen.*
Dom.o	Domíngo,	*Sunday.*
Ecc.o Ecc.a	Eclesiástico, ca,	*ecclesiastic.*
Enm.do, vále.	Enmendádo,	*amended, valid.*
En.o	Enéro,	*January.*
Es.mo Es.ma	Escelentísimo, ma,	*most excellent.*
Es.no p.co	Escribáno público,	*Not.y Public.*
Fho. fha.	Fécho, fécha,	*dated.*
Feb.o	Febréro,	*February.*
Frz, Frnz.	Fernández,	*Fernandez.*
Fol.	Fólio,	*folio.*
F.r	Fráy, Fréy,	*brother of certain relig-*
Fran.co	Francísco,	*Francis. [ious orders.*
Fern.do	Fernándo,	*Ferdinand,*
Gue. or gde.	Guárde,	*save, preserve.*
Gra.	Grácia,	*grace.*
Gen.l or gral.	Generál,	*general.*
Id. Yd.	Ídem,	*ditto.*
Igla.	Iglésia,	*church.*
Il.e	Ilústre,	*illustrious.*
Il.mo Il.ma	Ilustrísimo, ma,	*most illustrious.*
Inq.or	Inquisidór,	*inquisitor.*
Intend.te	Intendénte,	*intendant.*
Jhs.	Jesús,	*Jesus.*
Jph.	Joséf, José,	*Joseph.*
Jn.	Juán,	*John.*
L. L.*	Léyes,	*laws.*
Lib	Líbro,	*book.*
Lib.s lb.	Líbras,	*pounds.*
Lin.	Línea,	*line.*
Lic.do	Licenciádo,	*licentiate.*

---

* D. D. stands also for *Dónes*, plural of *Don.* The duplication of the initial letter of titles indicates the plural number.

M. P. S.	Múy poderóso Señór,	*most powerful Lord.*
M.ᵉ	Mádre,	*Mother.*
M.ᵒʳ	Mayór,	*elder, major.*
M.ˢ a.ˢ	Múchos áños,	*many years.*
Mag.ᵈ	Magestád,	*Majesty.*
Man.	Manuél,	*Manuel.*
May.ᵐᵒ	Mayordómo,	*Steward.*
M.º	Médio,	*Half.*
Mig.	Miguél,	*Michael.*
Minro.	Minístro,	*minister.*
Mrd.	Mercéd,	*favour, worship.*
Mrn.	Martín,	*Martin.*
Mras.	Muéstras,	*patterns.*
Mrnz.	Martínez,	*Martinez.*
Mro.	Maéstro,	*master.*
Mrs.	M.ⁱˢ , Maravedís,	*maravedis.*
Ms.	Múchos,	*many.*
MS.	Manuscríto,	*manuscript.*
MSS.	Manuscrítos,	*manuscripts.*
N. C. M.	Nro. Cat.º Monárca,	*our Cath. Mon.*
N. S	Nuéstro Señór,	*our Lord.*
N. S.ᵃ	Nuéstra Señóra,	*our Lady.*
Nro. nra.	Nuéstro, nuéstra,	*our.*
Nov.ᵉ , 9.ʳᵉ	Noviémbre,	*November.*
Obpo.	Obíspo,	*Bishop.*
Oct.ʳᵉ, 8.ʳᵉ	Octúbre,	*October.*
On. onz.	Ónza, ónzas,	*ounce, doubloons.*
Ord.ⁿ ord.ˢ	Órden, órdenes,	*order, orders.*
P. D.	Posdáta,	*postscript.*
P.ᵃ q.ᵉ	Pára que,	*for, in order that*
P.ᵉ	Pádre,	*father.*
P.º	Pédro,	*Peter.*
P.ʳ	Por,	*for, per, by.*
P.ˢ	Piés, pésos,	*feet, dollars.*
P.ᵗᵃ	Pláta,	*silver or plate.*
P.ᵗᵉ	Párte,	*part.*
P.ᵗᵒ	Puérto,	*port.*
Pag.	Página,	*page.*
Pag.ᵗᵒ	Pagaménto,	*payment.*
Pza.	Piéza,	*piece.*
Pl.	Plána,	*trowel, page.*
Pror.	Procuradór,	*attorney.*
Publ.º	Público,	*public.*

Prov.^{or}	Provisór,	*provisor.*
Pral.	Principál,	*principal.*
P.^{mo} p.^{do}	Próximo pasádo,	*last past.*
QQs.	Quintáles,	*quintals.*
Q. *or* q.^e	Que,	*that.*
Q.ⁿ	Quién,	*who.*
Q. S. M. B.	Quién sus mános bésa,	*W. K. Y. H.*
R.^l R.^{les} V.^{on}	Reál, reáles vellón,	*real, reales, silver coin.*
R.^{mo}, ^{ma}	Reverendísimo,	*most reverend.*
R. R.^{do} R.^{da}	Reveréndo, reverénda,	*reverend.*
P. M. Fr.	Pádre maéstro fráy,	*reverend father and*
R.^{bi}	Recibí,	*I received.* [*master.*
Rec.^o	Recíbo,	*receipt.*
Resp.	Respuésta,	*answer.*
S. S.^{to} Sta	San ó Sánto, Sánta,	*saint, holy.*
S. M.	Su magestád,	*his majesty.*
S.^r *or* Sor S.^{ra}	Señór, Señóra,	*Sir, Madam.*
S. S.^d	Su Santidád,	*his Holiness.*
SS. S.^{res}	Señóres,	*gentlemen, Messrs.*
S. S. S.	Su segúro servidór,	*your faithful servant.*
Seb.ⁿ	Sebastián,	*Sebastian.*
Sep.^{re} *or* 7.bre	Setiémbre,	*September.*
S.^{ria} Secret.ⁿ	Secretaría,	*secretary's office.*
S.^o Secret.^o	Secretário,	*secretary.*
Ser.^{mo} *or* ^{ma}	Serenísimo, ma,	*most serene.*
Serv.^o	Servício,	*service.*
Serv.^r	Servidór,	*servant.*
Spre.	Siémpre,	*always.*
Sig.^{te}	Siguiénte,	*following.*
SS.^{mo}	Santísimo,	*most holy.* [*ment.*
SS.^{mo}	Santísimo(el sacramén-	*the host, the holy sacra-*
SS.^{mo} P.^e	Santísimo pádre, [to)	*most holy father.*
SS.^{no}	Escribáno,	*notary, scrivener.*
S. S. P. P.	Sántos pádres,	*holy fathers.*
S. B. T. S.	Subteniéntes,	*sublieutenants.*
Súp.^{ca}	Súplica,	*entreaty, request*
Sup.^{te}	Suplicánte,	*petitioner.*
Super.^{te}	Superintendénte,	*superintendent.*
S. Y. Ú. O.	Sálvo yérro ú omisión,	*errors or omissions ex-*
Ten.^{te}	Teniénte,	*lieutenant.* ( ) [*cepted.*
Tesor.^o	Tesoréro,	*treasurer*
Tom.	Tómo,	*volume.*

Tpo.	Tiémpo,	*time.*
Ton.^a	Toneláda,	*ton.*
Tral.	Tribunál,	*tribunal.*
Usía, V. S.^a	Vuéstra Señoría,	*your lordship, honour.*
V. M.	Vuéstra Magestád,	*your Majesty.*
V. R.	Vuéstra Reál,	*your Royal.*
Ult.º	Último,	*last.*
V. V.ᵉ	Venerable,	*venerable.*
V. A.	Vuéstra Altéza,	*your highness.*
V. B.ᵈ	Vuéstra Beatitúd,	*your beatitude.*
V. I.	Vuéstra Il.ᵐᵃ,	*your grace.*
V. E *or* V. Ex.	Vueceléncia,	*your excellency.*
V. E. E.	Vueceléncias,	*your excellencies.*
V. G.	Vérbi grácia,	*for example.*
Vm. Vmd. V.	Vuéstra, vuésa mercéd,	*you, your worship, your*
Vd.*	or ustéd,	*favour.*
V. P.	Vuéstra Paternidád,	*your paternity.*
V. R.ᵃ	Vuéstra Reveréncia,	*your reverence.*
V. S.ᵃ, Usía,	V.ᵃ Señoría,	*·your lordship, honour.*
V. S. I.	Vueseñoría Ilustrísima,	*your most illustrious rev-*
V. S.ᵈ	Vuéstra Santidád,	*your holiness.* [*erence.*
V.ᵒⁿ	Reál vellón,	*real of bullion, coin.*
Vol.	Volúmen,	*volume.*
V. S. G.	Vuélva si gústa,	*please turn over.*
Vro. vra.	Vuéstro, vuéstra,	*your.*
X.ᵐᵒ	Diézmo,	*tenth and tithe.*
Xp.ᵗᵒ	Crísto,	*Christ.*
Xpt.ⁿᵒ	Cristiáno,	*Christian.*
Xptóbal.	Cristóbal,	*Christopher.*

* An *s* is added to these abbreviations when more than one person is addressed; and then they stand for *vuéstras mercédes, vuésas mercédes* or *ustédes,* in the plural.

SPANISH GRAMMAR.

INTRODUCTION

GRAMMAR is the art of speaking and writing correctly.

Speaking correctly is to speak according to established rules, as regards both the pronunciation of letters, syllables and words, and the arrangement and combination of these words among themselves.

Writing correctly is to write in conformity to the rules and usage adopted by the best writers.

We shall first consider words as sounds, show the letters that form them, and succinctly give the rules most proper to fix their pronunciation.

Considering them afterwards as signs of our thoughts, we shall examine their nature, and their accidental variations, the order they observe between themselves, and the rules of their union.

Most grammarians treat separately upon the rules of syntax. It has appeared to us more methodical, precise and simple, to place these rules in the chapters relating to each kind of words. From this it follows, however, that the examples we give for the understanding of the rules sometimes precede the knowledge, which they suppose of certain parts of speech. But those examples are always accompanied by the translation; which greatly diminishes a slight inconvenience, which a second reading of the grammar will remove, and which is abundantly compensated by the advantage of avoiding frequent repetitions and references, a multiplicity of which fatigues and discourages beginners.

2

CHAPTER I.

OF WORDS CONSIDERED AS SOUNDS.

Words, considered as sounds, are formed of letters and syllables. The only syllables that require explanation are *gue, gui; que, qui;* we shall speak of them at the letter *u,* next page, in which all the difficulty lies.

The Spanish language reckons twenty-eight letters. The following is the order and particular denomination of these letters:

ALPHABET,	a,	b,	c,	ch,	d,	e,	f,
Denomination.	ah,	bay,	thay,*	chay,	day,	a,	á-fay,§

ALPHABET,	g,†	h,	i,	j,†	k,	l,
Denomination.	hay,†	át-chay,	e,	hótah,†	kah,	á-lay,

ALPHABET,	ll,‡	m,	n,	ñ,‡	o,
Denomination.	á-lee-ay,	á-may,	á-nay,	á-nee-ay,	o,

ALPHABET,	p,	q,	r,	s,	t,	u,
Denomination.	pay,	koo,	áir-ray,	á-say,	tay,	oo,

ALPHABET,	v,	x,	y,	z,*
Denomination.	vay,	á-kiss,	e-gree-á-gah,	tháy-tah.

The letters are all of the feminine gender.

The Spanish language has five VOWELS, which are *a, e, i, o, u.* They are called vowels, because they have a perfect sound of themselves, without being joined to other letters.

The other letters are CONSONANTS; they are thus called, because they cannot form a perfect sound without the assistance of vowels.

---

* Pronounced as *tha* in the English word *thane; th* in *theft.*

§ In pronouncing the letters, lay the stress upon the vowels marked with the acute accent.

† *g* and *j* are guttural, and their pronunciation can be learned only from a master; the English combination under them conveys the nearest sound possible.

‡ *ll* and *ñ* are pronounced as the liquid *l* and *gn* in French; as in *treille,* vine-arbour; *régner,* to reign; Ex. in Spanish, *avellána,* filbert; *guadáña,* sithe.

OF THE PRONUNCIATION OF VOWELS.

A.—This letter is pronounced as *ah* in English. Ex *Amár*, to love; *álba*, dawn.

E.—This letter is pronounced as *a* in the alphabet in English. Ex. *Eclipse*, eclipse; *ve*, see thou.

Exceptions. Before *n*, *r*, *s*, *z*, in the same syllable, *e* is pronounced more open, as in the English words, *care*, *snare*. Ex. *ver*, to see; *desdén*, disdain; *verdadéro*, true; *espia*, spy; *vez*, time. On the contrary, in *verisimil*, probable, and similar cases, it is close, because *e*, in this last word, forms a part of the first syllable, and *r* begins the second.

I.—This vowel is pronounced as *e* in English, except when it is marked with the acute accent, then it is long, and pronounced like *ee* in English, as in the words, *todavía*, yet; *orígen*, origin; *sílaba*, syllable.

O.—The *o* is generally pronounced as in English; it is, however, necessary to observe, that it is sometimes open, sometimes close, and sometimes long. It is open,—1st,—in words of one syllable, when it is not immediately followed by another vowel, and before *n*, and *r* at the end of a syllable. Ex. *lo*, the, it; *no*, no, not; *vos*, you; *Don*, Mister; *dolór*, grief; *amór*, love.—2d.—At the end of words when it is accented; for example, in the third person of the singular of the preterite definite of regular and several irregular verbs. Ex. *Amó*, he loved; *temió*, he feared; *subió*, he went up. And this *o* must necessarily be distinguished by the pronunciation and the accent in the first conjugation, so as not to confound the first person of the present of the indicative *ámo*, I love, with the third of the preterite definite, *amó*, he loved. It is close when *o* ends a syllable of words of two or more syllables; Ex. *Dóña*, Mistress; *cóche*, coach; *cochéro*, coachman. It is long, whenever it is immediately followed by another vowel, as in *voy*,* go; *hoy*,* to-day; *doy*,* I give. In other cases it is close.

U.—*U* is pronounced *oo*. We except from this rule the syllables *que*, *qui*, *gue*, *gui*, in which the *u* is not sounded. Sometimes in the diphthong, *gue*, *gui*, the *u* preserves its sound of *oo*, as in *argüir*, to argue; *agüéro*, omen. Not to leave any doubt in this respect, the Spanish Academy writes the *u* with two dots whenever it must be pronounced *oo*, so

---

* See note at the bottom of the next page.

that it is very easy for any stranger to see, at the first glance, the difference of the pronunciation between *guérra*, war; and *vergüénza*, shame; *seguir*, to follow; and *argüír*, to argue.

Y.—This letter is sometimes a vowel and sometimes a consonant. It is a vowel when it is preceded by another vowel, making with it a diphthong, as in the words *ley,** law; *Rey,** King; *muy*, very. It is also a vowel, when it is a conjunctive particle. Ex. *Pan y água*, bread and water. In almost every other case it is a consonant, as in *sáya*, petticoat; *yérro*, error; *yúgo*, yoke; &c.

OF DIPHTHONGS.

A diphthong is the union of two vowels expressing a double sound, and pronounced by a single emission of the voice these are sixteen in number:

ai or ay.*	dábais,	you gave;	hay, —	there is, there are
au.	páusa,	pause;	cáusa,	cause.
ei or ey.*	réis, —	you see;	ley, —	law.
ea.	línea,	line;	Bóreas,	Boreas.
eo.	virgíneo,	virginal;	cutáneo,	cutaneous.
eu.	déuda,	debt;	déudo, —	kinsman.
ia.	grácia,	grace;	hácia,	towards.
ié.	ciélo,	heaven,	ciéno,	mud.
io.	précio,	price;	nécio, —	fool.
iu.	ciudád,	city;	viudo,	widower.
oe.	héroe,	hero;	áloe,	aloes.
oi or oy.*	sóis,	you are;	vóy, —	I go.
ua.	frágua, —	forge;	água, —	water.
ué.	duéño,	master;	suéño, —	dream.
uí or uy.*	ruído, —	noise;	muy, —	very.
uo.	árduo,	arduous;	mutuo,	mutual.

N. B. When in these combinations the *i* and *u* are accented, as in *brío, efectúa*, each vowel forms a distinct syllable.

The TRIPHTHONGS are four:

iai.	preciáis,	you value.	
ieis.	vaciéis,	you may empty.	
uai, uay *	santiguáis,	you bless.	Paraguáy.*
uei, uey.*	averigüéis,	you may search;	buéy, ox.

---

* The custom of using the letter *i* instead of *y* as a vowel is becoming more general. Ex. *Réyno, reynár*, are now spelt, *réino, reinár, &c.*

OF THE PRONUNCIATION OF THE CONSONANTS.

B.—*B*, in the beginning of a word, is always pronounced as in English. (See Obs. page 20.)

C.—*C* has the sound of *th* in English, as in the word *thane*, before *e* and *i*; and the sound of *k*, before *a, o, u*. Formerly the *c* with the *cedilla* (ç) was used, as in *çapá-lo*, shoe; *çutáno*, such a one; but it is no longer used, and the *z* has been substituted in its place: thus we now write *zapáto, zutáno*; double *cc* as in *dicción, ficción*, &c. pronounce *dick-theón, fick-theón*.

Ch.—These two letters are pronounced as in English in the word *check*; as *chico*, small; *chocoláte*, chocolate. In words derived from the ancient languages, it sounds like *k*, as *Cháribdis, Melchisedéch*. (See Obs. page 20.)

D.—*D* is pronounced in the beginning of a word, as in English; but when the *d* is between two vowels, it is as soft as the *th* in the words *though, the*. Ex. *Dádo*, a dye; *dédo*, finger. It is pronounced lisping at the end of a word, as *libertád, Madríd*. (See Obs. page 20.)

F.—*F* is pronounced as in English.

G.—*G* is pronounced as in English before *a, o, u*. It is guttural before *e, i*. Ex. *mugér*, woman; *elegír*, to elect Before *n* it has the Latin and English pronunciation. Ex. *dig-no*, worthy; *indig-no*, unworthy; *ig-noránte*, ignorant; *enig-ma*.

H.—The *H* is mute and only lightly aspirated before *ue*. Ex. *huéro*, egg; *huéso*, bone. The Academy suppresses it after the *t*; and uses *f* instead of *ph*. Ex. *Filosofía*, philosophy; *teátro*, theatre; *Filadélfia*, Philadelphia. The letter *h* has been retained in many words, though not pronounced; and in several it has taken the place of the letter *f*, formerly used. Ex. *fijo*, son; *facér*, to do; *fermosúra*, beauty, are now written *hijo, hacér, hermosúra*, &c.

J.—*J* is pronounced guttural before all the vowels. It is found before *e* and *i* only in the words *Jesús, Jerusalén, Jeremías*, and in the diminutives and derivatives of the nouns that terminate in *ja* or *jo*; as *pája, straw*; *pajíta*, little straw; *viéjo*, old man; *viejecíto*, little old man.

2*

K.—The *K* is admitted only in foreign words, and is pronounced as in English.

L.—This letter is pronounced as in English.

LL.—When *ll* occurs in a word, it is liquid, and pronounced as in the words *seraglio* and *William*, in English. Ex. *Llága*, wound ; *lléno*, full ; *cabállo*, horse ; *llegár*, to arrive ; *llovér*, to rain ; *llúvia*, rain.

M.—*M* and *N* are pronounced as in English.

N.—*N* having this mark (~) which the Spaniards call *n* with *tilde*, has the same sound as *n* in *onion, minion*, &c. Ex. *Señor*, Sir ; *niñéz*, childhood ; *enseñár*, to teach.

P and Q—are pronounced as in English.

R.—*R* preserves in Spanish its natural pronunciation. Ex. *razón*, reason ; *ríco*, rich ; and when it is double, both letters must be distinctly heard. Ex. *cár-ro*, cart ; *car-réra*, career ; *zúr-ra*, flogging. (See Obs. page 20.)

S.—*S* is always pronounced hard, like double *ss*, even between two vowels, as in *assembly*. Ex. *sábio*, wise ; *sébo*, tallow ; *famóso*, famous ; *espóso*, husband ; *sosiégo*, tranquillity.

T.—*T* never loses the sound it has in the alphabet, and is always hard. Ex. *tío*, uncle ; *tía*, aunt.

V.—The Spaniards often confound the sound of this letter with that of *b;* but the Academy disapproves of it, and recommends that it should be pronounced as the English and French. Ex. *valentía*, valour ; *vélo*, veil ; *vil*, vile ; *voluntád*, will ; *vuélo*, flight.

X.—*X* is pronounced like *s* when followed by a consonant, and it is lightly sounded *s* when followed by *ce, ci*. Ex. *extrangéro,** *extráño, excépto, excitár*, &c. It is pronounced like *ks* when it is found between two vowels, as *examinár, existír, séxo*. In a few words ending in *x*, it is somewhat guttural. Ex. *Relóx*,† watch; *box*, box-tree; *carcáx*, quiver. (See Obs. page 20.)

N. B The *x* is not *now* used as a guttural letter; the *j* is used in its place before the vowels *a, o, u,* and the *g* before *e* and *i*. (See Obs. page 20.)

---

* Now spelt *estrangéro, estráño, escépto, escitár*.
† Now written *relój, boj, carcáj,* &c.

Z.—The Z is only used now before *a*, *o*, *u*, and is pronounced like the *c* before *e* and *i*. Ex. *zapáto*, shoe; *zórra*, fox: *zúmo*, juice; and is always pronounced lisping after a vowel, as *juéz*, judge; *nuéz*, walnut.

Observations.

1st. The Spanish Academy, conforming to the pronunciation, has suppressed double consonants, when one alone is pronounced. In the Spanish books, printed within a few years, the double letters *ll*, *ss*, *ff*, *bb*, &c. are no longer found, and *cc*, *nn*, *rr*, only when both consonants are sounded; as in the words *accéso*, *ennoblecér*, *bárro*. Double *ll* is to be considered only as the sign of the liquid letter *l*, and not as a double consonant.

2d. But as Spanish books less modern have not followed fixed rules as respects not only doubling the consonants, but also the orthography, when the pronunciation does not indicate it in an evident manner, we inform beginners,—1st—that they ought to have recourse to the latest Dictionaries, (though it is to be regretted that these have as yet been printed and reprinted in England and in the United States most carelessly in this important point of view,) because it may be supposed that their authors have generally adopted the orthography of the Spanish Academy;—2d.—that, in consulting these Dictionaries, the scholar should remember, that, if he does not find the word at the first search, it is because its orthography has varied, and because the Spanish writers have often confounded, and do sometimes still confound the letters *b* and *v*; *s* and *c*; *c* and *ch*, and sometimes *q*; *c* and *q* in the syllables *qua*, *qüe*, *qüi*; *c* and *z*; *f* and *h*, in the beginning of a word; *i* and *y*; *j* and *g*, in the syllables *je* and *ji*. Some writers use the *j* entirely for the guttural sound, and never the *g* nor *x*; but we follow the decisions of the Academy and not the whims of every schemer. X, having had till lately the guttural sound, was confounded with *g*, before *e*, *i*; and with the *j*, which is always guttural before all vowels. Instead of looking in the Dictionary for *alvedrío*, *ferido*, *léxos*, *quándo*, *zélo*, *chîmia*, &c. he should look for *albedrío*, *herído*, *léjos*, *cuándo*, *célo*, *química*, &c. (See Syllabical Table and Observations, page 20. and directions, page 7.)

SYLLABICAL TABLE.

		Orthographical alterations made by the Royal Academy of Madrid, and now generally adopted by Spanish writers.	
ba,[1] be, bi, bo, bu,	ma, me, mi, mo, mu,		
ca, co, cu,	na, ne, ni, no, nu,		
ce, ci,	ña, ñe, ñi, ño, ñu,		
cha,[2] che, chi, cho, chu,	pa, pe, pi, po, pu,		
da,[3] de, di, do, du,	qua,[5] quo,	cua, cuo,	
fa, fe, fi, fo, fu,	que, qui,		
ga, go, gu,	qüe, qüi,	cue, cui,	
ge, gi,	ra,[6] re, ri, ro, ru,		
gue, gui,	rra, rre, rri, rro, rru,		
güe, güi,	sa, se, si, so, su,		
ha,[4] he, hi, ho, hu,	ta, te, ti, to, tu,		
ja, je, ji, jo, ju,	va, ve, vi, vo, vu,		
ka, ke, ki, ko, ku,	xa,[7] xe, xi, xo, xu,	ja, ge, gi, jo, ju,	
la, le, li, lo, lu,	xâ, xê, xî, xô, xû,	xa, xe, xi, xo, xu,	
lla lle, lli, llo, llu,	ya, ye, yi, yo, yu,		
	za, ze, zi, zo, zu,	za, ce, ci, zo, zu,	

IMPORTANT OBSERVATIONS.

[1] *B* is always hard at the beginning of a word, whatever letter may follow it. Ex. *baráto*, cheap; *bendito*, blessed, *brávo*, brave; *blánco*, white. In the middle of a word, between two vowels, *b* is softened into nearly a *v*. Ex. *bebér*, to drink; *subir*, to go up. *Bla, ble,* &c. are always pronounced hard, as in English, whatever place they occupy in a word. Ex. *hablár*, to speak; *establecér*, to establish. *Bra, bre,* &c. preceded by a *consonant,* are pronounced hard, as *hómbre*, man; *alámbre*, wire; but if preceded by a vowel, the *b* is generally softened into almost a *v*. Ex. *obrár*, to act; *abrir*, to open; *póbre*, poor.

[2] *Châ, chê,* &c. with a circumflex, as is stated in page 17, has heretofore been used with the sound of *kah, kai,* in words derived from the ancient languages; but now we use in the place of it, *ca, que, qui, co, cu;* as *quimia,* chemistry; *querubin,* cherubim; *Caríbdis,* Charibdis; *quilo,* chyle.

[3] The letter *d,* when preceded by a consonant is sounded hard. Ex. *endéble,* feeble; *enderezár,* to straighten; and *dra, dre,* &c. preceded by a vowel like *th* in *either.* Ex. *medrár,* to thrive; *adréde,* on purpose; *podrir,* to rot; *ladrón,* thief.

[4] Remember that the *h* is not aspirated.

[5] *Q* is changed into *c,* in all words where it is followed by *ua, uo, ue, ui,* and we write *cuándo,* when; *cuóta,* quota; *cuestión,* question; *cuociénte,* quotient.

[6] *R,* in the beginning and middle of words, is pronounced as in English, as *rio,* river; *erário,* treasury; but double *rr,* in Spanish, is pronounced a little stronger than the *r* in English at the beginning of a word, as *pérro,* dog; *cárro,* cart; *Pizárro.*

[7] *Xa,* &c. used to be guttural, and pronounced like the *j,* when the vowel fol-

OF THE ACCENT.

There is but one long syllable in each Spanish word. It is generally indicated by the acute accent placed upon the vowel. But this accent is suppressed, when the long syllable may be otherwise known, except in certain cases where use requires it should be preserved.

The following are the principal rules established by the Spanish Academy, for the use or suppression of the accent upon the vowel of the long syllable.

1st. The monosyllable must not be accented, because it is long from its nature.

Exceptions. We accent—1st.—the conjunctions *é*, and; *ó*, *ú*, or; and the preposition *á*, to.—2d.—The monosyllable *él*, he, him; *mí*, me, pronouns personal: *sí*, yes, oneself, affirmative particle or pronoun; *dé*, *sé*, and *vé*, (from the verbs *dar*, *sabér*, *ser*, *ver*, to give, to know, to be, and to see,) to distinguish these monosyllables from *el*, the, article; *mi*, my, pronoun possessive; *si*, if, conditional particle; *de*, of, preposition; *se*, himself, &c. pronoun; and *ve*, go thou, verb.

2d. The accent is suppressed in words of many syllables terminated by only one vowel, because their *penultima* is long from its nature.

Exceptions. 1st. In verbs, in the first and third person of the singular of the perfect and future of the indicative, the last syllable is long, and receives the accent. Ex. *amé*, I loved; *amó*, he loved; *amaré*, I shall love; *conocí*, I knew, *conocerá*, he shall know, &c. The accent remains,

---

lowing the *x* had not the circumflex accent over it, so (*á*.) The Spanish Academy, in the two last editions of their Dictionary, printed in 1817 and 1822, and in their last improved Treatise on Orthography, have used, instead of the guttural *x*, the letter *j*, before the vowels *a*, *o*, *u*; and the letter *g*, before *e* and *i*; but some writers use *j* for *x* before all the vowels. Ex. *jabón*, soap; *géfe*, chief; *Mégico*, Mexico; *júgo*, juice. The *x* is preserved only in those words, in which it is pronounced as *ks*. Ex. *axióma*, *exagerár*, pronounced *aksióma*, *eksagerár*. The *x* has also been changed into an *s* in all the instances in which it is followed by another consonant. Ex. *estrangéro*, stranger; *escépto*, except; *escitár*, to excite. The object of the Academy, in all the foregoing alterations, has been to simplify the orthography, and make it conform to the pronunciation as nearly as possible; therefore we have adopted these improvements in the orthography and pronunciation throughout this Grammar, Book of Exercises, and other publications.

even when we add a pronoun to some one of these words.
Ex. *cogíte*, I caught thee; *halléle*, I found him; *comeránlo*,
they will eat it. 2d. It is the same with the last syllable of
the words *allá*, there; *café*, coffee; *dejó*, he left; *Perú*,
Bercebú, *Tribú*, Tribe.

3d. In Spanish words of more than two syllables, the two
last are often short. We call words of this kind, *esdrújulos*,
dactyles. Some of them, as *cámara*, chamber; *espíritu*,
spirit; *santísimo*, most holy, take the accent upon the *antepenultima*, which is accented in the same manner in those
verbs which are made *esdrújulos* by the annexed pronoun,
as *mírame*, look at me; *óyeme*, hear me; which, without
the adjunction of the pronoun, would be written without an
accent, *mira*, look; *oye*, hear. Others, compounded of a
verb followed by two pronouns, and many adverbs, terminated in *mente*, have the accent upon the syllable preceding the
antepenultima. Ex. *búscamelo*, seek it for me; *díjoscnos*,
people told us; *fácilmente*, easily. Finally, certain adverbs
in *mente*, derived from words *esdrújulos*, receive the accent
upon the fifth syllable, reckoning from the last. Ex. *bárba-
ramente*, barbarously; *intrépidamente*, intrepidly; words derived from *bárbaro*, *intrépido*.

3d. The accent is suppressed upon the *penultima*, in words
of two syllables, terminated with two vowels, as *nao*, ship:
sea, let him be; *lea*, let him read; *mio*, mine; and in the
words terminated in *ia*, *ie*, *io*, *ua*, *ue*, *uo*, which, considering
the two vowels as diphthongs, are classed with dissyllables:
for instance, *India*; *Julio*, July; *agua*, water; *mutuo*, mutual; &c.

Exceptions. The first and third persons of the singular of
the perfects of the verbs deviate from this rule, since they always have, as we have said, the last syllable long and accented. We must then write *leí*, I read; *fié*, I trusted; *temió*,
he feared; *pidió*, he asked, &c.

4th. Words terminating in *y* preceded by a vowel, which
forms a diphthong, have no accent; their last syllable is always long. Ex. *Muley*, convoy, *Paraguay*.*

5th In words ending with two vowels, and of three or
more syllables, the position of the long syllable varies. 1st.
The last vowel is long, and takes the accent in the words

---

* See Note, page 10.

puntapié, a kick; *tirapié*, a strap; and in the first and third persons of the singular of the perfect of the indicative of verbs; as, *acarreé*, I carried; *continué*, I continued; *distribuí*, I distributed; *codició*, he coveted; *esceptuó*, he excepted. 2d. The penultima vowel is long, and receives the accent in the nouns and verbs terminated in *ae*, *ia*, *ie*, *io*, *ua*, *ue*, *uo*; for example, *provée*, he provides; *filosofía*, philosophy; *desafío*, challenge; *gradúo*, I graduate.

Exceptions. The accent is suppressed in all the persons ending in *ia*, of the imperfect of the indicative and 1st conditional tense, because the *i* is always long. For the same reason we do not accent the penultimate vowel of the terminations *ae*, *ao*, *au*, *ea*, *eo*, *oa*, *oe*, *oo*. However, sometimes these vowels form a diphthong; then the syllable that precedes them is long and receives the accent. Ex. *héroe*, hero; *línea*, line; *cutáneo*, cutaneous; *purpúreo*, purple coloured. If the final vowels *ia*, *ie*, *io*, *ua*, *ue*, *uo*, of words of three or more syllables, form diphthongs, it is also the preceding syllable which is long; but the accent is suppressed. Ex. *Esperiencia*, experience; *disturbio*, disturbance; *Nicaragua.*

6th. The last syllable of the words ending with a consonant is commonly long, and does not receive an accent. The accent is, on the contrary, marked, if the long syllable is the penultima, as in the words *árbol*, tree; *virgen*, virgin; *mártir*, martyr; *alférez*, ensign; or the antepenultima, as in *Júpiter*, *régimen*, *Aristóteles.*

Exceptions. 1st. The last syllable of any person singular of a verb, ending with a consonant, take the accent, if it be long. Ex. *amarás*, thou shalt love; *serás*, thou shalt be, &c.—2d.—In patronymick names terminated in *z*, as *Pérez*, *Sanchez*, *Fernandez*, the penultima is always long, and is not accented

7th. The plural of verbs and nouns follows the rule of their singular. The only exception is the plural *caractéres*, whose long accented syllable is not the same as in the singular, which is *carácter* on the penultima.

Observation.

See (pages 15, 17, 18,) what we have said of the accent circumflex and of the diæresis upon the *u*, signs formerly introduced by the Spanish Academy to fix the pronunciation in a few uncertain cases. The circumflex is now entirely suppressed, in consequence of depriving the *x* of its former guttural sound, and using the *j* and *g* in its place; and in consequence of using *ca*, *que*, *qui*, instead of *châ*, *chê*, *chî*, in words derived from the ancient languages. The diæresis is only used in *güe*, *güi*, to denote when the '*u* must be sounded separately from the *e* and *i*. (See Obs. page 20.)

OF PUNCTUATION.

Punctuation is in Spanish the same as in English. However, as it often happens in the Spanish language, that punctuation alone indicates the interrogative sense of the phrase; and that, if the period be long, the reader is informed too late by the note of interrogation which follows it, the Spanish Academy then makes use of a particular mark, causing the phrase to be preceded by the note of interrogation reversed. Ex. ¿ *No te espánta la cercanía de un precipício, que encubiérto con las apariéncias de vánas seguridádes, será pára ti tánto mas fatál cuánto ménos imaginádo?* Art thou not frightened at the vieinity of a precipice, which, concealed under the appearance of false security, will be the more fatal to thee, as it is less suspected?

If, in Spanish, we are not warned by the interrogative note, this phrase is only affirmative, *thou art not frightened*, &c. Its turn and the transposition of a pronoun do not announce at the outset, as in English, that the sense is interrogative. The same is true as respects the note of admiration in long periods, as ¡ *Válgame Diós, cuántas provincias y cuántas naciónes conquistó!* &c. Bless me, how many provinces and nations he conquered! &c.

CHAPTER II.

OF WORDS CONSIDERED AS SIGNS OF OUR THOUGHTS.

WORDS are divided into different classes, which Grammarians call Parts of Speech; which are, the Article, Noun, Pronoun, Verb, Participle, Adverb, Preposition, Conjunction, and Interjection. Of these parts of speech, the last four are invariable. The *article, noun, pronoun,* and *participle,* are declined; they have *genders, numbers,* and *cases.* The *verb* is conjugated; it has *modes, tenses, numbers,* and *persons,* as will be seen hereafter.

We shall speak of the *genders* and *numbers,* in the chapter of nouns to which they belong.

Though, in the Spanish language, nouns do not change their terminations in changing their relations, as they do in the Greek and Latin tongues, we shall, however, conform to the Grammar of the Spanish Academy, which admits six cases, to wit: the *nominative, genitive, dative, accusative, vocative,* and *ablative.*

The *nominative* is the case that denotes the noun or pronoun, which is the subject of a proposition.

The *genitive* denotes the person to whom belongs the object of which we speak.

The *dative* denotes the person or thing towards which the action of the verb is directed, or for which there results from it an advantage or disadvantage.

The *accusative* represents the person or thing which is the direct regimen of the verb or end of its signification without preposition, or preceded by one of those which govern this case; such as, *ánte, cóntra, éntre, hácia,* &c. *before, against, among, between, towards,* &c.

The *vocative* serves to call. We place in this case the persons to whom we address our speech.

The *ablative* serves to express the matter of or manner in which a thing is made; the cause from which it proceeds; or the instrument with which it is done. This case is always accompanied by one of the prepositions that govern it; such as *con, de, en, por,* &c. with, from, in, by, &c.

CHAPTER III.

OF THE ARTICLE.

The *Article* is a small word placed before nouns, or before any other word taking their place, to determine the person, the thing, or the action spoken of: therefore it is called definite or determinate.

The *article* has three genders in Spanish; the masculine, feminine, and neuter. For the masculine it is *el*, the; for the feminine *la*, the; and for the neuter *lo*, the. The two first have the two numbers, and the last has only the singular.

DECLENSION OF THE ARTICLES.

Masculine Article.

	Singular.						Plural.		
Nom.	el,	- - - - *the.*		*Nom.*	los,	- - - - *the.*
Gen.	del,*	- - *of the.*		*Gen.*	de los,	- -. *of the.*
Dat.	al,*	- - - *to the.*		*Dat.*	á los,	- - *to the.*
Acc.	el, al,†	- - - *the.*		*Acc.*	los, á los,†	- - *the.*
Abl.	del,*	- *from the.*		*Abl.*	de los,	- *from the.*

Feminine Article.

	Singular.						Plural		
Nom.	la,	- - - - *the.*		*Nom.*	las,	- - *the.*
Gen.	de la,	- - *of the.*		*Gen.*	de las,	- - *of the.*
Dat.	á la,	- - *to the.*		*Dat.*	á las,	- - *to the.*
Acc.	la, á la,†	- - *the.*		*Acc.*	las, á las,†	- - *the.*
Abl.	de la,	- *from the.*		*Abl.*	de las,	- *from the.*

Neuter Article.

Nom.	lo, - - - - *the.*	
Gen.	de lo, - - *of the.*	This article has no plural,
Dat.	á lo, - - *to the.*	and is used only before Adjec-
Acc.	lo, - - - - *the.*	tives and Participles passive.
Abl.	de lo, - *from the.*	

We have said in the definition of the article, that it must only be placed before nouns substantive, or *before any other part of speech that does their office;* from which must be concluded, that there are parts of speech that, without being substantives are sometimes employed as such. Really in these phrases *el leér me gústa,* reading pleases me; *preferír lo útil á lo agradable,* to prefer the useful to the agreeable; *ignorár el porqué,* to be ignorant of the why; *leér* is a verb,

---

* *Del* and *al* are contractions of *de el* and *á el*, which custom has introduced, and which the Academy has approved, in order to distinguish, by this contraction, the genitive, ablative, and dative of *el*, article, from the same cases of *él*, pronoun. Thus *del, al*, signify of or from the, to the; and *de él, á él*, signify of or from him, to him.

† See Note, page 31.

útil and *agradáble* are adjectives, and *porqué* is an adverb; but those words do the office of substantives, and it is for this reason that they take the article.

OF THE USE OF THE ARTICLES.

RULE I.—The article never admits of any elision in Spanish; but there are *a few* feminine nouns that, beginning with an *a*, take the masculine article *el*, instead of the feminine *la*, in order to avoid the disagreeable meeting of two *a*'s. Therefore we say *el água*, water; *el ála*, the wing; *el álma*, the soul; *el áma*, the mistress; *el áve*, the bird; *el águila*, the eagle; *el Álba*, the dawn; *el hámbre*, hunger; *la agua*, *la ala*, &c. would be too harsh. But it is necessary to observe,—1st.—that this change of article is admitted only in the singular, because the clashing of the two vowels does not take place in the plural.—2d,—if these nouns are accompanied by an adjective, this adjective must be put in the feminine: we say, *el água es fría; el ála derécha;* the water is cold; the right wing; and not *el água frío; el ála derécho*—3d.— observe that the nouns above mentioned are *nearly all* which usage has permitted to deviate from the general rule.

RULE II.—The article is placed in Spanish before nouns taken in a *universal sense*, even before proper names of regions, countries, rivers, winds and mountains, and should be repeated before each noun. Ex. *el óro*, gold; *la pláta*, silver; *el cóbre*, copper; *la Fráncia, de la Fráncia, á la Fráncia*, France, of France, to France; *la Castílla, de la Castílla, á la Castílla*, Castile, of Castile, to Castile; *el Ébro, el Tájo*, the Tagus, &c.; because the common nouns *región, província, río*, &c. are understood

Exceptions.—1st. Those countries are excepted which take their names from their capital cities. Ex. *Nápoles y Corfú son únos países múy favorecídos de la naturaléza*, Naples and Corfu are countries very much favoured by nature;—2d.—the names of countries which are under the regimen of the preposition *en*; as, *está en España*, he is in Spain; *vive en Fráncia*, he lives in France.—3d.—those nouns that serve to modify or qualify the preposition *de* with a noun that precedes; as, *el réino de Inglatérra*, the kingdom of England; *las ciudádes de Fráncia y de Alemánia*, the cities of France and Germany; *un tenedór de hiérro*, an iron fork; *úna casa de madéra*, a wooden house; and, lastly, the article is omitted before the names of countries, of which we speak of going to or returning from. Ex. *vuélvo de Prúsia*, I return from Prussia; *lléga de Polónia*, he arrives from Poland; *va á Mégico*, he goes to Mexico.

Remark 1st. Though the name of a country be under the regimen of the preposition *en* or *de*, it must be preceded by the article when it is personified, or when it is taken in a definite sense and in the whole extent of its signification. Ex. *La urbanidád de la Fráncia, el interés de la Inglatérra, la fertilidád de la Itália*, the politeness of France, the interest of England, the fertility of Italy.—2d.—The article is always placed before the names of certain distant countries; as, *llego del Japón, de la China, del Perú*, I arrive from Japan, from China, from Peru. We say; *Ir á índias*, or *á las índias; venír de índias*, or *de las índias*, to go to the Indies; to come from the Indies.

RULE III.—When the names of kingdoms and provinces are preceded in English by a verb expressing the idea of *coming, returning, going, coming back, sending* and *sending back*, the preposition *á* is used in Spanish, corresponding to the English *to*   Ex. *Ir á Fráncia*, to go to France; *volveré á Inglatérra*, I shall return to England, &c.;—on the contrary, *at, in, in the*, &c. are translated in Spanish, by *en*, when the preceding verb does not express any motion. Ex. *Está en París*, he is at Paris; *nació en Róma*, he was born in Rome; *estaré en cása*, I shall be in the house, or at home. We however say,—to be at the door, *estár á la puérta;* to wait for at the door, *esperár á la puérta*, &c.

RULE IV.—The nouns *Señór, Señóra, Señóres, Señóras, Señoríto, Señorítos, Señoríta, Señorítas*, Mister or Sir, Mistress or Madam, Gentlemen or Sirs, Masters, young Gentlemen, young Ladies, Miss, Misses, always take the article, except,—1st.—when they are preceded by one of the pronouns possessive *mi, tu*, my, thy, &c. and when they are in the vocative. We must then say: *el Señór del Cámpo, la señóra Sáncho, la señoríta Villégas, mi señóra Sáncho, el señoríto Quiróga; mi señoríto Quiróga; mi señoríta Villégas; cómo está vm.* señór don Francísco*, or, *señóra dóña Francísca?* Mister del Campo, Mistress Sancho, Master Quiroga, Miss Villegas, my lady Sancho, my young lady Villegas; how do you do, Sir Francis, or Lady Frances?

---

* See Abbreviations, page 12.

N. B. 1st. When we speak of, or to a person in high station, or to whom we owe respect, we use in Spanish these words; *señór don, señóra* or *señoríta dóña*, which must always be placed before christian names. Ex. *El señór don Pédro B.* My Lord Peter B.; *la señóra dóña María A.* My Lady Mary A.—It is necessary to remember that the words *Don* and *Dóña*, are *never* employed before a surname or family name. We shall then say, *El señór de Matallánas; la señóra de Villa Tórre;* and not, *el señór don de Matallánas; la señóra dóña de Villa Tórre.*

N. B. 2d. *Mi señóra, mi señoríta,* are expressions which indicate more deference than *la señóra, la señoríta.*

RULE V.—When one of the words, sir or mister, mistress or madam, my lord, my lady, *señór, señóra,* are accompanied with a title, the article is placed before that word, and not before the title. The marshal, *el señór mariscál;* the dutchess, *la señóra duquésa;* the bishop, *el señór obispo.* But if we use *mi señór, mi señóra,* the article is placed as in English. My lord the bishop, *mi señór el obispo, mi señóra la duquésa.*

RULE VI.—The neuter article is placed only before adjectives used as substantives, and taken in an absolute indeterminate case; as, *se débe preferír lo útil á lo agradáble,* one ought to prefer the useful to the agreeable. *Lo buéno es preferíble á lo hermóso,* the good is preferable to the beautiful.

CHAPTER IV.

OF NOUNS.

NOUNS are either *substantive* or *adjective.* The noun *substantive* expresses the name of a person or thing; the noun *adjective* expresses its quality. Ex. *Un hómbre dócto,* a learned man; *úna hermósa mugér,* a handsome woman; *hómbre* and *mugér,* man and woman, are substantives; *dócto* and *hermósa,* learned and handsome, are adjectives.

OF THE SUBSTANTIVE.

The substantive is either *common, proper,* or *collective.*

The substantive *common* is that which may be applied to several persons or several things; as, *generál,* general; *ciu*

3*

dád, city, *réino,* kingdom. One may say, *un generál Inglés, un generál Francés,* an English general, a French general; *la ciudád de Lóndres, la ciudád de París,* the city of London, the city of Paris; *el réino de Fráncia, el réino de Inglatérra,* the kingdom of France, the kingdom of England, &c.

The substantive *proper* expresses a separate idea, a single person or thing; as, *Nerón, París, Lóndres;* Nero, Paris, London.

The substantive *collective* is that which, though in the singular, presents to the mind several persons or things, either as making one whole, or as making part of a whole. The first is called *collective general;* as *egército, rebáño, florésta,* army, flock, forest. The second is called *collective partitive;* as, *trópa, infinidád,* troop, infinity, &c.

RULE VII.—The noun substantive *collective partitive* may govern the verb that follows it in the plural; but the noun substantive *collective general* never governs it in that number. We may then say, *entráron en Lóndres úna trópa, úna infinidád de ladrónes;* but we cannot say: *el egército pereciéron, el rebáño pececiéron;* say *el egército pereció,* &c.

GENDERS.

The *gender* originally denoted only the distinction of the sexes as male or female. The *masculine* designates man or the male. The *feminine* denotes woman or the female. Afterwards, by extension, we have attributed the masculine or feminine gender to other nouns, though they had no relation to either sex: the neuter has since been added to them in several languages.

There are three genders in the Spanish language: the *masculine, feminine,* and *neuter.* This last has only a relation to vague and indeterminate things: it is applicable only to adjectives, and has no plural. Ex. *Lo buéno, lo málo, lo jústo, ésto, aquéllo,* &c.; the good, the bad, the just, this, that, &c.

OF NUMBERS.

Numbers serve to designate one or many objects. There are two numbers, the *singular* and *plural.* The *singular* designates only one person or thing, as *hómbre,* man; *mugér,* woman; *libro,* book, *plúma,* pen. The *plural* designates many persons or things; as, *los hómbres,* men; *mugéres,* women; *libros,* books; *plúmas,* pens.

OF THE FORMATION OF THE PLURAL OF NOUNS.

The *plural* of nouns substantive and adjective is formed in Spanish in two different manners, according to the termination of the singular.

The nouns are terminated either with a *short vowel*, that is, *not accented*; or with a *long vowel*, that is, *accented*; or lastly, with a consonant.

RULE VIII. When the noun is terminated with a short vowel, the plural is formed by adding an *s* to the singular; Ex. *Cárta*, letter; *cártas*, letters; *lláve*, key; *lláves*, keys; *buéno*, *buéna*, good; *buénos*, *buénas*, good, &c.

When the noun terminates with an accented *í*, or with a consonant, the plural is formed by adding *es* to the singular. Ex. *Baladí*, *baladíes*, frivolous; *Alelí*, gilly-flower; *alelíes*, gilly-flowers; *alcalí*, *alcalíes*; *verdád*, truth; *verdádes*, truths; *razón*, reason; *razónes*, reasons; *hábil*, able; *hábiles*, able. *Maravedí* forms its plural in three ways. We say *maravedíes*, *maravedís*, and *maravedíses*.

N. B. The nouns, both substantive and adjective, which terminate with a *z* in the singular, change *z* into *c* to form their plural, with the addition of the letters *es:* Ex. *Luz*, light, *lúces; felíz*, happy, *felíces*, &c.

DECLENSION OF NOUNS.

Substantives masculine of a person, beginning with a consonant

Singular.

N.	el	pádre,	- - - - -	*the*	*father.*
G.	del	pádre,	- - - - -	*of the*	*father.*
D.	al	pádre,	- - - - -	*to the*	*father.*
A.	al	pádre,*	- - - - -	*the*	*father.*
V.		pádre,	- - - - -	*o*	*father.*
Ab.	del	pádre,	- - - - -	*from the*	*father.*

---

* Though the observation we are about to make belongs to the rules relative to the regimen of verbs, we have thought fit to give it here, in order to make known the reason of the difference that exists between the accusative of the nouns of persons and that of the nouns of things. Whenever a *rational being*, or *personified thing* is the object of this action of the active verb, the verb governs the noun in the compound (as it is called) accusative with the preposition *á*; and, as we have already said in speaking of the article, *al* is a contraction of the preposition *á* and of the article *el*. When on the contrary the object of the action of the active verb is a noun that expresses an inanimate thing, the verb governs it in the accusative without any preposition. See Rule LVI, page 153, which refers to this observation.

Plural.

N.	los	pádres,	- - - -	*the*	*fathers.*
G.	de los	pádres,	- - - -	*of the*	*fathers.*
D.	á los	pádres,	- - - -	*to the*	*fathers.*
A.	á los	pádres,	- - - -	*the*	*fathers.*
V.		pádres,	- - - -	*o*	*fathers.*
Ab.	de los	pádres,	- - - -	*from the*	*fathers.*

Substantive feminine of a person, beginning with a consonant:

Singular.

N.	la	mugér,	- - - -	*the*	*woman.*
G.	de la	mugér,	- - - -	*of the*	*woman.*
D.	á la	mugér,	- - - -	*to the*	*woman.*
A.	á la	mugér,	- - - -	*the*	*woman.*
V.		mugér,	- - - -	*o*	*woman.*
Ab.	de la	mùgér,	- - - -	*from the*	*woman.*

Plural.

N.	las	mugéres,	- - -	*the*	*women.*
G.	de las	mugéres,	- - -	*of the*	*women.*
D.	á las	mugéres,	- - -	*to the*	*women.*
A.	á las	mugéres,	- - -	*the*	*women*
V.		mugéres,	- - -	*o*	*women.*
Ab.	de las	mugéres.	- - -	*from the*	*women.*

Substantives feminine of a person, beginning with an *a*:

Singular.

N.	el	áma,	- - - -	*the*	*mistress.*
G.	del	áma,	- - - -	*of the*	*mistress.*
D.	al	áma,	- - - -	*to the*	*mistress.*
A.	al	áma,	- - - -	*the*	*mistress.*
V.		áma,	- - - -	*o*	*mistress.*
Ab.	del	áma,	- - - -	*from the*	*mistress.*

Plural.

N.	las	ámas,	- - - -	*the*	*mistresses.*
G.	de las	ámas,	- - - -	*of the*	*mistresses.*
D.	á las	ámas,	- - - -	*to the*	*mistresses.*
A.	á las	ámas,	- - - -	*the*	*mistresses.*
V.		ámas,	- - - -	*o*	*mistresses.*
Ab.	de las	ámas,	- - - -	*from the*	*mistresses.*

Substantive masculine of a thing:

Singular.

N.	el,	líbro,	- - - - -	the	book.
G.	del	libro,	- - - - -	of the	book.
D.	al	libro,	- - - - -	to the	book.
A.	el	líbro,*	- - - - -	the	book.
V.		líbro,	- - - - -	o	book.
Ab.	del	libro,	- - - - -	from the	book.

Plural.

N.	los	líbros,	- - - - -	the	books.
G.	de los líbros,		- - - - -	of the	books.
D.	á los líbros,		- - - - -	to the	books.
A.	los	líbros,	- - - - -	the	books.
V.		líbros,	- - - - -	o	books.
Ab.	de los líbros,		- - - - -	from the	books.

Substantive feminine of a thing:

Singular.

N.	la	cása,	- - - - -	the	house.
G.	de la cása,		- - - - -	of the	house.
D.	á la cása,		- - - - -	to the	house.
A.	la	cása,	- - - - -	the	house.
V.		cása,	- - - - -	o	house
Ab.	de la cása,		- - - - -	from the	house.

Plural.

N.	las	cásas,	- - - - -	the	houses.
G.	de las cásas,		- - - - -	of the	houses.
D.	á las cásas,		- - - - -	to the	houses.
A.	las	cásas,	- - - - -	the	houses.
V.		cásas,	- - - - -	o	houses.
Ab.	de las cásas,		- - - - -	from the	houses.

N. B. Neuter nouns never relate to persons but only to indeterminate things; as, *lo buéno, lo málo, lo útil, lo pasádo, lo escrito.* They have neither vocative case nor plural number, and are declined with the neuter article.

* See the preceding note, page 31.

DECLENSION OF A NEUTER NOUN.

N.	lo	útil,	- - - - - *the*	*useful.*
G.	de lo	útil,	- - - - - *of the*	*useful.*
D.	á lo	útil,	- - - - - *to the*	*useful.*
A.	lo	útil,	- - - - - *the*	*useful.*
Ab.	de lo	útil,	- - - - - *from the*	*useful.*

Remark. The neuter article is not placed indifferently before all adjectives employed as substantives, but only (as we have said in rule vi, p. 29) before those that are taken in a sense absolutely indeterminate. In this phrase, *el hómbre sábio prefiére siémpre lo útil á lo agradáble*, the wise man prefers always the useful to the agreeable; the neuter article is necessary before *útil* and *agradáble*, because those nouns do not express any determinate object. But in the following phrases, *el málo será castigádo*, the wicked shall be punished; *el azúl de éste páño es múy subído*, the blue of this cloth is very lively; one cannot make use of the neuter article, because the nouns substantive that are implied are sufficiently determinate; in truth, it is evident that *hómbre* is understood before *málo*, and *colór* before *azúl*, and in these cases the article takes the gender of the substantive to which it relates.

OF PROPER NOUNS, OR NAMES.

The proper names of men and women, of cities, towns, villages, months, &c. do not take any article, and are declined by the aid of the preposition *de* and *á*. *De* serves for the genitive and ablative, and *á* for the dative and for the accusative before proper names of men and women, and personified objects when governed by an active verb.

DECLENSION OF SOME PROPER NAMES.

N.	Pédro,	*Peter.*	*N.*	Ána,	*Ann.*
G.	de Pédro,	*of Peter.*	*G.*	de Ána,	*of Ann.*
D.	á Pédro,	*to Peter.*	*D.*	á Ána,	*to Ann.*
A.	á Pédro,*	*Peter.*	*A.*	á Ána,*	*Ann.*
Ab.	de Pédro,	*from Peter.*	*Ad.*	de Ána,	*from Ann.*
N.	António,	*Antony.*	*N.*	Lóndres,	*London.*
G	de António,	*of Antony.*	*G.*	de Lóndres,	*of London.*
D.	á António,	*to Antony.*	*D.*	á Lóndres,	*to London.*
A.	á António,*	*Antony.*	*A.*	✗ Lóndres,	*London.*
Ab.	de António,	*from Antony.*	*Ab.*	de Lóndres,	*from London.*

---

* See note, page 31.

OF NOUNS TAKEN IN A PARTITIVE SENSE.

Nouns taken in a partitive sense, often expressed in English by *some, any,* are always without an article in Spanish.

RULE IX. Whenever the noun, taken in a partitive sense, expresses an object vaguely and in an indeterminate sense, it does not take in Spanish a preposition nor an article. Ex. *Dáme pan,* give me bread; *cómo cárne,* I eat meat; *compraré manzánas,* I shall purchase apples; *bébo víno,* I drink wine; *véndo sídra,* I sell cider.

RULE X. When on the contrary the noun is taken *in a determinate sense,* it must be preceded by the genitive of the masculine or feminine article, singular or plural, according to the gender and number to which it belongs, or simply by the preposition *de,* if it does not admit the article. Ex. *Dáme del pan que has comprádo,* give me of the bread that thou hast purchased; *dáme de tu pan,* give me of thy bread. In the second example we use only the preposition *de,* because the possessive pronoun *tu* does not take the article.

RULE XI. If the noun taken in a determinate sense is in the plural, and it should be wished to express only the idea of *some, a few,* this should then be expressed by *únos, únas,* or *algúnos, algúnas;* according to the gender of the noun substantive. Ex. *Comeré únas ó algúnas ciruélas,* I shall eat plums, that is, *some* plums; *he comprádo algúnos líbros,* I have bought a few books, &c. But if the quantity, instead of being limited by the sense of *some,* is absolutely undetermined, then *some* is not expressed. Ex. *tiéne muy buénos líbros,* he has very good books. *Tenémos amígos,* we have friends.

DECLENSION OF THE INDEFINITE ARTICLE *un, úna; a* OR *an* IN ENGLISH.

Singular masculine.

N. & A.	un	amígo, - - -	a	friend.
G. & Ab.	de un amígo,	- - -	of or from a	friend.
D.	á un amígo,	- - -	to a	friend.

Plural.

N. & A.		amígos, - - -		friends.
G. & Ab.	de	amígos, - - -	of or from	friends.
D	á	amígos. - - -	to	friends.

Singular feminine.

N. & A.   úna   mónja, - - - - - - - - a nun.
G. & Ab. de úna mónja, - - - - - - - of a nun.
D.   á úna mónja, - - - - - - to a nun

Plural.

N. & A.   mónjas, - - - - - - - - nuns.
G. & Ab. de   mónjas, - - - - - - - - of nuns.
D.   á mónjas, - - - - - - - to nuns.

General observations upon the Genders.

The proper and appellative names of men, and male animals, as also the nouns that express arts, sciences, dignities,
professions, trades, &c. fit for men, are of the masculine gender; as, *hómbre*, man; *cabállo*, horse; *patriárca*, patriarch;
poéta, poet, &c.

Names of females, and of professions, trades, &c. fit for
females, are of the feminine gender. Ex. *mugér*, woman;
cábra, goat; *costuréra*, seamstress; *abadésa*, abbess, &c.

The names of kingdoms, cities, towns, and villages, generally take, says the Madrid Academy, the gender of the appellative nouns, expressed or understood, to which they refer.
For instance, *Tolédo* and *Madríd* are of the feminine gender,
because the feminine appellative nouns *ciudád* and *villa*, city
and town, are understood, the first before *Tolédo*, and the
second before *Madríd*. *Fuencarrál* is masculine, because
the masculine word *lugár*, village, is understood. The names
Cúba and *Moréa* are of the feminine gender because the appellative *ísla*, island, is understood before the first, and the
word *península*, peninsula, before the last. However, the
Academy adds, some of the names above mentioned, when
they are not joined to the common noun belonging to them,
follow the rule of their termination. Thus *España*, *Suécia*,
and almost all the names of countries ending in *a*, are feminine; *Ferról* and *Viséo* are masculine, though the appellative
noun of the two first be *réino*, kingdom; that of *Ferról*, ciudád, city; and that of *Viséo*, *villa*, town. The same is true
in regard to others, which practice will make known

OF THE GENDER OF NOUNS CONSIDERED WITH REGARD TO THEIR TERMINATIONS.

All nouns ending in *a*, are feminine, except *albacéa*, executor; *anagráma*, anagram; *antípoda*, antipodes; *axióma*, axiom; *clíma*, climate; *crísma*, chrism; *día*, day; *diléma*, dilemma; *diplóma*, diploma; *dógma*, dogma; *dráma*, drama; *epigráma*, epigram; *Etna*, Etna; *fa*, fa, (note of music;) *idióma*, idiom; *léma*, lemma; *maná*, manna; *mápa*, map; *poéma*, poem; *probléma*, problem; *sintoma*, symptom; *sistéma*, system; *sofísma*, sophism; *tapabóca*, slap given on the mouth; *téma*, theme; *teoréma*, theorem; and some others.

All those that terminate in *o*, are masculine, except *máno*, hand; and *náo*, vessel.

Those that terminate in *ción* or *tión*, are of the feminine gender, as *cuestión*, question; *meditación*, meditation; *acción*, action; *objeción*, objection, &c. These words are the same in both languages, except that in Spanish the *t*, of the termination *tion*, of the English word is changed into a *c*, when it has the sound of *sh*.

The nouns that in Spanish terminate in *tad* or *dad*, terminations that correspond to that of the Latin in *tas*, and to that of the English in *ty*, are of the feminine gender; as, *humanidád*, humanity; *puridád*, purity; *adversidád*, adversity. As to the nouns that have other terminations, they are subject to so many exceptions, that it is impossible to establish in regard to them satisfactory rules.

SUBSTANTIVES THAT ARE OF BOTH GENDERS, *according to the decision of the Academy.*

Albalá,	cocket, passport.
Anatéma,	anathema.
Árte,	art.
Azúcar,	sugar.
Canál,	canal.
Císma,	schism
Cútis,	skin
Dóte, dótes,	dowry, endowments
Embléma,	emblem
Hermafrodíta,	hermaphrodite.
Mar,	sea.

Márgen,	-	-	-	-	-	-	-	*margin, bank.*
Néma,	-	-	-	-	-	-	-	*seal*
Néuma,	-	-	-	-	-	-	*significant gesture.*
Órden,	-	-	-	-	-	-	-	*order.*
Puénte,	-	-	-	-	-	-	-	*bridge.*
Réuma,	-	-	-	-	-	-	-	*rheum.*
Tribú,	-	-	-	-	-	-	-	*tribe.*

N. B. Tribú, *tribe*, though of both genders, generally takes the masculine.

OF NOUNS ADJECTIVE.

Formation of the feminine of nouns adjective.

In the Spanish language, as in almost all others, the adjective agrees in gender and number with the substantive to which it relates. It is then necessary to know the manner in which the feminine is formed from the masculine. Of the formation of the plural, we have given the rules, when speaking of the numbers.

Nouns adjective, the termination of which is in *o*, form their feminine by changing *o* into *a*; as *buéno, buéna,* good; *álto, álta,* high, &c.

Those that terminate in the masculine, with any other letter, have generally but one termination for both genders. We say then, *un hómbre alégre,* a merry man; and *úna mugér alégre,* a merry woman; *un hómbre felíz,* a happy man; *úna mugér felíz,* a happy woman, &c.

N. B. The following nouns, terminating in the singular, with a consonant, are excepted from the above rule, the feminine being formed by adding an *a* to the masculine. *Haragán-a,* lazy; *holgazán-a,* idle; *mamantón-a,* a sucking child, *harón-a,* sluggish; *hampón-a,* vain; as also national adjectives, as *Francés-a,* French; *Inglés-a,* English; *Aragonés-a,* Aragonese; *Andalúz-a,* Andalusian, &c. (See in page 195, the table of names of countries, and national adjectives.) Among the adjectives of this last class, some are found that terminate in *a,* and do not undergo any change in the feminine, as *Pérsa,* Persian; *Moscovíta,* Muscovite, &c.

COLLOCATION AND AGREEMENT OF THE ADJECTIVE WITH THE SUBSTANTIVE.

1st. The adjective is generally placed in Spanish after the substantive. However, the Spaniards, like the French, consult taste and harmony in its collocation.

2d. The adjective must always agree in gender and number with the substantive that it qualifies.

3d. When an adjective relates to two singular substantives, it must be put in the plural.

4th. When an adjective serves to qualify in the same phrase several substantives of different genders, it is put in the plural and in the masculine

OF NOUNS DIMINUTIVE AND AUGMENTATIVE.

The Spanish language abounds, like the Italian language, in diminutives and augmentatives.

RULE XII. There are two kinds of diminutive nouns: 1st.—those that express tenderness, or the gentleness of any object whatever that is small; and their termination is in *ito* or *ico* for the masculine, *ita* or *ica* for the feminine, which are added to the nouns, whether adjective, or substantive, without altering any thing in them, when they terminate with a consonant, but suppressing the last letter, if it be a vowel. Ex. *pájaro* bird; *pajarito*, small or pretty little bird; *casa*, house; *casita*, small, or pretty little house; *señor*, sir; *señorito*, young gentleman, or master. From this rule should be excepted *buéno*, *buéna*, the diminutive of which is *bonito*, *bonita*, and which most often has only the meaning of *pretty*.

2. Those which denote contempt or pity, or which lessen the object without adding to it the idea of pretty, are generally terminated in *zuélo*, *illo* or *cillo*, for the masculine, *zuéla*, *illa*, or *cilla* for the feminine, according to the foregoing rule respecting diminutives. Ex. *pérro*, dog; *perrillo*, ugly little dog; *mugér*, woman; *mugercilla*, *mugerzuéla*, contemptible little woman; *hómbre*, *hombrecillo*, *hombrezuélo*, miserable little man.

There are other diminutives terminating in *éte*, *in*, *éjo*, &c. but they are comparatively little used.

RULE XIII. The augmentative nouns add to the positive the signification of the words *big* or *large*, and are formed by adding *on*, *ázo*, *onázo*, or *óte* for the masculine, and *óna*, *áza*, or *onáza*, for the feminine, following the same rule as the diminutives in regard to the termination. Ex. *hómbre*, man; *hombrón*, *hombrázo*, *hombronázo*, big or large man; *mugér*, woman; *mugeróna*, *mugeráza*, *mugeronáza*, big or large woman; *pérro*, dog; *perrón*, *perrázo*, *perronázo*, big or large dog; *gránde*, large; *grandón*, *grandóte*, *grandázo*, *grandonázo*, very big or large and without proportion.

DEGREES OF COMPARISON IN THE ADJECTIVES.

The adjectives may qualify the objects either absolutely, that is, without any relation to other objects, or relatively, that is, with relation to other objects. Hence arise three degrees of qualification, to wit: the *positive*, the *comparative*, and the *superlative*.

The *positive* is the adjective expressed without there being a comparison, as *buéno*, good; *málo*, bad.

The *comparative* serves to establish between the objects that are compared a relation of *superiority*, *inferiority* or *equality*.

The adjective is in the *superlative* when it expresses the quality either in a very high or in the highest degree; which forms two kinds of *superlatives*, the one *absolute*, and the other *relative*.

OF THE COMPARATIVES.

As a comparison may be made, not only by means of adjectives, but also by the aid of substantives, verbs and adverbs, we shall consider the comparatives in these four different cases. The Spanish language participates in this part of the Grammar, with the Latin tongue, and difficulties would doubtless be found in it, should we content ourselves with merely treating of comparatives in relation to adjectives.

OF COMPARATIVES CONSIDERED IN RELATION TO ADJECTIVES

RULE XIV. 1st. The comparative of *superiority* is always expressed by *mas*, more; and the *que* following, by *than*. Ex. He is more learned than you, *él es mas sábio* que *vm.*

2d. The comparative of *inferiority* is formed by *ménos*, less, followed by *que*, than, or by *no-tan*, not so, and the *as* following is rendered by *cómo*. Ex. He is less learned *than* his brother, or he is *not so* learned *as* his brother; *él es ménos dócto que su hermáno*, or *él no es tan dócto cómo su hermáno*.

3d. The comparative of *equality* is formed by *tan-cómo*, as-as; or *no-ménos que*, not less-than. Ex. You are as prudent *as* your sisters, *vm. es tan prudénte cómo sus hermánas*, or, you are *not less* prudent *than* your brothers, *vm. no es ménos prudénte que sus hermános*.

N. B. The following nouns are comparatives from their nature: *mayór*, larger, greater; *menór*, lesser, smaller; *mejór*, better; *peór*, worse; *superiór*, superior; *inferiór*, inferior. We also say, *el mayór*; *el menór*; *el mejór*, *el peór*; the largest, the greatest; the least, the smallest; the best, the worst; but then these adjectives become relative superlatives.

COMPARATIVE OF SUPERIORITY.

Of the comparative in relation to substantives, verbs, and adverbs.

RULE XV. This comparative before the substantive, the adverb, and after the verb, is rendered by *mas-que*, more-than, and admits no preposition after it. Ex. He has more prudence than you, *tiéne mas prudéncia que vm.*; she has more science than money, *tiéne mas ciéncia que dinéro*; we have more enemies than he, *tenémos mas enemígos que él*; I esteem thee more than Mary, *te estímo mas que á María*; we act more prudently than they, *obrámos mas prudénteménte que éllos*.

N. B. The foregoing rule perfectly agrees with the English construction.—*More than, less than*, followed by a noun of number, *one, two, three*, &c. are translated by *mas de* and *ménos de*. Ex. She has more than ten guineas, *tiéne mas de diéz guinéas*; she has more than seven brothers, *tiéne mas de siéte hermános*; we have less than a thousand dollars, *tenémos ménos de mil pésos*; less than 20 years, *ménos de 20 áños*.

Comparative of Inferiority.

RULE XVI. 1st. This comparative, considered in relation to substantives, may be expressed by *less* or *fewer-than*, or by *so much* or *so many-as*, preceded by the negative *not*.

Less-than is rendered by *ménos-que*. Ex. Less prudence than, *ménos prudéncia que*; fewer friends than, *ménos amígos que*, &c.—*Not so much* or *so many-as*, is expressed by *no-tánto,-a,-os,-as,—cómo*, according to the gender and number of the noun to which, *so much, so many* relate. Ex. I have not so much money as you, *no téngo tánto dinéro cómo vm.*; Peter has not so much ambition as John, *Pédro no tiéne tánta ambición cómo Juán*; Francis has not so

4 *

many books as his brother, *Francisco no tiéne tántos libros cómo su hermáno.*

2d. In relation to verbs; *less-than* is expressed by *ménos-que*; *not-so much* is expressed by *no-tanto*, and *as*, by *cuánto* or *cómo.* Ex. I do not love him *so much* as I esteem him, *no le quiéro tánto cuánto* or *cómo le estímo;* you study *less than* we, *vm. estúdia ménos que nosótros.*

3d. In relation to adverbs; *less-than* is rendered by *ménos-que,* and *not-so* or *not-so-as* by *no-tan-cómo.* Ex. They act less prudently than you, or they do not act so prudently as you, *óbran ménos 'prudénteménte que vm.,* or *no óbran tan prudénteménte cómo vm.*

N. B. Before participles passive, *so much-as; as much-as,* are rendered by *tan-cómo.* Ex. He is not so much esteemed as he, *no es tan estimádo cómo él.*—I am as much loved as she is, *sóy tan amádo cómo élla.*

Comparative of Equality.

RULE XVII. 1st. The comparative of equality, considered in relation to nouns substantive, is expressed by *as much-as, as many-as,* or by *not less-than.* *As much, as many,* is translated by *tánto,-a-os-as,* according to the gender and number of the substantive, and the following *as* by *cómo.* Ex. She has as much meekness as her sister, *tiéne tánta dulzúra cómo su hermána;* he acts with as much rigour as justice, *óbra con tánto rigór cómo justícia.* *Not less-than* is rendered by *no ménos-que.* Ex. I am not less hungry than you, *no téngo ménos hámbre que vm.;* we have not fewer protectors than friends, *no tenémos ménos protectóres que amígos.*

2d. In regard to verbs; *as much as* is expressed by *tánto cuánto* or *cómo.* Ex. I punish him as much as he deserves, *le castígo tánto cuánto* or *cómo meréce.*

Not-less than is always translated by *no-ménos que.* Ex. You do not eat less than his brother, *vm. no cóme ménos que su hermáno.*

3d. In relation to adverbs: *as-as* is rendered by *tan-cómo.* Ex. He sings as well as you, *cánta tan bién cómo vm.*

Not-less-than is translated by *no-ménos-que.* Ex. I do not write less correctly than he, *no escríbo ménos corréctamónte que él.*

Of Superlatives.

There are two kinds of superlatives, the one absolute and the other relative.

RULE XVIII. The first expresses a quality in the supreme degree, but without comparison, and then the adjective is preceded by *múy*, very; and if the adjective can form its superlative of itself, then, without having recourse to *múy*, we add to the positive *ísimo*, or *ísima*, *ísimos* or *ísimas*, according to the gender and number of the substantive to which it refers, cutting off the final letter of the adjective, if it ends with a vowel. Ex. Paris is a very beautiful city. *París es úna ciudád múy hermósa* or *hermosísima*.

The superlative absolute of adverbs is likewise formed by *múy*, or by changing *eménte* or *aménte* into *ísimaménte*. Ex *Prudént-eménte*, prudently, *prudent-ísimaménte*; *cándid-aménte*, candidly, *candíd-ísimaménte*.

N. B. 1st. It is proper to observe that there are adjectives and adverbs which do not admit the last form of the superlative; consequently when a doubt occurs whether it may be used with any adjective or adverb, the *surest way* will be to make use of *múy*, very, with the positive.

N. B. 2d. From the general rule of absolute superlatives must be excepted a few adjectives that cannot be subjected to it, as, *buéno*, good; *bonísimo*, very good; *fuérte*, strong; *fortísimo*, very strong. All those that terminate in *ble* change that syllable into *bilísimo*, for the superlative. Ex. *Amá-ble*, amiable, *ama-bilísimo*; *afáble*, *afa-bilísimo*. The following nouns are superlatives in their nature; *óptimo*, *pésimo*, *máximo*, *mínimo*, *ínfimo*, *suprémo*, very good, very bad, very great, very small, very low, supreme.

RULE XIX. The superlative relative expresses a quality in the highest degree, by comparison with other objects, and it is formed in English by one of these articles or pronouns, *the, of,* or *from the, to the; my, thy, his, her, its, our, your, their,* followed by *most, least, best, worst;* and in Spanish by one of these; *el, la, los, las; del, de la, de los* or *de las; al, á la, á los* or *á las; mi, tu, su, nuéstro, vuéstro, su, sus,* followed by *mas, ménos, mejór, peór;* and these articles and pronouns must agree in gender and number with the noun to which they relate. Ex. The most pure and constant pleasures, *los mas púros y constántes placéres*.

The adverb forms its superlative relative by *lo mas*, the most; *lo ménos*, the least; both which must always precede it. *Lo* is here a neuter article. *Lo mas sensible*, the most sensible.

Observations upon the Comparatives and Superlatives.

RULE XX. The comparatives govern the verb that follows the *que, than*. Ex. He is more learned than he appears, *él es mas dócto que paréce*, or *de lo que paréce*.

RULE XXI. When the substantive, to which the adjective in the superlative relative refers, is preceded by the definite article and is immediately followed by the adjective, then the article is not repeated before *mas* nor the adjective. Ex. He was prepared to deal the most terrible marks of his resentment, *quedó en disposición de usár de las demonstraciónes mas terríbles de su resentimiénto* (*Feijóo.*) But if the substantive is not immediately followed by *mas*, most, then the article must be repeated. Ex. *El hómbre que véo es el mas dócto*, the man I see is the most learned.

RULE XXII. The superlative relative governs the verb that follows the *que* in the indicative. Ex. The most powerful prince that has been, *el príncipe mas poderóso que ha habido*.

If, however, the verb, in English, is in the potential, we put it indifferently in the second or third conditionals. Ex. The best that he could find, *el mejór que hallàse* or *hallára*.

And if it is in the future, we put it in the future conjunctive, or in the present of the subjunctive. Ex. The least that I can or shall be able, *lo ménos que puéda* or *pudiére*. .

RULE XXIII. *Most* and *least* joined to a verb are rendered by *mas* and *ménos*. Ex. He is the man that I most love, *él es el hómbre que mas quiéro*.

This is the woman that I least esteem, *ésta es la mugér que menos estímo*.

RULE XXIV. 1st. *The more-the more*, (that is, *the more* repeated in different members of a sentence, the second being as a consequence of the first,) are expressed by *cuánto mas-tánto mas*. The more virtuous man is, the more happy he is, *cuánto mas virtuóso es el hómbre, tánto mas es feliz*.

2d. *The less-the less; the more-the less; the less-the more* are expressed by *cuánto ménos-tánto ménos; cuánto mas-tánto ménos; cuánto ménos-tánto mas*.

3d. *So much the more than, so much the less than,* are translated by *tánto mas que, tánto ménos que.*

Adjectives of number are words that serve for enumeration. We call them adjectives because their office is to modify, and because every noun that modifies is an adjective.
They are distinguished into two kinds, the *cardinals* and
ordinals.

The *cardinals* serve to designate absolutely and simply the
various numbers; the *ordinals* mark the order of persons or
things in relation to the numbers.

The cardinal numbers are;

úno, úna,	- - - - -	one,
dos,	- - - - -	two,
tres,	- - - - -	three,
cuátro,	- - - - -	four,
cínco,	- - - - -	five,
séis,	- - - - -	six,
siéte,	- - - - -	seven,
ócho,	- - - - -	eight,
nuéve,	- - - - -	nine,
diéz,	- - - - -	ten,
ónce,	- - - - -	eleven,
dóce,	- - - - -	twelve,
tréce,	- - - - -	thirteen,
catórce,	- - - - -	fourteen,
quínce,	- - - -	fifteen,
diéz y séis,	- - -	sixteen,
diéz y siéte,	- - - -	seventeen,
diéz y ócho,	- - -	eighteen,
diéz y nuéve,	- - - -	nineteen,
véinte,	- - - - -	twenty,
véinte y úno,	- - - -	twenty-one,
véinte y dos,	- - - -	twenty-two,
véinte y tres,	- - - -	twenty-three,
véinte y cuátro,	- - - -	twenty-four,
véinte y cínco,	- - - -	twenty-five,
véinte y séis,	- - - -	twenty-six,
véinte y siéte,	- - - -	twenty-seven,
véinte y ócho,	- - - -	twenty-eight,

véinte y núeve,	-	-	twenty-nine,
tréinta,	-	-	thirty,
cuarénta,	-	-	forty,
cincuénta,	-	-	fifty,
sesénta,	-	-	sixty,
seténta,	-	-	seventy,
ochénta,	-	-	eighty,
novénta,	-	-	ninety, .
ciénto,	-	-	a or one hundred,
dosciéntos-as,*	-	-	two hundred,
tresciéntos-as,	-	-	three hundred.
cuatrociéntos-as,	-	-	four hundred,
quiniéntos-as,	-	-	five hundred,
seisciéntos-as,	-	-	six hundred,
seteciéntos-as,	-	-	seven hundred,
ochociéntos-as,	-	-	eight hundred,
noveciéntos-as,	-	-	nine hundred,
mil,	-	-	a or one thousand,
dos mil,	-	-	two thousand,
mil y ciénto,	-	-	eleven hundred,
mil y dosciéntos-as,	-	-	twelve hundred,
cién mil,	-	-	a or one hundred thousand,
dosciéntos-as mil,	-	-	two hundred thousand,
millón,	-	-	million.

N. B. This last number is not an adjective, it belongs to the class of substantives.

priméro-a,†	-	-	first,
segúndo-a,	-	-	second,
tercéro-a,	-	-	third,
cuárto-a,	-	-	fourth,
quínto-a,	-	-	fifth,
sésto-a,	-	-	sixth,
séptimo-a,	-	-	seventh,
octávo-a,	-	-	eighth,
nóno-a,	-	-	ninth,
décimo-a,	-	-	tenth,
undécimo-a,	-	-	eleventh,
duodécimo-a,	-	-	twelfth,

* The masculine termination os is changed into as for the feminine.
† Priméro, m. priméra, f. &c.

décimo tércio, décima tércia,	thirteenth,
décimo cuárto, décima cuárta,	fourteenth,
décimo quínto, décima quínta,	fifteenth,
décimo sésto, décima sésta, -	sixteenth,
décimo séptimo, décima séptima,	seventeenth,
décimo octávo, décima octáva,	eighteenth,
décimo nóno, décima nóna, -	nineteenth,
vigésimo-a, - - -	twentieth,
vigésimo prímo-a-a, - -	twenty-first,
vigésimo segúndo-a-a, - -	twenty-second,
vigésimo tércio-a-a, - -	twenty-third,
trigésimo-a, - - -	thirtieth,
cuadragésimo-a, - - -	fortieth,
quincuagésimo,-a - - -	fiftieth,
sexagésimo-a, - - -	sixtieth,
septuagésimo-a, - - -	seventieth,
octogésimo-a, - - -	eightieth,
nonagésimo-a, - - -	ninetieth,
nonagésimo prímo, &c.-a-a, -	ninety-first,
centésimo-a, - - -	a or one hundredth,
ducentésimo-a, - - -	two hundredth,
trecentésimo-a, - - -	three hundredth,
cuadragentésimo-a, - -	four hundredth,
quingentésimo-a, - - -	five hundredth,
sexcentésimo-a, - - -	six hundredth,
septengentésimo-a, - -	seven hundredth,
octogentésimo-a, - - -	eight hundredth,
nonagentésimo-a, - - -	nine hundredth,
milésimo-a, - - - -	a or one thousandth,
antepenúltimo-a, - - -	antepenultima,
penúltimo-a, - - -	penultima,
último-a, postréro-a, - -	last.

Besides these two kinds of numbers, there are yet three others that belong to the class of substantives; these are the *collective, distributive* and *proportional.*

The *collective* numbers serve to denote determinate quantities, as, *a dozen,* úna docéna; *half a dozen,* úna média docéna; *a hundred of,* úna centéna; *a thousandth,* un millár; *a million,* un millón or cuénto.

The *distributive* serve to denote the different parts of a whole; as, the *half,* la mitád; the *third,* el tércio; *a fourth,* úna cuárta, &c

The *proportional* are those that serve to denote the pro
gressive increase of the number of things; as, the *double*, el
dúplo; the *quadruple*, el cuadrúplo; the *hundred fold*, el
centúplo, &c.

N. B.   All the cardinal numbers are indeclinable, except
úno, one, and the compounds of *ciénto;* for, we say *úno,
úna, dosciéntos, dosciéntas*, &c.   The ordinals form their
feminine by changing *o* into *a*, as adjectives.

ADJECTIVES WHICH, JOINED TO A SUBSTANTIVE, LOSE ONE OR MORE LETTERS IN THE SINGULAR ONLY.

RULE XXV. 1st. *úno*, one; *priméro*, first; *tercéro*, third;
postréro, last; *algúno*, some; *ningúno*, none; *buéno*, good;
and *málo*, bad, wicked, when they are followed by a substantive, lose the last vowel, but only in the masculine.   Ex
Un hómbre, one man; *el primér hómbre*, the first man, &c.
However, *tercéro* does not always lose it; for we say, *el
tercér día* or el *tercéro* día; and both manners of speaking are
admitted by the Academy.

2d. *Ciénto*, hundred, loses the last syllable in the singular
before a substantive.   Ex. *Cién hómbres*, a hundred men;
cién mugéres, a hundred women.

3d. *Gránde*, great, large, loses the last syllable before a
substantive masculine which begins with a consonant, whenever it signifies *great in merit, in qualities;* but if it only has
the signification of *large in extent, in dimensions*, or if the substantive that follows it begins with a vowel or an h, it loses
none of its letters.   We therefore say, *úna gran mugér*, a great
woman; *un gran cabállo*, a noble horse, if to these words
great, noble, we attach the idea of great in merit, in qualities;
but we must say, *úna gránde cása*, a large house; *un gránde
amígo*, a great friend; *un gránde almiránte*, a great admiral;
úna gránde hormíga, a large ant.

4th. *Sánto*, saint, loses only the last syllable before a proper
name masculine, but not before the feminine.   Ex. *San Pédro,
San Francísco; Santa María*, &c.   We except however from
this rule *Sánto Domíngo, Sánto Tomás, Sánto Toríbio*, and
Sánto Tomé.

N. B.   1st. It is not necessary, in order that this suppression of letters should take place, that the adjective be immediately followed by the substantive; for, if we must say
un hómbre, un libro, we must also say, *un hábil hómbre, un*

buén líbro, although in these examples *un* be separated from its substantive by an adjective.

If the substantive is not expressed, the adjective that relates to it, does not then lose any letter. Ex. *úno ó dos hómbres,* one or two men; *úno de ésos señóres,* one of those gentlemen. In the first example, the substantive *hómbre* is understood after *úno,* and in the second the word *señór;* thus we cannot say *un ó dos hómbres, un de ésos señóres.*

N. B. 2d. Whenever the word *ciénto* takes after it another number, it preserves all its letters: we must then say, *ciénto y dos, ciénto y cinco, ciénto y nuéve hómbres,* and not *cién y dos, cién y cinco, cién y nuéve hómbres.*

N. B. 3d. In speaking of sovereigns, and in quotations, we generally make use of ordinal numbers as in English, but the article *the* is not expressed in Spanish. Ex. Henry the Fourth, *Enrique Cuárto;* Chapter the Seventh, *Capítulo Séptimo.*

N. B. 4th. When in English the cardinal numbers are followed by *o'clock, hóra,* and one wishes to tell or ask the hour of the day, then the cardinal number must be preceded by the article *la* before *úna, hóra* is understood, and *las* before the other numbers, *hóras* being implied, and the expression *o'clock* is suppressed; and if the verb *to strike,* expressed in English, is translated into Spanish, it is rendered by *dar.* Ex. What o'clock is it? *que hóra es?* one o'clock, *la úna;* three o'clock, *las tres;* four o'clock, *las cuátro;* it has struck five o'clock, *las cinco han dádo;* it has just struck six o'clock, *las séis acában de dar;* seven o'clock is about striking, *las siéte están pára dar.*

Twelve o'clock at noon is translated by *las dóce, las dóce del día,* or *médio dia;* and *midnight* by *las dóce de la nóche,* or *média nóche.* In the following examples and others like them, *afternoon* is translated by *de la tárde,* and *in the evening* by *de la nóche.* Ex. At five o'clock in the afternoon, *á las cinco de la tárde;* at eight o'clock, at ten o'clock in the evening, *á las ócho, á las diéz de la nóche;* at six o'clock in the morning, *á la séis de la mañána;* at four o'clock in the morning, *á las cuátro de la mañána.*

N. B. 5th. The verb *it is,* taken impersonally in English in some of the preceding examples and the like, is not impersonal in Spanish; it agrees on the contrary in number with the noun *hóra, hour* understood, and the pronoun *it*, is never expressed. Ex. It is one o'clock, *es la úna;* it was two o'clock, *éran las dos;* it is half after three, *son las tres y média;* it wants a quarter of four, *son las cuátro ménos cuárto.*

N. B. 6th. In speaking of the days of the month, if we express the word *día*, day, it must be preceded by the article, and followed by the ordinal or cardinal number, but most commonly by the cardinal. Ex. The twelfth of January, *el dia dóce de Enéro.* If we suppress the word *día*, then we make use of the cardinal number, preceded by the preposition *á* or *en*. Ex. We are at the twelfth of January, *estámos á* or *en dóce de Enéro*. We also say *el priméro, el segúndo, &c. de Enéro*, and then the word *día* is understood; we never say el *úno* for the *first* of any month, but *priméro.*

DATES. *Madríd y Febréro* 20 *de* 1822. *Cambrigia,* 20 *de Júlio de* 1824. *Boston, á* 1.º *de* 7.*bre* 1827.

CHAPTER V.

OF PRONOUNS.

PRONOUNS hold the place of nouns, recall the idea of them, and prevent their repetition, which would render the speech languid. They are divided into *personal, possessive, demonstrative, relative, interrogative,* and *indefinite.*

OF PRONOUNS PERSONAL.

Pronouns personal denote persons, or hold the place of persons or personified things. Such, for the first person of the singular, are *yó, me, mí*, I, me; and, for that of the plural, *nos, nosótros, nosótras*, we, us. For the second person—sing. *tú, te, tí*, thou, thee;—Plur. *vos; vosótros, vosótras, os*, ye or you.

For the third person.—Sing. masc. *él*, he, him or it.—Masc. plur. *éllos*, they, them.—Fem. sing. *élla*, she or it; fem. plur. *éllas*, they or them.—Sing. masc. and fem. *le*, to him, to her, him. (*Le* is of both genders when it is in the dative, and of the masculine only, when in the accusative.) Sing. fem. *la*, her; plur. masc. and fem. *les*, to them; plur. masc. *los*, them; plur. fem. *las*, them.

There is another pronoun of the third person, which is *sí*, oneself, *se*, himself, herself, itself; it is of the three genders. In English *oneself* cannot relate but to the singular; *sí* in Spanish may be employed with both numbers without varying its termination. It is called reflective, because it denotes the relation of a person or thing to him, to her, or itself.

Among personal pronouns some are used only of persons, and others are used alike of persons and things. Those of the first person are only applied to persons or personified things; those of the third are indifferently used of persons and things.

Pronouns may be *nominatives*, and of the *direct* or *indirect regimen*.

They are *nominatives* when they are the subjects of the proposition. In this phrase, *yó háblo*, I speak; *yó*, I, is a pronoun nominative, because it is the subject of the proposition.

A pronoun is a *direct regimen*, when it is the object of the action expressed by the verb; and it is an *indirect regimen* when it is the end of the action expressed by the verb. In these phrases, *Diós le castigará*, God will punish him; *mi pádre te dará su opinión*, my father will give thee his opinion; *le* is the direct regimen, because it is the object of the punishment expressed by the verb *castigará*; and *te* put for *á tí* is the indirect regimen, because, instead of being the object of the action expressed by the verb *dará*, it is the end of it; the object is the thing given, that is, *his opinion*, and the end is the person to whom the opinion is to be given, that is, *to thee*.

Declension of personal pronouns.

PRONOUNS OF THE FIRST PERSON.

Singular of both genders.				Pron. as regimen.*				
N.	yó	-	-	*I.*				
G.	de mí,	-	-	*of me.*				
D.	á mí,	-	-	*to me.*	me,	-	-	-	*to me.*
A.	á mí,	-	-	*me.*	me,	-	-	-	*me.*
Ab	de mí,	-		*from me.*				

---

* We give to these pronouns the denomination of *pronouns used as a regimen*, (objective pronouns, direct and indirect,) because it appears to be more intelligible and conformable to true principles.

Plural masculine.   *Pron as Regimen.*

N	nos,* nosótros,	-	*we.*			
G.	de nosótros,	-	*of us.*			
D.	á nosótros,	-	*to us.*	nos,	- -	*to us.*
A.	á nosótros,	-	*us.*	nos,	- -	*us.*
Ab.	de nosótros,		*from us.*			

Plural feminine

N.	nos,* nosótras,	-	*we.*			
G.	de nosótras,	-	*of us.*			
D.	á nosótras,	-	*to us.*	nos,	- -	*to us.*
A.	á nosótras,	-	*us.*	nos,	- -	*us.*
Ab.	de nosótras,		*from us.*			

SECOND PERSON.

Singular of both genders.

N.	tú,†	-	-	*thou.*		
G.	de tí,	-	-	*of thee.*		
D.	á tí,	-	-	*to thee.*	te,	- - *to thee.*
A.	á tí,	-	-	*thee.*	te,	- - *thee.*
Ab.	de tí,	-		*from thee.*		

Plural masculine.

N.	vos,‡ vosótros,	*ye or*	*you.*			
G.	de vosótros,	-	*of you.*			
D.	á vosótros	-	*to you.*	os,	- -	*to you.*
A.	á vosótros,	-	*you.*	os,	- -	*you.*
Ab.	de vosótros,		*from you.*			

---

* *Nos* is only used by the King, Dignitaries, and Superior Officers and Tribunals in church and state, in their official capacity.

† We seldom use the pronoun *tú* in Spanish. However, masters use it in speaking to their domestics; man and wife; parents in speaking to their children, brothers to brothers, lovers to lovers, and friends to their friends; but except in these cases, it is not used in good company, and we make use for both genders of *ustéd* for the singular, and of *ustédes* for the plural, putting the following verb in the third person. *Ustéd* is an abbreviation of *vuéstra mercéd*, which signifies *your favour*, and *ustédes*, an abbreviation of *vuéstras mercédes, your favours*. If these pronouns are followed by an adjective that relates to them, this adjective must always take the gender of the person to whom we speak. Ex. Sir, are you well? *señór está vm. buéno?* Madam, I have been told that you are well, *señóra, me han dícho que vm. está buéna.* In conversation we pronounce *ustéd* and *ustédes*, but we write *vm.* and *vms.* (See Abbrev. page 12.)

‡ *Vos* is used with the Deity, Holy Virgin, Saints, Sovereigns and persons of high rank; and superiors use it also instead of *tú* with their inferiors.

Plural feminine.

Pron. as Regimen.

N.	vos, vosótras,	-	*you.*			
G.	de vosótras,	-	*of you.*			
D.	á vosótras.	-	*to you.*	os,	- -	*to you.*
A.	á vosótras,	-	*you.*	os,	- -	*you.*
Ab.	de vosótras,		*from you.*			

THIRD PERSON.

Singular masculine.

N.	él,*	-	-	*he, it.*		
✗ *G.*	de él,†	-	*of him, of it.*			
D.	á él,	-	*to him, to it.*	le, se,	- -	*to him.‡*
A.	á él,	-	-	*him, it.*	le, lo, - -	*him.‡*
✗ *Ab.*	de él,	*from him, from it.*				

Plural masculine.

N.	éllos,	-	-	*they.*		
G.	de éllos,	-	-	*of them.*		
D.	á éllos,	-	-	*to them.*	les, se, -	- *to them.‡*
A.	á éllos,	-	-	*them.*	les, los, -	- *them.‡*
Ab.	de éllos,	-	*from them.*			

---

* Instead of the pronouns of the third person singular and plural, masculine and feminine, if we address one or many persons to whom we owe much respect, we make use of *su merced*, and *sus mercédes*. Ex. *Su merced está buéno; sus mercédes están buénos*, you are well.

† Formerly we used to suppress the *e* of the preposition *de*, before *él* pronoun, as *dél, délla, déllos, déllas;* now this contraction is rejected by the Academy; it is suppressed before *el*, article. (See the note, page 26.)

‡ As it is easy to confound, in the use of these pronouns, those of the dative with those of the accusative, and as the Spaniards themselves confound them frequently, we have thought the following observations necessary.

A verb may have two regimens, one direct, and the other indirect. (See the difference of these two regimens, p. 55.) If the pronoun is the direct regimen, as in these phrases, *I see him, I respect her, I love them,* all these pronouns are in the accusative, and we must say, *lo véo, la respéto, los* or *las quiéro.* But, if it is the indirect regimen, as in the following phrases, *he wrote to him a letter, I gave them good advice,* the pronouns are in the dative, and we must say in Spanish, *le escribió úna cárta, les di buénos conséjos. Le, les,* serve in the dative or indirect case for both genders.

Singular Feminine.

Pron. as Regimen.

N.	élla, - - *she, it.*	
G.	de élla, - *of her, of it.*	
D.	á élla, - *to her, to it.* le, se, - - *to her* ‡	
A.	á élla, - - *her, it.* le, la, - - *her.* ‡	
Ab.	de élla, *from her, from it.*	

Plural Feminine.

N.	éllas, - - *they.*
G.	de éllas, - - *of them.*
D.	á éllas, - - *to them.* les, se, - - *to them.* ‡
A.	á éllas, - - *them.* les, las, - - *them.* ‡
Ab.	de éllas, - *from them.*

PRONOUN REFLECTIVE.

N.	se, - - - *one, people.* (Indef. Pronoun.)
G.	de sí, *of oneself, himself, herself,*
	itself, themselves.
D.	á sí, *to oneself, himself, herself, &c.* se, *to himself, &c.*
A.	á sí, - - - *oneself, &c.* se, *himself, &c.*
Ab.	de sí, - - *from oneself, &c.*

N. B. 1st. When the word *mismo, self,* is united to this pronoun, it agrees in gender and number with the noun or nouns to which the pronoun relates, as *sí mísmo, sí mísma,* &c. Ex. *Ellos háblan de sí mísmos,* they speak of themselves; *éllas se condénan á sí mísmas,* they condemn themselves.

N. B. 2d. *Se,* one, we, they, people, is often used as a nominative to the verb. Ex. *Se piénsa,* people think, or rendered by the passive voice; as, it is thought; *Se díce,* people say, or it is said.

N. B. 3d. The pronouns *mí, tí, sí,* ME, THEE, ONESELF, preceded by the preposition *con,* WITH, are changed in Spanish into *mígo, tígo, sígo,* which are united to the preposition. Ex. *conmígo,* with me; *consígo,* with him, with her, with them.

TABLE OF PRONOUNS AS REGIMEN OR OBJECTIVE.

		Dative,	Accusative
1st pers. sing. masc. and fem.	*to me, me,*	me,	me.
1st pers. plur. masc. and fem.	*to us, us,*	nos,	nos.
2d pers. sing. masc. and fem.	*to thee, thee,*	te,	te.
2d. pers. plur. masc. and fem.	*to you, you,*	os,	os.

‡ See the note on the preceding page.

		Dative.	Accusative.
3d.pers.sing.masc.& neut.	*to him, to it, him, it,*	le, se,	le, lo.
3d. pers. plur. masc.	*to them, them,*	les, se,	les, los.
3d. pers. sing. fem.	*to her, her,*	le, se,	le, la.
3d. pers. plur. fem.	*to them, them,*	les, se,	les, las.
3d. pers.pron.reflect.sing. & plur. masc. & fem.	*to himself, herself, itself, themselves.* }	se,	se.

ON THE CONSTRUCTION OF PRONOUNS AS REGIMEN, OR OBJECTIVE.

RULE XXVI. The PRONOUNS AS REGIMEN, *me, nos; te, os; le, lo, les, los; la, las, se,* must be placed after the verb, whenever it is in the *infinitive, imperative,* or a *gerund;* and in these cases they are united close to the verb, so as to form with it, at least in appearance, a single word. Ex. *No quiéro dárlo,* I will not give it; *dálo,* give it; *dándolo,* in giving it.

In all other cases, the general rule requires that they be placed before the verb. Ex. *Te digo,* I tell thee; *le escribirá,* he will write to him. We however find examples of *pronouns used as regimen* placed after verbs in other modes and tenses than those mentioned in the preceding rule; as, *digolo,* I say it; *harélo,* I shall do it; *sucédeme múchas véces,* it often happens to me. But as it is practice that must determine the propriety of this construction, it is best for the scholar to follow the general rule, until well versed in the language.

RULE XXVII. The *pronouns of indirect regimen,* TO HIM, TO HER, TO IT, and TO THEM, when they are accompanied by one of the pronouns of the direct regimen, *lo, la, los, las,* must be translated by *se.* Ex. *Se lo, se la daré,* I will give it to him, to her, to it, to them.

RULE XXVIII. We use also very elegantly the same pronoun *se,* when, besides the pronouns of direct regimen, *lo, la,* &c. the verb has a noun for an indirect regimen, and then *se* is merely an expletive. Ex. *Se lo prométo á vm.,* I promise it to you; *se* and *á vm.* stand for *to you* or *to your favour* separately, therefore it is a repetition to give clearness and force to the idea, often used in Spanish.

RULE XXIX. This pronoun *se* is also frequently used in Spanish to express the passive of verbs, as in these phrases; *se movió la tiérra,* the earth was shaken; *la tempestád se apaciguó,* the tempest was appeased; *se dóbla ó repíte el clamór*, the cries are increased or repeated. In these phrases *se* denotes that the verbs have a passive signification, though they retain the active termination. This is like the Latin; *terra movit; tempestas sedavit; clamor ingeminat.*

RULE XXX. When the pronoun *nos*, us, is a direct regimen, and is used immediately after the verb that governs it in the accusative, this verb, if it is in the first person of the plural, loses its final *s*. Ex. *Divertímonos*, we amuse ourselves; *amámonos*, we love one another; and in the imperative mode, if the second person of the plural is followed by *os*, you, it loses the *d*. Ex. *Cubríos*, cover yourselves

N. B. To give more clearness and energy to the phrase, we frequently place the pronoun, in Spanish, when it is the object of the action, both before and after the verb; and in this case one of the pronouns is always without the preposition, and the other is always preceded by the preposition *á*; as in the following phrases; *le estíman á él*, they esteem him; *me han escríto á mí*, they have written to me; *yó á tí no te quiéro*, I do not love thee. Also, when the verb has no other regimen but *you*, if this pronoun is rendered by *vuéstra mercéd*, or *vuéstras mercédes*, we often elegantly place before the verb one of these pronouns *le, lo, la, les, los, las*, according to the gender and number of the person or persons which the pronoun represents, and according to the case the verb governs. Ex. *No le básta á vm. el pretendér...* it is not sufficient for you to pretend ... *Yá lo han dícho, señóra; jamás la visitarán á vm.;* they have said it, madam; they never will visit you.

OF PRONOUNS POSSESSIVE.

The *pronouns possessive* serve to denote the possession of an object. They follow the rules of adjectives.

In order to render the use of these pronouns more clear and striking, we distinguish them into two kinds; those that are always joined to a noun and do not take an article; as *mi, tu, su,* &c. my, thy, his, &c. Ex. *Mi pádre*, my father; *tu mádre*, thy mother; *su hijo*, his son: and those that are not joined to the noun, and take the article: as, *el mío, el túyo, el súyo,* &c. mine, thine, his, &c.

OF PRONOUNS POSSESSIVE THAT ARE ALWAYS JOINED TO
NOUNS

These pronouns denote possession, either as respects one person or many.

Those which, in Spanish, relate only to one person, are, in the singular, *mi*, my; *tu*, thy; and in the plural, *mis*, my; *tus*, thy.

Those which denote that the possession relates to many, are *nuéstro*, masculine, *nuéstra*, feminine; *nuéstros*, masculine, *nuéstras*, feminine, our; *vuéstro*, masculine, *vuéstra*, feminine, your. For the third person in the singular, *su*, his, her, or their; and in the plural *sus*, his, her or their; and these pronouns of the third person may, in Spanish, relate to one possessor, or to many.

DECLENSION OF PRONOUNS POSSESSIVE.

N. B. The declension of these pronouns presenting no difficulty, it will be sufficient to decline the first and give the nominative of the others. They take no article.

SINGULAR AND PLURAL.

Masculine and feminine.

N.	mi, *sing.*	-	-	mis, *plur.*	-	-	-	my.
G.	de mi,	-	-	de mis,	-	-	-	of my.
D.	á mi,	-	-	á mis,	-	-	-	to my.
A.	mi, á mi,	-	-	mis, á mis,	-	-	-	my.
Ab.	de mi,	-	-	de mis,	-	-	-	from my.

When this pronoun *my* is used in calling, in addressing a person, or in exclamations, instead of *mi*, *mis*, we make use of *mío*, *mía*, *míos*, *mías*, without an article; they are placed after the noun to which they refer, and take its gender and number. Ex. *Amigo mío*, my friend; *hija mía*, my daughter; *amigos míos*, my friends, *hijas mías*, my daughters, &c.

SINGULAR AND PLURAL.

Masculine and feminine.

Tu,	-	-	-	tus,*	-	-	-	-	*thy.*
su,	-	-	-	sus,†	-	-	-	*his, her, its.*
nuéstro,	-	-	-	nuéstra, os, as,		-	-	*our.‡*
vuéstro,	-	-	-	vuéstra, os, as, -		-	-	*your.‡*
su,	-	-	-	sus,	-	-	-	-	*their.*

OF PRONOUNS POSSESSIVE NOT JOINED TO NOUNS.

These pronouns admit the masculine, feminine, and neuter termination, and relate, as well as the preceding, to one or more persons. Those that relate to a single person, are; *el mío,* masc. *la mía,* fem. sing *los míos,* masc. *las mías,* fem. plural, mine; *el túyo* masc. *la túya,* fem. sing. *los túyos, las túyas,* fem. plural, thine.

---

* We have said when speaking of personal pronouns, page 52, that *tú* and *vos* are not used in good society. It is the same with the possessive pronouns *tu* and *vuestro,* in the place of which we make use of *de vm.* in speaking to one person, and of *de vms.* in speaking to several: and we place before the noun substantive one of these articles *el, los, la, las,* according to the gender and number of the noun. Ex. Your son, that is, the son of your favour, or of your favours, *el hijo de vm.* or *de vms. (vm.* if we speak only to the father or to the mother; *vms.* if we speak to both.)

† When we speak of a person for whom we wish to show much respect, instead of *su* we make use of *su Merced, su Señoría, su Esceléncia,* according to the rank of the person; and such a phrase as the following; I have seen the Corregidor, and hope to obtain his protection (that is the protection of *his favour,*) is rendered in Spanish, *he visto al señór Corregidór, y espéro merecér la protección de su mercéd.*

‡ Though the pronouns *nuéstro* and *vuéstro* seem as though they ought to express the idea of more than one person, it happens sometimes that they relate only to one; for the king says *Nuéstro conséjo,* our council; and in speaking to a person distinguished for his rank and authority, we make use of *vuéstro, vuéstra.* We say for example, *Vuéstra Magestád, vuéstra Beatitúd, vuéstra Ilustrísima, vuéstra Altéza,* &c. Your Majesty, your Holiness, your Grace, your Highness, &c. We use the same pronouns *vuéstro* and *vuéstra,* in speaking to God, to the Holy Virgin, and the Saints. When *your* is turned by *of your favour* or *of your favours, de vm.* or *de vms.* we frequently use the pronouns *su* and *sus,* instead of the article before the substantive. Ex. *He recibído su cárta* (or *sus cártas*) *de vm.* or *de vms.* I have received your letter or your letters; i. e. the letter of your worship or worships, of your favour or favours.

Those that relate to several persons, are *el nuéstro*, masc. *la nuéstra*, fem. sing. *los nuéstros*, masc. *las nuéstras*, fem. plural, ours; *el vuéstro*, masc. *la vuéstra*, fem. sing. *los vuéstros*, masc. *las vuéstras*, fem. plural, yours; *el súyo*, masc. *la súya*, fem. his, hers, theirs; *los súyos*, masc. *las súyas*, fem. his, hers, theirs.

N. B. These pronouns are always preceded by the noun to which they relate, and with which they agree in gender and number; this noun is that which represents the object possessed, and not the possessor.*

The following declension will serve as a rule for those pronouns that are declined with the article.

DECLENSION OF THE PRONOUN, MÍO.

Singular masculine and feminine.

N.	el mío,	-	-	la mía,	-	-	*mine.*
G.	del mío,	-	-	de la mía,	-	-	*of mine.*
D.	al mío,	-	-	á la mía,	-	-	*to mine.*
A.	el *or* ál mío,	-	-	la mía *or* á la mía,	-	*mine.*
Ab.	del mío,	-	-	de la mía,	-	*from mine.*

Plural masculine and feminine.

N.	los míos,	-	-	las mías,	-	-	*mine.*
G.	de los mios,	-	-	de las mías,	-	-	*of mine.*
D.	á los míos,	-	-	á las mías,	-	-	*to mine.*
A.	los míos, *or* á los mios,		las mías, *or* á las mías,	*mine.*
Ab.	de los míos,	-	-	de las mías,	-	*from mine.*

The following pronouns are to be declined in the same manner.

Singular masculine and feminine.

el túyo,	-	-	-	la túya,	-	-	*thine.*
el súyo,	-	-	-	la súya,	-	*his, hers.*
el nuéstro,	-	-	-	la nuéstra,	-	-	*ours.*
el vuéstro,	-	-	-	la vuéstra,	-	-	*yours.*
el súyo,	-	-	-	la súya,	-	-	*theirs.*

* This rule requires a particular attention, because the English most always cause these pronouns to agree with the possessor and not with the object possessed. Ex. *Is that your sister's book ? No, it is mine ; here is hers ; hers*, pronoun, refers to *sister*, and not to *book;* in Spanish, on the contrary, we must say : *es éste el libro de su hermána de vm.?—No, es el mío; he aquí el súyo; súyo* is in the masculine because it refers to *libro* and not to *hermána*.

Plural masculine and feminine.

los túyos,	-	-	las túyas,	-	-	*thine.*
los súyos,	-	-	las súyas,	-	-	*his, hers.*
los nuéstros,	-	-	las nuéstras,	-	-	*ours.*
los vuéstros,	-	-	las vuéstras,	-	-	*yours.*
los súyos,	-	-	las súyas,	-	-	*theirs.*

N. B. With the neuter article we say, *lo mío*, what is mine; *lo túyo*, what is thine, &c. as with the adjectives.

RULE XXXI. These last pronouns, *mío, túyo, &c.* sometimes accompany a substantive, principally in exclamations, or when they are used in addressing a person, but then the substantive precedes the pronoun, and does not take an article. Ex. Father! *pádre mío!* mother! *mádre mía!* come, friend, &c. *ven, amigo mío, &c.*

RULE XXXII. When the verb *to be*, is taken in the sense of *to belong*, we use in Spanish as in English the possessive pronoun *mío*, mine, *túyo*, thine, &c. without the article, but this pronoun in Spanish agrees in gender and number with the thing possessed of which we speak. Ex. This book is mine, *éste líbro es mío;* this house is thine, his, theirs, ours, &c. *ésta cása es túya, súya, nuéstra, &c.*

N. B. 1st. When the verb *to be*, taken in the sense of *to belong*, is followed or preceded by another pronoun or by a noun, this noun or pronoun must be put in the genitive. Ex. This book is Mr. B's, *éste líbro es del señór B.;* this horse is my brother's, *éste cabállo es de mi hermáno;* whose house is this, *de quién es ésta cása?* (see the pronoun *cúyo*, Rule XXXIV, page 63.)

N. B. 2d. This same observation will apply to the possessive pronoun *yours*, after the verb *to be*, when instead of *vuéstro*, we should wish to employ *vm.* and *vms.* (*vuéstra mercéd* and *vuéstras mercédes*,) *your favour* and *your favours.* Thus, in this phrase; this book is yours; if I express *yours* by *de vm.*, I must say, *éste líbro es de vm.*, sing., *de ustédes*, plural.

RULE XXXIII. To translate *of mine, of thine, of his, &c.* the Spaniards use commonly the possessive pronouns *mío, túyo, súyo, &c.* placed as in English, but without the preposition *of.* Ex. A brother of his, *un hermáno súyo;* a friend of mine, *un amigo mío;* an uncle of his, of hers, of theirs, *un tío súyo.*

OF PRONOUNS DEMONSTRATIVE.

Pronouns demonstrative indicate, and place, as it were, under the eye, the person or the thing of which they hold the place. They are divided into three kinds.

The following pronoun designates the object that is neaı the person that speaks.

Singular maculine and feminine.

Este,   -   ésta, -   -   -   -   -   -   *this.*

Plural masculine and feminine.

Éstos,   -   éstas, -   -   -   -   -   -   *these.*

Neuter.

Ésto,   -   -   -   -   *this, this thing, any thing.*

N. B. We find in ancient authors, *aquéste, aquésta, aqués-tos, aquéstas, aquésto,* instead of *éste, ésta, &c.*

If the object is more distant from the person that speaks, than from the one to whom the speech is addressed, we make use of the following pronoun;

Singular masculine and feminine.

Ése,   -   ésa, -   -   -   -   -   -   *that.*

Plural masculine and feminine.

Ésos,   -   ésas, -   -   -   -   -   -   *those.*

Neuter.

Éso,   -   -   -   -   *that, that thing, any thing*

N. B. We also find *aquése, aquésa, aquésos, aquésas, aquéso,* for *ése, ésa, &c.*

The pronouns that follow, express a more distant object, both from the person who speaks, and from him to whom the speech is addressed.

X *Singular masculine and feminine.* X

Aquél, él,   aquélla, la,   -   *he, that,*   *she, that.*

Plural masculine and feminine.

Aquéllos, los, aquéllas, las,   -   -   *they,*   -   *those.*

Neuter.

Aquéllo,   éllo, lo,   -   -   -   *that,*   -   *it.*

There are also three other pronouns which are compounded of the preceding and of the adjective *ótro, ótra,* other. Viz

6

Masculine and feminine, singular and plural.

Estótro, estótra,	estótros, estótras,	*this other,*	*these others.*
Esótro, esótra,	esótros, esótras,	*that other,*	*those others.*
Aquél ótro, aque-lla ótra,	aquéllos ótros, a-quéllas ótras,	*that other,*	*those others.*

Neuter.

Estótro, esótro,   aquéllo ótro,   -   *this and that other.*

N. B. *He who, she who, they who,* or *that,* are translated by, él que *or* quién, la que, los *or* las que; or by aquél que, aquélla que, aquéllos *or* aquéllas que; and *that of,* by él de, aquél de; la de, aquélla de, &c.; and lo de, aquéllo de, by *that of, the thing of.*

What or *that which,* are translated by *lo que, aquéllo que.*

OF PRONOUNS RELATIVE.

Pronouns relative are those that relate to a noun or pronoun which precedes. Some take the article, others do not. The following do not take the article.

Singular masculine and feminine.

N.	que, quién,*	-	-	-	-	-	*who, that, which.*
G.	de quién,	-	-	-	-	*of whom, whose, &c.*
D.	á quién,	-	-	-	-	-	*to whom.*
A.	á quién *or* que,	-	-	-	-	-	*whom.*
Ab.	de quién,	-	-	-	-	-	*from whom.*

Plural masculine and feminine.

N.	que, quiénes,†	-	-	-	-	*who, that, which.*
G.	de quiénes,	-	-	-	-	*of whom, whose, &c.*
D.	á quiénes,	-	-	-	-	-	*to whom.*
A.	á quiénes,	-	-	-	-	-	*whom.*
Ab.	de quiénes,	-	-	-	-	-	*from whom.*

Neuter.

lo que,	-	-	-	-	-	-	*that which, what.*
de lo que,	-	-	-	-	-	-	*of what.*
á lo que,	-	-	-	-	-	-	*to what.*

* *Quién* and *quiénes* are applied only to persons and personified things ; *que* both to persons and things.

† We also use *quién* in the plural number, says the Grammar of the *Academy,* and it gives the following examples. *Los priméros con quién topámos éran los gimnosofistas,* the first whom we met were the gymnosophists. *Aquéllos siéte sábios á quién tánto veneró la Grécia,* those seven sages so much venerated by the Greeks.

N. B. *Whose* is translated by the pronoun *cúyo, cúya, cúyos, cúyas,* following the gender and number of the thing possessed, by which this pronoun *cúyo* must be immediately followed, if it is relative, but from which it is commonly separated by the verb, when it is interrogative. It always agrees with the object possessed, and never with the possessor.

CÚYO, CÚYA, CÚYOS, CÚYAS.

RULE XXXIV. The pronoun *cúyo* is relative and interrogative, and is used for *whose, of which;* but care should be taken to observe, as has been already said, that it agree with the thing possessed, and not with the possessor, and is applicable in Spanish to persons as well as to things. Ex. Whose book is this? *cúyo es éste libro?* Whose pens are those? *cúyas son ésas plúmas?* She is a lady whose qualities are known, *es úna señóra cúyas préndas son conocídas.* London the streets of which are so wide, *Lóndres cúyas cálles son tan ánchas.*

RULE XXXV. When the pronoun *that*, preceded by a noun or pronoun to which it relates, may be rendered by *of whom, in whom, by whom, for whom,* &c. it must be expressed by *de quién, á quién, en quién, por quién,* &c. Ex. It is of oneself that one ought to be afraid, *de sí mismo es de quién se ha de tenér miédo,* that is, *of whom,* &c. It is to God that we must have recourse, *es á Dios á quién es precíso de acudir,* that is, *to whom, &c.*

ANOTHER PRONOUN RELATIVE.

This pronoun is sometimes declined with the article and stands for animate and inanimate things.

Singular masculine and feminine.

N.	el cuál,	- -	la cuál,	- -	*which.*
G.	del cuál,	- -	de la cuál,	- -	*of which*
D.	al cuál,	- -	á la cuál,	- -	*to which*
A.	el cuál, al cuál,	-	la cuál, á la cuál,	-	*which*
Ab.	del cuál,	- -	de la cuál,	-	*- from which.*

Plural masculine and feminine.

N.	los cuáles,	- -	las cuáles,	- -	*which.*
G.	de los cuáles,	-	de las cuáles,	-	*of which*
D.	á los cuáles, -	-	á las cuáles, -	-	*to which*
A.	los cuáles, á los cuáles,	las cuáles, á las cuáles,	*which.*
Ab.	de los cuáles,	-	de las cuáles,	*- from which.*

Neuter.

N.	lo cuál, &c. -	-	-	-	*which, which thing.*

OF PRONOUNS INTERROGATIVE.

Pronouns interrogative are those which serve to interrogate, and are declined as follows.

Singular masculine and feminine.

N.	quién,	-	-	-	-	-	-	who.
G.	de quién,	-	-	-	-	-	-	of whom
D.	á quién,	-	-	-	-	-	-	to whom.*
A.	quién, á quién,	-	-	-	-	-	-	whom.
Ab.	de quién,	-	-	-	-	-	from whom.

Plural masculine and feminine

quiénes, &c. &c.   -   -   -   -   -   who

Neuter.

N.	que,	-	-	-	-	-	-	what.
G.	de que,	-	-	-	-	-	-	of what
D.	á que,	-	-	-	-	-	-	to what.
A.	que,	-	-	-	-	-	-	what.
Ab.	de que,	-	-	-	-	-	-from what.

Which? separate from the noun, is translated by *cuál, cuáles,* of both genders. Ex. You have read these books; which of the two do you prefer? *Vm. ha leído éstos libros, cuál de los dos prefiére? Cuál es su óbra?* Which is his work?

What, immediately followed by a noun, is rendered by *que* of both genders and numbers. Ex. What book do you read? *que libro lées?* What o'clock is it? *que hóra es?* What fruits will you buy? *que frútas comprará vm? Que hómbre ha rísto vm.?* What man have you seen?

Wherein is rendered by *en que.*

OF PRONOUNS INDEFINITE.

These pronouns are thus called, because they express an object vague and indeterminate. All those that are placed in this class are not always pronouns, strictly so called, but become adjectives when they are joined with nouns, and present some particulars which it is essential to make familiar.

---

* See Rule XXXIV, page 63, for the pronoun *cúyo,-a, os,-as.*

Nobody,	- - - - - -	*nádie, ningúno.*
None.	- - - - - -	*ningúno, ningúna.*
No, not any, (followed by a noun,) -		*ningúno, ningúna.*
Not one,	- - - - - -	*ni úno, ni úna.*
Neither,	- -	{ *ni úno ni ótro, ni úna ni ótra;* plural, *ni únos ni ótros, ni únas ni ótras.*
Both,	- - -	{ *ámbos-as, entrámbos, ámbos á dos;* *úno y ótro, úna y ótra;* plural, *únos y ótros, únas y ótras.*
Each, every, -	- - - - - - -	*cáda.*
Each one, every one,	- - -	*cáda úno, cáda úna.*

Every body, *Tódos*. *Otro, ótra,* another; *ótros, ótras,* others.

One another,	- -	{ *úno ótro, úna ótra ;* plural, *únos* *ótros, únas ótras.*
Of others,	- -	{ *de ótro, de ótros.* To others, *á ótro, á* *ótros;* and if *of others* is governed by a substantive, it is then translated by *agéno, agéna, agénos, agénas,* ac- cording to the gender and number of the noun to which it relates; as, the property of others, *el bién agéno, &c.*
Some one, somebody,	- - - -	*alguién, algúno.*
Some, (relating to a noun,)	- - -	*algúno-a, os-as.*
Some, (always joined to a noun,)		*únos, únas, algúnos, algúnas.*
Many; several,	- -	*múchos, múchas; vários, várias.*
Whosoever, whatsoever,	*cualquiér-a,* plur. *cualesquiéra.*	
Whoever, whosoever,	- - - -	*quienquiéra.*
Whenever,	- - - - - -	*siémpre que.*
Whatever,	- -	*cualquiéra-que; por mas que.*
However, howsoever,	*cualquiéra cósa que; por múcho que.*	

These pronoun govern the subjunctive.

Even, yet,	- - - - - -	*mismo, aún.*
Such a one,	- - - - -	*fuláno, a; zutáno, a.*
One says, *or it is said,*	- - -	*dicen or se* díce.*
They assure, *or it is assured,*	-	*Se asegúra or asegúran.*
People believe, *or it is believed,*	- -	*créen or se crée.*

OBSERVATIONS UPON THE INDEFINITE PRONOUNS.

RULE XXXVI. *Any one* and *any body* in interrogative phrases, or in phrases implying doubt, must be expressed in Spanish by *úno, algúno.* Of all those who know the motives of my conduct is there *any one* who has blamed it? *de tódos los que conócen los motívos de mis acciónes, hay acáso úno ó algúno que las háya condenádo?* I doubt that *any one* has blamed it, *dúdo que* algúno *la háya condenádo.* I doubt that *any one* be as wise as he, *dúdo que* algúno *séa tan sábio cómo él,* &c. This office suits him better than *any one else; éste empléo le conviéne mejór que á* cualquiér ótro.

RULE XXXVII. *Nobody, no person whatever,* is translated by *ningúno, nádie;* and *nothing whatever* is translated by *náda.* Ex. *Nobody whatever* has spoken ill of you to me, nádie *me ha habládo mal de vm.* Whatever genius one may have, one cannot, without application, excel in *any thing whatever, por mas* or *por múcho ingénio que úno ténga, en* náda *puéde sobresalír sin aplicación.*

RULE XXXVIII. In Spanish the following pronouns *nobody, none, not one, neither, nothing; nádie, ningúno, ni úno, ni úno ni ótro, náda,* require that the verb be preceded by the negative *no,* when they are placed after it; but this negative is suppressed when they precede it. Ex. He cannot excel in any thing, *en náda puéde sobresalír,* or *no puéde sobresalír en náda;* the first construction is the most elegant.

N. B. The adverbs *jamás, núnca,* never, follow the same rule.

CHAPTER VI.

OF VERBS.

The *verb* is that part of speech which is essentially the bond of our thoughts, the soul of all our reasonings, and the only one that has the property of pointing out the relation that they have with the present, past and future. Its office is to express actions, passions and situations.

There are six kinds of verbs, to·wit; the *active, passive, neuter, reflective, reciprocal* and *impersonal.*

The *active* verb is that of which the regimen is direct, or after which one may put *algúno, algúna cósa,* some one, some thing. *Amár,* to love, is an *active* verb, because we may say, *amár á algúno,* to love some one, *amár la virtúd,* to love virtue, and because in these two phrases the regimen is direct. *Buscár*, to seek, is also an *active* verb, because we may say, *buscár á algúno, buscár algúna cósa*, to seek somebody, to look for something.

The *passive* verb is that which is formed from the *active*, takes the direct regimen to form its subject, and always is followed by one of these prepositions, POR or DE; as, *el hómbre virtuóso es amádo* DE *tódos*, the virtuous man is loved by every body.

The *neuter* verb is that after which we cannot put *some one*, nor *some thing*, *algúno, algúna cósa*. *Existír, dormír*, to exist, to sleep, are neuter verbs, because we cannot say: *dormír á algúno, dormír algúna cósa*, to sleep some one, to sleep something.

The *reflective* verb is that of which the subject and the regimen are the same person, or *that* which is conjugated with two pronouns of the same person, expressed or understood; *Arrepentírse*, to repent, is a reflective verb, because in order to conjugate it, we must make use of two pronouns, and say; yo me *arrepiénto*, tú te *arrepiéntes*, él se *arrepiénte*, &c. or, me *arrepiénto*, te *arrepiéntes*, se *arrepiénte*, &c. (and then *yo, tú, él*, are understood,) I repent, thou repentest, he repents, &c.

The *reciprocal* verb* is that which expresses the action of several subjects that act one upon the other. Ex. *Los verdadéros amígos dében amárse y servírse únos á ótros*, true friends must love and serve one another.

The *impersonal* verb is that which is used, in all its tenses, only in the third person of the singular. *Tronár*, to thunder, is an impersonal verb, because it has in each tense only the third person. We say, *truéna, tronába, tronó, tronará*, &c. it thunders, it did thunder, it thundered, it will thunder; but we cannot say, I thunder, thou thunderest, we thunder, unless it be in a figurative sense.

Verbs may be *regular, irregular*, or *defective.*

The regular verbs, in the Spanish language, are those of which the radical letters are always the same, and of which

---

* In order that the verb should clearly express reciprocity, it is often necessary to add to it the following words, *úno á ótro, mútuamente, á porfía*, one another, mutually, in emulation of one another. In this phrase, *Cicero y António no dejában de alabárse úno á ótro*, Cicero and Anthony did not cease to praise one another; if we should not put *úno á ótro* there would be an equivocation which would leave a doubt of the reciprocity of the action.

the terminations are, in all the tenses, conformable to those of the verb that serves as a model for them.

We call those irregular which vary in the radical letters, or which do not agree, in all the tenses, with the terminations of the verb, that serves as a model.

N. B. We understand by *radical letters* those which precede the termination of the infinitive. We reckon only three conjugations in Spanish, the first has the infinitive terminated in *ar*, as *amár*, to love; the second has it in *er*, as *temér*, to fear; the third has it in *ir*, as *subír*, to go up. In these verbs all the letters that precede *ar*, *er*, and *ir*, that is, *am*, *tem*, and *sub*, are radical, and those that follow them in all the tenses, as well as in all the persons, form the terminations.

Lastly, we call those verbs defective, that want certain tenses or certain persons, which use does not admit.

There are besides *auxiliary* verbs, so called, because they serve to conjugate the others. The Spanish language reckons three, to wit; *habér* and *tenér*, to have; and *ser*, to be.

OF CONJUGATION.

To conjugate a verb, is to collect or recite all its terminations, as *ámo*, *ámas*, *áma*, &c. I love, thou lovest, he loves, &c.; *amába*, *amábas*, *amába*, &c. I did love, thou didst love, he did love, &c.

These different terminations form *modes*, *tenses*, *numbers* and *persons*.

OF MODES.

Modes are different manners of using the verb. There are five, *infinitive*, *indicative*, *conditional*, *imperative* and *subjunctive*.

The *infinitive* expresses indefinitely, and in a general manner the action or state that the verb designates. The infinitive is consequently neither susceptible of number nor person, as, *amár*, *temér*, *subír*, to love, to fear, to go up.

The *indicative* points out and indicates in a direct and absolute manner what we affirm of a person or thing, as, *ámo y témo al Diós que me crió, y cúya justícia recompensará á los buénos, y castigará á los málos;* I love and fear the God who created me, and whose justice will reward the good, and punish the wicked.

The *conditional* is the manner of expressing the affirmation depending upon a condition; as, *yo leería si tuviéra líbros*, I *should read* if I had books, *yo hubiéra escríto úna cárta ántes de comér, si no hubiése tenído la visíta del señór Cónde de Floridablánca*, I should have written a letter before dinner, if I had not had a visit from Count *de Floridablanca*.

The *imperative* expresses the action of commanding, praying or exhorting. This mode has but one tense that designates the present in relation to the action of commanding, and the future in relation to the thing commanded; as, *dáme éste líbro, give* me this book. *Veníd mañána, come* to-morrow. *Hágame vm. el favór de . . . do* me the favour of . . . This tense has no first person in the singular, because we do not command ourselves; but it has in the plural, because then it is rather others than ourselves that we address.

The *subjunctive* is a mode which, in order to make sense, requires to be preceded by another verb, expressed or understood, on which it depends. It depends upon it, because it makes sense with, and would not make any without it. These words, *quisiéra que viniése*, I should wish that he came or would come, make sense; but these, *que viniése*, that he came, alone and separate, would not make any.

OF TENSES.

We shall follow, in the division of tenses, the method received by the most esteemed and approved grammarians; and in order to obviate the very serious difficulties which the three futures and the three conditionals of the Spanish verbs present, we have thought it best to deviate from the plan followed by the Academy of Madrid. This plan may be excellent for the Spaniards who join, to the study of grammar, a constant practice; but it is too obscure for foreigners, as it deviates too much from the usage of other languages, and contains rules which are not sufficiently particular. Therefore, instead of comprising the two futures conjunctive, the second and third conditional in the subjunctive, we shall place the two futures in the indicative, we shall make a mode of the conditional that will have three terminations, and the subjunctive will have the tenses that it commonly has in other languages. This order has appeared to us the most proper to render obvious the relations that exist between the Spanish and English languages. (See N. B. 2d. &c. page 80.)

OF THE TENSES OF THE INFINITIVE.

The tenses of the infinitive are the *present*, the *preterite*, the *gerund* and the *participle*.

The present of the infinitive always designates the present time relative to the preceding verb; as, *le véo corrér*, I see him run; *le oí cantár*, I heard him sing; *le veré bailár*, I shall see him dance.

The preterite on the contrary denotes the past time relative to the preceding verb; as, *creia habérle vísto*, I thought I had seen him; literally, I thought to have seen him.

The gerund designates,—1st,—the state of the subject, the reason or foundation of the action, as in these phrases: *cánta durmiéndo*, he sings in his sleep; *el emperadór de Alemánia, temiéndo que la paz no duráse múcho tiémpo, licenció múy pócas trópas*, the emperor of Germany, fearing that the peace would not last long, disbanded only a few troops. In the first example, *durmiéndo*, expresses the state of the subject; and in the second, *temiéndo* expresses the reason or grounds of the action of the emperor.

2d. It denotes a manner or a mean of attaining an end, and then it is almost always preceded by the preposition *en*, in. Ex. *No espére el hómbre ser jamás felíz en dejándose arrastrár de sus pasiónes, no lo puéde ser sinó en dominándolas.* Let man never expect to be happy in giving himself up to his passions, he can only be so by subduing them.

3d. It serves to express a condition. Ex. *Siéndo ésto así, volveré á Fráncia*, this being so, I shall return to France.

4th. It is frequently used with the verb *estár*, to be, to show in a more positive manner that an action is, was, has been or will be done at the very time of which we speak. Ex. *Está escribiéndo*, he is writing; *estába escribiéndo*, he was writing; *estará escribiéndo*, he will be writing.

The *participle* is thus called, because it participates in the nature of the verb and that of the adjective. It is of the nature of the verb, because it has its signification and regimen. It is of the nature of an adjective, because it expresses a quality.

The *participles* are divided into present and past; into the present; as, *amánte, obediénte, oyénte;* into past;—as, *amádo, obedecído, oído*. The *participles of the present* have the termination in *ante*, as *amánte* for the first conjugation. Those of the second and third have it in *énte*, as *obediénte*, *oyénte*.

The participles present are in use only in part of the verbs; the greater part being rather verbal adjectives than participles, because they have not a regimen as their verbs. Ex *Oyénte*, hearing; *leyénte*, reading; are verbal adjectives, because we cannot say, *oyénte el sermón*, *leyénte líbros*, usage not permitting us to give a regimen to these participles.

The participles past of regular verbs have their terminations in *ádo*, for the first conjugation; and in *ído*, for the second and third. Those that do not follow this rule are irregular, and are found in their place in the alphabetical list which is subjoined. (See page 122.)

There are some verbs which have two participles past, the one regular and the other irregular. The first is always employed with the auxiliary verb *habér*, to have; the second is never joined to it, but follows the rule of adjectives, except *ingérto*, grafted; *préso*, caught; *prescríto*, prescribed; *provísto*, provided and *róto*, broken; which are used with the auxiliary *habér* just as well as the regular participle.

VERBS THAT HAVE TWO PARTICIPLES.

		Part. Regular.	Part. Irregular.
Ahitár,	*to surfeit,*	ahitádo,	ahíto.
Bendecír,	*to bless,*	bendecído,	bendíto.
Compelér,	*to compel,*	compelído,	compúlso.
Concluír,	*to conclude,*	concluído,	conclúso.
Confundír,	*to confound,*	confundído,	confúso.
Convencér,	*to convince,*	convencído,	convícto.
Convertír,	*to convert,*	convertído,	convérso.
Despertár,	*to awake,*	despertádo,	despiérto.
Elegír,	*to choose, to elect,*	elegído,	elécto.
Enjugár,	*to wipe,*	enjugádo,	enjúto.
Escluír,	*to exclude,*	escluído,	esclúso.
Espelér,	*to expel,*	espelído,	espúlso.
Espresár,	*to express,*	espresádo,	espréso.
Estinguír,	*to extinguish,*	estinguído,	estínto.
Fijár,	*to fix,*	fijádo,	fíjo.
Hartár,	*to satiate,*	hartádo,	hárto.
Incluír,	*to include,*	incluído,	inclúso.
Incurrír,	*to incur,*	incurrído,	incúrso.
Insertár,	*to insert,*	insertádo,	insérto.

		Part. Regular.	Part. Irregular.
Invertír,	to transpose,	invertído,	invérso.
Ingerír,	to ingraft,	ingerído,	ingérto.
Juntár,	to join,	juntádo,	júnto.
Maldecír,	to curse,	maldecído,	maldíto.
Manifestár,	to manifest,	manifestádo,	manifiésto.
Marchitár,	to wither,	marchitádo,	marchíto
Omitír,	to omit,	omitído,	omíso.
Oprimir,	to oppress,	oprimído,	opréso.
Perfecionár,	to perfect,	perfecionádo,	perfécto.
Prendér,	to seize, to arrest,	prendído,	préso.
Prescribír,	to prescribe,	prescribído,	prescríto.
Proveér,	to provide,	proveído,	provísto.
Recluír,	to confine,	recluído,	reclúso.
Rompér,	to break,	rompído,	róto.
Soltár,	to loosen or release,	soltádo,	suélto.
Suprimír.	to suppress,	suprimído,	supréso

There are other participles, the termination of which is passive and the signification active; such as the following.

Acostumbrádo,	-	-		accustomed
Agradecído,	-	-	-	grateful.
Atrevído,	-	-	-	bold.
Bién cenádo,	-	-	-	who has supped well.
Bién comído,	-	-	-	who has dined well.
Bién habládo,	-	-	-	who speaks well, well spoken.
Calládo,	-	-	-	discreet.
Cansádo,	-	-	-	tiresome.
Comedído,	-	-	.	prudent.
Desesperádo,	-	-	-	in despair.
Disimulado,	-	-	-	dissembling, hypocritical.
Entendído,	-	-	-	intelligent.
Esforzádo,	-	-	-	brave, intrepid.
Fingído,	-	-	-	deceitful, artful. [formed.
Leído,	-	-	-	who has read much, well in-
Medído,	-	-	-	cautious, circumspect
Mirádo,	-	-	-	prudent, regardful.
Moderádo,	-	-	-	moderate.
Negádo,	-	-	-	destitute of intelligence
Ocasionádo,	-	-	-	quarrelsome.
Osádo,	-	-	-	daring, undaunted,
Parádo,	-	-	-	slow, heavy.

Parecído,	-	-	-	resembling.
Partído,	-	-	-	liberal, who shares what he has.
Pausádo,	-	-	-	deliberate.
Porfiádo,	-	-	-	obstinate, stubborn.
Preciádo,	-	-	-	vain, presumptuous.
Precavído,	-	-	-	cautious.
Presumído,	-	-	-	presumptuous.
Recatádo,	-	-	-	considerate, discreet.
Sabído,	-	-	-	learned.
Sacudído,	-	-	-	rough, untractable.
Sentído,	-	-	-	sensitive, susceptible.
Sufrído,	-	-	-	enduring, patient.
Trascendído,		-	-	penetrating, keen-minded.
Valído,	-	-	-	confident, favourite.

All the participles have also a passive signification, and it is the sense of the phrase that determines which of the two significations we must adopt. We see, for example, that in these expressions, *hómbre leído,* a well read man; *mugér leída,* a well read woman; *libro leído,* a book that has been read; *cárta leída,* a letter that has been read; the participles *leído, leída,* have an active signification, when they refer to *hómbre* and to *mugér;* and passive, when they refer to *libro* and to *cárta.* Thus, if I say, *Pédro es un hómbre cansádo,* and *Pédro está cansádo de trabajár,* we see by the different use of the two verbs, *es, está,* (See upon these two verbs the Rule XLIX, page 95,) that the first of these phrases signifies, Peter is a *tiresome* man, and the second, Peter is *tired* of working.

OF THE TENSES OF THE INDICATIVE.

The Spaniards reckon eight tenses in the indicative, which are the *present,* the *imperfect,* the *preterite definite,* the *preterite indefinite,* the *preterite anterior,* the *pluperfect,* the *future absolute,* and the *future anterior.* We shall place in continuation of these two futures, the *future conjunctive simple,* and the *future conjunctive compound,* (though it seems they should belong to the subjunctive or conjunctive mode) so as the better to compare them together; and exhibit the difference between them. In the conjugation of the *irregular verbs,* we place the *future conjunctive* in its natural place in the subjunctive mode. This method will give ten tenses to the indicative in the regular conjugations.

7

The *present* denotes that a thing is, or is done at the moment we speak; as, *sóy*, I am; *ámo*, I love; *súbo*, I go up.

The *imperfect* denotes the past with relation to the present, and makes known that a thing was present in a past time; as, *yó escribia*, or *estába escribiéndo cuándo mi hermáno llegó*, I did write, or I was writing when my brother arrived.

The *imperfect* serves also to denote habitual actions, or actions often repeated in a past time; as, *yó iba á la comédia él áño pasádo dos véces cáda semána*, I went (used to go) last year to the play twice a week.

It serves also to express the qualities, either good or bad, of men who are no more; as, *Nerón éra un tiráno*, Nero was a tyrant; *Enríque cuárto éra un réy benéfico*, Henry the Fourth was a beneficent king.

The *preterite* may designate, either in a precise or only in a vague and indeterminate manner, that a thing has been done.

Thence arises two preterites; the *preterite definite* and the *preterite indefinite*. The *preterite definite* denotes a thing done at a time of which nothing more remains; as, *escribí ayér*, I wrote yesterday; *comí el lúnes último en cása del señór Pitt*, I dined on Monday last at the house of Mr. Pitt.

The *preterite indefinite* denotes a thing done at a time designated in an indeterminate manner, or at a time past but of which something yet remains; as, *la muérte de tu hermáno me ha afligído múcho*, the death of thy brother has afflicted me much; *he recibído ésta semána muchísimas visitas*, I have received this week a great many visits.

These two preterites cannot be indifferently used one for the other, it is essential to perceive clearly the difference that exists between them. In order that we may use the preterite definite, it is at least necessary that the time elapsed of which we speak should be a *whole* day; as, *fui ayér á la comédia*, I went yesterday to the play; *ví al réy la semána pasáda*, I saw the king last week. We cannot therefore say, *estudié ésta mañána; escribí hóy, ésta semána, éste mes, éste áño*, &c.; I studied this morning, I wrote to day, this week, this month, this year, &c. because the morning, the day, the week, the month, the year, are not entirely elapsed. On the contrary, in order that we may use the *preterite indefinite*, there must yet remain some part of the time past of which we speak; as, *he visto ésta mañána al primér pintór del réy de España,* I have seen this morning the first painter of the king of Spain; *hémos visto grándes evéntos en éste síglo,* we have seen great events in this century.*

There is still another preterite which is called *preterite anterior,* because it expresses a thing past before another in a time past; as, *después que húbe visto al réy, salí de Madrid,* after I had seen the king, I went out of Madrid.—This *preterite* is only used after the adverbs of time, *después que, luégo que, así que, cuándo,* after, as soon as, so soon as, when.

The *pluperfect* is compounded of two past tenses. It denotes a thing not only as past in itself, but also as past in regard to another thing which is also past; as, *yo había yá cenádo cuándo entró,* I already had supped when he came in.

N. B. The futures, as well as the conditionals, presenting to strangers considerable difficulty, we request them to pay to the following rules a particular attention.

OF THE FUTURES.

There are in the Spanish language four futures; the future simple or absolute; the future compound or anterior; the future conjunctive simple, and the future conjunctive compound.

The future absolute denotes that a thing will be, or will be done at a time which is yet to come; as, *sí, amaré siémpre al Diós que me crió,* yes, I shall always love the God who created me.

N. B. This future has often the signification of the *imperative,* in the second person; as, *amarás á Diós de tódo tu corazón,* thou shalt love God with all thy heart; *no robarás,* thou shalt not steal.

The *future anterior* denotes the future with relation to the past, making known that, at the time a thing will happen, another shall be past; as, *habré acabádo mi cárta cuándo tal ó tal cósa sucéda,* I shall have finished my letter when such or such a thing shall happen.

These two futures differ in this, that in the *future absolute* the time may or may not be determined; as, *iré, ó iré mañána á Bristól,* I shall go, or I shall go to-morrow to Bristol. On the contrary, in the future anterior, the period is neces-

---

* The above is the most proper way; however, Spaniards often use the Pret. Definite as in English for a period of time not entirely elapsed; as, *le encontré esta mañána,* I met him this morning, &c.

sarily determined; as, *habré comído cuándo vm. llégue*, I shall have dined when you arrive.

The *future conjunctive*, which is so called because it is always joined either to a conjunction or an adverb, or to a pronoun that governs it, serves to denote a future action always expressed in English by the present of the indicative, when the verb is preceded by the conjunction *si* or *cuándo*, if or when; sometimes by the present of the subjunctive when the verb is preceded by a conjunction that governs it in this mode, as, *ojalá, con tal que, así que, luégo que, dádo que, puésto que*, &c. and often by the future absolute or anterior.

Rules for using the future conjunctive.

RULE XXXIX. We use the future conjunctive when the verb is governed by the conjunction *si*, if; and when the phrase expresses a future action; as, *no te dígo que vívas, ni que muéras; víve si* PUDIÉRES, *y muére, si no* PUDIÉRES *mas*, I do not tell thee to live or to die; live, if thou canst; die, if thou canst not do better.

RULE XL. We make use of the future conjunctive whenever the verb is preceded by one of the pronouns *él que, los que, la que, las que, lo que*, he who, she that, &c.; or by the adjective *cuánto, a, os, as*, used in the sense of *tódo él que, tóda la que, tódos los que, tódas las que, tódo lo que; quién, quiénes*, (a pronoun relative) when it is used in the sense of one of the above pronouns *él que, los que*, &c. and finally, when the verb is governed by the adverb *cuándo*, if these pronouns, and this adjective and adverb are themselves preceded by another verb expressing an action, which the remainder of the phrase causes to depend on choice or chance; as, *elige, pués, de éstos 'dos partídos* él que *mas te* agradáre, choose then of these two measures that which will please thee most. *Tenémos yá determinádo hacér en obséquio súyo* tódo lo que alcanzáren *nuéstras fuérzas*, we have resolved to do in his behalf all that shall lie in our power.—*Sólo podrán ser delincuéntes*, los que *de rosótros nos* juzgáren *delincuéntes*, those only can be guilty, who, among you, shall judge us guilty. *Mánda*, lo que gustáres....*renuéva á nuéstro buén amigo mi fíno afécto, y á* cuántos *se* acordáren *de mí, dirás de mi párte* tódo lo que quisiéres, command what you please —renew to our good friend my sincere attachment, and say from me all that you please to all those who shall remember me. *Vm. lecrá éste libro cuándo quisiére,* you will read this book when you please. *Cuándo* quiéra ó quisiére *la fortú-na, seré rico.*—The compound tense of the future conjunctive follows the same rules.

N. B. 1st. The present of the subjunctive may be used in almost every one of the above-mentioned cases, instead of the future conjunctive.

2d. After the conjunction *si,* if, the verb expressing a future action is most frequently put in the future conjunctive.

3d. The conjunction *si,* if, &c. and the adverb *cuándo,* when, &c. are also used in the present, imperfect, and preterite of the indicative mode and their compound tenses, when we affirm, declare, in the present and past time. Ex. *Si téngo educa-ción, lo débo á mis maéstros; Cuándo tenía dinéro, tódos me pedian prestádo; si túvo sucéso, fué por mi ayúda.*

OF THE CONDITIONAL.

This mode has in the Spanish language three simple and three compound tenses, the terminations of which are in *ría, ra* and *se.* We shall call the three first, *conditionals present,* and the three others, *conditionals past.*

The *conditionals present* denote that a thing would be, or would be done in the present time under certain conditions; as *yó lecría* or *leyéra, si tuviéra* or *tuviése libros,* I would read if I had books.

The *conditionals past* denote that a thing would have been in a time past under certain conditions; as, habría, *or* húbiéra ído ayér á la comédia, *si* hubiéra or hubiése estádo buéno. I should have gone yesterday to the play, if I had been well.

Rules for the use of the conditional tenses.

RULE XLI. The first conditional, the termination of which is *ría* and *ra,* may be used indifferently whenever the verb is not governed by any conjunction; which is the case with one of the members in all conditional propositions; as, *leería* or *le-yéra tódo el dia, si mi existéncia no dependiéra or dependiése de mi trabájo.* I should read the whole day, if my support did not depend upon my labour. *El número de los póbres no sería* or *fuéra tan gránde, si fuéra or fuése menór él de los avúros,* the number of poor would not be so great, if that of misers were less considerable.

7*

RULE XLII. The second conditional, the termination of which is *ra*, and the third which is terminated in *se*, are used whenever the verb is governed by a conditional conjunction; as, *si*, if; *si no*, unless; *aunqué*, though; *bién que*, although; *dádo que*, granting that, &c. or by an interjection expressing a desire: Ex. *Aunqué* hubiéra *or* hubiése* *paz*, though peace should take place. *¡ Ojalá* fuéra *or* fuése *ciérto!* Would to God it were certain! If there be in the second member of these sentences, another conditional, we should make use of the first; as, *Si* hubiéra, *or* hubiése *buéna fé, sería mayór la solidéz de los contrátos*, if there should be good faith, the solidity of contracts would be greater.

RULE XLIII. The second conditional is used with elegance after the interrogative pronouns, when we use it with an exclamation, or to express surprise. Ex. *Quién lo creyéra? quién lo* imaginára? who would believe it? who would imagine it? *¿ Sin el auxilio de la escritúra, órgano de tódas las ciéncias, que* hubiéra *en el múndo sinó ignoráncia?* without the aid of writing, the organ of all the sciences, what would there be in the world but ignorance?

RULE XLIV. We use the second or third conditional after *cuándo*, though, and after the pronouns *él que, los que, la que, &c.* and after *cuánto, a, os, as*, (mentioned in Rule XL, page 76, when speaking of the future conjunctive,) when they themselves are preceded by a verb expressing an action, which the remainder of the phrase causes to depend on choice or chance; as *le díge que tomáse en mi huérta* tódo lo que, *or* cuánto quisiéra, I told him to take in my garden all that or whatever he should wish. *Prometió dárme* el *dinéro* que *yo* necesitára *or* necesitáse, he promised to give me the money that I might want.

RULE XLV. When a conditional phrase does not begin with a conjunction; such as, *si, aunqué, luégo que, &c.*, we may make use of the first and second conditional, and say; *fortúna sería* or *fuéra que lloviése; buéno sería* or *fuéra que lo mandásen.* (Grammar of the Academy.) But in such a case if there should be another conditional in the second member of the phrase, this last must take the third termination, as in the preceding examples. It is even necessary to

---

* Observe as a general rule throughout the Conjugations, that the terminations *ria, ra;* and *ra* and *se* may be used indifferently for one another, but never *ria* for *se*, nor *se* for *ria*. (See page 80.)

observe that in general, when a phrase begins with the second conditional and the first cannot be applied to the second member,* we must have recourse to the third, and not repeat the second; if, on the contrary, it begins with the third, we must, instead of repeating it in the second member, make use of the second: as, *obligádo me viéra yó sin dúda á enmudecér, ó me* contentára *con ser el débil éco de sus elevádas cláusulas, si los nuévos progrésos de la Académia no* abriésen *nuévo cámpo de asúntos al ingénio, no* ofreciésen *á la elocuéncia nuévas miéses, &c.* I should, without doubt, find myself obliged to keep silence, or content myself with being the feeble echo of his eloquent speeches, if the new progress of the Academy did not open to genius new subjects, and offer to eloquence new harvests, &c.

N. B. 1st. Whenever the conditional is expressed by means of the conjunction *si,* the verb that it governs is in English in the imperfect of the subjunctive, and this imperfect is always translated in Spanish by one of the two conditionals, according to the rules stated above, when the conjunction expresses a future condition; if on the contrary it expresses one already past, the verb is put in Spanish in the same tense as in English. Ex. *Si yó* fuéra *rico, socorrería á los póbres,* if I were rich, I would assist the poor; *si él éra póbre el áño pasádo, no éra cúlpa mía,* if he was poor last year it was not my fault. (See N. B. 3d. page 77.)

---

* Though Rule XLV. be extracted and faithfully translated from the Grammar of the Spanish Academy, we think it might lead to error, if we should not give it a little more clearness. We therefore observe,—1st.—that a conditional phrase must contain two propositions; the one principal, and the other subordinate. We call a principal proposition that after which we place the conjunction, and a subordinate proposition that which is placed after the conjunction. Each of those propositions may contain several members. In this phrase; *seria recompensádo, si fuéra diligénte,* he would be rewarded, if he were diligent; *he would be rewarded,* is the principal proposition. In the following, *seria recompensádo y tódos le estimarían, si estudiára con mas atención y fuéra mas amánte de la verdád,* he would be rewarded and every body would esteem him, if he should study with more attention and were more fond of truth; each of these propositions contains two members.—2.—That the Academy, in speaking of the second member, understands the whole subordinate proposition; for, if it contains several members, the same conditional must be used in each one of them; it is the same with the principal proposition as is seen in the example stated in Rule XLV, *obligádo me viéra, &c.* the first proposition of which terminates with these words, *á sus elevádas cláusulas,* and the second begins at *si los nuévos progrésos.* In the two members of the principal proposition, the verbs are in the second conditional, and in the subordinate proposition they are in the third.

N. B. 2d. It must be seen by the preceding rules and
examples, that the *second conditional is frequently used to hold
the place of the first and third;* for we may say indifferently
el tiémpo pudiéra *or* podria *ser mejór; hice que* viniéra *or*
viniése. *But it is not the same with the first and third;* they
are so opposed that one cannot be used for the other.
Therefore, to translate this phrase; I should wish to go to
Seville, we may say; *yó* querría *or* quisiéra *ir á Sevílla,* but
not *yó* quisiése *ir á Sevílla.*

The conditionals past follow the same rules as the conditionals present, and though the verb governed by the conjunction *si* should in English be in the pluperfect of the indicative, it must in Spanish be put in the second or third conditionals past. Ex. *Si lo* hubiéra *or* hubiése *sabido,* if I had
known it, or had I known it.

☞ The above N. B. 2d. is so true and important that the
conjugations will be improved in this edition by it, as far as
space will permit it without altering the paging.

USE OF THE IMPERATIVE.

RULE XLVI. The use of this mode in Spanish is not
entirely the same as in English. In the latter language, it
serves not only to command, pray, and exhort, but also to
forbid; the Spaniards on the contrary, express the prohibition
by means of the present of the subjunctive, and sometimes by
the future. Ex. *Nó hábles,* do not speak; *no me respóndas,*
do not answer me; *no mátes; no matarás;* do not kill; thou
shalt not kill.

N. B. The *first person plural of the* IMPERATIVE is always
like the *first of the plural* of the SUBJUNCTIVE PRESENT.

USE OF THE SUBJUNCTIVE.

This mode has four tenses, the *present,* the *imperfect,* the
preterite and the *pluperfect;* it expresses, as the indicative,
the *present, past,* and *future.*

Rules for using the tenses of the subjunctive.

As it is impossible to establish well defined rules to make
known in a sure manner the use of the tenses of the subjunctive, we cannot pretend to determine every case in which we
must make use of them; but we will endeavour to establish
rules, which will obviate the greatest part of the difficulties.

RULE XLVII. The verb that follows the conjunction *que,*

that, must be put in the indicative, when the verb preceding
it, expresses *affirmation* in a direct, positive and independent
manner; but it must be put in the subjunctive when the
preceding verb expresses *doubt,* surprise, fear, admiration,
uncertainty, desire, hope, will, permission, prohibition and
command. Thus we say; *sé que está málo,* I know that he is
sick; *los ateístas dícen que no háy Diós,* the atheists say that
there is no God; because the verb *sé* and *dicen* express a direct
and positive affirmation. But we must say; *no créo* or *dúdo
que esté málo,* I do not believe or I doubt that he is sick.
Los ateístas quiéren que no háya Diós, the atheists wish that
there may not be a God. *Deséo que* vénga, I desire that he
may come. *Me admíro que no háya llegádo,* I am surprised
that he is not arrived; because in these phrases the verbs preceding the conjunction express a doubt, desire or surprise

N. B. After *Ojalá, Plégue á Diós, &c.* conjunctions always
expressing a desire, the verb is put in the subjunctive.

RULE XLVIII. The relatives *que,* quién, cúyo,-a,-os,-as,
govern the subjunctive, when the phrase is interrogative or
negative, or when it expresses a doubt, desire or condition.
Ex. *No conózco úna sóla mugér, cúya álma séa mas sensible
que la de la señóra N.,* I do not know a woman whose soul is
more sensible than that of Madam N.

REMARK. See, 1st.—the N. B. in continuation of the rules
relative to the use of the tenses of the future conjunctive and
the rules that relate to it, (page 76;)—2d.—the successive
rules relative to those of the tenses of the conditional; and
3d.—under the head of conjunctions, those that govern the
subjunctive; (page 194.)

OF THE PERSONS AND NUMBERS OF VERBS.

Verbs have three persons. The pronouns personal are their
characteristics. The first person is that which speaks; as,
yó ámo, nosótros or *nosótras amámos,* I love, we love. The
second person is that to whom we speak; as, *tú ámas, vosótros*
or *vosótras amáis,* thou lovest, you love. The third person
is that of whom we speak; as, *él* or *élla áma, éllos* or *éllas
áman,* he or she loves, they love.

☞ In ancient authors, the termination of the second person
of the plural is in *des,* instead of *is.* Thus, they said and
wrote *amádes, amarédes; temédes, temíades; sufrídes, sufría-
des, &c.* instead of *amáis, amaréis; teméis, temíais; sufrís,
sufríais, &c.*

The verbs have both numbers; the singular is used when the verb has only a single person or thing for its nominative: as, *yó, tú, él, élla;* and the plural when it has many; as, *nosótros* or *nosótras, vosótros* or *vosótras, éllos* or *éllas.*

N. B. It is not the same with the Spanish language as with the English and French, in which the verb must always be preceded by the pronoun that governs it. In Spanish, as in Latin, the terminations generally distinguish the persons, consequently the pronouns are generally suppressed. We use them with advantage to add energy to the expression, as in these examples; *tú lo has hécho!* It is thou who hast done it! *yó lo mándo,* it is I who order it; *tú ríes é yó llóro,* thou laughest and I weep; *tú no quiéres hacérlo; pués, lo haré yó,* thou wilt not do it; well, I shall do it.

CONJUGATIONS.

The Spanish language, as we have already said, has but three conjugations, which are known by the termination of the infinitive. The first has the infinitive terminated in *ar,* as, *am-ár,* to love; the second in *er,* as, *tem-ér,* to fear; the third in *ir,* as *sub-ír,* to go up. It has besides three auxiliary verbs, which are so called because they serve to conjugate the other verbs in their compound tenses. These auxiliary verbs are *habér and tenér,* to have; and *ser,* to be. In conjugating the latter, we add to it *estár,* an irregular verb, translated by the same English verb, *to be,* being of such great use, that it is proper to study it, as soon as the auxiliary verbs are learnt.

Conjugation of the auxiliary verb HABÉR, *to have* *

INFINITIVE.

Present.	Habér,†	-	-	-	to have.
Preterite.	Habér habído,	-	-	-	to have had.
Gerund.	Habiéndo,	-	-	-	having.
Participle.	Habído,	-	-	-	had.

---

* This verb was used formerly as active, to express possession; and in this last acceptation it had the following imperative; *hábe tú.* (now out of use) *háya él, háyamos nosótros, habéd vosótros, háyan éllos.* Now the verb *habér* is seldom used but as an auxiliary or as an impersonal. See its conjugation for this last acceptation, page 120.

† *Haber,* followed by the preposition *de* and another verb in the infinitive, forms a future tense. Ex. *He de habér,* I am to have; *habia de tenér,* I was to have or possess; *habré de amár,* I shall have to love, &c. (See page 156.)

INDICATIVE.
Present.

Yó ho,	I have.
Tú has,	thou hast.
Él ha,	he has.
Nosótros hémos, or habémos,	we have.
Vosótros habéis,*	you have.
Éllos han,	they have.

Imperfect.

Yó había,	I had.
Tú habías,	thou hadst.
Él había,	he had.
Nosótros habíamos,	we had.
Vosótros habíais,*	you had.
Éllos habían,	they had.

Preterite definite.

Yó húbe,	I had.
Tú hubíste,	thou hadst.
Él húbo,	he had.
Nosótros hubímos,	we had.
Vosótros hubísteis,	you had.
Éllos hubiéron,	they had.

Preterite indefinite.

Yó he habído,	I have had.
Tú has habído,	thou hast had
Él ha habído,	he has had.
Nosótros hémos habído,	we have had.
Vosótros habéis habído,	you have had.
Éllos han habído,	they have had.

Preterite anterior.

Yó húbe habído,	I had had.
Tú hubíste habído,	thou hadst had.
Él húbo habído,	he had had.
Nosótros hubímos habído,	we had had.
Vosótros hubísteis habído,	you had had.
Éllos hubiéron habído,	they had had.

* See page 81, at the bottom, what we have said on the termination of the second person plural in ancient authors. Formerly the second person plural of all the verbs instead of terminating in *is* were terminated in *des*; they used to say *habédes, habíades,* &c.

Pluperfect.

Yó había habído,	-	-	-	*I had had.*	
Tú habías habído,	-	-	-	*thou hadst had.*	
Él había habído,	-	-	-	*he had had.*	
Nosótros habíamos habído,		-		*we had had.*	
Vosótros habíais habído,	-		-	*you had had.*	
Éllos habían habído,		-	-	*they had had.*	

Future absolute.

Yó habré,	-	-	-	-	*I shall or will have.*
Tú habrás,	-	-	-	-	*thou wilt have.*
Él habrá,	-	-	-	-	*he will have.*
Nosótros habrémos,	-		-	-	*we shall have.*
Vosótros habréis,	-		-	-	*you will have.*
Éllos habrán,	-	-	-	-	*they will have.*

Future anterior.

Yó habré habído,	-	-	-	*I shall have had.*
Tú habrás habído,	-	-	-	*thou wilt have had.*
Él habrá habído,	-	-	-	*he will have had.*
Nosótros habrémos habído,		-		*we shall have had.*
Vosótros habréis habído,	-		-	*you will have had.*
Éllos habrán habído,		-	-	*they will have had.*

Future conjunctive simple.

Si *or* cuándo,	-	-	-	-	*If or when,*
Yó hubiére,	-	-	-	-	*I have or shall have.*
Tú hubiéres,	-	-	-	-	*thou wilt have.*
Él hubiére,	-	-	-	-	*he will have.*
Nosótros hubiéremos,	-	-		*we shall have.*
Vosótros hubiéreis,	-	-	-	*you will have.*
Éllos hubiéren,	-	-	-	*they will have.*

Future conjunctive compound.

Si *or* cuándo,		-	-	-	*If or when.*
Yó hubiére habído,	-	-	-	*I have or shall have had*
Tú hubiéres habído,	-	-	-	*thou wilt have had.*
El hubiére habído,	-	-	-	*he will have had.*
Nosótros hubiéremos habído,		-		*we shall have had.*
Vosótros hubiéreis habído,		-		*you will have had.*
Éllos hubiéren habído,		-	-	*they will have had.*

CONDITIONALS.

First conditional present.

Yó habría or hubiéra*	- -	I should have.
Tú habrías,	- - - -	thou wouldst have.
Él habría,	- - - -	he would have.
Nosótros habríamos,	- - -	we should have.
Vosótros habríais,	- - -	you would have.
Éllos habrían,	- - - -	they would have.

Second and third conditionals present.

Si, or cuándo,	- - -	If or though.
Yó hubiéra or hubiése,	- -	I had or should have.
Tú hubiéras or hubiéses,	- -	thou wouldst have.
Él hubiéra or hubiése,	-	he would have.
Nosótros hubiéramos, or hubiésemos,	we had or should have.
Vosótros hubiérais or hubiéseis, -	you had or would have.
Éllos hubiéran or hubiésen,	-	they would have.

First conditional past.

Yó habría or hubiéra habído,	-	I should have had.
Tú habrías habído,	- -	thou wouldst have had.
Él habría habído,	- -	he would have had.
Nosótros habríamos habído,	-	we should have had.
Vosótros habríais habído, -	-	you would have had.
Éllos habrían habído, -	-	they would have had.

Second and third conditionals past.

Si, or cuándo,	- - -	If or though,
Yó hubiéra, or hubiese habído, -	I had or should have had.
Tú hubiéras, or hubiéses habído,	thou wouldst have had.
Él hubiéra, or hubiése habído, -	he would have had.
Nosótros hubiéramos, or hubiése- mos habído,	- - -	we had or should have had.
Vosótros hubiérais, or hubiéseis habído,	- - - -	you would have had.
Ellos hubiéran, or hubiésen habído,	they would have had.

---

* See pages 79 and 80 about the terminations of this and the following tense.

SUBJUNCTIVE.
Present.

Yó háya,	-	-	-	-	*I may have.*
Tú háyas,	-	-	-	-	*thou mayst have.*
Él háya,	. -	-	-	-	*he may have.*
Nosótros háyamos,	-	-	-		*we may have.*
Vosótros háyais,	-	-	-		*you may have.*
Éllos háyan,	-	-	-	-	*they may have.*

Imperfect.

Yó hubiése,	-	-	-	-	*I might have.*
Tú hubiéses,	-	-	-	-	*thou mightst have.*
Él hubiése,	-	-	-	-	*he might have.*
Nosótros hubiésemos,	-	-	-		*we might have.*
Vosótros hubiéseis,	-	-	-		*you might have.*
Éllos hubiésen,	-	-	-		*they might have.*

Preterite.

Yó háya habído,	-	-	-		*I may have had.*
Tú háyas habído,	-	-	-		*thou mayst have had.*
Él háya habído,	-	-	-		*he may have had.*
Nosótros háyamos habído,	-	-			*we may have had.*
Vosótros háyais habído,	-	-			*you may have had.*
Éllos háyan habído,	-	-	-		*they may have had*

Pluperfect.

Yó hubiése habído,	-	-			*I might have had.*
Tú hubiéses habído,	-	-			*thou mightst have had.*
Él hubiése habído,	-	-			*he might have had.*
Nosótros hubiésemos habído,	-				*we might have had.*
Vosótros hubiéseis habído,	-	-			*you might have had.*
Éllos hubiésen habído,	-	-			*they might have had.*

Conjugation of the auxiliary verb TENÉR, *to have, to hold, to possess.**

INFINITIVE.

Present.	Tenér,†	-	-	*to have, hold, possess.* .
Preterite.	Habér tenído,	-	-	*to have had.*
Gerund.	Teniéndo,	-	-	*having.*
Participle.	Tenído,	-	-	*had.*

* This verb is *auxiliary* and *active*. As *auxiliary* it is seldom used. As *active* it denotes possession, and must always be used to translate the verb *to have* when this verb is not auxiliary. We say, *he leído el libro,* I have read the book,

INDICATIVE.

Present.

Yó téngo,	-	-	-	-	*I have*, or *possess*.
Tú tiénes,	-	-	-	-	*thou hast*
Él tiéne, -	-	-	-	-	*he has*.
Nosótros tenémos,	-	-	-	*we have*.
Vosótros tenéis,	-	-	-	*you have*.
Éllos tiénen,	-	-	-	-	*they have*.

Imperfect.

Yó tenía, -	-	-	-	-	*I had*, or, *did possess*.
Tú tenías,	-	-	-	-	*thou hadst*.
Él tenía, -	-	-	-	-	*he had*.
Nosótros teníamos,	-	-	-	*we had*.
Vosótros teníais,	-	-	-	*you had*.
Éllos tenían,	-	-	-	-	*they had*.

Preterite definite.

Yo túve, -	-	-	-	-	*I had*, or *possessed*.
Tú tuvíste,	-	-	-	-	*thou hadst*.
Él túvo, -	-	-	-	-	*he had*.
Nosótros tuvímos,	-	-	-	*we had*.
Vosótros tuvísteis,	-	-	-	*you had*.
Éllos tuviéron, -	-	-	-	*they had*.

Preterite indefinite.

Yó he tenído, -	-	-	-	*I have had*, or *possessed*.
Tú has tenído, -	-	-	-	*thou hast had*.
Él ha tenído, -	-	-	-	*he has had*.
Nosótros hémos tenído,	-	-	*we have had*.
Vosótros habéis tenído,	-	-	*you have had*.
Éllos han tenído,	-	-	-	*they have had*.

Preterite anterior.

Yó húbe tenído,	-	-	-	*I had had*, or *possessed*.
Tú hubíste tenído,	-	-	-	*thou hadst had*.
Él húbo tenído,	-	-	-	*he had had*.
Nosótros hubímos tenído, -	-	*we had had*.
Vosótros hubísteis tenído, -	-	*you had had*.
Éllos hubiéron tenído,	-	-	*they had had*.

but we must say, *téngo un libro*, and not *he un libro*, I have a book; because in the first example the verb *to have* is auxiliary to the verb *to read*, and in the second it is active and denotes possession.

† *Tenér que* before an infinitive is *to have to*. Ex. *Téngo que salir*, I have to go out. (See page 156.)

Pluperfect.

Yó había tenído,	-	-	*I had had,* or *possessed.*
Tú habías tenído,	-	-	*thou hadst had.*
Él había tenído,	-	-	*he had had.*
Nosótros habíamos tenído,	-		*we had had.*
Vosótros.habíais tenído,	-		*you had had.*
Éllos habían tenído,	-	-	*they had had.*

Future absolute.

⟩

Yó tendré,	-	-	-	*I shall have,* or *possess.*
Tú tendrás,	-	-	-	*thou wilt have.*
Él tendrá,	-	-	-	*he will have.*
Nosótros tendrémos,	⁚	-	*we shall have.*
Vosótros tendréis,	-	-	-	*you will have.*
Éllos tendrán,	-	-	-	*they will have.*

Future anterior.

Yo habré tenído,	-	-	*I shall have had,* or *possessed.*
Tú habrás tenído,	-	-	*thou wilt have had.*
El habrá tenído,	-	-	*he will have had.*
Nosótros habrémos tenído,	-		*we shall have had.*
Vosótros habréis tenído,	-		*you will have had.*
Éllos habrán tenído,	-	-	*they will have had.*

Future conjunctive simple.

Si, *or* cuándo,	-	⁚	*If,* or *when,*
Yó tuviére,	-	-	-	*I have,* or *possess.*
Tú tuviéres,	-	-	-	*thou shalt have.*
El tuviére,	-	-	-	*he shall have.*
Nosótros tuviéremos,	-	-	*we shall have.*
Vosótros tuviéreis,	-	-	*you will have.*
Ellos tuviéren,	-	-	-	*they will have.*

Future conjunctive compound.

Si, *or* cuándo	-	-	*If,* or *when,*
Yó hubiére tenído,	-	-	*I have had.*
Tú hubiéres tenído,	-	-	*thou wilt have had*
El hubiére tenído,	-	-	*he will have had.*
Nosótros hubiéremos tenído,		*we shall have had.*
Vosótros hubiéreis tenído,	-	*you will have had.*
Éllos hubiéren tenído,	-	*they will have had.*

CONDITIONALS.

First conditional present.

Yó tendría, *or* tuviéra,	-	-	*I should have, or possess.*
Tú tendrías,	-	-	*thou wouldst have*
Él tendría,	-	-	*he would have.*
Nosótros tendríamos,	-	-	*we should have.*
Vosótros tendríais,	-	-	*you would have.*
Éllos tendrían,	-	-	*they would have.*

Second and third conditionals present.

Si, *or* cuándo,	-	-	*If, or though,*
Yó tuviéra, *or* tuviése,	-	-	*I should have.*
Tú tuviéras, *or* tuviéses,	-	-	*thou shouldst have.*
Él tuviéra, *or* tuviése,	-	-	*he should have.*
Nosótros tuviéramos, *or* tuviésemos,			*we should have.*
Vosótros tuviérais, *or* tuviéseis,			*you should have.*
Éllos tuviéran, *or* tuviésen,	-		*they should have.*

First conditional past.

Yó habría, *or* hubiéra tenído,	-		*I should have had.*
Tú habrías tenído,	-	-	*thou wouldst have had.*
Él habría tenído,	-	-	*he would have had.*
Nosótros habríamos tenído,	-		*we should have had.*
Vosótros habríais tenído,	-		*you would have had.*
Éllos habrían tenído,	-		*they would have had.*

Second and third conditionals past.

Si, *or* cuándo,	-	-	*If, or though,*
Yó hubiéra, *or* hubiése tenído,			*I had, or should have had.*
Tú hubiéras, *or* hubiéses tenído,			*thou wouldst have had.*
Él hubiéra, *or* hubiése tenído,			*he would have had.*
Nosótros hubiéramos, *or* hubiésemos tenído,	-	-	*we should have had.*
Vosótros hubiérais, *or* hubiéseis tenído,	-	-	*you would have had.*
Éllos hubiéran, *or* hubiésen tenído,	-	-	*they would have had.*

8 *

IMPERATIVE.

Present or future.

Ten tú,*	-	-	-	-	*have thou, or possess.*
Ténga él,	-	-	-	-	*let him have.*
Tengámos nosótros,		-	-	*let us have.*
Tenéd vosótros,*	-	-	-	*have you, or ye.*
Téngan éllos, -	-	-	-	*let them have.*

SUBJUNCTIVE.

Present.

Yó ténga,	-	-	-	-	*I may have, or possess*
Tú téngas,	-	-	-	-	*thou mayst have.*
Él ténga,	-	-	-	-	*he may have.*
Nosótros tengámos, -		-	-	*we may have.*
Vosótros tengáis,	-	-	-	*you may have.*
Éllos téngan, -	-	-	-	*they may have.*

Imperfect.

Yó tuviése,	-	-	-	-	*I might have, or possess.*
Tú tuviéses,	-	-	-	-	*thou mightest have.*
El tuviése,	-	-	-	-	*he might have.*
Nosótros tuviésemos,		-	-	*we might have.*
Vosótros tuviéseis, -		-	-	*you might have.*
Éllos tuviésen,	-	-	-	*they might have.*

Preterite.

Yó háya tenído,	-	-	-	*I may have had.*
Tú háyas tenído,	-	-	-	*thou mayst have had.*
El háya tenído,	-	-	-	*he may have had.*
Nosótros háyamos tenído,		-	*we may have had.*
Vosótros háyais tenído, -		-	*you may have had.*
Éllos háyan tenído, -		-	*they may have had.*

Pluperfect.

Yó hubiése tenído, -		-	-	*I might have had.*
Tú hubiéses tenído, -		-	-	*thou mightest have had.*
Él hubiése tenído, -		-	-	*he might have had.*
Nosótros hubiésemos tenído,		-	*we might have had.*
Vosótros hubiéseis tenído,		-	*you might have had.*
Éllos hubiésen tenído,	-	-	*they might have had.*

---

* In all the verbs, the 2d person, singular and plural, of the imperative, takes the termination of the 2d person, sing. and plur. of the present subjunctive, when used with a negation. Ex. *Have thou not*, no téngas. *Have ye not*, no tengáis.

Conjugation of the auxiliary verb SER, *and* ESTÁR,
meaning also TO BE.

INFINITIVE.

Present.	Ser,	estár,	*to be.*
Preterite	Habér sído,	habér estádo,	*to have been.*
Gerund.	Siéndo,	estándo,	*being.*
Participle.	Sído,	estádo,	*been.*

INDICATIVE.

Present

Yó sóy,	*or*	estóy,	- -	*I am.*
Tú éres,		estás,	- -	*thou art.*
Él es,		está,	-	*he is.*
Nosótros sómos,		estámos,	-	*we are.*
Vosótros sóis,		estáis,	- -	*you are.*
Éllos son,		están,	- -	*they are.*

Imperfect.

Yó éra,	*or*	estába,	- -	*I was.*
Tú éras,		estábas,	-	*thou wast.*
Él éra,		estába,	-	*he was.*
Nosótros éramos,		estábamos,	-	*we were.*
Vosótros érais,		estábais,	- -	*you were.*
Éllos éran,		estában,	- -	*they were.*

Preterite definite.

Yó fuí,	*or*	estúve,	- -	*I was.*
Tú fuíste,		estuvíste,	-	*thou wast*
Él fué,		estúvo,	-	*he was.*
Nosótros fuímos,		estuvímos,	-	*we were.*
Vosótros fuísteis,		estuvísteis,	-	*you were.*
Éllos fuéron,		estuviéron,	- -	*they were.*

Preterite indefinite.

Yó he sído,	*or*	estádo,	- -	*I have been.*
Tú has sído,		estádo,	-	*thou hast been*
Él ha sído,		estádo,	- -	*he has been.*
Nosótros hémos sído,		estádo,	- -	*we have been.*
Vosótros habéis sído,		estádo,	-	*you have been*
Éllos han sído,		estádo,	- -	*they have been.*

Preterite anterior.

Yó húbc sído,	or	estádo,	-	I had been.
Tú hubíste sído,		estádo,	-	thou hadst been.
Él húbo sído,		estádo,		he had been.
Nosótros hubímos sído,		estádo,		we had been.
Vosótros hubísteis sído,		estádo,	-	you had been.
Éllos hubiéron sído,		estádo,	-	they had been.

Pluperfect.

Yó había sído,	or	estádo,		I had been
Tú habías sído,		estádo,	-	thou hadst been
Él había sído,		estádo,	-	he had been.
Nosótros habíamos sído,		estádo,		we had been.
Vosótros habíais sído,		estádo,	-	you had been.
Éllos habían sído,		estádo,	-	they had been.

Future absolute.

Yo seré,	or	estaré,	-	I shall be.
Tú serás,		estarás,	-	thou wilt be.
El será,		estará,	-	he will be.
Nosótros serémos,		estarémos	-	we shall be.
Vosótros seréis,		estaréis,	-	you wilt be.
Ellos serán,		estarán,	-	they will be.

Future anterior.

Yó habré sído,	or	estádo,		I shall have been.
Tú habrás sído,		estádo,		thou wilt have been
El habrá sído,		estádo,	-	he will have been.
Nosótros habrémos sído,		estádo,	-	we shall have been.
Vosótros habréis sído,		estádo,	-	you will have been.
Ellos habrán sído,		estádo,	-	they will have been.

Future conjunctive simple.

Si, or cuándo,			-	If, or when,
Yó fuérc,	or	estuviére,	-	I be, or shall be.
Tú fuéres,		estuviéres,	-	thou wilt be.
Él fuérc,		estuviére,	-	he will be.
Nosótros fuéremos,		estuviéremos,		we shall be.
Vosótros fuéreis,		estuviéreis,	-	you will be.
Ellos fuéren,		estuviéren,	-	they will be.

Future conjunctive compound.

Si, or cuándo,			If, or when,
Yó hubiére sído,	or	estádo,	I have been.
Tú hubiéres sído,		estádo,	thou will have been.
El hubiére sido,		estádo,	he will have been.
Nosótros hubiéremos sído, estádo			we shall have been
Vosótros hubiércis sído,		estádo,	you will have been
Ellos hubiéren sído,		estádo,	they will have been.

CONDITIONALS.

First conditional present.

Yó sería or fuéra,	estaría or estuviéra,	I should be.
Tú serías,	estarías,	thou wouldst be.
El sería,	estaría,	he would be.
Nosótros seríamos,	estaríamos,	we should be.
Vosótros seriais,	estaríais,	you would be.
Éllos serían,	estarían,	they would be.

Second and third conditionals present

Si, or cuándo,		
Yó fuéra or fuése,	estuviéra or estuviése,	
Tú fuéras or fuéses	estuviéras or estuviéses,	If or though I were or should be, &c.
Él fuéra or fuése,	estuviéra or estuviése,	
Nosótros fuéramos or fué-semos,	estuviéramos or estuvié-semos,	
Vosótros fuérais or fuéseis,	estuviérais or estuviéseis,	
Éllos fuéran or fuésen,	estuviéran or estuviésen,	

First conditional past.

Yó habría sído,	or	estádo,	I should have been.
Tú habrías sído,		estádo,	thou wouldst have been.
Él habría sído,		estádo,	he would have been.
Nosótros habríamos sído,		estádo,	we should have been.
Vosótros habríais sído,		estádo,	you would have been.
Éllos habrían sído,		estádo,	they would have been.

Second and third conditionals past.

Si, or cuándo,		
Yó hubiéra, or hubiése sído,	or	estádo,
Tú hubiéras, or hubiéses sído,		estádo,
Él hubiéra, or hubiése sído,		estádo,
Nosótros hubiéramos, or hubiésemos sído,		estádo,
Vosótros hubiérais, or hubiéseis sído,		estádo,
Éllos hubiéran, or hubiésen sído,		estádo,

If or though I had been, or should have been, &c.

IMPERATIVE.

Present or future.

Sé tú,	*or*	está tú,	be thou.
Séa él,*		esté él,*	let him be.
Seámos nosótros,		estémos nosótros,	let us be.
Sed vosótros,		estád vosótros,	be you.
Séan éllos,*		estén éllos,*	let them be.

SUBJUNCTIVE.

Present.

Yó séa,	*or*	esté,	I may be.
Tú séas,		estés,	thou mayst be.
Él séa,		esté,	he may be.
Nosótros seámos,		estémos,	we may be.
Vosótros seáis,		estéis,	you may be.
Éllos séan,		estén,	they may be.

Imperfect.

Yó fuése,	*or*	estuviése,	I might be.
Tú fuéses,		estuviéses,	thou mightest be.
Él fuése,		estuviése,	he might be.
Nosótros fuésemos,		estuviésemos,	we might be.
Vosótros fuéseis,		estuviéseis,	you might be.
Éllos fuésen,		estuviésen,	they might be.

Preterite.

Yó háya sído,	*or*	estádo,	I may have been.
Tú háyas sído,		estádo,	thou mayst have been.
Él háya sído,		estádo,	he may have been.
Nosótros háyamos sído,		estádo,	we may have been.
Vosótros háyais sído,		estádo,	you may have been.
Éllos háyan sído,		estádo,	they may have been.

Pluperfect.

Yó hubiése sído,	*or*	estádo,	I might have been.
Tú hubiéses sído,		estádo,	thou mightest have been.
Él hubiése sído,		estádo,	he might have been.
Nosótros hubiésemos sído,		estádo,	we might have been.
Vosótros hubiéseis sído,		estádo,	you might have been.
Éllos hubiésen sído,		estádo,	they might have been.

---

* *Séa vm.*, be you, sing.—*Séan vms.*, be you, plural,—and so on; use the third person in polite style in *all* the tenses of *all* the verbs. See note 2d. page 52.

Rules on the verbs SER and ESTÁR.

RULE XLIX. The verb *to be* cannot be translated in Spanish indifferently by *ser* or by *estár*. *Ser,* joined to an adjective, gives it sometimes an entirely different meaning from that which *estár* would give it. It is consequently necessary to understand well the use of these two verbs. We observe then, that we must use the verb *ser,*—1st.—whenever we speak of qualities essential to the subject;—2d.—of qualities relating to the mind or to the heart;—3d.—whenever we speak of an art, a dignity, an employment, a trade, &c. or of the dimensions of an object;—4th.—for the conjugation of the passive verbs;—5th.—when it is used for *to belong,* and when it is used impersonally: Ex. *Sóy hómbre,* I am a man ; *sómos mortáles,* we are mortal ; *son buénas géntes,* they are good people ; *son instruídos,* they are learned ; *sóis prudéntes,* you are prudent ; *éran caritatívos,* they were charitable, *ser álto, chíco, górdo, fláco,* to be tall, short, fat, lean; *ser réy, primér minístro, generál, juéz, pintór, sástre, zapatéro,* &c, to be a king, prime minister, a general, a judge, a painter, a tailor, a shoe-maker, &c.; *ser amádo, aborrecído,* to be loved, hated; *de quién es éste aníllo?* es de *María,* whose ring is this? it is Mary's; *yó sóy,* it is I; *tú éras,* it was thou; *él fué,* it was he; *nosótros serémos,* it will be we; *vosótros seríais,* it would be you, &c.

We make use, on the contrary, of *estár,*—1st.—whenever we speak of the state of health;—2d.—of being in any place;—3d.—of an emotion or of a sudden and transient sensation;—4th,—a manner or state of being. Ex. *Estár buéno ó málo,* to be well or ill; *estár en cása, en el jardín, en el cámpo,* to be at home, in the garden, in the country; *estár enfadádo,* to be offended; *estár conténto,* to be content.

Nevertheless, in the following examples and other similar ones, we can make use of *ser* or of *estár* indifferently; *ser* or *estár del mísmo parecér,* to be of the same opinion; *ser corregidór* or *estár de corregidór en Madríd,* to be corregidor at Madrid. We must however observe in the second example, that if we make use of *estár,* this verb must be followed by the particle *de,* for, *estár corregidór, alcálde,* would not be Spanish, as it is never immediately followed by a substantive.

N. B. *Ser buéno, ser málo,* signifies to be good, to be bad; *estár buéno, estár málo,* signifies to be well or ill; *estár me-*

jór, to be better, to be better in health; *estár peór*, to be more sick, to be worse.

RULE L. The verb *estár* is often used as in English *to be*, before another verb to signify in a more positive manner that an action is doing, has been done, or will be done, at the very moment in which we speak, or of which we speak; and then the verb which follows is put in the gerund. Ex. *Está escribiéndo*, he writes, that is, he is writing; *estába escribiéndo*, he wrote, that is, he was writing; *entónces estarán escribiéndo*, they will write then, that is, they will then be writing. (See the *Appendix* in page 459, for more particular remarks on *Ser* and *Estár*, *Habér* and *Tenér*.)

A GENERAL SCHEME OF THE TERMINATIONS OF REGULAR VERBS IN THEIR SIMPLE TENSES.

The figures 1, 2, 3, signify the *first*, *second* and *third* conjugations.

All the regular verbs of each conjugation are easily conjugated by changing the terminations *ar*, *er*, *ir*, of the infinitive into those expressed as follows.

INFINITIVE MOOD.

Present.	*Gerund.*	*Participle.*	*If there is an active part.*
1. ar,	ándo,	ádo,	ánte,
2. er,			
3. ir,	iéndo,	ído,	iénte *or* yénte,*

INDICATIVE.
Present.

	Singular.			*Plural.*		
1.	yó,	tú,	él.	nosótros,	vosótros,	éllos.
	o,	as,	a.	ámos,	áis,	an.
2.	o, ·	es,	e.	émos,	éis,	en.
3.				ímos,	ís,	en.

Imperfect.

1.	ába,	ábas,	ába.	ábamos,	ábais,	ában.
2.	ía,	ías,	ía.	íamos,	íais,	ían.
3.						

Preterite definite.

1.	é,	áste,	ó.	ámos,	ásteis,	áron.
2.	í,	íste,	ió.	ímos,	ísteis,	iéron.
3.						

* See 5th and 6th observations preceding the Conjugation of the Irregular verbs, page 122.

Future absolute.

1. aré, arás, ará. arémos, aréis, arán.
2. cré, crás, crá. erémos, eréis, erán
3. iré, irás, irá. irémos, iréis, irán.

Future conjunctive simple.

1. áre, áres, áre. áremos, áreis, áren.
2.
3. } iére, iéres, iére. iéremos, iéreis, iéren.

CONDITIONALS.

First conditional present.

1. aría,* arías, aría. aríamos, aríais, arían.
2. ería, erías, ería eríamos, eríais, erían.
3. iría, irías, iría. iríamos, iríais, irían.

Second and third conditionals present.

1. ára,* áras, ára. áramos, árais, áran.
2.
3. } iéra, iéras, iéra. iéramos, iérais, iéran.

1. áse,* áses, áse. ásemos, áseis, ásen.
2.
3. } iése, iéses, iése. iésemos, iéseis, iésen.

IMPERATIVE MOOD.

1. a, e. émos, ad, en.
2.
3. } e, a ámos, { ed, an.
id, an.

SUBJUNCTIVE MOOD.

Present.

Singular. Plural.

1. { yó, tú, él. nosótros, vosótros, éilos.
e, es, e. émos, éis, en.
2.
3. } a, as, a. ámos, áis, an.

Imperfect.

1. áse, áses, áse. ásemos, áseis, ásen.
2.
3. } iése, iéses, iése. iésemos, iéseis, iésen.

* See the rules about the use of these conditional tenses, pages 77 to 80, inclusive.

PARADIGMS OF THE THREE CONJUGATIONS.

First conjugation in AR.

INFINITIVE.

Present	Am-ár,	-	-	-	to love.
Preterite.	Habér amádo,	-	-	to have loved.
Gerund.	Amándo,	-	-	-	loving.
Participle.	Amádo,	-	-	-	loved.

INDICATIVE.

Present.

Yó ámo, - - - - -	I love, or do love.
Tú ámas, - - - - -	thou lovest.
Él áma, - - - - -	he loves.
Nosótros amámos, - - -	we love.
Vosótros amáis, - - - -	you love.
Éllos áman, - - - -	they love.

Imperfect.

Yó amába, - - - - -	I did love.
Tú amábas, - - - -	thou didst love.
Él amába, - - - - -	he did love.
Nosótros amábamos, - - -	we did love.
Vosótros amábais, - - -	you did love.
Éllos amában, - - - -	they did love.

Preterite definite.

Yó amé, - - - -	I loved.
Tú amáste, - - - -	thou lovedst.
Él amó, - - - -	he loved.
Nosótros amámos, - - -	we loved.
Vosótros amásteis, - - -	you loved.
Éllos amáron, - - - -	they loved.

Preterite indefinite

Yó he amádo, - - - -	I have loved.
Tú has amádo, - - -	thou hast loved.
Él ha amádo, - - - -	he has loved.
Nosótros hémos amádo, - -	we have loved.
Vosótros habéis amádo, - -	you have loved.
Éllos han amádo, - - -	they have loved.

Preterite anterior.

Yó húbe amádo, - - -	I had loved.
Tú hubíste amádo, - - -	thou hadst loved.
Él húbo amádo, - - - -	he had loved.

Nosótros hubímos amádo, - - we had loved.
Vosótros hubísteis amádo, - - you had loved.
Éllos hubiéron amádo, - - they had loved.

Pluperfect.

Yó había amádo, - - - I had loved.
Tú habías amádo, - - - thou hadst loved.
Él había amádo, - - - he had loved.
Nosótros habíamos amádo, - - we had loved.
Vosótros habíais amádo, - - you had loved.
Éllos habían amádo, - - - they had loved.

Future absolute.

Yó amaré, - - - - I shall love.
Tú amarás, - - - - thou wilt love.
Él amará, - - - - he will love.
Nosótros amarémos, - - - we shall love.
Vosótros amaréis, - - - you will love.
Éllos amarán, - - - - they will love

Future anterior.

Yó habré amádo, - - - I shall have loved.
Tú habrás amádo, - - - thou wilt have loved.
Él habrá amádo, - - - he will have loved.
Nosótros habrémos amádo, - - we shall have loved.
Vosótros habréis amádo, - - you will have loved.
Éllos habrán amádo, - - - they will have loved.

Future conjunctive simple.

Si, *or* cuándo, - - - If *or* when,
Yó amáre, - - - - I love *or* shall love.
Tú amáres, - - - - thou wilt love.
Él amáre, - - - - he will love.
Nosótros amáremos, - - - we shall love.
Vosótros amárcis, - - - you will love.
Éllos amáren, - - - - they will love.

Future conjunctive compound

Si, *or* cuándo, - - - If, *or* when,
Yó hubiére amádo, - - - I have loved.
Tú hubiéres amádo, - - - thou wilt have loved.
Él hubiére amádo, - - - he will have loved.
Nosótros hubiéremos amádo, - we shall have loved.
Vosótros hubiéreis amádo, - - you will have loved.
Éllos hubiéren amádo, - - - they will have loved

CONDITIONALS.

First conditional present.

Yó amaría or amára, - -	I should love.
Tú amarías, - - - -	thou wouldst love.
Él amaría, - - - -	he would love.
Nosótros amaríamos, - -	we should love.
Vosótros amaríais, - - -	you would love.
Éllos amarían, - - -	they would love.

Second and third conditionals present.

Si, or cuándo, - - -		If, or though,
Yó amára or	amáse, -	I should love.
Tú amáras	amáses, -	thou wouldst love.
El amára	amáse, -	he would love.
Nosótros amáramos	amásemos, -	we should love.
Vosótros amárais	amáseis, -	you would love.
Éllos amáran	amásen, -	they would love.

First conditional past.

Yó habría or hubiéra amádo, -	I should have loved.
Tú habrías amádo, - - -	thou wouldst have loved.
El habría amádo, - - -	he would have loved.
Nosótros habríamos amádo, -	we should have loved.
Vosótros habríais amádo, - -	you would have loved.
Éllos habrían amádo, - -	they would have loved.

Second and third conditionals past.

Si, or cuándo,		
Yó hubiéra, or	hubiése amádo,	If or though,
Tú hubiéras,	hubiéses amádo,	I had loved,
El hubiéra,	hubiése amádo,	or should have
Nosótros hubiéramos,	hubiésemos amádo,	loved, &c
Vosótros hubiérais,	hubiéseis amádo,	
Éllos hubiéran,	hubiésen amádo,	

IMPERATIVE.

Present or future.

Áma tú,* - - - - -	love thou.
Áme él, - - - - -	let him love.

* Verbs in the imperative require the pronouns governed close after them, when used affirmatively; and before them, as usual, when used negatively; Ex. *Love me,* ámame; *do not love me,* no me ámes; *Receive us,* recibidnos; *ao not receive us,* no nos recibáis.

Amémos nosótros,	-	-	*let us love.*
Amád vosótros,		-	*love ye.*
Ámen éllos,	-	-	*let them love.*

SUBJUNCTIVE.

Present.

Yó áme,	-	-	-	*I may love.*
Tú ámes,	-	-	-	*thou mayst love.*
Él áme,	-	-	-	*he may love.*
Nosótros amémos,	-	-		*we may love.*
Vosótros améis,	-	-	-	*you may love.*
Éllos ámen,	-	-	-	*they may love.*

Imperfect.

Yó amáse,	-	-	-	*I might love.*
Tú amáses,	-	-	-	*thou mightest love.*
Él amáse,	-	-	-	*he might love.*
Nosótros amásemos,	-	-		*we might love.*
Vosótros amáseis,	-	-		*you might love.*
Éllos amásen,	-	-	-	*they might love.*

Preterite

Yó háya amádo,	-	-	*I may have loved.*
Tú háyas amádo,	-	-	*thou mayst have loved*
Él háya amádo,	-	-	*he may have loved.*
Nosótros háyamos amádo,	-		*we may have loved.*
Vosótros háyais amádo,		-	*you may have loved.*
Éllos háyan amádo,	-	-	*they may have loved.*

Pluperfect.

Yó hubiése amádo,	-	-	*I might have loved.*
Tú hubiéses amádo,	-	-	*thou mightest have loved*
Fl hubiése amádo,	-	-	*he might have loved.*
Nosótros hubiésemos amádo,			*we might have loved.*
Vosótros hubiéseis amádo,		-	*you might have loved.*
Éllos hubiésen amádo,	-	-	*they might have loved.*

Second conjugation in ER.

INFINITIVE.

Present.	Tem-ér	-	-	*to fear.*
Preterite.	Habér temído	-		*to have feared.*
Gerund.	Temiéndo,		-	*fearing.*
Participle.	Temído,	-	-	*feared.*

9*

INDICATIVE.

Present.

Yó témo,	-	-	-	-	*I fear.*
Tú témes,	-	-	-	-	*thou fearest.*
Él téme,	-	-	-	-	*he fears.*
Nosótros temémos,		-	-	*we fear.*
Vosótros teméis,	-		-	-	*you fear.*
Éllos témen,	-	-	-	-	*they fear.*

Imperfect.

Yó temía,	-	-	-	-	*I did fear.*
Tú temías,	-	-	-	-	*thou didst fear.*
Él temía,	-	-	-	-	*he did fear.*
Nosótros temíamos,		-	-	*we did fear.*
Vosótros temíais,	-		-	-	*you did fear.*
Éllos temían,	-	-	-	*they did fear.*

Preterite definite.

Yó temí,	-	-	-	-	*I feared.*
Tú temiste,	-	-	-	-	*thou fearedst.*
Él temió,	-	-	-	-	*he feared.*
Nosótros temímos,		-	-	*we feared.*
Vosótros temísteis,	-	-	*you feared.*
Éllos temiéron,	-	-	-	*they feared.*

Preterite indefinite.

Yó he temído,	-	-	-	*I have feared.*
Tú has temído,	-	-	-	*thou hast feared.*
Él ha temído,	-	-	-	*he has feared.*
Nosótros hémos temído,		-	*we have feared.*
Vosótros habéis temído,	-	-	*you have feared.*
Ellos han temído,	-	-	*they have feared*

Preterite anterior.

Yó húbe temído,	-	-	-	*I had feared.*
Tú hubíste temído,	-	-	*thou hadst feared.*
Él húbo temído,	-	-	-	*he had feared.*
Nosótros hubímos temído,	-	*we had feared.*
Vosótros hubísteis temído,	-	*you had feared.*
Éllos hubiéron temído,	-	-	*they had feared.*

Pluperfect.

Yó había temído,	- - -	I had feared.
Tú habías temído,	- - -	thou hadst feared.
El había temído,	- - -	he had feared.
Nosótros habíamos temído,	- -	we had feared.
Vosótros habíais temído,	- -	you had feared.
Éllos habían temído,	- - -	they had feared.

Future absolute.

Yó temeré,	- - -	I shall fear.
Tú temerás,	- - - -	thou wilt fear.
Él temerá,	- - - -	he will fear.
Nosótros temerémos,	- -	we shall fear.
Vosótros temeréis,	- -	you will fear.
Éllos temerán,	- -	they will fear.

Future anterior.

Yó habré temído,	- - -	I shall have feared.
Tú habrás temído,	- - -	thou wilt have feared.
Él habrá temído,	- - -	he will have feared.
Nosótros habrémos temído,	- -	we shall have feared.
Vosótros habréis temído,	- -	you will have feared.
Éllos habrán temído,	- - -	they will have feared.

Future conjunctive simple.

Si, or cuándo,	- - -	If, or when,
Yó temiére.	- - - -	I shall fear.
Tú temiéres,	- - - -	thou wilt fear.
Él temiére,	- - - -	he will fear.
Nosótros temiéremos,	- - -	we shall fear.
Vosótros temiéreis,	- - -	you will fear.
Éllos temiéren,	- - - -	they will fear.

Future conjunctive compound.

Si, or cuándo,	- - -	If, or when,
Yó hubiére temído,	- - -	I have feared.
Tú hubiéres temído,	- - -	thou wilt have feared
Él hubiére temído,	- - -	he will have feared.
Nosótros hubiéremos temído,	-	we shall have feared.
Vosótros hubiéreis temído,	- -	you will have feared.
Éllos hubiéren temído,	- -	they will have feared.

CONDITIONALS.

First conditional present.

Yó temería, *or* temiéra,	-	I should fear.
Tú temerías,	- - -	thou wouldst fear.
Él temería,	- - -	he would fear.
Nosótros temeríamos,	- -	we should fear.
Vosótros temeríais,	- - -	you would fear.
Éllos temerían,	- - -	they would fear.

Second and third conditionals present.

Si, *or* cuándo,	- - -	If, *or* though,
Yó temiéra *or* temiése,	- -	I feared.
Tú temiéras *or* temiéses,	- -	thou shouldst fear.
Él temiéra *or* temiése,	- -	he should fear.
Nosótros temiéramos *or* temiésemos,	we should fear.
Vosótros temiérais *or* temiéseis,	you should fear.
Éllos temiéran *or* temiésen,	-	they should fear.

First conditional past.

Yó habría *or* hubiéra temído,	-	I should have feared.
Tú habrías temído,	- - -	thou wouldst have feared.
Él habría temído,	- - -	he would have feared.
Nosótros habríamos temído,	-	we should have feared.
Vosótros habríais temído,	-	you would have feared
Éllos habrían temído,	- -	they would have feared.

Second and third conditionals past.

Yó hubiéra *or* hubiése temído,	
Tú hubiéras, *or* hubiéses temído,	If, *or* though, I
Él hubiéra, *or* hubiése temído,	had feared, or
Nosótros hubiéramos, *or* hubiésemos temído,	should have
Vosótros hubiérais, *or* hubiéseis temído,	feared, &c.
Éllos hubiéran, *or* hubiésen temído,	

IMPERATIVE.

Present or future.

Téme tú,	-	-	-	fear thou.
Téma él,	-	-	-	let him fear.
Temámos nosótros,	-	-	-	let us fear.
Teméd vosótros,	-	-	-	fear ye.
Téman éllos,	-	-	-	let them fear.

SUBJUNCTIVE.

Present.

Yó téma,	-	-	-	-	I may fear.
Tú témas,	-	-	-	-	thou mayst fear.
El téma,	-	-	-	-	he may fear.
Nosótros temámos,	-	-	we may fear.
Vosótros temáis,	-	-	-	you may fear.
Ellos téman,	-	-	-	they may fear.

Imperfect.

Yó temiése,	-	-	-	I might fear.
Tú temiéses,	-	-	-	thou mightest fear.
Él temiése,	-	-	-	-	he might fear.
Nosótros temiésemos,	-	-	we might fear.
Vosótros temiéseis,	-	-	you might fear.
Éllos temiésen,	-	-	-	they might fear.

Preterite.

Yó háya temído,	-	-	-	I may have feared.
Tú háyas temído,	-	-	thou mayst have feared.
Él háya temído,	-	-	-	he may have feared.
Nosótros háyamos temído,	-	we may have feared.
Vosótros háyais temído,	-	you may have feared.
Éllos háyan temído,	-	-	they may have feared.

Pluperfect.

Yó hubiése temído,	-	I might have feared.
Tú hubiéses temído,	-	-	thou mightest have feared
Él hubiése temído,	-	-	he might have feared.
Nosótros hubiésemos temído,	-	we might have feared.
Vosótros hubiéseis temído,	-	you might have feared.
Éllos hubiésen temído,	-	-	they might have feared.

Third conjugation in IR.

INFINITIVE.

Present.	Sufr-ír,	-	-	to suffer.
Preterite.	Habér sufrído,	-	to have suffered.
Gerund.	Sufriéndo,	-	-	suffering.
Participle.	Sufrído,	-	-	suffered.

INDICATIVE.

Present.

Yó súfro,	-	-	-	-	-	I suffer.
Tú súfres,	-	-	-	-	-	thou sufferest.
Él súfre✗	-	-	-	-	-	he suffers.
Nosótros sufrímos,		-	-	-		we suffer.
Vosótros sufrís,	-	-	-	-		you suffer.
Éllos súfren,	-	-	-	-		they suffer.

Imperfect.

Yó sufría,	-	-	-	-	-	I did suffer.
Tú sufrías,	-	-	-	-	-	thou didst suffer.
Él sufría,	-	-	-	-	-	he did suffer.
Nosótros sufríamos,		-	-	-		we did suffer.
Vosótros sufríais,		-	-	-		you did suffer.
Éllos sufrían,		-	-	-		they did suffer.

Preterite definite.

Yó sufrí,	-	-	-	-	-	I suffered.
Tú sufriste,	-	-	-	-	-	thou sufferedst.
Él sufrió,	-	-	-	-	-	he suffered.
Nosótros sufrímos,		-	-	-		we suffered.
Vosótros sufrísteis,		-	-	-		you suffered.
Éllos sufriéron,		-	-	-		they suffered.

Preterite indefinite.

Yó he sufrído,	-	-	-	-	I have suffered.
Tú has sufrído,	-	-	-	-	thou hast suffered.
Él ha sufrído,	-	-	-	-	he has suffered.
Nosótros hémos sufrído,		-	-		we have suffered.
Vosótros habéis sufrído,		-	-		you have suffered.
Éllos han sufrído,	-	-	-	-	they have suffered

Preterite anterior.

Yó húbe sufrído,	-	-	-	-	I had suffered.
Tú hubíste sufrído,		-	-	-	thou hadst suffered.
Él húbo sufrído,	-	-	-	-	he had suffered.
Nosótros hubímos sufrído,		-	-		we had suffered.
Vosótros hubísteis sufrído,		-	-		you had suffered.
Éllos hubiéron sufrído,		-	-		they had suffered.

Pluperfect.

Yó había sufrído,	-	-	-	*I had suffered.*
Tú habías sufrído,	-	-	-	*thou hadst suffered.*
El había sufrído,	-	-	-	*he had suffered.*
Nosótros habíamos sufrído,		-		*we had suffered.*
Vosótros habíais sufrído,	-	-		*you had suffered.*
Éllos habían sufrído,	-	-	-	*they had suffered*

Future absolute.

Yó sufriré,	-	-	-	-	*I shall suffer.*
Tú sufrirás,	-	-	-	-	*thou wilt suffer.*
Él sufrirá,	-	-	-	-	*he will suffer.*
Nosótros sufrirémos,	-	-	-		*we shall suffer.*
Vosótros sufriréis,	-	-	-		*you will suffer.*
Éllos sufrirán,	-	-	-	-	*they will suffer.*

Future anterior.

Yó habré sufrído,	-	-	-	*I shall have suffered.*
Tú habrás sufrído,	-	-	-	*thou wilt have suffered.*
Él habrá sufrído,	-	-	-	*he will have suffered.*
Nosótros habrémos sufrído,		-		*we shall have suffered.*
Vosótros habréis sufrído,	-	-		*you will have suffered.*
Éllos habrán sufrído,	-	-	-	*they will have suffered.*

Future conjunctive simple.

Si, *or* cuándo,	-	-	-	*If, or when,*
Yó sufriére,	-	-	-	*I suffer.*
Tú sufriéres,	-	-	-	*thou wilt suffer.*
El sufriére,	-	-	-	*he will suffer.*
Nosótros sufriéremos,	-	-	-	*we shall suffer.*
Vosótros sufriéreis,	-	-	-	*you will suffer.*
Ellos sufriéren,	-	-	-	*they will suffer.*

Future conjunctive compound.

Si, *or* cuándo,	-	-	-	*If, or when,*
Yó hubiére sufrído,	-	-	-	*I shall have suffered.*
Tú hubiéres sufrído,	-	-	-	*thou wilt have suffered.*
Él hubiére sufrído,	-	-	-	*he will have suffered.*
Nosótros hubiéremos sufrído,		-		*we shall have suffered.*
Vosótros hubiéreis sufrído,	-	-		*you will have suffered.*
Éllos hubiéren sufrído,	-	-	-	*they will have suffered.*

CONDITIONALS.

First conditional present.

Yó sufriría, *or* sufriéra. - - - I should suffer.
Tú sufrirías, - - - - thou wouldst suffer.
El sufriría, - - - - he would suffer.
Nosótros sufriríamos, - - we should suffer.
Vosótros sufriríais, - - you would suffer.
Ellos sufrirían, - - - they would suffer.

Second and third conditionals present.

Si *or* cuándo, - - *If*, or though,
Yó sufriéra, *or* sufriése, - I suffered.
Tú sufriéras, *or* sufriéses, - thou shouldst suffer.
El sufriéra, *or* sufriése, - - he should suffer.
Nosótros sufriéramos, *or* sufriésemos, we should suffer.
Vosótros sufriérais, *or* sufriéseis, you should suffer.
Éllos sufriéran, *or* sufriésen, - they should suffer.

First conditional past.

Yó habría *or* hubiéra sufrído, - I should have suffered.
Tú habrías sufrído, - - thou wouldst have suffered
El habría sufrído, - - - he would have suffered.
Nosótros habríamos sufrído, - we should have suffered.
Vosótros habríais sufrído, . - you would have suffered.
Éllos habrían sufrído, - - they would have suffered.

Second and third conditionals past.

Si, *or* cuándo,
Yó hubiéra, *or* hubiése sufrído,
Tú hubiéras, *or* hubiéses sufrído,
Él hubiéra, *or* hubiése sufrído,   *If*, or though,
Nosótros hubiéramos, *or* hubiésemos sufrído,   I had suffered,
Vosótros hubiérais, *or* hubiéseis sufrído,   or should have
Éllos hubiéran, *or* hubiésen sufrído,   suffered, &c.

IMPERATIVE.

Present or future.

Súfre tú, - - - - suffer thou.
Súfra él, - - - - let him suffer.
Sufrámos nosótros, - - let us suffer.
Sufríd vosótros, - - - suffer you.
Súfran éllos, . - - - let them suffer.

SUBJUNCTIVE.

Present.

Yó súfra, - - - -	*I may suffer.*
Tú súfras, - - - -	*thou mayst suffer.*
El súfra, - - - -	*he may suffer.*
Nosótros sufrámos, - -	*we may suffer.*
Vosótros sufráis, - - -	*you may suffer.*
Éllos súfran, - - - -	*they may suffer.*

Imperfect.

Yó sufriése, ☉ - - -	*I might suffer.*
Tú sufriéses, - - -	*thou mightest suffer.*
Fl sufriése, - - - -	*he might suffer.*
Nosótros sufriésemos, - -	*we might suffer.*
Vosótros sufriéseis, - -	*you might suffer.*
Éllos sufriésen, - - -	*they might suffer.*

Preterite.

Yó háya sufrído, - - -	*I may have suffered.*
Tú háyas sufrído, - - -	*thou mayst have suffered.*
Él háya sufrído, - - -	*he may have suffered.*
Nosótros háyamos sufrído, -	*we may have suffered.*
Vosótros háyais sufrído, -	*you may have suffered.*
Éllos háyan sufrído, - -	*they may have suffered.*

Pluperfect.

Yó hubiése sufrído, - -	*I might have suffered.*
Tú hubiéses sufrído, - -	*thou mightest have suffered.*
Él hubiése sufrído, - -	*he might have suffered.*
Nosótros hubiésemos sufrído, -	*we might have suffered.*
Vosótros hubiéseis sufrído, -	*you might have suffered.*
Éllos hubiésen sufrído, - -	*they might have suffered.*

PARADIGM OF THE PASSIVE VERBS.

Observation. The passive verbs are conjugated always and in all their tenses, with the auxiliary *ser*, to be; and with the participle past of the *active* verb, which takes the gender and number of the subject.

INFINITIVE.

Present.

Ser amád-o *or* a, os *or* as, - - *to be loved.*

Preterite.

Habér sído amád-o *or* a, os *or* as, - *to have been loved.*

Participle present.

Siéndo amád-o *or* a, os *or* as, - *being loved.*

Participle past.

Habiéndo sído amúd-o *or* a, os *or* as, *having been loved.*

INDICATIVE.

Present.

Yó sóy, tú éres, él *or* élla es amádo *or* amáda. — *I am, thou art, he or she is loved.*

Nosótr-os *or* as sómos, vosótr-os *or* as sóis, éllos *or* éllas son amad-os *or* as. — *We are, you are, they are loved.*

Imperfect.

Yó éra, tú éras, él *or* élla éra amádo *or* amáda. — *I was, thou wast, he or she was loved.*

Nosótr-os *or* as éramos, vosótr-os *or* as érais, éllos *or* éllas éran amádos *or* amádas. — *We were, you were, they were loved.*

Preterite definite.

Yó fuí, tú fuíste, él *or* élla fué amádo *or* amáda. — *I was, thou wast, he or she was loved.*

Nosótr-os *or* as fuímos, vosótr-os *or* as fuísteis, éllos *or* éllas fuéron amádos *or* amádas. — *We were, you were, they were loved.*

Preterite indefinite.

Yó he, tú has, él *or* élla ha sído amádo *or* amáda. — *I have, thou hast, he or she has been loved.*

Nosótr-os *or* as hémos, vosótr-os *or* as habeís, éllos *or* éllas han sído amádos *or* amádas. — *We have, you have, they have been loved.*

Preterite anterior.

Yó húbe, tú hubíste, él *or* élla húbo sído amádo *or* amáda.	*I had, thou hadst, he or she had been loved.*
Nosótr-os *or* as hubímos, vosótr-os *or* as hubísteis, éllos *or* éllas hubiéron sído amádos *or* amádas.	*We had, you had, they had been loved.*

Pluperfect.

Yó había, tú habías, él *or* élla había sído amád-o *or* a.	*I had, thou hadst, he or she had been loved.*
Nosótr-os *or* as habíamos, vosótr-os *or* as habíais, éllos *or* éllas habían sído amádos *or* amádas.	*We had, you had, they had been loved.*

Future absolute.

Yó seré, tú serás, él *or* élla será amád-o *or* a.	*I shall be, thou wilt be, he or she will be loved.*
Nosótros serémos, vosótros seréis, éllos *or* éllas serán amád-os *or* as.	*We shall be, you will be, they will be loved.*

Future anterior.

Yó habré, tú habrás, él *or* élla habrá sído amád-o *or* a.	*I shall have, thou wilt have, he or she will have been loved.*
Nosótr-os *or* as habrémos, vosótr-os *or* as habréis, éllos *or* éllas habrán sído amád-os *or* as.	*We shall have, you will have, they will have been loved.*

Future conjunctive simple.

Si, *or* cuándo, Yó fuéro, tú fuéres, él *or* élla fuéro amád-o *or* a. Nosótr-os *or* as fuéremos, vosótr-os *or* as fuéreis, éllos *or* éllas fuéren amád-os *or* as.	*If, or when, I am loved, or I shall be loved, &c.*

Future conjunctive compound.

Si, *or* cuándo, Yó hubiére, tu hubiéres, él *or* élla hubiére sído amád-o *or* a. Nosótr-os *or* as hubiéremos, vosótr-os *or* as hubiércis, éllos *or* éllas hubiéren sído amádos *or* as.	*If, or when, I have been loved, or I shall have been loved, &c.*

CONDITIONALS.

First conditional present.

Yó sería *or* fuéra, tú serías, él *or* ella sería amád-o *or* a. Nosótr-os *or* as seríamos, vosótr-os *or* as seríais, éllos *or* éllas serían amád-os *or* as.	*I should be, thou wouldst be, he or she would be loved. We should be, you would be, they would be loved.*

Second and third conditionals present.

Si, *or* cuándo, Yó fuéra *or* fuése, tu fuéras *or* fuéses, él *or* élla fuéra *or* fuése amád-o *or* a. Nosótr-os *or* as fuéramos *or* fuésemos, vosótr-os *or* as fuérais *or* fuéseis, éllos *or* éllas fuéran *or* fuésen amád-os *or* as.	*If, or though, I were loved, or I should be loved, &c.*

First conditional past.

Yó habría *or* hubiéra, tú habrías, él *or* élla habría sído amád-o *or* a. Nosótr-os *or* as habríamos, vosótr-os *or* as habríais, éllos *or* éllas habrían sído amád-os *or* as.	*I should have, thou wouldst have, he or she would have been loved. We should have, you would have, they would have been loved.*

Second and third conditionals past.

Si, *or* cuándo,
Yó hubiéra *or* hubiése, tú hubiéras *or* hubiéses, él or élla hubiéra *or* hubiése sído amád-o *or* a,
Nosótr-os *or* as hubiéramos *or* hubiésemos, vosótr-os *or* as hubiérais *or* hubiéseis, éllos *or* éllas hubiéran *or* hubiésen sído amád-os *or* as.

If, or though, I had been loved, or I should have been loved, &c.

IMPERATIVE.

Sé amád-o *or* a,	*Be thou loved.*
Séa amád-o *or* a,	*Let him be loved.*
Seámos amád-os *or* as,	*Let us be loved.*
Sed amád-os *or* as,	*Be ye loved.*
Séan amád-os *or* as	*Let them be loved.*

SUBJUNCTIVE.

Present.

Yó séa, tú séas, él *or* élla séa amád-o *or* a,
Nosótr-os *or* as seámos, vosótr-os *or* as seáis, éllos *or* éllas séan amád-os *or* as.

I may be, thou mayst be, he or she may be loved. We may be, you may be, they may be loved.

Imperfect.

Yó fuése, tu fuéses, él *or* élla fuése amád-o *or* a.
Nosótr-os *or* as fuésemos, vosótr-os *or* as fuéseis, éllos *or* éllas fuésen amád-os *or* as.

I might be, thou mightest be, he or she might be loved. We might be, you might be, they might be loved.

Preterite.

Yó háya, tú háyas, él *or* élla háya sído amád-o *or* a,

Nosótr-os *or* as háyamos, vosótr-os *or* as háyais, éllos *or* éllas háyan sido amád-os *or* as

I may have, thou mayst have, he or she may have been loved. We may have, you may have, they may have been loved.

10*

Pluperfect.

Yó hubiése, tú hubiéses, él or
  élla hubiése sído amád-o
  or a,

Nosótr-os *or* as hubiésemos, vosótr-os *or* as hubiéseis, éllos
  or éllas hubiésen sído amád-
  os *or* as

*I might have, thou mightest
have, he or she might
have been loved.*

*We might have, you might
have, they might have been
loved.*

PARADIGM OF NEUTER VERBS.

Observation. These verbs take in Spanish as an auxiliary
in their compound tenses, the verb *habér*, to have, and the
participle is indeclinable. In their simple tenses they are
conjugated like the verbs of the conjugation to which they
belong.

INFINITIVE.

Present.   Llegár,*   *To arrive.*
Preterite.   Habér llegádo,   *To have arrived.*
Gerund.   Llegándo,   *Arriving.*
Participle.   Llegádo,   *Arrived.*

INDICATIVE.

Present.

Llég-o, as, a, ámos, áis, an.   *I arrive, &c.*

Imperfect.

Lleg-ába, ábas, ába, ábamos,
  ábais, ában.   *I did arrive, &c*

Preterite definite.

Lleg-ué,† áste, ó, ámos, ásteis,
  áron.   *I arrived, &c.*

---

* This verb without being irregular, takes an *u* after the *g* in all the persons in
which it is immediately followed by an *e*. This rule applies to all the verbs that
end in *gar*. (See N. B. 4th, page 121.)

† We suppress the pronouns, the use of which the Spaniards generally dispense
with, in speaking as well as in writing, the preceding conjugations giving examples
enough of them.

Preterite indefinite.

He llegádo, - - - - *I have arrived.*
Has llegádo, - - - - *thou hast arrived.*
Ha llegádo, - - - - *he has arrived.*
Hémos llegádo, - - *we have arrived.*
Habéis llegádo, - - *you have arrived.*
Han llegádo, - - - - *they have arrived.*

Preterite anterior.

Húbe, hubíste, húbo, hubímos, hubísteis, hubiéron llegádo. *I had, thou hadst, he or she had, we had, you had, they had arrived.*

Pluperfect.

Había, habías, había, habíamos, habíais, habían llegádo. *I had, thou hadst, he or she had, we had, you had, they had arrived.*

Future absolute.

Lleg-aré, arás, ará, arémos, aréis, arán. *I shall or will arrive, &c.*

Future anterior.

Habré, habrás, habrá, habrémos, habréis, habrán llegádo. *I shall have, thou wilt have, he or she will have, we shall have, you will have, they will have arrived.*

Future conjunctive simple.

Si, or cuándo, Lleg-áre, áres, áre, áremos, áreis, áren. *If, or when, I arrive, or shall arrive, &c.*

Future conjunctive compound.

Si, or cuándo, Hubiére, hubiéres, hubiére, hubiéremos, hubiéreis, hubiéren llegádo. *If, or when, I have or shall have arrived, &c. if or when we have, or shall have arrived, &c.*

CONDITIONALS.

First conditional present.

Lleg-aría or lleg-ára, arías, aría, aríamos, aríais, arían *I should or would arrive, &c.*

Second and third conditionals present.

Si, *or* cuándo,	*If*, or *though, I arrived* or *should arrive, &c.*
Lleg-ára *or* áse, áras *or* áses, ára, *or* áse.	
Lleg-áramos *or* ásemos, árais *or* áseis, áran *or* ásen.	*If*, or *though, we arrived* or *should arrive, &c.*

First conditional past.

Habría, *or* hubiéra, habrías, habría, habríamos, habríais, habrían llegádo.	*I should have, thou wouldst have, he or she would have, we should have, you would have, they would have arrived.*

Second and third conditionals past.

Si, *or* cuándo,	*If*, or *though, I had* or *should have arrived, &c.*
Hubiéra *or* hubiése, hubiéras *or* hubiéses, hubiéra *or* hubiése.	
Hubiéramos *or* hubiésemos, hubiérais *or* hubiéseis, hubiéran *or* hubiésen llegádo.	*If*, or *though, we had* or *should have arrived, &c.*

IMPERATIVE.

Present or future.

Llég-a tú,	-	-	-	-	*arrive thou.*
Llég-ue él,	-	-	-	-	*let him arrive.*
Lleg-uémos nosótros,		-	-		*let us arrive.*
Lleg-ád vosótros,	-		-	-	*arrive ye.*
Llég-uen éllos,	-		-	-	*let them arrive.*

SUBJUNCTIVE.

Present.

Lllég-ue, ues, ue, uémos, uéis, uen.	*I may arrive, &c.*

Imperfect.

Lleg-áse, áses, áse, ásemos, áseis, ásen.	*I might arrive, &c.*

Preterite.

Háya, háyas, háya, háyamos, háyais, háyan llegádo.
I may have arrived, &c. we may have arrived, &c.

Pluperfect.

Hubiése, hubiéses, hubiése, hubiésemos, hubiéseis, hubiésen llegádo.
I might have arrived, &c we might have arrived, &c.

PARADIGM OF REFLECTIVE AND RECIPROCAL VERBS.

Observation. Reflective and reciprocal verbs have no conjugation peculiar to them. In the simple tenses they are conjugated like the verbs of the conjugation to which they belong; and they form the compound tenses with the auxiliary *habér* and not *ser;* and the participle past is indeclinable. Nevertheless, as the double pronoun, which is found in all the tenses and in each person, might present some difficulties, we shall conjugate some tenses of the verb *congratulárse,* to congratulate oneself, which will suffice both for reflective and reciprocal verbs; observing however, that the reciprocal verbs can be such only in the three persons plural, because reciprocity cannot exist but between two persons at least. In these persons, *yó me congratúlo, tú te congratúlas, él se congratúla,* I congratulate myself, thou congratulatest thyself, he congratulates himself, the verb is reflective; and in *nosótros nos congratulámos, vosótros os congratuláis, éllos se congratúlan,* the verb can be either reflective or reciprocal; it is reciprocal if these words *únos á ótros,* each other, *mútuaménte,* mutually, can be joined to the verb: it is reflective if these words are neither expressed nor understood.

INFINITIVE.

Present.

Congratulárse,* . *to congratulate oneself.*

Preterite.

Habérse congratuládo, *to have congratulated oneself.*

---

* All verbs require the regimen or objective pronouns to be placed close after them in the *present* and *gerund,* and after the auxiliary in the compound tenses of the *Infinitive* mode, whether used affirmatively or negatively; Ex. *No alabárse,* not to praise oneself; *no conociéndose,* not knowing himself; *no habérse alabádo,* not to have praised oneself; *no habiéndose conocido,* not having known himself.

Gerund.

Congratulándose,   *congratulating oneself.*

Compound gerund.

Habiéndose congratuládo,   *having congratulated oneself.*

Participle.

Congratuládo,   *congratulated.*

INDICATIVE.
Present.

Yó me congratúlo,	*I congratulate myself.*
Tú te congratúlas,	*thou congratulatest thyself.*
Él se congratúla,	*he congratulates himself.*
Nosótros nos congratulámos,*	*we congratulate ourselves.*
Vosótros os congratuláis,	*you congratulate yourselves.*
Éllos se congratúlan,	*they congratulate themselves.*

The other simple tenses follow the same order.

Preterite indefinite.

Yó me he congratuládo,	*I have congratulated myself.*
Tú te has congratuládo,	*thou hast congratulated thyself.*
Él se ha congratuládo,	*he has congratulated himself.*
Nosótros nos hémos congratuládo,	*we have congratulated ourselves.*
Vosótros os habéis congratuládo,	*you have congratulated yourselves.*
Éllos se han congratuládo.	*they have congratulated themselves.*

All the compound tenses follow the same order.

IMPERATIVE.

Congratúlate,	*congratulate thyself.*
Congratúlese, ·	*let him congratulate himself.*
Congratulémonos,*	*let us congratulate ourselves.*
Congratuláos,*	*congratulate yourselves.*
Congratúlense,	*let them congratulate themselves.*

---

* The *s* of the first person plural, and the *d* of the second, when used affirmatively, are *always* suppressed in the *imperative*, in reflective and reciprocal verbs; and the *s* of the first person plural of the tenses of the *indicative* mode, when the reflective pronoun is placed after it, is also elegantly suppressed. Ex. *Amámonos*, we love ourselves; *divertímonos*, we amused ourselves; *compadecerémonos*, we shall compassionate.

PARADIGM OF THE IMPERSONAL VERBS
INFINITIVE.

Present.	Granizár, - -	*to hail.*
Preterite.	Habér granizádo,	*to have hailed.*
Gerund.	Granizándo, -	*hailing.*
Participle.	Granizádo, - -	*hailed.*

INDICATIVE.

Present.	Graníza, - -	** it hails.*
Imperfect.	Granizába, - -	*it did hail.*
Pret. def.	Granizó, - -	*it hailed.*
Pret. indef.	Ha granizádo, -	*it has hailed.*
Pret. ant.	Húbo granizádo,	*it had hailed.*
Pluperfect.	Había granizádo,	*it had hailed.*
Fut. abs.	Granizará, - -	*it will hail.*
Fut. ant.	Habrá granizádo,	*it will have hailed.*
Fut. conj.	Cuándo granizáre,	*when it shall hail.*
F. conj. past.	Cuándo hubiére gra-nizádo,	*when it shall have hailed.*

CONDITIONALS.

Present.	Granizaría or granizára, *it would hail.*	
Past.	Habría *or* hubiéra gra-nizádo,	*it would have hailed.*

SUBJUNCTIVE.

Que

Present.	Graníce, - -	*that it may hail.*
Imperfect.	Granizáse, - -	*that it might hail.*
Preterite.	Háya granizádo,	*that it may have hailed.*
Pluperfect.	Hubiése granizádo,	*that it might have hailed.*

Conjugation of the impersonal verb SER MENES-TÉR, *to be requisite or necessary.*

INFINITIVE.

Present.	Ser menestér, -	*to be necessary.*
Gerund.	Siéndo menestér,	*being necessary.*
Participle.	Sído menestér, -	*been necessary.*

INDICATIVE.

Present.	Es menestér, - -	*it is necessary.*
Imperfect.	Éra menestér, -	*it was necessary.*
Pret. def.	Fué menestér, -	*it was necessary.*
Fut. abs.	Será menestér, -	*it will be necessary.*
Fut conj.	Cuándo fuére menester,	*when it shall be necessary.*

---

* The Pronoun *it* nominative of impersonal Verbs is not expressed in Spanish.

CONDITIONAL.

Sería *or* fuéra menestér, -   -   *it would be necessary.*

SUBJUNCTIVE.

Present.   Séa menestér, - -   *it may be necessary.*
Imperfect.   Fuése menestér, -   *it might be necessary.*

The compound tenses of this verb are formed as in English, except that the pronoun *it* is not expressed in Spanish as may be seen throughout the impersonal verbs; Ex. It has been necessary, *ha sído menestér, &c.*

Conjugation of the impersonal verb HABÉR.

INDICATIVE.

Present.   Háy,*   -   -   -   *there is, there are.*
Imperfect. Había, -   -   -   *there was, there were.*
Pret. def. Húbo,   -   -   -   *there was, there were.*
Fut. abs.   Habrá, -   -   -   *there shall or will be.*
Fut. conj. Si hubiére, -   -   *if there be or shall be.*

CONDITIONAL.

Habría *or* hubiéra, -   -   -   *there would or should be.*

SUBJUNCTIVE.

Present.   Háya,   -   -   -   *there may be*
Imperfect. Hubiése,   -   -   *there might be.*

N. B. This impersonal is used thus, that is to say, in the third person singular, even with a substantive in the plural; as, *háy un hómbre*, there is a man; *húbo mugéres*, there were women. The compound tenses are formed by adding the participle *habído*, to the simple tenses. Ex. *Ha habído*, there has or there have been; *había habído, &c.*

LIST OF SOME IMPERSONAL VERBS.

Infinitive.	*3d. pers. of the pres. of the Ind.*
Amanecér, *to begin to be day-light.*	Amanéce, *it begins to be day-light.*
Anochecér, *to begin to grow dark.*	Anochéce, *it begins to grow dark.*

---

* *Hay* loses the letter *y* when this word is placed at the end of a phrase. Ex. For *háy un áño*, we also say, *un áño ha*, it is one year or a year ago. We often use *hacér* for *habér*, as an impersonal verb; as, *háce diéz áños que murió*, it is ten years since he died, or he has been dead these ten years.

Escarchár, *to freeze, to glaze,** Escárcha, *it freezes, it glazes.*
Granizár, *to hail,*   Graníza, *it hails.*
Helár, *to freeze,*   Hiéla, *it freezes.*
Llovér, *to rain,*   Lluéve, *it rains.*
Lloviznár, *to drizzle,*   Llovízna, *it drizzles.*
Nevár, *to snow,*   Niéva, *it snows.*
Relampagueár, *to lighten,*   Relampaguéa, *it lightens.*
Tronár, *to thunder,*   Truéna, *it thunders.*

Observation. Amanecér and *anochecér* have sometimes the three persons; then they signify to arrive, to be, to find one-self at the dawn of day or at the fall of night in a certain condition. Ex. *Mi pádre amaneció en Paris: amaneció el cámpo lléno de rocío:* are, as if I said, *mi pádre llegó á Paris cuándo amaneció: el cámpo estába lléno de rocío cuándo amaneció,* my father arrived at Paris when the day dawned: the fields were covered with dew at the dawn of day. *Mi amigo amaneció póbre, é yó anochecí rico,* that is to say, *mi amigo se halló póbre cuándo amaneció, é yó me hallé rico cuándo anocheció,* my friend was poor when the sun rose, and I was rich when the sun set; *vm. anocheció buéno, y amaneció málo,* you went to bed well, and rose sick.

List and conjugations of the irregular verbs, arranged in alphabetical order.

IMPORTANT OBSERVATIONS.

N. B. 1st. The verbs marked thus† are little used.

2d. The third conditional not differing at all in its terminations from the imperfect of the subjunctive, we have thought it useless to conjugate it in the conditional, and we have contented ourselves with giving it in the subjunctive.

3d. We place in the subjunctive mode the future conjunctive simple for the sake of distinctness and regularity.

4th. There are some verbs which undergo slight alterations, either in their radical letters, or in their terminations; but they are not on that account irregular; they only undergo these changes to preserve in the other tenses the pronunciation analogous to that which they have in the present of the infinitive. Of this number are,—1st,—the verbs ending in *car,* which change the *c* into *qu* when it must be followed by an *e:* as, *buscár,* to seek, *busqué,* I sought; *búsque, búsques, búsque, &c.* that I may seek, that thou mayst seek, that

---

* Speaking of dew or rain that glazes what it falls upon by freezing.

11

he may seek, &c.—2d.—Those ending in *gar* and *guir* which
take an *u* after the *g* before *e* and *i*; as, *llegár*, to arrive; *llegué*, I arrived: *distinguir*, to distinguish; *distingo*, *distinga*;
and drops it before *a* and *o*. See *seguir*, p. 148.—3d.—Several ending in *cer* and *cir* which change the *c* into *z* before *a*
and *o*; as, *vencér*, to conquer; *vénzo*, I conquer; *resarcír*, to
repair; *resárzo*, I repair.—4th.—For the same reason *delin-
quír*, to do wrong, changes *qu* into *c* before *a* and *o*. Ex. *De-
línco*, *delínca*, *delincámos*;—and *escogér*, to choose, changes
the *g* into *j* before *a* and *o*. Ex. *Escójo*, *escója*.—5th.—The
verbs which terminate in *eér*, as, *creér*, to believe; *leér*, to
read; *poseér*, to possess; *proveér*, to provide; in those terminations which contain an *i*, change it into *y* whenever it is
to be joined with another vowel; as, *creí*, *creyó*; *leí*, *leyé-
ron*; *poseí*, *poseyére*; *proveí*, *proveyéremos*, &c.—6th.—We
must make the same change in the verbs ending in *uir*,
when the *u* and the *i* make a part of two different syllables.
Thus, *huír*, to fly, makes in the third person of the preterite
definite, *huyó*; *argüir* makes *arguyó*; *constituír* makes
constituyó, &c.

N. B. 1st. The *tenses* and *persons* which are *irregular*
are laid down in *italics*, and *only* the *first person* of the tenses
which are *regular* or run off *uniformly irregular* throughout
the tense, is expressed.

N. B. 2d. The verbs that are referred to page 71, only,
have no other irregularity than is there stated: *p.* will stand
for *page* and *pages*.

A.

Inf. Pres.	Aborrecér,	*to hate, to abhor.*
Gerund.	Aborreciéndo,	*hating.*
Participle.	Aborrecído,	*hated.*

Ind. Pres.	*Aborrézco*, aborréces, aborréce, }	*I hate* or
	aborrecémos, aborrecéis, aborrécen, }	*abhor.*
Imperfect.	Aborrecía, &c.	*I did abhor.*
Pret. def.	Aborrecí, &c.	· *I hated.*
Future.	Aborreceré, &c.	*I shall* or *will hate.*
Condition.	Aborrecería *or* aborreciéra, &c.	{ *I should* or { *would hate.*
Imperat.	*Aborréce, aborrézca*, aborrezcámos, aborrecéd, *aborrézcan*.	*hate thou,* &c.
Sub. pres.	{ Que *aborrézca, aborrézcas, aborrézca,* { *aborrezcámos, aborrezcáis, aborréz-* { *can.*	{ *that I hate* { or *may* { *hate.*

Imperfect. Que aborreciése, &c, *that I hated,* or *might hate.*
Future. Si aborreciére, &c. *If I hate or shall hate.*

N. B. The irregularity of this verb, and of all like it in *ecér*, and of those ending in *océr*, *acér*, and *ucír*, consists in taking a *z* before *c* in the first person singular of the present indicative, in all those of the present subjunctive, in the first of the plural, and in the third of the singular and plural of the imperative. The verbs *hacér* and *cocér*, and their compounds are the only exceptions to this rule; the first has other irregularities, and both are found conjugated in their alphabetical order.

Abrír, *to open, is irregular only in the participle* abiérto.

Infinitive.	Absolvér,	*to absolve.*
Gerund.	Absolviéndo,	*absolving.*
Participle.	*Absuélto,*	*absolved.*

Ind. pres. Absuélvo, absuélves, absuélve,
absolvémos, absolvéis, absuélven, } *I absolve,* or *do absolve.*

Imperfect. Absolvía, &c. *I did absolve.*

Pret. def. Absolví, &c. *I absolved.*

Future. Absolveré, &c *I shall* or *will absolve*

Condition. Absolvería *or* absolviéra, &c. *I should* or *would absolve.*

Imperative. *Absuélve, absuélva,* } *absolve thou,*
absolvámos, absolvéd, *absuélvan.* } &c.

Subj. Pres. Que absuélva, absuélvas, absuélva, } *that I absolve*
absolvámos, absolváis, *absuélvan,* } *or may absolve.*

Imperfect. Que absolviése, &c. *that I absolved* or *might absolve.*

Future. Cuándo absolviére, &c. *when I absolve* or *shall absolve.*

Abstraér, *to abstract, to make an abstraction.* See traér, p. 149.
Acaecér, *to happen, (impersonal.)* See aborrecér, p. 122.

Infinitive.	Acertár,	*to succeed, to hit the mark.*
Gerund.	Acertándo,	*succeeding.*
Participle.	Acertádo,	*succeeded.*

Ind. pres. Aciérto, aciértas, aciérta,
Acertámos, acertáis, *aciértan* } *I succeed,* or *hit the mark.*

Imperf. Acertába, &c. *I did succeed.*

Pret. def. Acerté, &c. *I succeeded.*

| *Future.* | Acertaré, &c. | *I shall* or *will succeed.* |
| *Condit.* | Acertaría *or* acertára, &c. | *I should* or *would succeed.* |

Imperat.	*Aciérta, aciérte,* acertémos, acertád, *aciérten,*	} *· succeed thou,* &c.
Sub. pres.	Que *aciérte, aciértes, aciérte,* acertémos, acertéis, *aciérten,*	} *that I succeed,* or *may succeed.*
Imperf	Que acertáse, &c.	*that I succeeded,* or *might succeed.*
Future.	Si acertáre, &c.	*if I succeed,* or *shall succeed.*

Inf. pres.	Acordár,	*to agree, to resolve.*
Gerund.	Acordándo,	*agreeing.*
Participle.	Acordádo,	*agreed.*
Ind. pres.	*Acuérdo, acuérdas, acuérda,* Acordámos, acordáis, *acuérdan.*	} *I agree,* or *do resolve.*
Imperf.	Acordába, &c.	*I did agree.*
Pret. def.	Acordé, &c.	*I agreed.*
Future.	Acordaré, &c.	*I shall* or *will agree.*
Condit.	Acordaría, acordára, &c.	*I should* or *would agree.*
Imperat.	*Acuérda, acuérde,* acordémos, acordád, *acuérden.*	} *agree thou, &c*
Sub. pres.	Que *acuérde, acuérdes, acuérde,* acordémos, acordéis, *acuérden.*	} *that I agree,* or *may agree.*
Imperf.	Que acordáse, &c.	*that I agreed* or *might agree.*
Future.	Cuándo acordáre, &c.	*when I agree or shall agree.*

Acordárse, *to remember.*   See acordar, p. 124.
Acordár á úno, *to make one remember*   Idem.
Acostár, *to put to bed.*   Idem.
Acostárse, *to go to bed.*   Idem.
Acrecentár, *to increase.*   See acertár, p. 123.

Inf. pres.	Adherír,	*to adhere.*
Gerund.	Adhiriéndo,	*adhering.*
Participle.	Adherído,	*adhered.*
Indic. pres	*Adhiéro, adhiéres, adhiére,* adherímos, adherís, *adhiéren.*	} *I adhere,* or *do adhere.*
Imperf.	Adhería &c	*I did adhere.*
Pret. def.	Adherí, adheríste, *adhirió,* adherímos, adherísteis, *adhiriéron.*	} *I adhered.*
Future	Adheriré, &c.	*I shall* or *will adhere*

Condit. Adheriría, *or adhiriéra,&c. I should, or would adhere.*

Imperat. Adhiére, adhiéra, } *adhere thou, &c.*
adhirámos, adheríd, adhiéran, }

Sub. pres. Que adhiéra, adhiéras, adhiéra, } *that I adhere,*
adhirámos, adhiráis, adhiéran, } *or may adhere.*

Imperf. Que adhiriése, *&c. that I adhered, or might adhere.*

Future. Si adhiriére, *&c.   if I adhere, or shall adhere*

Adestrár, *to guide, to teach.*   See acertár, p. 123.
Adolecér, *to fall or to be sick.*   See aborrecér, p. 122.
Adormecér, *to lull asleep.*   Idem.
Advertír, *to perceive, observe, advise.*   See adherír p. 124.
Adquerír, *or* adquirír, *to acquire.*   Idem.
Aducír, *to adduce.*   See conducír, p. 129
†Agorár, *to augur, to conjecture.*   See acordár, p. 124
Agradecér, *to take a thing kindly, to acknowledge a benefit, to
    thank.*   See aborrecér, p. 122.
Ahitár, *to surfeit.*   See p. 71.
{ Alentár, *to encourage.*   See acertár, p. 123.
{ Alentárse, *to take courage.*   Idem.
Almorzár, *to breakfast.*   See acordár, p. 124.
Amanecér, (verb. imp.) *to grow daylight.* See aborrecér, p. 122.
†Amentár, *to shoot an arrow.*   See acertár, p. 123.
Amolár, *to sharpen, to whet.*   See acordár, p. 124.
†Amortecérse, *to faint, to lose courage.* See aborrecér, p. 122.

Inf. pres.   Andár,   *to walk, to go.*
Gerund.   Andándo,   *walking.*
Participle.   Andádo,   *walked.*

Ind. pres. Ándo, &c.   *I walk, or do walk.*
Imperf. Andába, &c.   *I did walk.*
Pret. def. Andúve, anduvíste, andúvo, } *I walked.*
    anduvímos, anduvísteis, anduviéron, }
Future. Andaré, &c.   *I shall or will walk.*
Condit. Andaría *or* anduviéra, *&c.   I should or would walk.*
Imperat.   Ánda, ánde, andémos, &c.   *walk thou, &c.*
Sub. pres. Que ánde, &c.   *that I walk, or may walk.*
Imperf. Que anduviése, *&c.   that I walked, or might walk.*
Future. Cuándo anduviére, *&c. when I walk, or shall walk.*

Anochecér, *to begin to grow dark.*   See aborrecér, p. 122.
Anteponér, *to prefer.*   See ponér, p. 143
Antevér, *to foresee*   See ver. p. 151.

Apacentár, *to lead sheep to grass.*   See acertár, p. 123.
Aparecér, *to appear.*   See aborrecér, p. 122.
Apercibír, *to prepare, to get ready.*   See pedír, p. 142.
Apetecér, *to wish, to long for.*   See aborrecér, p. 122.
Aplacer, *to please.*   See placer, p. 142.
Apostár, *to lay a wager.*   See acordár, p. 124.
Aporcár, *to cover with earth,* (*cclery, &c.*)   Idem.
Aportár, *to make a harbor*   Idem.
Apretár, *to tighten.*   See acertár, p. 123.
Aprobár, *to approve.*   See acordár, p. 124.
†Arbolecér, *to become a tree.*   See aborrecér, p. 122.
Apovrecér, *to impoverish.*   Idem
Arrendár, *to let to a tenant;—to tie* (*a horse*) *by the reins*
     See acertár, p. 123.
Asentír, *to consent, assent.*   See adherír, p. 124.
Arrepentírse, *to repent,* (refl. v.)   See adherír, p. 124.
Ascendér, *to ascend.*   See entendér, p. 135.
Asentár, *to sit down, to place, to resolve, to register.*   See
     acertár, p. 123.
Aserrár, *to saw.*   See acertár, p. 123.
Asestár, *to aim or point at.*   Idem.
Asír, *to seize, to take root,* (*speaking of plants, or figuratively speaking of persons,*) *has no irregularity but in the following tenses, which are very little used. Indicat. pres.* Asgo, áses áse, asimos, asís, ásen. *Imperat.* Ase, ásga, asgámos, asíd, ásgan. *Subj. pres.* Ásga, ásgas, ásga, asgámos, as gáis, ásgan.
Asolár, *to pull down, to destroy.*   See acordár, p. 124
Asoldár, *to furnish one with money*   Idem.
Asonár, *to assemble by the sound of bells, to tune.*   Idem.
Atendér, *to apply oneself, to consider, to regard.*   See entendér, p. 135.
†Atenér, *to keep pace with another—to keep one's word.*   See tenér, p. 86.
Atentár, *to attempt—to form an enterprise against the laws in a capital concern.*   See acertár, p. 123
†Aterecérse, *to get benumbed, to stiffen with cold.*   See (r. v.) aborrecér, p. 122.
Aterrár, *to throw down on the ground.*   See acertár, p. 123.
Atestár, *to fill up.*   Idem.
Atormecérse, *to get benumbed.*   See aborrecér, p. 122.
Atraér, *to attract, to draw over to oneself.*   See traér, p. 149
Atravesár, *to pierce, bore, or cross.*   See acertár, p. 123

†Atronár, *to thunder,* (*verb. imp.*) See acordár, p. 124.

{ Avenír, *to happen, to come unexpectedly, to reconcile a dif-*
ference. See venír, p. 150.
Avenírse, *to agree, to be suitable, agreeable.* (refl. v.) Idem.

{ Aventár, *to fan, to winnow.* See acertár, p. 123.
Aventárse, *to be frightened,* (*speaking of a flock.*) Idem.

{ Avergonzár, *to make one ashamed.* See acordár, p. 124.
Avergonzárse, *to be ashamed.* (refl. v.) Idem.

B.

Inf. pres.	Bendecír,	*to bless.*
Gerund.	*Bendiciéndo,*	*blessing.*
Participle.	*Bendíto,*	*blessed.*

See p. 71.

Ind. pres. Bendígo, *bendíces, bendíce,* ben-
decímos, bendecís, *bendícen.* } *I bless, or do bless.*

Imperf. Bendecía, &c. *I did bless*

Pret def. Bendíge, *bendigíste, bendijo, bendi-*
gímos, bendigísteis, bendigéron, } *I blessed.*

Future. Bendeciré, &c. *I shall or will bless.*

Condit. Bendeciría, or *bendigéra, &c. I should or would bless.*

Imperat. *Bendíce, bendíga,*
bendigámos, bendecíd, *bendígan,* } *bless thou, &c.*

Sub. pres. Que *bendíga, &c.* *that I bless, or may bless.*

Imperf. Que *bendigése, &c.* *that I blessed, or might bless.*

Future. Si *bendigére, &c.* *if I bless, or shall bless.*

C.

Inf. pres.	Cabér,	*to fall to, to happen, to be contained.*
Gerund.	Cabiéndo,	*being contained.*
Participle.	Cabído,	*been contained.*

Ind. pres. Quépo, *cábes, &c.* *I am contained.*

Imperf. Cabía, &c. *I was contained.*

Pret. def. Cúpe, *cupíste, cúpo, &c.* *I was contained.*

Future. Cabré, *&c.* *I shall or will be contained*

Condit. Cabría, or *cupiéra, &c.* *I should or would be con-*
tained.

Imperat. Cábe, quépa,
quepámos, cabéd, quépan, } *be thou contained, &c.*

Sub. pres. Que quépa, *&c.* *that I be or may be contained.*

Imperf. Que cupiése, *&c.* *that I was or might be contained.*

Future. Cuándo cupiére, *&c.* *when I be, or shall be contained*

Inf. pres.	Caér,	*to fall.*
Gerund.	Cayéndo,	*falling.*
Participle.	Caído,	*fallen.*

Ind. pres.	Cáigo, cáes, &c.	. *I fall or do fall*
Imperf.	Caía, &c.	*I did fall*
Pret. perf.	Caí, caíste, cayó, caímos, caísteis, cayéron, *I fell.*
Future.	Caeré, &c.	*I shall or will fall.*
Condition.	Caería or cayéra,	*I should or would fall.*
Imperat.	Cáe, *cáiga,* caigámos, caéd, *cáigan,*	} *fall thou, &c.*
Sub. pres.	Que cáiga, &c.	*that I fall, or may fall.*
Imperf.	Que cayése, &c.	*that I fell or might fall.*
Future.	Si cayére, &c.	*if I fall, or shall fall.*

Calentár, *to warm, to heat.*   See acertár, p. 123
Canecér, *to grow grayhaired.*   See aborrecér, p. 122.
Carecér, *to want, to be in want of.*   Idem.
Cegár, *to blind, to become blind.*   See acertár, p. 123.
{ Ceñír, *to girdle, to surround.*   See . . . pedír, p. 142.
{ Ceñírse, *to girdle oneself; to limit oneself; to restrict oneself.* (refl. v.)   Idem.
Cernér, *to sift, to pass flour through a sieve—to blossom,* (speaking *of vines, of grain, &c.*)   See entendér, p. 135.
Cerrár, *to shut, to lock up.*   See acertár, p. 123.
Cimentár, *to cement, to lay the foundation.*   Idem.

Inf. pres.	Cocér,	*to cook, to bake.*
Gerund.	Cociéndo,	*cooking.*
Participle.	Cocído,	*cooked.*

Ind. pres.	Cuézo, cuéces, cuéce, cocémos, cocéis, cuécen,	} *I bake or do bake.*
Imperf.	Cocía, &c.	*I did cook.*
Pret. perf.	Cocí, &c.	*I baked.*
Future.	Coceré, &c.	*I shall or will cook.*
Condit.	. Cocería or cociéra, &c	*I should or would bake.*
Imperat.	Cuéce, *cuéza,* cozámos, cocéd, *cuézan,*	} *bake thou, &c.*
Sub. pres.	Que *cuéza, cuézas, cuéza,* cozámos, cozáis, *cuézan,*	} *that I bake, or may bake.*
Imperf.	Que cociése, &c.	*that I baked, or might bake.*
Future.	Cuándo cociére, &c.	*when I bake, or shall bake.*

N. B. This verb has the same irregularities as *Absolvér;*

hut we have conjugated it on account of the *z* which it takes instead of the *c* before *a* and *o*, and its regular part. past; that we may refer to it for the conjugation of similar verbs.

Colár, *to strain, to filter a liquor.* See acordár, p. 124.
Colegír, *to collect, to conclude, to deduce.* See pedír, p. 142.

  N. B. It changes *g* into *j* before *a* and *o*. See p. 122. Obs. 4.

Colgár, *to hang, to suspend.* See acordár, p. 124.
†Comedír, *to reflect, to think, to premeditate.* See pedír, p. 142.
Comedírse, *to become polite, to be ruled by reason.* (r. v.) Idem.
Comenzár, *to begin.* See acertár, p. 123.
Compadecérse, *to have pity.* (refl. v.) See aborrecér, p. 122.
Compelér, *to compel.* See p. 71.
Componér, *to compose, adjust.* See ponér, p. 143.
Comparecér, *to appear.* See aborrecér, p. 122.
Competír, *to rival, to compete.* See pedír, p. 142.
Complacér, *to please one, gratify.* See aborrecér, p. 122.
Comprobár, *to prove, to confirm.* See acordár, p. 124.
Concebír, *to conceive.* See pedír, p. 142.
Concertár, *to concert.* See acertár, p. 123.
Concluír, *to conclude.* See p. 71.
Concordár, *to adjust, to conciliate, to be conformable, like.*
  See acordár, p. 124.
Condescendér, *to condescend.* See entendér, p. 135.
Condolér, *part. past.* condolído, *to sympathize.* See absolvér, p. 123.

  N. B. Some of these irregular verbs have regular part. past; in such a case they are noted down.

Inf. pres Conducír, *to conduct, to lead.*
Gerund. Conduciéndo, *conducting.*
Participle. Conducído, *conducted.*

Ind. pres. Condúzco, condúces, &c. *I conduct.*
Imperfect. Conducía, &c. *I did conduct.*
Pret. def. Condúge, condugíste, condújo, condu- } *I conduct-*
  gímos, condugísteis, condugéron, } *ed.*
Future. Conduciré, &c. *I shall or will conduct.*
Condition. Conduciría *or* condugéra, &c. } *I should, or would conduct.*
Imperative. Condúce, condúzca, } *conduct*
  condúzcamos, conducid, condúzcan. } *thou, &c.*

Sub. pres. Que condúzca, &c.   *that I conduct or may conduct.*
Imperf.   Que condugése, &c. $\begin{cases} \textit{that I conducted, or} \\ \textit{might conduct.} \end{cases}$
Future.   Si condugére, &c.   *if I conduct, or shall conduct.*

Conferír, *to confer.*   *See* adherír, p. 124.
Confesár, *to confess, to own.*   *See* acertár, p. 123.
Confundír, *to confound.*   *See* p. 71.
Conmovér, *part. past.* conmovído, *to excite. See* absolvér, p. 123.
Conocér, *to know.*   *See* aborrecér, p. 122
Conseguír, *to obtain.*   *See* pedír, p. 142.
Consentír, *to consent.*   *See* adherír, p. 124.
Consolár, *to console.*   *See* acordár, p. 124.
Consonár, *to agree, to be in tune.*   Idem.
Constreñír, *to constrain.*   *See* pedír, p. 142.
Contár, *to count, relate.*   . *See* acordár, p. 124.
Contenér, *to contain.*   *See* tenér, p. 86.
Contendér, *to contest, to dispute.*   *See* entendér, p. 135.
Contradecir, *to contradict.*   *See* decir, p. 131. N. B. *They differ only in the second person singular of the imperative which is* CONTRADICE, *and not* CONTRADÍ.
Contrahacér, *to counterfeit.*   *See* hacér, p. 138.
Contraér, *to contract.*   *See* traér, p. 149.
Contravenír, *to act contrary, counterrene.*   *See* venír, p. 150.
Controvertír, *to controvert.*   *See* adherír, p. 124.
Convalecér, *to be convalescent.*   *See* aborrecér, p. 122.
Convencér, *to convince.*   *See* p. 122.
Convenír, *to agree.*   *See* venír, p. 150.
Convertír, *to convert.*   *See* adherír, p. 124 and 71.
Corregír, *to correct.*   *See* pedír, p. 142.
Costár, *to cost.*   *See* acordár p. 124.
Crecér, *to grow.*   *See* aborrecér, p. 122
Cubrír, *to cover,—irregular only in the part. past.* cubiérto.

D.

	Inf. pres.	Dar,	*to give.*
	Gerund.	Dándo,	*giving.*
	Participle.	Dádo,	*given.*

Ind. pres. Dóy, das, &c.   *I give.*
Imperfect. Dába, &c.   *I did give.*
Pret. def. Dí, diste, dió, dímos, dísteis, diéron.   *I gave.*
Future.   Daré, &c.   *I shall or will give.*

Condition.	Daría or *diéra*,	*I should or would give.*
Imperat.	Da, dé, démos, dad, den,	*give thou, &c.*
Sub. pres.	Que dé, &c.	*that I give, or may give.*
Imperf.	Que *diése, &c.*	*that I gave, or might give.*
Future.	Cuándo *diére, &c.*	*when I give, or shall give.*

Decaér, *to decay.*'   *See* caér, p. 128.
Decentár, *to cut, to take away a part.*   *See* acertár, p. 123.

	Inf. pres.	Deçír,	*to tell, to say.*
	Gerund.	Diciéndo,	*saying.*
	Participle.	Dícho,	*said.*
Ind pres.	Dígo, díces, díce, decímos, decís, dícen,		} *I say or do say.*
Imperf.	Decía, &c.		*I did tell*
Pret. def.	Dige, digíste, díjo, digímos, digísteis, digéron.		} *I said*
Future.	Diré, dirás, &c.		*I shall or will tell*
Condition.	Diría or digéra, &c.		*I should or would say*
Imperat.	Di, díga, digámos, decíd, dígan,		*tell thou, &c*
Sub. pres.	Que díga, &c.		*that I say or may say.*
Imperf.	Que digése, &c.		*that I told, or might tell.*
Future.	Si digére, &c.		*if I tell, or shall say.*

Deducír, *to deduct.*   *See* conducír, p. 129.
Defendér, *to defend.*   *See* entendér, p. 135.
Deferír, *to defer, to delay.*   *See* adherír, p. 124.
Degollár, *to decapitate, cut the throat.*   *See* acordár, p. 124.
Demolér, *part. past.* demolído, *to demolish. See* absolvér, p. 123
Demostrár, *to demonstrate.*   *See* acordár, p. 124.
Denegár, *to deny; to refuse.*   *See* acertár, p. 124.
Denostár, *to use any one ill, abuse.*   *See* acordár, p. 124.
Deponér, *to depose, to resign.*   *See* ponér, p. 143.
Derrengár, *to break the back.*   *See* acertár, p. 124.
Derretír, *to melt.*   *See* pedír, p. 142.
Desabastecér, (úna pláza,) *to strip a place of provisions*
                                                              See aborrecér, p. 122.
Desacertár, *to err, to mistake.*   *See* acertár, p. 124.
Desacordár, *to disagree.*   *See* acordár, p. 124.
Desadormecér, *to awake.*   *See* aborrecér, p. 122
Desalentár, *to discourage*   *See* acertár, p. 124.
Desaparecér, *to disappear.*   *See* aborrecér, p 122

Desapretár, *to loosen, to unbind.*   *See* acertár, p. 123.

Desaprobár, *to disapprove.*   *See* acordár, p. 124.

Desasosegár, *to disturb.*   *See* acertár, p. 123.

Desatendér, *to be inattentive.*   *See* entendér, p. 135.

Desatentár, *to trouble, to act giddily.*   *See* acertár, p. 123.

†Desatravesár, *to disentangle.*   Idem.

Desavenír, *to disagree, to be of a contrary opinion.*   *See* venír, p. 150.

Descaecér, *to decay, to lose one's strength.*   *See* aborrecér, p. 122.

Descendér, *to descend.*   *See* entendér, p. 135.

Desceñír, *to ungirdle.*   *See* pedír, p. 142.

†Decimentár, *to undermine the foundation.*   *See* acertár, p. 123.

Descolgár, *to take down; to slacken.*   *See* acordár, p. 124

Descollár, *to surpass in height, to be taller.*   Idem.

Descomedírse, *to grow unpolite, to take too much liberty.* (r. v.)   *See* pedír, p. 142.

Descomponér, *to disorder, to discompose.*   *See* ponér, p. 143

Desconsentír, *to refuse one's consent.*   *See* adherír, p. 124.

Desconcertár, *to confound, to derange.*   *See* acertár, p. 123.

Desconocér, *to disown.*   *See* aborrecér, p. 122.

Desconsolár, *to afflict, to grieve.*   *See* acordár, p. 124.

Descontár, *to discount.*   Idem.

Descubrír, *to discover—is irregular only in the participle past,* descubiérto.

Desdecír, *to give the lie. See* decír, p. 131. *except for the second person singular of the imperative, which is* desdíce *and not* desdí.

Desentendérse, *to feign ignorance.* (r. v.) *See* entendér, p. 135.

Desencerrár, *to set at liberty.*   Idem.

Desengrosár, *to diminish, lessen.*   *See* acordár, p. 124.

Desentendér, *to pretend ignorance.*   *See* entendér, p. 135.

Desenterrár, *to unbury, disinter.*   *See* acertár, p. 123.

Desentorpecér, *to awaken, to quicken.*   *See* aborrecér, p. 122.

Desenvolvér, *to unwrap, to develope.*   *See* absolvér, p. 128.

Deservír, *to clear the table, to oblige, to hurt. See* pedír, p. 142.

Desfallecér, *to faint away.*   *See* aborrecér, p. 122.

Desflaquecér, *to weaken, to languish.*   Idem.

Desflocár, *to ravel, (cloth.)*   *See* acordár, p. 124.

Desfogárse, *to vent one's passion.* (refl. v.)   Idem.

Desguarnecér, *to unfurnish.*   *See* aborrecér, p. 122.

Deshacér, *to undo.*   *See* hacér, p. 138.

Deshelár, *to thaw.*   *See* acertár, p. 123.
Desherrár, *to unfetter, to unshoe (a horse.)*   Idem.
Desléir, *to dilute, to temper.*   *See* pedír, p. 142.

Inf. pres. Deslucír, *to tarnish, to deface.—Gerund.* Deslucién-
do.—*Part.* Deslucído.—*Indic. pres. Deslúzco,* deslúces &c.
—*Imperat.* Deslúce, deslúzca, desluzcámos, deslucíd, des-
lúzcan.—*Sub. pres* deslúzca, &c.—*See* N. B. p. 123.

N. B. All the other tenses are regular and are conjugated
like *sufrír.*

Desmembrár, *to dismember.*   *See* acertár, p. 123.
Desmentír, *to contradict.*   *See* adherír, p. 124.
Desobedecér, *to disobey.*   *See* aborrecér, p. 122.
Desollár, *to skin.*   *See* acordár, p. 124.
Desovár, *to spawn, (speaking of fishes.)*   Idem.
Despedír, *to send away, dismiss.*   *See* pedír, p. 142.
Despedirse, *to take leave of. (r. v.)*   Idem.
Desempedrár, *to take up the stones, unpave. See* acértar, p. 123.
Despernár, *to cut off the legs.*   Idem.
Despertár, *to awake.*   Idem, and p. 71.
Desplacér, *to displease.*   *See* aborrecér, p. 122.
Desplegár, *to display; to unplait.*   *See* acertár, p. 123.
Despoblár, *to unpeople, depopulate.* *See* acordár, p. 124.
Desteñír, *to discolour.*   *See* pedír, p. 142.
Desterrár, *to exile, to banish.*   *See* acertár, p. 123.
Destorcér, *to untwist, to straighten.* *See* cocér, p. 128.
Destrocár, *to exchange back again.*   *See* acordár, p. 124.
Desvanecérse, *to faint away.*   *See* aborrecér, p. 122.
Desvergonzárse, *to lose all shame; to want respect.*   *See*
                                      acordár, p. 124.
Detenér, *to stop, detain.*   *See* tenér, p. 86.
†Detraér, *to remove, to detract.*   *See* traér, p. 149.
Devolvér, *to return, to give back.*   *See* absolvér, p. 123.
Dezmár, *to decimate or tithe.*   *See* acertár, p. 123.
Diferír, *to differ.*   *See* adherír, p. 124.
Digerír, *to digest.*   Idem.
Disentír, *to dissent.*   Idem
Disolvér, *to dissolve.*   *See* absolvér, p. 123
Disponér, *to dispose.*   *See* ponér, p. 143
Distraér, *to distract, to divert the attention.* *See* traér, p. 149
Divertír, *to divert.*   *See* adherír, p. 124.

{ Dolér, *to feel pain*, part. past. *dolído. See* absolvér, p. 123.
{ Dolérse, *to be sorry, to repent; to feel for others' pain; to*
  compassionate. part. past. *dolído.* (r. v.)   Idem.

Inf. pres.	Dormír,	*to sleep.*
Gerund.	Durmiéndo,	*sleeping.*
Participle.	Dormído,	*slept.*

Ind. pres. Duérmo, duérmes, duérme, } I *sleep, or do sleep.*
          dormímos, dormís, *duérmen,* }

Imperf. Dormía, &c.   *I did sleep.*

Pret. def. Dormí, dormíste, *durmió,*   }
          dormímos, dormísteis, *durmiéron.* } *I slept.*

Future. Dormiré, &c.   *I shall or will sleep.*

Condit. Dormiría *or* durmiéra, &c. I *should or would sleep.*

Imperat.   Duérme, duérma,   }
          durmámos, dormíd, *duérman,* } *sleep thou, &c.*

Sub. pres. Que *duérna,* duérmas duérma, } *that I sleep or may*
          durnámos, durmáis, *duérman,* } *sleep.*

Imperf. Que *durmiése,* &c.   *that I slept or might sleep.*

Future. Cuándo *durmiére,* &c.   *when I sleep or shall sleep.*

E.

Elegír, *to choose, to elect.*   *See* pedír, p. 142 and 71.

N. B. This verb changes *g* into *j* before *a* and *o* to preserve the guttural pronunciation of the infinitive.

Embestír, *to attack, to assail.*   *See* pedír, Idem.
Embravecérse, *to become furious.* (r. v.) *See* aborrecér, p. 122.
Embrutecérse, *to become brutish.* (r. v.)   Idem.
Empedrár, *to pave.*   *See* acertár, p. 123.
Empezár, *to begin.*   Idem.
Emplumecér, *to begin to have feathers. See* aborrecér, p. 122
Empobrecér, *to grow poor.*   Idem.
Emporcár, *to dirt.*   *See* acordár, p. 124.
Encabellecér, *to begin to have hair.*   *See* aborrecér, p. 122
Encallecér, *to form a callus.*   Idem.
Encalvecér, *to become bald.*   Idem.
Encanecér, *to grow grayhaired by old age.* Idem.
Encarecér, *to raise the price, to exaggerate.* Idem.
Encendér, *to light a fire, kindle.*   *See* acertár, p 123
Encensár, *to perfume with incense.*   Idem.

Encerrár, *to shut in, enclose.*   *See* acertár, p. 123.
Encomendár, *to recommend.*   Idem.
Encrudecérse, *to become cruel.* (r. v.)   *See* aborrecér, p. 122.
Encruelecér, *to irritate, to render cruel.*   Idem.
Encontrár, *to meet, to find.*   *See* acordár, p. 124.
Encordár, *to put strings and cords (to an instrument.)*   Idem.
Encubertár, *to cover with a blanket.*   *See* acertár, p. 123.
Endentecér, *to breed teeth.*   *See* aborrecér, p. 122.
Endurecér, *to grow hard.*   Idem.
Enfervorecér, *to heat, to incite.*   Idem.
Enflaquecér, *to grow lean.*   Idem.
Enfurecérse, *to become furious.* (r. v.)   Idem.
Engrandecér, *to aggrandize, to enlarge.*   Idem.
Engreírse, *to adorn oneself, to grow vain.* (r.v.) *See* pedír, p. 142.
Engrosár, *to grow big.*   *See* acordár, p. 124.
Enjugár, *to wipe.*   *See* p. 71.
Enloquecér, *to become mad.*   *See* aborrecér, p. 122.
Enlucír, *to whiten, to do over with plaster.* *See* deslucír, p. 133.
Enmendár, emendár, *to correct, amend.*   *See* acertár, p. 123.
Enmocecér, *to grow young again.*   *See* aborrecér, p. 122.
Enmohecérse, *to grow mouldy.* (r. v.)   Idem.
Enmudecér, *to grow dumb, to be silent.*   Idem.
Ennegrecér, *to grow black, to blacken.*   Idem.
Ennoblecér, *to ennoble.*   Idem
†Ennudecér, *to set or to knit, (speaking of grain, &c.)*   Idem
Enrarecér, *to rarefy, to become thin.*   Idem.
Enriquecér, *to enrich.*   Idem.
Enrodár, *to break upon the wheel.*   *See* acordár, p. 124.
Ensangrentár, *to make bloody.*   *See* acertár, p. 123.
Ensoberbecérse, *to grow proud.* (r. v.) *See* aborrecér, p. 122.
Entallecér, *to shoot or bud.*   Idem.

Inf. pres.	Entendér,	*to understand.*
Gerund.	Entendiéndo,	*understanding.*
Participle.	Entendído,	*understood.*

Ind. pres. Entiéndo, entiéndes, entiénde,   { *I understand, or*
    entendémos, entendéis, entiénden,   { *do understand.*
Imperf. Entendía, &c.   *I did understand.*
Pret. def. Entendí, &c.   *I understood.*
Future. Entenderé, &c.   *I shall or will understand.*
Condit. Entendería or entendiéra, &c. { *I should or would*
    { *understand.*

Imperat.	*Entiénde, entiénda,*	⎱	*understand*
	entendámos, entendéd, *entiéndan,*		*thou,* &c.
Sub. pres.	Que *entiénda, entiéndas, entiénda,*	⎰ *that I under-*	
	entendámos, entendáis, *entiéndan.*	*stand or may*	
		understand.	
Imperf.	Que entendiése, &c.	*that I understood or*	
		might understand.	
Future.	Si entendiére, &c.	*if I understand or*	
		shall understand.	

Enternecér, *to soften, to touch, to move.* See aborrecér, p. 122.

Enterrár, *to bury.* See acertár, p. 123.

Entomecér or entumecér, *to swell, to stupify.* See aborrecér, p. 122.

Entontecérse, *to become dull, foolish.* (r. v.) Idem.

Entorpecérse, *to become heavy, lazy.* (r. v.) Idem.

Entrelucír, *to glimmer.* See deslucír, p. 135.

Entreoír, *to hear imperfectly.* See oír, p. 141.

Entretenér, *to entertain.* See tenér, p. 86.

Entristecér, *to vex, to make sad.* See aborrecér, p. 122.

Entullecér, *to lose the use of one's limbs.* Idem.

Entumecérse, *to swell, to grow angry (speaking of the sea.)* (r. v.) Idem.

Envanecér, *to make vain, proud.* Idem.

Envegecér, *to grow old.* Idem.

Enverdecér, *to paint in green.* Idem.

Envestír, *to invest.* See pedír, p. 142.

Envolvér, *to wrap up, to involve.* See absolvér, p. 123.

Equivalér, *to be of equal value.* See valér, p. 150

Inf. pres.	Erguír,	*to erect, to raise*
Gerund.	Irguiéndo,	*erecting.*
Participle.	Erguído,	*erected.*

Ind. pres.	Yérgo, yérgues, yérgue, erguimos, erguís, yérguen,	⎱ *I erect, or do erect.*
Imperf.	Erguía, &c.	*I did erect.*
Pret. def.	Erguí, erguíste, irguió, erguímos, erguísteis, irguiéron,	⎱ *I erected.*
Future.	Erguiré, &c.	*I shall or will erect.*
Condit.	Erguiría or irguiéra, &c.	*I should or would erect.*
Imperat.	Yérgue, yérga, irgámos, erguid, yérgan,	⎱ *erect thou,* &c.

Sub. pres.	Que *yérga, yérgas, yérga,* }	*that I erect, or may*
	irgámos, irgáis, yérgan, }	*erect.*
Imperf.	Que *irguiése,* &c.	*that I erected or might erect.*
Future.	Cuándo *irguiére, &c.*	*when I erect or shall erect.*

Inf. pres.	Errár,	*to err.*
Indic. pres.	Yérro, yérras, yérra, }	
	errámos, erráis, yérran, }	*I err or do err.*
Imperat.	Yérra, yérre, }	
	errémos, errád, yérren, }	*err thou, &c.*
Sub. pres.	Que *yérre, yérres, yérre,* }	
	errémos, erréis, yérren, }	*that I err or may err.*

N. B. All the other tenses are regular.

---

†Escalentár, *to warm.*	*See* acertár, p. 123.
Escarmentár, *to correct oneself by experience.*	Idem.
Escarnecér, *to mock one.*	*See* aborrecér, p. 122.
†Esclarecér, *to clear up, to light.*	Idem.
Escluír, *to exclude.*	*See* p. 71.
Escocér, *to smart, to itch painfully.*	*See* cocér, p. 128.
Escribír, *to write.* (*It has no irregularity but in the participle past,* escríto.)	
Esforzár, *to animate, to encourage.*	*See* acordár, p. 124.
Espelér, *to expel.*	*See* p. 71.
Espresár, *to express.*	Idem.
Estinguír, *to extinguish.*	Idem.
Establecér, *to establish.*	*See* aborrecér, p. 122.
Estregár, *to scour, rub.*	*See* acertár, p. 124.
Estremecérse, *to shudder.* (r. v.)	*See* aborrecér, p. 122.
Estreñír, *to bind, to press close, to squeeze.*	*See* pedír, p. 142.
Espedír, *to dispatch, to expedite.*	Idem.
Esponér, *to expose.*	*See.* ponér, p. 143.
Estár, *to be, to stand.*	*See* p. 91.
Estendér, *to spread.*	*See* entendér, p. 135.
Estraér, *to export, to extract*	*See* traér, p. 149.

F.

Fallecér, *to die.*	*See* aborrecér, p. 122.
Favorecér, *to favour.*	Idem.
Fechár, *to date;* part. fechádo, *fécho*	*the 2d.* part. *only irr.*
Fenecér, *to finish, to die, to settle.*	*See* aborrecér, p. 122.
Fijár, *to fix.*	*See* p. 71.
Fortalecér, *to fortify.*	*See* aborrecér, p. 122.

Forzár, *to force.*   *See* acordár, p. 124
Fregár, *to wash, to clean, to furbish (plate.) See* acertár, p. 123.
Freír, *to fry. Part.* Frito.   *The rest like* pedír, p. 142.

G.

Gemír, *to groan.*   *See* pedír, p. 142.
Gobernár, *to govern.*   *See* acertár, p. 123
Guarnecér, *to furnish.*   *See* aborrecér, p. 122.

H.

Habér, *(Impersonal.)—Indic. pres.* Hay *and* Ha, *there is
there are. The rest like the auxiliary verb* habér, *with
this difference, that the former has only the third person
singular. (See the impersonal verbs,* p. 120.)
N. B. The abverb *there* is never expressed in this impersonal verb in Spanish.

Inf. pres.	Hacér,	*to do, to make.*
Gerund.	Haciéndo,	*making.*
Participle.	Hécho,	*done.*

Ind. pres. Hágo, háces, &c.   *I do or make.*
Imperf.   Hacía, &c.   *I did do or make.*
Pret. def. Hice, hicíste, hízo,   ⎱ *I did or made*
             hicímos, hicísteis, hiciéron, ⎰
Future.   Haré, harás, hará,   ⎱ *I shall or will do or*
             harémos, haréis, harán,   ⎰ *make.*
Condition. Haría, *or* hiciéra, &c.   *I should or would do.*
Imperat.   Haz, hága,   ⎱
                hagámos, hacéd, hágan,   ⎰   *do thou, &c.*
Sub. pres. Que hága, hágas, hága,   ⎱ *that I do or may do.*
             hagámos, hagáis, hágan,   ⎰
Imperf.   Que hiciése,   *that I made, or might make.*
Future.   Si hiciére, &c.   *If I do or shall do.*

Hacérse, *to make oneself, to become.* (r. v.)   *See* Idem.
Hartár, *to satiate.*   *See* p. 71.
Hedér *to stink.*   *See* entendér, p. 135.
Hedrár, *to dig about a vine.*   *See* acertár, p. 123.
Helár, *to freeze, (impersonal.)*   Idem.
Hendér, *to cleave or split.*   *See* entendér, p. 135.
Heñír, *to knead.*   *See* pedír, p. 142.
Herir, *to wound, to strike.*   *See* adherír, p. 124.
Herrár, *to shoe or to bind with iron work. See* acertár, p. 123.
Hervír, *to boil.*   *See* adherír, p. 124.
Holgár, *to repose, to do nothing.*   *See* acordár, p. 124.

Hollár, *to trample under feet, to tread.*   *See* acordár, p. 124.
Humedecér, *to moisten.*   *See* aborrecér, p. 122.

I.

Impedír, *to prevent.*   *See* pedír, p. 142.
Imponér, *to impose.*   *See* ponér, p. 143
Infernár, *to damn, to disquiet*   *See* acertár, p. 123.
Incluír, *to include, enclose.*   *See* p. 71.
Incurrir, *to incur.*   Idem.
Indisponér, *to indispose, to vex, to render incapable.*   *See* ponér, p. 143.
Incensar, *to incense, perfume.*   *See* encensár, p. 134.
Inducír, *to induce.*   *See* conducír, p. 129.
Inferír, *to infer.*   *See* adherír, p. 124.
Insertár, *to insert.*   *See* p. 71.
Intervenír, *to intervene.*   *See* venír, p. 150.
Introducír, *to introduce.*   *See* conducír, p. 129.
Invernár, *to winter.*   *See* acertár, p. 123.
Invertír, *to transpose, to subvert the order.*   *See* adherír, p. 124 and 71.
Investír, *to invest.*   *See* pedír, p. 142.
Ingerír, *or* engerír, *to graft a tree. Part.* ingérto *or* engérto.   *See* adherír, p. 124 and 71.

Inf. pres.	Ir,	*to go.*
Gerund.	Yéndo,	*going.*
Participle.	ído,	*gone.*
Ind. Pres.	Vóy, vas, va, vámos, váis, van,	*I go or do go.*
Imperf.	íba, &c.	*I did go.*
Pret. def.	Fuí, fuíste, fué, fuímos, fuísteis, fuéron,	*I went.*
Future.	Iré, &c.	*I shall or will go.*
Condition.	Iría, *or* fuéra, &c.	*I should or would go.*
Imperat.	Vé, váya, vámos, id, váyan,	*go thou, &c.*
Subj. Pres.	Que váya, váyas, váya, váyamos, váyais, váyan,	*that I go or may go.*
Imperfect.	Que fuése, fuéses, fuése, fuésemos, fuéseis, fuésen,	*that I went or might go.*
Future.	Cuándo fuére, &c.	*when I go or shall go.*

N. B. *All the compound tenses of this verb are conjugated with the verb* habér *and not* ser. *We translate then,* I have *or* am gone, I had *or* was gone, &c. *by* he ído, había ído, *and not by* Sóy ído, éra ído, *as in times of yore.*

J.

Inf. Pres.   Jugár,   *to play.*

Ind. pres. Juégo, juégas, juéga,   }
        jugámos, jugáis juégan, }   *I play.*
Imperat.   juéga, juégue,   )
        juguémos, jugád, juéguen,) *play thou, &c.*
Sub. pres. Que juégue, juégues, juégue, } *that I play or may*
        juguémos, juguéis, juéguen, }   *play.*

N. B. All the other tenses are regular.

Juntár, *to join.* See p. 71.

L.

Lucír, *to shine.* See deslucír, p. 133.

LL.

Llovér, *to rain,* (impers.) *Part.* Llovído. See absolvér, p. 123.

M.

†Magrecér, *to grow lean.*   *Part.* Magrecído. *See* aborrecér, p. 122.

Maldecír, *to curse.* See bendecír, p. 127 and 71.
Manifestár, *to manifest.* See acertár, p. 123 and 71.
Mantenér, *to maintain.* See tenér, p. 86.
Marchitár, *to wither.* See p. 71.
Medír, *to measure.* See pedír, p. 142.
Mentár, *to mention, to name.* See acertár, p. 123.
Mentír, *to lie.* See adherír, p. 124.
Merecér, *to merit* See aborrecér, p. 122.
Merendár, *to eat a collation between dinner and supper.* See acertár, p. 123.
Mohecérse, *to grow mouldy.* (r. v.) See aborrecér, p. 122.
Molér, *to grind.* *Part.* molído. See absolvér, p. 123.
Mordér, *to bite.* *Part.* mordído. Idem.
Morír, *to die.* *Part.* muérto. See dormír, p. 134.
Mostrár, *to show.* See acordár, p. 124.
Movér, *to move, to affect.* *Part.* movído. See absolvér, p. 123.

N.

Nacér, *to be born.* See aborrecér, p. 122
Negár, *to deny, to refuse.* See acertár, p. 123.
Negrecér, *to blacken, to become black.* See aborrecér, p. 122.
Nevár, *to snow,* (impers.) See acertár, p. 123.

O.

Obedecér, *to obey.*   *See* aborrecér, p. 122.
Oscurecér, *or* obscurecér, *to obscure, darken.*   Idem.
Obtenér, *to obtain.*   *See* tenér, p. 86.
Ofrecér, *to offer.*   *See* aborrecér, p. 122.

Inf. pres.	Oír,	*to hear.*
Gerund.	Oyéndo,	*hearing.*
Participle.	Oído,	*heard.*

Ind. pres. óigo, óyes, óye, }
 oímos, oís, óyen, }   *I hear or do hear.*

Imperfect. Oía, &c.   *I did hear.*

Pret. def. Oí, oíste, oyó, }
 oímos, oísteis, oyéron, }   *I heard.*

Future. Oiré, &c.   *I shall or will hear.*

Condition. Oiría or oyéra, &c. -   *I should or would hear.*

Imperat.   Oye, óiga, }
 oigámos, oíd, óigan, }   *hear thou, &c.*

Sub. pres. Que óiga, &c.   *that I hear, or may hear.*

Imperfect. Que oyése, &c.   *that I heard, or might hear.*

Future. Si oyére, &c.   *If I hear or shall hear.*

Inf. pres.	Olér,	*to smell, or scent.*
Gerund.	Oliéndo,	*smelling.*
Participle.	Olído,	*smelt.*

Ind. pres. Huélo, huéles, huéle, }
 olémos, oléis, huélen, }   *I smell or do smell.*

Imperat.   Huéle, huéla, }
 olámos, oléd, huélan, }   *smell thou, &c.*

Sub. pres. Que huéla, huélas, huéla, } *that I smell or may*
 olámos, oláis, huélan, } *smell.*

N. B. All the other tenses are regular.

Omitír, *to omit.*   *See* p. 71.
Oponér, *to oppose.*   *See* ponér, p. 143.
Oprimír, *to oppress.*   *See* p. 71.

P.

Pacér, *to feed, to graze.*   *See* aborrecér, p. 122.
Padecér, *to suffer, to endure.*   Idem.
{ Parecér, *to appear.*   Idem.
{ Parecérse, (refl. v.) *to resemble.*   Idem.

Inf. pres.   Pedír,   *to ask, to beg.*
Gerund.   Pidiéndo,   *asking.*
Participle.   Pedído,   *asked.*

Ind. pres.	Pído, pídes, píde, pedímos, pedís, píden, }	*I ask, or do ask.*
Imperfect.	Pedía, &c.	*I did ask.*
Pret. def.	Pedí, pedíste, pidió, pedímos, pedísteis, pidiéron, }	*I asked.*
Future.	Pediré, &c.	*I shall or will ask.*
Condit.	Pediría or *pidiéra, &c.*	*I should or would ask.*
Imperat.	Píde, pída, pidámos, pedíd, pídan, }	*ask thou, &c.*
Sub. pres.	Que pída, &c.	*that I ask or may ask.*
Imperf.	Que pidiése, &c.	*that I asked or might ask.*
Future.	Cuándo pidiére, &c.	*when I ask or shall ask.*

Pensár, *to think.*	See acertár, p. 124.
Perdér, *to lose.*	See entendér, p. 135.
Perecér, *to perish.*	See aborrecér, p. 122.
Perfeccionár, *to perfect.*	See p. 71.
Perniquebrár, *to break the legs.*	See acertár, p. 124.
Perseguír, *to persecute, to pursue.*	See pedír, p. 142.
Pertenecér, *to belong.*	See aborrecér, p. 122.
Pervertír, *to pervert.*	See adherír, p. 124

Inf. pres.   Placér,   *to please.*

Ind. pres.	Me pláce,	*it pleases me.*
Imperfect.	Placía,	*it did please.*
Pret. def.	Plúgo,	*it pleased.*
Sub. pres.	Que plégue,	*that it may please.*
Imperf.	Que pluguiése, or *pluguiéra,*	*that it might please.*
Future.	Si *pluguiére,*	*if it shall please.*

N. B. *Placér*, is only used in the above tenses and persons, and as an Interject. : Ex. *Plégue* á Diós ! May it please God!

Plegár, *to plait or fold.*	See acertár, p. 124.
Poblár, *to people.*	See acordár, p. 124.

Inf. pres.	Podér,	*to be able, can, may.*
Gerund.	Pudiéndo,	*being able.*
Participle.	Podído,	*been able.*

Ind. pres.	Puédo, puédes, puéde, podémos, podéis, puéden,	} *I am able, or I can.*
Imperf.	podía, &c.	*I was able, or could.*
Pret. def.	Púde, pudíste, púdo, pudímos, pudisteis, pudiéron	} *I was able, or could.*
Future.	Podré, &c.	*I shall or will be able.*
Condition.	Podría, or pudiéra, &c.	*I should or would be able.*
Imperat.	(*wanting.*)	
Sub. pres.	Que puéda, puédas, puéda, podámos, podáis, puédan,	} *that I can, or may be able.*
Imperfect.	Que pudiése, &c.	*that I could or might be able.*
Future.	Cuándo pudiére, &c.	*when I can or shall be able.*

Inf. pres.	Podrír,	*to rot.*
Gerund.	Pudriéndo,	*rotting.*
Participle.	Podrído,	*rotten.*

Ind. pres.	Púdro, púdres, púdre, podrímos, podrís, púdren,	} *I rot or do rot.*
Imperf.	Podría, &c.	*I did rot.*
Pret. def.	Podrí, podríste, *pudrió,* podrímos, podrísteis, *pudriéron,*	} *I rotted.*
Future.	Pudriré, &c.	*I shall or will rot.*
Condit.	Podriría *or pudriéra,* &c.	*I should or would rot.*
Imperat.	Púdre, púdra, pudrámos, podríd, púdran,	} *rot thou, &c.*
Sub. pres.	Que púdra, &c.	*that I rot or may rot.*
Imperfect.	Que pudriése, &c.	*that I rotted or might rot.*
Future.	Si pudriére, &c.	*if I rot or shall rot.*

N. B. Most tenses and persons of the above verb can only be used figuratively.

Inf. pres.	Ponér,	*to put, to place.*
Gerund.	Poniéndo,	*putting.*
Participle.	Puésto,	*put, or placed.*
Ind. pres.	Póngo, pónes, &c.	*I put or do put.*
Imperf.	Ponía, &c.	*I did put.*
Pret. def.	Púse, pusíste, púso, pusímos, pusísteis, pusiéron,	} *I put or placed*

Future.	Pondré, &c.	*I shall,or will put.*
Condit	Pondría, or pusiéra, &c.	*I should or would put.*
Imperat.	Pon, pónga,	
	pongámos, ponéd, póngan,	*put thou,* &c.
Sub. pres.	Que pónga, &c.	*that I put or may put.*
Imperf.	Que pusiése, &c.	*that I put or might put*
Future.	Cuándo pusiére, &c.	*when I put or shall put.*

Predecír, *to predict.*   See decír, p. 131
Preferír, *to prefer.*   See adherír, p. 124.
Prendér, *to capture, to arrest.*   See p. 71.
Prevér, *to foresee.*   See vér, p. 150.
Proponér, *to propose.*   See ponér, p. 143.
Proscribír, *to proscribe.*   See p. 71.
Presentír, *to have a forecast*   See adherír, p. 124.
Presuponér, *to presuppose.*   ` See ponér, p. 143.
Prevalecér, *to prevail.*   See aborrecér, p. 122.
Prevenír, *to anticipate, to prepare.*   . See venír, p. 150.
Prevér, *to foresee.*   See vér, p. 151.
Producír, *to produce.*   See conducír, p. 129.
Proferír, *to utter.*   See adherír, p. 124.
Promovér, *to promote, to elevate.*   *Part.* promovído. See
Probár, *to prove.* See acordár.   [absolvér, p. 123.
Proponér, *to propose.*   See ponér, p. 143.
Proscribír, *to banish, is irregular only in the participle past,*
   proscríto.
Proseguír, *to pursue, to continue.*   See pedír, p. 142.
Probár, *to prove, to experience, to taste, to try.*   See acordár,
                                                           p. 124.
Provenír, *to proceed, to issue.*   See venír, p. 150.
Proveér, *to provide.*   See N. B. 5th, p. 121, and 71.

Q.

Quebrár, *to break, to dash in pieces; to fail, to be a bank-*
   rupt.   See acertár, p. 123.

Inf. pres.	Querér,	*to will, love, wish or want.*
Gerund.	Queriéndo,	*willing.*
Participle.	Querído,	*willed.*
Ind. pres.	Quiéro, quiéres, quiére,	*I will, love, wish,*
	querémos, queréis, quiéren,	*or want.*
Imperf.	Quería, &c.	*I did wish.*
Pret. def.	Quíse, quisíste, quíso,	*I willed or wished,*
	quisímos, quisísteis, quisiéron,	*or loved.*

Future.	Querré, &c.	*I shall* or *will wish.*
Condition.	Querría, or quisiéra, &c.	*I should* or *would wish.*
Imperat.	Quiére, quiéra, querámos, queréd, quiéran, }	*love thou,* &c.
Sub. pres.	Que quiéra, quiéras, quiéra, querámos, queráis, quiéran, }	*that I love,* or *may love.*
Imperfect.	Que quisiése, &c.	*that I wished* or *might wish.*
Future.	Si quisiére, &c.	*if I wish* or *shall wish.*

R.

Rebolcár *or* revolcár, *to tumble, to welter.* See acordár, p. 124.
Recaér, *to fall again.* See caér, p. 128.
Recluír, *to confine.* See Obs. 6th, p. 122, and p. 71.
Recocér, *to bake again, boil again.* See cocér, p. 128.
Recomendár, *to recommend.* See acertár, p. 123.
Reconocér, *to acknowledge, know again.* See aborrecér, p. 122.
Reconvalecér, *to recover from an illness.* Idem.
Recordár, *to remember, to call to mind.* See acordár, p. 124.
Recostárse, *to lie or lean on one side.* (r. v.) Idem.
Recordárse, *to remember, recollect.* (r. v.) Idem,
Recrecér, *to grow again.* See aborrecér, p. 122.
Reducír, *to reduce.* See conducír, p. 129.
Referír, *to relate; to refer,* in this last sense it is regular.
See adherír, p. 124.
Reflorecér, *to blossom again.* See aborrecér, p. 122.
Reforzár, *to strengthen, to reinforce.* See acordár, p. 124.
Regár, *to water, to irrigate.* See acertár, p. 123.
Regír, *to govern.* See pedír, p. 142.
Regoldár, *to belch.* See acordár, p. 124.
Rehacér, *to do again.* See hacér, p. 138.

Inf. pres.	Reír,	*to laugh.*
Gerund.	Riéndo,	*laughing.*
Participle.	Reído,	*laughed.*
Ind. pres.	Río, ríes, ríe, reímos, reís, ríen, }	*I laugh* or *do laugh*
Imperf.	Reía, &c.	*I did laugh*
Pret. def.	Reí, reíste, rió, reímos, reísteis, riéron, }	*I laughed.*
Future.	Reiré, &c.	*I shall* or *will laugh.*
Condit.	Reiría, or riéra, &c.	*I should* or *would laugh.*
Imperat.	Ríe, ría, riámos, reíd, rían, }	*laugh thou,* &c.

Sub. pres.	Que ría, &c.	*that I may laugh.*
Imperfect.	Que riésc, &c.	*that I might laugh.*
Future.	Cuándo riére, &c.	*when I laugh*, or *shall laugh.*

Relucír, *to shine, glitter.*   See deslucír, p. 133.
Remanecér, *to appear, to come in suddenly, to remain.*   See aborrecér, p. 122.
Remendár, *to mend, to patch.*   See acertár, p. 123.
Remordér, *to bite again, to cause remorse.*   Part. remordído.   See absolvér, p. 123.
Removér, *to remove, to change place.*   Part. removído.   Idem.
Renacér, *to be born again, to revive.*   See aborrecér, p. 122.
{ Rendír, *to return, to subject, to enslave.*   See pedír, p. 142.
} Rendirse, *to surrender oneself.* (r. v.)   Idem.
Renegár, *to deny, disown, curse.*   See acertár, p. 123.
Renovár, *to renew.*   See acordár, p. 124
Reñír, *to scold, to quarrel.*   See pedír, p. 142.
Repetír, *to repeat.*   Idem.
Reponér, *to put again.*   See ponér, p. 143.
Reprobár, *to reprove.*   See acordár, p. 124.
Requebrár, *to cajole or wheedle.*   See acertár, p. 123
Requerír, *to require.*   See adherír, p. 124.
Resentírse, *to resent, to be sensible of.* (r. v.)   Idem
Rescontár, *to balance one part of an account with another.*   See acordár, p. 124.
Resollár, *to breathe.*   Idem.
Resolvér, *to resolve.*   See absolvér, p. 123
Resonár, *to resound.*   See acordár, p. 124
Restablecér, *to repair, or restore.*   See aborrecér, p. 122.
Retemblár, *to have continual tremblings.*   See acertár, p. 123.
Retenér, *to detain, retain.*   See tenér, p. 86.
Retentár, *to be threatened with a relapse,* (*speaking of sickness.*)   See acertár, p. 123.
Reteñír, *to dye again.*   See pedír, p. 142.
Retorcér, *to twist again, to retort*   See cocér, p. 128.
{ Retrnérse, *to take refuge, shelter.* (r. v.)   See traér, p. 149.
} Retraér, *to withdraw, to draw towards oneself.*   Idem.
Retrotraér, *to antedate, to trace back a thing to a time previous to its existence.*   Idem
Revenírse, *to be contracted, to yield.* (r. v.)   See venír, p. 150
Reventár, *to burst.*   See acertár, p. 123.
Revér. *to see again*   See vér, p. 150.

Reverdecér, *to grow green again.* ... *See* aborrecér, p. 122.
Revertér, *to return, to overflow.* ... *See* entendér, p. 135
Revestír, *to invest.* ... *See* pedír, p. 142.
Revolár, *to fly again.* ... *See* acordár, p. 124
Revolcárse, *to wallow oneself.* (r. v.) ... Idem
Revolvér,*to stir, to disturb, to overthrow, to turn over.* ... *See* absolvér, p. 123
Rodár, *to roll.* ... *See* acordár, p. 124
Rogár, *to pray, desire.* ... Idem
Rompér, *to break.* ... *See.* p. 71

S.

Inf. pres.	Sabér.	*to know things.*
Gerund.	Sabiéndo,	*knowing.*
Participle.	Sabído,	*known.*

Ind Pres.	Sé, sábes, &c.	*I know or do know.*
Imperf.	Sabía, &c.	*I did know*
Pret. def.	Súpe, supiste, súpo, supímos, supísteis, supiéron,	*I knew.*
Future,	Sabré, &c.	*I shall or will know.*
Condition.	Sabría or supiéra, &c.	*I should or would know.*
Imperat.	Sábe, sépa, sepámos, sabéd, sépan,	*know thou, &c.*
Subj. Pres.	Que sépa, &c.	*that I know or may know*
Imperfect.	Que supiése, &c.	*that I knew or might know.*
Future.	Si supiére, &c.	*if I know or shall know.*

Sabér bién, *to relish, (speaking of meat, fruit, &c.) See* sabér.

	Inf. pres Salír,	*to go out, to walk out.*
	Gerund. Saliéndo,	*going out.*
	Participle. Salído,	*gone out.*
Ind. pres.	Sálgo, sáles, &c.	*I go or do go out.*
Imperf.	Salía, &c.	*I did go out.*
Pret def.	Salí, &c.	*I went out.*
Future.	Saldré, &c.	*I shall or will go out.*
Condition.	Saldría or saliéra, &c.	*I should or would go out.*
Imperat.	Sal, sálga, salgámos, salíd, sálgan,	*go thou out, &c.*
Sub. pres.	Que sálga, sálgas, sálga, salgámos, salgáis, sálgan,	*that I go out, or may go out.*
Imperf.	Que saliése, &c.	*that I went out or might go out.*
Future.	Cuándo saliére, &c.	*when I go out or shall go out.*

Satisfacér, *to satisfy.*   *See* hacér, p. 138
Segár, *to reap, to mow.*   *See* acertár, p. 123
Seguír, *to follow.*   *See* pedír, p. 142.

N. B. This verb and its compounds lose the *u* before *a* and
o: we say consequently *sigo* and *siga* and not *siguo* and *sigua.*

Sembrár, *to sow, to strew.*   *See* acertár, p. 123.
Sentár *to lay down.*   Idem.
Sentárse, *to sit down.* (refl. v.)   Idem.
Sentír, *to feel, to perceive, to regret.*   *See* adherír, p. 124.
Ser, *to be.*   *See* p. 91.
Serrár, *to saw.*   *See* acertár, p. 123.
Servír, *to serve.*   *See* pedír, p. 142.
Sobreponér, *to place above.*   *See* ponér, p. 143.
Sobresalír, *to surpass in height, to excel, &c.* *See* salír, p. 147.
Sobrevenír, *to come in unlooked for*   *See* venír, p. 150.
Soldár, *to solder, settle.*   *See* acordár, p. 124.

Inf. pres.	Solér,	*to be wont* or *accustomed to*
Gerund.	Soliéndo,	*being wont to.*
Participle.	Solído,	*accustomed to.*
Indic. pres.	Suélo, suéles, suéle, solémos, soléis, suélen,	*I am wont to.*
Imperat.	Suéle, suéla, solámos, soléd, suélan,	*be accustomed to.*
Sub. pres.	Que suéla, suélas, suéla, solámos, soláis, suélan,	*that I be* or *may be wont to.*

N. B. This verb is seldom used except in the *Ind. pres.*
and *Imperfect*, which last tense is regular.

Soltár, *to loosen, to release.*   *See* acordár, p. 124. and 71.
†Solvér, *to solve, to resolve. Part.* Solvído. *See* absolvér, p. 122.
Sonár, *to sound, to ring, to appear.*   *See* acordár, p. 124.
Sonárse, (las naríces,) *to blow one's nose.* (r. v.)   Idem.
Soñár, *to dream.*   Idem.
Sonreír, *to smile.*   *See* reír, p. 145.
Sosegár, *to repose.*   *See* acertár, p. 123.
Sosegárse, *to tranquillize oneself.* (r. v.)   Idem.
Sostenér, *to support.*   *See* tenér, p. 86.
Soterrár, *to inter, to bury.*   *See* acertár, p. 123.
Subarrendár, *to underlet.*   Idem.
Sustraér, *to subtract.*   *See* traér, p. 149.
Suponér, *to suppose*   *See* ponér, p. 143.

Suprimír, *to suppress.*   *See* p. 71.

Suspendér, *to suspend,* suspendído, *suspénso,* the 2d partic.:
    only irreg.

Sustituír, *to substitute,* sustituído, *sustitúto,*   idem.

T.

Temblár, *to tremble.*   *See* acertár, p. 123.

Tendér, *to spread, to extend.*   *See* entendér, p. 135.

Tenér, *to have, to possess, to hold*   *See* p. 86.

Teñír, *to dye.*   *See* pedír, p. 142.

Tentár, *to tempt, to feel.*   *See* acertár, p. 123.

Torcér, *to twist, to turn, to alter.*   *See* cocér, p. 128.

Tostár, *to roast.*   *See* acordár, p. 124.

Traducír, *to translate.*   *See* conducír, p. 129.

Inf. pres.	Traér,	*to bring.*
Gerund.	Trayéndo,	*bringing.*
Participle.	Traído,	*brought.*

Ind. pres.	*Tráigo,* tráes, &c.	*I bring* or *do bring.*
Imperf.	Traía, &c.	*I did bring.*
Pret. def.	*Tráje, trajíste, trájo.*	} *I brought.*
	Trajímos, trajísteis, trajéron,	
Future.	Traeré, &c.	*I shall* or *will bring.*
Condit.	Traería, or *trajéra, &c.*	*I should* or *would bring.*
Imperat.	*Tráe, tráiga,*	} *bring thou, &c.*
	traigámos, traéd, *tráigan,*	
Sub. pres.	Que *tráiga, &c.*	*that I bring* or *may bring.*
Imperf.	Que *trajése, &c.*	*that I brought* or *might bring.*
Future.	Si *trajére, &c.*	*if I bring* or *shall bring.*

N. B. Formerly *traér* had *trúje,* and *trujése* instead of
those laid down in *pret. def.* and *imp. subj.*

Trascendér, *to go, to pass beyond.*   See entendér, p. 135.

Trascendér, *to discover, to penetrate, to comprehend.*   Idem.

Trascolár, *to strain, to filter.*   See acordár, p. 124.

Trascordárse de, *to forget.* (r. v.)   Idem.

Trasegár, *to put topsy turvy, to turn up.*   See acertár, p. 123.

Trasoñár, *to dream, to be out of one's mind.* See acordár, p. 124.

Trasponér, *to transpose.*   *See* ponér, p. 143.

Travesár, *to traverse.*   *See* acertár, p. 123.

Trocár, *to exchange.*   *See* acordár, p. 124.

N. B. This verb changes *c* into *qu* before *e. See* p. 121 & 122.

Tronár, *to thunder.*   *See* acordár, p. 124.

Tropezár, *to stumble, to make a false step. See* acertár, p. 123.

13*

V.

Inf. pres.	Valér,	*to be worth.*
Gerund.	Valiéndo,	*being worth.*
Participle.	Valído,	*been worth.*
Ind. pres.	*Válgo,* váles, &c.	*I am worth.*
Imperf.	Valía, &c.	*I was worth.*
Pret. def.	Valí, &c.	*I was worth.*
Future.	*Valdré, &c.*	*I shall be worth.*
Condit.	*Valdría* or valiéra, &c.	{ *I should or would be worth.*
Imperat.	Vúle, válga, valgámos, valéd, válgan,	} *be thou worth, &c.*
Sub. pres.	Que válga, &c.	*that I be or may be worth.*
Imperf.	Que valiése, &c.	*that I was or might be worth.*
Future.	Cuándo valiére,	*when I be or shall be worth.*

Inf. pres.	Venír,	*to come.*
Gerund.	Viniéndo,	*coming.*
Participle.	Venído,	*come.*
Ind. pres.	*Véngo,* viénes, viéne, venímos, venís, viénen,	} *I come or do come.*
Imperf.	Venía, &c.	*I did come.*
Pret. def.	*Víne,* viníste, víno, vinímos, vinísteis, viniéron,	} *I came.*
Future.	*Vendré, &c.*	*I shall or will come.*
Condit.	*Vendría,* or viniéra, &c.	*I should or would come.*
Imperat.	Ven, vénga, vengámos, veníd, véngan,	} *come thou, &c.*
Sub. pres.	Que vénga, &c.	*that I come or may come*
Imperf.	Que viniése, &c.	*that I came or might come*
Future.	Si viniére, &c.	*if I come or shall come*

Venírse, (refl. v.) *to come away.*   See venír, above

Inf. pres.	Ver,	*to see.*
Gerund.	Viéndo,	*seeing.*
Participle.	Vísto,	*seen.*
Ind. pres.	*Véo,* ves, &c	*I see or do see.*
Imperf.	Veía, &c.	*I did see.*
Pret. def.	Ví, &c.	*I saw.*
Future.	Veré, &c.	*I shall or will see.*
Condit.	Veria *or* viéra, &c.	*I should or would see.*

Imperat.	Ve, véa, }	see thou, &c.
	reámos, ved, véan, }	
Sub. pres.	Que véa, véas, &c.	that I see or may see.
Imperf.	Que viése, &c.	that I saw or might see.
Future.	Cuándo viére, &c.	when I see or shall see.

N. B. In the above verb the *v* is the only radical letter.
See *Temér* second regular conjugation.

Vertér, *to pour, to shed.*	See entendér, p. 135.
{ Vestír, *to dress, to clothe.*	See pedír, p. 142.
{ Vestírse, *to dress oneself.* (r. v.)	Idem.
Volár, *to fly,* (*with wings.*)	See acordár, p. 124.
Volcár, *to turn, to overthrow.*	Idem.
{ Volvér, *to come back, to return; to turn, to send back.*	
{	See absolvér, p. 123.
{ Volvérse, *to become, to change oneself, to return, to go back.*	
{	(r. v.) Idem.
Yacér, *to lie down, to be fixed.* (def. v.) See aborrecér, p. 122.
Zaherír, *to upbraid, to blame.*	See adherír, p. 124.

AGREEMENT OF VERBS WITH THEIR SUBJECT.

We call that the *subject* of which we affirm some thing,
and that the *attribute* which is affirmed of it. When we say;
el réy es benéfico, the king is beneficent; the word *réy* is
the subject of which we affirm the quality of *benéfico*, which
is the attribute.

Rule LI. The subject is always either a noun or pronoun.
When it is a pronoun, it is almost always suppressed in Spanish, both when the phrase is affirmative and negative, as we
have already stated in the N. B. upon the *persons* and *numbers* of verbs, page 82. If I have to translate in Spanish the
words *I love, thou lovest, they love,* I suppress the pronouns,
and say, *ámo, ámas, áman;* the termination of each of these
persons sufficiently indicates the pronoun that belongs to it,
and which is implied.

Exception. We often express the pronoun to give more
energy to the phrase. We must also express it whenever *its*
suppression would leave an ambiguity in speech. Ex. *¡ Yó
lo dígo, tú lo has hécho!* I say it, thou hast done it! *Pédro me
quiére, é yo le aborrézco, &c.* Peter loves me, and I hate him, &c.

Rule LII. The subject, whether a noun or pronoun, is
commonly placed before the verb. Ex. *Tu pádre llóra y tú
ríes,* thy father weeps and thou laughest.

1st Exception. In interrogative and imperative phrases

the subject is always placed after the verb. Ex. *¿ Que pre-ténden pués los nuévos reformadóres con su soñáda igual-dád?* What then do the new reformers pretend with their chimerical equality? *Háblen las naciónes dónde se viéron táles trastórnos; háble la misma Fráncia,.....*let the nations where were seen such overturnings, let France herself speak.

2d EXCEPTION. The subject is also placed after the verb, in the incidental phrase denoting that we quote the words of some one. Ex. *Si tenéis, decía* LUÍS XI *á su hîjo, si tenéis la desdicha de llegár á ser réy, acordáos de que os debéis tódo entéro á la felicidád de vuéstros conciudadános;* if you have, said Louis XI to his son, if you have the misfortune to be a king, remember that you owe yourself entirely to the happi-ness of your fellow citizens.

3d EXCEPTION. This inversion is also made with great advantage whenever it gives elegance, energy, sweetness or harmony to speech. Ex. *¡ Dichósos los pádres que tiénen buénos hîjos!* Happy the fathers who have good children! *¡Feliz el réino dónde víven los hómbres en paz!'* Happy the kingdom where men live in peace! These phrases are much more energetic than if we said, *los pádres que tiénen buénos hîjos son dichósos; el réino dónde los hómbres víven en paz es feliz.*

RŮLE LIII. Every verb must be of the same number and person as its subject. Ex. *Yó no sé lo que dígo, lo que hágo, &c.* I do not know what I say, what I do, &c. *Tu hermáno no estúdia; tus hermános no estúdian;* thy brother does not study; thy brothers do not study. In the first example, *sé, dígo* and *hágo* are in the singular number and in the first person, because the pronoun *yó,* expressed before the first verb, and understood before the others, is in the singular and first person. In the second, *estúdia* is in the third per-son of the singular, because its subject *hermáno* is of that person and number, &c.

Of the regimen of verbs.

The regimen of a verb is a word that immediately depends on it, and which restrains or determines its signification.

A verb may have for its regimen three kinds of words, an-other verb, a substantive or a pronoun.

Of the verb as a regimen.

A verb governs another in the infinitive either with or without a preposition; as, *quiéro estudiár,* I wish to study;

las lénguas dében apreydérse por princípios, languages must be learned by principles; *véngo de comér,* I come from din- ner; *vóy á paseár,* I am going to walk; *estúdia pára intru- írse,* he studies to instruct himself, &c.

RULE LIV. In Spanish, the verb *temér,* to fear, when we do not wish the thing expressed by the second verb; the verbs *dudár,* to doubt; *negár,* to deny, forming a negative member of a phrase; and the verb *impedir,* to prevent; *prohibír,* to forbid; require the verb, which they govern, to be in the subjunctive mood, with the conjunction *que. Témo que vénga,* I fear he will come. *No niégo que ténga razón,* I do not deny that he is right. *Impidió que saliésen,* he prevented their go- ing out. (*See* Rule XLVII. p. 81.)

RULE LV. In Spanish, a verb governs another in the infinitive by the aid of the following prepositions; *á, de, con, en, hásta, por, pára, éntre, tras, sóbre, sin,* to, of or from, with, in or into, till or even, by, for, between, after, on or up- on, without. Ex. *Irémos á paseár después de comér,* we shall go to walk after dinner; *véngo de almorzár,* I come from breakfast; *gásto la mayór párte del tiémpo en jugár y divertírme,* I spend the greatest part of my time in playing and amusing myself.

N. B. It often happens that we elegantly use in Spanish the infinitive with the article *el,* when governed by another verb: Ex. *Me gústa el leér novélas,* I like to read novels.

The Spanish verb *acabár,* to finish, followed by the prepo- sition *de,* and governing the following verb in the infinitive, means that a thing has just been done or happened. Ex. *Acábo de oír buénas notícias,* I have just heard good news. *Pédro acabába de salír,* Peter had just gone out.

Andár and *ir,* to go, govern the verb that follows them, in the following phrases and others like them, in the gerund, without a preposition. Ex. *Van* or *ándan cantándo por las cálles,* they go singing in the streets. *Lo irán diciéndo á tó- dos,* they will go telling it to every one. *Andaré paseándo,* I shall be walking.

Of the noun substantive as regimen of the verb.

RULE LVI. All active verbs govern in Spanish the noun substantive, which is the immediate object of the action that is expressed, in the accusative with the preposition *á,* if this noun expresses a rational being or personified object; and without a preposition in all other cases. Ex. *amár á Diós,* to love God; *el réy quiére á su primér minístro*, the king loves his prime minister. *Amár la virtúd*, to love virtue. *aborrecér el vício*, to hate vice.

N. B. Sometimes the harmony of the sentence requires the particle *á* to be suppressed. Ex. *¡dichósos los pádres que tiénen buénos hijos!* happy the parents who have good children! And sometimes *á* is used before an inanimate object for the sake of clearness and euphony. Ex. *Fernándo sitió y tomó á Granáda*, Ferdinand besieged and took Granada.

There are some active verbs which govern two nouns at the same time, but under different relations. One of these nouns is the immediate object of the action expressed by the verb, and the other is the end to which it tends. That which is the end of it, is always governed by the preposition *á*. Ex. *Daré un líbro á Pédro*, I shall give a book to Peter. The word *líbro* is the object of the action expressed by the verb *daré*, and *Pédro* is the end to which it tends.

Neuter verbs in general have no regimen, because their signification does not extend beyond themselves; as, *nacér*, to be born; *vivír*, to live; *crecér*, to grow; *dormír*, to sleep.

Reflective and reciprocal verbs govern the personal pronouns which they have for their regimen in the accusative and dative, and these pronouns are placed before or after the verb, according to the rules of objective pronouns. *See* pages 55 and 56. Ex. *Arrepentírse* to repent; *se arrepiénte* or *arrepiéntese*, he repents; *se dá* or *dáse*, he gives himself.

Of objective pronouns, or those which are the regimen of verbs.

As we already have given all the rules respecting pronouns, we refer the reader to pages 54, 55, 56.

Observations upon verbs.

1st. The adverbs *but* or *only*, used with a verb are rendered in Spanish by *sólo* or *sólaménte*, or by the adverb *no* placed before the verb, and *sinó* after the same verb. Ex. I have *but* one thousand dollars, sólo *téngo mil pésos*, or, no *téngo sinó mil pésos*.

2d. The Spaniards, in order to express the repetition of an action, generally make use of the verb *rolvér*, (which is equivalent to the English word *again*,) always followed by the preposition *á*, which governs the following verb in the infinitive; and *rolvér* is put in the tense and person in which the English verb is, which expresses the repetition of the action. Ex. I shall read again this book, *volveré á leér éste libro;* I saw him again, *rolví á vérle.*

3d. The pronoun *it,* placed in English before the verb *to be,* is most always suppressed in Spanish; and sometimes it is translated by the pronouns *él, élla, éllo,* for clearness sake.

It is often suppressed,—1st.—in these modes of speaking; *it is enough, it is little, it is too much, it is dear; is it enough? is it little? &c. es bastánte, es póco, es demasiádo, es cáro, es bastánte? es póco? &c.*—2d.—In answers. Ex. Who has said that? it is I, it is you, it is Peter, it is he, &c. *Quién ha dicho éso? yó sóy, es vm., es Pédro, es él, &c.* Or, by suppressing the verb and the pronoun *it,* we may say: *yó, vm., Pédro, él, &c.*—3d.—When the verb *to be* is followed by a noun substantive having after it the pronoun relative *who* or *that,* quien, que, then these pronouns are translated by *él que, la que, los que, las que,* see p. 62, according to the gender and number of the noun to which they refer. Ex. It was the Spaniards who conquered Mexico, *fuéron los Españóles los que conquistáron á Mégico.*

In the following phrase, and others of the same nature, in which the verb becomes the nominative of the verb *to be,* we elegantly use the article *el* before the verb, and suppress the pronoun *it.* Ex. It is not an easy thing to know men, *no es cósa fácil el conocér á los hómbres.* To know how to be silent is a great virtue, *el sabér callár es úna gránde virtúd.* To despise the sciences is not to know their value, *el despreciár las ciéncias no es conocér su valór.*

In these modes of speaking: *it is I who, it is thou who, it is he who, &c.* have, hast, or has done it or said it, we suppress the pronoun *it,* and place the pronoun personal before the verb, which is put in the same person as the pronoun that precedes it, and *who* is translated by the relative pronoun quién, plural, quiénes. *Yó sóy, tú éres, él, élla es,* quién *lo ha hécho,* quién *lo ha dicho, nosótros sómos* quienes, it is I, thou, he, she, who has done it, it is we who, &c.

4th. *To have like, to come very near,* are translated by *estár á pique de, estár en púnto de, estár pára* or *faltár póco pára que.* Ex. I had like to have been killed, *estúve á pique,* or *á púnto de matárme.* Thy brother came very near falling, *póco faltó pára que tu hermáno cayése.* I came very near writing to thee this morning, *estúve pára escribírte ésta mañána.*

N. B. The *que* after *faltár* governs the following verb in the subjunctive, as may be seen in the above example.

Of the agreement of the participle past with the subject and with its regimen.

The participle past may be constructed ·with *habér, tenér, ser, llevár* or *ir.*

RULE LVII.—Whenever the participle past is constructed with the verb *habér*, it neither takes gender nor number. Therefore we say; *éllos* or *éllas han comprádo libros*, they have bought books. *Los libros que hémos leído*, the books we have read.

> N. B. *Habér de, tenér que*, and *debér*, are in English *to have to, to be to, to be obliged to*, and are often rendered by the defective verbs *must* and *ought to*. Ex. *He de, téngo de, débo trabajár*, I have to, I am to, I must, &c. work. *Téngo que hablár*, I have to speak: and so on through all the tenses and persons.

RULE LVIII.—When the participle past is constructed with the verb *tenér* used as *auxiliary*, which is done to give more precision and energy to the sentence, then it takes neither gender nor number. Ex. *Téngo habládo á su mádre*, I have spoken to his mother. *Tenía olvidádo mis trabájos*, I had forgotten my troubles. *Me tuviéron abochornádo*, they had put me to the blush.

RULE LIX.—If the verb *tenér*, when it serves to construct the participle past, is used as an *active* verb, that participle agrees in gender and number with its direct regimen. Ex. *Téngo escrita úna cárta á mi hijo*, I have written a letter to my son. *La cása que mi tío tiéne compráda*, the house that my uncle has bought. *¿ Tenían empezádas las óbras?* had they begun the works? *Tenía consentída su venída*, &c.

> N. B. 1st. This last rule is applicable to the verb *llevár* when used for the auxiliary *habér*, this last expresses only a simple action, but the former expresses the state of a thing. Ex. *Yá llevába gastádos múchos pésos*, he had already spent many dollars. *Llevará puésta la espáda*, he will have on the sword. *Yá lleváis entendidas las órdenes*, you now are acquainted with the orders. *No lléva camino determinádo*, &c.
>
> N. B. 2d. *Andár* and *ir* are also used in the same manner for the auxiliary *ser*. Ex. *Múchos ándan ocupádos en frioléras*, many are occupied with trifles. *Íbamos cási muértos de cansáncio*, we were almost dead with fatigue. *Andában ocupádos en leér*, &c.
>
> N. B. 3d. *Andár* and *ir* are also used for *estár*, to denote precision and force before a gerund or participle active. Ex. *Los maéstros me andában enseñándo á esgrimír y á montár á cabállo*, the masters were teaching me to fence and ride a horse. *La primavéra fué acercándose* or *se fué acercándo*, the spring was drawing near or went on approaching. *Ándan requebrándo*, they are making love.

RULE LX.—When the participle past is constructed with the verb *ser* or *estár*, it always takes the gender and number of its subject. Ex. *Las riquézas son apetecídas*, riches are sought after. *Los málos serán castigádos*, the wicked shall be punished. *Élla está sentáda*, she is seated.

RULE LXI.—The *neuter, reflective* and *reciprocal* verbs form their compound tenses with the auxiliary verb *habér*, to have; and the participle past is always invariable when used with said auxiliary; therefore we say, *han salído*, they have or are gone out; *nos hémos alabádo*, we have praised ourselves; *Pédro y Juán se han amádo siémpre*, Peter and John have always loved one another.

N. B. *Morír* and *morírse*, to die, to be dying, is conjugated in the compound tenses, either with *habér*, preceded by two pronouns of the same person, one the subject and the other the direct regimen, or with *estár* or *ser;* in the first case the participle is invariable; in the second, it takes the gender and number of the subject. Ex. *Élla se ha muérto*, she has died. *Éllos son*, or *están muértos*, they are dead; *mi mádre es muérta*, or *está muérta*, or *se ha muérto*, my mother is dead, or has died.

CHAPTER VII.

OF ADVERBS.

The *adverb* is an indeclinable part of speech, which serves to modify the signification of another word, or express a circumstance of it; its collocation depends generally in speech like the adjective in relation to the substantive, on force and euphony.

N. B. *Simple adverbs* are generally placed after the verbs. *See* N. B. page 256.

Adverbs are simple or compound. They are simple, when they are expressed in one single word, and compound, when they are expressed in several. They are distinguished as adverbs of *place, time, order, quantity, comparison, manner, doubt, affirmation* and *negation*.

Adverbs of *place* serve to denote distances and the situations of persons or things; as *aquí*, or *acá*, here where I am; *ahí*, there where you are; *allí* or *allá*, there where he is, where she is, where they are; *acullá*, there, on the other side, on the side opposite to where you are; *cérca*, near; *léjos*, far; *dónde*, where, (without motion;) *á dónde*, where, (with motion); *déntro*, in, within; *fuéra*, out, without; *arríba*, up,

14

up stairs; *abájo*, down, down stairs; *delánte*, before; *detrás*, behind; *encima*, over, above; *debájo*, under, below.

Adverbs of *time* are those which express some relation to time, as *hóy*, to day; *ayér*, yesterday; *mañána*, to-morrow; *ahóra*, now; *luégo*, soon; *tárde*, late; *tempráno*, early; *présto*, quick; *prónto*, quickly; *siémpre*, always, ever; *jamás*, or *núnca*, never; *yá*, already; *miéntras*, in the mean time.

Adverbs of *order* express the manner in which things are arranged, in regard to one another, as *priméraménte*, firstly; *ántes*, before; *despues*, afterwards: *en lugár*, in lieu, &c.

Adverbs of *quantity* serve to denote the quantity of objects, or their value; as, *múcho*, much; *póco*, little; *álgo*, somewhat; *múy*, very; *hárto*, *bastánte*, enough, sufficiently; *tan*, so-as. N. B. *Tan* is always used for *tánto* before a *participle passive*. Ex. ¿ *Quién es* TAN (and not *tánto*) *amádo cómo él?* Who is *so* or *as much* beloved as he? *tánto*, so much; *cuánto*, how much.

Adverbs of *comparison* serve to compare objects together; as, *mas*, more; *ménos*, less; *mejór*, better; *peór*, worse; *múy*, very.

N. B. This last adverb *múy* placed before a participle past stands for *much*, *very much*, in English. Ex. *Estóy múy conténto*, or *satisfécho*, I am *much* or *very much* pleased, He was *much* esteemed, *éra múy estimádo*.

Adverbs of *manner* express how and in what manner things are done; they commonly hold the place of a preposition and a noun; as, *prudénteménte*, prudently; *elegánteménte*, elegantly; which are put for *con prudéncia*, *con elegáncia*, with prudence, with elegance, &c. They are also called adverbs of *quality*, because they are almost all formed from adjectives, the property of which is to qualify; the adverbs formed from adjectives are terminated in *mente* which is added to the feminine of those that terminate in *o*, and to the masculine of those that have another termination, without altering any thing in it; as, *constánte*, constant; *constánteménte*, constantly; *sutíl*, subtle; *sutíl-ménte*, artfully; *ríco*, rich; *rica-ménte*, richly; *álto*, high; *álta-ménte*, highly, &c.

There are others, which, not being derived from adjectives, cannot follow this rule, such as, *bién*, well; *mal*, ill; *así*, thus, *callandico*, silently; *pasíto á páso*, softly, &c.

There are in Spanish only two adverbs of *doubt*, these are, *acáso*, *quizá*, perhaps.

Adverbs of *affirmation* are; *sí*, yes; *ciértaménte*, *ciérto*, certainly, to be sure; *por ventúra, tal vez*, per chance; *ver-dadéraménte*, truly; *indubitáblcménte*, undoubtedly, &c.

Adverbs of *negation* are; *ningúno*, no one; *nádie*, no-body; *no*, no, not; *náda*, nothing, &c. and are always placed in Spanish in simple tenses before the verb, and in compound tenses before the auxiliary.

Observations upon jamás, núnca, no, mas, ménos, *and* múy.

1st. *Jamás* is used in the same sense as *núnca;* thus, we say; *jamás le hablaré*, I never shall speak to him; *jamás ví tal cósa*, I never saw any thing like. It is often joined to *núnca, por siémpre*, or *pára siémpre*, to give more strength and energy to the phrase; as *núnca jamás lo haré*, I never shall do it; *por siémpre* or *pára siémpre jamás me acor-daré de tí*, I shall forever remember thee. We see by these examples that, when it is joined to *núnca*, it signifies *never;* and that on the contrary, it has the signification of *eternally*, when it is joined to *por siémpre*, or *pára siémpre*. N. B. *Ja-más* is EVER, in English, in interrogations. Ex. Do you ever read? *¿ Lée vm. jamás?* Has he ever seen? *¿ Ha jamás vísto?*

2d. *No* does not always serve to deny; this word serves sometimes on the contrary to give more force to the affirma-tion and to make the opposition that exists between the two objects compared more striking; as, *mejór es la virtúd que no las riquézas*, virtue is preferable to riches.

REMARK. Two *negative* adverbs do not always destroy each other in Spanish; on the contrary, they often serve in familiar conversation to add to the strength of the negation. Consequently we say; no *he vísto á nádie*, I have seen no-body. No *háy* ningúno, there is nobody; and not *no he vísto algúno; no háy algúno;* but care must be taken to observe that, in order to make use in the same phrase of this double negation, *no* must precede the verb, and the other ne-gative must follow it, as in the above examples. If any other negative than *no* precede the verb, *no* is not expressed. We say, and very properly; jamás *oí voz mas harmoniósa*, I nev-er heard a more harmonious voice; náda *quiéro*, I wish for nothing; but we cannot say, *jamás no oí voz mas harmoni-ósa; no náda quiéro*. Finally, it is necessary to suppress the negative *no*, and place the negative adverb before the verb, or separate the two negatives in such a manner that *no* should precede the verb, and the other negative word should follow it; as, jamás *te hablaré* or, no *te hablaré* jamás,

I never shall speak to thee; nádie *te quiére*, or, no *te quiére* núdie, nobody loves thee; the first construction is the most elegant. *Ningúno*, nobody, not any body, none, not any one. *Ningúno me gústa*, none pleases me.

3d. When several adverbs terminating in *ménte*, are found in the same phrase, all of them except the last, lose the termination *ménte*. The object of this rule is to avoid repetitions disagreeable to the ear. Instead therefore of saying; *háblan sábiaménte y elocuéntemente; escríbe cláraménte, concisaménte y elegántemente*, we say, *háblan sábia y elocuénteménte; escríbe clára, concisa y elegántemente;* they speak wisely and eloquently; he writes clearly, concisely and elegantly.

4th. *Mas*, more; *ménos*, less; are also used to qualify substantives. Ex. *El es mas hómbre*, or, *ménos hómbre que su hermáno*, he is more a man or less a man than his brother.

5th. *Múy* serves also to qualify substantives. Ex. *Múy amígo mío*, very much my friend; *múy señór mío*, dear sir; *muy cabálléro*, very much a gentleman; *múy señóra mía*, dearest madam, lady.

CHAPTER VIII.

OF PREPOSITIONS.

Prepositions serve to express or denote the different relations which persons or things have with each other; they are fixed and invariable; and have neither gender nor number. Alone, they make no sense; and in order that they may signify something, it is necessary that they be followed by a regimen expressed or understood.

The prepositions most used in the Spanish language are the following; *á, ánte, con, cóntra, de, désde, en, éntre, hácia, hásta, pára, por, según, sin, sóbre, tras;* to *or* at, before, with, against, of *or* from, since, in, between *or* among, towards, till *or* until, for, by *or* for, according to, without, upon, behind *or* after. They have in Spanish the same use as in English, except the prepositions *pára, por, sóbre* and *tras* which require some observations.

Observations upon pára *and* por, *for*, by.

The English preposition *by* presents no difficulty, it is always rendered in Spanish by *por*. Ex. The world has been created *by* God; *el múndo fué criádo* por *Diós*.

But it is not the same with the English preposition *for*, it is sometimes rendered by the preposition *pára*, and sometimes by the preposition *por;* and we cannot use indifferently one for the other. The following rules will direct the learner respecting the use to be made of the words *pára* and *por*, according to the different cases.

Rule LXII.—The preposition *for* is translated by *pára* when it denotes,—1st.—that an action is directed towards a person or thing. Ex. This letter is *for* John, *ésta cárta es pára Juán.*—2d.—Motion towards a place. Ex. I set out for Italy, *sálgo pára Itália.*—3d.—A particular time, or fixed term, to which an action is referred. Ex. We shall leave it *for* to-morrow, *lo dejarémos* pára *mañána.*—4th.—The relation that a person or thing has with another. Ex. He has not done it ill *for* a beginner; pára *un principiánte no lo ha hécho mal.*

N. B. 1st. When the preposition *for* serves to express the end that we propose, it may be translated, either by *pára* or *por*, we say; I work *to* gain, *trabájo* por *or* pára *ganár.*

2d. *To be about*—is translated by *estár pára*, and the following verb is put in the present of the infinitive. Ex. I am about setting out, *estóy* pára *partír.*—*In respect to*—in comparison with*—are translated by *pára con*,—Ex. What is the creature *in comparison with*, or *in respect to* his creator? *Quién es la criatúra* pára con *su criadór?*—*Among* is elegantly rendered in the following phrase, and others like it, by *pára éntre*. Ex. *Among* friends compliments are always useless, pára éntre *amígos los cumplimiéntos son siémpre escusádos.*—*Pára* is also used before some adverbs, for we say, pára ahóra *lo quiéro*, I wish for it *now;* pára cuándo *vénga*, *when* he shall come; pára déntro *de un mes*, *within* a month; pára entónces *lo verémos*, we shall *then* see him.

Rule LXIII.—The preposition *for* is translated by *por* when it serves to express,—1st.—the time that a thing has lasted or will last. Ex. I leave Madrid *for* one month, *sálgo de Madríd* por *un mes.*—2d.—When it is equivalent to *in favor of.* Ex. I shall speak *for* thy brother, *hablaré* por *tu hermáno.*—3d.—When it signifies *in the place of*, as *substitute of.* Ex. I attend *for* my friend, *asísto* por *mi amigo.*—4th.—When it serves to express an exchange. I would give my coat *for* thine, *daría mi vestído* por *el túyo.*

14*

We also use the preposition *por* in the following modes of speaking; *in* the morning, *por la mañána;* in the afternoon, *por la tárde;* such a thing is not yet done, *tal cósa está por hacér;* to go for, *ir por;* he goes *for* wine, *va por víno;* to pass for, *estár tenído* por;—he passes *for* a wicked man, *está tenído* por *málo;* to come for, *venír* por; he came for them, *víno por éllos.*

Observations upon sóbre and tras.

These prepositions *sóbre* and *tras* are frequently used before verbs, which they govern in the infinitive. Ex. Sóbre *ser réo convícto, quiére que le prémien,* he has been found guilty, and yet he wishes to be rewarded. Tras *ser culpádo, es él que mas levánta el grílo,* he is guilty, and yet raises his voice the loudest. *Ir tras,* to go *after.*

Prepositions which, in Spanish, govern the following nouns in the genitive.

Before, *antes*—Before the time, *ántes del tiémpo.*
After, *después*—After you, *después de vm.*
Within, *déntro*—Within two years, *déntro de dos áños.*
Except, *fuéra*—Except my father, *fuéra de mi pádre.*
Besides, *además*—Besides the money, *además del dinéro.*
Near, *cérca*—Near the door, *cérca de la puérla.*
Across, *por el médio*—Across the fields, *por el médio de los cámpos.*
At, in the, *en cása*—At my brother's, *en cása de mi hermáno;* at home, *en mi cása;* in thy house, *en tu cása;* at our home, *en nuéstra cása.*
Notwithstanding, in spite of, *á pesár de*—In spite of you, *á pesár de vm.*
Opposite, *frénte á, en frénte de*—Opposite his house, *en frénte de su cása.*
By the side of, *al ládo*—By the side of the king, *al ládo del réy.*
Behind, *detrás*—Behind the chest of drawers, *detrás del armário.*
Upon, *encíma*—Upon the bed, *encíma de la cáma.*
Under, *debájo*—Under the bridge, *debájo del puénte.*

The following prepositions govern the dative.

As respects, *en órden á*—As respects what you say, *en órden á lo que vm. díce.*

Adjoining, *júnto* — Adjoining the garden, *júnto al jardín.*
Concerning, *locánte* — Concerning this affair, *locánte á ésta pendléncia.*

Almost all the other prepositions govern the noun in Spanish in the same case as in English.

In addition to the preceding directions for the use of prepositions, we ought not to omit the following table taken from the Grammar of the Spanish Academy, which teaches at once how the prepositions govern and are governed. We advise young students to commit this table to memory.

TABLE.

A.

Abalanzárse á los peligros	to rush *on* dangers
abandonárse á la suérte	to abandon oneself *to* chance
abocárse *con* algúno	to confer *with* any one
abochornárse *de* álgo	to be chagrined *with* any thing
abogár *por* algúno	to plead *for* any one
abordár (úna náve) *á, con* ótra	to board (one ship) another
aborrecible *á* las géntes	hateful *to* the people
aborrecido *de* tódos	detested *by* all
abrasárse *en* deséos	to be inflamed *with* desires
abrirse *á, con* los amigos	to open oneself *to* one's friends
abstenérse *de* la frúta	to abstain *from* fruit
abundár *de, en* riquézas	to abound *with* or *in* riches
aburrido *de* las desgrácias	weary *with* misfortunes
abusár *de* la amistád	to abuse friendship
acabár *de* venir	to be just come
acaecér *á* algúno	to happen *to* any one
acaecér *en* tal tiémpo	to happen *at* such a time
acalorárse *en, con* la dispúta	to grow warm *in* a dispute
accedér *á* la opinión de ótro	to accede *to* another's opinion
accesible *á* tódos	accessible *to* all
acertár *á, con* la cása	to find out, to hit the house
acogérse *á* sagrádo	to take shelter *in* a church
acomodárse *á, con* ótro dictámen	to conform oneself *to* another opinion
acompañárse *con* ótros	to keep company *with* others
aconsejárse *con, de* sábios	to take advice *with* wise men
acontecér *á* los incáutos	to happen *to* the unwary
acordárse *de* lo pasádo	to remember the past
acordárse *con* los contrários	to agree *with* the opponents
acostumbrárse *á* trabájos	to accustom oneself *to* trouble
ácre *de* génio	austere *in* temper, disposition
acreditárse *de* nécio	to prove oneself a fool

acreditárse con, pára algúno	to get credit with one
acreedór á la confiánza	worthy of confidence
acreedór de algúno	any one's creditor
actuárse de, en los negócios	to acquaint oneself with business
acusár (á algúno) de algún delito	to accuse (any one) of any crime
acusárse de las cúlpas	to accuse oneself of faults
adelantárse á ótros	to be in advance of others, to take the lead of others
adherírse á ótro dictámen	to adhere to another opinion
adolecér de algúna enfermedád	to be ill of some disorder
aferrárse en, con su opinión	to be fixed in one's own opinion
aferrárse (úna náve) con ótra	to grapple (one ship) another
aficionárse á, de algúna cósa	to be fond of any thing
afirmárse en lo dícho	to affirm what has been said
agéno de verdád	foreign to truth
agradáble al paladár	agreeable to the palate
agradecído á los benefícios	grateful for benefits
agraviárse de algúno	to be affronted with any one
agraviárse de la senténcia	to appeal from the sentence
agregárse á ótros	to unite oneself to others
ágrio al gústo	sour to the taste
agúdo de ingénio	witty, or sharp of intellect
ahitárse de manjáres	to surfeit oneself with food
ahogárse en el mar	to be drowned in the sea
ahorcajárse en las espáldas	to get astride upon the back
ahorrár de razónes	to spare words
ahorrárse (no) con ningúno	not to spare any one
airárse con algúno	to be angry with any body
ajustárse á la razón	to be right inclined
ajustárse con algúno	to make it up with any one
alabárse de valiénte	to boast of bravery
alargárse á la ciudád	to hasten to the city
alegrárse de álgo	to be rejoiced at any thing
alejárse de su tiérra	to leave one's country
alimentárse de, con yérbas	to subsist upon herbs
alimentárse de esperánzas	to feed oneself with hopes
alindár con ótra heredád	to be contiguous to another's estate
allanárse á lo justo	to submit to what is just
álto de cuérpo	tall in stature
amáble á tódos	amiable to all
amancebárse con los líbros	to be fond of books
amánte de algúno	a lover of some one
amañárse á escribír	to be clever in writing
amoróso con los súyos	kind with one's relations
amparárse de álgo, de algúna cósa	to take possession of any thing
áncho de bóca	wide mouthed
andár con el tiémpo	to accommodate oneself to time
andár de cápa	to walk with a cloak on
andár en pléitos	to be litigious
andár á gátas	to go all fours
andár por tiérra	to be humbled to the ground
angósto de mánga	tight sleeved
anhelár á, por mayór fortúna	to covet better fortune
anticipárse á ótro	to anticipate another

aovár *en* la ribéra	to lay eggs *on* the sea-shore
aparár *en* la máno	to receive *with* the hand
aparecérse *á* algúno	to present oneself suddenly *before* any one
aparecérse *en* el camino	to present oneself suddenly *on* the road
aparejárse *pára* el trabájo	to prepare *for* work
apartárse *de* la ocasión	to separate oneself *from* the occasion
apartárse *á* un ládo	to retire *on* one side
apasionárse *á, de, por* algúno	to be enamoured *with* any one
apeárse *de* su opinión	to change one's opinion
apechugár *con* algúna cósa	to undertake any thing *with* spirit
apecingár *por* los peligros	to brave dangers
apedreár *con* las palábras	to abuse any one *with* words
apegárse *á* algúna cósa	to adhere *to* any thing
apelár *de* la senténcia	to appeal *from* the sentence
apelár *á* otro médio	to have recourse *to* another measure
apercibírse *de* ármas	to provide oneself *with* arms
apercibírse *á, pára* la batálla	to get ready *for* battle
apetecible *al* gústo	desirable *to* the palate
apetecído *de, por* tódos	desired *by* all
apiadárse *de* los póbres	to have compassion *on* the poor
aplicárse *á* los estúdios	to apply oneself *to* study
apoderárse *de* la haciénda	to take possession *of* the property
apostár *á* corrér	to lay a wager *on* a race
apresurárse *á* venír	to make haste *to* come
apresurárse *por* algúna cósa	to make haste *for* something
apretár *por* la cintúra	to take fast hold *by* the waist
aprobárse *en* algúna facultád	to be approved in any faculty
aprobádo *de* cirujáno	approved *as a* surgeon
apropiádo *pára* el oficio	adapted *to* the office
apropiárse *á* si	to appropriate *to* oneself
apropincuárse *á* algúno	to approach any one
aprovechár *en* la virtúd	to improve *in* virtue
aprovechárse *de* la ocasión	to seize the opportunity
ápto *pára* el empléo	fit *for* the employment
apurádo *de* médios	exhausted *of* means
aquietárse *en* la dispúta	to grow quiet *in* the dispute
ardér *en* deséos	to burn *with* desires
ardérse *en* quiméras	to be full *of* quarrels
armárse *de* paciéncia	to arm oneself *with* patience
arrebozárse *con* álgo	to muffle oneself up *in* any thing
arrecirse *de* frío	to be benumbed *with* cold
arreglárse *á* las léyes	to conform *to* the laws
arregostárse *á* algúna cósa	to be inclined *to* any thing
arremetér *á, con, cóntra* el múro	to assault the wall
arrepentírse *de* las cúlpas	to repent *of* sins, faults
arrestárse *á* tódo	to be enterprising *in* every thing
arribár *á* tiérra	to arrive *at* land, *on* shore
arrimárse *á* la paréd	to lean *against* the wall
arrinconárse *en* cása	to confine oneself *at* home
arrogárse (álgo) *á* si mismo	to appropriate (any thing) *to* oneself

arrojárse á peleár	to rush on to fight
arropárse con la cápa	to cover oneself with a cloak
arrostrár á, con los peligros	to face dangers
asárse de calór	to be scorched with heat
ascendér á ótro empléo	to ascend to another office
asegurárse de su contrário	to shelter oneself from one's enemy
asentír á ótro dictámen	to assent to another's opinion
asesorárse con letrádos	to seek council from learned men
asistír á los enférmos	to assist the sick
asistír en tal cása	to attend such a house
asociárse á, con ótro	to associate oneself with another
asomárse á, por la ventána	to look out at the window
aspárse á gritos	to be exhausted with clamourings
aspárse por algúna cósa	to torment oneself for any thing
áspero al gústo	rough to the taste
áspero en las palábras	rude in conversation
aspirár á mayór fortúna	to aspire to better fortune
atárse á úna sóla cósa	to tie oneself to one thing alone
atemorizárse de, por álgo	to be afraid of something
atendér á la conversación	to attend to the conversation
atenérse á lo segúro	to keep to the safe side
aténto con sus mayóres	respectful to one's superiors
atestiguár con ótro	to testify with another
atinár á, con la cása	to hit upon the house
atollárse en los caminos	to stick fast in the road
atraér á sí	to attract to oneself
atrevérse á cósas grándes	to animate oneself to great things
atrevérse con tódos	to dare every body
atribuír á ótro	to attribute to another
atribulárse en, con los trabájos	to be afflicted with labor, troubles
atropellárse en las acciónes	to overhasten actions
atufárse en la conversación	to take pet in conversation
atufárse por póco	to be affronted at a trifle
aunárse con ótro	to unite oneself with another
ausentárse de Madrid	to absent oneself from Madrid
avecindárse en algún puéblo	to take one's abode in any town
avenirse con tódos	to agree with all
aventajárse á ótros	to gain the advantage over others
avergonzárse á pedír	to be ashamed at asking
avergonzárse de álgo	to be ashamed of any thing
averiguárse con algúno	to agree with any one
aviárse de rópa	to furnish oneself with clothes
avocár (algúna cósa) á sí	to call a cause from an inferior court to one's own

B.

Balanceár á tal párte	to vibrate on such a side
balanceár en la dúda	to fluctuate in doubt
balár por dinéro	to clamour for money
bamboleár én la maróma	to dance on the rope
bañárse en água	to bathe oneself in water

barár *en* tiérra	to run aground
barheár *con* la paréd	to reach a wall *with* one's chin
bastardeár *de* su naturaléza	to degenerate *from* his nature
bastardeár *en* sus acciónes	to be degenerated *in* one's actions
batallár *con* los enemígos	to fight *with* the enemy
bajár *á* la cuéva	to go down *to* the cellar
bajár *de* la tórre	to descend *from* the tower •
bajár *de* la autoridád	to recede *from* authority
bajár *hácia* el válle	to descend *towards* the valley
bájo *de* cuérpo	low *in* stature
benéfico *á, pára* la salúd	beneficial *to* the health
blanco *de* cútis	of a white complexion
blándo *de* cortéza	of a soft skin, bark
blasfemár *de* la virtúd	to blaspheme *against* virtue
blasonár *de* valiénte	to boast *of* bravery
bordár (álgo) *de, con* pláta	to embroider (any thing) *in* or *with* silver
bordár (álgo) *al* tambór	to embroider *on a* tambour frame
bordár *de* pasádos	to embroider *with* a needle
bostezár *de* hámbre	to gape *through* hunger
bóto *de* púnto	blunt *at* the point
boyánte *en* la fortúna	to be very fortunate
bramár *de* coráge	to roar *with* anger
breár *á* chásco	to vex *with* tricks
bregár *con* algúno	to struggle *with* any one
brindár *con* regálos	to offer presents
brindár *á* la salúd de algúno	to toast *to* any one's health
buéno *de, pára* comér	good *to* eat
bufár *de* ira	to swell *with* anger
bullir *en, por* tódas pártes	to move *in* all parts
burlárse *de* álgo	to make a jest *of* any thing

C.

Cabér *de* piés	to be able to stand in *on* one's feet
cabér *en* la máno	to be contained *in* the hand
caér *á, hácia* tal párte	to fall *on* such a side
caér *de* lo álto	to fall *from* on high
caér *en* tiérra, *en* cuénta, *en* error, *en* tal tiémpo, *en* lo que se dice	to fall *upon* the earth, to comprehend, to fall *into* a mistake, to fall out at such a time, to understand what is said
caér *por* páscua	to fall *at* Easter
caér *sóbre* los enemígos	to fall *upon* the enemy
calárse *de* água	to wet oneself through *with* water
calentárse *á* la lúmbre	to warm oneself *at* the fire
calificár *de* dócto •	to qualify any one *as* a learned man
callar (la verdád) *á* ótro	to conceal (the truth) *from* another
callár *de, por* miédo	to be silent *from* fear
calumniár (á algúno) *de* injústo	to calumniate (any one) *as* unjust
calzárse *á* algúno	to lead another *by* the nose

cambiár (algúna cósa) *con, por* ótra — to exchange (one thing) *for* another
caminár á, *pára* Sevílla — to travel *to* Seville
caminár á pié — to travel *on* foot
caminár *por* el mónte — to walk *along* the mountain
cansárse *de, con* el trabájo — to fatigue oneself *with* the labor
cansárse *de* pretendér — to be tired *of* pretending
cansárse *en* el camíno — to be tired *on* the road
capáz *de* cién arróbas — capable *of* holding a hundred arrobas *

capáz *de, pára* el empléo — capable *for* the employment
capitulár *con* el enemígo — to capitulate *with* the enemy
capitulár (á algúno) *de* mal juéz — to reproach (any one) *as* a bad judge
cargárse *de* razón — to insist *upon* one's opinion
casár (úna persóna ó cósa) *con* ótra — to couple (one person or thing) *with* another
catequizár (á algúno) *pára* algúna cósa — to persuade (any one) *to* any thing
causár (perjuício) á álgúno — to cause (prejudice) *to* any one
cautivár (á algúno) *con, por* beneficios — to overcome (any one) *with* favours
cavár (la imaginación) *en* algúno — any one to think (seriously)
cavár (con la imaginación) *en* algúna cósa — to think (deeply) *on* any thing

cazcalcár *de* úna párte á ótra — to go lounging *about*
cedér á ótro, á la autoridád — to yield *to* another, *to* authority
cedér *en* beneficio de algúno — to resign *in* another's favour
censurár (algúna cósa) *de* mála — to blame (any thing) *as* bad
ceñirse á lo posíble — to keep *within* bounds
chancearse *con* algúno — to joke *with* any one
chapuzár (álgo) *en* el água — to sink (any thing) *in* the water
chíco *de* cuérpo — small *in* person
chocár á algúno — to provoke any one
chocár *con* ótro — to strike one *against* another
circunscribirse á úna cósa — to confine oneself *to* one thing
clamár á Diós — to call *on* God
clamár *por* dinéro — to cry out *for* money
clamoreár *por* los muértos — to ring a peal *for* the dead
coartár (la facultád) á algúno — to restrict (the power) *of* any one
cobrár (dinéro) *de* los deudóres — to recover (money) *from* debtors
colegír *de, por* los antecedéntes — to infer *from* the antecedents
coligárse *con* algúno — to make an alliance *with* any one
columpiárse *en* el áire — to swing *in* the air
combatir *con, cóntra* el enemígo — to fight *against* the enemy
combinár (úna cósa) *con* ótra — to combine (one thing) *with* another
comedírse *en* las palábras — to be civil *in* words
comenzár á decír — to begin *to* say
comérse *de* envídia — to pine *with* envy
compatíble *con* la justícia — compatible *with* justice
compensár (úna cósa) *con* ótra — to compensate (one thing) *with* another

---

* Four *arróbas* make a quintal.

competir *con* algúno — to vie *with* any one
complacérse *de, en* algúna cósa — to be pleased *with* any thing
componérse *con* los deudóres · — to compound *with* debtors
componérse *de* buéno y málo — to be made *of* good and bad
comprár (algúno) *al, del* vendedór — to buy (any one) *from the* seller
comprensible *al* entendimiénto — comprehensible *to the* understanding

comprobár (álgo) *con* instruméntos — to prove (any thing) *with* instruments
comprometérse *con* algúno — to render oneself answerable *to* any one

comprometérse *en* juéces árbitros — to compromise *by* arbitration
comunicár (luz) *á* algúna párte — to communicate (light) *to* any part
comunicár (úno) *con* ótro — to commune (one) *with* another
concebir (algúna cósa) *en* el ánimo — to comprehend (something)
concebir (úna cósa) *por* buéna — to conceive (any thing) *as* good
concedér (álgo) *á* ótro — to yield (any thing) *to* another
conceptuár (á algúno) *de, por* sábio — to look upon (any one) *as* a wise man
concertár (úna cósa) *con* ótra — to concert (one thing) *with* another
concordár (la cópia) *con* el originál — to make the copy agree *with* the original

concurrír *á* algún fin — to concur *to* some end
concurrír *á* algúna párte — to meet *at* some place
concurrír *con* ótros — to concur *with* others
concurrír (múchos) *en* un dictámen — to agree (many) *in* one opinion
condenár (á úno) *á* galéras — to condemn (one) *to* the galleys
condenár (á úno) *en* las cóstas — to condemn (one) *in* the costs
condescendér *á* los ruégos — to condescend *to* entreaties
condescendér *con* la instáncia — to condescend *to* the instance
condolérse *de* los trabájos — to be grieved *with* the troubles
conducir (álgo) *á* tal párte — to conduct (any thing) *to* such a place
conducir (úna cósa) *al* bién de ótro — to conduce (something) *to* another's good

confabulárse *con* los contrários — to converse *with* one's enemies
confederárse *con* algúno — to ally oneself *to* any one
conferir (úna cósa) *con* ótra — to compare one thing *with* another
conferir (un negócio) *con, entre* los amígos — to confer on any business *with* friends
confesár (el delíto) *al* juéz — to confess (one's crime) *to* the judge
confesárse *á* Dios — to confess *to* God
confesárse *con* algúno — to acknowledge *to* any one
confesárse *de* sus cúlpas — to confess one's sins
confiár (úna cósa) *á* úna persóna — to entrust (any thing) *to* any one
confiár *en, de* algúno — to rely *upon* any one
confinár (á algúno) *á* tal párte — to confine (any one) *to* such a place
confinár (España) *con* Fráncia — to lie adjacent (Spain) *to* France
confirmárse *en* su dictámen — to be confirmed *in* one's opinion
conformárse *con* el tiémpo — to conform *to* the times
confórme *á, con* su opinión — conformable *to* his opinion
confrontár *con* algúno — to confront *with* any one
confrontár (úna cósa) *con* ótra — to confront (one thing) *with* another
confundirse *de* lo que se ve — to be confounded *with* what one sees
confundirse *en* sus juícios — to be thrown (one's senses) *into* confusion

15

congeniár *con* algúno	to be congenial *to* any one
congraciárse *con* ótro	to ingratiate oneself *into* another's favour
congratulárse *con* los súyos	to congratulate oneself *with* one's own friends
congratulárse *de* algúna cósa	to rejoice *in* any thing
congeturár (álgo) *de, por* señáles	to conjecture (any thing) *by* signs
conmutár (álgo) *con* ótra cósa	to barter (one thing) *for* another
conmutár (un vóto) *en* ótra cósa	to exchange (a vow) *into* another thing
consagrárse *á* Diós	to consecrate oneself *to* God
consentir *en* álgo	to agree *to* any thing
consolárse *con* sus pariéntes	to be comforted *with* one's friends
conspirár *á* algúna cósa	to aspire *to* any thing
conspirár *cóntra* algúno	to conspire *against* any one
conspirár *en* un inténto	to enter *into* a conspiracy
constár (el tódo) *de* pártes	to be composed (the whole) *of* parts
constár *por* escríto	to appear *in* writing
consultár *á* algúno pára un empléo	to propose any one for an employment, office
consultár *con* letrádos	to consult *with* learned men
consumádo *en* úna facultád	to be consummate *in* a faculty
contaminárse *con* los viciósos	to pervert oneself *with* the vicious
contaminárse *de* heregías	to contaminate oneself *with* heresies
contemporizár *con* algúno	to temporize *with* any one
contendér *con* algúno	to contend *with* any one
contendér *sóbre* algúna cósa	to dispute *upon* any thing
contenérse *en* su obligación	to hold *to* one's contract, duty
contestár *á* la pregúnta	to answer one's question
contraér (álgo) *á* un asúnto	to apply (something) *to* a subject
contrapesár (úna cósa) *con* ótra	to counterpoise (one thing) *with* another
contraponér (úna cósa) *á* ótra	to put (one thing) *against* another
contrapuntárse *con* algúno	to compare oneself *with* any one
contrapuntárse *de* palábras	to scold *at* one another
contravenír *á* la ley	to transgress *against* the law
contribuír *á* tal cósa	to contribute *to* such a thing
contribuír *con* dinéro	to contribute money
convalecér *de* la enfermedád	to recover *from* illness
convencérse *de* la razón	to be convinced *by* reason
convenír *con* ótro	to agree *with* another
convenír *en* algúna cósa	to agree *upon* any thing
conversár *con* algúno	to converse *with* any one
conversár *en* matérias de estádo	to converse *on* affairs of state
convertír (la haciénda) *en* dinéro	to convert (goods) *into* money
convertírse *á* Diós	to be converted *to* God
convidár (á algúno) *á* comér	to invite (any one) *to* dine
convidár (á algúno) *con* dinéro	to offer money *to* any body
convidárse *á* los trabájos	to be ready *to* work
convocár *á* júnta	to convene a meeting
cóoperár (con ótro) *á* algúna cósa	to cooperate *in* any thing
correrse *de* vergüénza	to be ashamed

correspondér á los beneficios	to be grateful
correspondérse con los amigos	to correspond *with* friends
cotejár (la cópia) con el originál	to compare (the copy) *with* the original
crecér en virtúdes	to increase *in* virtues
creciclo de cuérpo	tall *in* stature
creér en Diós	to believe *in* God
creérse de algúna cósa	to be convinced *of* any thing
cuchareteár en tódo	to intermeddle *in* every thing
cuidár de álgo, de algúno	to take care *of* something, *of* some one
culpár (á úno) de omíso	to blame (any one) *for* negligence
cumplir con algúno	to discharge one's obligation *to* any body
cumplir con su obligación	to perform one's duty
curárse de algúna enfermedád	to be cured *of* any disorder
curárse en salúd	to take care of oneself *in* health
curtírse al áire	to tan *by* the air
curtido del sol	tanned *by* the sun

D.

dar (álgo) á algúno	to give (something) *to* any body
dar (á algúno) de pálos	to beat (any one) *with* a stick
dar de blánco	to hit *the* mark
dar en manías	to be foolish, whimsical
dar por visto	to suppose any thing *as* seen
dárse á estudiár	to give oneself *to* study
dárse al diántre	to despair
dárse por vencido	to acknowledge oneself *as* conquered
debér (dinéro) á algúno	to be indebted *to* any body
decaér de su autoridád	to fall *from* one's authority
decír (álgo) á ótro	to say (any thing) *to* another
decír (bién) con úna cósa	to agree (one thing) *with* another
decír (bién) de algúno	to speak (well) *of* any one
declarárse á algúno	to declare oneself *to* any body
declarárse por un partido	to declare oneself *for* a party
declinár á, hácia tal párte	to incline *towards* such a side
declinár en bagéza	to degenerate
dedicár (tiémpo) al estúdio	to employ (one's time) *in* study
dedicárse á la virtúd	to devote oneself *to* virtue
defendér (á úno) de sus contrários	to defend (any body) *from* his enemies
deferir (al parecér) de ótro	to adopt another's opinion
defraudár (álgo) de la autoridád de ótro	to usurp (a little) another's authority
degenerár de su nacimiénto	to degenerate *from* one's ancestors
delánte de algúno	before any body
delatárse al juéz	to accuse oneself *to* a judge
deleitárse con la vísta	to be pleased *with* seeing
deleitárse en oír	to delight *in* hearing

deliberár *sóbre* tal cósa	to deliberate *upon* any thing
déntro *de* cása	within the house
dependér *de* algúno	to depend *upon* any body
deponér (á algúno) *de* su empléo	to depose (any body) *from* his employment
depositár (álgo) *en* algúna párte	to deposit (any-thing) *in* any place
derivár *de* ótro autoridád	to derive authority *from* another
derrenegár *de* algúna cósa	to detest any thing
desabrirse *con* algúno	to have a difference *with* any body
desabrochárse *con* algúno	to divulge one's secret *to* another
desagradecido *á* algún beneficio	ungrateful *for* any benefit
desahogárse (con algúno) de su péna	to communicate (to another) one's trouble
desapropiárse *de* álgo	to alienate any thing
desavenirse *con* algúno	to disagree *with* any one
desavenirse (únos) *de* ótros	to disagree (some) *with* others
desayunárse *de* algúna noticia	to take notice *of* any news
descabezárse *en, con* algúna cósa	to labor hard in vain *on* any thing
descalabazárse *en* algúna cósa	to puzzle one's wits to find out any thing
descansár *de* la fatiga	to relieve oneself *from* fatigue
descantillár (álgo) *de* algúna cósa	to break off the corner *of* any thing
descargárse *de* algúna cósa	to clear oneself *from* any thing
descartárse *de* algún encárgo	to excuse oneself *from* any charge
descendér *á* los válles	to descend *to* the vallies
descendér *de* buén lináge	to come *of* a good family
descolgárse *de, por* la murálla	to creep down the wall
descollár *sóbre* ótros	to surpass others
descomponérse *con* algúno	to disagree *with* any one
desconfiár *de* algúno	to mistrust any one
desconocido *á* los beneficiós	ungrateful *for* benefits
descontár (álgo) *de* algúna cósa	to discount one thing *from* another
descubrirse *con* algúno	to disclose oneself *to* any one
descuidárse *de, en* su obligación	to neglect one's obligation, duty
desdecir *de* su carácter	to deviate *from* one's character
desdecir *de* lo dícho	to retract what one has said
desdeñárse *de* algúna cósa	to disdain any thing
desembarázárse *de* estórbos	to get rid *of* obstacles
desembarcár *de* la náve	to unship, unload *from* the vessel
desembarcár *en* el puérto	to land *in* the harbour
desenfrenárse *en* vícios	to abandon oneself *to* vices
desertár *de* las bandéras	to desert the standard
desesperár *de* la pretensión	to despair *of* one's pretension
desfalcár (álgo) *de* algúna cósa	to deduct *from* another thing
desgajárse *de* los móntes	to fall *from* the mountains
deshacérse *á* trabajár	to work hard, *with* anxiety
deshacérse *de* algúna cósa	to get rid *of* any thing
deshacérse *en* llánto	to burst *into* tears
desmentir *á* algúno	to give any one the lie
desmentir (úna cósa) *de* ótra	to contradict (one thing) another
desnudárse *de* pasiónes	to divest oneself *of* passions
despedirse *de* algúna cósa	to take leave *of* any thing

despeñárse *de* un mónte	to fall headlong *from* a mountain
despertár *á* algúno	to awake any one
despertár *del* suéño	to awake *from* sleep
despicárse *de* la ofénsa	to be revenged *of* an affront
despoblárse *de* génte	to become unpeopled
desposárse *con* algúno	to marry any one
desprendérse *de* álgo	to get rid *of* something
déspués *de* llegár, *de* algúno, *de* algúna cósa	after arriving, after any one, after any thing
desquiciár (á algúno) *de* su podér	to deprive (any one) *of* his authority
desquitárse *de* la pérdida	to make up *for* one's loss
desterrár (á úno) *de* su pátria	to banish (any one) *from* his country
destrizárse *á* llorár	to consume oneself *with* weeping
destrizárse *de* enfádo	to consume oneself *with* anger
desvergonzárse *con* algúno	to take liberties *with* any body
desviárse *del* camíno	to lose one's way
desvivírse *por* álgo	to be anxious *for* something
detenérse *en* dificultádes	to be stopped *by* difficulties
determinárse *á* partír	to take the resolution *to* set out
detrás *de* la iglésia	behind the church
devolvér (la cáusa) *al* juéz	to return the cause *to* the judge
dejár (úna mánda) *á* algúno	to leave (a legacy) *to* any one
dejár *de* escribír	to leave off writing
dejár (álgo) *en* máno de ótro	to deposit something *in* the hands of another
diferír (álgo) *á*, *pára* ótro tiémpo	to defer (any thing) *to* another time
dignárse *de* concedér álgo	to condescend *to* grant any thing
dimanár (úna cósa) *de* ótra	to emanate (one thing) *from* another
discernír (úna cósa) *de* ótra	to discern (one thing) *from* another
disgustárse *de*, *con* algúna cósa	to be disgusted *with* any thing
disponér *de* los biénes	to dispose *of* goods
disponérse *á* caminár	to prepare oneself *to* travel
disputár *de*, *sóbre* algúna cósa	to dispute *about*, *on* any thing
disentir *de* ótro dictámen	to dissent *from* another's opinion
distár (un puéblo) *de* ótro	to be distant (one town) *from* another
distinguír (úna cósa) *de* ótra	to distinguish (one thing) *from* another
distraérse *de*, *en* la conversación	to wander *from*, *in* conversation
disuadir (á algúno) *de* algúna cósa	to dissuade (any one) *from* any thing
dividír (úna cósa) *de* ótra	to divide (one thing) *from* another
dividír *en* pártes	to divide in parts
dividir *éntre* múchos	to divide *between* several
dividir *por* mitád	to divide *into* halves
dolérse *de* los pecádos	to repent *of* sins
dotádo *de* ciéncia ·	endowed *with* learning
dudár *de* algúna cósa	to doubt any thing
durár *hásta* el inviérno	to last *till* winter
durár *por* múcho tiémpo	to last a long time
dúro *de* cortéza	of a rough skin, bark

15*

E.

Echár (álgo) *de, en, por* tiérra	to throw (any thing) *from, on* the earth
echár (olór) *de* sí	to exhale (an odour) *from* oneself
elevárse *á, hásta* el ciélo	to be exalted *to* the skies
elevárse *de* la tiérra	to be elevated *from* the earth
embarcárse *en* negócios	to be involved *in* business
embobárse *con, de, en* algúna cósa	to be stupified *with* any thing
emboscárse *en* el mónte	to lie *in* ambush *on* a hill
embutir (algúna cósa) *de* algodón	to inlay (any thing) *with* cotton
embutir (úna cósa) *en* ótra	to inlay (one thing) *in* another
enmendárse *con* la corrección	to be amended *by* correction
enmendárse *de, en* algúna cósa	to correct oneself *in* any thing
empapárse *en* água	to be soaked *with* water
emparejár *con* algúno	to put one on a level *with* any one
emparentár *con* algúno	to be related *to* any one
empeñárse *en* úna cósa	to pledge oneself *to* a thing
empeñárse *por* algúno	to take part *for* another
empleárse *de* algúna cósa	to employ oneself *about* a thing
enagenárse *de* algúna cósa	to alienate any thing
euamorárse *de* algúno	to be enamoured *with* any one
enamoricárse *de* algúno	to fall in love *with* any one
encallár (la náve) *en* aréna	to run (a ship) *on* shore, or on the sand
encaminárse *á* algúna párte	to direct one's course *to* any part
encaramárse *en, por, sóbre,* la paréd	to climb up the wall
encarárse *á, con* algúno	to face another
encargárse *de* algún negócio	to charge oneself *with* any business
encasquetárse (álgo) *en* la cabéza	to be obstinate *in* maintaining any thing
encastillárse *en* algúna párte	to fortify oneself *in* any place
encajárse *en, por* algúna párte	to busy oneself *in* any thing
encenagárse *en* vícios	to become vicious
encendérse *en* íra	to kindle *with* anger
encerrárse *en* su cása	to shut oneself up *in* one's house
encharcárse *en* água	to drink too much water
encomendárse *á* Diós	to commend oneself *to* God
enconárse *con* algúno	to be irritated *against* any one
enfermár *del* pécho	to have a pain *in* the breast
enfrascárse *en* la dispúta	to entangle oneself *in* a dispute
engolfárse *en* cósas gráves	to be absorbed *in* important things
engreírse *con* la fortúna	to become vain *with* fortune
enlazár (algúna cósa) *con* ótra	to tie (one thing) close *to* another
enredárse (úna cósa) *con, en* ótra	to interweave (one thing) *with* another
ensayárse *á, pára* algúna cósa	to try *to* do any thing
ensayárse *en* algúna cósa	to become expert *in* any thing
entendér *de* algúna cósa	to understand any thing
entendér *en* sus negócios	to understand one's business
enterárse *de* algúna cósa	to be well informed *of* any thing
enterárse *en* algún negócio	to be well acquainted *with* any business

entrár *en* algúna párte	to enter any place
entregár (álgo) *á* algúno	to deliver (something) *to* some one
entremetérse *en* cósas de ótro	to meddle *with* another's affairs
enviár (álgo) *á* algúno	to send (something) *to* some one
equivocárse (úna cósa) *con* ótra	to mistake (one thing) *for* another
equivocárse *en* álgo	to be mistaken *in* any thing
escapárse *de* la prisión	to escape *from* prison
escapárse *por* la ventána	to escape *through* the window
escarmentár *de*, *con* algúna cósa	to take warning *at* any thing
escarmentár *en* cabéza agéna	to take warning *at* another's expense
escondérse *en* algúna párte	to hide oneself *in* any place
escondérse *de* algúno	to hide *from* any one
escáso *de* médios	limited *in* means
escribir (cártas) á algúno	to write (letters) *to* any one
esculpir *en* brónce	to engrave *on* brass
esmerárse *en* algúna cósa	to exert oneself *in* any thing
espantárse *de* álgo	to be terrified *at* any thing
estampár *en* papél	to print *on* paper
estár *á* la órden de ótro	to be under another's direction
estár *de* viáge	to be *on* a journey
estár *en* algúna párte	to be *in* some place
estár *en* ánimo de	to have a mind to
estár *en* lo que se háce	to know what is doing
estár *pára* salir	to be ready *to* go out
estár *por* algúno	to be *in favour of* any one
estár (algúna cósa) *por* sucedér	to be (something) *near* happening
estrechárse *con* algúno	to become intimate *with* any one
estrechárse *en* los gástos	to restrain oneself *in* one's expenses
estrellárse *con* algúno	to fall out *with* any one
estrellárse *en*, *contra* algúna cósa	to dash oneself *against* any thing
estribár *en* algúna cósa	to be supported *in* any thing
escedér (úna cósa) *á* ótra	to excel (one thing) another
escedér (úna cantidád) *en* mil reáles	to exceed (a sum) *by* one thousand rials
escéptuar (á algúno) *de* algúna cósa	to except (any one) *from* any thing
escluir (algúno) *de* algúna párte ó cósa	to exclude (any one) *from* any place or thing
escusárse *con* algúno	to apologize *to* any one
escusárse *de* hacer algúna cósa	to excuse oneself *from* doing any thing
exhortár (á algúno) *á* tal cósa	to exhort (any one) *to* such a thing
eximir (á algúno) *de* algúna cósa	to exempt (any one) *from* any thing
exonerár (á algúno) *de* su empléo	to dismiss (any one) *from* his place
espelér (á algúno) *de* algúna párte	to expel (any one) *from* any place
espérto *en* las ártes	skilled *in* the arts
estraér (úna cósa) *de* ótra	to extract (one thing) *from* another
estraviárse *de* la carréra	to deviate *from* one's purpose

F.

fácil *de* digerír	easy *to* digest
faltár *á* la palábra	to fail *in* one's promise
faltár *de* algúna párte	to be missing, wanting.

fálto *de* juicio — wanting *in* sense

fastidiárse *de* manjáres — to be disgusted *with* victuals

fatigárse *de, en, por* algúna cósa — to long *for* something

favoráble, *á, pára* algúno — favourable *to* some one

favorecérse *de* algúno — to avail oneself *of* any one

fiárse *de, en* algúno — to confide *in* any one

fiár (álgo) *á* algúno — to trust (any thing) *to* any one

fiél *á, con* sus amígos — faithful *to* one's friends

fijár (álgo) *en* la paréd — to fix (any thing) *in* the wall

flexíble *á* la razón — pliant *to* reason

fluctuár *en, éntre* dúdas — to fluctuate *in* doubt

fortificárse *en* algúna párte — to strengthen oneself *in* any place

franqueárse *á, con* algúno — to open oneself *to* any one

frisár (úna persóna ó cósa) *con* ótra — to be like (a person or thing) *with* another

fuéra *de* cása — out *of* the house

fuérte *de* condición — high, strong *in* temper

fundárse *en* razón — to be founded *in* reason

G.

girár (úna létra) *á* cárgo de ótro — to draw (a bill) *upon* another

girár *de* úna párte *á* ótra — to reel *from* one side *to* another

girár *por* tal párte — to turn *to* such a side

girár *sóbre* úna cása de comércio — to draw *upon* a commercial house

gloriárse *de* algúna cósa — to boast *of* any thing

górdo *de* tálle — fat or thick set

gozár *de* algúna cósa — to relish any thing

graduár, (úna cósa) *de, por* buéna — to pronounce (any thing) *as* good

grangeár (la voluntád) *á, de* algúno — to gain (the affection) *of* any one

guardárse *de* algúno, *de* algúna cósa — to guard oneself *from* any one, *from* any thing

guarecérse *de* algúna persóna ó cósa — to shelter oneself *from* any person or thing

guarecérse *en* algúna párte — to take shelter *in* any place

guarnecér (úna cósa) *con, de* ótra — to garnish (one thing) *with* another

guiádo *de* algúno — guided *by* any one

guiárse *por* algúno — to guide oneself *by* any one

guindárse *por* la paréd — to suspend oneself *by* the wall

gustár *de* algúna cósa — to like any thing

H.

hábil *en* papéles — skilful *in* documents

hábil *pára* el empléo — qualified *for* the employment

habilitár (á úno) *en, pára* algúna cósa — to fit up (any body) *to* do any thing

habitár *con* algúno — to dwell *with* any one

habitár *en* tal párte — to dwell *in* such a place

habituárse *á, en* algúna cósa — to accustom oneself *to* something

hablár *con, por* algúno — to speak *with*, or *for* any one

hablár *de, en, sobre* algúna cósa — to speak *of, about* any thing

hablár *en* griégo — to talk gibberish or Greek

hacér *á* tódo — to be handy *at* any thing

nacér *de* valiénte	to pretend *to* courage
hacér *pára* sí	to provide *for* oneself
hacér *por* algúno	to do *for* any one
hacérse *con* buénos libros	to furnish oneself *with* good books
hallár (algúna cósa) *en* tal párte	to find (any thing) *in* such a place
hallárse, *á*, *en* la fiésta	to be present *at* the feast
hartárse *de* comída	to satiate oneself *with* food
henchír (el cántaro) *de* água	to fill (the pitcher) *with* water
herír (á algúno) *en* la estimación	to hurt (any one) *in* his reputation
herído *de* la injúria	wounded *by* injury
hermanár (úna cósa) *con* ótra	to match (one thing) *with* another
hervír (un lugár) *de*, *en* génte	to swarm (a place) *with* people
hincárse *de* rodíllas	to kneel down
hocicár *en* algúna cósa	to stumble *on* any thing
holgárse *con*, *de* algúna cósa	to rejoice *at* any thing
huír *de* algúna persóna ó cósa	to fly *from* any person or thing
humanárse *á* algúna cósa	to lower oneself *to* any thing
humanárse *con* los inferióres	to be condescending *to* inferiors
humillárse *á* algúna persóna ó cósa	to humble oneself *to* any person or thing.
hundír (algúna cósa) *en* el água	to plunge (any thing) *into* the water
hundirse *en* un pantáno	to sink *in* a bog

I

idóneo *pára* algúna cósa	fit *for* any thing
iguál *á*, *con* ótro	equal *to*, *with* another
iguál *en* fuérzas	equal *in* forces
igualár (úna cósa) *á*, *con* ótra	to make (one thing) equal *with* another
imbuír (á algúno) *de*, *en* algúna cósa	to imbibe (any one) *with*, *in* any thing
impelér (á algúno) *á* algúna cósa	to compel (any one) *to* any thing
impelido *de* la necesidád	impelled *by* necessity
impenetráble *á* los mas perspicáces	impenetrable *to* the most perspicacious
impenetráble *en* el secréto	impenetrable *in* secrecy
impetrár (álgn) *de* algúno	to obtain (any thing) *of* any one
implicárse *con*, *en* algúna cósa	to intermeddle *in* any thing
imponér (péna) *á* algúno	to impose (penalties) *on* any one
imponérse *en* algúna cósa	to instruct oneself *in* any thing
importár *á* algúno	to be of importance *to* any one
importunádo *de*, *por* ótro	importuned *with*, *by* another
importunár (á algúno) *con* pretensiónes	to importune (any one) *with* pretensions
impresionár (á algúno) *cóntra* ótro	to impress (any one) *against* another
imprimir (algúna cósa) *en* el ánimo	to imprint (any thing) *on* the mind
imprópio *de*, *en*, *pára* su edad	unbecoming his age
impugnár algúna cósa *á* algúno	to impugn any one *in* any thing
impugnádo *de*, *por* múchos	impugned *by* many
imputár (la cúlpa) *á* ótro	to impute (the fault) *to* any one

inaccesíble á los pretendiéntes	inaccessible to pretenders
inapeáble de su opinión	obstinate in one's opinion
incansáble en el trabájo	untiring in work
incapáz de remédio	incapable of remedy
incesánte en sus taréas	incessant in one's labours
incidír en cúlpa	to fall again into a fault
incitár (á algúno) á su defénsa	to incite (any one) to one's defence
incitár (á algúno) cóntra ótro	to incite any one against another
inclinár (á algúno) á la virtúd	to incline (any one) to virtue
incluír en el número	to include in the number
incompatíble con el mándo	incompatible with the command
incomprensíble á los hómbres	incomprehensible to men
inconsecuénte en algúna cósa	inconsistent in any thing
inconstánte en su procedér	inconsistent in one's proceedings
incorporár (úna cósa) á, con, en ótra	to incorporate (one thing) with another
increíble á, pára múchos	incredible to many
incumbír (úna cósa) á algúno	to be incumbent (any thing) on any one
incurrír en delítos	to incur crimes
indecíso en resolvér	undecided in resolving
indignárse con, cóntra algúno	to be angry with any one
indisponér (á úno) con ótro	to indispose (one) with another
inducír (á algúno) á pecár	to induce (one) to sin
inductivo de error	leading to error
indultár (á algúno) de la péna	to pardon (any one) the punishment
infatigáble en el trabájo	indefatigable in labour
infécto de heregías	infected with heresies
inferiór á ótro	inferior to another
inferior en algúna cósa	inferior in any thing
inferír (úna cósa) de, por ótra	to infer (one thing) from another
inficionádo de péste	infected with the plague
infiél á su amígo	unfaithful to one's friend
inflexible á la razón	inflexible to reason
inflexíble en su dictámen	inflexible in one's opinion
influir en algúna cósa	to have an influence over any thing
informár (á algúno) de, sóbre algúna cósa	to inform (any one) of any thing
infundír (ánimo) á, en algúno	to infuse (courage) in any one
ingráto á los beneficios	ungrateful for favours
ingráto con los amígos	ungrateful to friends
inhábil pára el empléo	unfit for the employment
inhabilitár (á algúno) pára algúna cósa	to disable any one for any thing
inhibír (al juéz) de, en el conocimiénto	to inhibit (any judge) from taking cognizance
insensíble á las injúrias	insensible to injuries
inseparáble de la virtúd	inseparable from virtue
insertár (úna cósa) en ótra	to insert (one thing) in another
insinuár (úna cósa) á algúno	to insinuate (any thing) to any one
insinuárse con los poderósos	to insinuate oneself into the favour of the great

insípido *al* gústo	insipid *to* the taste
insistír, *en, sóbre* algúna cósa	to insist *on* any thing
inspirár (algúna cósa) *á* algúno	to inspire (another) *with* any thing
instruír (á algúno) *de, en, sóbre* algúna cósa	to instruct (any one) *in* any thing
intercedér *con* algúno por ótro	to intercede *with* any one for another
interceder *por* ótro con algúno	to intercede *for* another with any one
interesárse *con* algúno por ótro	to interest oneself *with* any one for another
interesárse *en* algúna cósa	to interest oneself *in* any thing
internárse *con* algúno	to creep *into* another's favours
internárse *en* algúna cósa ó lugár	to penetrate *into* any thing or place
interpolár (únas cósas) *con* ótras	to mingle (one thing) *with* another
interponér (su autoridád) *con* algúno	to interpose (one's authority) *with* any one
intervenír *en* las cósas	to intervene *in* things
intervenir *por* algúno	to intervene *for* any one
introducirse *con* los que mándan	to introduce oneself *to* those who command
introducirse *en, por* algúna párte	to intrude oneself *into* any place
invadido *de, por* los contrários	invaded *by* the enemies
invernár *en* tal párte	to winter *in* such a place
invertir (el caudál) *en* ótro úso	to invest stock *into* another use
ingerír (un árbol) *en* ótro	to ingraft (one tree) *on* another
ir de (Madríd) *á, hácia* Cádiz,	to go (from Madrid) *towards* Cadiz
ir *cóntra* algúno	to go *against* any body
ir *por* el camino	to go *in* the way, road
ir *por* pan	to go *for* bread
ir *tras* algúno	to go *after* one

J.

jactárse *de* algúna cósa	to boast *of* any thing
jugár *á* tal juégo	to play *at* such a game
jugár (únos) *con* ótros	to play (one) *with* another
jugár (algúna cósa) *con* ótra	to move (one thing) *with* another
juntár (úna cósa) *á, con* ótra	to join (one thing) *to* another
justificárse *de* algún cárgo	to justify oneself *from* any charge
juzgár *de* algúna cósa	to judge *of* any thing

L.

ladeár (úna cósa) *á* tal párte	to incline (a thing) *on* such a side
ladeárse (algúno) *á* ótro partído	to be inclining *to* another party
lamentárse *de* la desgrácia	to lament the misfortune
lanzár (álgo) *á, cóntra* algúno	to fling (something) *at* any one
lárgo *de* cuérpo	tall *in* stature
lárgo *de* mános	liberal *with*, free *with*
lastimárse *con, en* úna piédra	to hurt oneself *against* a stone
lastimárse *de* algúno	to take pity *on* any one

leér (los pensamiéntos) *á* algúno	to read (the thoughts) *of* any one
léjos *de* la tiérra	far *from* land
levantár (las mános) *al* ciélo	to raise (the hands) *to* heaven
levantár (algúna cósa) *del* suélo	to raise (any thing) *from* the ground
levantár (algúna cósa) *en* álto	to raise (any thing) *on* high
libertár (á algúno) *de* peligro	to deliver (any one) *from* danger
librár (á algúno) *de* riésgos	to free (any one) *from* risk
lidiár *con* algúno	to contend *with* any one
ligár (úna cósa) *con* ótra	to tie (one thing) *with* another
ligéro *de* piés	lightfooted
limitár (las facultádes) *á* algúno	to limit any one's powers
limitádo *de* taléntos	of slender talents
lindár (úna posesión) *con* ótra	to be adjoining (a possession) *to* another
llevár (álgo) *á* algúna párte	to carry (something) *to* any place
llevárse *de* algúna pasión	to be carried away *by* some passion
luchár *con* algúno	to wrestle *with* any one
ludir (úna cósa) *con* ótra	to rub (one thing) *against* another

M.

malquistárse *con* algúno	to make oneself hated *by* any one
manár (água) *de* úna fuénte	to spring (water) *from* a fountain
mánco *de* úna máno	maimed *of* one hand
mancomunárse *con* ótros	to unite oneself *with* others in the execution of any thing
mandár (algúna cósa) *á* algúno	to command (any thing) *to* any one
manifestár (algúna cósa) *á* algúno	to manifest (any thing) *to* any one
mantenér (conversación) *á* algúno	to maintain conversation *with* one
mantenérse *de* yérbas	to live *upon* herbs
mantenérse *en* paz	to live *in* peace
maquinár *cóntra* algúno	to plot *against* any one
maquinár *en, sóbre* algúna cósa	to contrive any thing
maravillárse *de* algúna cósa	to wonder *at* any thing
mas *de* cién ducádos	more *than* a hundred ducats
matárse *en* trabajár	to kill oneself *with* labour
matárse *por* conseguir algúna cósa	to strive *to* obtain any thing
matizár *con, de* colóres	to shade *with* colours
mediáno *de* cuérpo	of a middling stature
mediár *con, por* algúno	to intercede *for* any one
mediár *éntre* los contrários	to mediate *between* enemies
medirse *con* sus fuérzas	to act according *to* one's abilities
medirse *en* las palábras	to weigh one's words
medrár *en* la haciénda	to thrive *in* riches
mejorár *de* empléo	to better one's employment
mejorár (á algúno) *en* tércio y quínto	to meliorate (any one's fortune) *in* a third and fifth part
menór *de* edád	under age, minor
ménos *de* cién ducádos	less *than* a thousand ducats
merecér *á, de, con* algúno	to merit *from* any one
mesurárse *en* las acciónes	to be cautious *in* one's actions
metér (dinéro) *en* el cófre	to put (money) *into* the chest

metér (á algúno) *en* empéño	to put (one) *under* the necessity of doing a thing
metér (úna cósa) *éntre* ótras cósas	to put (one thing) *among* others
metérse *á* gobernár	to set oneself *to* govern
metérse *á* caballéro	to affect the character and dignity of a knight, a gentleman
metérse *con* los que mándan	to meddle *with* those who command
metérse *en* los peligros	to expose oneself *to* dangers
mezclár (úna cósa) *con* ótra	to mix (one thing) *with* another
mezclárse *en* negócios	to meddle *in* business
mirár (la ciudád) *á* oriénte	to face (the city) the east
mirár *por* algúno	to look *for* any one's interest
mirárse *en* algúna cósa	to regard oneself *in* any thing
moderárse *en* las palábras	to be moderate *in* words
mofárse *de* algúno	to make game *of* any one
mojár (algúna cósa) *en* água	to wet (something) *in* water
molérse *á* trabajár	to fatigue oneself *with* working
molído *de* andár	fatigued *with* walking
molestár (á úno) *con* visítas	to trouble (any one) *with* visits
molésto *á* tódos	troublesome *to* all
montár *á* cabállo	to mount *on* horseback
montár *en* múla	to mount a mule
montár *en* cólera	to get *into* a passion
morár *en* pobládo	to dwell *in* a settled place
morir *de* póca edád	to die *at* an early age
morír *de* enfermedád	to die *of* a sickness
morírse *de* frío	to be dying *with* cold
morírse *por* lográr algúna cósa	to long *for* obtaining any end
motejár (á algúno) *de* ignoránte	to stigmatise any one *as* ignorant
motivár (la providéncia) *con* razónes	to persuade (a measure) *by* reasons
movérse *de* úna párte á ótra	to move *from* one side to another
múchos *de* los preséntes	many *of* those present
mudár (algúna cósa) *á* ótra párte	to remove (any thing) *to* another place
mudár *de* inténto	to change one's intention
mudárse *de* cása	to remove *from* a house
murmurár *de* algúno	to murmur *against* any one

N.

nacér *con* fortúna	to be born *to* a fortune
nacér (algúna cósa) *de* algúna párte	to spring (any thing) *from* any part
nacér *en* las málvas	to be born *of* low parents
nacér *pára* trabájos	to be born *to* labour, trouble
nadár *en* el río	to swim *in* the river
navegár *á* Indias,	to sail *to* the Indies
negárse *á* la comunicación	to deny oneself *to* company
nímio *en* su procedér	over-nice *in* one's conduct
ningúno *de* los preséntes	none *of* the present
nivelárse *á* lo jústo	to level oneself *to* justice

16

nombrár (á algúno) *pára* el empléo

to appoint (any one) *to* the employment,
  office.

notár (á algúno) *de* habladór

to censure (any one) *as* a talker

notificár (algúna cósa) *á* algúno

to notify (any thing) *to* any one

O.

obligár (á algúno) *á* algúna cósa

to oblige (any one) *to* any thing

obstár (úna cósa) *á* ótra

to hinder (one thing) another

obstinárse *en* algúna cósa

to be obstinate *in* any thing

obtenér (algúna grácia) *de* algúno

to obtain (a favour) *from* any one

ocultár (algúna cósa) *á, de* algúno

to conceal (any thing) *from* any one

ocupárse *en* trabajár,

to be occupied *with* work

ofendérse *con, de* algúna cósa

to be offended *at* any thing

ofrecér (algúna cósa) *á* algúno

to offer any thing *to* any one

ofrecérse *á* los peligros

to offer oneself *to* dangers

olér (úna cósa) *á* ótra

to have the smell (one thing) *of* another

olvidárse *de* lo pasádo

to forget the past

opinár *en, sóbre* algúna cósa

to hold an opinion *on* any thing

oprimír á algúno *con* el podér

to oppress (another) *by* power

optár *á* los empléos

to be a candidate *for* offices

ordenárse *de* sacerdóte

to be ordained *as* a priest

orillár *á* algúna párte

to draw *near* any side

P.

pactár (algúna cósa) *con* ótro

to contract (something) *with* another

pagár *con* palábras

to pay *with* words

pagár *en* dinéro

to pay *in* cash

pagárse *de* buénas razónes

to be satisfied *with* good reasons

paladeárse *con* algúna cósa

to please one's palate *with* any thing

paliár (algúna cósa) *con* ótra

to palliate one thing *with* another

pálido *de* semblánte

pale-faced

palmeár *á* algúno

to cheer any one *with* the hands

parár *á* la puérta

to stop *at* the door

parár *en* cása

to stay *at* home

parárse *á* descansár

to stop *to* rest oneself

parárse *con* algúno

to stop *with* any one

parárse *en* algúna cósa

to stop *at* any thing

párco *en* la comida

sparing *in* eating

parecér *en* algúna párte

to appear any where

parecérse *á* ótro

to resemble another

participár (álgo) *á* algúno

to communicate (any thing) *to* any one

participár *de* algúna cósa

to partake *of* any thing

particularizárse *con* algúno

to be singular *with* any one

particularizárse *en* algúna cósa

to signalize oneself *in* any thing

partír *á* Itália

to set off *to* Italy

partír (álgo) *con* ótro

to share (any thing) *with* another

partír *en* pedázos

to break *into* pieces

partír *éntre* amígos

to share *between* friends

partir *por* mitád	to divide *in* halves
partir *por* entéro	to divide *by* tens
partirse *de* España	to set off *from* Spain
pasár *á* Madríd	to go *to* Madrid
pasár *de* Sevílla	to go *beyond* Seville
pasár *éntre* móntes	to pass *between* mountains
pasár *por* el camíno	to pass *by* the road
pasár *por* éntre árboles	to pass *between* trees
pasár *por* cobárde	to pass *for* a coward
pasárse (algúna cósa) *de* la memória	to slip the memory (any thing)
pasárse (la frúta) *de* madúra	to begin (the fruit) to decay
pasárse (algúno) *de* létras	to become (some one) a scholar,
paseárse *con* ótro	to take a walk *with* another
paseárse *por* el cámpo	to walk *in* the country
pecár *cóntra* la léy	to transgress the law
pecár *de* ignoránte,	to sin *through* ignorance
pecár *en* algúna cósa	to be faulty *in* any thing
pecár *por* demasía	to sin *through* excess
pedir (algúna cósa) *á* algúno	to ask (any thing) *of* any one
pedir *con* justicia	to ask *with* justice
pedir *cóntra* algúno	to bring an action *against* any one
pedir *de* justicia	to claim *in* law
pedir *en* justicia	to sue *at* law
pedir *por* Diós	to beg *for* God
pedir *por* algúno	to ask *for* any one
pegár (úna cósa) *á* ótra	to apply (one thing) *to* another
pegár (úna cósa) *con* ótra	to join (one thing) *with* another
pegár *cóntra*, *en* la paréd	to fasten *against* the wall
pelárse *por* algúna cósa	to be anxious *for* any thing
peligrár *en* algúna cósa	to be in danger *in* any thing
peloteárse *con* algúno	to scuffle *with* any one
penár *en* la ótra vída	to suffer *in* the other life
penár *por* algúna persóna ó cósa	to suffer *for* any person or thing
pendér *de* algúna cósa	to depend *upon* any thing
penetrár *hásta* las entráñas	to penetrate *to* the entrails
penetrádo *de* dolór	penetrated *with* grief
pensár *en*, *sóbre* algúna cósa	to think *of*, *upon* any thing
perdér (álgo) *de* vísta	to lose sight *of* any thing
perdérse (algúno) *de* vísta	to excel *in* an eminent degree
perdérse *en* el camíno	to lose one's way
perecér *de* hámbre	to perish *with* hunger
perecérse *de* rísa	to die *with* laughing
perecérse *por* algúna cósa	to die *for* any thing
peregrinar *por* el múndo	to wander *through* the world
perfumár *con* inciénso	to perfume *with* incense
permanecér *en* algúna párte	to remain *in* any place
permitir (algúna cósa) *á* algúno	to permit (any thing) *to* any one
permutár (úna cósa) *con*, *por* ótra	to exchange (one thing) *for* another
perseguído *de* enemígos	pursued *by* enemies
perseverár *en* algún inténto,	to persevere *in* any design
persuadir (algúna cósa) *á* algúno	to persuade any one *of* (any thing)
persuadirse *á* algúna cósa	to be persuaded *of* any thing

persuadírse *de*, *por* las razónes de ótro	to be persuaded *by* another's reasons
pertenecér (úna cósa) á algúno	to belong (any thing) *to* any one
pertrechárse *de* lo necesário	to provide oneself *with* necessaries
pesárle (á algúno) *de* lo que ha hécho	to regret (any one) what he has done
pesádo *en* la conversación	dull *in* conversation
pescár *con* réd	to fish *with* a net
piár *por* algúna cósa	to long *for* any thing
picár *de*, *en* tódo	to excel *in* every thing
picárse *de* algúna cósa	to pique oneself *upon* any thing
pintiparádo á algúno	like *to* any one exactly
plagárse *de* grános	to be plagued *with* pimples
plantár (á algúno) *en* algúna párte	to set (any one) *in* any place
plantárse *en* Cádiz	to be settled *in* Cadiz
poblár *de* árboles	to fill *with* trees
poblár *en* buén paráge	to settle *in* a good situation
poblárse *de* génte	to be peopled *with* persons
ponderár (úna cósa) *de* gránde	to exaggerate (any thing) *as* great
ponér (á úno) á oficio	to put (any one) *in* business
ponér (algúna cósa) *en* algúna párte	to put (any thing) somewhere
ponér (á algúno) *por* corregidór	to appoint (any one) *as* corregidor
ponérse á escribír	to set oneself *to* writing
porfiár *con* algúno	to be positive *with* any one
portárse *con* decéncia	to conduct oneself *with* decency
posár *en* algúna párte	to lodge *in* any place
poseído *de* temór	possessed *by* fear
postrádo *de* la enfermedád	prostrated *by* sickness
postrárse á los piés de algúno	to prostrate oneself *at* another's feet
postrárse *en* cáma	to be confined *to* one's bed
postrárse *en* tiérra	to kneel down *on* the ground
precedido *de* ótro	preceded *by* another
preciárse *de* valiénte	to pique oneself *upon* courage
precipitárse *de*, *por* algúna párte	to be precipitated *from* any place
preferído á ótro	preferred *to* another
preferído *de* algúno	preferred *by* any one
preguntár (algúna cósa) á algúno	to ask any one (any thing)
prendárse *de* algúno	to be taken *with* any one
prendér (las plántas) *en* la tiérra	to take root (plants) *in* the earth
preocupárse *de* algúna cósa	to be prepossessed *with* any thing
preparárse á, *pára* algúna cósa	to prepare oneself *for* any thing
preponderár (úna cósa) á ótra	to preponderate (one thing) *over* another
prescindír *de* algúna cósa	to lay aside any thing
presentár (algúna cósa) á algúno	to present (any thing) *to* any one
presentar (á úno) *pára* úna prebénda	to present any one *for* a prebend
preservár (á algúno) *de* dáño	to preserve (any one) *from* injury
presidír á ótros	to preside *over* others
presidír *en* un tribunál	to preside *in* a tribunal

PREPOSITIONS.

presidido *de* útro	presided *by* another
prestár (dinéro) *á* algúno	to lend (money) *to* any one
prestár (la diéta) *pára* la salúd	to contribute (the diet) *to* health
prestár *sóbre* prénda	to lend *on* security
presumir *de* dócto	to set up *for* a man of learning
prevalecér (la verdád) *sóbre* la mentíra	to prevail (truth) *over* falsehood
prevenir (algúna cósa) *á* algúno	to advise another *of* (any thing)
prevenírse *de* lo necesário	to provide oneself *with* necessaries
prevenírse *para* un viáge	to prepare oneself *for* a journey
priméro *de*, *éntre* tódos,	first *among* all
pringárse *en* algúna cósa	to intermeddle *in* any thing
privár (á algúno) *de* lo súyo	to deprive (any one) *of* his own
privár *con* algúno	to be intimate *with* any one
probár *á* saltár	to try *to* jump
probár *de* tódo	to taste *of* every thing
procedér *á la* elección	to proceed *to* the election
procedér *con*, *sin* acuérdo	to proceed *with* or *without* circumspection
procedér *cóntra* algúno	to proceed *against* any one
procedér (úna cósa) *de* útra	to proceed (one thing) *from* another
procesár (á úno) *por* delítos	to proceed against a man *for* crimes
procurár *por* algúno	to procure *for* any one
proejár *cóntra* las ólas	to row *against* the waves
profesár *en* religión	to profess *in* religion
prometér (algúna cósa) *á* algúno	to promise (any thing) *to* any one
promovér (á algúno) *á* algún cárgo	to promote (any one) *to* any office
propasárse *á*, *en* algúna cósa	to overshoot one's mark *in* any thing
proponér (algúna cósa) *á* algúno	to propose (any thing) *to* any one
proponér (á algúno) *en* primér lugár	to propose (any one) *in* the first place
proporcionár (á algúno) *pára* algúna cósa	to fit (any one) *for* any thing
proporcionárse *á* las fuérzas	to proportion oneself *to* one's strength
proporcionárse *pára* algúna cósa	to fit oneself *for* any thing
prolongár (el plázo) *á* algúno	to prolong (the credit) *to* any one
prorumpir *en* lágrimas	to burst *into* tears
proveér (la pláza) *de* víveres	to furnish (the fortress) *with* provisions
proveér (el empléo) *en* algúno	to provide any one *with* (an employment)
provenír *de* ótra cósa	to proceed *from* something else
provocár *á* íra	to provoke *to* anger
provocár (á algúno,) *con* malas palábras	to provoke (any one) *by* scurrilous language
próximo *á* morír	at the point *of* death
pujár *por* algúna cósa	to strive *for* any thing
purgárse *de* sospécha	to clear oneself *from* suspicion

16 *

Q.

cuadrár con el encárgo	to fit for the employment
cuadrár (algúna cósa) á algúno	to fit (any thing) any one
cuál de los dos	which of the two
quebrantár (los huésos) á algúno	to break any one's bones
quebrár (el corazón) á algúno	to break any one's heart
quedár de asiénto	to remain or reside in a place
quedár de piés	to remain standing
quedár en cása	to tarry at home
quedár (camíno) por andár	to have to proceed farther
quedár por algúno	to be bail for any one
quedár por cobárde	to be reputed a coward
quedár (úna cósa) por mía	to fall (any thing) to my share
quedárse en el sermón	to stop short in a discourse
quejárse á algúno	to complain to any one
quejárse de algúno	to complain of any one
querellárse á, ánte el juéz	to lay one's complaint before the judge
querellárse de su vecino	to complain of one's neighbour
quemár con málas razónes	to inflame one with invective
quemárse de algúna palábra	to be offended with any word
quemárse por algúna cósa	to heat oneself for any thing
querído de sus amigos	beloved by one's friends
quién de éllos	which of them
quitár (algúna cósa) á algúno	to take (any thing) from any one
quitár (algúna cósa) de algúna párte	to take (any thing) from any place
quitárse de quiméras	to free oneself from whims

R.

rabiár de hámbre	to be very hungry
rabiár por comér	to long to eat
radicárse en la virtúd	to be fixed in virtue
raér de algúna cósa	to scrape from any thing
rallár (las trípas) á cualquiéra	to importune (the intestines) any one
rayár con la virtúd	to excel in virtue
razonár con algúno	to converse with any one
rebalsárse (el água) en algúna párte	water to stagnate in any place
rebatir (úna cantidád) de ótra	to deduct (a sum) from another
rebajár (úna cantidád) de ótra	to abate one sum from another
recaér en la enfermedád	to relapse into sickness
recalcárse en lo dícho	to be firm in what has been said
recatárse de algúno	to be cautious of any one
recavár (algúna cósa) de, con algúno	to obtain (any thing) from any one
recetár (medicínas) á, pára algúno	to prescribe (medicines) for any one
recetár cóntra algúno	to make a charge against any one
recibír (algúna cósa) de algúno	to receive (any thing) from any one
recibír á cuénta	to receive on account
recibír (á algúno) en cása	to receive (any one) at home

recibírse *de* abogádo	to be admitted *as* a counsellor
récio *de* cuérpo	of a strong constitution
reclinárse *en, sóbre* algúna cósa	to lean *upon* any thing
recluir (á algúno) *en* algúna párte	to shut (any one) up *in* any place
recobrárse *de* la enfermedád	to recover oneself *from* sickness
recogérse á cása	to retire home
recomendár (algúna cósa) *á* algúno	to recommend (any thing) *to* any one
recompensár (agrávios) *con* benefícios	to recompense wrongs *with* benefits
reconcentrárse (el ódio) *en* el corazón	to concentrate (hatred) *in* the heart
reconciliár (á úno) *con* ótro	to reconcile (one) *with* another
reconvenir (á algúno) *con, de, sóbre* algúna cósa	to charge (any one) *with* any thing
recostárse *en, sóbre* la sílla	to recline *on* a seat
recudir (á algúno) *con* el suéldo	to pay (any one) his wages
redondeárse *de* déudas	to pay off one's debts
reducir (algúna cósa) *á* la mitád	to reduce (any thing) *to* the half
redundár *en* benefício	to conduce *to* the benefit
referírse *á* algúna cósa	to refer oneself *to* any thing
refocilárse *con* algúna cósa	to be refreshed *with* any thing
refugiárse *á, en* sagrádo	to take refuge *in* some sacred place
reglárse *á* lo jústo	to conform *to* what is right
regodeárse *en, con* algúna cósa	to delight oneself *in* any thing
reirse *á* carcajádas	to laugh heartily
reirse *de* algúno	to make a jest *of* any one
remirárse *en* algúna cósa	to examine oneself *in* any thing
reemplazár (á algúno) *en* su empléo	to take the place (of any one) *in* his employment, office
rendírse *á* la razón	to yield *to* reason
renegár *de* algúna cósa	to apostatize *from* any thing
repartir (algúna cósa) *á, éntre* algúnos	to share (any thing) *among* several
representárse (algúna cósa) *á* la imaginacion	to represent any thing *to* one's imagination
resbalárse *de* las mános	to slip away *from* the hands
resentirse *de* algúna cósa	to resent any thing
residir *de* asiénto *en* algúna párte	to be settled *in* any place
residir *en* la córte	to reside *at* court
resolvérse *á* algúna cósa	to resolve *upon* any thing
respondér *á* la pregúnta	to answer the question
restár (úna cantidád) *de* ótra	to remain (one sum) *from* another
restituirse *á* su cása	to return *to* one's house
resultár (úna cósa) *de* ótra	to result (one thing) *from* another
retirárse *á* la soledád	to retire *into* solitude
retirárse *del* múndo	to retire *from* the world
retraérse *á* algúna párte	to take refuge any where
retraérse *de* algúna cósa	to escape *from* any thing
retrocedér *á, hácia* tal párte	to recede *towards* such a place
reventár *de* risa	to burst *with* laughter
reventár *por* hablár	to burst *with* a desire of speaking
revestirse *de* autoridád	to be invested *with* authority
revolcárse *en* los vícios	to wallow *in* vice
revolvér *cóntra, hácia, sóbre* el enemígo	to return *to* the enemy

robár (dinéro) á algúno — to rob any one *of* (money)
rodár (el cárro) *por* tiérra — to overset (a cart)
rodeár (á algúno) *por* tódas pártes — to encompass (any one) *on* all sides
rodeár (úna pláza) *con, de* murállas — to surround (a place) *with* walls
rogár (algúna cósa) á algúno — to beg (any thing) *of* any one
rompér *con* algúno — to break off *with* any one
rompér *por* algúna .párte — to break *in* any place
rozárse (úna cósa) *con* ótra — to rub (one thing) *against* another
rozárse *en* las palábras — to stammer *in* one's speech

S.

sabér *á* víno — to taste *like* wine
sabér *de* trabájos — to be acquainted *with* trouble
sacár (úna cósa) *á* la pláza — to take (any thing) *to* the market
sacár *de* algúna párte — to take any thing *from* any place
sacár *en* limpio — to clear up all doubts, to copy fair
sacrificár (algúna cósa) *á* Diós — to sacrifice (any thing) *to* God
sacrificárse *por* algúno — to sacrifice oneself *for* any one
salir *á* algúna cósa — to co-operate *in* any thing
salir *con* la pretensión — to obtain one's aim
salir *cóntra* algúno — to go out *against* any one
salir *de* algúna párte — to go out *from* any place
salir *por* fiadór — to appear *as* security.
saltár (úna cósa) *á* la imaginación — strike (any thing) the imagination
saltár *de* el suélo — to leap *from* the ground
saltár *de* gózo — to leap *with* joy
saltár *en* tiérra — to leap *on* the ground, *on* shore
salvár (á algúno) *del* peligro — to save (any one) *from* danger
sanár *de* la enfermedád — to recover *from* sickness
satisfacér *por* las cúlpas — to atone *for* one's faults
satisfacérse *de* la dúda — to be satisfied *for* the doubt
segregár (á algúno) *de* algúna párte — to separate (any one) *from* any place
segregár (úna cósa) *de* ótra — to separate (one thing) *from* another
seguírse (úna cósa) *de* ótra — to follow (one thing) *from* another
semejár, ó semejárse (úna cósa) *á* ótra — to liken (one thing) *to* another, to resemble
sentárse *en* la mésa — to sit down *to* table
sentárse *á* la sílla — to sit down *in* the chair
sentenciár (á úno) *á* destiérro — to condemn (one) *to* exile
sentírse *de* álgo — to be sensible *of* any thing
separár (úna cósa) *de* ótra — to separate (one thing) *from* another
ser (úna cósa) *á* gústo de tódos — to be (any thing) *to* the taste of all
ser (úna cósa) *de, pára* algúnos — to be (any thing) *to* or *for* some one
servir *de* mayordómo — to serve *as* a steward
servir *en* palácio — to be a servant *in* a palace
servirse *de* algúno — to make use *of* any one
sincerárse *de* algúna cósa — to clear oneself *from* something
sisár *de* la cómpra — to curtail *from* the purchase
sitiádo *de* enemigos — besieged *by* enemies

situár *por* hámbre — to lay siege *by* means of hunger

situárse *en* algúna párte — to station oneself *in* any place

sobrellevár (los trabajos) *con* paciéncia — to undergo (labours or troubles) *with* patience

sobrellevár (á algúno) *en* sus trabájos — to assist (any one) *in* his labours or troubles

sobrepujár (á algúno) *en* autoridád — to exceed (any one) *in* authority

sobresalír *en* gálas — to surpass *in* dress

sobresalír *éntre* tódos — to excel *among* all

sobresaltárse *de* algúna cósa — to be started *at* any thing

sojuzgádo *de* enemígos — subdued *by* enemies

sometérse *á* algúno — to submit *to* any one

sonár (algúna cósa) *á* huéca — to sound (any thing) hollow

sonár (algúna cósa) *hácia* tal párte — to sound (any thing) *towards* such a side

sórdo *á* las vóces — deaf *to* the cries

sórdo *de* un oído — deaf *with* one ear

sorprendér (á algúno) *en* algúna cósa — to surprise (any one) *with* any thing

sorprendérle *en* algúna cósa — to surprise him *in* any thing

sorprendído *de* la bulla — surprised *by* the noise

sospechár (algúna cósa) *de* algúno — to suspect any one *of* (any thing)

sospechóso *á* algúno — suspected *by* any one

subdividir *en* pártes — to subdivide *into* parts

subir *á* algúna párte — to go up *to* any place

subir *de* algúna párte — to go up *from* any place

subir *sóbre* la mésa — to get *upon* the table

subrogár (úna cósa) *en* lugár de ótra — to substitute (one thing) *instead* of another

subsistír *del* auxílio agéno — to subsist *by* others' aid

subsistír *en* el dictámen — to continue *in* an opinion

sustituír, *á, por* algúno — to substitute *for* any one

sustituír (un podér) *en* algúno — to substitute (a power) *to* any one

sustraérse *de* la obediéncia — to withdraw oneself *from* subordination

sucedér (á algúno) *en* el empléo — to succeed (any one) *in* an employment, office

sufrir (los trabájos) *con* paciéncia — to suffer (troubles) *with* patience

sugerír (algúna cósa) *á* algúno — to suggest (any thing) *to* any one

sujetárse *á* algúno, ó algúna cósa — to subject oneself *to* any one, or any thing

sumergír (algúna cósa) *en* el água — to plunge (any thing) *in* the water

sumirse *en* algúna párte — to sink *in* any place

sumíso *á* la voluntád — submissive *to* the will

supeditádo *de* los contrários — subdued *by* the enemies

superiór *á* sus enemígos — superior *to* one's enemies

superiór *en* lúces — superior *in* talents

suplicár *de* la senténcia — to petition *against* the sentence

suplicár *por* algúno — to entreat *for* any one

suplir *por* algúno — to supply *for* any one

surgir (la náve) *en* el puérto — to ride (the vessel) at anchor *in* the port

surtír *de* víveres — to supply *with* victuals

suspénso *de* oficio — suspended in the exercise *of* one's employment, office

suspirár *por* el mándo — to aspire *after* command
sustentárse *con* yérbas — to feed *upon* herbs
sustentárse *de* esperánzas — to sustain oneself *with* hopes

T.

tachár (á algúno) *de* ligéro — to accuse (any one) *of* levity
temblár *de* frío — to tremble *with* cold
temído *de* múchos — feared *by* many
temeróso *de* la muérte — fearful *of* death
temíble *á* los contrários — dreadful *to* his enemies
templárse *en* comér — to be temperate *in* eating
tenér (á úno) *por* ótro — to take (one) *for* another
tenérse *en* pié — to keep oneself *on* foot
teñir *de* azúl — to dye *in* blue
tirár *á, hácia* tal párte — to draw *on* such a side
tirár *por* tal párte — to draw *towards* such a side
tiritár *de* frío — to shiver *with* cold
titubeár *en* algúna cósa — to waver *in* any thing
tocár (la heréncia) *á* algúno — to fall (the inheritance) *to* any one
tocár *en* algúna párte — to touch *on* any where
tocádo *de* enfermedád — touched *with* disease
tomár *con, en* las mános — to take *with,* or *in* the hands
tomár (úna cósa) *de* tal módo — to take (any thing) *in* such a manner
tomár (úna cósa) *á* úno — to take (any thing) *from* any one
torcído *de* cuérpo — deformed *in* body
tornár *á* algúna párte — to turn *to* such a side
tornár *de* algúna párte — to turn *from* such a side
trabajár *en* algúna cósa — to work *in* any thing
trabajár *por* algúna cósa — to contend *for* any thing
trabajár *por* ótro — to work *for* another
trabár *de* algúno — to seize *on* any one
trabár (úna cósa) *con* ótra — to join one thing *with* another
trabár *en* algúna cósa — to fall *on* any thing
trabárse *de* palábras — to engage *in* words
trabucárse *en* las palábras — to mistake *one's* words
traér (algúna cósa) *á* algúna párte — to bring (any thing) *to* any place
traér (algúna cósa) *de* algúna párte — to bring any thing *from* any place
traficár *en* drógas — to deal *in* drugs
transferir (algúna cósa) *á* ótro tiémpo — to transfer (any thing) *to* another time
transferírse *á* tal párte — to transport oneself *to* such a place
transfigurárse *en* ótra cósa — to transform oneself *into* another thing
transformár (úna cósa) *en* ótra — to transform (one thing) *into* another
transitár *por* algúna párte — to pass *by* any place
transpirár *por* tódas pártes — to transpire *on* all sides
transportár (algúna cósa) *á* algúna párte — to transport (any thing) *to* any place
transportár (algúna cósa) *de* algúna párte — to transport (any thing) *from* any place

traspasár (alguna cósa) á algúno — to transfer (something) *to* another
traspasádo *de* dolór — transfixed *with* grief
trasplantár (de úna párte) á ótra — to transplant (from one place) *to* another

tratár *con* algúno — to treat *with* any one
tratár *de* algúna cósa — to treat *of* any thing
tratár *en* lánas — to deal *in* wool
traveseár *con* algúno — to banter *with* any one
triunfár *de* los enemigos — to triumph *over* the enemy
trocár (úna cósa) *por* ótra — to change (one thing) *for* another
tropezár *en* algúna cósa — to stumble *on* any thing

U.

último *de* tódos — the last *of* all
uncír (los buéyes) *al* cárro — to yoke (the oxen) *to* the cart
uniformár (úna cósa) con ótra — to make (one thing) uniform *with* another

unír (úna cósa) *á, con* ótra — to unite (one thing) *with* another
unírse *en* comunidád — to unite *in* a community
unírse *éntre* sí — to be united *between* themselves
úno *de, éntre* múchos — one *among* many
útil *á* la pátria — useful *to* the country
útil *pára* tal cósa — useful *for* such a thing
utilizárse *en, con* algúna cósa — *to* draw advantage *of* any thing

V.

vacár *al* estúdio — to attend *to* study
vaciárse *de* algúna cósa — to be emptied *of* any thing
vaciárse *por* la bóca — to be openmouthed
vacilár *en* la elección — to hesitate *in* one's choice
vacilár *éntre* la esperánza y el temór — to vacillate *between* hope and fear
vacío *de* entendimiénto — addle-headed
vagár *por* el múndo — to wander *through* the world
valérse *de* algúno, *de* algúna cósa — to avail oneself *of* any one, or any thing

valuár (úna cósa) *en* tal précio — to value (any thing) *at* such a price
vanagloriárse *de* algúna cósa — to be puffed up *with* pride for any thing

vecíno *al* tróno, — near the throne
vecíno *de* António — near Anthony
velár *á* los muértos — to watch the dead
velár *sóbre* algúna cósa — to watch *over* any thing
vencérse *á* algúna cósa — to conquer oneself *in* any thing
vencído *de* los contrários — conquered *by* the enemy
vendérse *á* algúno — to sell oneself *to* any one
vengárse *de* ótro — to revenge oneself *on* another
venír *á, de, por* algúna párte — to come *to, from,* or *by* any place
venír *con* algúno — to come *with* another
vérse *con* algúno — to meet any one
vérse *en* altúra — to find oneself *in* such a latitude, or high station

vestir *á* la móda	to dress *in* the fashion
vestirse *de* páño	to be dressed *in* cloth
vigilár *sóbre* sus súbditos	to watch *over* one's subjects
violentárse *á, en* algúna cósa	to be violent *in* any thing
visible *á, pára* tódos	visible *to* all
vivir *á* su gústo	to live *to* one's taste
vivir *con* algúno	to live *with* any one
vivir *de* limósna	to live *by* alms
vivir *por* milágro	to live *by* a miracle
vivir *sóbre* la haz de la tiérra	to live *without* care
volár *al* ciélo	to fly *to* heaven
volár *por* el áire	to fly *in* the air
volvér *á, de, hácia, por* tal párte	to return *to, from, towards, by* such a place
volvér *por* la verdád	to defend the truth
votár *en* el pléito	to vote *in* the trial
votár *por* algúno	to vote *for* any one

Z.

zabullírse ó zambullírse *en* el água	to plunge *into* the water
zafárse *de* algúna persóna ó cósa	to escape any one or any thing
zambucárse *en* algúna párte	to hide oneself *in* any place
zambuzárse *en* água	to dive *into* water
zapateárse *con* algúno	to scuffle *with* any one
zozobrár *en* la torménta	to sink *or* founder *in* the storm

---

CHAPTER IX.

OF CONJUNCTIONS.

Conjunctions serve to join phrases, or parts of phrases together. They are indeclinable like the prepositions and adverbs. They are distinguished into *copulative, disjunctive, restrictive, adversative, conditional, causative* and *comparative.*

The *copulative* conjunctions serve to bring together several words or several members of a phrase under the same affirmation or negation.

Those denoting affirmative are,

1st. *Y, é,* and, Ex. *El valór y el honór son las dos principáles dótes que caracterízan al héroe,* valour and honour are the two principal qualities that characterize a hero. *El señór B. es un hómbre cruél é injústo,* Mr. B. is a cruel and unjust man.

2d. *También,* also. Ex. *Yá que vm. lo quiére, lo quiéro también,* since you wish it, I also wish it.

3d. *Que*, that; Ex. *Yá sé que vm. es amigo mio*, I know already that you are my friend.

RULE LXIV.—*And* is translated in Spanish by *é*, and not by *y*, when the following word begins with an *i* or *y*; as, we shall go out at five o'clock, and go to the play, *saldrémos á las cinco, é irémos á la comédia;* right and left, *derécho é izquiérdo.*

The conjunctions that denote a negation are; *ni*, nor; *tampóco*, neither. Ex. *Ni reír, ni llorár puédo*, I can neither laugh, nor weep. *Yá que no sáles, tampóco yó saldré*, since thou dost not go out, I shall not neither.

The *disjunctive* conjunctions denote an alternative, or distinction; as, *ó, ú*, or; Ex. *Juan ó Francisco*, John or Francis; *entrár ó salír*, to go in or out; *úno ú ótro*, one or the other; *Diéz ú ónce*, ten or eleven.

RULE LXV.—*Or* is translated in Spanish by *ú*, if the following word begins with an *o*. Ex. *Siéte ú ócho hómbres*, seven or eight men; *Poéta ú oradór*, poet or orator.

The *restrictive* conjunctions restrict, in any manner whatever, an idea or a proposition; as, *sinó*, only, except. Ex. *No téngo náda que decírle, sinó que lo quiéro*, I have nothing to tell him, except that I wish it.

The *adversative* conjunctions connect two propositions, denoting an opposition in the second as respects the first; as, *mas, péro*, but; *no obstánte*, nevertheless, yet, however; *cuándo*, when; *aunqué, bién que*, though. Ex. *Quisiéra salír, mas no puédo*, I should wish to go out, but I cannot. *El dinéro háce á los hómbres rícos, péro no dichósos*, money makes men rich, but not happy. *Hábla la verdád, no obstánte nádie le crée*, he speaks the truth, yet nobody believes him. *No haría úna injustícia, cuándo le importára un tróno*, he would not commit an injustice, though it might be worth to him a throne. *No es imprudénte, bién que*, or *aunqué parézca sérlo*, he is not imprudent, though he appears to be so.

The *conditional* conjunctions connect two members of speech by a supposition, or by denoting a condition: as, *si*, if; *cómo, con tal que*, provided. Ex. *Si aspíras á ser dócto, estúdia con perseveráncia*, if thou aimest at being learned, study with perseverance. *Sabrás ésta fábula á las dóce, cómo* or *con tal que la estúdies*, thou wilt know this fable at noon, provided thou study it.

The *causative* conjunctions serve to denote the cause of a

17

thing, or the reason for which it has been done, as *porqué*, because; *pués, pués que*, since. Ex. *Débe el hómbre evitár la ociosidád, porqué es la mádre de tódos los vícios*, man must shun idleness, because it is the mother of all vices. *Leeré éste líbro, pués vm. me díce que es buéno*, I shall read this book, since you tell me that it is good.

The *comparative* conjunctions serve to denote a relation or parity between two objects, or two propositions, such as, *cómo*, as; *así cómo*, just as; Ex. *La belléza es cómo la flor que se marchíta el mísmo día que la vió nacér*, beauty is as the flower that withers the same day that saw it bloom.

OF THE CONJUNCTIONS THAT GOVERN THE SUBJUNCTIVE.

The conjunctions which govern in the subjunctive the verb that follows them, are, *pára que*, in order that; *afín de que*, to the end that; *á no ser que, á ménos que*, unless; *ántes que*, before that; *cáso que, en cáso que*, in case that; *aunqué*, though; *aún cuándo*, although; *bién que*, though; *hásta que*, till, until; *dádo que*, grant, or suppose that; *con tal que, cómo quiéra que*, provided that; *por mas que, por múcho que*, however, whatever; *siémpre que*, whenever; *Ojalá*, would to God; Ex. *Bién que*, or *aunqué la ambición séa un vicio, es no obstánte la báse de muchísimas virtúdes*, though ambition be a vice, it is nevertheless the basis of a great many virtues. *Por mas sábios que séan, no conócen la cáusa de éste efécto*, however enlightened they be, they do not know the cause of this effect. *El maéstro se afána pára que* or *afín de que adelánten sus discípulos*, the master exerts himself to the end that his scholars may improve.

N. B. As we frequently make use of the second future and of the second and third conditionals, with the above conjunctions, see the rules 39, 40, 42, 43, 44, and 45, *page* 76 *and following*.

CHAPTER X.
OF INTERJECTIONS.

INTERJECTIONS serve to express an emotion, or an affection of the mind, or to awake attention. *Ah! áy! he! O! Hóla! ta! chito! éa! sus! tále!* The affections of the mind may be of grief, sadness, contempt, indignation, joy, or astonishment; to express them we may indifferently make use of the following interjections, *ay! ah! O!* for, if we say,—*¡áy*

que péna! oh, what pain! *¡ah, que desgrácia!* oh, what
misfortune ! *¡o desdichádo de mí!* alas, unhappy me! we
may also say,—*¡áy, que gózo!* ha, what delight ! *¡áh, que
alegría!* ha, what joy ! *¡o, felíces de nosótros!* ha, how
happy we are ! *¡O ciélo!* oh heavens ! *Ha! he! hóla!*
and *to!* serve to awaken attention. *He!* is also used to
show that we have not understood what has been said. *Hóla*
is sometimes an interjection of admiration, and *to* is hardly
ever used except to call a dog; it is an abbreviation of *tóma*
take.—*Chito,* hush, serves to impose silence. *Éa, vámos,*
and *sus,* come, come on, are used to animate and excite courage.—*Táte, guárda!* take care ! serves to prevent one's
doing or saying something. *Vira!* huzza ! *Hóla!* holla !
ho ho ! *Ótra vez!* encore ! *váya!* come ! *Quédo!* softly !
Vóto á! zounds ! *héteme aquí!* here I am ! *he aquí!* here
is, here are ! *he allí!* there is ! *héle aquí!* here he is !
héla allí! there she is ! *hélo, héla, hélos, hélas,* here it is, &c.

NAMES OF COUNTRIES, ISLANDS, CAPES AND SEAS.

Nouns.		Adjectives.	
Africa,	*África.*	African,	*Africáno.*
Algiers,	*Argél.*	Algerine,	*Argelino.*
America,	*América.*	American,	*Americáno*
Anseatic (cit-ies,)	*Anseáticas (ciudádes,)*	Anseatic,	*Anseático.*
Antilles, (the)	*Antíllas, (las)*		
Arabia,	*Arábia.*	Arabian,	*Arabe, arábigo.*
Andalusia,	*Andalucía,*	Andalusian,	*Andalúz.*
Asia,	*Ásia.*	Asiatic,	*Asiático.*
Austria,	*Áustria.*	Austrian,	*Austriáco.*
Asturias,	*Astúrias.*	Asturian,	*Asturiáno.*
The Azores,	*Las Azóras.*		
The Atlantic,	*El Atlántico.*		
The Baltic,	*El Báltico.*		
Barbary,	*Berbería, (cós-ta de.)*	Berberisk,	*Berberísco.*
Botany Bay,	*Bahía Botánica.*		
Bavaria,	*Baviéra.*	Bavarian,	*Bávaro.*
Biscay,	*Vizcáya.*	Biscayan,	*Vizcaíno.*
Bohemia,	*Bohémia.*	Bohemian,	*Bohémo.*
Bolívar, Bo-lívia,	*Bolívia*	Bolivian,	*Boliviáno, Bo-livéño.*

Brazil,	*Brasíl.*	Brazilian,	*Brasiléro.*
Great Britain,	*Gran Bretáña.*	British,	*Británico.*
Brittany,	*Bretáña.*	Briton,	*Bretón.*
Burgundy,	*Borgóña.*	Burgundian,	*Borgoñés.*
British Channel (the,)	*(La) Máncha.*		
Canary Islands,	*Canárias (Íslas.)*		
Cape of Good Hope,	*Cábo de Buéna Esperánza.*		
Cape Horn,	*Cábo de Hórnos.*		
Catalónia,	*Cataluña.*	Catalonian,	*Catalan.*
China,	*China.*	Chinese,	*Chino, Chinésco.*
Castile (Old and New,)	*Castilla (la viéja y nuéva.)*	Castilian,	*Castelláno.*
Cantábria,	*Cantábria.*	Cantabrian,	*Cántabro.*
Chili,	*Chile.*	Chilian,	*Chiléno.*
Colombia,	*Colómbia.*	Colombian,	*Colombiáno.*
Córdova,	*Córdoba.*	Cordovese,	*Cordobés.*
Corsica,	*Córcega.*	Corsican,	*Córso.*
Dauphiny,	*Delfinádo.*	Dauphin,	*Delfíno.*
Denmark,	*Dinamárca.*	Dane,	*Dinamarqués.*
Deux Ponts,	*Dos Puéntes.*		
Egypt,	*Egípto.*	Egyptian,	*Egípcio.*
Extremadura,	*Estremadura,*	Estremadurian,	*Estreméño.*
Europe,	*Európa.*	European,	*Européo.*
England,	*Inglatérra.*	English,	*Inglés.*
Fernandez mássafuéro, (island,) *Fernández mas á fuéra.*			
Finland,	*Finlánda.*	Finlander,	*Finlandés.*
Finisterre (Cape) *Finistiérra, (Cábo.)*			
Flanders,	*Flándes.*	Flemish,	*Flaménco.*
France,	*Fráncia.*	French,	*Francés.*
Franche Comté, *Fránco Condádo.*			
Georgia,	*Jórgia.*	Georgian,	*Jorgiáno.*
Galicia,	*Galícia.*	Galician,	*Gallégo.*
Germany,	*Alemánia.*	German,	*Alemán.*
Granada,	*Granáda.*	Granadine,	*Granadíno.*
Greenland,	*Groenlánd.*	Greenlander,	*Groenlandés.*
Greece,	*Grécia.*	Greek,	*Griégo.*
Guatemala,	*Guatemála.*	Guatemalean,	*Guatemattéco.*
Holland,	*Holánda.*	Hollander or Dutch,	*Holanaés.*
Hungary,	*Hungría.*	Hungarian,	*Húngaro.*
Iceland,	*Islánda.*	Icelandic,	*Islandés.*
Ireland,	*Irlánda.*	Irish,	*Irlandés.*
Indies (East and West,) *Índias (Orientáles y Occidentáles.)*			
Ionian (Islands,) *Iónicas (Íslas.)*			

Italy,	*Itália.*	Italian,	*Italiáno.*
Japan,	*Japón.*	Japanese,	*Japonés.*
Leon,	*Leon.*	Leonese,	*Leonés.*
Lombardy,	*Lombardía.*	Lombard,	*Lombárdo.*
Levant,	*Levánte.*	Levantine,	*Levantíno.*
Madeira,	*Madéra.*		
Mauritius,	*Maurício.*		
Malta,	*Málta.*	Maltese,	*Maltés.*
Mediterranean,	*Mediterráneo.*		
Mexico,	*Mégico.*	Mexican,	*Megicáno.*
Montaña,		Mountaineer,	*Montañés.*
Morocco,	*Marruécos.*	Moorish,	*Móro, Marruéco.*
Murcia,	*Múrcia.*	Murcian,	*Murciáno.*
Navarre,	*Narárra.*	Navarrese,	*Navárro.*
Newfoundland,	*Térra Nóva.*		
Normandy,	*Normandia.*		
Norway,	*Norvéga.*	Norwegian,	*Norvegiáno.*
Naples,	*Nápoles.*	Neapolitan,	*Napolitáno.*
Netherlands,	*Paises bájos.*	Dutch,	*Holandés*
Pacific(Ocean,)	*Pacífico (Océano.)*		
Palatinate,	*Palatinádo.*	Palatine,	*Palatíno.*
Persia,	*Pérsia.*	Persian,	*Pérsa, Persiáno.*
Peru,	*Perú.*	Peruvian,	*Peruáno.* ·
Picardy,	*Picardía.*		
Piedmont,	*Piamónte.*	Piedmontése,	*Piamontés.*
Poland,	*Polónia.*	Pole,	*Poláco.*
Portugal,	*Portugál.*	Portuguése,	*Portugués.*
Provinces (United,)	*Províncias (Unídas.)*		
Provinces (of River la Plate,)	*Províncias (del río de la Pláta.*		
		Argentine,	*Argentíno.*
Prussia,	*Prúsia.*	Prussian,	*Prusiáno.*
Porto Rico,	*Puérto Ríco.*	Porto Rican,	*Puérto Riqué- ño, Porténo*
Rhodes,	*Ródas.*	Rhodian,	*Rodiáno.*
Ragusa,	*Ragúsa.*	Ragusian,	*Ragusés.*
Red (Sea,)	*Rójo, Berméjo.* (mar)		
Russia,	*Rúsia.*	Russian,	*Rúso.*
Salvador,			*Salvadoréño.*
St. Vincent (Cape,)	*San Vicénte, (Cábo.)*		
St. Domingo	*Sánto Domingo.*		
Sardinia,	*Cerdéña.*	Sardinian,	*Sárdo.*
Savoy,	*Savóya.*	Savoyard,	*Savoyárdo.*

17*

Saxony,	*Sajónia.*	Saxon,	*Sajón.*
Scotland,	*Escócia.*	Scotch,	*Escocés.*
Sicily,	*Sicília.*	Sicilian,	*Siciliáno*
Sweden,	*Suécia.*	Swede,	*Suéco*
Switzerland,	*Suíza.*	Swiss,	*Suízo.*
Sound (the,)	*Súnda. (la)*		
Spain,	*España.*	Spanish, Span- iard,	*Español.*
Tartary,	*Tartária.*	Tartar,	*Tártaro.*
Table Bay,	*Bahía de Tábla.*		
Turkey,	*Turquía.*	Turk,	*Túrco.*
United States,	*Estádos Únidos*	American,	*Americáno*
Valencia,	*Valéncia.*	Valencian,	*Valenciáno*
Venezuéla,	*Venezuéla.*	Venezuélian,	*Venezoláno*
Zealand,	*Celánda.*	Zealander,	*Celandés.*

NAMES OF CITIES, MOUNTAINS AND RIVERS.

Aix-la-Chap- elle,	*Aquisgrána.*	Cherbourg,	*Cherbúrgo.*
Alicant,	*Alicánte.*	Cologne,	*Colónia.*
Alps. (the)	*Álpes (los.)*	Coblentz,	*Coblénza.*
Antwerp,	*Ambéres.*	Constantino- ple,	*Constantinó- pla.*
Antioch,	*Antióquia.*	Copenhagen,	*Copenhágue.*
Andes. (the)	*Ándes (los.)*	Corunna,	*Corúña.*
Amazon. (the)	*Amazónas (las.)*	Chimborazo,	*Chimborázo.*
Appenines. (the)	*Apeninos (los.)*	Dover,	*Dúvre.*
		Dresden,	*Drésde.*
Basle,	*Basiléa.*	Downs (the,)	*Dúnas. (las)*
Bayonne,	*Bayóna.*	Danube (the,)	*Danúbio. (el)*
Berne,	*Bérna.*	Edinburgh,	*Edinbúrgo.*
Bordeaux,	*Burdéos.*	Florence,	*Floréncia.*
Bilboa,	*Bilbáo*	Genoa,	*Génova.*
Boulogne,	*Bolóña.*	Geneva,	*Ginébra.*
Breslaw,	*Bresláo.*	Gibraltar (Straits of,)	*Gibraltár.(Es- trécho de)*
Bruges,	*Brújas.*		
Brussels,	*Brusélas.*	Hague (the,)	*Háya. (la)*
Buenos Ayres,	*Buénos Áires.*	Hamburgh,	*Hambúrgo.*
Cairo,	*Cáiro. (el)*	Havana,	*Habána.*
Calais,	*Calés.*	Leipzig,	*Lípsia.*
Cape François,	*Guaríco. (el)*	Liege,	*Liéja.*

Leghorn,	*Liórna.*	Pyrenees (the,)	*Pirinéos. (los)*
Lille,	*Líla.*	Providence,	*Providéncia.*
London,	*Lóndres.*	Prague,	*Prága.*
Lyons,	*León (de Frán-*	Roncesvaux,	*Roncesválles.*
	cia.	Rome,	*Róma.*
Lisbon,	*Lisbóa.*	Rhone (the,)	*Rhódano. (el)*
Marseilles,	*Marsélla.*	Saragóssa,	*Zaragóza.*
Mountain	*Siérra (Moré-*	Stockholm,	*Stocólmo.*
(Brown)	*na.)*	Seville,	*Sevílla.*
Mentz,	*Magúncia.*	St. Andero,	*Santandér.*
Meuse,	*Mósa.*	Seine (the,)	*Séna. (la)*
Nile (the,)	*Nílo. (el)*	Scheld (the,)	*Escáldo. (el)*
New York,	*Nuéva York.*	Trent,	*Trénta.*
New Orleans,	*Nuéva Orleáns.*	Thames (the,)	*Tamísa. (la)*
Petersburgh	*Petersbúrgo.*	Venice,	*Venécia.*
(St.)	*(San)*	Vienna,	*Viéna.*
Philadelphia,	*Filadélfia.*	Warsaw,	*Varsóvia.*

CHRISTIAN NAMES, MOST USED.

Albert,	*Albérto.*	Candid,	*Cándido.*
Alexander,	*Alejándro.*	Casimir,	*Casimíro.*
Alexis,	*Aléjo.*	Catherine	*Catalína.*
Alphonso,	*Alfónso.*	Charles,	*Cárlos.*
Ambrose,	*Ambrósio.*	Charlotte,	*Carlóta.*
Andrew,	*Andrés.*	Christopher,	*Cristóbal.*
Ann,	*Ána.**	Clement,	*Cleménte.*
Antony,	*António.*	Cornelius,	*Cornélio.*
Athanasius,	*Atanásio*	Dyonisius,	*Dionísio.*
Augustin,	*Agustín.*	Dominico,	*Domíngo.*
Augustus,	*Augústo.*	Dorothy,	*Dorotéa.*
Bartholomew,	*Bartolomé.*	Edward,	*Eduárdo.*
Basil,	*Basílio.*	Elisha,	*Eliséo.*
Baptist,	*Bautísta.*	Eugene,	*Eugénio.*
Benedict,	*Beníto.*	Eusebius,	*Eusébio.*
Bernard,	*Bernárdo.*	Eustach,	*Eustáquio.*
Blaise,	*Blas.*	Eleonor,	*Leonór.*
Boniface,	*Bonifácio.*	Faustus,	*Fáusto.*
Camillus,	*Camílo.*	Ferdinand,	*Fernándo.*

---

* N. B. Though the last syllable of *Sánto* before a christian name is generally suppressed, this is only in the masculine, for it is not in the feminine, the letter *o* is only changed into *a* as in adjectives. *See* page 48. Ex. *Sánta Ána, Sánta Catalína,* &c.

Florent,	*Floréncio.*	Matthew,	*Matéo.*
Francis,	*Francisco*	Maurice,	*Mauricio.*
Frederic,	*Federico.*	Michael,	*Miguél.*
Fulgence,	*Fulgéncio.*	Moses,	. *Moisés.*
Gaetan,	*Cayetáno.*	Narcissus,	*Narciso.*
George,	*Jórge.*	Nathan,	*Natán.*
Godfrey,	*Godefrédo.*	Nicasius,	*Nicásio.*
Gregory,	*Gregório.*	Oliver,	*Olivério.*
Grace,	*Grácia.*	Patrick,	*Patrício.*
Helen,	*Eléna.*	Paul,	*Páblo.*
Henry,	*Enrique.*	Philip,*Felipe,Filipode Macedónia.*	
Hugh,	*Húgo.*	Peter,	*Pédro.*
Hyacinthus,	*Jacinto.*	Pius,	*Pío.*
Ignatius,	*Ignácio.*	Rachael,	*Raquél.*
Isabel,	*Isabél.*	Raphael,	*Rafaél.*
Isidorus,	*Isidóro.*	Raymond,	*Raimúndo.*
James,	*Jáime, Jacóbo,*	Remy,	*Remígio.*
	Diégo, San-	Reynold,	*Reináldo.*
	tiágo.	Roch,	*Róque.*
Januarius,	*Genáro.*	Richard,	*Ricárdo*
Jeremy,	*Jeremías.*	Robert,	*Robérto.*
Jonathan,	*Jonatás.*	Roger,	*Rogério.*
John,	*Juán.*	Sarah,	*Sára.*
Jane,	*Juána.*	Sophia,	*Sofía.*
Jerome,	*Gerónimo.*	Susan,	*Susána.*
Joachim,	*Joaquín.*	Stephen,	*Estéban.*
Joseph,	*José.*	Sixtus,	*Sésto.*
Josephine,	*Josefína.*	St. Telmo,	*San Télmo.*
Joshua,	*Josué.*	Thaddeus,	*Tadéo.*
Lawrence,	*Lorénzo.*	Theodore,	*Teodóro.*
Lazarus,	*Lázaro.*	Theresa,	*Terésa.*
Leander,	*Leándro.*	Thomas,	*Tomás.*
Lucy,	*Lucía.*	Theophilus,	*Teófilo.*
Luke,	*Lúcas.* .	Timothy,	*Timotéo.*
Lewis,	*Luís.*	Victoria,	*Victória.*
Mark,	*Márco.*	Victorianus,	*Victoriáno.*
Marcellus,	*Marcélo.*	Vincent,	*Vicénte.*
Margaret,	*Margaríta.*	William,	*Guillérmo.*
Mary & Maria,	*María.*	Walter,	*Gualtéro.*

END OF THE FIRST PART.

A

GRAMMAR

OF THE

SPANISH LANGUAGE,

WITH

PRACTICAL EXERCISES.

THE FIRST PART

Containing *essential Observations and Directions* with respect to Ancient and Modern Orthography; A List of the Abbreviations which are frequently found in writing and books; A Treatise on Pronunciation and Alterations in Orthography, founded upon the latest Rules established by the Academy of Madrid; Comparative Rules of the Spanish and English Languages; A general Scheme of the Terminations of Regular Verbs; An alphabetical List of the Irregular Verbs, conjugated in their order; A Table, illustrating the use of Prepositions in Spanish; Lists of the Names of different Countries, Islands, Capes, Seas, Rivers, Cities, and Christian Names.

THE SECOND PART

Containing a Collection of Exercises interlined; A Vocabulary; Familiar Phrases and Dialogues; Spanish Extracts; Literary and Mercantile Correspondence and Documents; A Treatise on Spanish Versification; and an Appendix upon SER and ESTAR. *The whole* carefully accented, to facilitate the pronunciation.

BY M. JOSSE.

REVISED, AMENDED, IMPROVED, AND ENLARGED

BY F. SALES, A. M.,

Instructer of French and Spanish at Harvard University, Cambridge.

SIXTEENTH AMERICAN EDITION.

" PEU DE PRÉCEPTES, ET BEAUCOUP DE PRATIQUE."

SECOND PART.

BOSTON AND CAMBRIDGE:

JAMES MUNROE AND COMPANY.

1860.

SPANISH EXERCISES,

ADAPTED

TO THE FUNDAMENTAL PRINCIPLES ESTABLISHED BY THE
ACADEMY OF MADRID.

WITH

References to the rules which are to serve for their translation; notes explanatory of the idiomatic differences between the two languages, and of all the important difficulties.

EXPLANATION of the SIGNS which are found in the Spanish Exercises.

m. Masculine
f. Feminine.
n. Neuter.
p. Plural.
irr. Irregular.
* The star denotes that the word, under which it is found, must not be translated.

1-2-3-4 &c. The numbers indicate the order in which words must be placed in Spanish.

Two or three English words, having the same number, are expressed by the same number.

Spanish under them between parentheses, thus ( )

Two or more English words put within a parenthesis, thus ( ) are expressed by the Spanish placed under them.

The gender of nouns is not laid down when the article definite is not required; but is, however, put down, whenever there is an adjective or a pronoun agreeing with the noun, independently of any article.

N. B. Having made known, in all the Exercises, the rules to which they relate, we advise the scholar never to translate before he has read over carefully the rules and examples referred to. If he consults them with attention, we feel confident that he will easily overcome any difficulties the translating may present.

EXERCISE I.

See Rules I. and II. and the gender of nouns, p. 27, 28, of the Grammar.

The man, the woman, the child, the husband,
hómbre, m. *mugér,* f. *niño,* m. *marído,* m.
the wife and the maid. The book, the paper,
espósa *y* *criáda,* f. *líbro,* m. *papél,* m.
the pen, the ink and the penknife. The table,
plúma, f. *tínta,* f. *cortaplúmas,* m. (1) *mésa,* f
the chair, the chamber, the door and the window,
sílla, f. *cuárto,* m. *puérta,* f. *ventána,* f.

(1) The noun *cortaplúmas* is the same in both numbers; we say *el cortaplúmas,* and *los cortaplúmas.*

The　city,　the　house,　the　palace　and　the　shop.
　　ciudád, f.　　　*cása,* f.　　　*palácio,* m.　　　　　*tiénda,* f.
The　country,　the　husbandman　and　the　shepherd.
　　cámpo, m.　　　*labradór,* m.　　*y* .　　　　*pastór,* m.
The　grass,　the　hay,　the　straw　and　the　corn.
　　yérba, f.　　　*héno,* m.　　*pája,* f.　　　　*trigo,* m
The sheep, the fleece, the cow, the milk and the butter.
　　ovéja, f.　　*tusón,* m.　　*váca,* f.　　*léche,* f.　　*mantéca,* f.
The heifer, the calf and the bull.　　The oak, the elm,
　　becérra, f.　　*ternéro,* m.　　　*tóro,* m.　　*encína,* f. *ólmo,* m.
the poplar and the willow.　The chestnut tree, the apple tree,
　　álamo, m.　　*sáuce,* m.　　　*castáño,* m.　　　*manzáno,* m.
and the pear tree.　The chestnut, the apple and the pear
　　　　perál, m.　　　　*castáña,* f.　*manzána,* f.　　*péra,* f.
The　cock,　the　hen,　and　the　chicken.　The　horse,
　　gállo, m.　*gallína,* f.　　　　*póllo,* m.　　*cabállo,* m.
the mare and the jack.　　The loaf, the meat, the fish,
　　yégua, f.　　　*ásno,* m.　　　*pan,* m.　*cárne,* f. *pescádo,* m.
the　wine,　the' cider　and　the　beer.　The　chocolate,
　　víno, m.　　*cídra,* f.　　　' *cervéza,* f.　　*chocoláte,* m
the tea and coffee.　The sugar, the salt, and the pepper.
　　té, m.　*café,* m.　　*azúcar,* m. *sal,* f.　.　*pimiénta,* f.
France,　Germany,　Russia,　Navarre,　Biscay　and
Fráncia, f. *Alemánia,* f. *Rúsia,* f. *Navárra,* f. *Vizcáya,* f.
Andalusia.　　The　dawn,　(1)　the　mistress,　the　soul,
Andalucía, f.　　　*álba,* f.　　　　*áma,* f.　　　*álma,* f.
the　bird,　the　wing,　the　eagle　and　the　water;
　. *áve,* f.　　　*ála,* f.　　　*águila,* f.　　　　*água,* f.
the speech, hunger, Africa, and Asia. (2)
　　hábla, f. *hámbre,* f.

EXERCISE II.

See Rule II. page 27; Rules III. and IV. page 28; the two N. B. following, and Rules V. and VI. page 29.

The　kingdom　of　France;　the　king　of　England;　the
　　réino, m.　　　　　　　　*réy,* m.

---

(1) The following are nearly all the nouns that take the article *el* for *la* before a vowel or an *h.* See 1st Rule, p. 27.

(2) *See* names of countries, &c. page 195 and following.

queen of Portugal. The province of Navarre. The
réina, f.   *província*, f.
bay of Biscay. I (shall go) to Italy. Thou (wilt come) to
bahía, f.   *Yó iré*   *Tú   vendrás*
England. He (will return) to Spain   I (shall send) to
          Él   volverá   *Yó   enviaré*
Catalonia. I am in the garden. He (will be) at home. (1.)
          Yó estóy   jardín m. *Él   estará*
We   (shall be) in the cellar. Mr. de Campo, Madam
Nosótros estarémos,   *bodéga* f. *Señór*   *Señóra*
Solís and Miss Rosas   The servant of the Count de
      Señorita   *criádo*, m.   *Cónde*, m.
Noroña, and the chambermaid of the marchioness de
Noróña   *camaréra*, f.   *marquésa*, f.
Montehermoso. Sir, the Countess is in the garden. Miss
              Condésa f. *está*.
Frances Pedreras. ●The bishop of Saint Andero. (2) Mr.
Francisca   *obíspo*, m.   *Don*
Francis Peredo, secretary of the consulate of the city of
Francisco   *secretário* ˉ   *consuládo*, m.
Saint Andero. Mr. Velasco, knight of the royal order of
                        caballéro   *reál órden*, f.
Charles Third, member of the supreme (3) council of
Cárlos Tercéro, *miémbró*   *suprémo*   *conséjo*, m·
Castile and of the royal academy of history. The good,
Castilla   *académia*, f. *história*, f. *buéno* n.
the beautiful, the useful, and the agreeable. The sweet,
    béllo, n.   *útil*, n.   *agradáble*, n.   *dúlce*, n.
the sour, the bitter and the savoury.
    ágrio, n. *amárgo*, n.   *sabróso*, n.

EXERCISE III.

See Rule VIII. page 31, and the gender of nouns considered in regard to their terminations, &c. page 37.

The men, the women, the children, the husbands, the
wives, and the servants. The books, the pens and the pen-

---

(1) In this phrase and others similar, the word *cása* never takes an article. Consequently, we say: *estár en cása, ir á cása;* to be at home, to go home, and not *elsár en la cása; ir á la cása.*
(2) See names of Cities, &c. page 198.
(3) Adjectives generally follow substantives. See p. 38.

knives. The chambers, the tables, the chairs, the doors, and
the windows. The towns, the houses, the palaces and the
shops. The fields, the husbandmen and the shepherds
The sheep and the cows. The heifers, the calves and the
bulls. The oaks, the elms, the poplars and the willows.
The chestnut trees, the apple trees and the pear trees. The
cocks, the hens and the chickens. The horses, the mares,
and the asses. The roses and the gillyflowers.

rósa, f.   aleli, m.

The maravedis, the sous, and the louis. The rubies
    maravedí, m. suéldo, m.   luís, m.   rubí, m.
are precious stones of a red[2] colour.[1] The kingdoms
son   * encendido
of France and Spain; the provinces of Normandy and
Picardy. (1) Messrs. Peter and John Pineda. My ladies de
             Pédro   Juán
Isla. The (young ladies) Mary and Frances de Villatorre.
        Señorita, f.
The sisters of the young ladies Floridablanca. The
    hermána, f.
brothers of the Count de Meléndez Valdés. The poem
hermáno, m.   Cónde, m.
of the Araucana, by Alonzo de Ercilla. The climates.
    Araucána, f.   Alónso   clíma, m.
The dogmas of religion. The epigrams of Messrs.
    dógma, m.   religión, f.   epigráma, m.
John de Iriarte and Joseph Iglesias. Truth is
                  José   verdád f. es
a celestial[2] manna.[1] An action worthy of praise. The
  (2) celéste maná, m.   acción, f. dígno   alabánza.
ambition of men. Canals and bridges. The humanity
ambición, f.   canál, m. & f.   puénte, m. & f.   humanidád, f.
and generosity of [2]sensible souls.[1] The purity of the
    generosidád, f.   sensible álma, f.   puréza, f.
heart.   Constancy in adversity. The amiability, the
corazón, m. constáncia, f. en adversidád, f.   amabilidád, f.
simplicity, and the goodness of Mrs. Wilson.
simplicidád, f.   bondád, f.

---

(1) See page 195, and following.
(2) Úno always drops the o, when it is followed by a masculine substantive.
Úna, feminine of úno never drops any letter. (See Rule XXV, page 48.)

EXERCISE IV.

See the formation of the feminine of nouns adjective, their collocation, and their agreement with the substantive, page 38 and 39.

The climate of Spain is (1) warm.   The houses
          es   caliénte.   cása, f.
of Paris are high.   The English women are handsome
 Paris son álto   Inglés mugér, f.   hermóso
Emulation is a passion worthy of a noble soul.   Virtue is
emulación, f.   pasión, f. digno   nóble álma, f. virtúd, f.
amiable   Idleness is despicable.   Bread is dear.   Man
amáble.   peréza, f.   despreciáble.   pan, m.   cáro.
is mortal.   Prudence is a precious virtue.   Madam Vial is
mortál. prudéncia, f.   precióso
a charming woman.   Miss Peredo is sensible, charitable,
 agradáble   sensible   caritativo
pretty and well educated.   Holland is a rich country.
líndo   bién   criádo.   es   rico pais, m.
The sister of the corregidor is happy and his brother is
        corregidór, m. es felíz   su
unhappy.   The cousin of Peter is slothful, and the niece
infelíz.   príma, f.   haragán   sobrína, f.
of Andrew is idle.   My Lord (2) the prince of Peace is
 Andrés holgazán.   príncipe, m.   Paz. f.
a Biscayan, and my lady the duchess of Almaviva is an
* Viscaíno,   duquésa, f.   *
Andalusian.   The wife of Mr. Charles Ponteverde is an
Andalúz.   espósa, f. Don   *
Aragonese.   The servant of the Spanish consul is an
Aragonés.   criáda, f.   Español cónsul, m.
English woman.   The father, the mother and the
Inglés   pádre, m.   mádre, f.
children are sick.   The brother and sister are idle.
niño, m. están   son
The ink, the pens and the paper are dear.   The window
and the door are shut.   The house is high, large and well
     estár cerrádo.   es álto, gránde   bién

---

(1) See Rule XLIX page 95, when we ought to translate the verb *to be* by *ser*, and when by *estár;* and the Appendix page 459.
(2) See Rule V. page 29.

adorned.   The (vegetable garden) (the fruit garden) and
adornádo.   *huérta,* f.   *huérto,* m.
the parterre of the duke de Alcudia are well cultivated.   The
jardin de flóres, m.   *son   cultivádo.*
country (1) house of the father of Miss Louisa Alameda, is
                                             Luisa   es
pretty but small.
lindo péro pequéño.

EXERCISE V.

See Rules IX. X. and XI. page 35.

The English drink beer, good wine, excellent tea, and
          *bében cervéza, buéno víno,*m. *escelénte*
eat potatoes.   I have (2) sugar, coffee, and cream.   Bread,
cómen patáta. Yó téngo   azúcar,·café   `   náta
meat and water are things necessary to man.   We have
          cósa, f. *necesário*   *tenémos*
pens, paper and ink.   Take of the bread and butter of
plúma, papél,   tínta. Tóma   ,   mantéca, f.
Nicolas.   I (will give²)you¹ some cherries that I have bought
Nicolás.   daré te   guínda, f. *que he comprádo.*
To-morrow I (shall make) visits: I (shall go) to see some
mañána   haré   visíta   iré   á ver á
friends.   Mr. Augustin Vial has² lent³ me¹ some books.
amígo, m. *Don Agustín   ha prestádo me   líbro,* m.
The father of Miss Puente has good friends and
                    Señoríta   amígo, m.
excellent protectors.   The friend of Madam Torres
escelénte   protectór.   amíga, f.
gives wise and prudent advice to your sister.   I have
da   sábio   prudénte conséjo   tu   téngo
white stockings, blue shoes, and a gray hat.
blánco média, f. *azúl zapáto,* m.   *párdo sombréro,* m.

-----

(1) The word *country* is *pais, región;* and is rendered by *campáña* (cham-
paign) only when we speak of a great extent of level, open country; in the other
cases, it is rendered by *cámpo.* We say then a country house, *úna cása de cámpo;* also, *úna Quínta.* The fields are rich, *son rícos los cámpos; un bello
pais,* a fine country.

(2) The verb *to have* is rendered by *tenér* whenever it denotes the possession
of an object, and by *habér* when it is an auxiliary. See the *notes to the conjugation of these two verbs,* pages 82 and 86, and the Appendix page 459.

EXERCISE VI.

See Rules XII. XIII. XIV. XV. XVI and XVII,
pages 39, 40, 41, 42.

The brother of Charles Martinez de Irujo, Secretary of
      Cárlos   *Secretário*
the embassy to London has a pretty little country house,
embajáda, f. en   *tiéne*
and the son of *his Excellency* (1) *my lord* the Marquis
del Campo has a pretty little parrot and a pretty little
            papagáyo, m.
cage. This young gentleman is well educated. I have a
jáula, f.   *criádo,*   *téngo al*
few pretty little birds and a pretty little squirrel Mr. D. is
gúnos   *ardilla f.*
an ugly little man and his wife is an ugly little woman.
         su espósa
Peter is more wise and more prudent than John; but less
    sábio . *prudénte*   *Juán*
ingenious than he. Mr. de Casa Nueva is richer than his
hábil   *él*
cousin, but his cousin is not so proud as (2) he. The
primo, m.   *orgullóso*
city of London is more populous than that of Paris.
   Lóndres   *pobládo*   *la*
The streets of London are wider than those of Madrid.
  cálle, f.   *áncho*   *las*
He is more lazy than his brother. I am more tranquil
   perezóso   *Estóy* *tranquílo*
here than in the garden. She is not so happy as her
aquí
sister. Madam Costillas is not so old as Madam Delpuente.
        viéjo   •
What a large woman! what a large, ugly man! The
que *⁕*   *⁕*

---

(1) *His excellency my lord* cannot be translated literally in Spanish: translate as if it was *the most excellent lord* and say *el escelentísimo señór*—and
add *Don* when the christian name of the person is expressed.

(2) See, in the grammar, after Rule XIV, page 40, the note relative to the
manner of translating *as* in the different degrees of comparison.

Spanish soldier is not less brave than the Turk. The
Biscayans and the Catalonians are brave and (1) intrepid.
Vizcaíno   *Catalán,* m.   *valiénte*   *intrépido*
You are as lively as he. He is as learned as his eldest[2]
Tú éres   *vivo*   *él*   *dócto*   *mayór*
brother.[1] I am more (of a) man than Thomas.
        soy   *

EXERCISE VII.

Upon the preceding Rules.

Mary is as amiable as her sister. We are as poor as
                                    sómos   *póbre*
they. They are as rich as thy father. I have as many (2)
éllas, f. *Éllos son*   *téngo*
friends as thou. She has as many admirers as
            tú.   *Élla*   .   .   *adoradór,* m.
formerly. Thy brother has as many books as I. Thy
ántes.
brother has more children than thou. We have more
pleasures than labour. They have more than ten
placér   *trabájo.*   *liénen*   *diéz*
guineas. (3) I have written more than ten letters (to-day.)
guinéa.   *he escríto*   *cárta hóy*
My brother is more than twenty years old. I am not
        tenér   *véinte áño* *   *tenér*
more than twelve years old. Thou hast less pride than
        dóce   *   *orgúllo*
they. Thou art not so (4) tall as I. Peter is not so old as
éllos.   *álto*   *viéjo*
his friend. He does not eat less meat than bread. He
                     cóme
drinks less water than wine. Red wine is less agreeable
bébe   *tínto*   *agradáble*
to the taste than white. (5) This little chamber is prettier
     gústo, m.   *blánco,* m. *Éste*   *cuárto*
than mine. This small apple is better than the others.
               manzána, f.   *ótro.*

---

(1) See Rule LXIV, page 193.
(2) *As many,* before a substantive, is rendered by the adjective *tánto-a, os-as.*
See Rule XVII, page 42.
(3) See the N. B. of Rule XV, page 41.
(4) See the collocation of the negation, page 159.
(5) This adjective is used here substantively.

We have not so much fruit in our garden this year as
   tenémos,   *frúta,* f.   *éste áño*
last year. Mr. B has not so much wit as the Countess de
último   *ingénio,* m.
la Puebla. I have less money than the Marquis of D.;
           dinéro   *Marqués*
but I have as much honour and not less religion than he.
        honór, m   *religión*   *él*
The garden and parterre of the Marquis de Mondéjar,
huérta, f.   *Jardín,* m.
knight of the royal order of Charles Third, are large
caballéro   *reál órden,* f.   *Tercéro son*
than ours. (1) The wine of Mr. V. is bad, but that of
nuéstro.   *málo*   *él*
Mrs. P. is worse. Peter studies as much as his brother,
                   estúdia
and makes greater progress than he. Miss Sophia Mar-
   háce   *mayór*   *progréso*   *Sofía*
tinez talks much more than her sister Frances, but her
   hábla múcho   *Francísca*
sister talks better than she. More (than) I can count.
        élla.   *de lo que*   *puédo*

EXERCISE VIII.

Continuation of the degrees of Comparison.—See Rules XIV, XV, XVI, XVII, XVIII and XIX, and the N. B. of Rule XVIII, pages 40, 41, 42, 43.

The lazy sleep more and do not work as much as the
       duérmen   *   trabájan
diligent. I translate better English into French than
diligénte.   *tradúzco*   *el*   *en*
French into English. (2) The French dance better than
el   *báilan*
the Spaniards. The Biscayans, the Andalusians, and the
                   Andalúz, m.
Catalonians are excellent soldiers, and pass for the best,
           soldádo   *pásan por*

---

(1) See the N. B. of Rule XIV, page 41.
(2) In this phrase the adjectives *English* and *French,* used as substantives, take the masculine article which agrees with the word *idióma* understood, after the preposition *en* the article is not repeated. (*See* the remark following the declension of the neuter article page 34.)

the most courageous and the most faithful in the kingdom.
      valeróso   *léal*   *de* (1)*

The Spanish mountaineers are very strong and almost all
      montañés, m.   *fuérte*   *cási tódo*

very tall. Lille, capital of French Flanders, is a very
  álto. *Líla* *capitál*   *Flándes*, f. sing.

handsome city. The new house of the Spanish consul is
 hermóso   *nuévo*   *cónsul*

very large and very well ornamented. The youngest[2]
  grande   *adornádo*.   *menór*

sister[1] of Mr. Henry Milbourne is very pretty and very
        Don Enríque   *boníto*

amiable. John's cousin speaks very correctly, and writes
            primo, m. *hábla*   *corréctaménte* (2) *escríbe*

very elegantly. Lying is the most abject of all vices.
 elegánteménte. *Mentíra*, f. -   *bájo*   *vício*, m.

The marquis de la Roja is my best friend and your most
  Marqués   *mi*   *vuéstro*

cruel enemy. The Luxembourg was not the least pleasant
 cruél enemígo.   *Luxembúrgo*   *améno*

of the walks in (1) Paris. The wise man will[1] always[2] act[1]
 paséo, m.   * *siémpre obrará*

very prudently. My brother studies the history of Eng
               estúdia   *história*, f.

land as often as he can. The dog is a very faithful (3)
   á menúdo   *puéde*.

animal, and perhaps the most faithful of all animals.
animál, m.   *quizá*

Your sister is very amiable, and a very good woman. (4)
Vuéstro

The servant of my (brother-in-law) is very strong. (4)
  criádo, m.   *cuñádo*

EXERCISE IX.

*See Rules XX, XXI, XXII, XXIII, XXIV, and the
preceding, page 44.*

The good employment of time is one of the things that
       empléo, m.   *tiémpo*, m.

---

(1) *In* after the superlative is translated by the article *de, del, de la,* &c.
(2) See note 3d. page 160.
(3) The superlative absolute of *fiél* is irregular, it is *fidelísimo*.
(4) See the N. B. 2d. of Rule XVIII, page 43.

contribute most (1) to the happiness of man. The
contribúyen   *dicha.* f.
amateurs   say that Mr. de la Motte is one of those who
aficionádo, m. *dicen*   *los   que*
have laboured most for the academy of Music. Francis
han trabajádo   pára   académia, f. *música,* f.
is the most learned man in the city, and Philip the most
                dócto   de
(2) ignorant man in the kingdom.   Temperance renders
   ignoránte   de   *Sobriedád,* f. *háce*
the most simple food very agreeable. The most innocent
        simple aliménto, m. *agradáble.*   *inocénte*
pleasures are always the most pure and the most constant.
placér, m. *son siémpre   púro   *   *constánte.*
The daughter of the Count de Colomera is the hand-
       hija   Conde, m.
somest woman in Madrid.   The most barbarous nations.
        de Madríd.   *bárbaro puéblo,* m.
The most just commandment. Charles is one of the most
       justo mandamiénto, m. *Cárlos es*
learned men in Paris. He is my best friend. Socrates
was one of the most enlightened philosophers of his
éra   *esclarecído   filósofo,* m.   *su*
century. Peter, Paul and Antony are three good children,
síglo.   *Páblo   António son tres   muchácho,* m.
but Antony is the best of all. Mr. B. is the most prudent
man that I have seen. (3) The cousin of the Cardinal
                vísto   *Cardenál*
de Lorenzana is the most learned man that has appeared
                    sábio   *parecído*
at Rome. Miss Villegas is more amiable than I thought.
en Róma.   *de lo que   creía*
(4) The flatterer is always more dangerous than he
          aduladór, m.   *peligróso de lo que*
appears. Ingratitude will[1] always[2] be[1] the vice the most
paréce. Ingratitúd, f.   *será*
unworthy of a well-bred and sensible man. The Count
indigno   bién nacído   sensíble

---

(1) See Rule XXIII, page 44.
(2) See Rule XXI, page 44.
(3) See Rule XXII, page 44.
(4) See Rule XX, page 44.

de Fernan-Núñez is the man whom I esteem[2] the most,
                                          estímo   *

and Mrs. A. is the woman whom I respect[2] the least!
                                      .respéto,   *

The richer a man is, the more he desires to be so. The
                                  deséa,   *   *sérlo*

lazier he (shall be,) the more ignorant will[1] he be.[1] The
perezóso   será   ignoránte   será

shorter time is, the more precious it is. The more
bréve   precióso

scarce a thing is, the dearer it is. The more just and
ráro   jústo

beneficent a prince is, the more faithful are the subjects;
benéfico   vasállo, m.

and the more faithful the subject is, the more constant
                                          constánte

and secure is the happiness of the kingdom. The less
      segúro es   dicha, f.

laborious man is, the less he enriches himself.
trabajadór   se enriquéce.

EXERCISE X.

*See the numerical adjectives, and Rule XXV, as well as
the N. B. which relates to it, from page 48 to 50.*

I have only one sister, four brothers, one uncle, five aunts
téngo   tío, m.   tía

and eight nieces. France was, before the revolution,
      sobrína   éra   ántes de   revolución, f.

(that is) before the new division decreed by the
ésto es   nuévo división, f. decretádo por

national assembly, divided, in regard to religion,
nacionál asambléa, f. dividido en cuánto   religión, f.

into eighteen archbishoprics, and subdivided into one
*en   arzobispádo   subdividido   *

hundred and twelve bishoprics. As to the civil
                obispádo.   en cuánto á   civíl

administration, it was divided into thirty-two governments
*administración, f. *(1) éra   gobiérno*

or provinces. In regard to justice, it was divided into four
ó província   justícia, f.

-----

(1) *It*, the pronoun, subject of a verb, is generally suppressed.

great councils and thirteen parliaments. (There were) then
    conséjo   *parluménto*   *había entónces*
in France thirty-nine academies and literary societies;
             y   *académia*   *literário sociedád*, f.
fifteen in the north, eight in the middle, and sixteen in the
        nórte, m.   *céntro*, m.
south.   The academies of Paris, which were the principal
médiodía, m.   *principál*
ones, were seven (in number,) (1) the French academy,
*   *
the academy of Inscriptions and Belles-Lettres, the academy
         inscripción, f.   *Béllas Létras,*
of Sciences, the academy of Painting and Sculpture, the
ciéncia, f.   *pintúra,*   *escultúra,*
academy of Architecture, the academy of Surgery, and the
     arquitectúra   *cirugía*
academy of Writing.   The French revolution commenced in
     escritúra,   *principió*
one thousand seven hundred and eighty-nine.   The king-
*   *   *y*
dom of France was the most ancient of all the modern
         éra   *antíguo*   *modérno*
States.   It commenced in the year four hundred and
estádo, m. * principió*
twenty; (*there are reckoned in it*) sixty-seven kings: the
           se cuénta   *en él*   *y*   *réy,*
first was Pharamond, and the last Louis the Sixteenth.
     Faramúndo
The large house next mine, is not new.   Saint Ignatius,
      vecíno de   *Ignácio.*
founder of the Jesuits, was a Spaniard.
fundadór   *Jesuíta*, m. *éra* *

EXERCISE XI.

Continuation of the preceding rules and of the N. B. which
relates to them.

Louis the fourteenth was one of the greatest kings of
               fué
France, and merited the epithet of Great.   Peter the
       mereció   *epiléto*, m.

---

(1) Instead of expressing *in number*, translate this phrase as if it was *seven* only: and say, *éran siéte.*

(2) The capital *Y* is always used for the capital *I* in writing in Spanish, but not in print.

first, czar or emperor of Russia, was a mathematician,
     czar   *emperadór*   *Rúsia*   *   *matemático,*
a philosopher, a great general, an excellent admiral, a
*   *filósofo*   *   *   *almiránte,* *
profound politician, an historian, pilot, architect;
insigne   *político,*   *   *historiadór, pilóto, arquitécto,*
in a word, he was a rare genius, a wonderful genius.
en úna palábra   *ingénio,* m. *portentóso*
Clovis first, fifth king of France, and the first christian
                                           cristiáno
king, began to reign towards the end of the year four
    principió á reinár   *cérca*   *del fin,*
hundred and eighty-one: he reigned thirty years. Of
       *   *y*   *reinó*
all the reigns of the kings of France, the longest has
    reinádo, m.   ·   *lárgo*
been that of Louis fourteenth, the sixty-fifth king: it
    él   *   *
lasted seventy-two years. Charles fifth was
duró
contemporary of Francis first, king of France, and the pope,
contemporáneo *Francisco*   *pápa,* m.
Sixtus fifth was that of the great Henry fourth. George
Sésto   *éra²*   *lo¹*   *Jórge*
third, king of England, was crowned in² Westminster abbey¹
             fué coronádo   *abadía,* f.
the twenty-second of September one thousand seven hun-
                       *
dred and sixty-one. James second, banished to France,
   *   *Santiágo*   *desterrádo*
died the sixth of August one thousand seven hundred and one.
murió   *Agósto*   *
I received on Monday last (1) a letter from my friend Mr.
       el   *lúnes*   *cárta,* f.
Abel: it was delayed fifteen days, see the date of it: (2)
   *   *atrasádo de*   *ved*
Paris, twenty-second of June one thousand eight hundred and
           Júnio *

---

(1) The names of the week take the article, then we must say: *el lúnes último,*
or *pasádo; on* is not expressed in Spanish in such cases.

(2) *Of it* must not be translated, or we must turn it by *su,* which corresponds
to *its* in English; its date, *su fécha.*

three. What o'clock is it?(1) Sir, it is eleven, or three
   Que

quarters past eleven. (Give me) my watch, it is twelve
 cuárto   * Dáme* (2)

o'clock and you said it was but (3) eleven. Where wast
    tú decías   *En dónde estábas*

thou at ten o'clock? I was at home. (4) Well, return,
       estába   *Bién vuélve*

at one o'clock. Sir, it is one o'clock. I know it: go to
              Yó sé² lo¹ véte (5)

Mr. Arco's, and (tell him) that I expect him here at nine
      dile   *espéro le aquí á*

o'clock in the morning, or at four o'clock in the afternoon.
 de mañána, f.   *de tárde,* f.

He (will tell) thee (no doubt) whether he can come in the
 dirá² te¹ sin dúda si puéde venír

morning or in the evening. (6)

EXERCISE XII.

*On the pronouns personal and possessive, and on the auxiliary
verbs* ser *and* estár, *to be;* habér *and* tenér, *to have.*

See in the Grammar the declension of these pronouns,
page 51 and following, 57 and following; the conjugation of
the auxiliary verbs, page 82 and following; the observations on
habér and *tenér* at the beginning of their conjugation, and Rule
XLIX, relative to the different uses which must be made of *ser*
and *estár*, to be, page 95; and the Appendix, page, 459, &c.

---

(1) See the *N. B.* 4th and 5th of Rule XXV, page 49. ·
(2) *Dáme* is a compound of the verb and pronoun; it is the same with *véte*
and *dile*. Custom has willed, that whenever the pronoun governed by the verb, is
put after it, it should be joined to the verb. Instead then of writing, *da me, di le,*
we write *dáme, dile,* it happens even very frequently that two pronouns are joined to
the same verb as in these phrases: send it to me, *enviamelo;* I wish to tell it to you,
quiéro decirselo; bring me some there, *tráigame algúnos alli.*
(3) Translate *that it was but,* as if it was, *that it was only, que éran sólo.*
But or only adverbs, *sólo* or *sinó* in Spanish.
(4) See Rule III. page 28.
(5) To Mr. Arco's *is, á la cása del Señór Árco.*
(6) Translate these phrases, *por la mañána, ó por la tárde.*

N. B. We place the objective pronouns after the exercises on the three regular conjugations, persuaded that the scholar will find less difficulty in them after having familiarised himself with the auxiliaries and regular verbs.

Infinitive.

To have a new coat.   To be tall,   short,   fat,   lean.
         vestído, m.   *álto, pequéño, górdo, fláco.*
Having good friends, good patronage. (1).   Having been out
        protección, f.   *fuéra.*
of temper.   To be sick or well (2).   To have been
    humór
indisposed.   To be occupied.   To have genius.   To be
indispuésto.   *ocupádo.*   *ingénio.*
wise, prudent, amiable.   Having had patience.   Having been
                paciéncia.
Consul of the French republic.   To have been a Senator.
                   * *Senadór.*
To be Corregidor of the City of Cadiz.   To be in the
    Corregidór
country.   To have been all day at home.
cámpo, m.   *el.*

Indicative present.

I have a book of geography and one of mathematics, (3).
        geografía   *matemática,* sing.
I am very happy, and my brother is very unhappy.   We
have excellent wine and they have no beer.   You were
                cervéza.
diligent last year, and now you are lazy.   They have a large
        ahóra.
garden (4) and many flowers; they are very well cultivated.
jardín, m.   *flor,* f.   *cultivádo.*
Thou hast more money than I, but I have more goods
      dinéro   *péro*   *mercaderías*
than thou.   Thou art more learned than thy brother, but thy
brother is less proud than thou.

---

(1) See Rule XI. page 35.
(2) See Rule XLIX. page 95.
(3) See Rule XXV. page 48.
(4) See Rule XXV. note 3, page 48.

EXERCISE XIII.

Imperfect.

I had and I have still the works of the best Spanish[2]
           todavía   *óbra*, f.
authors.[1] Thou hadst the grammar and dictionary of the
autór, m.   *gramática*, f.   *diccionário*, m.
academy; thou wast well pleased. We had also the
académia, f.   *conténto.*   *también*
poetical works of the Count de Noróña and Mr. John Me-
poético, óbra, f.   *Don*
léndez Valdés, the two best modern[2] Spanish[3] poets.[1] That
work was a history and was very well written.
    ser   *estár*

Preterite definite.

Thou wast very well satisfied with the poem of the Count
             satisfécho de   *poéma*, m.
de Noróña on death, and with the odes of Anacreon by
     sóbre muérte. f.   *de*   *óda*, f. *Anacreón por*
Meléndez Valdés: they are truly excellent poetry. We
                        poesía
had fine weather yesterday. Thy cousin had a rich
  béllo   *ayér.*   *primo*, m.
present. My brothers and sisters were charitable; they
presénte, m.   *caritatívo;*
had compassion on the unfortunate. My mother (was in
  compasion de   *tenér*
trouble) last week, she was very sad; we pitied her
pesadúmbre   *tenér lástima de*

Preterite indefinite.

I have had much vexation, and I have been very sick.
         vejación, f.
Thou hast had three *masters*, (1) and thou hast been well
instructed. They have had (a great deal of) money. They
instruido   *múcho*   *dinéro.*
have been prodigal. My neighbour has been very sick.
    pródigo   *vecíno*

---

(1) *Master*, when used to signify a man who has people dependent upon him, a
landlord, owner or master of a house or an estate, must be translated by *amo* or
duéño; but when it expresses the idea of a man who teaches some art or science,
then it is rendered by *maéstro.*

Preterite anterior.

When I had been fifteen days in the town of Bilboa.
villa, f.   Bilbáo
When we had had our passport. When the wine had been an
pasapórte, m.
hour in the bottle. (As soon as) you had been a month
botélla, f.   Luégo que   mes, m
at Paris. After he had had his money.
en   Después que   dinéro

EXERCISE XIV.

Pluperfect

I had had a reward for diligence, and thy brother had
prémio, m. de diligéncia
had the first reward for memory. My master (1) had been
de memória.
satisfied with me; I had been diligent and attentive. Thy
satisfécho de   aténto
brothers and thy sisters had been studious, they had had
estudióso
praises. We had been rash. Thou hadst had much bold-
elógio.   temerário   osa-
ness. They had been timid. We had had good motives.
día, f.   tímido.   motívo.

Future absolute.

Our cousins will have to-morrow new pens and good paper,
they will be occupied. My sister and I will be diligent. We
shall have friends. The English will always be good
siémpre
seamen. The French will[2] perhaps[3] never[1] be[2] as powerful as
marinéro   quizá   jamás   poderóso
they on the sea; but they will[2] always[3] be[2] more[4] so[1] on land.
    por * mar;   mas   lo por liérra.
Thou wilt be taller than thy friend Francis, but thy friend
álto
will be more fat than thou.
górdo

---

(1) See the note in the preceding page.

Future anterior.

I shall have had my books. Thou wilt have been happy.
libro, m.   *feliz.*

We shall have been more civil. The enemies will not
cortés   *enemigo,* m.

have been victorious; they will not have had any success;
victorióso;   *algún sucéso;*

they will have been conquered. General B. will have been
vencído.

victorious. You will have had generals, commanders, in a
victorióso   *comandánte,*

word, courageous and intrepid chiefs, and you will have
palábra, f. *corajúdo*   *géfe,*

been yourselves valorous and invincible.
  vosótros mísmos   *invencíble.*

EXERCISE XV.

See Rule XXXIX. and XL. p. 76. *Future conjunctive
simple and future conjunctive compound. Mind well!*

If I have money, they (will rob me of it.) (1) I am sure
      me lo robarán   *segúro*

that *if I have* patience, I shall have success. Thou wilt be
   paciéncia,

rewarded *if thou art* attentive. *If* the war *is* long, many
recompensádo   *guérra,* f. *lárgo,*

towns will be destroyed *If* the enemy *has* the imprudence
   arruinádo.   *imprudéncia,* f.

to put his threats in execution he will be vanquished, *if*
de ponér amenáza egecución,   *vencído,*

you *are* all, in the moment of attack, faithful to your
     moménto, m. *atáque,* m. *fiél*

prince, to your country, to the laws of honour. I (shall obtain)
    pátria, f.   *léy,* f. *honór,* m.   *lograré*

the pardon of my fault, (as soon as) my uncle *shall have*[2]
  perdón, m.   *cúlpa, luégo que*   *tio*

solicited[3] it[1]
solicitár lo.

---

(1) In this phrase and others similar, we put in the second future only the verb
governed by the conjunction. These are italicised to strike the eye of the student.

First, second, and third conditionals present.   See Rules XLI. XLII. XLIII. XLIV. and XLV. pages 77 and 78.

I should have better patronage than thy friend.   You
protección
would have more scholars *if* you *were* more learned.
discípulo   instruído.
Their father would be happier *if* he *was* less avaricious.
feliz   aváro.
Man would be less unhappy *if* he *was* less ambitious.   Thou
infeliz   ambicióso.
wouldst not be sick *if* thou *wast* more prudent.   Who
quién
would have believed *that* the war *would have* lasted ten
creído   durádo.
years?   It would be just *that* he *should be* severely
jústo   severaménte
punished.   Your children would not be so ignorant, *if* they
castigádo.   *ignoránte*
were more studious.   Although we *should have* peace, I
estudióso. Aunqué   paz,
(should not go) to England.   I should be better (1) *if* I
no iría
were in the country.   They would be more active and
activo
dexterous *if* they *were* younger.
diéstro   *jóven.*

EXERCISE XVI.

On the first, second, and third conditionals present and past.   See Rules XLI. XLII. XLIII. XLIV. and XLV pages 77 and 78.

The day would have been much finer, *if* the sun *had* not
dia, m.   sol, m.
been so hot.   The writings of Voltaire would have been
ardiénte.   óbra, f.

---

(1) *To be well or ill,* is translated as if it was *to be good or bad, estár buéno, estár málo; and to be better, estár mejór, to be worse, estár peór.* See page 95, and Appendix 459.

generally admired *if* the*y* *had* contained a wiser and
gencrálménte admirádo si   *contenido*
more religious philosophy. *If* the works of Rousseau *were*
religióso   *filosofía,* f.   *óbra,* f.
more moral, they would be less dangerous, and would not
              peligróso,
have done (so much) harm. *If* your husband *was* less
causádo tánto   *mal.*
violent and less jealous, you would be happier. *If* men
violénto   *zelóso,*
were not so unjust, the number of the unfortunate would not
injústo,   *número*   *infortunádo,* m.
be so great. The effects of the revolution would not have
gránde.   *efécto,* m.
been so cruel, *if* the depravity of manners *had* not been
         depravación, f.   *costúmbres,* f.
so great in England, *if* licentiousness *had* not been (so much)
          licéncia, f.   *tan* (1)
countenanced, *if* irreligion *had* not been so general (2). *If*
favorecido,   *irreligión,* f.   *generál.*
the Spanish language, *if* its beauties, its riches, *were* more
      léngua, f.   *belléza,*   *riquéza,*
known, the literature of this country would have more
conocido,   *literatúra,* f.   *país,* m.
amateurs. *If* your brother *was* better informed than you
aficionádo.   *fué*   *instruido*
last year (3), it was your fault (4). The miser would
                   aváro, m.
never be contented, *if* he *had* not in his coffers treasures to
              cófre tesóro pára
feed   his insatiable cupidity.
alimentár   *insaciáble codícia.*

---

(1) See Adverbs of quantity, page 158; *tan* instead of *tánto.* '
(2) See Rule XLV. p. 78.
(3) See the N. B. 1st. Rule of XLV. p. 79. and try to remember it.
(4) The pronoun *It* must not be translated in this phrase; therefore say, *éra culpa vuéstra.* See page 119.

EXERCISE XVII.

Imperative. (1)

Have, my friends (2), patience and perseverance. Let
                    paciéncia   *perseveráncia.*
him have a good dictionary, and a grammar better than yours.
                    diccionário, m. *gramática*, f.
Let them be less lazy.   Let the virtuous man be rewarded,
                                    virtuóso   *recompensádo*
let the wicked man be punished. (3) Let me have prudence
      málo   *castigádo.*   *prudéncia.*
and wisdom. Let your brother be more discreet, and let
  sabiduría.   *discréto*
them have more prudence. Have pity on the poor and
                                    lástima de póbre, m. pl.
unfortunate.   Be good, charitable, and beneficent.
desdichádo, m. pl.   *caritativo*   *benéfico.*

Subjunctive present.

That I may have riches. (4) That I may be generous. That
Que
I may not be ambitious. Although we may not be avaricious.
                    ambicióso.   *aunqué*   *avariénto*
(In order that) he may have servants, and that he may not
      pára que   *criádo*
be unhappy.   In order that our enemies may not have
any partisans in this country, and that we may be victorious.
* *partidário*   *éste*
Although our troops may have excellent officers. In order
            trópas, f.   *oficiál.*
that we may all be friends of our king and of our country.
                                              pátria, f.

---

(1) See the note to the conjugation of the auxiliary verb *habér.* p. 82 of the grammar.
(2) See Rule XXXI, p. 60.
(3) In English, when the verb is in the third person of the imperative, and has a noun for its nominative, this noun always precedes it; on the contrary in Spanish, it is always placed after the verb; Ex. say or write; *séa el hómbre virtuóso, &c.*
(4) See Rule XLVII, p. 81; and Conjunctions, p. 194.

Be not thou so negligent.(1) Be not you a slanderer. **Have**
,   * *maldiciénte.*
thou no pride.   Be not impious.   Have not envy.
   orgúllo.   *impio.*   *envidia*

*Imperfect.**

Provided that I might have friends. Although the Count de
Naranja might not be prodigal. (Would to God) that their chil-
            ser pródigo.   *ojalá*
dren might not be libertine. Before your father and your uncle
            disolúto.   *ántes que*
had a garden. Before thou wast at Madrid. That the kingdom of England might not be in danger. In order that the
                      estár   peligro.   *afin de   que*
traitors were arrested; in case that they were in prison. (2)
traidór, m   *en cáso que*   *cárcel,* f.

EXERCISE XVIII.

*Preterite.**

Although I *have* had the pleasure of . . . Unless your father
Bién que   *gústo,* m.   *á ménos que*
has had news from your mother.   Grant that he *has* been
   noticia,   *Dádo que*
ill treated.   I do not believe that the marchioness de Angosse
maltratádo..   *créo*   *marquésa,* f.
has ever been pretty, nor that her daughter *has* ever been ugly.
   jamás   lindo   *féo*
Your sister is very gay, although she *has* been sick (so long.)
          alégre   *tánto tiémpo.*
Miss de Costillas has been very amiable, before she *has* had
                               ántes que
(so many) admirers.   The number of wise and virtuous men
      adorador.   *número,* m. *sábio*   *virtuóso*
is very small, however much they *have* always been esteemed.
   reducído, por mas que   *estimádo.*

*Pluperfect.**

If I *had* had good wine, I should not have been so sick.
Although the war *had* been very long, the peace lasted *but*
aún cuándo   *lárgo*   *paz,* f. *duró*

---

(1) See Rule XLVI. p. 80. * Observe the subjunctive mode.
(2) *In prison* must be translated as if it was *in the prison.*

one year. (1)   Your children would not have been very good
yesterday, were it not that they *had* been punished the day
   ayér   (*á no ser que*)   *castigár* *día,* m.
preceding.   Your nephew was very ignorant before he *had*
precedénte.   *sobrino,* m. *éra*   ·   *ántes que*
been at the   university.   Whenever I *should have* met him.
   en   *universidád,* f. *Siémpre que*

EXERCISE XIX.

ON THE REGULAR VERBS.

*Indicative present, imperfect, preterite definite, preterite
indefinite, preterite anterior and pluperfect.*

I speak to men of my country.   Thou answerest thy father.
hablár   *país,* m.   *respondér á*
He (comes up) *to* (2) speak to his *master.* (3)   We did
     subir
speak of the revolution of Constantinople.   We did answer
the Marquis de las Rojas.   You *call* my son and my daugh-
                   llamár
ter (4); but they refuse to come up.   I fasted, last year,
       rehusár de   *ayunár*
every Friday.   I drank nothing but water, and thou fearedst
tódos los viérnes. bebér   *sinó*   *temér*
that I should be sick. (5)   He allowed his children games
                   permitír á *hijos* *juégo*
of exercise and dexterity.   The governor of the City of
egercício   *destréza.*   *gobernadór,* m.
Cadiz supped yesterday with the Commissary *of the Navy.* (6)
   cenár   *Comisário,* m. *
We pretended that the Corregidor was sick; but to-day I
pretendér   *hóy*

---

(1) *But,* taken in the sense of *only,* is translated into Spanish by *sólo* or *sólaménte,* or by *no* placed before the verb and *sinó* placed after this same verb. See
p. 155 of the grammar, what relates to it.

(2) *See on the prepositions the important rules which relate to* por *and*
pára, page 160 and following of the grammar.

(3) See Exercise XIII, page 219, note 1.

(4) See Rule LVI, page 154.

(5) See Rule LIV, page 153.

(6) The article *the* must not be translated in this phrase; we say, *el comisário
de marina, de guérra,* and not *de la marina, de la guérra*

am sure that he is well, (1) that he judged yesterday a
estár segúro •   *juzgár*
criminal and sentenced him to be whipped. I bought
réo, m. *condenár* *á* *azotár.* *comprár*
yesterday two dozen of pears, and we have eaten them
     docéna *péra,*   *comér*
already. John, why hast thou breakfasted so late? Sir,
 yá   *porqué*   *almorzár* *tárde?*
(it was) eight o'clock when I took my *cup* of chocolate. (2)
éran   *tomár*   *chocoláte.*
Thou frightenedst me when thou *knockedst* at my door. (3)
  espantár *cuándo*
My father was very well satisfied with me when he had
         satisfécho de
spoken to my masters, and he rewarded me. We had dined,
       recompensár   *comér,*
sung and danced when Miss Peredo arrived. We had
cantár *bailár*   *llegár.*
promised to write to my aunt. Messrs. Isla and Valdés had
prometér de escribír   *tía.*
procured an excellent place for a son of Madam de Legarra.
procurár   *empléo*   *Madáma*

EXERCISE XX.
Rule XXXIX. and XL. page 76.

*Future absolute, future anterior, future conjunctive simple, and future conjunctive compound.**

If the next winter *is* as cold as the last, the poor will
   inviérno, m. *frío* *último,* *pl.*
suffer very much. We will remedy the evil if it *is* possible.
padecér   *remediár* *mal,* m. * posíble.*
Shalt thou not sell (4) thy wine this year? He will shear
  vendér   *esquilár*

(1) See Exercise XV, page 222, note 1. * See note. page 221.
(2) *Cup,* speaking of chocolate, is translated by *gícara* and not by *táza.*
(3) *To knock at the door* is translated by *llamár á la puérta* and not by *pegár á la puérta.*
(4) In interrogative phrases, when the nominative of the verb is one of the personal pronouns, the pronoun is suppressed in Spanish; and in conversation the interrogation is caused to be understood by the inflexion of the voice.

his sheep (in the) beginning of the spring. Thy father
ovéja, pl.   al   principio,   primavéra, f.
has assured me that *if* thou *art* diligent and *studiest* with
  asegurár   .   estudiár con
attention, thou shalt have the gold watch (1) that he has prom-
atención   óro relój, m.
ised thee. The physician has advised me not to (go out)
              médico, m.   aconsejár   no² de¹ salír
to-morrow, if the sun *is* as hot as it has been to-day. I shall
mañána,   sol, m.   ardiénte lo   hóy
speak to your sister, when she *shall have* received the visit
                                      recibír   visíta, f.
and the good advice of her aunt. We shall not omit, in this
              conséjo, m.   omitír
critical circumstance, (any thing) that prudence, duty and
crítico circunstáncia, f.   náda   de lo que obligación, f.
honour *shall prescribe* (to us) for the safety of our country.
honór, m.   prescribír nos pára seguridád, f.
They will write (to me) all that *shall happen* (to them)
              escribír me   tódo lo que   acontecér   les
while I *shall be* absent. Thou wilt do, my child, all that
miéntras   ausénte.   harás   tódo lo que
thy masters *shall command* thee: thou wilt (be silent) when
              mandár   callár
they shall speak (2) and thou wilt answer when they *shall*
question thee. *If* thou *breakfastest* to-morrow with the
interrogár   almorzár
Marquis de las Estrellas, thou wilt not forget, I hope, to
                        olvidár, lo esperar de
speak of my law-suit. Tell Mr. Joseph Mor de Fuentes
              pléito, m. Di' á Don
when thou *shall meet* him, that I wish to write to his son,
              encontrár   deseár * escribír
but I (don't know) where he lives.
      ignorár   dónde   vivír.

---

(1) Turn it *watch of gold*, and so all similar dictions.
(2) See Rule XL. page 76.

EXERCISE XXI.

See Rules XLI, XLII, XLIII, XLIV and XLV, and the N. B, 1st. and 2d. pages 77, 78, 79, 80.

First, second and third conditionals present and past. *

If man *occupied himself* (1) a little more with his own
       ocupárse   *un póco*   *de*   *própio*
affairs, and *meddled* a little less with those (*of others*), he
negócio, m. *metérse*(2)   *los*   *agéno* (3)
would live happier. *If* men (*gave themselves up*) less to
    vivír   *entregárse*
their passions, if they *would* (*suffer themselves to be*
  pasión,   *dejárse*
persuaded) more by the counsels of reason and of virtue, *if*
persuadír mas   *conséjo*, m. *razón*, f.
they *respected*, as they ought, the sacred rights of
    respetár cómo   *lo debér*   *sagrádo derécho*, m.
innocence, in a word, *if* they *respected* themselves, the
inocéncia, f. *en úna palábra*   *respetárse á si mismos*
manners *would* not *be* so corrupted, the victims of crime
costúmbre, f.   *corrompér víctima*, f. *crímen*, m.
would not *be* in so great a number, and the most cutting
           en   *   número*   *agúdo*
remorse *would* not *torment* their souls. (4) The archbishop
of Toledo permitted yesterday the Countess de Almaviva
    Tolédo
and her children to take in his garden whatever they *pleas-*
    híjos   *de tómar*   *todo lo que*
ed. (5) If I *wrote* the revolution of Algiers, if I *painted* its
                                              pintár
injustices, its cruelties and its horrors under the reign of
injustícia   *crueldád*   *horrór*   *en*   *reinádo*
the cannibal Roland, I *should use* colours as black
ántropófago, m. *Rolándo*   *usár* (6) *colór*   *négro*

---

(1) Rule XLII, p. 77. * Be particular in this exercise.
(2) *To meddle with* is translated as if it was *to put oneself in,* consequently *with those* must be rendered by *en los.*
(3) *Others* is rendered in Spanish by *agéno,-a,-os,-as,* which, as an adjective, agrees with the substantive, or its substitute to which it relates. (See pronouns indefinite, p. 65 of the grammar.)
(4) Rule XLII, p. 77.
(5) Rule XLV, p. 78. to please, *gustár*.
(6) *Usár* takes the preposition *de;* say then, *de colóres.*

as was his soul.   I *should esteem* Mr. B. *if* he *loved* more
    lo   estimár (1)

his wife, *if* he *treated* her with more attention and kindness,
              tratár   la con   atención   bondád

and *if* he *loved himself* (2) a little less.   Who *would* ever
    si   amárse á sí mismo   Quién

have imagined, before having seen it, that Cæsar *would*
    pensár, ántes de habérlo visto   ·   César

have perished by the hand of Brutus. (3)   It *would be*
    muérto de   Brúto.   *

good and useful (4) that all governments *should protect*
           útil   gobiérno, m.   protegér

the arts and sciences.   If I *was* rich, if I *was* powerful,
    árte, f.   ciéncia.   poderóso

I would fly to the assistance of *all those who should implore*
       volár   socórro, m   los que   implorár

my assistance. (5)   He promised to lend me all the books
    asisténcia.   de prestárme (6)

that he *should buy*.   If the French were brave before the
       comprár.   éran   ántes de

revolution (7) they are not less so now.
             lo

EXERCISE XXII.

See Rule *XLVII. XLVIII. page* 81.

*Imperative; present, imperfect, preterite and pluperfect of the
subjunctive.*

My friends, the enemy threaten you;   show who you
                amenazár os;   mostrár

---

(1) See Rule LVI, page 154.

(2) *Himself*, a personal pronoun, being directly governed by the active verb *to love*, and the pronoun after the verb being an energetic repetition of *se*, placed before, a turn often used in Spanish, it must be preceded by the preposition *á;* say then *se amára á sí mismo*.   (See Rule LVI, p. 154.)

(3) See Rule XLIII, p. 78.

(4) Rule XLV, page 78, and observe that placing *good* and *useful* before the verb, the phrase is infinitely better in Spanish.

(5) See Rule XLIV, p. 78.

(6) The verb *to lend*, being in the infinitive, the pronoun *me* must be placed after *prestár* and be joined to it; *prestárme* is then a compound of the verb and the pronoun.   (See Rule XXVI, p. 55.)

(7) See the N. B. 1st of the Rule XLV, p. 79.

are: (take up) arms, fly to meet him, attack him with
  tomár *árma volár*   *le* *atacár*
courage, fight with intrepidity, and the victory is *yours.* (1)
 valór, combatir *intrepidéz,*   *victória,* f.
Let us prove to our neighbours, that, if they have valor, we
  probár *recíno,* m.   *tienen* (2).
have (at least) as much as they. Let them fear the
  á lo ménos
patriotism of a nation ready to shed even the last
patriotísmo, m. *nación,* f. *prónto derramár hásta*
drop of its blood for its government and its liberty. God
góta, f. *sángre pára* *gobiérno*   *libertád. Diós*
grant that the war *may* not *last* long. Speak more softly,
quiéra   *durár múcho.*   *bájo,*
thou hast already interrupted me twice. Let us promise to
    yá interrumpír dos véces.   *prometér de*
study, and let us study with more attention, and our master
estudiár   *maéstro*
will be pleased. Eat some cherries, they are very good.
  conténto. *comér* *guínda,* f.
Open the door for my father, he has already knocked
Abrír *puérta,* f. *á*   *llamár*
twice. I wish the physician *may cúre* our poor patient. I
  deseár *médico,* m. *curár*   *enférmo,* m.
fear that my father and mother *will* not *pardon* my sister the
            perdonár
fault that she has committed. I hoped that you *would have*
cúlpa, f. *que*   *cometér.* *esperár*
permitted your son to *come* and dine *with me.* (3) They
      de venír *á comér*
sang and danced, although I *was speaking* to you. He
cantár *bailár* *aunqué*
would have (been offended) (4) if we *had* revealed his secret.
    enfadárse

---

(1) See Rule XXXII, page 60.
(2) See Rule XL, N. B. 3rd, p. 77.
(3) The verbs *to come, to go, to return,* venír, ir, volvér, followed by another verb, requires in Spanish to be followed by the preposition *á,* which is placed immediately before the verb which it governs. See for the manner of translating *with me, with thee, with oneself,* the N. B. 3d, following the personal pronouns, p. 54 of the Grammar.
(4) The verb *to be offended* being reflective in Spanish is conjugated in the compound tenses with the verb *habér* and not *ser.* (See Rule LXI. page 157.)

Let us never speak ill of (any body.) Let us always respect
    mal *nádie*   *siémpre respetár*
the reputation of (*every body*.) My son continued to study,
     tódos   *continuár*
although he *had* dismissed his master. I shall sup with
     despedir   *cenár*
appetite, although I *have* dined well. He is always in good
apetito   *de*
humour, provided he *drinks* and *eats* well. Though you
humór, m. *con tal que* *bebér* *comér bién.*
(*fall* in a passion) very often without reason, I remain cool.
 enfadárse   *á menúdo*   *mantenérse seréno.*

OBSERVATIONS.

In all the preceding exercises, we have made it our duty,
in order to render the labour easier to the scholar, to follow
all the rules in their order, to cite them even in almost all the
phrases and to refer to them as often as possible, persuaded
that there can be no better way of familiarising the scholar
with the principles of a language, than by obliging him to
have recourse to them, to study them and to reflect on them
at the very moment he makes the application of them.
Now that we have already been over the greatest part of
these rules, we think it will not be useless to exercise oneself anew on the same rules by the translation of some exercises which will embrace them all. We shall not cite them,
in order to render it necessary to consult with a more consid-
erate and deeper attention the grammar and notes of the preceding exercises. We shall pass afterwards to the other rules.

EXERCISE XXIII.

On the preceding Rules.

A state is not flourishing but by the purity of its laws,
estádo, m. *no floreciénte sinó* *puréza*, f. *léy,*
the security of its commerce, the holiness of its religion,
      comércio,   *santidád*, f.
and the respect and love which the sovereign inspires in
   respéto, m. *amór*   *soberáno*, m. *inspirár á*
his subjects. The intimacy of two virtuous hearts is the
  vasállo. *intimidád*, f.   *corazón*, m.
gordian knot which nobody can untie. The unhappy
gordiáno núdo, m. *que* *nádie* *desatár* *infeliz*

person is not wholly (to be pitied,) if virtue remains to
   entéraménte de compadecérse,   *quedár*
him in his misfortune. Romances are a poison for the
   infortúnio *novéla,* f. *venéno,* m. *pára*
heart, they corrupt it (by degrees,) and finish by
   corrompér *póco á póco*   *acabár por*
destroying entirely all its sensibility. Maternal tenderness
destruír del tódo sensibilidád, f. *maternál ternúra,* f.
is a debt that all mothers ought to pay to nature. Let
 déuda, f. *mádre,* f. *déber* * pagár naturaléza,* f.
us regulate our gifts by prudence, and our desires by
 reglár don, m, *confórme á*
wisdom. Esteem is durable only when it is founded on
sabiduría, f.   *duráble cuándo fundárse sóbre*
virtue. A sensible heart receives, (soon or late,) even in
   sensíble *recibír tárde · ó tempráno aún*
this world its reward. To speak little, to observe much, to
 múndo, m. *recompénsa.* *   póco* * *observár múcho,* *
think maturely, and act prudently, are almost certain
pensár madúraménte, obrár prudénteménte, cási ciérto
proofs of innocency of soul, rectitude of mind and purity of
prueba, f. *inocéncia,* f. *álma,* f. *rectitúd,* f. *ingénio,* m. *puréza,* f.
manners.
costúmbres, f.

EXERCISE XXIV.
On the preceding Rules.

M. de la Rochefoucault says with much reason that
      dice con   *razón,* f.
self-love is the greatest of all flatterers. Silence is the
amór própio, m. *mayór* *aduladór,* m. *siléncio,* m.
safest part for him who mistrusts himself. The world
seguro párte, f. *él que desconfiár de*
rewards more frequently the appearances of merit than
recompensár   *apariéncia,* f. *mérito,* m.
merit itself. Avarice is more opposed to economy than to
 mismo.   *opuésto economía,* f.
liberality. Envy is more irreconcileable than hatred.
liberalidád, f. *envídia,* f.   *irreconciliáble* *ódio,* m.
The soul is an emanation of the Divinity. The soul,
   emanación f. *divinidád,* f.

' thought and the faculty of speaking, says the Count de
pensamiénto, m.   *facultád. f.*
Buffon, do not depend on the form, nor organization of
              dependér de   fórma, f.   *organización,* f.
the body, *they* are gifts which the Creator has granted
   cuérpo, m. *   don,* m.   *concedér*
solely to man, and not to other animals. The clearest
únicaménte   *ótro animál,* m.   *cláro*
proof of this truth, is that although the ourang-outang has
pruéba, f.   *aunqué   orang-utángo*
the body, the limbs, the senses, the brain and the tongue
              miémbro, m. sentído, m.   *léngua,* f.
   entirely   similar to those of man, nevertheless he
entéraménte semejánte   los   sin embárgo
speaks not, he thinks not. The empire of man over ani-
              piénsa   império   sóbre
mals is a lawful empire that no revolution (1) can
              legítimo   que ningúno   puéde
destroy; it is the empire of mind over matter, and it is not
*destruir *   *espíritu,* m. *matéria,* f.
   only a right given by nature, and a power
sólaménte derécho, m. *dádo por naturaléza,* f.   *poder,* m.
founded on its unalterable laws,   but   a gift of God, by
fundár   inalteráble léy, sinó también   Diós,
which man can at every moment perceive the excellence of
el cuál   puéde   cáda instánte reconocér   esceléncia, f.
his being. (*There are*) many Jews in Asia and in Africa.
   ser, m.   *Háy   Judío,* m.
The catholic religion reigned alone before the French revo-
   católico   dominár sólo ántes de
lution, in Italy, in France, in Spain, in several States of
   Itália,   *múcho estádo*
Germany and in the greatest part of Poland. France is the
              mayór párte   Polónia.
most ancient of the kingdoms of Europe. Germany was[1]
   antiguo   réino, m.   *Európa.*
formerly[2] called[1] Germania from these Teutonic words, *ger*
   ántes llamárse Germánia   teutónico voz, f.
and *man,* which signify man of courage, (warlike.)
              que significár   valór,   guerréro

---

(1) See Rule **XXXVIII**, page 66.

EXERCISE XXV.
On the preceding Rules.

Mr. Benedict Jerome Feijóo of the order of Saint Ben-
Don Benito   Gerónimo   órden, m. *San*
edict, and member of the council of his majesty, was the
           miémbro,   conséjo, m.   *magestád,*
first of all the Spanish writers who *dared* (1) to attack
                    escritór, m. *atrevérse   atacár*
openly the prejudices of his nation.   Mr. Thomas de
abiértaménte   preocupación, f.   *Don Tomás*
Iriarte is a Spanish poet justly celebrated; his translations
of Virgil and Horace are excellent, and his literary fables
    Virgílio   Horácio   *literário fábula,* f.
are productions of the most subtle genius and of the most
    producción   *sutíl ingénio,* m.
delicate   taste.   The Spanish language is very rich; it is
delicádo gústo, m.   *léngua,* f.
much more noble,   much more majestic and much more
múcho   *majestuóso*
expressive than the Italian language.   The Don Quixote of
espresívo   *Italiáno*   *Quijóte*
Michael Cervantes is the best romance that has ever been
Miguél   *novéla,* f.   *jamás*
written.   All those who have read the poem of the Araucana
escríto.   *los   que   leído   poéma,* m.   f.
by Ercilla, make   a pompous panegyrick of this work,
por   hácen   pompóso   elógio, m.   *óbra,* f.
particularly of the speech of *Colocolo* so much (2) extolled
particularménte   arénga, f.   .   *celebrádo*
by Voltaire; it (is found) (3) in the second Canto.   The more
          * *hallárse*   *Cánto,* m.
foreigners cultivate the Spanish language, the more beautiful
estrangéro, m. *cultivár*   .
they find it.   Lope de Vega is a very great poet, and without
                                                       sin
doubt the best that Spain has produced.   Charles fourth,
dúda   *producír.*   *Cárlos*

---

(1) If we translate *to dare* by *atrevérse,* a reflective verb, we must place the
pronoun as usual before the verb and say; *se atrevió á.*

(2) See Adverbs of quantity, p. 158.

(3) See Passive verbs, p. 55, Rule XXIX.

Catholic king of Spain, (was born) at Naples, the twelfth
Católico   nacér   en Nápoles,
(1) of November of the year one thousand seven hundred
           *

and forty-eight, and began to reign the fourteenth of
*   y   principiár
December of the year one thousand seven hundred and
diciémbre   *   *
eighty-eight: he was proclaimed king at Madrid the seven-
    y   proclamár   en
teenth of February of the following year.   (What day)[1] of the
    febréro   siguiénte   Á cuántos
month[3] is it[2]?   To day is the 19th of June.   I have received
    estámos
a letter   dated   Cadiz the 9th April, 1827.
    con fécha de   de   de   de.

EXERCISE XXVI.

On the preceding Rules and on Rules XXXI, XXXII. and
XXXIII. page 60.

At what hour did[1] my mother[2] dine[1] yesterday?   At one
          comió
o'clock.   At what hour did she (take a collation?) (2)   At
        merendár
six o'clock and she supped at nine.   When dost thou expect,
    cenár   esperár
my friend, to receive news from thy son?   I desire very
    * recibír noticia   descár
much to know how he does; he is a good child.   One of
múcho * sabér cómo   estár   muchácho, m.
my friends, who arrived (the day before yesterday) from
       llegár   ánte ayér
Madrid, has assured me that he was very well last week.
    asegurár me que   semána, f.
(Here are) very handsome houses.   Yes, my friend, they are
He aquí   sí
truly very handsome; the first belongs to the Marquis de
ciértaménte   Marqués, m.

_____

(1) The twelfth may be translated by *en dóce de* or by *el día dóce de.*
(2) We have said in the N. B. on the persons and numbers of the verbs, page 82, that the nominative personal pronouns are almost always suppressed in Spanish: this rule must be observed, whether the phrase be interrogative or not.

Blanco, the second is mine, the third is my brother's, and the
fourth the Count de Isla's; this large garden is also his, and
the other is mine. Let us (go into) mine, we will gather
                                entrár en   cogér
some flowers. Who would have thought that the weather
algúno flor, f.   Quién   creér   tiémpo
would have been so fine to-day? If thy brother had more
patience, he would have more success in his undertakings.
                                fortúna   emprésa, f.
If (any one) asks for me, (take care) to answer that I
        preguntár por   cuidádo   de
am not at home. If the Irish - - instead of attacking the
                Irlandés, m. en lugár de   atacár
city of Dublin by day, had attacked it by night, Ireland
            de día,   de nóche, Irlánda, f.
would have run great perils; for, it appears, that the
            corrér   peligro; pués * parecér
malcontents were well provided with arms and ammunition
malconténto, m.   proveér   de árma   munición
I speak of the insurrection of the end of July of the year
            insurrección, f.   fin, m.   Júlio
one thousand eight hundred and three. Book the eighth,
 *   *
Chapter the twelfth, page 82. On the 15th of July next.
capítulo, m.*   página, f.   *   próximo.

EXERCISE XXVII.
On the preceding Rules.*
Study, be diligent and docile, and your masters will reward
estudiár   dócil   premiár
you; but, if you are lazy, they will punish you. I do not
                                    castigár
understand what the countess has said, although she has
comprendér lo que   dícho,
repeated it thrice. We should have invited thy friend to
 repetir lo   convidár
dine with thee, if he had come (1) yesterday to the party. If
            venir   tertúlia, f.
you consoled the afflicted, if you assisted the unfortunate,
            afligído, m.   socorrér   póbre, m.

(1) The verb to come, venír, being a neuter verb, is not conjugated in Spanish
in the compound tenses with the auxiliary ser but with habér. (See Rule LXI,
page 157.) * N. B. Verbs in italic are governed in the subjunctive mode.

if you *shared* with them your superfluity, you would thus
    repartír éntre   *supérfluo,* m.   *así*
acquire treasures of benedictions.   M. Luis de la Plata
    tesóro   *bendición*   *Don*
pretends (to be) very poor, although he *is* the richest man in
    ser   *póbre*   *de*
the city.   I shall dine (to-morrow) with my friend the count
               mañána
de Isla, (there will be) (a great many) *people,* and after din-
             habrá   *múcha*   *génte*   *despúes de co-*
ner we shall play cards and we shall dance all night; we
mér   *jugár á los náipes*   *bailár*   *nóche,* f.
shall sing also; and I wish very *much* (1) that the Marquis
    tambièn   *deseár*
de Mondejar and the duchess de Almodóvar *would sing* (pres.
subj.) the duet of Zemire and Azor.   Mr. Charles Tuerto
    dúo, m.   *Don*
bought a house last week, and he sold it at ten o'clock in
              semána, f.   *vendér la*   *de*
the morning.   Where didst thou dine yesterday?   At thy
   mañána, f.   *Dónde*   *en cása de*
brother's, and I shall dine to-morrow with the Duke de
Alcudia, at his country house.   Hast thou breakfasted? yes,
    en   *almorzár*   *sí*
my friend; I breakfasted at eight o'clock, or half past
eight. (2) Francis the first, died the 31st of March, 1547,
                    *   *falleció*
(at the age) of 52 years.
    de edád   ———

EXERCISE XXVIII.
On the preceding Rules.

The Swiss are very strong, very courageous and very
    Suízo, pl.
faithful men.   A band of robbers *attacked* the Count de
            trópa, f. *ladrón* *atacár*
Fernan Nuñez and the Marchioness de Ariza, and *obliged*
                 Marquésa   *obligár*
them to give all their money and their jewels. (3) I lost
les á dar   *jóya.*   *perdér*

---

(1) *Múcho* is indeclinable when joined to a verb, and is declined thus *múcho-a-os-as* when joined to a substantive.
(2) Say, at eight and a half struck, *á las ócho y média dádas.*
(3) See Rule VII, page 30.

yesterday my little dog, hast thou found him?   No: if I had
                    hallár lo
found him, I should have sent him (to thee)   immediately.
              enviár lo   te   *inmediátaménle.*
Hast thou seen the little country house that my mother has
           visto
bought?   It is very pretty, we shall always have in the   yard
comprár   *   pátio,* m.
a large dog capable of frightening the most daring robbers.
     pérro, m. *capáz de amedrentár*   *osádo   ladrón*
A mother said one day to her children: practise virtue,
          decía   *híjo   practicár*
detest vice, love study, be generous without prodigality,
aborrecér   *estúdio*   *sin   prodigalidád*
wise and religious without affectation, and you will be happy,
     religióso   sin   afectación,
not only in this life, but also in the life (to come.)   The
sólaménte en   *mas tambien*   *futúro.*
miser is a martyr of the devil or an anchorite who,
aváro   *mártir*   *demónio,* m. *ó   anacoréta,* m. *que*
by his abstinence and his continual inquietudes, acquires
    abstinéncia   *contínuo angústia,* f. *adquirir*
rights to hell; his heart is always divided between the
derécho infiérno, m.   *partir*
desire of preserving and that of accumulating.   He is
deséo, m.   *conservár*   *él*   *amontonár*   *tenér*
hungry and eats not, he is thirsty and drinks not, he
hámbre   *comér*   *tenér sed*   *bebér*
(has need) of repose and takes none, he is *never* free (1)
necesitár * *descánso*   *no lo tomár*   *libre*
from alarms.   Before the revelation, the[2] whole[1] universe was
sobresálto. ántes de   revelación, f.   *todo univérso,* m.
a temple of idols: each vice was a divinity.   Your
témplo, m.   *ídolo cáda vício*   *deidád,* f.
garden is well cultivated, its walks are delightful.   It is not
huérta, f.   *cálle,* f.   * *son*
riches which make us happy, but the use we make of them.
                     que se háce

---

(1) See the observations, p. 159 of the grammar.

EXERCISE XXIX.

ON PRONOUNS.

*See Rules XXVI. XXVII. XXVIII. XXIX. and
XXX. pages 55 and 56.*

I will send thee (to-morrow morning) the books I promised
    enviár   mañána por la mañána   que
thee; if they please thee, I advise thee to buy them; thou
        gustár   aconsejár   de comprár
wilt find them at the Book-Store of Messrs. Perkins and Mar-
hallár   en   librería, f.
vin. Mr. Luis de Villa Real has assured us that Miss Sophia
Don   asegurár   Sofía
Hermosa is at Cadiz: write to her, and invite her to come
             escribír   . convidár   de venír
and pass some time with us. I have received two letters for
á pasár   recibir   pára
my brother. I will send (1) *them to him* at his country
house without opening them. I will write to him myself
           abrir   yó mísmo
to-morrow, and I will enclose these two letters in mine.
                      encerrár   éstas
Let us defend ourselves, (2) *my friends,* (3) let us defend
    defendérse
ourselves with courage against the enemy who attacks us
          con   coráge cóntra   ·   que acometér
and pretends to conquer us; let us repulse him with vigour,
   *pretendér ***   *vencér   rechazár*
and let us force him to confess that our valour and our
        obligár (4)   *confesár*
attachment to our country, and to the religion of our fathers
apégo, m.   *antepasádos*

---

(1) See the very important, Rule XXVII, p. 55.

(2) See Rule XXX, page 56.

(3) In the apostrophes : *my friend, my friends, my father, my mother, my
brother, my sister,* &c.—the possessive pronoun may be suppressed, excepting
when they are accompanied with a sentiment of joy or sorrow ; in these cases the
pronoun is expressed with advantage, and is placed after the noun ; and instead of
the pronoun *mi,* we make use of *mio* without an article. (See Rule XXXI,
p. 60.)

(4) See the N. B. 4th which precedes the list of the irregular verbs, p. 121 of
the Grammar.

render us invincible. Thy brothers are very unjust and very
hácen invencible. *múy injústo*
ungrateful. A thousand times I have succoured them in
ingráto. * *vez socorrér*
their misfortunes, never has Madam Vial assisted them,
infortúnio, *asistir*
nevertheless, they love her, they see her, and it appears that
no obstánte * *tratár* * *parecér*
they detest me. (1) I have received letters for her, and I
detestár
will send them to her, without opening them.
enviár *abrír*

EXERCISE XXX.
On the preceding Rules.

Somebody advised Philip, the father of Alexander,
Algúno aconsejár á Filipo * *Alejándro*
to banish from his dominions a man who had spoken ill of
de echár estádo que
him; I shall (take good care not) to do it, answered he,
guardárse bién de hacér respondér
he would go every where and *speak ill* of me. When a
ir (por tódas pártes) á decír mal cuándo
Roman general triumphed, a herald said to him from
románo generál, m. triunfár, heráldo, m. decír de
time to time, remember that thou art mortal. Let us
cuándo en cuándo, acuérdate mortál.
always submit with resignation to the decrees of
siémpre sometérse resignación decréto, m.
providence. Lend me thy book, I will return it to thee
providéncia, f. Prestár volvér
to-morrow; *do not refuse* it to me. (2) No, I cannot refuse
mañána rehusár puédo
it to thee. Lend thy fan to thy sister, and present it to
abanico presentár
her politely. Thou knowest Mrs. D. T. S.; the count and
cortésménte conocér
I were speaking (3) of her; and we said that she is well
decír

---

(1) See the N. B. of Rule XXX. page 56.
(2) See Rule XLVI. page 80.
(3) See Rule L. page 95.

informed, that she speaks several languages and that she is
instruído,   *múcho   léngua,* f.
very amiable. All those who know her say (the same)
          Tódos   los   que   *ótro tánto*
of her. Where is Mr. de A.? Do not speak to me of him,
          Dónde
I detest him. Here are pears and apples, eat some, they
   detestár   *He   aquí péra   manzána   algúno,*
are excellent. I shall buy *some* more to-morrow and I will
                     comprár
send you *some*. (Idle men) are a burden to themselves.
             *perezóso   *   *molésto*

EXERCISE XXXI.

On the preceding Rules.

If they *carry* thy brother's servant to prison, he will[1] not
Si   llevár   *criádo,* m. *cárcel,* f.
(come out[1]) *of it* to-morrow. He is already there. I assure
   saldrá   *yá   allí.   asegurár*
you that I shall[2] not[1] go[2] to see him there The viscount de
              iré   ver   allá.   vizcónde
Isla has bought a country house. I shall dine with him
   comprár
to-morrow: he[1] will[3] speak[3] (to me)[2] of it[4]; it is new,
large, and well ornamented; it is a palace. My son learned
             *adornádo   *   *palácio,* m.   *aprendér*
last year all the fables of La Fontaine, but he has already
          fábula, f.   *yá*
forgotten the greatest part of them. Twelve robbers were
olvidár   mayór   *ladrón*
stopped last month in the wood of V.... they were tried
arrestár   *bósque,* m.   *juzgár*
(the day before yesterday) by the criminal tribunal, which
          ánteayér   por   criminál tribunál, m. *que*
condemned six of them to be hanged. (How many) children
                     ahorcár   cuánto   hijo
has your sister? she has two, one son and one daughter.
Thy (pocket handkerchiefs) are very handsome, but I have
          pañuélo, m.   *mas*
some that are at least as handsome and as good.
   que   á lo ménos

(Shall we go) to the garden to-day? go *there* now if you
  Irémos   *jardin,* m.   *id*   *ahóra*
wish: (as for me,) I shall not go; for, I come from it.
querér *yó.*   *   *pués*   *él*
John, open my chest, thou wilt find in it ten louis, take
  abrír armário, m.   *hallár*   *luís,* m. *tomár*
them, I give them to thee. (There were) yesterday fifty
  dóy   *había*
persons at the party at Madam Vial's. I wished to write
  en   *en cása de*   *quería* *
to them. Bring them to me thither.
     allí

EXERCISE XXXII.

On the pronouns demonstrative, relative, interrogative and
indefinite, and on the preceding Rules.

Whose garden is this? (1) Whose houses are these?
Whose palace is this? This garden is *mine,* (2) these houses
are the *prime minister's,* (3) and the palace is the king's.
    primér ministro
Who is *there.* (4) *Some one* knocks at the door; John,
           llamár á
open it. Give me this book and take that, I shall send to
abrír *dar*   *tomár*   *enviár*
them this cage and this bird. This man is (looking for) thee.
 jáula, f. *pájaro,* m.   *buscár*
He who was speaking to thee is one of my best friends, and
she who is with him is the friend of thy sister. Has thy son
paid too dear for his hat? Yes, he paid twenty-five
pagár   *por sombréro,* m. *sí*
shillings for it. The (young man) *whose* talents (5) we ad-
chelines por   *jóven*   *taléntos,* m.
mire is hardly twenty-five years old: he will be without
 tenér apénas,   *   *sin*
doubt one of the first painters in Europe. Of all vices, that
dúda   *pintór,* m. *de*   *vício,* m. *él*
which degrades man most is intemperance. Who[2] are[3]
 degradár   *borrachéra,* f.

---

  (1) See Rule XXXIV. page 63.
  (2) See Rule XXXII. page 60.
  (3) See Rule XXXII. N. B. 2d. page 60.
  (4) *There,* is not translated in this phrase.
  (5) See Rule XXXIV. page 63.

you⁴ speaking⁵ of?¹ of those of whom we were speaking
two minutes ago, of those two gentlemen whose credulity
      ha,   *caballéro*   *credulidád*, f.
you condemned (so much).—Yes, yes, I condemned their
   condenár   *tánto*
credulity, and I shall endeavour to undeceive them on the
               procurár * *desengañár*   *sóbre*
conduct of their sons.—Well; open their eyes on the
condúcta, f.
scandalous conduct of these poor (young people) who, if
escandalóso   *jóven*
their parents do not *correct* them, will run insensibly to
    pádres   *castigár*   *corrér*
their ruin. My history is long, his is short, theirs the best.
  pérdida,   *lárgo*   *córto.*

EXERCISE XXXIII.

On the preceding Rules.

Hast thou seen this parterre? (Look at) these flowers.
    vísto   *jardin*, m. *Mirár*   *flor*, f.
this and that are, in my opinion, the two handsomest.
         á   *parecér,*   *hermóso*
Here is a rose the colour (1) *of which* I admire. This is
He aquí   *colór*, m.
not less handsome; it is fresher than that the brilliancy
            *   *frésco*   *aquélla*   *brillo*, m.
of which you admire (so much.) If the Turkish fleet attack
               Túrco flóta, f. *atacár*
that of the English, it will find men *to whose* courage and
la   *Inglés.* *   *hallár*   *valór*, m.
superiority, she may be obliged to yield. I advise thee,
        * *podrá* *obligár de cedér,* *aconsejár*
my friend, to study grammar, the rules *of which* are so
        de estudiár gramática, f. *régla,* f.
necessary. I shall speak to-morrow to those gentlemen, and
necesário.   *señór*
(shall tell) them to present a petition to the prime minister
 diré   *de presentár súplica,* f.   *primér*

---

(1) See Rule XXXIV. page 63.

whose power equals almost that of the king. He who
    podér, m. *igualár*   *él*   *aquél*
was speaking to me yesterday, when my father came into
                                    entrár en
my room, is much more learned than thou thinkest. (1)
 cuárto, m.   *instruído de lo que*   *piénsas*
What seekest thou? Whom[2] are[3] these[5] ladies[6] looking[4]
      buscár   *señóra mirár*
at?[1] What[2] are[3] they[4] talking[5] about?[1] (Here are) two
    que   *acérca de*   *He aquí*
pinks: *which* of the two (2) shall I give thee? This pleases
clavél, m.   *dar*   *gustár*
me more than that. And what sayest thou of these tulips?
                   dices   *tulipán,* m.
They are superb: I shall take some (*of them.*) Take, my
    magnífico   *tomár algúno*   *
friend, as many as you wish (*of them.*) (3) *I am very glad*
             quiéras   *
that they please thee.(4) Those ladies dance elegantly.
  gustár   *primorósaménte.*

EXERCISE XXXIV.

On the preceding pronouns.

At *what* hour shall we dine? (5) At[1] half[4] after[3] two.[2]
                                média   *y*
Shall we play after dinner? Yes.—At *what* game?.
  jugár después de   *Sí*   *juégo*
At chess. Somebody asking one day a (witty man) if he
 ajédrez, m.   *preguntár*   *ingénio*
was a nobleman, (the latter) answered: Noah had three sons,
  *   *nóble*   *éste*   *respondér: Noé*

---

(1) See Rule XX. page 44.

(2) See after the declension of the interrogative pronouns, page 64 of the grammar, the manner of translating *which* in Spanish.

(3) *As many as*, instead of being translated by *tánto-a-os-as cómo* is rendered much better in this phrase and others similar by *cuánto-a-os-as.*

(4) *I am very glad that* must be translated as if it was *I rejoice very much that* . . . *me alegro múcho de que* . . . and the following verb must be put in the present of the subjunctive.

(5) See after pronouns interrogative (page 64 of the grammar) how we must translate *what,* &c.

I do not know *from which* I have descended. Knowest
      sé   *descendér.*   *Conocér*
thou *any* of these gentlemen, *any* of these ladies? Have you
               caballéro,
any of these works? Replace all these portraits, *each* in
              óbra, f. *volvéd á ponér*   *retráto,* m.
its place. (We must) give to *each one* what belongs to him.
  lugár. Es menestér   *lo que pertenecér*
Alexander wished that the[2] beasts[3] even[1] and the walls of the
Alejándro quíso   *animál,* m. *aún*   *murálla,* f.
cities should testify *each* in their way, their grief for the
ciudád, f.   *manifestár*   *á*   *módo,*   *pesár,* m. *por*
death of Hephestion. *Each* country has its customs.
    Efestión.   *país*
(Let us put) *every thing* in its place. I doubt if *any one*
pongámos   *dudár que algúno*
has ever known men better than La Bruyére. Has *any one*
   jamás conocér   *alguién*
ever spoken more ingenuously than La Fontaine? His house
(would suit) him better than *any body.* Do not unto *others,*
convendría   *á cualquiéra. Hagáis á*
what you would not that they (should do) (unto you.)
        queréis   *hágan*   *os*
(*Some people*) do not open their mouths but at the expense
  algúno   *abrír la bóca,* sing. *sinó á* * *espénsas*
of *others.* *He who* has no education resembles a body
                        educación semejárse á
. without a soul. We always love those who admire us.
   sin * *álma.*   *querér*

EXERCISE XXXV.
On the preceding Rules.

The people always suffer from the wars which princes
  puéblo, m. pl.   *sufrír,* pl.   *príncipe,* m.
make against *each other.* They have killed *each*
se hácen los únos á los ótros.   *matárse*
other. Many are deceived (1) in wishing to deceive others.
                   en queriéndo *
It is said the Greeks have beaten the Turks completely.

---

(1) Instead of *are deceived,* say; *see themselves deceived,* se ven engañádos

However rich you be, be polite with every body.
por mas   *que*   *cortés*

Whatever you write (1) avoid useless repetitions.
Cualquiéra cósa que   *evitár inútil repetición.*

To *whomsoever* we speak, we ought to be civil. We ought
quiénquiéra que   *debér* *

never to speak ill of (any body) in their absence. In
nádie   *auséncia.*   *á*

whatever he *employs* himself (2) he always works with
dedicárse   *trabajár*

taste. Those who do not occupy themselves in *any thing*
gústo.   *ocupárse*   *náda de*

good and useful, appear to me very despicable. Customs
útil,   *parecér*   *despreciáble. costúmbre,* f.

are not the *same* in all countries. We ought not to associate
país, m.   * *frecuentár*

with the impious, we ought *even* to avoid them as public
*   * *evitár*   *público*

pests. (No one) knows whether he is worthy of love or hatred.
péste, f.   *nádie sáber si*   *digno amór ódio.*

(3) *None* of these ladies (will go) to the play. The treaties
irá   *comédia,* f.

are null. The good man has² (no where)¹ a more tranquil
núlo.   (*en ningúna parte*)

retreat, where he can be more at liberty than in his soul.
retíro, m. *dónde puéde*   *en*

No reverse (ought to) disturb true friendship. One is not
contratiémpo debér alterár   *úno*

always - master of his passions. (There are) defects that
duéño   *pasión.*   *Háy*   *deféto*

we conceal carefully. When *we* have had the misfortune
ocultár cuidadósaménte.   *desdícha,* f.

to offend any body, *we* ought to labour to make him
de ofendér á alguién,   *trabajár hacér*

forget the displeasure that we have caused him. What do
olvidár disgústo, m.   *causár*

they say of the negotiations? *They* affirm that peace is made.
se díce   *negociación,* f.   *asegurár*   *hécho*

---

(1) See the pronouns indefinite, pages 65 and 66 of the grammar.
(2, See the N. B. 4th, relative to verbs ending in *car* and **gar**, which precedes
the irregular verbs. Grammar pages 121 and 122.
(3) See Rule XXXVIII. page 66.

OBSERVATIONS.

The second person singular, as well as that of the plural, being very little used in good society, and as they cannot be made use of but in speaking to a friend or to a person over whom we have authority (*see the observation on the pronoun of the second person, after its declension,* page 52,) it will be proper to begin in the following exercise to substitute the words *vm.* and *vms.* for the pronouns of the second persons, which is not difficult.

When the pronoun *you* is addressed to one person only, it is changed into *your favour, vuéstra mercéd,* which is abbreviated to *ustéd* and is written VM., (See page 12) and when it is addressed to more than one person, it is changed into *your favours, vuéstras mercédes,* which is abbreviated to *ustédes,* and written VMS. In the first case the verb is put in the third person singular, and in the second, in the third of the plural.

VM. and VMS. are of both genders, that is to say, they are used equally in speaking to men and women.

It is well to observe that the words VM. and VMS. are not repeated in Spanish as often as *you* in English; we do not repeat them excepting when they are so distant that it would be difficult to know them as nominatives to the verb. Ex. *You* say that *you* know and that *you* love Miss Villegas, that is, *your favour* says that he knows and loves Miss Villegas; VM. *dice que conóce y áma á la Señoríta Villégas.* And if the pronoun *you* is followed by this possessive pronoun *your,* it must be rendered by the pronouns of the third person *his, her* and *their,* SU or SUS. Ex. *You* have sold all *your* gold and silver plate, that is, *your favour* has sold all *his* or *her* gold and silver plate; VM. *ha vendído tóda* SU *vagilla de óro y de pláta. Your* when not preceded by *you* is changed into these words *of your favour,* which are preceded by the substantive to which *your* refers, and this substantive takes the masculine or feminine, singular or plural article, according to its gender and number. Ex. *Your* brother came to see me, SU *hermáno* DE VM. *víno á vérme,* that is, *the* brother *of your favour, &c.* I have received *your* letter, *he recibído* LA *cárta* DE VM., that is, I have received *the* letter *of your favour* or *worship.*

In addressing God and speaking to crowned heads, and Grandees, we make use of the second person plural in Spanish. Ex. *O Diós, vos sóis mi verdadéro pádre.*——ADMITÍD,

O Gran Cárlos, con benigno róstro, con oidos propícios, y cómo prénda de nuéstro afécto, de nuéstra veneración, lealtád y rendimiénto á la Magestád, éste escrito, que con tánta mayór confiánza dedicámos á vuéstro nómbre, cuánto conocémos que náda os es mas gráto y decoróso, náda paréce mas reál y mas digno de un Borbón que los pensamiéntos capáces de fomentár y ennoblecér las ártes y la sabiduría.—Academical discourse.

In the first part of the exercises we have enabled the scholar to exercise himself on all the parts of speech, from the article to the auxiliary verbs and the three regular conjugations inclusively. We have introduced in it very few neuter, reflective and reciprocal verbs, because our intention has always been to begin this second part with exercises on the rules that belong to them. We have also avoided, as much as possible, introducing irregular verbs in the first part in order to give the scholar time to study them. Their great number is enough to frighten one at the first glance; but we are soon encouraged, if we reflect,—1st.—that the four hundred and eighty-three or eighty-four irregular verbs are reduced, in a manner, to thirty-five, by which all the others are conjugated:—2d.—that they are almost all regular in their irregularities. Indeed, if we examine one or two of these verbs, we shall find that a little reflection renders the difficulty very trifling. *Acordár*, to remind, to accord, to resolve, is irregular; the irregularity consists in changing the *o* into *ué* in the three persons singular and the third plural of the three present tenses, that is, of the present of the indicative, of the present of the imperative, and of the present of the subjunctive. All the other persons and all the other tenses are regular. The irregularity of the verb *aborrecér* to abhor, consists in placing a *z* before the *c* whenever the latter is to be followed by an *o* or an *a:* the *o* and *a* are found only in the three present tenses as above stated; there is then no irregularity but in these three tenses, and all the others are regular. Let the scholar study these verbs attentively and judiciously, and they will not present any serious difficulty.—In the following exercises, we shall make known the irregular verbs by these letters, *irr*, whenever they are in a person subject to irregularity, and they will be found in their places in the Alphabetical List, beginning at page 122, which cannot be too often consulted by students, and which, it is presumed, will be found by far more complete than in any other Grammar.

EXERCISE XXXVI.

On the neuter, reflective, reciprocal, and impersonal verbs.
See Rule LXI. page 157.

I have walked all day. My brother and sister have
            paseárse (1)
amused themselves very much in the garden of the English
divertírse, irr
Consul. My uncle has assured me that you (were angry)
                                        enfadárse
yesterday with the prime minister. The Germans have
            primér   *Alemán,* m.
defended themselves well against the English. The French
defendérse
had fought like desperadoes. Your mother will be
peleár cómo desesperádo.   *habér*
(gone out) when we shall arrive. The dancing² master¹ of
salír   *llegár.*   *báile*
Mr. Luis Angelo had arrived when we entered. I should
Don Luís   *entrár.*
have repented very much having spoken to Messrs.
arrepentírse   *de*
de Callenuéva if they had been pronounced guilty. Rejoice,
                declarár culpáble. alegrárse, (2)
my children, your father is much better, (3) he is out of
                                        fuéra
danger. My nephew does not cease to torment and afflict
            sobríno   *dejár de atormentárse*
himself. It rained, hailed, lightened and thundered
    *   llovér, granizár, relampagueár   tronár*
yesterday almost all day. (There were) yesterday more than
            *cási   día,*m.   *húbo*
sixty persons at the party at the Countess de Torillo's, and
            en   en cása de
to-morrow (there will be) at least two hundred at Madam
                á lo ménos   *Madáma*
Terranueva's. I have met neither of them this morning.

(1) The pronoun *se* which is found joined to the verb in the infinitive, always
denotes that it is reflective, or reciprocal. See page 117.
(2) See Note page 118.
(3) See the N. B. of Rule XLIX. page 95.

EXERCISE XXXVII.

On the neuter, reflected, reciprocal, impersonal and irregular verbs.

Messrs. Cojo and Giboso disputed on Monday last (1) for
  disputárse *   *
about an hour. Your cousin *told* me yesterday that his
cérca de   *primo decír,* irr.
mother would not return from her (country seat) till
                        volvér   *quinta*   *ántes de*
next week, although she had already arrived. I *abhor*
próximo   *aborrecér,* irr.
and my sister abhors like me false philosophy. I desire that
                    cómo yó   *filosofía,* f.   *deseár*
you would *abhor* (Subj. pres.) (2) it also. *Can* you, Sir, do
                                            Podér, irr.   *hacér*
me the pleasure to lend me ten louis? I *cannot:* if I *could* I
  favór, m. *de prestár*   *luis*
would *do* it willingly. - - The servant of Mr. Cáñas
hacér, irr. *de buéna gána.*   *criádo,* m
has been judged and declared innocent. What do you
        juzgár   *declarár*
think of what I have *told* you? At what hour do you
pensár, irr   *decír,* irr.   *Á*
wish that your children should - - *breakfast.*? (2) I
querér, irr.   *almorzár,* irr.
breakfast at seven o'clock, and I *wish* that they should breakfast, and that you should all[2] breakfast[1] at eight. Go, my
                                                      ir, irr.
children, go and study till breakfast is (subj. pres.) ready.
        á   *hásta que almuérzo,* m.   *prónto*
I *know* that it will not be so *before* half an hour. (3) None
sabér, irr.   *   *estár lo*   *
can - recollect without horror the bloody[2] scenes[1]
podér, irr. *acordárse* *sin*   *horrór de*   *sangriénto escéna,* f.
which the revolution of Morocco *produced* in the years one
                                          producír, irr.   *de*

---

(1) The days of the week take the article, say therefore; *el lúnes último,* or *pasádo:* on is not expressed in such cases in Spanish.
(2) See Rule XLVII. page 81.
(3) *Before* is here translated by *ántes de*.....say *ántes de média hóra; an* is suppressed.

thousand five hundred and eighty-two and eighty-three.

*   *y*   *y*

I *say* and I *repeat* it every day that our posterity will
  decír, irr.   *repetír*, irr.   *niéto*, pl. m.
scarcely believe such atrocities. I bring you, gentlemen, a
apénas   *creér*   *atrocidád*   *traér*, irr.
book that you will read with pleasure; I desire that you
             leér   *gústo;*   *deseár*
would bring me also, or that you would send me that
               también,   *enviár*   *él*
which you have promised me. I (go out) every day about
       prometér   *salír*, irr.   *hácia*
one o'clock: do me the favour to send it to me before that
            hacér, irr.   *de*   *ántes de*
hour. It is not right that many *should suffer* for a few.
       razón.   *padecér*, irr.   *únos pócos.*

EXERCISE XXXVIII.
Continuation of the preceding Rules.

The[1] truly[3]   christian[4] man[2] *blesses* the hand of
  verdaderaménte   *cristiáno*   *bendecír*, irr.
God, even when it chastens him: let us *follow* his *example,*
  aún cuándo *   *castigár*   *seguír*, irr. *egémplo,* m
and let us *bless*, (in the midst) of our misfortunes the God of
             en médio   *infortúnio,* m.
goodness who has given us being and who preserves it to us.
            dar   *ser,* m.   *conservár*
I fear this child will *fall*, (1) tell him *to stop*. (2). Your
          caér, irr.   *decír*, irr. *detenérse*, irr.
father *wishes* that you should *conduct* your sister to
      querér, irr.   *conducír*, irr.
school by the same road that you conducted her yes-
escuéla, f. *por*   *mismo camino,* m.
terday. I *say* and I *repeat* every day that nothing is (3)
            repetír, irr. *cáda*   *náda*
so rare, as a true friend. In summer, almost all Spaniards
                  veráno,   *cási*
sleep (after dinner;) it is the heat which requires that
dormír, irr. *después de comér* *   *exigír*

---

(1) Put *caér* in the subj. pres. See Rule XLVII. page 81.
(2) Translate the phrase as if it was, *tell him that he stop*, pres. sub.
(3) See Rule XXXVIII. page 66 and 159.

they should *do* it.   It lightens and *thunders* often in
     hacér, irr.   *   *tronár*, irr. *á menúdo*
Spain; it *rains* there very rarely in the southern
    *   *rára vez*   *médiodía*,m.
provinces, and in the nothern provinces the rain is almost
província, f.   *nórte*, m.   *llúvia*, f.
continual *from* the month of October till the end of April.
contínuo désde *mes*, m.   *octúbre hásta*   *fin*, m. *abríl*
Where are[1] you[2] going,[1] Margaret?   I (am going) into the
Á dónde   *ir*, irr. *Margaríta?*   *en*
garden, I shall gather some flowers, and I *shall go* and carry
        cogér   *flor*, f.   *á llevár*
them to the Countess de Dupuy; I should desire you
                             deseár
would *come* with me, but I fear that your mother (1) does
  venír, irr.
not *wish* you (2) to (go out).—I (am going) to ask her.—
     que vm.   *salír*, irr.   *preguntárselo.*
Well, go and *return* quickly.   My mother *consents*
Bién,   *volvér*, irr. *prónto*,   *consentír*,irr.
that (2) I should *go* with you, provided that (2) I *bring* her
en que   *con tal* *que*   *traér*, irr.
some flowers, and that (2) we do not (go out) before (2) I
                    salír, irr. *ántes que*
know my lesson in geography.   Is it possible that so many
sabér,irr. *leción de geografía.*
honourable people should say it and believe it? (2)
  honrádo génte f. *decír*, irr.

EXERCISE XXXIX.

See Rules LI. LII. LIII and LIV. pages 151, 152, 153.

I (*have just* heard) that the countess de Villegas has lost a
   acábo de oír
son, it is the queen's surgeon who has killed him.   The Mar-
   *   réina*, f. *cirujáno*, m.   *morír*, irr.   *Mar-*
chioness de Costillas is also dead, and she (is to be buried)
quésa   *se ha de enterrár*

---

(1) *Your mother*, is politely translated in Spanish *su señóra mádre: your father, su señór pádre*, &c.
(2) See conjunct. that govern the subj. page 81, and 194.

the day after to-morrow at her country seat. I am very poor
en cása de cámpo
and thou art very rich. (1) *I am not more indebted* (2) to
Philip my father, said often Alexander, ·than to Aristotle,
Filipo decía Alejándro· Aristótcles,
my preceptor; if I owe my life to one, I owe virtue to the
preceptór; debér al
other. Do you believe what (was told you) this morning?
creér le decían
What? that Mr. Peredo is dead? I believe and I know²
muérto sabér, irr.
even¹ that he is very well.(3) What is my son doing? He is
aún hacér?
writing.(3)—Where is he? He is in his room.—And this
escribir. dónde cuárto
morning what was he doing when you were with him? He
was studying geography. I thought that he was drawing.—
geografía, f. *creér* irr. *dibujár.*
No, sir, but he will do it while you are breakfasting. I fear
miéntras almorzár. temér
that you deceive me. Let us go and write the letters of
engañár ir, irr. *á escribír*
which I spoke (to thee.) Sir, I have *written* them. (4)
escribír, irr.
(There are) some men who *repeat* (5) (everywhere) all that
habér, impers. *repetír,* irr. *(por tódas pártes)lo que*
they hear. We will go and dine *when* you *please.* (6) Let
oír, irr. *á gustár.*
us go and walk first, we shall dine with more appetite. My
á priméro apetíto
son (*has just* arrived) from the wharf, where he has beer.
acúba de llegár muélle, m, *dónde*
walking an hour and a half. Do not forget, Francis, that I
* *olvidár, Francísco,*
have *ordered* thee to return to-morrow.(7)He(is just gone out.)
mandár de volvér mañana salír

---

(1) See the exception to Rule LI. p. 152 at the top.
(2) Say: I do not owe more . . . . *No débo mas.*
(3) See Rule L. p. 93.
(4) See Rule LIX. p. 156.
(5) Say; *que ándan repitiéndo,* or *que van repitiéndo,* for *who repeat.*
(6) See Rule XL. p. 76.
(7) See Rule LVIII. p. 156.

EXERCISE XL.

On the preceding Rules and on Rules LVII. LVIII.
LIX. LX. and LXI. pages 156, 157.

The Spaniards were conquered but never subdued.
                       vencér   *sojuzgár*

I have all the works of Mr. Thomas de Iriarte, I have
                 óbra, f.   *Don Tomás*

read them, and they please me very much. (I *like* also
              gustár   *Me gustan*

very much (1) the writings of Calderon and Lope de
                    óbra, f.

Vega: I bought them fifteen days ago, and I paid very
       comprár   *ha,*   *pagár*

dear for them. Spanish books were so scarce in Boston
   por   *escáso,*

that the lovers of that language could hardly procure any.
  aficionádo á   *podér*   *encontrár*

I should wish to read the poem of la Araucana by Alonso
    querér, irr.   *Alónso*

de Ercilla; but I do not *know* if I shall (be able)
                 sabér, irr.   *podér,* irr.

to find it in this city. I do not believe that you can find
* *encontrár*   *creér*

it at the bookstores; but one of my friends, who has in his
                 librería, f.

library ten or twelve thousand volumes of the best French,
bibliotéca   *tómo*

English, Spanish, German and Italian works, has often
                    óbra, f.

spoken to me of this poem; I will ask (him for it,) *telling*
                 pedir   *se lo decír,* irr.

him that you wish to read it; and I am persuaded that, if
   deseár *   estár persuadido*

he *has* it, he will not refuse it to me. (How much) do you
      rehusár   *cuánto*

think I have paid for the four hundred bottles of Burgundy
  pagár por   *botélla,* f.

wine that I have bought? One hundred and twenty pounds
          *   libra*

---

(1) The verb *to like*, *gustár*, is used impersonally: as, *le gústa la música Italiána*, he likes Italian music. *Nos gústa el Españól*, we like the Spanish. *Les gústa el vino tinto*, they like red wine.

sterling?   They did not cost me but one hundred pounds,
esterlína?   *costár* irr.   *
they are not dear.   The wine being so old and so good, I
                               ráncio
would[1] willingly[2] have[1] paid a hundred and fifty pounds.
    de buéna gána
The letter which I have *written* to your mother to announce
    cárta, f.   *escribír,* irr.   *pára anunciár*
to her that Miss Sidney is dead, will be delivered to-morrow
                                                entregár
to Mr. Montague, who (*is going*) to see her at her country
                          ir, irr.   *en*
house, and has offered to carry it to her.   You live and you
              ofrecér de llevár
have killed your friend!   The supper finished, the guests
    morir, irr.   *céna.*f. *acabár,*   *convidádo,* m.
(took leave.)
despedírse, irr

                    ———

EXERCISE XLI.

On the Adverbs, the Prepositions, and the preceding
  Rules.   See page 157 and the following observations on
  adverbs.

N. B. In Spanish the adverbs are generally placed after
the verb; except the *negative* and *interrogative* adverbs,
which are placed before the verbs, and before the auxiliaries
in compound tenses.

The arts and sciences have *never* been more cultivated
          árte, f.   *ser*   *cultivár*
than they are now: but never also have they been more
          lo ahóra:
encouraged than they are.   (There is) *no* country where
    protegér   *lo*   *háy*
the laws are more just and wise, and where justice is
              séan   *séa*
administered with less partiality than in France.   The vir-
administrár   *parcialidád*
tuous man is more estimable reduced even to the most
                                  reducído   *aún*
extreme misery, than the man without honour and without
estrémo miséria, f. *   sin*
religion, living in the greatest opulence.   It is not riches
          vivir   *mayór*   *opuléncia,* f. * No son*

that command esteem, but honour and virtue. Indigence
grangeár estimación, f. mas si   indigéncia, f.
was never, and never can be criminal, *but* by being the
                              criminál, sólo con ser
effect of crime. There is nothing so common as the name
efécto, m. crímen, m.   común
of friend; nothing however so rare as true friendship.
                  sin embárgo   amistád, f.
(It is said) that the Hon. Mr. W. speaks *learnedly, prudently*
 se dice   dóctaménte,
and *eloquently*. (1) Professor E. writes and speaks correctly
elocuénteménte
and elegantly.   Modesty, candor and virtue are, in a
 elegánteménte   candór, m.
woman, preferable to beauty. (2) When we hear men say
          mejór   hermosúra. f.   oír.irr.   decír
to us every day: gentlemen, we are wholly yours; we are
          cáda   Señór   de vm.
entirely devoted to your service: let us believe that it is
          adicto   creér   *
almost always as if they said: we might (be useful) to you,
cási   decír,irr. podér, irr.   servír
but (we will do nothing about it.)
        no lo harémos

EXERCISE XLII.

*On the Conjunctions and preceding Rules. See Rules
LXII. LXIII. LXIV. and LXV. pages* 161, 162, 193.

William second, king of England, was killed while
                                       matár estándo
hunting, with an arrow, *by* Walter, his favourite, in the
en cáza,   de   saetázo   Gualtéro,   valído
year eleven hundred and one. Now united, now separate;
    de mil ciénto   Yá júntos   apartádos,
now they extend their bodies, now they contract them. The
ahóra   tendér, irr.   encogér

---

(1) See p. 160 of the Grammar, 3d. observ.
(2) Translate this phrase as if it was: *modesty, &c.* **are** *better* **in a** *woman*
than beauty.

battle of Masura in Egypt (was fought) in the year twelve
batálla, f. *Masúra*,   *dárse*, irr.   *mil dos*
hundred and fifty.   Saint Louis, king of France, after hav-
cientos   • *después de*
ing fought with a heroic courage, was made prisoner *by* the
     pelear   *valór*, m.   *hacér*, irr.
army of the Saracens commanded *by* Malec Sala. Having
     egército, m. *Sarracéno*   *mandár*
been ransomed, he resumed the conquest of the Holy[2] Land;[1]
     rescatár,   *volvér á*   *conquísta*, f. *Sánto Tiérra*, f.
but the plague having introduced itself into his army, the
          péste, f.   *introducírse*
greatest part of his troops perished with it, and he perished
mayór   *perecér*   *de*
(with it) himself.   Punishments (ought to) be *for* the
     * él mismo   castígo*, m.   · *debér*
wicked, the rewards *for* the good.   I shall (be absent)
málo, m. *recompénsa*, f.   *ausentárse*
next week *for* some days, and on my return my son can
          por   *á*   .*vuélta*   *podrá*
depart *for* Madrid, or if he prefers it, delay his journey *till*
salir   *preferír*, irr. *dejár*   *viáge pára*
Spring. (1) (Every body) says that, *for* a (young man) of
la   *tódos*, pl.   *decír*, irr.   *jóven*, m.
fourteen, your nephew is prodigiously learned. Your father
     años, *sobríno*   *instruído*.
is *on the point* of (2) (setting out) for the capital: he
                    partír
intends   to speak to the minister *for* your brother and to
tenér ánimo de   *minístro*, m.
endeavour to obtain a place *for* him. Mr. D. speaks Latin,
*procurár * lográr empléo*, m.
French, Spanish, *and* English. (3) Charles and Ignatius, his
                              Ignácio,
brothers, are also very learned. Do you know where Mr.
     también   *dócto*.   *sabér*, irr.
Francis Ordoñez is now?   No, sir; I know that he is no
               ahóra

---

(1) See pages 160 and 161 of the grammar, the different modes of using *por*
and *pára*.
(2) See the N. B. 2d of Rule LXII. page 161.
(3) See Rule LXIV. page 193.

longer a canon of the Cathedral of Saint Andero; and I
mas   * canónigo   catedrál, f.
believe that he is archbishop *or* bishop (1) As rapid tor-
creér   arzobíspo   obíspo   Cuál
rents, &c. so those brave warriors, &c. As two hungry
        así   Cuál hambriénto
lions, &c. so the battalions, &c.
        tal   ———

EXERCISE XLIII.

On the Conjunctions, the Interjections, and the preceding Rules.

I shall not (go out) to day *unless* it ceases raining. *Al-*
        salír, irr.   * dejár de llovér.
though beauty is much (sought for) in women, yet it is very
        múy   deseádo   con tódo
often .dangerous and   productive of very great
       peligróso   productívo
evils. This war will be very long, *unless* the powers of the
                                    poténcia, f.
north coalesce. The Spanish Academy has established *for*
nórte.m.ligárse.(2)   establecér
pronunciation clear and precise rules, that there might
pronunciación,f. cláro   precíso régla, f. afin que*
not remain the least doubt on so essential a point. *Woe*
        quedár   dúda f.   *Ay*
to those who suffer themselves (to be dragged away) by the
de   dejárse   arrastrár   de
torrent of passions! *Alas!* I am ruined. (How unfortunate
torrénte, m. pasión,f.   estár perdér.   desdichádo
I am!) *courage! courage!* after the combat,   victory.
de mí! espíritu!   combáte, m.   victória, f.
Passing (last evening) in the street of Saint Charles, I heard
 Pasár ayér nóche   cálle, f.   Cárlos oír,irr.
repeated on all sides these cries: *fire! fire!* I hastened my
repétir por   párte, f.   gríto, m.   adelantár el
steps, and on entering the neighbouring street, I met a
páso   al entrár en   vecíno   encontrár
poor woman, who melted into tears and did not cease to
            deshacérse en lágrimas   cesár de
repeat these words: My God, how unfortunate I am! *Ah!*
        voz, f.   cuán

(1) See Rule LXV. page 193.
(2) See Grammar, page 121, N. B. 4.

my child, my poor child! where art thou? the house of this
woman was then almost reduced to ashes, and the child
        entónces   cási   reducír   ceníza,
whom she lamented had been a victim to the flames, it was
        *llorár   * víctima de   llámа, f.* tenér*
only three years old. (Poor little one!) exclaimed I, what
        *   Pobrecíto!   esclamár*
sorrow, what a misfortune for a mother! I endeavoured to
*dolór,   * desdícha   procurár   *
console her, I gave her some money; but all was useless:
consolár   dar, irr.   dinéro
she was inconsolable; ah! said she to me, thanking me,
        inconsoláble;   decír, irr.   dar grácias
(God grant)   you   may   never experience a similar
*Diós quiéra que   esperimentár * semejánte*
misfortune One obtains by arms (if not) more riches,
 desdícha   alcanzár.   si no
at least more honour than by Letters.
á lo ménos   létras, f.

EXERCISE XLIV.
On the preceding Rules.

Madam Luisa de Legarra arrived yesterday from Madrid, and brought me letters from some of my friends. I
      traér, irr.   algúno
shall go and walk, after dinner, and Mary will come with
 ir á   venir, irr.
me. For whom is that ribbon? for me or for thee? it is for
             cínta, f.
thee, I shall buy another for me; dost thou know Miss M....?
                   conocér
do I know her! certainly; and I assure thee that I love her
si   ciértaménte; asegurár   querér, irr.
and esteem her very much. And dost thou love me also?(1)
Yes, I love thee (very much) and shall never forget thee.
        muchísimo   olvidár
What did the Marquis de Rojas want? He asked me how
                querér? preguntár
you did, and then he (went away.) I received last week
 estár,   después   irse, irr.   recibír
a letter from Mr. John Roca; it ended thus: and do me the
     *Don   *acabár   hacér, irr.*

---

(1) See the N. B. of Rule XXX. page 66.

favour to believe that I am *forever* (1) your sincere friend,
*favór,*m. *de creér*
&c. You know him, (as well as) his brother Augustus.
                            cómo también   *Augústo.*
Well, tell me if you have ever known men more worthy of the
bién, decír, irr.   *jamás*
esteem and affection of those who associate with them.—
*estimación,*f. *aféclo,*m.   *frecuentár **
Never; and I assure you that I love them both with all my
Núnca; .   asegúrar   *á ámbos de*
heart. I say as much of them and I say it with pleasure.
            ólro tánto   *gústo*
The man who has passed his youth in *amusing himself,* (2)
                pasár   juventúd
repents of it (sooner)³ or² (later.)¹   My children spend
    éllo tempráno   *lárde*   *pasár*
two or three hours every day in studying history. (2) Playing
                        á   *jugár*
and walking, you will not inform yourself.   A man of
                        instruírse
genius (ought to) cultivate his talents to (render himself)
ingénio   debér   *talénto,*m. *pára   hacérse*
useful to society. I *like reading and study.* (3) I do not
        *sociedád,*f. *me gústa*
like the company of Miss B., I fear she will come. (4)
                            que   venír.

EXERCISE XLV.

On the preceding Rules and a few Idioms.

My husband solicits the place of officer in the queen's
                solicitár   empléo, m. *oficiál*
regiment; but I fear that the king will refuse it to him. (4)
*regimiénto,*m.   *rehusár*
The Governor promised us yesterday to come to-day to the
                promelér   *de*
party, but we fear that his occupations will prevent (4)
*terlúlia,*f.   *ocupación*   *impedír,*irr.

---

(1) See these words, page 159, Note 1st.
(2) See Rule LV. page 153.
(3) See Rule LV. and the N. B. that follows it, page 153
(4) See Rule XLVII, page 81.

our having the pleasure to see him.   (Is there) any news?
que tengámos   de ver   Háy   noticia,f.
No, there is *none.* (1) (How many) persons are there below?
                                                abájo?
(How many) ladies and (how many) gentlemen?   There
                                          caballéro?
are ten ladies and nineteen gentlemen; and there were
yesterday forty-two persons (at) the Marchioness de
                              en cása de
Torillo's; the assembly was very brilliant.   (*It is*) a great
              asambléa, f.   *brillánte.*   *es*
misfortune for a man not² to¹ have³ friends.⁴ (2)   Who
desdícha, f.   *el*
has done that? *It is* I. (2)   Who has written this letter?
hacér,irr.   *cárta*,f.
It is you, I believe.   Read, my child, and *read again* (3)
            creér.   Leér,
the maxims of La Rochefoucault, they are fine and suitable
    máxima, f.   *hermóso   própio*
to give a very great knowledge of the human heart.   I
á dar   conocimiénto, in.
cannot (go out) to-day, *I have too bad a headache.* (4)
podér, irr. *salír*
Sir, your father (has but just) gone out, (5) he will return
                  acabár de   *volvér*
(in) two hours.   The archbishop of Toledo *was like to*
déntro de   *estár pára*
die (6) (last evening) of an indigestion.   (It is) only an hour
morír   anóche   *indigestión*, f. *háy*
since the Marchioness de Costillas told me of it.   I have
que   *decír*,irr. *

---

(1) See Rule XXXVIII, page 66.

(2) See page 155 and 156 of the grammar, 3d observation.

(3) See page 155 of the grammar, 2d observation.

(4) To translate these words, we must render them in this manner, *the head
pains me too much; me duéle demasiádo la cabéza.* These modes of speaking; to *have a pain in the eyes, in the teeth, &c.* are rendered in the same manner; as, *me dolía un ójo, un diénte, &c.* I had a pain in one eye, a tooth, &c.

(5) *To have* or *to be but just,* is *acabár de,* governing the next verb in the
present of the infinitive. Ex. *Acábo de salír,* I have just gone out.

(6) See page 156; 4th observation.

written two lines to him to express to him (how much)
escribír, irr. *renglón*   *pára espresár*
I am grieved by this accident. (1) I am very much grieved
me pésa *
(by it) myself; I shall go and see him after dinner. Do me
    *   *á*   *después de Hacér*, irr.
then the favour to tell him that this evening we will go,
pués favór, m.*de*   *nóche*, f.
seven or eight friends (of us) and keep him company. Do
            *   *á hacér*
you give credit to what he says? This coat suits him well.
  dar se   *caér*
I shall go and meet him. We are attached to you.
    á recibír   *tenér cariño*
(Be so good as to) introduce me. We(enjoy the good graces)
  Servírse   *gozár del favór*
of the king. I (shall be much indebted) to you for that fa-
          debér múcho
vour. (It is in vain for) you to say so. Let us forbear speak-
      Por mas que   subj. pres. *dejár de*
ing of that. They have learnt that lesson by heart. You
                de memória.
tire my patience. Let us take a draught. He has (resigned)
apurár   *echár trágo*   *hacér dejación de*
his office. You (murder the language.) He understood
  empléo.   *hablár chapurrádo*   *entendér*
about that (of course.) She was well pleased with herself.
  de yá se sábe.   *estár múy pagádo de sí*
Let us take a walk. I have bespoken a pair of shoes. I
      dar vuélta, f.   *mandár hacér*
have missed my aim. Look out of the window. I
no salír bién con su inténto.   *asomárse á*
had like to die. For whom do you take me? I regret the
estár á píque de. por   *tenér echár á ménos*
time lost. This dish has no taste. I will extricate them
      guisádo, m. *sabér á náda.*   *sacár de apriéto.*
There does not grow coffee in Europe, but wheat and grapes
  *   *criárse*   *mas sí*

(1) Say: how much *grieves me* this accident; and so, in all the tenses used
as impersonal verbs; as, *le pesába*, he was grieved; *nos pesará*, we shall be
grieved; *me ha pesádo*, I have been grieved; *nos gustó*, we liked; *les ha gustádo*, they have liked; *te habría gustádo*, thou wouldst have liked, &c. I am in
a hurry, *estóy de prisa.*

A VOCABULARY,

Containing such words as most frequently occur in familiar conversation, and ought therefore to be known by students

———

N. B. In nouns of the same gender and number as the preceding one, the space of the article to be applied is left blank.

The parts of the human body.
Las pártes del cuérpo humáno.

La cabéza,	head.
coronílla,	crown of the head.
molléra,	mould of the head.
frénte,	forehead.
Las siénes	temples.
La oréja	ear.
ternílla,	gristle.
céja,	eyebrow.
cuénca del ójo,	corner of the eye.
El lagrimál,	
blánco del ójo,	white of the eye.
celébro, or cerébro,	brain.
cogóte,	back of the neck.
huéco de la oréja,	hollow of the ear.
tímpano del oído,	drum of the ear.
Los párpados,	eye-lids.
Las pestáñas,	eye-lashes.
La niña del ójo,	eye-ball.
téla del ójo,	film of the eye.
megílla,	cheek.
bóca,	mouth.
encía,	gum.
léngua,	tongue.
naríz,	nose.

La púnta de la naríz,	tip of the nose.
Las ventánas de la naríz,	nostrils.
Los cáños de la naríz,	gristle of the nose.
diéntes,	teeth.
colmíllos,	eye teeth.
Las muélas,	grinders.
El nérvio óptico,	the optic nerve.
lábio,	lip.
paladár,	palate.
La quijáda,	jaw.
cervíz,	hinder part of the neck.
núca,	nape of the neck.
gargánta,	throat.
barríga,	belly.
máno,	hand.
muñéca,	wrist.
pálma de la máno,	palm of the hand.
bárba,	chin.
Las bárbas,	beard.
costíllas,	ribs.
La íngle,	groin.
Las coyuntúras de los dédos,	joints of the fingers.
Los dédos de los piés,	toes.
El gaznáte,	gullet.
séno,	bosom.

El pécho,	breast.	*The interior parts of the human body.*—Pártes interióres del cuérpo humáno.	
estómago,	stomach.		
pélo,	hair.		
véllo,	down.		
cuéllo,	neck.	El murecíllo, músculo, }	muscle.
brázo,	arm.		
códo,	elbow.	nérvio,	nerve.
sobáco,	arm-pit.	tendón,	tendon, sinew.
espinázo,	back-bone.	La grása, or gordúra,	fat.
omblígo,	navel.	membrána,	membrane.
La yéma del dédo,	brawn of the finger.	véna,	vein.
		artéria,	artery.
úña,	nail.	ternílla,	gristle.
rodílla,	knee.	El huéso,	bone.
piérna,	leg.	meóllo,	
pantorrílla,	calf of the leg.	La medúla, }	marrow.
espinílla,	shin-bone.	El tuétano,	
plánta del pié,	sole of the foot.	cásco, la calavéra,	skull
		Las espiníllas,	shin bones
gargánta del pié,	instep.	La espaldílla,	shoulder-bone
piél; cútis, m. & f.	skin.	canílla del brázo,	arm-bone.
El pulgár,	thumb.	El huéso sácro, or }	rump
dédo índice,	fore-finger.	La rabadílla	bone.
dédo del corazón,	middle finger.	El esqueléto,	skeleton.
		corazón,	heart.
dédo anulár,	fourth finger.	Los bófes, pulmónes, }	lungs.
dédo meñíque, or auriculár, }	little finger.	liviános,	lights.
		El hígado,	liver.
múslo,	thigh.	bázo,	spleen.
jarréte,	ham.	Los riñónes,	kidneys.
tobíllo,	ancle.	sésos,	brains.
pié,	foot.	El estómago,	stomach.
talón,	heel.	La bóca del estómago,	pit of the stomach.
Las espáldas,	back.		
Los hómbros,	shoulders.	Los lómos,	loins.
ládos,	sides.	Las trípas,	guts.
El cuéro,	hide.	Los intestínos,	intestines.
pelléjo,	skin.	La mádre, la matríz, El útero, }	womb.

23

La vegíga,	bladder.
sángre,	blood.
cólera	choler.
fléma,	phlegm.
El quílo,	chyle.
La léche,	milk.
salíva	spittle.

The five senses.—Los cínco
sentídos.

La vísta,	sight.
El oído,	hearing.
olfáto,	smell.
gústo,	taste.
tácto,	feeling.

Ages.—Edádes.

La niñéz,	childhood.
infáncia.	infancy.
puerícia,	boyishness.
adolescéncia,	adolescence.
juventúd,	youth.
virilidád,	manhood.
senectúd, } vejéz, }	old age.

Qualities of the body.—Calidádes del cuérpo.

La salúd,	health.
fuérza,	strength.
debilidád.	'weakness
hermosúra,	beauty.
fealdád,	ugliness.
El gárbo,	good presence.
brío,	sprightliness.
ríco tálle,	fine stature.

Defects in the human body.—
Deféctos del cuérpo humáno.

La fealdád,	deformity.
Las arrúgas,	wrinkles.
pécas,	freckles.
lagáñas,	blear eyes.
La verrúga,	wart.
El lunár,	mole.
La núbe en el ójo,	a pearl in the eye.
Las cosquíllas,	tickling.
La cataráta,	. cataract.
ceguedád, or } ceguéra, }	blindness.
magrúra,	leanness.
El ciégo,	blind.
tuérto,	one-eyed.
cójo,	lame.
La cojéz,	lameness.
El tartamúdo,	stammerer.
La corcóva,	crookedness.
El cálvo,	bald.
rómo,	flat-nosed.
estropeádo,	crippled.
tullído,	benumbed.
zúrdo,	left-handed.
bízco, bisójo,	squinting.
mánco,	maimed of one hand or arm.
múdo,	dumb.
sórdo,	deaf.

---

*Virtues and vices, good and
bad qualities of men.*—
Virtúdes y vícios, buénas
y málas calidádes de los
hómbres.

El recatádo,	cautious, modest.
diéstro,	dexterous.
dócil,	docile.

El galán,	*gallant.*	El misericordióso,	*merciful.*
símple,	*harmless.*	paciénte,	*patient.*
agúdo,	*sharp.*	religióso,	*religious.*
vívo,	*sprightly.*	ambicióso,	*ambitious.*
sutíl,	*subtle.*	avariénto,	*covetous.*
chocarréro,	*buffoon.*	aváro,	*miser.*
nécio,	*foolish.*	sobérbio,	*proud.*
astúto,	*crafty.*	hipócrita,	*hypocrite.*
lóco,	*mad.*	cohárde,	*coward.*
malicióso,	*malicious.*	holgazán,	*lazy, idle.*
temeróso	*fearful.*	altívo,	*haughty.*
espantadízo,	*easy to be*	chismóso,	*tale-bearer.*
	frightened, skittish.	aduladór,	*flatterer.*
valiénte,	*brave*	golóso,	*glutton.*
tónto,	*stupid.*	desleál,	*treacherous.*
fantástico,	*fantastical.*	desagradecído,	*ungrate-*
embustéro,	*deceitful.*		*ful.*
groséro,	*clownish.*	inhumáno,	*inhuman.*
revoltóso,	*mutinous.*	insolénte,	*insolent.*
bién criádo,	*well-bred.*	lujurióso,	*lewd.*
cortés,	*courteous.*	porfiádo,	*obstinate.*
gráve,	*grave.*	perezóso,	*slothful.*
jústo,	*just.*	prúdigo,	*prodigal.*
prudénte,	*discreet.*	váno,	*vain.*
desvergonzádo,	*impudent.*	mugeriégo,	*given to*
fogóso,	*fiery.*		*women.*
impertinénte,	*impertinent.*	atrevído,	*bold.*
importúno,	*troublesome.*	colérico,	*passionate.*
ligéro,	*light.*	rabióso,	*outrageous.*
descuidádo,	*careless.*	alégre,	*merry.*
temerário	*rash.*	ufáno,	*arrogant.*
afáble,	*affable.*	indecíso,	*irresolute.*
amigáble,	*friendly.*	zelóso,	*jealous.*
bizárro,	*brave.*	adúltero,	*adulterer.*
caritatívo,	*charitable.*	rufián,	*ruffian.*
cásto,	*chaste.*	matadór,	*killer, murderer.*
constánte,	*constant.*	salteadór,	*highwayman.*
devóto,	*devout.*	juradór,	*swearer.*
diligénte,	*diligent.*	calumniadór,	*slanderer.*
fiél,	*faithful.*	murmuradór,	*censurer.*
generóso,	*generous.*	hechicéro,	*sorcerer.*
humílde,	*humble.*	trampóso,	*cheat.*

El incestuóso,	*incestuous.*	El pan de cebáda,	*barley bread.*
ladrón,	*thief.*		
ratéro,	*pickpocket.*	pan de avéna,	*oaten bread.*
mentiróso,	*liar.*	pan de míjo,	*millet bread.*
perjúro,	*perjurer.*	pan de maíz,	*indian corn*
pérfido,	*perfidious.*		*bread.*
profáno,	*profane.*	pan de levadúra,	*leavened*
rebélde,	*rebel.*		*bread.*
sacrílego,	*sacrilegious.*	bizcócho,	*biscuit.*
traidór,	*traitor.*	La migája de pan,	*crumb of*
malvúdo,	*wicked.*		*bread.*
		mása,	*dough.*
		tórta,	*cake* or *loaf.*

Of eating and drinking.—
Del comér y bebér.

		rósca,	*roll.*
La comída,	*dinner.*	El buñuélo,	*fritter.*
céna,	*supper.*	La empanáda,	*meat pie.*
El almuérzo,	*breakfast.*	cárne,	*meat.*
La meriénda,	*luncheon.*	tárta ó el pastelíto,	*tart.*
colación,	*collation.*	El cocído,	*boiled meat*
El banquéte,	*entertainment.*	asádo,	*roasted meat*
convidádo,	*guest.*	estofádo,	*stewed meat*
convíte,	*feast.*	La cárne fríta,	*fried meat.*
La hámbre,	*hunger.*	carbonáda,	*broiled meat.*
séd,	*thirst.*	pepitória	*giblets.*
El borrácho,	*drunkard.*	El picadíllo,	*hash.*
buén bebedór,	*hard drinker.*	La cecína,	*hung meat.*
buén apetíto }	*good appetite.*	El perníl, el jamón,	*ham.*
Las buénas gánas, }		carnéro,	*mutton.*
El glotón,	*glutton.*	La váca,	*beef.*
pan,	*bread.*	El cordéro,	*lamb.*
pan blánco,	*white bread.*	La ternéra,	*veal.*
pan candiál,	*the whitest bread.*	El puérco,	*pork.*
		cabríto,	*kid.*
pan bázo,	*brown bread.*	tocíno,	*bacon.*
molléte,	*hot loaf.*	La piérna de carnéro,	*leg of mutton.*
pan frésco,	*new bread.*	El brazuélo de carnéro,	*shoulder of mutton.*
pan de tódo trígo,	*wheaten bread.*	lómo,	*loin.*
		pécho,	*breast.*
pan de centéno,	*rye bread.*	Las mános de carnéro,	*sheep's trotters.*

La ruéda de ternéra — *fillet of veal.*

asadúra, — *the pluck.*

salchícha, — *sausage.*

El salchichón, — *big sausage.*

La morcílla, — *blood pudding.*

longaníza, — *long sausage.*

El pastél, — *pie, pastry.*

cáldo, — *broth.*

La sópa, — *soup.*

El potáge, — *pottage.*

Las pápas, } — *any sort of*
púches, } — *pap.*

El písto, — *jelly broth.*

La cárne fiámbre, — *cold meat.*

léche, — *milk.*

náta, — *cream.*

El suéro, — *whey.*

La mantéca, — *butter.*

El quéso, — *cheese.*

quéso frésco, — *new cheese.*

requesón, — *curds.*

cuájo, — *rennet.*

La cuajáda, — *milk hardened with rennet.*

El huévo, — *the egg.*

La yéma de huévo, — *the yolk of an egg.*

clára de huévo — *the white of an egg.*

El huévo blándo, — *soft egg.*

huévo dúro, — *hard egg.*

huévo frésco, — *new egg.*

huévo en cáscara, — *egg in the shell.*

huévo cocído, — *boiled egg.*

huévo asádo, — *roasted egg.*

huévo estrelládo, — *fried egg.*

huévo huéro, — *addle egg.*

El huévo empolládo, — *egg with a chicken in it.*

Los huévos de pescádo, — *the spawn of fish.*

huévos megídos, — *yolks of eggs stewed with wine and sugar.*

huévos y torréznos, — *collops and eggs.*

huévos revuéltos, — *buttered eggs.*

La tortílla de huévos, — *omelet.*

Los huévos de faltriquéra, — *yolks of eggs in shells of sugar.*

huévos hiládos, — *sweet eggs spun out.*

El sazonamiénto, — *seasoning.*

La salmuéra, — *brine.*

Las espécias, — *spices.*

La pimiénta, — *pepper.*

El gengíbre, — *ginger.*

Los clavíllos, — *cloves.*

La canéla, — *cinnamon.*

nuez moscáda, — *nutmeg.*

flor de espécia, — *mace.*

mostáza. — *mustard.*

El agráz, — *verjuice.*

vinágre, — *vinegar.*

acéite, — *oil.*

La sal, — *salt.*

El azúcar, — *sugar.*

Los escabéches, — *pickles.*

dúlces — *sweetmeats*

almíbares, — *preserves.*

El almíbar, — *sugar boiled.*

jarábe, — *syrup.*

Los confítes, — *comfits.*

Las consérvas, — *conserves.*

mermeláda, — *marmelade.*

peráda, — *pears preserved.*

Las alcorcíllas, } aniseed su-
  pastíllas,   }   gar.
La naranjáda,   candied or-
                    anges.
El turrón,   sweetmeat.
Los barquíllos ó las suplica-
  ciónes   sweet wafers.
  buñuélos,   puffs.
La bebída,   drink.
El víno,   wine.
  víno púro, •   pure wine.
  víno vuélto,   pricked wine.
  víno moscatél, muscatell
                    wine.
  vínto tínto,   red wine.
  víno blánco,   white wine.
  víno alóque,   pale wine.
  víno claréte, claret wine.
  víno dúlce   y picánte,
                sweet and tart wine.
  víno añéjo,   old wine.
  víno ligéro,   light wine.
  vinázo,   strong wine.
  malvasía,   malmsey.
  água pié,   mixture of must
                   and water.
La hez del víno, wine lees.
El aguardiénte,   brandy.
La cervéza,   beer.
  sídra,   cider.
  alója,   mead, metheglin.
El chocoláte,   • chocolate.
  té,   tea.
La horcháta,   orgeat.
  limonáda,   lemonade.
  mistéla,   anise brandy.
El café, · _____   coffee.

Of Clothes.—De los vestídos.

El páño,   cloth.
  páño fíno,   fine cloth.

El páño tundído, shorn cloth.
La grána,   }
  escarláta,   }   scarlet.
  rája,   rash cloth.
El sayál,'   sackcloth.
La frísa,   frieze.
  estaméña,   serge.
  estófa,   stuff.
El tafetán,   taffety.
  ráso, ráso líso, satin.
  tércio pélo,   velvet.
  damásco,   damask.
  brocádo,   brocade.
  gorgorán,   grogram.
La gása,   gauze.
Las laníllas,   drugget.
El cendál,   crape.
  camelóte,   camblet.
La téla de óro, cloth of gold.
El trípe,   shag.
  algodón,   cotton.
  fustán,   fustian.
La muselína,   muslin.
El líno,   flax.
  liénzo,   linen.
  cambrái,   cambrick.
La holánda,   holland.
El ruán,   French linen
  cáñamo.   hemp.
  terlíz,   ticken.
  calicút,   calico.
  fiéltro,   felt
  angéo,   canvass
La lóna,   sailcloth
  bayéta,   baize
  lúna,   wool.
El estámbre,   worsted.
La séda,   silk.
El bocací,   buckram.
Úna jóya,   a jewel
  hebílla,   a buckle.
Los alamáres,   loops on coats.

Un ojál,	a button-hole.	Úna agujéta,	a point.
La bordadúra,	embroidery.	faltriquéra,	a pocket.
Un botón,	a button.	Un bolsillo,	a purse.
Úna fránja, } Un fléque, }	a fringe.	Las médias,	stockings.
		lígas,	garters.
Las púntas, } Los encáges, }	lace.	Los zapátos,	shoes.
		escarpínes,	pumps, socks.
Úna cínta,	a ribbon.	Las chinélas,	slippers.
Un listón,	a broad ribbon.	Un borceguí,	a buskin.
pasamáno,	gold or silver lace.	Las bótas, ·	boots.
		poláinas,	spatterdashes.
ribéte,	an edging.	espuélas,	spurs.
sombréro,	a hat.	Los púños,	wristbands.
La cópa del sombréro,	the crown of the hat.	Las vuéltas,	ruffles.
		Los vuélos,	cuffs.
ála ó fálda del sombréro,	the brim of the hat.	Un tahalí,	a shoulder-belt.
		Únos tíros,	a waist-belt.
El torzál ó la trencílla,	the hat-band.	Úná espáda,	a sword.
		dága,	a dagger
El plumáge,	feathers.	cápa,	a cloak.
Un bonéte,	a cap.	casúca,	a coat.
górro de nóche,	a night-cap.	Un guánte,	a glove.
		ceñidór,	a girdle.
Úna górra,	an old fashioned cap.	Úna pelúca,	a round wig.
		Un peluquín,	a bag wig.
caperúza,	a sort of cap.	pañuélo,	a pocket hand-kerchief.
montéra,	a hunting cap.		
camísa,	a shirt.	Úna rópa, } Un ropón, } Úna báta, }	a gown.
almílla, chúpa,	a waist-coat.		
Los calzoncíllos,	drawers.	rópa de levantár,	a morning gown.
Un jubón,	a doublet.		
Úna mánga,	a sleeve.	Un pellíco, } Úna zamárra, }	a shepherd's jerkin.
mánga perdída,	a hanging sleeve.		
Las faldíllas de jubón,	the skirts of a jacket.		

For women.—**Pára mugéres.**

Los calzónes,	breeches.	Un tocádo, } Úna cófia, } escófia, }	a head-dress, a cap.
Úna valóna,	a tucker, a band.		
Un corbatín,	a neckcloth.		
cuéllo,	a collar.		
coléto,	a buff coat.	Un mánto,	a veil.

Úna sáya, basquíña,	a black gown or petticoat.	Únos zarcíllos, pendiéntes,	ear-rings. pendants.
Un guardapiés, Únas enáguas,	an upper petticoat.	La gargantílla,	neck-lace.
Un avantál, devantál,	an apron.	Únas maníllas, Únos brazalétes,	bracelets.
guárda sol, quíta sol,	a parasol.	Únas sortíjas, Únos anillos,	rings.
parágua,	an umbrella.	Las pedrerías,	precious stones.
relój,	a watch.	Un abaníco,	a fan.
Únas tablíllas,	tables.	Las calcétas,	thread stockings.
Un espéjo,	a looking-glass.	El peinadór,	combing cloth.
Úna bugéta,	a little box.	Los pañáles,	swaddling clouts.
Un manguito,	a muff.	Úna fája,	a band, a roller.
Úna cotílla,	stays.	Los juguétes,	play-things.
camísa,	a shift.	Úna cúna,	a cradle.
mantilla,	a mantle.	áma de léche,	a wet nurse.
báta,	a gown.		
Un chapín,	a clog.	Los díges,	toys.

[*The beasts, fowls, fishes, fruits, herbs, roots, &c. that are eatable, will be found under their respective names.— Los animáles, áves, péces, frútas, yérbas, raíces, &c. comestíbles, se hallarán debájo de sus nómbres respectívos.]

Beasts.—Béstias.		Un corderíco,	a lambkin.
		búrro,	
Úna béstia mánsa	a tame beast.	borríco, ásno,	an ass.
béstia feróz,	a wild beast.	Úna búrra, borríca,	a she ass.
El ganádo,	cattle.	Un puérco, marráno,	a hog.
ganádo mayór,	large cattle.	lechón, lechoncíllo,	a pig.
		jabalí,	a wild boar.
Un tóro,	a bull.	Úna háca,	a pony, a
ternéro ó becérro,	a calf.	haquílla,	colt.
Úna ternéra,	a heifer.	Un búfalo	a buffalo.
Un buéy,	an ox.	úna yégua,	a mare.
carnéro,	a sheep.	yegüecílla,	a young mare.
Úna ovéja,	an ewe.	Un cabállo,	a horse
Un cordéro,	a lamb.	caméllo,	a camel.

Un gáto, a cat.
garañón, a stallion.
cabállo castrádo, a gelding.
cabállo entéro, a stone-horse.
cabállo corredór, a race-horse.
cabállo de máno, a led horse.
cabállo de pósta, a post horse.
cabállo de alquilér, a hackney horse.
cabállo rebélde, a restive horse.
cabállo desbocádo, a hard-mouthed horse.
cabállo medróso, a starting horse.
cabállo tropezadór, a stumbling horse.
cabállo que sacúde, a jolting horse.
cabállo asmático, a broken winded horse.
cabállo indómito, a horse that cannot be tamed.
cabállo saltadór, a leaping horse.
cabállo báyo, a bay horse.
báyo castáño, a chestnut bay.
báyo oscúro, a brown bay,
báyo dorádo, a bright bay.
picázo, a pyed horse.
rúcio rodádo, a dapple grey.
de colór de gamúza, cream colour.
alazán, a sorrel.

Un alazán tostádo, a dark sorrel.
ovéro, a speckled white horse.
rubicán, a grey horse.
Úna cábra, a she goat.
Un cabríto, a kid.
cabrón, a he goat.
pérro, a dog.
pérro de cáza, a hound.
pérro de muéstra, a setter.
sabuéso, a blood hound.
podénco, mongrel grey hound.
perdiguéro, a pointer.
pérro calládo, a hound that does not open well.
pérro bájo, a terrier.
gálgo, a greyhound.
lebrél, a sort of fierce dogs resembling greyhounds, common in Ireland.
pérro ventór, a finder.
pérro de água, or lamedíllo, a water-dog.
mastín, a mastiff.
pérro de pastór, a shepherd's dog.
pérro veladór, a house dog.
perríllo de fálda, a lap-dog.
aláno ó dógo, a bull-dog.
barbadíllo, a spaniel.
pérro raposéro, or jatéo, small setting dog for fox hunting.
gózque, } a little dog, a
gozquéjo, } turnspit.
conéjo, a rabbit.
Úna hacanéa, a pad.
Un muléto, a young mule.

Un múlo,   a he mule.
Úna múla,   a she mule.
Un pótro,   a colt.
    pollíno,   an ass's colt.
    ciérvo,   a stag.
    venádo,   a deer.
    gámo,   a fallow deer.
    cachórro de ciérvo, a fawn.
Las ástas de ciérvo, the horns
                    of a deer.
El rástro ó las pisádas de ci-
    érvo,   the track of a stag.
Úna comadréja,   a weasel.
Un tejón,   a badger.
Úna gamúza,   a wild goat.
    cábra montés, a roebuck.
Un gáto de algália, a civet-cat.
Úna dáma,   a doe.
    ardílla,   a squirrel.
Un elefánte,   an elephant.
Úna fuína,   a martin.
    gardúña,   a pole-cat.
Un móno,   a monkey.
    gímio,   an ape.
    armínio ó armíño,   an er-
                         mine.
    erízo,   a hedge-hog.
Úna liébre,   a hare.
    liebrecílla,   a leveret.
Un lirón.   a dormouse.
Úna ráta,   a rat.
    zórra ó rapósa,   a fox.
Un ratón,   a mouse.
    tópo,   a mole.
Úna hiéna,   a hyena.
Un leopárdo,   a leopard.
    león,   a lion.
Úna leóna,   a lioness.
Un leoncíllo,   a lion's whelp.
    lóbo,   a wolf.
    lóbo cervál,   a lynx.
    óso   a bear.

Un osíllo,   a bear's cub.
Úna pantéra,   a panther.
Un rinocerónte, a rhinoceros.
    tígre,   a, tiger.
    jabalí, puérco montés,   a
                     wild boar.
Las navájas ó los colmíllos de
    jabalí,   the tusks of a wild
                        boar.
El cochiníllo de jabalí,   the
                pig of a wild boar.
La jabalína,   a wild sow.

Creatures that creep on the
    earth.—Animáles que se
    arrástran.

Úna serpiénte,   a serpent.
    serpiénte aláda, a flying
                       serpent.
Un dragón,   a dragon.
    aspíd,   an asp.
Úna culébra,   a snake.
Un cocodrílo,   a crocodile.
    caimán,   an alligator.
Úna lagartíja,   }
    salamanquésa,   } a lizard.
Un lagárto,   }
Una víbora.   a viper.
Un viborézno, a young viper.

Amphibious   creatures.—Ani-
    máles anfíbios.

Un bívaro or castór, a beaver
                     or castor.
Úna nútria, or nútra, an otter.
Un hipopótamo,   a river-
                       horse.
Úna tortúga,   a tortoise

Un galápago, *a land tortoise.*
Una fóca marína, *sea calf.*

Insects.—Sabandíjas.

Una aráña,	*a spider.*
arañuéla,	*a little spider.*
carcóma,	*a wood worm.*
orúga,	*a caterpillar.*
Un aradór,	*a hand-worm.*
sápo,	*a toad.*
escarabájo,	*a beetle.*
caracól,	*a snail.*
Una hormíga,	*an ant, a pis-mire.*
rána,	*a frog*
Un gríllo,	*a cricket.*
revoltón,	*an insect that spoils grape vines.*
piójo,	*a louse.*
Una liéndre,	*a nit.*
púlga,	*a flea.*
chínche,	*a bug.*
langósta,	*a locust.*
Un escorpión, ⎫ alacrán, ⎭	*a scorpion.*
Una tarántula,	*a tarantula.*
polílla	*a moth.*
mósca,	*a fly.*
avíspa,	*a wasp.*
Un avispón,	*a large wasp.*
Una abéja,	*a bee.*
Un moscón, ⎫ Una moscárda, ⎭	*an ox-fly.*
Un zángano,	*a drone.*
tábano,	*a hornet.*
Una mósca de bérro,	*gad fly.*
cigárra,	*a balm cricket.*
lucérna or luciérnaga,	*a glow worm.*
Una maripósa,	*a butterfly.*

Una vaquílla de diós, *a lady-bird.*
Un zancúdo, *a gnat.*
enjámbre, *a swarm.*

Birds.—Áves.

Una águila,	*an eagle.*
Un aguilúcho,	*an eaglet.*
buítre,	*a vulture.*
esmerejón,	*a merlin.*
gavilán,	*a sparrow-hawk.*
mochuélo,	*a horn owl.*
halcón,	*a falcon.*
torzuélo, ⎫ halcón, ⎭	*a male falcon, or hawk.*
girifálte,	*a ger-falcon.*
alcotán,	*a lanner.*
sácre,	*a sacre, a kind of hawk.*
Una gárza,	*a heron.*
garzóta,	*a small heron.*
Un miláno,	*a kite.*
cuérvo,	*a crow or raven.*
Una cornéja,	*a jack-daw.*
calándria,	*a lark.*
Un aguzaniéve,	*a wagtail.*
canário,	*a canary bird.*
gilguéro,	*a linnet*
Un mírlo, ⎫ Una mérla, ⎬ mírla, ⎭	*a blackbird.*
Un pinzón,	*a chaffinch.*
ruiscñór,	*a nightingale*
verderón,	*a green-bird.*
papagáyo, ⎫ lóro, ⎬ Una cotórra, ⎭	*a parrot.*
urráca,	*a magpie.*
Un grájo,	*a daw.*
Una lechúza,	*an owl.*
Una chóva,	*a chough.*

Un murciélago,   *a bat.*
Un mochuélo,   *horn-owl.*
Úna comáya,   *a night-crow.*
Un grájo, *a jackdaw* or *chough.*
Úna chotacábras,   *a goat-sucker.*
Un ánade,   *a wild duck.*
Úna cercéta,   *a teal.*
Un chorlíto,   *a grey-plover.*
cuérvo maríno,   *a cormorant.*
páto,   *a duck.*
gánso, }   *a goose.*
ánsar, }
ansarón,   *a large goose.*
cernícalo, *a kestrel, small hawk.*
Úna fúlga,   *a moor-hen.*
Un avión,   *a martin.*
Una gabióta,   *a gull.*
Un somorgujón,   *a diver.*
Úna chócha, }   *a wood-*
gallinaciéga, }   *cock.*
Un tórdo,   *a sea thrush.*
estorníno,   *a starling.*
Úna codorníz,   *a quail.*
Un capón,   *a capon.*
gállo,   *a cock.*
Úna gallína,   *a hen.*
Un póllo,   *a chicken.*
Úna pólla,   *a pullet.*
Un pávo, }   *a turkey.*
Úna páva, }
Un francolín, *a godwit, moor-cock.*
faisán,   *a pheasant.*
zorzál,   *a thrush.*
horteláno,   *an ortolan.*
gorrión,   *a sparrow.*
palómo,   *a pigeon.*
Úna perdíz,   *a partridge.*
palóma,   *a dove.*
tórtola,   *turtle dove.*

Un pichón, }   *a young pig-*
palomíno, }   *eon.*
Un alción,   *a king-fisher.*
Úna golondrína,   *a swallow.*
Un avestrúz,   *an ostrich.*
Úna cigüéña,   *a stork.*
Un cuclíllo,   *a cuckoo.*
císne,   *a swan.*
petorójo,   *a robin red-breast.*
Úna grúlla,   *a crane.*
pezpíta,   *a wagtail.*
Un frailecíllo,   *a lapwing.*
Úna oropéndola,   *a witwall.*
Un vencéjo,   *a martlett.*
abejarúco,   *a bee eater.*
Úna avútárda,   *a bustard.*
Un mírlo, *black bird, an ousel.*
pelicáno,   *a pelican*
feníx,   *a phœnix.*
píca madéra, *a woodpecker.*
píco vérde, *a green beak.*
chorlíto,   *a plover.*
reyezuélo,   *a wren.*
mérgo,   *a puffin*

Parts of a bird.—Pártes de úna Áve.

El píco,   *the beak.*
Úna plúma,   *a feather.*
El plumón,   *the down.*
ála,   *wing.*
Los cañónes, }   *quills.*
Las plúmas, }
El pié,   *the foot.*
La cola,   *the tail.*
El búche,   *the craw.*
Las gárras, } *claws, or tal-*
úñas, }   *ons*
La rabadílla,   *the rump.*
pechúga,   *the breast.*
entrepechúga, *the flesh of the bridge.*

Fishes.—Péces.

Un albúrno,	*a bleak.*
sábalo,	*a shad.*
úna anchóva,	*an anchovy.*
anguíla,	*an eel.*
balléna,	*a whale*
Un bárbo,	*a barbel.*
méro,	*a halibut.*
lúcio,	*a pike.*
úna cárpa,	*a carp*
Un calamár,	*a calamary.*
talpáire,	*a miller's thumb.*
cabállo marino,	*a sea-horse.*
cóngrio,	*a conger.*
delfín,	*a dolphin.*
dorádo,	*a gilt-back.*
La doradílla,	*the gold-fish.*
Un lenguádo,	*a sole.*
úna langósta,	*a lobster.*
Un esturión,	*a sturgeon.*
góbio,	*a gudgeon.*
arénque,	*a herring.*
úna óstra, óstia,	*an oyster.*
lampréa,	*a lamprey.*
langostín,	*a prawn.*
lobína,	*a bass.*
sárda,	*a mackerel.*
marsópa,	*a porpoise.*
El abadéjo, La merlúza, El bacalláo,	*cod-fish.*
úna alméja,	*a muscle.*
ortíga pez,	*a stinging fish.*
pérca,	*a perch*
Un púlpo,	*a polypus.*
úna ráya,	*a thornback.*
líza,	*a skate.*
úna sardína,	*a pilchard.*
Un salmón,	*salmon.*

úna trúcha,	*trout*
gíbia,	*cuttle fish.*
ténca,	*a tench.*
Uu atún,	*a tunny-fish.*
úna tremiélga,	*a torpedo.*
Un rodabállo,	*a turbot.*

Parts of a fish.—Pártes de un pez.

El hocico,	*the snout.*
Las agállas,	*the gills.*
álas,	*the fins.*
escámas,	*the scales.*
espínas,	*the bones.*
La cóncha,	*the shell.*
Los huévos de pez,	*the hard roe.*
La léche,	*the soft roe.*

Trees.—Árboles.

Un albaricóque,	*an apricot-tree.*
alméndro,	*an almond-tree.*
durázno,	*a peach-tree.*
guíndo,	*a cherry-tree.*
cerézo,	*a heart cherry-tree.*
castáño,	*a chestnut-tree.*
cídro,	*a citron-tree.*
membrilléro,	*a quince-tree.*
serbál,	*a service-tree.*
Úna pálma,	*a palm-tree.*
higuéra,	*a fig-tree.*
Un azuféifo,	*a jujub-tree.*
granádo,	*a pomegranate-tree.*
limón,	*a lemon-tree.*
morál,	*a mulberry-tree.*
níspero,	*a medlar-tree.*
avelláno,	*a hazel-nut-tree.*

24

Un nogál,	a walnut-tree.	La zárza,	the blackberry bush.
olívo, aceitáno,	an olive-tree.	hiniésta,	broom.
acebúche,	a wild-olive-tree.	úva espína,	gooseberry-bush.
narúnjo,	an orange-tree.	adélfa,	rose bay.
albérchigo, pérsigo,	a peach-tree.	yédra,	ivy.
ciruélo,	a plum-tree.	El brúsco,	butcher's broom.
perál,	a pear-tree.	La regalíz,	liquorice
manzáno,	an apple-tree.	El alhocígo,	the pistachio-tree
álamo négro,	black-poplar-tree.	roméro,	rosemary.
		rosál,	rose-tree.
álamo blánco,	white-poplar-tree.	La sabína,	savin.
		El tamaríz,	tamarisk-tree.
cédro,	a cedar-tree.	La alhéña,	privet.
alíso,	an alder-tree.	víña,	vine.
úna encína,	ever-green-oak.	lubrúsca,	wild vine.
Un róble,	an oak-tree.	úna párra,	a wall vine.
El córno,	the cornel-tree.	El mírto, arrayán	myrtle.
ciprés,	the cypress-tree.	úna párra de corínto,	currant-tree.
ébano,	the ebony-tree		
árce,	the maple-tree.		
La háya,	the beech-tree.	Fruits.—Frútas.	
El frésno,	the ash-tree.	Un albericóque,	an apricot.
acébo,	the holly-tree.	úna alméndra,	an almond.
téjo,	the yew-tree.	Un madróño,	a wild strawberry.
laurél,	the laurel-tree.		
alcornóque,	the cork-tree.	durázno,	a peach.
ólmo,	the elm-tree.	úna guínda,	a cherry.
píno,	the pine or fir-tree.	ceréza,	a heart-cherry.
Un plántano,	a plantain-tree.	castáña,	a chestnut.
sáuce, saúz,	a willow-tree.	cídra,	a citron.
tílo, úna téja,	a linden-tree.	Un membríllo,	a quince.
		úna sérba,	service-apple.
		Un dátil,	date
		hígo,	a fig.
Shrubs.—Mátas.		úna bréva,	early fig.
El ágno cásto,	agnus castus.	azufáifa,	a jujub.
alméz,	the lote-tree.	granáda,	a pomegranate.
bálsamo,	the balsam.	Un limón,	a lemon.
boj,	the box-tree.	úna móra,	a mulberry.
La mádresélva,	the honey-suckle.	níspola,	a medlar.
		avellána,	a filbert.

Úna nuéz, *a walnut.*
aceitúna, *an olive.*
naránja, *an orange.*
ciruéla, *a plum.*
ciruéla pása, *a prune.*
péra, *a pear.*
bergamóta, *a bergamot.*
manzána, *an apple.*
camuésa, *a pippin.*
manzána de San Juán, *St. John's apple.*
Un melón, *a melon.*
Úna bellóta, *an acorn.*
algarróba, *a carob.*
alcapárra, *a caper.*
zarzamóra, *a blackberry.*
Un tamaríndo, *a tamarind.*
piñón, *a nut of pine trees.*
Úna úva, *a grape.*
cáscara de nuéz, &c. *a shell of ◦ nut, &c.*
téla de granáda, *film of a pomegranate.*
Un pimpóllo, *a sucker, or sprout of a vine.*
sarmiénto, *a twig of a vine.*
La yéma de víña, *the bud of a vine.*
Los zarcíllos de la vid, *the tendrils of a vine.*
Un pámpano, *a vine branch.*
renuévo, *a young shoot of a vine.*
racímo de úvas, *a bunch of grapes.*
Úna pepíta de la úva, *a grape-stone.*
Podár, *to prune a vine.*
Cavár, *to lay open the roots.*
Rodrigár, *to prop a vine.*
El rodrigón, *the prop.*

Terciár la víña, *to dig a third time about a vine.*
Rozár, *to weed.*
úna raíz, *a root.*
Las hébras de raíz, *the fibres of a root.*
arraigár, *to take root.*
El trónco, *the trunk of a tree.*
Un renuévo, *a sprig.*
La cortéza del árbol, *the bark.*
El zúmo, *the sap.*
móho, *the moss.*
rámo, *the branch.*
úna hója, *a leaf.*
El huéso de frúta, *the stone of fruit.*
Las mondadúras de frúta, *the parings of fruit.*
El pezón, *the stalk*
ingerír, *to ingraft.*
ingerír de cañúto, *to inoculate.*
Un ingérto, *a graft.*
La pepíta, *the seed of fruit.*

Corn and its parts.—Trígos y sus pártes.

El trígo, *wheat.*
El candiál, *the best wheat.*
trígo rubión, *red wheat*
La escándia, *bearded wheat.*
El herrén, *meslin.*
La espélta, *spelt.*
El centéno, *rye*
La cebáda, *barley.*
avéna, *oats.*
El arróz, *rice.*
míjo, *millet.*
maíz, *Indian corn.*
Las legúmbres, *pulse.*
Un averjón, *a large vetch.*
Los garbánzos, *Spanish peas.*

Las judías, *kidney-beans.*
Los guisántes, *peas.*
úna húba, *a horse-bean.*
lentéja, *a lentil.*
Un altramúz, *a lupine.*
Un frijól, *French bean.*
Las cicérchas, *wild tares.*
La cáscara, *the shell.*
El holléjo, *the husk.*

Roots, plants, and herbs.—
Raíces, plántas, é yérbas.
El agénjo, *wormwood.*
ápio, *celery.*
ájo, *garlick.*
enéldo, *dill.*
anís, *aniseed.*
La alegría, *sesame.*
Los armuélles, *orach or golden flowers.*
úna alcachófa, *an artichoke.*
Un espárrago, *asparagus.*
El abrótano, *southernwood.*
La acélga, *white beet.*
Un blédo, *a blite.*
La borrája, *borage.*
Las zanahórias, *carrots.*
El peregíl, perifóllo, } *chervil.*
Un hóngo, úna séta, } *a mushroom.*
chirivín, *a parsnep.*
chicória, endívia, escaróla, } *succory, endive.*
col, bérza, *a cabbage.*
Un repóllo, *round head cabbage.*
úna bérza créspa, *a savoy.*
Un brotón, *a sprout.*
úna coliflór, *a cauliflower.*
calabáza *a pumpkin*
Un pepíno, *a cucumber.*

Un culántro, *coriander.*
culantríllo, *capillaire.*
peregíl maríno, *samphire*
mastuérzo, *garden cresses.*
úna escalóna, *a scallion.*
espináca, *spinage.*
Un hinójo, *fennel.*
hoblón, *hops.*
úna lechúga murciána, ó cerrája, *a wild-jagged lettuce.*
lechúga créspa, *a curled lettuce*
Un nábo, *a turnip.*
nabál, *a turnip field.*
úna cebólla, *an onion.*
acetósa, acedéra, } *sorrel.*
romáza, *long sorrel.*
El peregíl, *parsley.*
Un puérro, *a leek*
úna verdológa, *purslain.*
únos ruipónces, *rampions.*
úna roquéta, *rocket.*
rúda, *rue.*
sálvia, *sage.*
criadílla de tiérra, *a truffle.*
mejorána, *sweet marjoram.*
Un agaríco, *agarick.*
úna agrimónia, *agrimony.*
El acíbar, *juice from the aloes.*
La angélica, *angelica.*
celidónia, *celandine.*
betónica, *betony.*
bistórta, *snakewort.*
manzanílla, *camomile.*
El culantríllo de pózo, *maiden hair.*
La centinódia, *centinody.*
verbásca, El gordolóbo, } *wolf blade, or great lung wort.*

La amapóla, *poppy.*
El díctamo, *dittany.*
La coníza pulguéra, *fleabane.*
El eléboro *hellebore.*
tártago, *spurge.*
La genciána, *gentian.*
El camédrio, *germander.*
La gráma, *dog's grass.*
yérba puntéra, *house-leek.*
El beléño, *hen bane.*
marrúbio, *hore hound.*
La matricária, *feverfew.*
Las málvas, *mallows.*
La coróna de réy, *melilot.*
El torongíl, *balm.*
mercuriál, *mercury.*
Las milhójas, ⎫
Un milenránia, ⎭ *mill-foil.*
El corazoncíllo, *St. Johns wort, or grass.*
nárdo, *spikenard.*
tabáco, *tobacco.*
orégano, *wild marjoram.*
La higuéra, *fig-tree.*
parietária, *pellitory.*
cepacabállo, ⎫ *ground*
uña de cabállo, ⎭ *thistle.*
adormidéra, *poppy.*
rósa montés, *peony.*
El plántano, *plantain.*
polipodio, *polypody.*
agenúz, ⎫ *bishopswort.*
La neguílla, ⎭
cidronéla, *balm mint.*
El poléo, *pennyroyal.*
La sanguinária, *bloodwort.*
sanícula, *sanicle.*
El satirión, *ragwort.*
La saxifrága, *saxifrage.*
escabiósa, *scabwort.*

La escamonéa, *scammony.*
cebólla albarrána *wild onion.*
séna, *senna.*
yérba cána, *groundsel.*
valeriána, *valerian.*
verbéna, *vervain.*
El llantén, *grass plantain.*
siéte en ráma, *sept-foil.*
muérdago, *misletoe.*
acánto, ⎫ *bears-foot.*
La blánca urcína, ⎬
yérba gigánta, ⎭
El acónito, *wolfsbane.*
Las óvas del mar, *sea weed.*
La cóla de cabállo, *horse-tail.*
El espliégo, ⎫ *lavender.*
La alhucéma, ⎭
El amór del horteláno, ⎫ *bur-dock.*
los lampázos, ⎭
El peregíl de água, *water-parsley.*
El tamaríz silvéstre, *tamarisk shrub.*
asarabácara, *asarabacca.*
calaménto, *calamint.*
La cáña, *the reed.*
doradílla, *spleenswort.*
El cáñamo, *hemp.*
líno, *flax*
La cicúta, *hemlock.*
El comíno, *cummin.*
La yérba de ciérva, *hart's fodder.*
El helécho, *fern.*
La palomílla, *fumitory.*
Los amóres sécos, ⎫ *clover grass.*
El treból, ⎭
El yésgo, *danewort, dwarf elder.*
júnco, *rush*

24*

La cerrája, *sow-thistle.*
mandrágora, *mandrake.*
yérba móra, *nightshade.*
correhuéla, *knot-grass.*
ortíga, *nettle.*
El ruibárbo, *rhubarb.*
lepídio, *pepperwort.*
El alazór, ⎫
azafrán, ⎭ *saffron.*
La jabonéra, *soap-wort.*
alfálfa, *darnel or cockle.*
La albaháca, *sweet basil.*
yérba buéna, *mint.*
El serpól, *wild thyme*
tomíllo, *thyme.*

———

Flowers.—Flóres.

El amaránto, *amaranth.*
La anémone, *anemone.*
El jacínto, *hyacinth.*
jazmín, *jessamine.*
junquíllo, *jonquil.*
La azucéna, *the lily.*
máya, *the daisy.*
El narcíso, *daffodil.*
clavél, la clavellína. *the plant, also, the pink.*
alelí, *gilliflower.*
La espadáña, *flag-flower.*
campanílla, *blue-bottle.*
velloríta, *the cowslip.*
El ranúnculo, *ranunculus.*
La rósa, *the rose.*
cién hójas, *the hundred leaf rose.*
caléndula, *marigold.*
El girasól, *sun-flower.*
tulipán, *the tulip.*
La violéta, *the violet.*
Un capúllo, *a rose bud.*

Colours.—Colóres
Adjectives agree with Substantives.

Morádo, *purple.*
Un colór de auróra, *aurora colour.*
Blánco *white.*
Colór de ladríllo, *brick-colour.*
Azúl, *blue.*
Azúl celéste, *light blue.*
Azúl turquí, *dark blue.*
Columbíno, *dove colour.*
Cetríno, *lemon colour.*
Colór gamúza, *light yellow.*
Colór deceréza, *filemot.*
Colór encendído, *flame colour.*
Colór de fuégo, *fire colour.*
Carmesí, *crimson.*
Párdo, *grey.*
Ceniciénto, *ash-colour.*
Amaríllo, *yellow.*
Encarnádo, ⎫
Colorádo, ⎬ *red.*
Rójo, ⎭
Escarláta, Grána, *scarlet.*
Leonádo, *tawny.*
Négro, *black.*
Anaranjádo, *orange colour.*
Accitunádo, *olive colour.*
Colór de rósa, *rose-colour.*
Bermejón, *reddish.*
Vérde, *green.*
El matíz de colóres, *the shade of colours.*
Colór de mar, *sea-green.*

———

Parts of a kingdom.—Pártes de un réino.

úna província, *a province.*
ciudád, *a city.*
vílla, *a town.*
aldéa, *a village.*
Un lugár, *a small place.*

Parts of a city.—Pártes de úna ciudád,

Úna cása,	a house.
tiénda,	a shop.
iglésia,	a church.
capílla,	a chapel.
Un altár,	an altar.
palácio,	a palace.
hospitál,	an hospital.

La cása de la vílla, or del a-yuntamiénto, *the town house.*
Un tribunál, *a court of justice.*

arsenál,	an arsenal.
Úna académia,	an academy.
Un colégio,	a college.
Úna cálle,	a street.
Un callejón,	an alley.

Úna calléja, callejuéla, *a lane.*

Un mercádo,	a market.
Úna carnicería,	a slaughter-house.
encrucijáda,	a cross way.
lónja, bólsa,	an exchange.
cárcel,	a prison.

Los múros, las murállas, *walls.*

puértas,	gates.
fortificaciónes,	fortifications.
Úna pláza,	a square.
plazuéla,	a little square.

Of the inhabitants of cities. &c.
De los moradóres de úna ciudád, &c.

Un niño,	a child.
muchácho,	a boy.
Una muchácha,	a girl.
Un mózo, mocíto,	a youth.
hómbre,	a man.
Úna mugér,	a woman.
Un viéjo,	an old man.
Úna viéja,	an old woman.
Un cójo,	lame of one leg.

Un mánco,	lame of one hand.
ciégo,	blind.
sórdo,	deaf.
zúrdo,	left-handed.
magistrádo,	a magistrate.
nóble, hidálgo, }	a nobleman.

caballéro, *knight, or gen-tleman.*

tendéro,	a shopkeeper.
mercadér,	a trader.
comerciánte, } negociánte, }	a mer-chant.

El poblácho, } vulgácho, } La plébe, } the populace, the mob.

canálla,	the rabble.
Un artesáno,	a tradesman.
mecánico,	a mechanic.
jornaléro,	a journeyman.
labradór,	a farmer.

Úna labradóra, *a farmer's wife, or daughter.*

Un aldeáno,	a countryman.
Úna aldeána,	a countrywo-man.
Un pícaro,	a rogue.
esclávo,	a slave.
platéro,	a goldsmith.
libréro,	a bookseller
impresór,	a printer.
barbéro,	a barber.

mercadér de séda, *a mercer.*
mercadér de liénzo, *a lin-en-draper.*
mercadér de páño, *a wool-len-draper.*

sástre,	a tailor.
Úna costuréra,	a seamstress.
batéra,	a mantua-maker.
Un sombreréro,	a hatter.
calcetéro,	a hosier.
zapatéro,	a shoemaker.

Un remendón,	a patcher, a cobbler.
herréro,	a blacksmith.
albéitar,	a farrier.
cerrajéro,	a smith.
Úna lavandéra,	a laundress.
comádre, partéra,	a midwife.
Un partéro,	a man-midwife.
médico,	a physician.
embustéro,	a cheat.
charlatán,	a quack.
cirujáno,	a surgeon.
sacamuélas,	a dentist.
silléro,	a saddler.
carpintéro,	a carpenter.
peón,	a labourer.
albañíl,	a bricklayer.
pintór,	a painter.
panadéro,	a baker.
carnicéro,	a butcher.
frutéro,	a fruiterer.
Úna verduléra,	an herb, vegetable woman.
Un pasteléro,	a pastry-cook.
tabernéro,	a vintner.
cervecéro,	a brewer.
mesonéro,	an innkeeper.
relojéro,	a watchmaker.
pregonéro,	a crier.
joyéro,	a jeweller.
boticário,	an apothecary.
buhonéro,	a pedlar.
vidriéro,	a glazier.
carbonéro,	a collier.
jardinéro,	a gardener.
letrádo,	a lawyer.
procuradór,	a solicitor, an attorney.
abogádo,	a counsellor at law.
juéz,	a judge.
carceléro,	a jailer.
Un verdúgo,	a hangman.
ceréro,	a wax chandler.
ganapán, esportilléro, mandadéro,	a porter.
remendón de vestídos,	a botcher.
tatarabuélo,	a grandfather's grandfather.
bisabuélo,	great grandfather.
abuélo,	a grandfather.
pádre,	a father.
Úna mádre,	a mother.
Un híjo,	a son
úna híja,	a daughter
Un niéto,	a grandson.
bizniéto,	a great grandson.
hermáno,	a brother
cuñádo,	a brother in law.
padástro,	a step-father.
úna madrástra,	a step-mother.
Un suégro,	a father in law.
úna nuéra,	a daughter in law.
Un yérno,	a son in law.
prímo hermáno,	a cousin-german.
tío,	an uncle.
sobríno,	a nephew.
prímo segúndo,	a second cousin.
marído,	a husband.
úna mugér,	a wife.
Un nóvio,	a bridegroom.
úna nóvia,	a bride.
Un desposádo,	one betrothed.
ahijádo,	a godson.
padríno,	a godfather.
úna madrína,	a godmother.
Un compádre, úna comádre,	a father and mother in God.
Un compañéro,	a partner.
camaráda,	a companion.

Un cofráde, *a brother of the same pious society.*
mellízo, *a twin.*
Úna cofradía, *a guild or society.*
tertúlia, *a society, a club.*
comunidád, *a community.*
Un huérfano, *an orphan.*
soltéro, *a bachelor.*
heredéro, *an heir.*
áyo, *a tutor.*
curadór, *a guardian.*
Úna víuda, *a widow.*
Un hermáno de léche, *a foster brother.*
híjo de la piédra, espósito, ó echadízo, *a foundling.*
níño supuésto, *a supposititious child.*
bastárdo, *a bastard.*
híjo naturál, ó de ganáncia, *a natural son.*
úna doncélla, *a maiden.*
mugér casáda, *a married woman.*
parída, *a lying-in woman.*
enferméra, *a nurse.*
áma de lláves, *a housekeeper.*
mancéba, *a concubine.*

———

Of a house and all that belongs to it.—De úna cása, y tódo lo perteneciénte á élla.
úna cása, *a house.*
Un solár, *a ground of a house.*
cimiénto, *a foundation.*
úna paréd, *a wall.*
Un tabíqu', *a light wall.*
pátio, *a court, or yard.*
La facháda, *the front.*
Un álto, andár, *a story or floor.*
portál, *a porch.*

úna ventána, *a window.*
Un entresuélo, *a low floor.*
zaquizamí, *a cockloft, a dirty house.*
ciélo, *ceiling.*
ciélo de cáma, *cover of a bed.*
desván, *a garret.*
artesón, *an arched ceiling.*
úna bóveda, *a vault.*
escaléra, *a stair-case.*
Un escalón, *a step.*
tejádo, *a roof.*
Las téjas, *tiles.*
Los ladríllos, *bricks.*
Las pizárras, *slates.*
La puérta, *the door.*
Un pasadízo, *a passage.*
corrál, *a court-yard.*
trascorrál, *a back-yard.*
úna cámara, *a chamber.*
Un aposénto, *an apartment.*
úna piéza, *a room.*
Un cuárto *a chamber.*
úna estáncia, *a sitting room.*
antecámara, *an antichamber.*
trascuádra, *a backroom.*
sála, *a hall,*
Un salón, *a large hall.*
corredór, *a gallery.*
retréte, *a closet.*
estúdio *a study.*
armário, *a press.*
úna alhacéna, *a cupboard.*
Un guárda rópa, *a wardrobe.*
úna alcóva, *an alcove.*
Un balcón, miradór, *a balcony.*
úna azotéa, *the flat roof of a house, a terrace.*
ún camaranchón, *a cockloft.*
úna tórre, *a tower.*
bodéga, *a cellar.*
Un sótano, *a vault*

Un repostéro, *a larderer.*
úna repostería, *a restorator.*
despénsa, *a pantry.*
cocína, *a kitchen.*
caballeríza, *a stable.*
perrería, *a dog kennel.*
Un palomár, *a dove house.*
gallinéro, *a hen roost.*
jardín, *a garden.*
párque, *a park.*
La priváda, necesária, *the privy.*
coronílla del edifício, *the top of the building.*
El rípio, *rubbish.*
úna rípia, *a lath, a shingle.*
El aléro de tejádo, *the eaves of the roof.*
La canál, *the canal, the gutter.*
El umbrál, *the threshold.*
Los bastidóres de la puérta, *the frames of the door.*
El postígo, *the wicket, the by-door.*
Los quícios ó góznes, *hinges.*
úna cerradúra, *a lock.*
Un candádo, *a padlock.*
El pestíllo, *the bolt of a lock.*
Un cerrójo, *a bolt.*
úna lláve, *a key.*
ventanílla, *a little window.*
aldába, *a knocker.*
La tránca de úna puérta *the bar of a door.*
Las guárdas de la lláve, *the wards of a lock.*
El cañúto de úna lláve, *the pipe of a key.*
La vidriéra, *the glass of a window.*
Las réjas de úna ventána, *the bars of a window.*

úna escaléra de caracól, *a winding stair-case*
Los rellános, ó las mesétas de escaléra, *the landing-places of the stairs.*
El descánso de úna escaléra, *the resting place of stairs.*
úna gráda, un escalón, *a step*
escaléra secréta, *back-stairs.*
víga, *a beam.*
Un cuartón, *a girder, or large joist.*
úna tábla, *a board.*
Un crucéro, *a trimmer.*
ladríllo, *a brick.*
La paréd maéstra, *the main wall.*
paréd de en médio, *the party wall.*
úna paréd de cal y cánto, *a wall of lime and stone.*
Un tabíque, *a partition wall.*
La cal, *lime or plaster.*
argamása *mortar.*
encostradúra de úna paréd, *the plaster of a wall.*
El yéso, *fine white lime.*
jalbégue, *white wash.*
úna mésa, *a table.*
Un bánco, *a bench.*
úna sílla *a chair.*
sílla de brázos, *an arm-chair.*
Un taburéte, *a chair without back or arms to it.*
sitiál, *a stool.*
banquíllo, *a little bench.*
úna cája, *a box.*
árca, un arcón, *a chest.*
Un cajón, *a case of drawers.*
tirradór, *a drawer.*
escritório, *a scrutoire.*

úna cáma, a bed.
Un lécho, a couch.
úna armadúra or un maderáje de cáma, a bedstead.
El ciélo de cáma, the bed's tester.
Las cortínas de cáma, the bed-curtains.
El rodapiés, the fringe of a table, a bed.
Un tapéte, úna alfómbra, a carpet.
Las sábanas, the sheets.
El cobertór, counterpane.
Las almohádas, pillows.
La tapicería, tapestry.
úna pintúra, a picture.
Un espéjo, a looking-glass.
candeléro, a candlestick.
Las despabiladéras, snuffers.
úna aráña, a branch of crystal to hold many candles.
La yésca, tinder.
úna pajuéla, a match.
Un pedernál, a flint.
eslabón the steel to strike fire with.
orinál, a chamber-pot.
colchón, a mattress.
colchón de plúmas, feather bed.
úna cólcha, a quilt or coverlet.
Un cátre, a cot.
úna cáma de campáña, a field bed.
La testéra de cáma, the bed's head.
Las colúmnas de cáma, the bed posts.
Un gergón. a straw-bed.
úna estéra, a mat.
Un calentadór de cáma, a warming-pan.

úna chimenéa, a chimney.
Un respiradéro, ó cajón de chimenéa, the flue of a chimney.
Los moríllos, the andirons.
El fuélle, the bellows.
Las tenazás, the tongs.
úna pála or un badíl, a shovel.
Un guardafuégo, a screen, a fender.
biómbo, a folding-screen.
atizadór, a poker.
úna ólla, a porridge-pot.
cobertéra, a pot-lid.
El ása, the ear of a pot.
Un puchéro, a pipkin.
cucharón, a ladle.
úna caldéra, a kettle.
Un escalfadór, } a chafing
braseríllo, } dish.
Las trébedes, a trevet.
Un horníllo, a cooking-stove.
hórno, an oven.
úna sartén, a frying-pan.
Un cázo, a saucepan.
úna cazuéla, a little pan.
espumadéra, a skimmer
Las parríllas, a gridiron.
Un coladéro a sieve.
rállo, a grater.
úna mechéra, a larding pin.
Un asadór, a spit.
úna aceitéra, alcúza, an oil-pot.
vinagéra, a cruet.
Un almiréz, mortéro, a mortar.
úna máno de mortéro, a pestle.
redóma, a vial.
Un sumidéro, a sink.
cántaro, a pitcher.
bacín, a close stool pan.
úna albórnia, a great earthen pan.

úna herráda, ⎱ a bucket or
Un cúbo, ⎰ pail.
úna cúba, a tub.
La legín, coláda, lye.
El jabón, soap.
La levadúra, leaven.
úna rodilla, a coarse cloth.
Un estropájo, a dishclout.
La pála del hórno, the peel of
the oven.
harína, meal, flour.
El salvádo, bran.
úna artésa, a trough.
Los mantéles, table cloths.
úna servilléta, a napkin.
Un aguamaníl, a water-jug.
úna almofía, an earthen bowl.
toálla, a towel.
Los plátos, the plates.
Un cuchíllo, a knife.
tenedór, a fork.
saléro, a salt cellar.
pláto gránde, a large dish.
úna escudílla, a porringer.
cuchára, a spoon.
Un tajadór, a chopping block.
járro, a jug, a mug.
úna táza, a cup.
salvílla, a salver.
Un flásco, a flask.
úna botélla, a bottle.
Un váso de vídrio, a tumbler.
úna fuénte, un gran pláto, a
dish, a basin.
Un mónda diéntes, ⎱ a tooth-
escárba diéntes, ⎰ pick.
mayordómo, a steward.
trinchánte, a carver.
secretário, a secretary.
camaréro, a chamberlain.
dispenséro, a purveyor.
capellán, a chaplain.
limosnéro, an almoner.

Un páge, a page.
lacáyo, a footman.
cochéro, a coachman.
mózo de cabállos, a groom
caballerízo, a gentleman
of the horse.
copéro, a cup-bearer
maéstre sála, a sewer.
bodeguéro, ⎱
repostéro, ⎰ a butler.
halconéro, a falconer.
cocinéro, a cook.
galopín, a scullion.
portéro, a porter.
El huésped, ⎱ the host or
úmo de casa, ⎰ landlord.

Of country affairs.—De las
cósas del cámpo.

úna alquería, a farm house.
quínta, a country house
Un quintéro, a farmer.
boyéro, ⎱
vaquéro, ⎰ a cowkeeper.
porquéro, a swine-herd.
pastór, a shepherd.
zurrón, a scrip.
cayádo, a shepherd's
crook.
úna hónda, a sling.
Un horteláno, ⎱
jardinéro, ⎰ a gardener.
cavadór, a digger.
viñadéro, a vine dresser.
arúdo, a plough.
úna azáda, a spade.
Un azadón, a pick-axe.
labradór, a husbandman.
úna estéva, ⎱ a plough
mancéra, ⎰ handle.
réja de arádo, a plough
share.
El rastríllo, the harrow.

Un sembradór, *a sower.*
escardadór, *a weeder.*
rozadór, *a weeding-hook.*
segadór, *a reaper.*
una guadáña, *a sithe.*
Un tríllo, mayál, *a flail.*
úna hórca, *a fork.*
Un biéldo, *a winnowing fan.*
pescadór, *a fisherman.*
úna red barredéra, *a drag-net.*
vára, cáña pára pescár, *a fishing rod.*
Un sedál de cáña, *a fishing-line.*
anzuélo, *a fish-hook.*
cazadór, *a huntsman.*
cébo, *a bait.*
La líga, *bird lime.*
úna jáula, *a cage.*
Un obréro, ⎫ *a day labour-*
jornaléro, ⎭ *er.*
asnéro, *a keeper of asses.*
cabréro, *a goat-herd.*
paisáno, *a countryman.*
cámpo, *a field.*
lómo, *a ridge.*
Un súrco, *a furrow.*
El trígo en yérba, *green corn.*
La tiérra incúlta, *land untilled.*
Un mónte, ⎫ *a mount, or*
úna montáña, ⎭ *mountain.*
cuésta, *a declivity.*
Un colládo, *a hill.*
cérro, *a high ridge of hills.*
válle, *a valley.*
abísmo, *an abyss.*
úna zánja, *a trench, a ditch.*
lagúna, *a lake.*
Un pantáno, *a marsh.*
úna llanúra, *a plain.*
péña, róca, *a rock.*
Un peñásco, *a ridge of rocks.*

Un despeñadéro, *a precipice.*
úna sélva, *a forest.*
Un bósque, *a grove, a wood.*
úna esplanáda, *esplanade.*
máta, *a bush.*
zárza, *a bramble.*
espína, *a thorn.*
Un prádo, *a meadow.*
vergél, huérto, *an orchard.*
úna huérta, *a kitchen-garden.*
Un jardín, *a flower-garden.*
úna éra en un jardín, *a bed, a plot in a garden.*
gloriéta, *a bower.*
almáciga, *a seed plot.*
bóveda de párras, *a vine arbour.*
Un laberínto, *a labyrinth.*
úna grúta, *a grotto.*
cascáda, *a cascade.*
fuénte, *a fountain.*
Un chórro de água, *a spout of water.*
El pilón de úna fuénte, *the basin of a fountain.*
Un encañádo, *a conduit of water.*
acuedúcto, *an aqueduct.*
La hortalíza, *garden vegetables.*
úna plánta, *a plant.*
El camíno reál, *the highway.*
úna sénda, veréda, *a path.*
pisáda, un rástro, *a footstep, a track.*
cabalgadúra, *a beast of burden.*
Un carromáto, *a wagon.*
cárro, *a cart.*
úna ruéda, *a wheel*
El ráyo de úna ruéda, *the spoke of a wheel.*

25

Las llántas,	the tire or rim.
pínas,	the felloes of a wheel.
El cúbo de úna ruéda,	the nave of a wheel.
ége,	the axle tree.
La pezonéra,	the pin of a wheel.
úna calésa,	a chaise
litéra,	a litter.
Las ándas,	a bier, the shafts.
Un cóche,	a coach.
úna carróza,	an awning.
césta,	an osier basket.
rástra, nárria,	a sledge,
canásta,	a twig-basket.
espuérta,	a bass-basket.
Un chirrión,	a dung-cart.
úna banásta,	a great hamper.
alfórja,	saddle bag, wallet.
bólsa,	a purse.
Un costál, sáco,	a sack, bag.
úna maléta,	a portmanteau.
Un talégo,	a bag.
úna balíja,	a cloak-bag.
Un zurrón,	a budget or pouch.

Of the church, and things belonging to it.—De la Iglésia, y cósas pertenecientes á élla.

La náve,	the nave, aisle of a church.
El cimbório,	the dome.
La cúpula,	the cupola.
El pináculo,	the pinnacle.
córo,	the choir.
La capílla.	the chapel.
Un atríl,	a stand or desk.
La sacristía,	the vestry.
El campanário,	the belfrey, steeple.
úna campána,	a bell.

El badájo,	tongue of the bell, or clapper.
La lengüéta,	
píla,	the font.
El hisópo,	the sprinkler.
confesionário,	the confession box.
úna tribúna,	a tribune or gallery.
El cimentério,	the church yard.
osário,	the charnel-house.
Un altár,	an altar.
frontál,	a forepart of an altar.
ornáto,	an ornament.
El tabernáculo,	the tabernacle, ciborium.
sagrário,	
Un pálio,	a pall, a canopy.
El mantél del altár,	the altar-cloth.
Un misál,	a mass-book.
úna sotána,	a cassock.
sobrepellíz,	a surplice.
Un roquéte,	a short surplice.
bonéte,	a bonnet, a cap.
úna mítra,	a mitre.
Un báculo,	a crosier.
patriárca,	a patriarch.
arzobíspo,	an archbishop
obíspo,	a bishop
obispádo,	a bishoprick
úna diócesis,	a diocese
Un coadjutór,	coadjutor.
sufragáneo,	suffragan.
sacerdóte,	a priest.
El sacerdócio,	priesthood.
Un diácono,	a deacon.
subdiácono,	a subdeacon.
acólito,	an acolyte.
lectór,	a reader.
clérigo,	a clergyman.
preládo,	a prelate.
abád,	an abbot

Úna abadésa, *an abbess.*
abadía, *an abbey.*
Un canónigo, *a canon.*
deán, *a dean*
prevóste, *a provost.*
arcediáno, *an archdeacon*
chántre, *a chanter.*
maéstro de córo, *a master of the choir.*
cantór, *a singer.*
sacristán, *a vestry keeper.*
prebendádo, *a prebendary.*
cúra, *a curate, a parson.*
Úna parróquia, *a parish.*
Un vicário, *a vicar.*
oficiál, *an officer.*
promotór, *a promoter.*
Úna encomiénda, *a commandry.*
El bautísmo, *baptism.*
La confirmación, *confirmation.*
El matrimónio, *matrimony.*
Comulgár, *to receive the sacrament.*
Los órdenes sácros, *holy orders.*
Úna ceremónia, *a ceremony.*
La rúbrica, *the rubric.*
El rituál, *the ritual.*
oficio divíno, *divine service.*
saltério, *the psalter.*
Un sálmo, *a psalm.*
La antífona, *antiphon.*
úna lección, *a lesson.*
Un versículo, *a verse.*
sermón, *a sermon.*
La meditación, *meditation.*
oración vocál, *vocal prayer.*
oración mentál, *mental prayer.*

Predicár, *to preach.*
Catequizár, *to catechise.*
Enterrár, *to inter.*
Sepultár, *to bury.*
La escomunión, *excommunication.*
suspensión, *suspension.*
Un entredícho, *an interdict.*
La irregularidád, *irregularity.*
Descomulgár, *to excommunicate.*
úna catedrál, *a cathedral church.*
La conventuál, *the church of a convent*
úna parroquiál, *a parish church.*
El adviénto, *advent.*
La cuarésma, *lent.*
Las témporas, *ember-weeks.*
úna vigília, *a vigil, an eve.*
Un ayúno, *a fast.*

Things relating to War.—
Cósas pertenecléntes á la guérra.
La artillería, *artillery.*
úna piéza de artillería, } *a cannon.*
Un cañón, }
El tren de artillería, *the train of artillery.*
La bóca de cañón, *the mouth of a cannon.*
El fogón, *the touch-hole.*
La culáta del cañón, *the breech of a gun.*
curéña, } *the carriage of a gun.*
El afúste, }
Cargár, *to load.*
Apuntár, *to aim at, to level.*
Disparár, *to fire.*
Un tíro de cañón, *a cannon-shot.*

Desmontár un cañón,	to dismount a gun.
Enclavár un cañón,	to spike a gun.
úna culebrína,	a culverin.
Un falconéte,	a falconet.
Un pedréro,	a swivel, paterero.
cañón entéro,	a whole cannon.
médio cañón,	half cannon.
petárdo,	a petard.
úna bómba,	a bomb.
bombárda,	a bomb-ketch.
Un mortéro,	a mortar-piece.
Úna granáda,	a grenade.
Un mosquéte,	a musket.
úna carabína,	a carabine.
escopéta,	a gun, a fire-lock.
pistóla,	a pistol.
bála,	a ball, a bullet.
La pólvora,	powder.
úna mécha,	a match.
Un pedernál,	a flint.
úna flécha,	an arrow.
Un dárdo,	a dart.
úna jabalína,	a boar-spear.
hónda,	a sling.
Un árco,	a bow.
úna hácha de ármas,	a battle-axe.
lánza,	a lance.
alabárda,	a halberd.
partesána,	a partisan.
píca,	a pike.
Un alfange,	a scimitar.
úna espáda,	a sword.
El púño de la espáda,	the handle of a sword.
pómo de la,	the pommel of.
La guarnición de la hója,	the hilt of the blade.
Un puñál,	a poniard
úna bayonéta,	a bayonet.
Un yélmo,	a casque.
úna celáda,	a helmet.
dága, .	a dagger.
Un morrión,	a murrion.
La viséra,	the visor of a helmet.
El gorjál,	the gorgerin.
La góla,	▪ the gorget.
Un péto,	a breast-plate.
úna coráza,	a cuiras.
El espaldár,	the back-plate.
Un coseléte,	a corslett.
brazaléte,	an armlet.
escarcéla,	armour from the waist to the thighs.
únas hinojéras,	armour for the knees.
Un broquél,	a buckler.
escúdo,	a shield.
úna adárga,	a target.
cóta de málla,	a coat of mail.
Un generál,	a general.
teniénte generál,	a lieutenant general.
sargénto mayór de batálla,	a major general
coronél,	a colonel.
sargénto mayór,	a lieutenant colonel
capitán,	a captain.
teniénte,	a lieutenant.
cornéta,	a cornet.
alférez,	an ensign.
sargénto,	a serjeant.
cábo,	a corporal.
cuadrilléro,	a commander of a squad.
soldádo,	a soldier.
caudíllo,	a chieftain.
tambór,	a drum, drummer

Un pífano,	a fife.	Un vivandéro,	a sutler.
úna trompéta,	a trumpet.	partído,	a party.
Un atabál, timbál,	kettle drum.	Los corredóres,	the scout
soldádo de á cabállo,	a trooper.	Batír el cámpo,	to scout
soldádo de á pié, infánte,	a foot soldier.	Los batidóres,	discoverers.
granadéro,	a grenadier.	La murálla,	rampart
dragón,	a dragoon.	Los múros,	walls
piquéro,	a pike-man.	úna alména,	turret, battle-ment.
mosquetéro,	a musqueteer.	El parapéto,	the parapet.
fusiléro,	a fusileer.	Un castíllo,	a castle.
La infantería,	the infantry.	fuérte,	a fort.
caballería,	the cavalry.	úna fortaléza,	a fortress.
Un artilléro,	a gunner.	fortificación,	a fortifica-tion.
bombardéro,	a bombard-ier.	tórre,	a tower.
ingeniéro,	an engineer.	ciudadéla,	a citadel.
minéro,	a miner.	Un bastión,	a bastion.
gastadór,	a pioneer.	úna cortína,	a curtain.
zapadór,	a sapper.	medía lúna,	a half moon.
úna centinéla,	a centinel.	tronéra,	an embrasure.
La vanguárdia,	the vanguard.	Un terraplén,	a platform.
Ei cuérpo de batálla,	the main body of the army.	caballéro,	a cavalier.
La retaguárdia,	the rear.	rebellín,	a ravelin.
El cuérpo de resérva,	the corps de reserve.	La cóntra escárpa,	counter-scarp.
cuérpo de guárdia,	the corps de guard.	úna barréra,	a barrier.
ála,	the wing of an army.	fálsa brága,	a fausse braye.
Un batallón,	a battalion.	Un fóso,	a ditch.
regimiénto,	a regiment.	repécho,	a breast work.
úna compañía de cabállos,	a troop of horse.	úna garita,	a centry box
compañía de infantería,	a company of foot.	casamáte,	casemate
hiléra,	a rank.	galería, Un corredór,	gallery
fila,	a file.	La estráda cubiérta, El camíno cubiérto,	the cov-ertway.
Un escuadrón,	a squadron.	Un cestói, gavión,	a gabion.
mochiléro,	baggage man.	úna estacáda,	a palisade.
bagáge,	a baggage.	Un redúcto,	a redoubt.
		úna ataláya,	a beacon, a watch tower

Úna mánta,   *a mantelet or moveable pent house.*

fagína,   *a fascine.*

mína,   *a mine.*

Úna cóntra-mína,   *a counter-mine.*

trinchéra,   *a trench.*

El reál,   *the royal camp.*

Las vituállas,   *provisions.*

municiónes,   *ammunition.*

Un bisóño, reclúta,   *a recruit.*

pecoréro,   *a marauder.*

Úna cóntra márcha,   *a counter-march.*

escaramúza,   *a skirmish.*

batálla,   *a battle.*

Un sítio,   *a siege.*

cuartél mayór,   *head quarters.*

Úna encamisáda,   *a camisado.*

salída,   *a sortie, sally.*

Batír,   *to batter.*

Úna brécha,   *a breach.*

escaláda,   *an escalade.*

Un asálto,   *an assault.*

La llamáda, *the call, chamade.*

capitulación, *the capitulation.*

guarnición, *the garrison.*

Tocár la cája,   *to beat the drum.*

Levantár génte, *to raise men.*

Pagár el suéldo, el pre, *to pay the soldiers.*

Batír la estráda, *to scour the country.*

Levantár el sítio, *to raise the siege.*

Marchár á bandéras desplegádas, *to march with flying colours.*

Reforzár el egército, *to reinforce the army.*

Tocár á recogér,   *to sound a retreat*

Entregár úna pláza, *to surrender a place.*

Commercial terms.—Vóces mercantíles.

Un abarcadór, *a monopoliser*

Abaratár,   *to cheapen*

Abonár,   *to credit*

Acarreár,   *to convey*

El acarréo, pórte,   *carriage.*

Aceptár úna létra,   *to accept a bill.*

Úna acción,   *a share, stock.*

La acción de empujár ó tirár,   *hallage.*

Un acreedór, *creditor;* acreedór hipotecúrio, *mortgagee;* él que da la hipotéca *mortgager;* acreedór importúno, *a dun;* valísta, ó acreedór por vúle, *creditor by a note or bill.*

La aduána,   *custom-house.*

Un ajúste, *bargain;* ajúste de cuéntas,   *a settlement.*

á la buélta,   *carried over.*

almacén, *store-house, ware house, magazine.*

Úna almonéda, *a public sale, an auction.*

Alquilár, arrendár,   *to hire.*

Úna áncla de la esperánza, *a sheet anchor.*

Á quién su podér hubiére, *to his or their assigns.*

Úna arbitración, senténcia de juéces árbitros, *umpirage.*

Las árras, ó la dóte, *earnest money.*

Un arrendadór, *a farmer that hires.*

El arrendamiénto, *hiring, farming.*
Arrendár, *to undertake, to farm.*
Un arríbo, *an arrival.*
Un aseguradór, *an insurer.*
Asegurár, *to insure.*
Un asiénto, *a contract, an entry.*
La avería, *average.*
avería y cápa, *primage and hat money.*
Un balánce, sáldo, *a balance.*
bánco, *bank.*
banquéro, *banker.*
Baráto, *cheap.*
Los biénes própios, *real or personal property.*
biénes habídos y por habér, *goods had and to be had.*
Un calabróte, *a short cable.*
cámbio, *exchange, change.*
Negociár úna létra de cámbio, *to negotiate a bill of exchange.*
Un capitál, caudál, *stock, capital.*
Cargár el temporál, *to befall a heavy storm.*
Cáro, *dear.*
Úna cárta cuénta, *a bill of sale.*
cárta, *letter;* el pórte de cártas, *postage;* portadór, *bearer, penny-postman.*
Cárta de mareár, *sea-chart.*
Cerrár úna cárta, *to make up a letter.*
Cárta de guía, *a passport.*
Cárta de sanidád, *bill of health.*
úna maléta pára cártas, *mail.*
Un caudál, *a treasure, a stock.*
caudál destinádo, *a fund.*
La cája, *cash;* un cajéro, *cashier, cash-keeper;* dinéro en cája, *cash on hand.*

El líbro de cája, *cash-book.*
Un certificádo, *certificate.*
Certificár, *to certify.*
Un ciénto, *cent;* dos ó tres &c. por ciénto, *two or three &c. per cent.*
El cobradór, *receiver;* cobrár, *to receive;* cobradór de sísa, *exciseman;* —de deréchos de muélle, *wharfinger.*
La comisión, *commission.*
Un compañéro, *partner.*
Úna compañía, *. partnership.*
cómpra, *purchase;* un compradór, *buyer, purchaser;* compradór, ó vendedór de acciónes, *stock-jobber.*
Un compromíso, *compromise.*
La comunicación, *intercourse.*
El conocimiénto, *bill of lading.*
La consignación, *consignment.*
El consúmo, *consumption.*
Contádo (dinéro de contádo) *ready money.*
El contenído, *contents.*
Un contrabandísta, *smuggler.*
contrabándo, *contraband.*
Úna contráta de fletaménto, *a charter party of freight.*
contribución, *an assessment or tribute.*
cópia, *a copy*
Un corredór, *or corredór de oréja, broker;* —de cámbios, *exchange-broker.*
El corréo, *the post office.*
La correspondéncia, *correspondence.*
Un correspondiénte, *a correspondent.*
Corriénte, *current.*
La costúmbre, *custom*

El crédito, credit.

La cuénta, bill, account; sumár úna cuénta, to cast up an account; pedír cuénta, to call to an account; pagár á cuénta, to pay a part of an account.

Los dáños, damages.

La dáta ó fécha, date.

dar, ó dejár á fléte, to let out a vessél on freight.

Debájo de cubiérta, under deck.

El derécho,. duty, custom; deréchos de entráda, duties of importation; dros. de estracción, of exportation.

Los deréchos de embárque ó desembárque, wharfage.

La descárga, unlading.

El descuénto, discount; devolución de dros. de entráda, drawback.

Un desembólso, disbursement.

Desempaquetár, to unpack.

Estivár, to stow.

Estivadór, stower

Estíva, stowage.

Despachár to sell, send, dispatch; despachár un corréo, to send an express; despachár mercaderías, to sell goods; despácho de aduána, clearance, cocket; despácho, expedition.

Je tódo nos hacémos cárgo, we have taken due notice of all.

La déuda, debt.

El deudór, debtor.

El diézmo, tenth, tithe; diezméro, tithe gatherer.

El dinéro, money; dinéro contádo ó de contádo, ready money; dinéro cercenádo, ó cortádo, clipped money; dinéro en cája, cash; dinéro prestádo, money lent

Un domicílio, a domicil.

Úna tripulación, a crew.

Tripulár, to man.

Únas árras, a pledge.

Los dros. municipáles, town's fees.

Un duplicádo, duplicate.

duéño, ámo, owner.

Únos eféctos, effects.

Un envoltório, ó úna arpilléra, wrapper.

empéño, pawn, obligation.

Encima·de la bárra, over the bar.

Un endosadór, an endorser encargádo de, agent for. endóso, endorsement.

En testimónio de verdád, in testimonium veritatis.

La entráda, entry; dros. de entráda, duties of entry.

El equivalénte, equivalent. escásos de despácho, dull of sale.

Escribír, to write; la escritúra, hand-writing, bond, engagement; escritúra de arrendamiénto, lease; un escritório, counting-room.

Estrenar, to hansel.

La exigéncia, exigency. estracción, exportation.

Un estrúcto, extract, abridgement

estractór, extractor.

La estorsión, extortion.

Un factór, factor

Úna factúra, invoice.

factoría, factory.

La fálta, *fault, want, error.*
fálta de pagaménto, *non-payment.*
Un fárdo, *a bale.*
fárdo pequéño, *a truss.*
Úna féria, *a fair.*
Un fiadór, abóno, *surety, bail.*
fiadór hipotecário, *mortgager.*
fiél medída ó péso, *standard measure, or weight.*
únas fijadéras pára papéles, *files for papers.*
Fletár, *to freight a ship.*
El fléte, *freight.*
fletadór, *freighter.*
fóndo, ó caudál, ó acción, *funds, stock, or share.*
forcéjo, *struggle.*
ganadór, *gainer.*
La ganáncia, *gain.*
El ganapán, *porter.*
Los gástos, *charges, expenses.*
géneros, *goods.*
Las guárdas, *custom-house officers;* guárdas vijiadóres, *tides-men, tide-waiters.*
úna gruésa ó múcha mar, *a heavy sea.*
Un guárda de navío, *a tidesman, inspector.*
úna guía, *a permit.*
haciénda ruín, *trash of goods.*
arpilléra, ⎫
Un envoltório, ⎰ *wrapper.*
Hílo acarréto, *packthread.*
úna hipotéca, *a mortgage.*
júnta de sanidád, *board of health.*
El impórte; impórte líquido, *proceeds, net proceeds.*

Insolvénte, insolvéncia, *insolvent, insolvency.*
El interés, *interest.*
introductór de géneros, *importer of goods.*
inventário, *inventory.*
juéz, *judge.*
juéz árbitro, *referee, umpire, arbitrator.*
Los júros, *fees, annuity.*
El lácre, *sealing-wax.*
úna láncha, *a lighter.*
lancháda, embarque en láncha, *lighterage.*
úna létra de cámbio, *a bill of exchange, a draft;* cámbio séco, *usurious contract;* dar ó tomár á cámbio, *to lend or borrow on interest;* sacár, librár, ó tirár úna létra, *to draw a bill;* aceptár úna létra *to accept a bill.*
Un legájo de cártas, *a bundle of letters.*
Un líbro de tiénda, *shop book;* borradorcíllo, *small note-book for memoranda;* borradór, *a day-book,* diário ó jornál, *a journal;* libro mayór, *a ledger;* copiadór, ó líbro de cópias de cártas, *a letter-book;* líbro de muéstras, *a pattern book.*
La licéncia, *license, permit.*
lósa vidriáda, *Dutch ware.*
maléta pára cártas, *mail.*
Un marchánte, *a customer.*
marinéro, *seaman.*
Las mercaderías, ⎫ *goods,*
mercancías, ⎰ *wares.*

Un mercadér por mayór, *a wholesale dealer.*
monopolísta, *monopolist.*
puérto, *a port or harbour.*
Un muélle, *wharf;* deréchos de muélle, *wharfage;* su cobradór, *its wharfinger.*
Un negociánte de géneros estrangéros, *importer of foreign goods.*
Un negociánte de acciónes *a stock-jobber.*
Úna obléa, *a wafer.*
obligación, *a bond.*
obligaciónes, *contracts.*
Un ofrecedór, *bidder;* mayór oferénte, *higher bidder.*
La orílla, *the shore.*
Pagár á cuénta, *to pay on account;* un pagaménto, *payment;* fálta de págo, *non-payment;* un pagaré, *a promissory note.*
Un paquéte, *parcel.*
paquéte de cártas, *a packet of letters.*
Pára las cóstas de, *for the costs of.*
Pedír cuénta, *to call to an account.*
Las pérdidas, *losses.*
El péso brúto, *gross weight.*
péso límpio de réy, *net weight.*
póco mas ó ménos, *thereabout.*
úna petáca, *bundle, hamper, roll.*
póliza de segúros, *policy of insurance.*
ponér las cósas en órden, *to set things in order.*
El portadór, *bearer;* porta-

dór de cártas, *penny-post man;* cárta de espéra, *letter of respite.*
Los pórtes, *porterage.*
El précio, *price, rate;* la subída de précio, *enhancement, rise of price.*
El prémio, *premium, interest.*
Un préstamo, dinéro prestádo, *a loan, money lent.*
El primáge, párte de flétes de navío, *primage.*
úna promésa, *a promise.*
protésta, *a protest.*
Protestár úna létra, *to protest a bill or draft.*
Protestár úna, dos y tres y las mas véces en derécho necesárias.....*to protest in the most effectual manner possible against....*
El provécho, *profit.*
La puntualidád, *punctuality.*
Un quebrádo, *a bankrupt.*
úna quiébra, *a bankruptcy.*
Que se dirá, *which will be mentioned*
La quinquillería, *hardware.*
Un quintál, *a hundred weight.*
úna quitánza, *a release.*
El recámbio, *re-exchange.*
recíbo, *receipt.*
Regateár, *to cheapen.*
La remésa, *the remittance.*
rénta, *income.*
riquéza, *wealth.*
El riésgo, *risk.*
Rompér sóbre la cósta, *to break on the shore.*
La rópa, *clothes.*
sóbra de haciénda, *refuse of goods.*

Sacár las mercaderías, *to un-stow.*

Sáno de quílla y costádos, *light, staunch and strong.*

El segúro, *insurance.*

Sellár úna cárta, *to seal a letter.*

Ser de cuénta de, *to be on account of.*

La sísa, *excise.*

Su cobradór, *the exciseman.*

Un sobrescríto, *a superscription.*

sobrestánte de tiérra, *land-overseer.*

La sobrestáda, *demurrage.*

subásta, almonéda, *sale by auction.*

El remáte,

Sumár úna cuénta, *to cast up an account.*

La subída de précio, *enhancement, rise*

suscripción, *subscription.*

El suscriptór, *the subscriber.*

Surgír, *to ride at anchor.*

Un talégo de monéda, *a bag of money.*

La tára, *the tare, tret.*

tasación, *the set rate.*

tása, *assize.*

Un tendéro, *a shop-keeper.*

Ponér tiénda, *to open a shop.*

úna tiénda, *a shop.*

Un tenedór de líbros, *a book-keeper.*

La tonelería, *cooperage.*

Un tratánte, *a trader.*

negociánte, *a merchant.*

Tratár *to deal or trade.*

Un tráto, ó negócio, *intercourse, business, or traffick.*

Un tribúto, *tribute.*

truéque, *barter, exchange.*

Trocár, *to barter.*

Un vendedór, *seller.*

La vénta, *sale.*

Un valór, *a value, worth.*

Los vigiádores de réntas, *inspectors, tides-men.*

úna cumplída, las restántes de ningún valór, *one being fulfilled, the others to stand void.*

Un úso, 60 *days usance.*

La usúra, *usury.*

Un usuréro, *a usurer.*

La gérga, *coarse cloth.*

Un gergón, *a large coarse sack*

Navigation.—Navegación.

Un navío, úna náve ó náo, *a ship.*

de línea, *of the line.*

Un navío de guérra, *a man of war.*

Un navío marchánte ó úna fragáta, *a merchant ship.*

Un navío ligéro, *a light vessel.*

úna galéra, *a galley.*

galeáza, *a galeasse.*

Un galeón, *a galleon.*

úna galeóta, *a galleot.*

fragáta de guérra, *a frigate.*

Un saíque, *a saick.*

úna carráca, *a carrack.*

Un fúste, *a fuste.*

úna pináza, *a pinnace.*

bárca de paságe, *a ferry-boat.*

goléta *a schooner.*

canóa, *a canoe.*

pirágua, *a pirogue.*

góndola, *a light boat.*

Un esquífe, *a skiff.*

úna balándra, *a sloop.*

Un bergantín,   *a brig.*
 quéche,   *a ketch.*
úna láncha, un bóte, *a launch.*
 barquéta, ⎫
 barquílla, ⎬ *a boat.*
Un batél,   ⎭
 bagél,bárco,búque, *vessel.*
úna bálsa, *a raft, a float.*
La capitúna, *the admiral ship.*
 almiránta, *the vice-admiral.*
 armáda, *the royal fleet.*
 flota, *the fleet of merchant-*
        men.
úna escuádra, *a squadron.*
Abórdo,   *aboard.*
La pópa, *the poop, stern.*
 próa, *the prow or head.*
úna tartána, *a tartan.*
Un brulóte, *a fireship.*
 patáche, *a tender, a petach.*
úna falúca, falúa, *a felucca.*
 bárca, *a coasting fishing*
      vessel
La sentína, *the well.*
El lástre,   *ballast.*
 mástil, árbol, *the mast.*
 árbol mayór,. *the main-*
       mast.
La gábia, *the round top.*
El trinquéte, *the fore-mast.*
La mesána, *the mizen-mast.*
La carlínga del árbol, *the step*
     of the mast.
 vérga, cnténa *the yard.*
El estribór,   *starboard.*
 babór,   *larboard.*
Gobernár el navío, *to steer.*
El barlovénto, *windward.*
 sotavénto,   *leeward.*
Remolcár,   *to tow.*
Escoltár, convoyár, *to convoy.*
úna véla,   *a sail.*
 véla mayór, *the main-sail.*

La véla de gábia, *the top-sail.*
El juanéte, *the top-gallant-*
       sail.
La véla de mesána, *the mizen-*
       sail.
 véla de trinquéte, *the fore*
       sail.
 cevadéra, *the sprit sail.*
 véla latína, *latine sail.*
Un rémo,   *an oar.*
La pála de rémo, *the blade.*
Un práctico,   *a pilot.*
Las tronéras, *the port holes.*
 empavesádas, *nettings.*
Enarbolár,   *to hoist.*
Tremolár,   *to waive*
Un pabellón,   *a flag.*
 gallardéte, *a pendant.*
 estandárte, *standard.*
úna banderóla, *a banner.*
 bandéra, *the colours.*
La brújula, *the compass.*
 púnta de la próa, *the stem.*
 puénte, cubiérta, *the deck.*
Las escotíllas, *the hatches.*
El timón,   *the helm.*
La quílla,   *the keel.*
úna áncla, áncora, *an anchor.*
 amárra,   *mooring.*
 maróma,   *a rope.*
Un cáble,   *a cable*
La sónda, *the sounding lead.*
Un pilóto,   *a mate.*
 guardián, *a boatswain.*
 marinéro,   *a sailor.*
 corsário,   *a privateer.*
 armadór, *a ship-owner.*
úna cámara,   *a cabin.*
Un camaróte,   *a berth.*
úna torménta, *a tempest.*
 borrásca,   *a storm.*
 bonánza, *fair weather.*
 cálma,   *calm.*

El viénto en pópa, *the wind full astern.*

viénto lárgo, *fair wind.*

Cogér el·viénto, *to ply to windward.*

Ir á la bolína, *to tack upon a wind.*

Írse á fóndo, á píque, *to sink.*

The year and its parts, &c.— El áño y sus pártes, &c.

Un áño, *a year.*

Un mes, *a month.*

Úna semána, *a week.*

Un día, *a day.*

Úna nóche, *a night.*

La mañána, *the morning.*

La tárde, *the evening.*

Úna hóra, *an hour.*

Un minúto, *a minute.*

Un moménto, *a moment.*

La primavéra, *the spring.*

El veráno, *the summer.*

El otóño, *the autumn.*

El inviérno, *the winter.*

La salída del sol, *the sun-rising.*

El ponérse del sol, *the sun-setting.*

La auróra, *the dawn.*

El mediodía, *noon.·*

La média nóche, *midnight..*

Un cuárto de hóra, *a quarter of an hour.*

Úna média hóra, *half an hour.*

Tres cuártos de hóra, *three quarters of an hour.*

Hóy, *to-day.*

Ayér, *yesterday.*

El día ántes de ayér, *the day before yesterday.*

El día después de mañána, *the day after to-morrow.*

---

*The months,—*Los méses.— *are masculine.*

Enéro, *January.*

Febréro, *February.*

Márzo, *March.*

Abríl, *April.*

Máyo, *May.*

Júnio, *June.*

Júlio, *July.*

Agósto, *August.*

Setiémbre, *September.*

Octúbre, *October.*

Noviémbre, *November.*

Diciémbre, *December.*

---

*The days of the week.—*Los días de la semána,—*are masculine.*

Lúnes, *Monday.*

Mártes, *Tuesday.*

Miércoles, *Wednesday*

Juéves, *Thursday.*

Viérnes, *Friday.*

Sábado, *Saturday.*

Domíngo, *Sunday.*

The holidays of the year.— Días de fiésta del áño.

El primér día del Áño, *New Year's day.*

El día de Réyes, *Twelfth-tide.*

La Cuarésma, *Lent.*

Las Cuátro témporas, *the Ember-weeks.*

El domíngo de Rámos, *Palm-Sunday.*

El Viérnes Sánto, *Good-Friday.*

26

La páscua de resurrección, *Easter-day.*
páscua del Espíritu Sánto, *Whit-Sunday.*
El día de Difúntos, *All-Souls-day.*
día de tódos los Sántos, *All-Saints-doy.*
La páscua de navidád, *Christmas.*
vigília, *the vigil, the Eve.*

Winds,—Viéntos,—*are masculine.*

El nórte, *north wind.*
sud ó sur, *south wind.*
éste, } *east wind.*
levánte, }
poniénte, oéste, *west wind.*
nordéste, *north-east wind.*
noroéste, *north-west wind*
sudéste, *south-east wind*
sudoéste, *south-west wind*

Table of the current Money in Spain.—Tábla de las Monédas de España.

La piéza mas pequéña de monéda de España se lláma Maravedí, del cuál resulta la Tábla siguiénte,

Copper, or Billion.—*Cóbre, ó vellón.*

2 maravedíses *hácen,* un ochávo.
2 ochávos, un cuárto.
2 cuártos, úna móta, ó dos cuártos.

Silver.—*Pláta.*

*8 1-2 cuártos, un reál.
†10⅜ diez cuártos y médio y un maravedí.
‡17 cuártos, 2 reáles.
§21 1-4 cuártos, 2 1-2 reáles.
‖34 cuártos, 4 reáles ó úna peséta,

¶42 1-2 cuártos, 5 reáles ó peséta columnária.
85 cuártos, 10 reáles o médio dúro.
170 cuártos, 20 reáles ó un péso dúro.

Gold.—*óro.*

20 reáles, escudillo de óro.
40 reáles, dóble escudíllo de óro.
80 reáles, doblón de óro.
160 reáles, média ónza de óro, ú 8 pésos dúros.
320 reáles, úna ónza, ó 16 pésos dúros.

---

* 5 Cents. † 6 1-4 Cents. ‡ 10 Cents. § 12 1-2 Cents. ‖ 20 Cents, or a pistareen. ¶ 25 Cents. In *ci-devant* Spanish America, copper money is as yet unknown; dollars, half dollars, quarters, eighths and sixteenths of a dollar, and the gold coins above mentioned, are only in use.

Military words of command.—Palábras militáres de Mandamiénto.

Fórmense,	*fall in.*	Césen el fuégo,	*cease firing.*
Atención,	*attention.*	Márchen,	*march.*
Ármas al hómbro,	*shoulder.*	Álto,	*halt.*
	arms.	Línea á la izquiérda,	*left into line.*
Fíjen bayonétas,	*fix bayonets.*	Conversión á la derécha,	
Presénten las ármas,	*present arms.*		*right wheel.*
Aparéjen,	*make ready.*	Conversión á la izquiérda,	*left wheel.*
Presénten,	*present.*	Conversión atrás á la derécha,	
Fuégo,	*fire.*		*right backwards wheel.*
Cében,	*prime.*	Conversión atrás á la izquiérda,	*left backwards wheel.*
Cárguen,	*load.*		
Sáquen baquéta,	*draw ramrods.*	Á la derécha frénte,	*right face.*
Atáquen,	*ram down cartridge.*	Á la izquiérda frénte,	*left. face*

FAMILIAR PHRASES.

Senténcias Córtas y Familiáres.—*Short and Familiar Phrases.*

I. *Acérca de pedir álgo.*

I. About asking any thing.

Le suplíco, le ruégo, déme vm.; hágame el favór de dárme
I beseech you, pray, give me; do me the favour to give me

Tráigame
Bring me

Se lo agradézco
I thank you for it

Le dóy las grácias
I give you thanks

Váya á buscárme tal cósa
Go and fetch me such a thing

Luégo, en éste instánte
Presently, this moment

Querído Señór, hágame vm. éste gústo
Dear Sir, do me this pleasure

Concédame, señóra, ésta grácia
Madam, grant me this favour.

Se lo suplíco
I beseech you for it

Se lo pído encarecídaménte
I earnestly ask it of you

II. *Espresiónes tiérnas.*	II. Tender expressions.
Mi vída	*My life*
Mi querído, mi querída	*My dear, my beloved*
Mi álma	*My soul*
Mi duéño,	*My lore, my lord or master*
Mi queridíto, mi queridita	*My little darling, little dear*
Mi corazoncíto	*My little heart*
Lúmbre de mis ójos,	*Dear sweet heart, light of my eyes*
Ciélo mío, níña de mi álma	*My heaven, pupil of my soul*
Híja de mi corazón	*My dearest child, child of my heart*
Ángel mío	*My angel*
Estrélla mía	*My star*
Bién mío	*My blessing*
III. *Acérca de agradecér y cumplimentár, y mostrár amistád.*	III. About thanking and complimenting, and showing friendship.
Víva ustéd múchos áños	*I thank you, may you live many years*
Le devuélvo las mas vívas grácias	*I return you the most heartfelt thanks*
Gustóso lo haré	*I will do it cheerfully*
De tódo mi corazón	*With all my heart*
De múy buéna gána	*Heartily, with a very good will*
Lo estímo	*I am obliged for it*
Sóy de vm.	*I am yours*
Sóy su servidór	*I am your servant*
Su múy humílde servidór	*Your very humble servant*
Vm. me favoréce múcho	*You are very obliging, you favour me much.*
Se tóma vm. demasiádo trabájo	*You take too much trouble*
No hállo ningúno en servírle	*I find none in serving you*
Es vm. múy aténto y múy cortés	*You are very civil and polite*
¿Que deséa vm.? ¿que me mánda vm.?	*What do you wish? what do you command me?*
Ordéneme con tóda libertád	*Command me with full liberty*
Sin cumplimiénto	*Without compliment*

Sin ceremónia	*Without ceremony*
Le ámo de corazón	*I love you sincerely*
Con el álma y la vída	*With my soul and life*
É yo correspóndo á vm. có-mo débo	*And I return it to you as I ought*
Hága cuénta sóbre mí	*Rely or depend upon me*
Mándeme vm.	*Command me*
Hónreme con sus precéptos	*Honour me with your com-mands*
Tiéne vm. álgo que man-dárme?	*Have you any thing to com-mand me?*
No tiéne vm. sinó hablár	*You have but to speak*
Dispónga de su servidór	*Dispose of your servant*
Sólo aguárdo sus precéptos	*I only wait your commands*
Demasiádo honór me háce	*You do me too much honour*
Degémonos de cumplimiéntos	*Let us forbear compliments*
Éntre amígos honrádos, se es-cúsan cumplimiéntos	*Between honest friends, com-pliments are excused*
Al Señor Don—le béso las mános	*Present or give my respects to Mr. D—. or I kiss the hands of Mr. D—.*
Déle vm. múchas espresiónes mías	*Remember my love to him, give him many expressions of mine*
No faltaré	*I will not fail*
Póngame vm. á los piés de la Señóra	*Present my humble respects to my lady, or put me at the feet of Madam*
Múchas memórias á la Se-ñoríta	*Remember me to Miss, or ma-ny remembrances to Miss*
Páse vm. adelánte, le vóy á seguír	*Walk before, I am going to follow you*
Después de vm., Cabálléro	*After you, Sir*
Sé bién lo que le débo	*I know well what I owe you*
Vámos, Señór, páse vm.	*Come, Sir, pass on*
Lo haré pára obedecérle	*I will do it to obey you*
Pára sólo agradárle	*Only to please you*
No sóy amígo de tántas cere-mónias	*I am not fond of so many ceremonies*
No sóy cumplimentéro	*I am not ceremonious*
Es lo mejór	*It is the best*
Tiéne vm. razón	*You are in the right*

26*

IV. *Acérca de afirmár, negár, consentír, &c.*

IV. About affirming, denying, consenting, &c.

Es verdád	*It is true*
Es ésto verdád?	*Is this true?*
Demasiádo verdád	*Too true*
Pára tratár verdád	*To tell the truth*
En efécto, es así	*Really, it is so*
Quién lo dúda?	*Who doubts it?*
No háy dúda	*There is no doubt*
Créo que es así	*I believe it is so*
Créo que no	*I believe not*
Dígo que sí	*I say it is*
Dígo que no	*I say it is not*
Apuésto que sí	*I lay it is*
Vu que no	*I lay it is not*
Por mi vída	*Upon my life*
Á fe de caballéro	*As I am a gentleman*
Á fe de hómbre de bién	*As I am an honest man*
Por mi honór	*Upon my honour*
Créame vm.	*Do believe me*
Se lo puédo decír	*I can tell it to you*
Se lo puédo afirmár	*I can affirm it to you*
Apostúra álgo	*I could bet something*
Se búrla vm.?	*Do you jest?*
Hábla vm. de véras?	*Do you speak in earnest?*
Lo dígo múy de véras	*I say it quite in earnest*
Lo adivinó vm.	*You guessed at it*
Lo acertó vm.	*You hit it*
Bién le créo	*I truly believe you*
Se le puéde creér	*One may believe you*
Éso no es imposíble	*That is not impossible*
Pués, en hóra buéna	*Well, let it be so, well and good*
Póco á póco	*Softly, fair and softly*
No es verdád	*It is not true*
Aquéllo es fálso	*That is false*
Náda de éso háy	*There is no such thing*
Es inciérto	*It is untrue, uncertain*
Es mentíra	*It is a lie*
Es úna falsedád	*It is a falsehood*
Me burlába, chanceába	*I did jest, I was joking*
Lo decía de chánza	*I said it in jest, joking*
Séa en hóra buéna	*Let it be so; well and good*
No me opóngo á éllo	*I do not oppose it*

Estámos de acuérdo	*We are agreed, in accord*
Dícho y hécho	*Said and done*
No lo quiéro	*I will not have it, I do not want it, I do not wish for it*

V. *Acérca de consultár, ó considerár.*	V. About consulting, or considering.
¿Que se ha de hacér?	*What is to be done?*
¿Que harémos?	*What shall we do?*
Que me díce vmd. que hága?	*What do you tell me to do?*
Que remédio háy pára éso?	*What remedy is there for that?*
Que partído hémos de tomár?	*What course are we to take?*
Hagámos ésto ó éso	*Let us do this or that*
Hagámos úna cósa	*Let us do one thing*
Mejór será que yó....	*It will be better that I....*
Aguárde vm. un póco	*Wait a little*
No sería mejór, si?....	*Would it not be better, if?...*
Dégeme hacér	*Let me do*
Si estuviéra en su lugár	*Were I in your place, if I were, &c.*
Es lo mísmo	*It is the same*
Viéne á salír á lo mísmo	*It comes to turn out to the same*

VI. *Del comér y del bebér.*	VI. About eating and drinking
Téngo buén apetíto	*I have a good appetite*
Téngo hámbre	*I am hungry*
Me muéro de hámbre	*I am starving, dying with hunger*
Me paréce que ha tres días que náda he comído	*It seems to me that it is three days I have eaten nothing*
Cóma vm. álgo	*Eat something*
Que gústa vm. comér?	*What do you like to eat?*
Comiéra un póco de cualquiéra cósa	*I could eat a little of any thing*
Déme vm. álgo de comér	*Give me something to eat*
He comído bastánte	*I have eaten enough*
Estóy satisfécho	*I am satisfied*
Quiére vm. comér aún mas?	*Will you eat still more?*
No téngo mas apetíto	*I have no more appetite*
Téngo sed	*I am dry, I have thirst*
Me muéro de sed	*I am dying with thirst*
Téngo múcha sed	*I am very thirsty*
Déme vmd. de bebér	*Give me to drink*

Víva vm. múchos áños	I thank you, may you live many years
Gustóso bebería úna copíta de víno, un váso de água	I could drink with pleasure a glass of wine, a tumbler of water
Béba vm. pués	Drink then
He bebído bastánte	I have drank enough
No puédo bebér mas	I can drink no more
Mi sed está apagáda	My thirst is allayed, extinct

VII. *Del ir, venír, movérse, &c.* — **VII.** Of going, coming, stirring, &c.

De dónde viéne vm.?	Whence do you come?
Á dónde va vm.?	Where do you go?
Véngo de—Vóy á—	I come from—I am going to—
Súba, báge	Come up, come down
Éntre vm., sálga vm.	Come in, go out
Páse vm. adelánte	Come forward
No se muéva, no se menée	Do not move, do not stir
Estése ahí	Stay there
Acérquese de mí	Come near to me, approach me
Retírese vm.	Retire, withdraw
Váyase	Go away, begone
Váya un póco atrás	Go back a little
Vénga vm. acá	Come hither, here
Aguárde vmd. un ráto	Wait a little
Espéreme, aguárdeme	Wait for me, stay for me
No váya tan de prísa	Do not go so fast
Va vm. múy á prísa	You go very fast
Quítese de delánte de mí	Get away from before me
No me tóque vm.	Do not touch me
Dége éso	Leave that
Porqué?	Why?
Así lo quiéro	I wish it so
Estóy bién aquí	I am well here
La puérta está cerráda	The door is shut
Ahóra está abiérta	Now it is open
Ábra vm. la puérta	Open the door
Ábra vm. la ventána	Open the window
Ciérre la ventána	Shut the window
Vénga vm. por aquí	Come this way
Váya vmd. por allá	Go that way
Páse vmd. por aquí	Pass this way

Páse por allá	*Pass that way*
Que búsca vm.?	*What do you look for?*
Que perdió vm.?	*What did you lose?*

VIII. *Del hablár, decír, obrár, &c.*	VIII. Of speaking, saying, acting, &c.
Háble vm. álto	*Speak loud*
Hábla vm. múy bájo	*You speak very low*
Con quién hábla vm.?	*With whom do you speak?*
Me hábla vm.?	*Do you speak to me?*
Dígale álgo	*Tell him something*
Hábla vm. Español?	*Do you speak Spanish?*
Sábe vm. el Castelláno?	*Do you know the Castilian?*
Álgo lo entiéndo y háblo	*I understand and speak it a*
Que díce vm.?	*What do you say?* [*little*
Que ha dícho vm.?	*What have you said?*
No dígo náda	*I say nothing*
No he dícho náda	*I have said nothing*
Cálle vm.	*Hold your tongue, be silent*
Cállome	*I am silent, I hold my tongue*
Élla no quiére callár	*She will not hold her tongue*
No háce mas que hablár y charlár	*She does nothing but prattle and tattle*
He oído decír, que—	*I have heard, that—*
Me lo han dícho	*They have told me so*
Lo dícen por ahí	*They say so abroad*
Tódos lo dícen	*Every one says so*
El Señór A. me lo díjo	*Mr. A. told it me*
Madáma no me lo ha dícho	*The lady has not told it me*
Se lo díjo á vm.?	*Did he tell it to you?*
Se lo díjo élla?	*Did she tell it to you?*
Cuándo lo oyó vm. decír?	*When did you hear it said?*
Hóy me lo han dícho	*To-day, they have told it to me*
Quién se lo díjo?	*Who told it to you?*
No lo puédo creér	*I cannot believe it*
Que díce él?	*What does he say?*
Que díce élla?	*What does she say*
Que le ha dícho?	*What has he said to you*
No me díjo náda	*He said nothing to me*
No me ha dícho notícia algúna	*He has not told me any news*
El Señór B. me díjo nuévas	*Mr. B. told me news*
No se lo díga vm.	*Do not tell it to them*
Se lo diré	*I will tell it him*

No se lo diré	*I will not tell it to her*
No le díga vm. palábra	*Say not a word to her*
• Se lo callaré	*I will keep it from him*
Cállelo vm. bién	*Keep it well to yourself*
Ha dícho vm. éso?	*Have you said that?*
No, no lo he dícho	*No, I have not said it*
No lo díjo vm.?	*Did you not say so?*
No lo han dícho?	*Have they not said so?*
Que está vm. haciéndo?	*What are you doing?*
Que ha hécho vm.?	*What have you done?*
No hágo náda	*I do nothing*
No he hécho náda	*I have done nothing*
Acabó vm.?	*Have you done? did you finish?*
No acabó vm.?	*Have you not done? did you not finish?*
Que está haciéndo él?	*What is he doing?*
Que háce élla?	*What does she do?*
Que quiére vm.? que mánda vm.?	*What do you wish? what do you command?*
Que es lo que le háce fálta?	*What is it that you want?*
Que píde vm.?	*What do you ask?*
Respóndame	*Answer me*
Porqué no me respónde vm.?	*Why don't you answer me?*

IX. *Del oír, escuchár, &c.*	IX. Of hearing, listening, &c
Óiga vm., Don. N.	*Hearken, Mr. N.*
Óigo, señór	*I hear, Sir*
Me óye vm.?	*Do you hear me?*
No le óigo	*I do not hear you*
No le puédo oír	*I cannot hear you*
Háble mas álto	*Speak louder*
Óiga, vénga acá	*Hark ye, come hither*
Óigole	*I hear you*
Escúchole	*I listen to you, I hearken to you.*
Estése quiéto	*Be quiet, be still*
No hága ruído	*Do not make a noise*
Que ruído es éste?	*What noise is this? [speak*
No nos podémos oír hablár	*We cannot hear one another*
Que zámbra árma vm. allá!	*What a thundering noise you make there!*
Me quiébra la cabéza	*You break my head*
Me atúrde vm.	*You stun me*
Es vm. muy molésto	*You are very troublesome*

X. *Del entendér, y compren-*
dér.

X. Of understanding and com-
prehending.

Le entiénde vm. bién? — *Do you understand him well?*

Ha entendído vm. lo que ha dícho? — *Have you understood what he has said?*

Entiénde vm. lo que díce? — *Do you understand what he says?*

Me entiénde vm.? — *Do you understand me?*

Le entiéndo bién — *I understand you well*

No le entiéndo — *I do not understand you*

Entiénde vm. el Españól? — *Do you understand Spanish?*

No lo entiéndo — *I do not understand it*

Lo entiéndo un póco — *I understand it a little* [it?

Lo entiénde el Señór? — *Does the gentleman understand*

No lo entiénde — *He does not understand it*

Me ha entendído vm.? — *Have you understood me?*

No le he entendído — *I have not understood you*

Ahóra le entiéndo — *Now I understand you*

Cuándo no hábla vm. tan de prísa — *When you do not speak so fast*

Él no pronúncia bién — *He does not pronounce well*

Paréce tartamúdo — *He seems a stammerer*

No se le entiénde lo que díce — *One does not understand what he says*

XI. *Acérca de preguntár.*

XI. About asking a question.

Cómo díce vm.? — *How do you say?*

Que es ésto? que háy? — *What's this? what is there?*

Que se díce? — *What do people say?*

Que quiére decír éso? — *What means that?*

Que quiéren éllos decír? — *What do they mean?*

De que sírve aquéllo? á que buéno? — *What is the use of that? what's it good for?*

Que le paréce? que tal? — *What do you think of it? how do you like it?*

Á que viéne aquéllo? — *To what purpose comes that?*

Dígame vm., se puéde sabér? — *Tell me, may one know?*

Se le puéde preguntár? — *May one ask you?*

Que me pregúnta vm.? — *What do you ask of me?*

Cómo, Señór? — *How, sir?*

Que se ha de hacér? — *What is to be done?*

Que deséa vm.?	*What do you wish?*
Que gústa vm.?	*What do you choose?*
Lo que quisiére	*What you please*
Suplícole me respónda	*I beg of you to answer me*
Porqué no me respónde?	*Why don't you answer me?*

XII. *Acérca de sabér.*	XII. About knowing or having a knowledge of things.

Sábe vm. éso?	*Do you know that?*
No lo sé	*I do not know it*
No sé náda de éllo	*I know nothing of it*
Élla bién lo sabía	*She knew it well*
Acáso no lo sabía él?	*Did he not perchance know it?*
Supuésto que lo supiése	*Suppose he knew it*
No sabrá náda de éllo	*He shall know nothing of it*
Que! no ha sabído náda de éllo?	*What! has he known nothing of it?*
No súpo jamás de ésto	*He never knew of this*
Ántes de vm. lo sabía yó	*I knew it before you*
Es así ó no?	*Is it so or not?*
No que lo sépa yó	*Not that I know of*

XIII. *Del conocér, olvidár, y acordárse.*	XIII. Of knowing or being acquainted with persons, forgetting and remembering.

Lo conóce vm.?	*Do you know him?*
La conóce vm.?	*Do you know her?*
Los conóce vm.?	*Do you know them?*
Las conózco	*I know them*
No les conózco	*I do not know them*
Nos conocémos	*We are acquainted*
No nos conocémos	*We do not know one another*
No le conóce vm. á él?	*Do you not know him?*
Créo que le he conocído	*I believe I have known him*
Le he conocído á élla	*I have known her*
Nos hémos conocído	*We have known one another*
Les conózco de vísta	*I know them by sight*
La conózco de nómbre	*I know her by name*
Él me conocía muy bién	*He knew me very well*
Me conóce vm.?	*Do you know me?*
He olvidádo su nómbre	*I have forgotten your name*
Me ha olvidádo vm.?	*Have you forgotten me?*

Le conóce á vm. élla? — *Does she know you?*
Le conóce á vm. el Señór? — *Does the gentleman know you?*
Paréce que no me conóce — *It seems he does not know me*
Bién me conóce el Señór — *The gentleman knows me well*
Yá no me conóce — *He knows me no more*
Me olvidó del tódo — *He quite forgot me*
Yá no me conóce élla — *She knows me no more*
Téngo el honór de ser conocído de él — *I have the honour to be known to him*
Se acuérda vm. de éso? — *Do you remember that?*
No se me acuérda, no me acuérdo de éllo — *I do not remember it, I do not recollect it*
Múy bién lo téngo presénte. — *I do remember it very well*
Hágaselo acordár — *Remind him of it*

XIV. *De la edád, de la vída, de la muérte, &c.* — **XIV.** Of age, life, death, &c.

Que edád tiéne vm.? — *How old are you?*
Que edád tiéne su hermáno? — *How old is your brother?*
Téngo véinte y cínco áños — *I am five and twenty*
Tiéne véinte y dos áños — *He is twenty-two years old*
Tiéne vm. mas áños que yó — *You are older than I*
Empiéza á envejecér — *He begins to grow old*
Que edád tendrá vm.? — *How old may you be?*
Estóy buéno que es lo esencial — *I am well, that is the main thing*
Está vm. casádo? — *Are you married?*
Cuántas véces ha estádo vm. casádo? — *How many times have you been married?*
Cuántas mugéres ha tenído vm.? — *How many wives have you had?*
Tiéne vm. aún pádre y mádre vívos? — *Have you a father and mother still alive?*
Mi pádre murió — *My father is dead*
Mi mádre se ha muérto — *My mother is dead*
Dos áños ha que perdí á mi pádre — *I lost my father two years ago*
Mi mádre se ha vuélto á casár — *My mother has married again*
Cuántos híjos tiéne vm.? — *How many children have you?*
Cuátro téngo — *I have four*
Híjos ó híjas, varónes ó hémbras? — *Sons or daughters, males or females?*

27

Téngo un híjo y tres híjas	I have one son and three daughters
Cuántos hermános tiéne vm.?	How many brothers have you?
No téngo ningúno vívo	I have none living, alive
Tódos se han muérto	They have all died
Tódos hémos de morír	We must all die
Cáda hóra es un páso hácia el túmulo	Every hour is a step towards the grave

XV. *De úna áya y su Señoríta.* — **XV.** Of a governess and her young lady.

Está vm. aún en la cáma?	Are you in bed still?
Duérme vm.?	Do you sleep? are you asleep?
Despiérte; que pesáda es vm.!	Awake; how heavy you are!
Es vm. múy dormilóna	You are very sleepy
No está aún despiérta?	Are you not awake yet?
Levántese ligéro, présto	Rise quickly, soon
Acáso es yá hóra de levantárse?	Is it perchance already time to rise?
Sin dúda lo es	It is so undoubtedly
Luégo darán las nuéve	Nine o'clock will presently strike
Está vm. levantáda?	Are you up, risen?
Está su hermána levantáda?	Is your sister up?
Vámos, despáche vm.	Come, make haste
Porqué no se da mas prísa?	Why do you not make more haste?
Cuidádo	Take care
Se caerá vm.	You will fall
Por póco se cáe	You came near falling
Acérquese de la lúmbre	Come near or draw near the fire
Abríguese bién	Clothe yourself warm
Se resfriará vm.	You will catch cold
Yá estóy acatarráda	I have a cold already
Vístase luégo	Dress yourself directly
Péinese	Comb your hair
Póngase las médias	Put on your stockings
Cálcese los zapátos	Put on your shoes
Tóme ésta camísa blánca	Take this clean chemise
Lávese las mános, la bóca, y la cára	Wash your hands, your mouth, your face
Límpiese los diéntes	Clean your teeth
Sus péines están súcios	Your combs are dirty

Acordóneme la cotílla	*Lace my stays*
Ayúdeme vm.	*Help me*
Porqué no me asíste?	*Why don't you help me?*
Acabó vm. yá?	*Have you already done?*
Aún no	*Not yet*
Que enfadósa es vm.!	*How tedious you are!*
Díga sus oraciónes	*Say your prayers*
Háble álto	*Speak loud*
Empiéce	*Begin*
Vámos adelánte	*Let us go on, forward*
Acábe vmd.	*Make an end, finish*
Adónde está su líbro de oraciónes?	*Where is your prayer-book?*
Tráiga su Bíblia	*Bring your Bible*
Búsquela présto, prónto	*Look for it quick, soon*
Léa vm. un capítulo	*Read a chapter*
A dónde acabó vm. ayér?	*Where did you leave off, finish yesterday?*
Aquí me paré	*I stopt here*
No tiéne vm. bién su líbro	*You do not hold your book well*
Léa póco á póco	*Read slowly, by degrees*
Deletrée ésa voz	*Spell that word*
Vm. lée múy de prísa	*You read very fast*
No lée vm. bién	*You do not read well*
Lée múy despácio	*You read very slow*
No aprénde vm. náda	*You learn nothing*
No obsérva náda	*You observe nothing*
No estúdia vm.	*You do not study*
No aprovécha náda	*You do not improve any*
Es vm. múy perezósa	*You are very idle*
Que murmúra vm. allá?	*What do you mutter there?*
Vuélva á empezár	*Begin again*
No sábe vm. su lección	*You do not know your lesson*
Ésta es su lección	*This is your lesson*
Déme ótra lección	*Give me another lesson*
Porqué me hábla vm. Inglés?	*Why do you speak English to me?*
Háble vm. siémpre Españól	*Speak always Spanish*
Quiére vm. almorzár?	*Will you breakfast?*
Que gústa vm. pára su almuérzo?	*What will you have, or do you wish for your breakfast?*
Comerá vm. pan y mantéca?	*Will you eat bread and butter?*

Díga vm. lo que quiére mas	*Say what you like best*
Acábe de almorzár	*Finish breakfasting*
Almorzó vm. yá?	*Have you breakfasted already?*
Tóme su labór	*Take your work*
Muéstreme su labór	*Show me your work*
Éso no está buéno	*That is not right*
Rehága tódo aquéllo	*Do all that again*
Tiéne úna agúja buéna?	*Have you a good needle?*
Tiéne vm. hílo?	*Have you any thread?*
Dége su labór	*Leave your work*
Váya á jugár un póco,	*Go and play a little*
Vuélva á trabajár cuándo há-ya jugádo	*Come again to work when you have played*
Váya á paseárse en el jardín	*Go and walk in the garden*
No se caliénte	*Do not overheat yourself*
Vuélva présto, prónto	*Come again quickly, soon*
Es hóra de comér	*It is dinner-time*
Siéntese á la mésa	*Sit down to the table*
Vámos, tóme vmd. úna sílla	*Come, take a chair*
Póngase la servilléta	*Put on your napkin*
Dónde están su cuchíllo, su tenedór y su cuchára?	*Where are your knife, your fork and your spoon?*
Réce úntes de empezár	*Say grace before you begin*
Cóma vm. sópa	*Eat some soup*
Gústa vm. carnéro?	*Will you have some mutton?*
Quiére górdo ó mágro?	*Will you have fat or lean?*
Le gústa la gordúra?	*Do you like fat?*
Le gústa á vm. sálsa?	*Do you like sauce?*
Dígame su gústo	*Tell me your taste*
Cóma, no cóme vm.	*Eat, you do not eat*
He aquí úna úla de póllo	*Here is the wing of a chicken*
Cóma vm. pan con su cárne	*Eat bread with your meat*
Ha bebído vm.?	*Have you drank?*
Pída de bebér	*Ask for drink*
Es ésta cárne sabrósa?	*Is this meat agreeable?*
Quiére vm comér mas?	*Will you eat more?*
Ha comído vm. bastánte?	*Have you eat enough?*
Le gusta el quéso?	*Do you like cheese?*
Dé vm. las grácias	*Give thanks*
Váya á bailár	*Go to dance*
Ha bailádo vmd.?	*Have you danced?*
Egercítese bién	*Exercise yourself well*

Váya, dánce vm. un minuéte	*Come, dance a minuet*
No dánza vm. bién	*You do not dance well*
Téngase derécha	*Stand, hold yourself upright*
Levánte la cabéza	*Hold up your head*
Hága la cortesía	*Make a curtsey*
Míreme vmd	*Look at me*
Que está vm. mirándo?	*What are you looking at?*
Se fué su maéstro?	*Is your master gone?*
Ha acabádo vm. yá?	*Have you done already?*
Váya ahóra á cantár	*Go now and sing*
Lléve su líbro consígo	*Carry your book with you*
Vuélva á trabajár cuándo há-ya acabádo	*Come again to work when you have done, finished*
Ha cantádo vm.?	*Have you sung?*
Tiéne lección nuéva?	*Have you a new lesson?*
Cánte vm. úna ariéta	*Sing an air, arietta*
Cánte vm. úna canción	*Sing a song*
Cánta vm. bonítaménte	*You sing prettily*
Tóque vm. el cláve ó piáno fórte, la hárpa	*Play on the harpsichord or forte piano, the harp*
Ahóra la guitárra espańóla	*Now the Spanish guitar*
Su príma no vále náda	*Your treble string is good for nothing*
Está su guitárra templáda?	*Is your guitar in tune?*
Sábe vm. templárla?	*Do you know how to tune it?*
Aún está destempláda	*It is still out of tune*
No tiéne vm. bién su guitárra	*You do not hold your guitar well*
Váya vm. á aprendér el Espańól y el Francés	*Go and learn Spanish and French*
Dónde está su gramática?	*Where is your grammar?*
Búsque su líbro	*Look for your book*
Que lección tiéne vm.?	*What lesson have you?*
Que diálogo ha leído?	*What dialogue have you read?*
Repíta su lección	*Repeat your lesson*
No la sábe vm.	*You do not know it*
Náda ha aprendído	*You have learned nothing*
Léa delánte de mí	*Read before me*
No pronúncia vm. bién	*You do not pronounce well*
Aprendió vm. su lección de memória?	*Have you learned your lesson by heart?*
No tiéne vmd. memória	*You have no memory*

27 *

No tóma vm trabájo	*You take no pains*
Que quiére pára merendár? —pára cenár?	*What will you have for luncheon? for supper?*
Vénga á cenár	*Come to sup*
No se engolosíne en la frúta	*Do not eat fruit greedily*
Estará vm. mála	*You will be sick*
La frúta no le siénta bién	*Fruit does not suit you*
Es tiémpo de acostárse	*It is time to go to bed*
Desnúdese luégo	*Undress yourself presently*
Réce	*Say your prayers*
Levántese mañána tempráno	*Rise early to-morrow*

XVI. *Del paséo.*   XVI. Of walking.

Háce múy béllo tiémpo	*It is very fine weather*
Éste día cláro y seréno convída al paséo	*This clear and serene day invites to walk*
No paréce núbe algúna	*There does not appear any cloud*
Vámos á paseár	*Let us go and walk*
Vámos á tomár el áire	*Let us go and take the air*
Quiére vm. dar úna vuélta?	*Will you take a turn?*
Gústa vm. venír conmígo?	*Do you wish to come with me?*
Respóndame, dígame si, ó no	*Answer me, tell me yes or no*
Vámos pués, me gústa	*Let us go then, I wish it*
Le acompañaré	*I will accompany you*
A dónde irémos?	*Where shall we go?*
Vámos al Párque	*Let us go to the Park*
Vámos á los prádos	*Let us go to the meadows*
Irémos en cóche?	*Shall we go in a coach?*
Cómo le gustáre	*As you please*
Vámonos á pié	*Let us go on foot*
Tiéne vm. razón	*You are in the right*
Éso es saludáble	*That is healthy, wholesome*
Se gána apetíto andándo	*Walking gets one an appetite*
Ánimo, vámos, andémos	*Cheer up, come, let us walk*
Por dónde irémos?	*Which way shall we go?*
Por dónde quisiére	*Which way you please*
Por aquí ó por allí?	*This way or that way?*
Vámos por aquí	*Let us go this way*
Á máno derécha, á la derécha	*On the right hand, to the right*
Á máno izquiérda, á la izquiérda,	*On the left hand, to the left*

Quiére vm. ir por água?	*Will you go by water?*
A dónde está el bárco?	*Where is the vessel?*
A dónde están los barquéros?	*Where are the boatmen?*
Éntre vm. en el bóte	*Step into the boat*
Sólo atravesarémos el río	*We will just cross the river*
El água está múy mánsa y apacíble	*The water is very smooth ana calm*
Empiéza á movérse	*It begins to move*
A dónde quiére vm. desembarcár, abordár?	*Where will you land, board?*
Estámos cérca de la orílla	*We are near the shore, the bank*
Pára tú el bóte	*Stop the boat*
Pasémos la vísta sóbre éstos cámpos y prádos	*Let us cast our sight upon these fields and meadows*
Que verdúra tán hermósa !	*What a fine green!*
Éstos prádos están esmaltádos con variedád de flóres	*These meadows are enamelled with a variety of flowers*
Que prospécto tan hermóso!	*What a beautiful prospect!*
Éste lugár es múy améno	*This place is very pleasant*
Los árboles échan flóres	*The trees are blooming*
Los rosáles empiézan á echár capúllos	*The rose-bushes begin to bud, or throw out buds*
Aún no están abiértas éstas rósas	*These roses are not blown open yet*
Créce el trígo	*The corn grows*
Prométen múcho los pánes	*The cornfields are very promising*
Las espígas son múy lárgas	*The ears are very long*
Yá el trígo está madúro	*The wheat is already ripe*
Ésta es úna bélla llanúra	*This is a fine plain*
Éstas sómbras son múy apacíbles	*These shades are very pleasant*
Que tódo tan hermóso!	*What a fine whole!*
Me paréce que estóy en un paraíso terrenál	*Methinks I am in an earthly paradise*
No óye vm. la dúlce melodía de las áves?	*Do you not hear the sweet melody of birds?*
El cánto suáve del ruíseñór?	*The sweet · warbling of the nightingale?*
Aún no estámos en Máyo	*We are not yet in May*
Ánda vm. demasiádo présto	*You walk too quick, fast*
No le puédo seguír	*I cannot follow you*
No puédo ir tan de prísa	*I cannot go so fast*

No me es posíble alcanzárle	*Is it not possible for me to overtake you*
Es vm. un póbre caminánte	*You are a sorry walker*
Le suplíco, ánde un póco mas despácio	*Pray, go a little slower*
Descansémos un ráto	*Let us rest a little, a while*
No vále la péna	*It is not worth the while*
Está vm. cansádo?	*Are you tired?*
Estóy molído	*I am fatigued*
Acostémonos en la yérba	*Let us lie down upon the grass*
Me témo que esté húmeda	*I am afraid it is damp*
Cómo puéde ser? no ha llovído	*How can it be? it has not rained*
Básta la humedád de la nóche	*The dampness of the night is sufficient*
Ni aún quiéro sentárme en el suélo	*Nor will I even sit upon the ground*
Pasémos pués á ésa sélva, florésta	*Let us proceed then to that wood, forest*
Entrémos en ése bosque	*Let us go into that grove*
Que sítio tán gustóso!	*What a delightful place!*
Que idóneo pára estudiár!	*How fit for study!*
He aquí tres paséos	*Here are three walks*
Que bién plantúdos están éstos árboles!	*How well these trees are planted!*
Se inclínan únos hácia ótros	*They bend towards each other*
Éstos árboles hácen bélla sómbra	*These trees make a fine shade*
Que espésa está ésa arboléda!	*How thick that grove is!*
Los ráyos del sol no la puéden penetrár	*The sun-beams cannot pierce through it*
He aquí hermósos huértos	*Here are fine orchards*
Háy múcha frúta	*There is a great deal of fruit*
Véo manzánas, péras, avellánas, guíndas	*I see apples, pears, filberts, cherries*
Ántes quisiéra nuéces ó castáñas	*I had rather have walnuts or chestnuts*
Éstos albaricóques y pérsigos me hácen venir el água á la bóca	*These apricots and early peaches make my mouth water*
Bién me comiéra duráznos y algúnas de éstas ciruélas	*I could really eat peaches and some of these plums*

Cuánto cuésta la líbra de guíndas?	*How much costs a pound of cherries?*
Ócho cuártos y médio	*Five cents*
Comprémos algúnas	*Let us buy some*
Me témo que nos mojémos	*I am afraid we shall get wet*
Repáro que el tiémpo empiéza á anublárse	*I observe the weather begins to grow cloudy*
Volvámonos	*Let us go back, let us return*
Empiéza á ser tárde	*It begins to be late*
Se póne el sol	*The sun is setting*
No córra vm.	*Do not run*
Aguárdeme un póco	*Stay for me a little*
Vámos, vámos, si estuviére cansádo, descansará cenándo	*Come, come, if you be weary, you will rest yourself at supper*
Y aún mejór en la cáma	*And yet better in bed.*

XVII. *Del tiémpo* — XVII. Of the weather

Que tiémpo háce?	*How is the weather?*
Háce buén tiémpo?	*Is it fine weather?*
Háce mal tiémpo?	*Is it bad weather?*
Háce calor?	*Is it hot?*
Háce frío?	*Is it cold?*
Lúce el sol?	*Does the sun shine?*
Háce béllo tiémpo	*It is fine weather*
Háce mal tiémpo	*It is bad weather*
El tiémpo está séco, húmedo, nubládo, lluvióso, tempestuóso, ventóso	*It is dry, damp, cloudy, rainy, stormy, windy weather*
Es tiémpo inconstánte y variáble	*It is unsettled and changeable weather*
Háce grán calór, múcho frío	*It is very hot, very cold*
El tiémpo está cláro y seréno	*It is clear and serene weather*
Lúce el sol	*The sun shines*
Háce ún tiémpo oscúro	*It is dark weather*
Háce nubládo, el ciélo está cargádo de núbes	*It is cloudy, the sky is overcast*
Las núbes son múy espésas	*The clouds are very thick*
Lluéve?	*Does it rain?*
No, créo que no	*No, I believe not*
Empiéza á llovér	*It begins to rain*
Aún no lluéve	*It does not rain yet*
Présto lloverá á cántaros	*It will soon rain in torrents*

Yá lluéve	It rains already
Sólo es un aguacéro	It is but a shower
Pasará luégo	It will be over presently
Me témo que tendrémos água	I am afraid we shall have rain
No téma vm., no ténga miédo	Do not fear, be not afraid
Es úna núbe que pása	It is a flying cloud
Tódo el día lloverá	It will rain all day
Múcho lo dúdo	I question it much
Présto acabará de llovér	It will soon cease to rain
Pongámonos al abrígo	Let us put ourselves under shelter
No hay náda que temér	There is nothing to fear
Sólo es água	It is but water
Tiéne vm. miédo del água?	Are you afraid of water?
Sólo témo echár á perdér mi vestído	I fear only to spoil my clothes
Yá tenémos água	It rains already
No debémos salír con éste tiémpo	We must not go out in such weather
Graníza ó apedréa	It hails
Graníza múy récio	It hails very hard
Ahóra niéva	Now it snows
Que! niéva?	What! does it snow?
Míre vm. ésos grándes cópos	Look at those great flakes
Hiéla también?	Does it freeze also?
No, que deshiéla	No, it thaws
Créo que hiéla múy fuérte	I think it freezes very hard
Es hiélo múy dúro	It is a very hard frost
El hiélo se derríte	The ice is melting
La niéve se háce água	The snow melts away
Cáe aguaniéve	There is a sleet falling
Córre úna borrásca gránde	There blows a great storm
Truéna	It thunders
Relampaguéa	It lightens
Sólo alúmbran los relámpagos	The flashes of lightning alone give light
Córre múcho viénto	The wind blows hard
Háce múcho viénto	The wind blows high
El viénto viéne múy frío	The wind blows very cold
Se mudó el viénto	The wind is changed
El viénto cáe	The wind falls
Pasó la torménta	The storm is over
El tiémpo se aclára	The weather clears up

El ciélo empiéza á aclarárse	*The sky begins to clear up*
Se ábre el tiémpo, empiéza á serenárse	*The weather settles, it begins to be fair again*
Divídense las núbes; desaparécen y desvanécense póco á póco	*The clouds divide or break asunder; they disappear and vanish by degrees*
Yá vémos lucír el sol	*We now see the sun shine*
Véo el árco íris, el árco celéste	*I see the rainbow*
Es señál de buén tiémpo	*It is a sign of fair weather*
Háce úna neblína múy espésa	*There is a very thick mist*
No nos podémos ver	*We cannot see one another*
He allí úna niébla que se levánta	*There is a fog rising*
Péro el sol empiéza á disipárla	*But the sun begins to disperse it*

XVIII. *De la hóra.*	XVIII. Of the time of day.
Que hóra es?	*What o'clock is it?*
Véa vm. que hóra es	*See what o'clock it is*
Dígame que hóra es	*Tell me what o'clock it is*
No sábe vm. que hóra es?	*Don't you know what o'clock it is?*
Es tempráno	*It is early*
No es tárde	*It is not late*
Nos volverémos á cása?	*Shall we return home?*
Háy bastánte tiémpo	*There is time enough*
Sólo es médio día, sólo son las dóce del día	*It is but mid-day, only twelve o'clock, (at noon)*
Es cérca de la úna	*It is near one*
Ahóra dió la úna	*It struck one now*
Es la úna y cuárto	*It is a quarter past one*
Es la úna y média	*It is half an hour past one*
Es la úna y tres cuártos	*It is three-quarters past one*
Es cérca de las dos, ó darán las dos	*It is near two, or it is upon the stroke of two*
No he oído el relój	*I have not heard the clock*
Han dádo las séis	*It has struck six*
Son las siéte al sol	*It is seven by the sun*
Acában de dar las siéte	*It struck seven just now*
Las ócho han dádo	*It has struck eight*
Cérca de las diéz	*About ten o'clock*
Es cérca de las dóce de la nóche, ó média nóche	*It is near twelve o'clock, **or** midnight*
Cómo lo sábe vm.?	*How do you know it?*

Da el relój	*The clock strikes*
Lo óye vm. dar?	*Do you hear it strike?*
No créo que séa tan tárde	*I do not think it is so late*
Míre su relój de faltriquéra	*Look at your watch*
Adelánta múcho	*It goes very fast*
Atrása demasiádo	*It goes too slow*
No ánda, está parádo	*It does not go, it is stopped*
Déle vm. cuérda	*Wind it up*
Véa vm. que hóra es al relój de sol	*See what o'clock it is by the sun-dial*
Los cuadrántes no concuérdan	*The sun-dials do not agree*
La máno está quebráda	*The hand is broken*
Dónde está su relój de repetición?	*Where is your repeater? or repeating watch?*
No lo hállo, está estraviádo	*I do not find it, it is mislaid*

XIX. *De las estaciónes del año.*

XIX. Of the seasons of the year.

Que estación le gústa mas?	*What season do you like best?*
La primavéra es la mas agradáble de tódas	*Spring is the most pleasant of all*
Tóda la naturaléza se aníma	*All nature is animated*
El tiémpo está muy suáve, templádo	*The weather is very mild, temperate*
Ni háce demasiádo calór, ni demasiádo frío	*It is neither too hot, nor too cold*
Enamóran entónces tódos los animáles, ó árden en amór	*All creatures then make love, or burn with love*
No háy primavéra éste áño	*There is no spring this year*
Los tiémpos están revuéltos	*The times are disordered*
Es un inviérno moderádo	*It is a moderate winter*
Náda adelánta	*Nothing comes forward*
La estación está muy atrasáda	*The season is very backward*
Tenémos un estío muy caluróso, tiémpo abochornádo	*We have a very hot summer, sultry weather*
Oh, que calór!	*How hot it is!*
Háce un calór escesívo	*It is excessively hot*
Que tiémpo tan pesádo,	*What heavy weather!*
No puédo con tánto calór	*I cannot endure so much heat*
Estóy traspirándo, sudándo, hécho água	*I am perspiring, sweating, all over in a perspiration*
Me muéro de calór	*I am dying with heat*
Jamás túve tánto calór	*I never was so hot*

Es múy béllo tiémpo pára los frútos de la tiérra	It is very fine weather for the fruits of the earth
Tendrémos múcho héno	We shall have a great deal of hay
La cosécha será múy abundánte	The harvest will be very plentiful
Háy abundáncia de frúta	There is abundance of fruit
Tódos los árboles han producído múcho	All the trees have produced much
Nos háce fálta un póco de água	We are in want of a little rain
La cosécha está cérca	Harvest time draws near
Empiézan á segár los trígos	They begin to reap the wheat
Se han segádo los prádos	The meadows have been mowea
Es menestér recogér los pánes	We must take in the corn
Estámos en la canícula	We are in dog-days
Pasó yá el veráno	The summer is already gone
El otóño, la caída de las hójas, le ha sucedído	Autumn, the fall of the leaves, has taken its place
La vendímia se acérca	Vintage draws near
Hermósa vendímia tenémos	We have a fine vintage
Vendimiarémos en tres ó cuátro días	We shall gather grapes in three or four days
Los vínos serán buénos ésto áño	Wines will be good this year
Las víñas han dádo bién	The vines have borne well
El víno será baráto	Wine will be cheap
Es precíso recogér los frútos atrasádos	We must gather the late produce
Las manzánas y péras de inviérno	Winter apples and pears
Los días se han acortádo múcho	The days have grown very short
Las mañánas son frías	The mornings are cold
El inviérno viéne acercándose	Winter comes on drawing near, approaching
Múy présto es nóche	It is very soon night
Las tárdes son lárgas	The evenings are long
Empiéza la lúmbre á recreár á la tardecíta	Fire begins to be pleasant at dusk, early in the evening
No me gústa el inviérno	Winter does not please me
Los días son múy bréves	The days are very short

28

Yá no es de día á las cínco	*It is no longer light at five*
No se ve á las cínco	*One does not see at five*
Empiéza á anochecér á las cuátro	*It begins to grow dark at four*
Amanéce á las siéte	*The day breaks at seven*
No se sábe en que pasár el tiémpo	*One knows not in what to spend one's time*
Éste inviérno es múy frío, múy áspero	*This is a very cold, very sharp winter*
Se acuérda vm. del gránde inviérno?	*Do you remember the hard winter?*
Jamás vi inviérno tan frío	*I never saw so cold a winter.*
Empiézan á crecér los días	*The days begin to lengthen*
Los días son un póco mas lárgos	*The days are a little longer*
Cási no hémos tenído inviérno	*We almost have had no winter*
La primavéra yá viéne á regocijár la naturaléza	*The spring comes already to revive or rejoice nature*

XX. *De la ida á la escuéla.*   **XX.** Of going to school.

De dónde viéne vm.?	*From whence do you come?*
De cása. De mi cása.	*From home. From my house.*
Adónde va, vm. tan de prísa?	*Where are you going so fast?*
Vóy á la escuéla	*I am going to school*
Vénga conmígo	*Come with me*
Aguárde un poco	*Stay a little*
Vámonos, le suplíco	*Let us go, I pray you*
Porqué juéga vm. andándo?	*Why do you play as you go?*
No se entreténga	*Do not amuse yourself.*
Llegarémos bastánte présto	*We shall arrive soon enough*
Que hóra es?	*What o'clock is it?*
Cérca de las siéte	*Almost seven*
Aún no ha dádo el relój	*The clock has not struck yet*
Despachémos	*Let us make haste*
Quién viéne ahí?	*Who comes there?*
Es úno de nuéstros condiscípulos	*It is one of our schoolfellows*
Irémos los tres júntos	*We will go all three together*
Vámonos á prísa	*Let us go away fast*

XXI. *En la escuéla.*   **XXI.** In the school.

Siéntese en su lugár	*Sit down in your place*
Cuélgue su sombréro	*Hang up your hat*

A dónde está su líbro?	*Where is your book?*
Léa su lición	*Read your lesson*
Estúdie su lición	*Study your lesson*
Apréndа su lición de memória	*Get your lesson by heart*
Náda háce sinó jugár	*You do nothing but play*
Le anotaré	*I will set you up*
Se lo diré al maéstro	*I will tell it to the master*
Acabó vm.?	*Have you done?*
Aún no he acabádo	*I have not finished yet*
Que está escribiéndo?	*What are you writing?*
Escríbo mi egercício	*I am writing my exercise*
Tódo lo he escríto	*I have written it all*
No me muéva	*Do not jog me*
Hága me un póco de lugár	*Make a little room for me*
Vm. tiéne bastánte lugár	*You have room enough*
Váya atrás un póco	*Go a little farther*
Un póco mas arríba	*A little higher*
Álgo mas abájo	*A little lower*
Sírvase de dárme un líbro	*Be pleased to give me a book*
Adónde empezámos?	*Where do we begin?*
Hásta dónde decímos?	*How far do we say?*
Hásta aquí	*Thus far, so far*
Cuál es su taréa?	*Which is your task?*
De quién es éste líbro?	*Whose book is this?*
Sábe vm. su lición de memória?	*Do you know your lesson by heart?*
Aún no	*Not yet*
Apúnteme vm.	*Do prompt me*
Ha de leérla tres véces	*You must read it three times*
Quién lo ha dícho?	*Who has said so?*
El Señór A. lo mandó	*Mr. A. ordered it*
Tiéne vm. plúma y tínta?	*Have you pen and ink?*
Escríba vm. su egercício	*Write your exercise*
Lo escribió vm. mal	*You wrote it ill*
Léa vm. su lición	*Read your lesson*
Díga su lición	*Say your lesson*
Le azotarán	*You will be flogged*
Meréce vm. azótes	*You deserve a whipping*
Porqué lléga vm. tan tárde?	*Why do you arrive so late?*
Túve que hacér	*I had to do*
Que negócio le detúvo?	*What business detained you?*
Á que hóra se levantó?	*At what hour did you rise?*
Á las ócho	*At eight o'clock*

Porqué se levantó tan tárde?	*Why did you rise so late?*
Es vm. un flojón	*You are a sluggard*
Quédese en su sítio	*Remain in your place*
Quítese de mi lugár	*Get away from my place*
Porqué me rempúja así?	*Why do you push me so?*
Quién le tóca?	*Who touches you?*
No se enóge vm.	*Do not be angry*
Me quejaré al maéstro	*I will complain to the master*
Dígaselo, si quisiére	*Tell it to him, if you will*
Póco me impórta	*I care little*
Señór, no me quiére dejár quiéto	*Sir, he won't let me alone*
Me agarró el líbro de las mános	*He snatched the book from my hands*
Háce búrla de mí	*He makes fun of me*
Me tiró de los cabéllos	*He pulled me by the hair*
Me da patádas	*He kicks me*
Me empúja fuéra de mi lugár	*He thrusts me out of my place*
No háy tal	*There is no such thing*
Que búlla es ésta?	*What noise is this?*
Tómen éste muchácho y dénle úna máno de azótes	*Take this boy and give him a good whipping*
Señór, perdóneme vm.	*Sir, pardon me*
Suplícole, Señór, perdóneme ésta sóla vez	*Pray, Sir, forgive me this once alone*
Pórtese pués mejór en adelánte	*Behave then better for the future, hereafter*

———

Diálogos Familiáres, Españóles é Ingléses.
Familiar Dialogues, Spanish and English.

Diálogo I. *Acérca de saludár é informárse de la salúd de algúno.*	Dialogue I. Of saluting and inquiring after any one's health
Buénos días, Señór	*Good morning, good day, Sir*
Yó se los deséo á vm.	*I wish you the same*
Buénas tárdes, Caballéro	*Good afternoon, good evening, Sir*
Buénas nóches, Señór	*Good night, Sir*
Servidór de ustéd	*Your servant*
Cómo está vm.?	*How do you do?*
Buéno, pára servír á vm.	*Very well, to serve you*

Cómo va? cómo lo pása?	How goes it? How are you?
Siémpre al servício de vm.	Always at your service
Y á vm., Señór, cómo le va?	And you, Sir, how is it with you?
Múy bién, grácias á Diós	Very well, thank God
Estóy buéno pára servír á vm.	I am very well at your service
Vámos pasándo; así así	Pretty well; so so
Me alégro múcho de vérle	I am very glad to see you
Me alégro de vérle con salúd	I rejoice to see you in health
Agradézcoselo infiníto	I thank you very much for it
Viva vm. múchos áños	I am obliged to you
Cómo está el Señór su hermáno?	How does your brother do?
Estába buéno la última vez que le ví	He was well the last time I saw him
Está buéno, grácias á Diós	He is well, thank God
Créo que le va bién	I believe he is well
Ayér nóche estába buéno	He was well last night
Me alégro de éso	I am very glad of it
Dónde está?	Where is he?
En el cámpo	In the country
En la ciudád	In the city
En cása	At home
Ha salído póco háce	He is just gone out
Se alegrará de ver á vm.	He will be glad to see you
Celebrará múcho sabér que vm. góza de perfécta salúd	He will be very happy to hear you enjoy perfect health
Vm. le favoréce múcho	You are very kind to him
También encontrará vm. con el mas síncero reconocimiénto	You will also meet with a most sincere return
Sóy su servidór	I am his servant
Cómo está la Señoríta?	How is the young lady?
Está buéna	She is well
Créo que está muy buéna	I believe she is very well
No está muy buéna	She is not very well
Está álgo malíta	She is a little unwell
Ayér mañána estába indispuésta	She was indisposed yesterday morning
Héla aquí que viéne	Here she is coming
Señoríta, á los piés de vm.	Miss, your most humble servant

28*

Servidóra de vm., Señór	Sir, I am your servant
Cómo ha estádo vm., désde que no le he vísto?	How have you been, since I saw you last?
Siémpre bién, grácias á Diós	Always well, thank God
Cómo se hálla vm.?	How do you find yourself?
Entéraménte bién	Quite well
Me da gústo de sabérlo	I am pleased to know it
De corazón lo agradézco	I thank you heartily
Péro cómo le va ahóra?	But how is it with you now?
Mediánaménte	Tolerably
No he pasádo buéna nóche	I have not passed a good night
Lo siénto muchísimo	I am very sorry for it
Es un dolór	I regret it very much
Yó le compadézco múcho	I sympathise much with you
No puédo yó lisongeárme múcho de salúd	I cannot boast much in point of health
Que ha tenído vm.?	What has been the matter with you?
Mi estómago ha estádo álgo descompuésto	My stomach has been a little out of order
Paréce que está vm. buéna ahóra	It seems you are now well
Así así, púra servír á vm.	So so, at your service
Cómo están en cása?	How do they do at home?
Están nuéstros amígos de la córte, del cámpo, de la ciudád, de la vílla, buénos?	Our friends at court, in the country, in the city, in town, are they well?
Tódos están buénos, ménos mí mádre	They are all well, except my mother
Que le duéle?	What ails her?
Que enfermedád tiéne?	What is her complaint?
Tiéne calentúra, dolór cólico, tos	She has a fever, the colic, a cough
Le duéle la cabéza	She has the head-ache
Désde cuándo?	How long since?
Désde média nóche empezó á padecér	Since midnight she began to suffer
Deséo que se mejóre prónto	I wish her to improve speedily
Puédo yó servírla de álgo?	Can I serve her in any thing?
Puéde mandárme con tóda satisfacción	She may command me with full confidence
La Señóra núnca ha dudádo del favór de vm.	Madam never has doubted your goodness

Suplíco á vm. que no me ol-víde	*I beg you will not forget me*
Éso quéda de mi cuénta	*That lies to my account*
Ha múcho tiémpo que está mála?	*Is it long since she has been ill?*
No ha múcho	*It is not long*
Deséo que se mejóre	*I wish you may grow better*
La Señóra sábe múy bién el favór de vm.	*My lady is very sensible of your kindness*
Se alegrará de ver á vmd.	*She will be glad to see you*
Sóy múy servidór súyo	*I am her very humble servant*
Siénto no tenér tiémpo de vérla hóy	*I am sorry I have not time to see her to day*
Siéntese vmd. un ráto	*Sit down a little while*
De véras no puédo	*Indeed I cannot*
Está vm. múy de prísa?	*Are you in great haste?*
Volveré mañána	*I will come again to-morrow*
No puéde vm. esperár un póco?	*Cannot you wait a little?*
Téngo negócios urgéntes	*I have earnest business*
Sólo véngo pára sabér cómo estában vms.	*I only come to know how you were*
Rínda vm. mis respétos á su hermáno	*Present my best regards to your brother*
Encomiéndeme á mi Señóra su mádre	*Present my respects to my lady your mother*
Sus órdenes serán- puntuál-ménte obedecídas	*Your orders shall be punctu-ally obeyed*
Dígale vm. cuánto siénto sa-bér su indisposición	*Tell her how sorry I am to know her indisposition*
Lo haré sin fálta	*I shall do it without fail*
Váya vm. con Diós	*Farewell, go with God*
Quéde vm. con Diós	*Good bye, remain with God*
Estímo múcho ésta visíta	*I thank you for this visit*
Buénas nóches, Cabálléro	*Good night, good evening, Sir*
Señóra, felíces nóches	*Good night, Madam*

Diál. II. *Acérca del hablár Español.*	Dial. II. Of speaking Span-ish.
Aprénde vm. el Español?	*Do you learn Spanish?*
Sí, Señór, algún tiémpo háce	*Yes, Sir, some time since*
Yó me empéño en aprendérlo	*I endeavour to learn it*
Vm. háce múy bién	*You do very well*

Es úna léngua múy útil y hermósa

It is a very useful and very fine language

Es también múy graciósa, lléna de sal y espresión

It is also very witty, full of humour and expression

Me han dícho también que es mas varoníl y copiósa que la Francésa

I have been told it is also more manly and copious than the French

No obstánte, la Francésa es mas de móda

Notwithstanding, the French is more in fashion

Si los Españóles hubiéran cultivádo su léngua cómo los Ingléses, en éstos dos últimos síglos, sin dúda que sería múcho mas de móda

Had the Spaniards cultivated their language as the English have, in these two last centuries, no doubt it would be much more in fashion

Por la superioridád de su dicción, y la suavidád de su estílo

For its superiority of diction, and suavity of style

Porqué su pronunciación no tiéne mas de 27 sonídos

Because its pronunciation has only twenty-seven sounds

Porqué cáda létra se débe pronunciár

Because every letter is to be pronounced

Y cási siémpre con el mísmo sonído que en el Alfabéto

And almost always with the same sound as in the alphabet

Porqué su pronunciación se puéde esplicár suficiénteménte en úna página de duodécimo (véase página 20)

Because its pronunciation may be sufficiently explained in a duodecimo page, (See page 20)

También se puéde adquirír con facilidád en úna hóra

It may also be easily acquired in an hour

No háy estudiánte que en la priméra lección no la puéda con facilidád aprendér

There is no learner that in the first lesson may not easily learn it

Está en su podér, con 8 lecciónes, el leérla corrién·eménte, y con 20 entendér perféctaménte cualquiér líbro con la ayúda de un buén diccionário

It is in his power, with eight lessons, to read it fluently, and with twenty to understand perfectly any book with the help of a good dictionary

No tiéne declinación sinó pára los artículos y pronómbres

It has no declension but for the articles and pronouns

No tiéne mas de tres vérbos auxiliáres

It has no more than three auxiliary verbs

Cási constánteménte guárda la natural precedéncia de las palábras

It preserves almost constantly the natural precedence of words

La preposición núnca se encuéntra sinó delánte de su própio cáso

The preposition never is met with but before its own case

Tódas sus irregularidádes se puéden con facilidád corregír

All its irregularities may be easily corrected

Por ésto la léngua Españóla es la mas própia pára aprendérse por árte

For this reason the Spanish language is •the most proper to be learned by art

Y la mas proporcionáda pára los colégios, tratádos, comércio y tráto generál

And the most proper for Colleges, treaties, commerce and general intercourse

Tóda su brillantéz se descubrió en el síglo 16°—

All its brilliancy appeared in the 16th century

Y entónces se hablába mas comúnménte que ningúna ótra léngua

And it was then more commonly spoken than any other language

Los autóres Españóles de aquél síglo hiciéron entónces y aún hácen ahóra, así en vérso cómo en prósa, úna múy brillánte figúra

The Spanish writers of that century then made and yet make, both in verse and prose, a very brilliant figure

Ahóra también háy múchos líbros nuévos

There are also now many new books

Escrítos en el reinádo de Cárlos III.

Written in the reign of Charles III.

Que yó no cíto, porqué son múchos

Which I do not quote, because they are very numerous

La priméra lección me mostró lo múy fácil que es ésta léngua

The first lesson convinced me of the great facility of this language

Por mí, yó gústo múcho de élla

For my part, I like it very much

Porqué facilíta nuéstros médios de fomentár el mas impórtánte comércio que poséemos

Because it facilitates our means of encouraging the most important trade we possess

Dígo él de España y las Américas

I mean that with Spain and North and South America

Péro no empiéce vm. sin un hábil maéstro

But do not begin without an able master

Porqué un mal hábito no es fácil de dejár

Because an evil habit is not easily removed

Se díce, que vm. hábla múy bién el Españól

It is said, that you speak the Spanish very well

Entiéndolo mediánaménte

I understand it pretty well

Que líbros lée vm. pára aprendér el Españól?

What books do you read to learn Spanish?

Los Rudiméntos de la Léngua Española por Sáles

The Rudiments of the Spanish Language by Sales

La Gramática de Jossé, y los Egercícios por el mísmo Autór, edición de Sáles

The Grammar of Josse, and the exercises by the same Author, Sales' edition.

És amánte de España y su ríca y bélla literatúra

He is fond of Spain and its rich and beautiful literature

Léo también la Colména, las Cártas Marruécas y poesiás seléctas de CADALSO, y un tómo de Comédias Famósas escogídas por el mísmo Editór.

I read also the Colména, the Cártas Marruécas and select poems of CADALSO, and a volume of comédias famósas by the same Editor.

Porqué no lée vm. Don Quijóte?

Why do you not read Don Quixote?

Mi maéstro me díjo que no éra líbro pára principiántes

My master told me this was not a book for beginners

Que razón tiéne?

What is the reason?

Porqué háy en él múchos módos de hablár y refránes

Because it contains a great many idioms and proverbs

De que diccionário se sírve vm.

What dictionary do you make use of?

De él de Neumán en 2 tómos 8vo., ó de él del mísmo, en 1v. 18vo.

Of the dictionary of Neuman, 2v. 8vo., or that of the same in 1v. 18mo.

Que apréndo vm. de memória?

What do you get by heart?

Apréndo algúnas vóces del vocabulário de ésta Gramática

I learn some words in the vocabulary of this Grammar

Dígame vm., cómo se llámă aquéllo?

Tell me, how is that called?

Créo que se lláma ——

I believe it is called ——

Múy bién, y ésto?
Very well, and this?

Péro no estúdia vm. algúna cósa además de vóces?
But do you not study any thing else besides words?

Sí Señór, los egémplos de las réglas de la gramática
Yes, Sir, the examples of the rules of the grammar

El libro de egercícios, fráses familiáres y diálogos de la referída Gramática
The book of exercises, familiar phrases and dialogues of said Grammar

Va vm. aprendiéndo bién
You are learning well

Agradézco á vm. que me aliénte
I thank you for encouraging me

Pronúncio bién?
Do I pronounce well?

Bíllaménte, elegánteménte ·
Beautifully, elegantly

Sólo le fálta mas práctica
You only want more practice

Náda se adquiére sin trabájo
Nothing is acquired without pains

Por póco que se aplíque vmd., sabrá múy présto el Español
However little you apply, you will very soon know the Spanish

Estóy convencído de éllo
I am convinced of it

Me han dícho que vm. entendía múy bién el Idióma Castelláno
I have been told you understood well the Castilian language

Quisiéra que fuése verdád
I should wish it were true

Supóngo que deséa vm. sabér ésta hermósa léngua
I suppose you have a mind to know this fine language

Lo ha de suponér así; porqué, en efécto, lo deséo
You ought to suppose it so; for, indeed, I wish it

Bién, le vóy á enseñár el módo de hablár en póco el Español
Well, I am going to teach you the way to speak Spanish in a short time

Se lo agradeceré múcho
I shall be much obliged to you

El método mas fácil pára aprendér úna léngua, es hablárla á menúdo
The easiest way to learn a language, is to speak it frequently

Péro pára hablárla, es menestér sabér álgo de élla
But to speak it, one must know something of it

Yá sábe vm. bastánte
You know enough already

Sólo sé algúnas palábras de las mas necesárias, y algúnas senténcias bréves
I know but a few words most necessary, and some short phrases

Ésto básta pára empezár á hablár
This is enough to begin to speak

Si éso fuéra así, présto sabría la léngua	If it were so, I should soon know the language
No ténga vm. dúda de éllo	Have no doubt of it
No entiénde vmd. lo que le dígo?	Do not you understand what I say to you?
Lo entiéndo y compréndo múy bién	I understand and comprehend it very well
Péro hállo múcha dificultád en hablár	But I find much difficulty to speak
No téngo facilidád en hablár	I have no facility in speaking
Ésto viéne con el tiémpo	This comes in time
Téngo cortedád de hablár, por temór de esponérme á decír disparátes	I am bashful to speak, for fear of exposing myself to speak nonsense.
No se enfáde por ésto	Be not discouraged for that
Póca paciéncia téngo	I have little patience
Háce múcho tiémpo que vm. apréode?	Is it long since you have been learning?
Dos méses ha que empecé	It is two months since I began
Es múy córto tiémpo	It is a very short time
No le díce su maéstro que debiéra siémpre hablár?	Does not your master tell you that you should always speak?
Múy á menúdo me lo díce	He tells me so very often
Porqué pués, no quiére vm. hablár?	Why will you not speak then?
Con quién he de hablár?	With whom shall I speak?
Con tódos los que le háblen	With all those that speak to you
Quisiéra hablár, péro no me atrévo	I should wish to speak, but I dare not
Créame vm., séa atrevído, háble siémpre, bién ó mal	Believe me, be confident, speak always, well or ill
Sóbre tódo, no omíta vm. ocasión de hablár cuándo la encuéntre	Above all, omit no occasion of speaking when you find it
Hablándo es, cómo aprendémos á hablár	It is by speaking that we learn to speak
Ha pensádo vm múy bién	You have judged very right
Seguiré pués su conséjo	I shall follow your advice then
Hará vm. múy bién	You will do very well

Diál. III. *Pára hablár Inglés*	Dial. III. To speak English
Señór, es vm. Español?	Sir, are you a Spaniard?
Sí, Señór, pára servírle	Yes, Sir, at your service

De que paráge de España es vm.?

What part of Spain are you from?

De Madríd, de Toledo, de Sevílla, &c.

From Madrid, Toledo, Seville, &c.

De que ciudád?

Of what city?

De Cádiz

Of Cadiz

Cuánto tiémpo háce que está vm. en Inglatérra?

How long have you been in England?

Háce mas de un año

It is more than a year

Hábla vm. Inglés?

Do you speak English?

Háblolo un póco

I speak it a little

Péro mas entiéndo de lo que háblo

But I understand it better than I speak

La léngua Inglésa es múy dificultósa pára los Españóles

The English language is very difficult for Spaniards

La Españóla no es difícil pára los Ingléses

The Spanish is not difficult for Englishmen

Estóy persuadído de lo contrário

I am persuaded of the contrary

Con dificultád lo créo

I hardly believe it

La esperiéncia nos lo muéstra tódos los días

Experience shows it to us every day

La pronunciación del Español es múcho mas fácil que la del Inglés

The pronunciation of the Spanish is a great deal easier than that of the English

Éllos pronúncian tódas las létras cómo las escríben

They pronounce all the letters as they write them

Conózco á vários Ingléses que pronúncian múy bién el Castellano

I know several Englishmen who pronounce the Spanish very well

Apénas se podrá hallár un Español éntre ciénto que pronúncie bién el Inglés

One can hardly find one Spaniard in a hundred who pronounces English well

Los Ingléses se cómen la mitád de sus vóces

The English clip or eat up half their words

Dan un sólo sonído á três ó cuátro létras

They give a single sound to three or four letters

Péro en Español cáda létra tiéne su sonído

But in Spanish each letter has its sound

29

De suérte que la dificultád no paréce iguál de ámbos ládos

So that the difficulty does not seem equal on both sides

El Españól tiéne la ventája

The Spanish has the advantage

Y aún la dificultád es ménos pára la génte móza

And the difficulty is yet less for young people

Porqué los jóvencs son cómo céra blánda, en que se impríme fácilménte tódo

Because young people are like soft wax, on which one easily impresses every thing

Diál. IV. *Del hacér úna visíta por la mañána.*

Dial. IV. Of making a morning visit.

Quién está ahí?

Who is there?

Génte de paz, ábra vmd. la puérta

A friend, people of peace, open the door

Dónde está tu úmo?

Where is your master?

Está en la cáma

He is in bed

Duérme aún?

Does he sleep yet?

No, Señór, está dispiérto

No, Sir, he is awake

Está levantádo?

Is he up?

Aún no; quiére vm. entrár en su cuárto?

Not yet; will you step into his chamber?

Aún en la cáma?

Still in bed?

Me recogí anóche tan tárde, que no me he podído levantár mas tempráno

I retired so late last night, that I could not get up earlier

Que hízo vm. después de cenár?

What did you do after supper?

Cómo pasó vm. la nóche?

How did you spend the evening, the night?

Jugámos á los náipes

We played at cards

Á que juégo?

At what game?

Jugámos á los ciéntos

We played at piquet

Es un juégo múy de móda

It is a game much in fashion

Luégo nos fuímos al báile

Afterwards we went to the ball

Hásta que hóra se estúvo vmd. allí?

Till what o'clock were you there?

Hásta média nóche

Till midnight

Á que hóra se acostó vmd.?

What time did you go to bed?

Á la úna de la nóche

At one in the morning

No estráño que vm. se levánte tan tárde — *I do not wonder you rise so late*

Que hóra puéde ser? — *What o'clock may it be?*

Que hóra le paréce que es? — *What o'clock do you think it is?*

Han dádo las diéz — *It has struck ten*

Levántese vm. présto — *Rise quickly*

Darémos úna vuélta en el párque luégo que esté vmd. vestído — *We will take a turn in the Park as soon as you are dressed.*

Diál. V. *Del almorzár.* — Dial. V. Of breakfasting.

Quiére vm. almorzár? — *Will you breakfast?*

Es tiémpo de desayunárse? — *Is it breakfast time?*

Que gústa vm. pára su almuérzo? — *What do you wish for your breakfast?*

Pan y mantéca? — *Bread and butter?*

Mollétes caliéntes? — *Hot loaves?*

Léche? tostádas? chocoláte? — *Milk? toasts? chocolate?*

No; tódo éso es buéno pára niños — *No; all that is fit for children*

Tráiganos ótra cósa — *Bring us something else*

Gústan vms. de jamón? — *Do you wish for ham?*

Sí, tráigalo, que cortarémos úna tajáda — *Yes, bring it, and we will cut a slice of it*

Pónga úna servilléta en la mésa, y dénos plátos, cuchíllos y tenedóres — *Lay a cloth upon the table, and give us plates, knives and forks*

Láve los vásos — *Rinse the tumblers*

Dé un asiénto al Señór — *Give the gentleman a seat*

Tóme vm. úna sílla y siéntese — *Take a chair and sit down*

Acérquese de la lúmbre — *Come near the fire*

Estaré bién aquí, no téngo frío — *I shall be well here, I am not cold*

Gústan vms. de huévos fréscos? — *Will you have new laid eggs?*

Han de ser pasádos por água ó frítos? — *Must they be boiled or fried?*

Quíte ése pláto gránde — *Take that dish away*

Cóma vm. salchicha — *Eat sausage*

Probémos el víno — *Let us taste the wine*

Destápe ésa botélla — *Uncork that bottle*

No téngo tirabuzón — *I have no corkscrew*

Déme de bebér — *Give me to drink*
Cómo lo hálla vm.? — *How do you like it?*
Que le paréce á vm.? — *What do you think of it?*
Es buéno, no es málo — *It is good, it is not bad*
Dé de bebér al Señór — *Give the gentleman to drink*
Acábo de bebér — *I have just drank*
No cóme vm. — *You do not eat*
Tánto he comído, que no tendré gánas á médio día — *I have eaten so much, that I shall have no appetite at noon*
Se búrla vm.? náda cási ha comído — *Do you jest? you have eaten almost nothing*

Diál. VI. *Ántes de la comída.* — ***Dial. VI.** Before dinner.*

Es yá tiémpo de comér? — *Is it already dinner time?*
Son cérca de las tres — *It is near three o'clock*
Es hóra de comér — *It is time to dine*
Se atrasó hóy la comída hásta las cuátro — *Dinner was delayed to-day till four*
Quiére vm. hacér hóy peniténcia con nosótros? — *Will you make penance with us to-day?*
Si vm. quiére cenár bién, vénga á comér á mi cása — *If you wish to sup heartily, come and dine at my house*
Pónga la mésa, el mantél — *Lay the table, the cloth*
Tráiga la comída — *Bring the dinner*
Pónga los saléros y los plátos en la mésa — *Put the salt-cellars and plates upon the table*
Láve ó límpie los vúsos — *Wash or cleanse the tumblers*
Póngalos sóbre el aparadór — *Set them upon the side-board*
Córte únos pedacítos de pan — *Cut a few slices of bread*
Pónga las síllas al rededór de la mésa con sus almohadíllas — *Set the chairs round the table with their cushions*
Quién asíste á la mésa? — *Who waits at the table?*
Han venído tódos los convidádos ó huéspedes? — *Are all the invited persons or guests come?*
Aún no, algúnos fáltan — *Not yet, some are missing*
Dónde están los cuchíllos tenedóres y cucháras? — *Where are the knives, forks, and spoons?*
Están sóbre el aparadór — *They are upon the side-board*
Sólo le he convidádo pára gozár de su compañía — *I have invited you only to enjoy your company*
Hará vm. peniténcia — *You will make penance*
Mánde servír la comída — *Order the dinner to be served*

Aún no está prónta	*It is not yet ready*
Yá está la comída en la mésa	*The dinner is already on the table*
Sólo aguárdan á vm., Señór	*Sir, they only wait for you*
Tocáron la campána	*They rung the bell*
Siéntese vm. á la mésa	*Sit down to the table*
Tóme el primér asiénto	*Take the first seat*
No permitiré que esté sentádo allí	*I will not suffer you to sit there*
Aquí se sentará vm.	*You will sit here*
En verdád que no lo haré	*Indeed I shall not do it*
Vámos, degémonos de cumplimiéntos	*Come, let us forbear compliments*
Pára que tánta ceremónia?	*Why so much ceremony?*
Mas llanéza se ha de usár éntre los amígos	*More freedom should be used among friends*
Váya un póco mas atrás, que tengámos lugár	*Go a little farther back, that we may have room*
Bién cabémos tódos	*There is room enough for all*
Es menestér que quepámos	*We must all find place*
Tenémos mas compañía de lo que pensábamos	*We have more company than we thought*
Fáltan aquí dos cubiértos*	*Two covers are wanted here*
Muchácho, vé á buscár dos servillétas	*Boy, go and fetch two-napkins*

Diál. VII. *Comiéndo.* — Dial. VII. At dinner.

Le gústa á vm. la sópa á la Francésa?	*Do you like soup after the French fashion*
Sí, cómo el cáldo esté bién hécho	*Yes, provided the broth is well made*
Á mí, déme vm. de nuéstra buéna ólla	*As for me, give me some of our good ólla †*
Vénga un póco de pan caséro	*Bring a little household bread*
Tóme vm. pan blánco	*Take white bread*
Mas quiéro éste	*I like this better*
Éste pan está mohóso	*This bread is mouldy*
Péro éste es múy sabróso	*But this is very sweet*
Muchácho, dános pan tiérno	*Boy, give us new bread*

---

* *Cubiérto* means a plate, napkin, knife, fork and spoon, altogether.

† *Ólla*, a Spanish dish made of beef, mutton, bacon, vegetables, &c. &c.

29 *

Ráspa éste pan	Rasp this bread
Quiére vm. la cortéza de encíma ó de debájo?	Do you wish the upper or under crust?
Gústa vm. de éste cocído?	Will you have some of this boiled meat?
Si vm. gústa ó gustáre	If you please
Me serviré á mí mísmo	I will help myself
Dános el pláto gránde	Give us the dish
Ésta cárne es múy sustanciósa	This meat is very juicy
Sí, lo créo	Yes, I think so
No cóme vm., Señór	Sir, you do not eat
Perdóneme vm., que cómo túnto cómo dos	Excuse me, I eat as much as two
Que buénos princípios!	What a fine first course!
Por mí, yó alábo éste convíte comiéndo bién	For my part, I commend this entertainment by eating well
Péro aún no ha bebído vm.	But you have not drank yet
Muchácho, da de bebér al Señór	Boy, give the gentleman some drink
Écha de bebér	Pour some drink
Lléna la cópa	Fill the glass
Señóra, bríndo por la salúd de vm.	Madam, I drink your health
Buén provécho hága á vmd.	Much good may it do you
Señór, á la salúd de sus amígos	Sir, to the health of your friends
Á tódos sus gústos	To all your pleasures
Á sus inclinaciónes	To your inclinations
Múcho favór me háce vm.	You are very kind
Cómo hálla vm. ésta cervéza?	How do you like this beer?
Es bastánte buéna	It is pretty good
Quiéro probárla	I wish to taste it
La hállo múy amárga	I find it very bitter
Me quejaré al cervecéro	I will complain to the brewer
Quíte tódo ésto del médio	Take away all these things
Sírvan los segúndos princípios	Serve up the second course
Es vm. buén bebedór y mal comedór	You are a great drinker and a small eater
No ve vm. que cómo y bébo bién?	Do you not see I eat and drink well?
Vámos, Señór, cóma vm. de lo que gustáre mas	Come, Sir, eat of what you like most
No téngo apetíto	I have no appetite

Que le paréce de ésta léngua de buéy, del picadíllo, del guisádo?	*What do you say to this neat's tongue, to the minced meat, to the fricassee?*
Quiére vm. que le sírva de éstas perdíces, de ése capón, de los póllos, ó gallinétas?	*Shall I help you to a piece of these partridges, of that capon, of the chickens or woodcocks?*
Lo que á vm. le gustáre	*What you please*
Que quiéro vmd. mas, un alón ó úna piérna?	*Which do you like best, a wing or a leg?*
Pára mí es tódo úno	*It is all one to me*
Cóma vm. algúnos rábanos pára aguzár el apetíto	*Eat some radishes to sharpen your appetite*
La hámbre es la mejór sálsa	*Hunger is the best sauce*
Yá he comído desmasiádo	*I have eaten too much already*
Dénos mostáza	*Give us some mustard*
Dónde está el mostacéro?	*Where is the mustard-pot?*
Yá ve vm. que mésa tenémos	*You see now what table we keep*
No gastámos delicadéza	*We use no daintics*
Ésto no se lláma comér	*This is not called eating*
Téngo múcha sed	*I am very thirsty*
Déme úna cópa de víno	*Give me a glass of wine*
Vámos, Señór, por la salúd del Presidénte	*Come, Sir, to the health of the President*
Víva el Egército y la Armáda!	*Huzza for the Army and Navy!*
Víva el Gobernadór!	*Huzza for the Governour!*
Le corresponderé con múcho gústo	*I will pledge you with a great deal of pleasure*
Bebámos tódos	*Let us all drink*
El víno es múy esquisíto	*The wine is very exquisite*
Que le paréce ésta empanáda de pichónes?	*How do you like this pigeon pie?*
Está múy buéna y múy bién sazonáda	*It is very good and very well seasoned*
Sábe vm. trinchár?	*Can you carve?*
Trincho mediánaménte	*I carve pretty well*
Le serviré á vm.	*I will help you*
Conózco lo que le gústa	*I know what you like*
Acertaré con su gústo	*I shall hit your taste*
Á tódos sírve vm. y se olvída de sí mísmo	*You help every body and forget yourself*
Quíte ése pláto, vénga el ótro	*Take away that dish, bring the other*

Nos da vm. úna comída de Réy, en lugár de un convíte de amígo
You give us a king's dinner, instead of a friendly entertainment

Pruébe de éstas alcachófas
Try these artichokes

Dáme ése cuchíllo
Give me that knife

Ésta cárne está fría
This meat is cold

Recaliéntala en el braséro
Warm it again on the chafing dish

Hágame el favór de un póco de morcílla
Favour me with a piece of pudding

Ésta cárne está crúda
This meat is rare

Córteme vmd. un póco de váca
Cut me a small piece of beef

Quiére vm. carnéro, váca ó ternéra?
Will you have mutton, beef or veal?

Lo que gustáre, Señór
What you please, Sir

Asádo ó cocído?
Roasted or boiled meat?

Cóma vm. zanahórias, nábos, chirivías y bérza ó col
Eat some carrots, turnips, parsneps and cabbage

Tóme vm mostáza
Take some mustard

Le daré brazuélo ó piérna de carnéro?
Shall I help you to some shoulder or leg of mutton?

Mas quiéro un póco de lómo de ternéra
I prefer a piece of the loin of veal

Váya éste pláto al rededór de la mésa
Let this dish go round the table

Yá ve vm., Señór, cómo nos tratámos
Sir, you now see, how we fare

Éste es el mejór pláto de la mésa guisádo con mantéca
This is the best dish at table dressed with lard

Aún no se le ha llegúdo
It has not yet been touched

Vóy á probár de él
I am going to taste it

Buén provécho hága á vmd.
Much good may it do you

Le gústa á vmd. la léche cocída, la mantequílla?
Do you like boiled milk, butter?

Gústo múcho de cuajáda, náta y quéso frésco
I am very fond of curds, cream and new cheese

Cóma vm. de éste manjár blánco
Eat of this blanc-manger

Váya un póco del estofádo
Take some of the stewed meat

Las empanádas de cárne nútren mas que las de manzánas
Meat pies nourish more than apple-pies

Que béllos póstres! — *What a fine dessert.*

La frúta correspónde á tódo lo demás — *The fruit corresponds with all the rest*

Ha recogído vm. las frútas mas esquisítas de la estación — *You have collected the most exquisite fruits of the season*

Ésta pásta ó mása es muy ligéra y bién hécha — *This pastry is very light and well made*

La tórta es múy buéna — *The tart is very good*

Dáme cervéza fuérte — *Give me some strong beer*

Da un pláto límpio al Señór — *Give a clean plate to the gentleman*

Siénto no tengámos álgo mejór — *I am sorry we have nothing better*

He comído múy bién — *I have dined very well*

Créo que tódos han acabádo — *I think every body has done*

Degémos la mésa — *Let us leave the table*

Quíta la mésa — *Remove the table*

Démos grácias á Diós — *Let us say grace*

Vámos á dar un paséo en el jardín — *Let us go and take a turn in the garden*

Vámos en hóra buéna — *Let us go with all my heart*

Téngo múcho suéño — *I am very sleepy*

Sóy múy amígo de hacér la siésta — *I am very fond of taking a nap after dinner*

Diál. VIII. *Pára comprár líbros.* — Dial. VIII. To buy books

Tiéne vm. algún líbro nuévo? — *Have you any new book?*

Sí, Señór; que espécie de líbros quiére vm.? — *Yes, Sir; what sort of books do you wish?*

Le gústan á vm. libros de história, de matemáticas, de filosofía, de teología, de medicína, de derécho? — *Will you have books of history, mathematics, philosophy, theology, physic, or law?*

No, Señór, búsco líbros de poesía — *No, Sir, I am looking for poetical works*

Le puédo proveér de éllos en tódas lénguas — *I can furnish you with them in all languages*

Pués téngo tódos los poétas Griégos, Latínos, Españóles, Portuguéses, Italiános, Francéses, é Ingléses — *For I have all the Greek, Latin, Spanish, Portuguese, Italian, French, and English poets*

Múchos téngo yó de éstos

I have many of them

Que poétas necesíta vm. pués comprár?

What poets do you want then to purchase?

Virgílio en Latín, las comédias de Calderón, y el Teátro de Feijóo en Español

Virgil in Latin, the plays of Calderon, and the Theatre of Feijóo in Spanish

Tiéne vmd. el Paraíso Perdído de Miltón, ó las óbras dramáticas de Shakspeáre en Inglés?

Have you Milton's Paradise Lost, or the plays of Shakspeare in English?

Téngo menestér de la Gramática Italiána y Egercícios de Vergáni, de la Bibliotéca Italiána de Buttúra, y diccionário de Gráglia.

I have need of Vergani's Italian Grammar and Exercises, Buttura's Bibliotéca Italiana and Graglia's Dictionary.

Tiéne vmd. la Gramática Española é Inglésa de Jossé, y la de la Académia?

Have you the Spanish and English Grammar of Josse, and that of the Academy?

Tiéne vmd. la História de Inglatérra, de Fráncia, de España y de Itália?

Have you the History of England, France, Spain and Italy?

Tódos ésos líbros téngo

I have all those books

De que tamáño son?

Of what size are they?

Los téngo en Fólio, Cuárto, Octávo y Duodécimo

I have them in Folio, Quarto, Octavo and Duodecimo

Hágame vm. el favór de enseñármelos

Do me the favour to show them to me

Los quiére vm. encuadernádos en badána, becérro, ó cordobán?

Will you have them bound in sheep, calf, or morocco leather?

Los quiére vm. dorádos é intituládos?

Will you have them gilt on the back and lettered?

No háy necesidád de éso

There is no occasion for that

No los cómpro pára adórno, sinó pára leérlos

I do not buy them for ornament, but to read them

Ésta encuadernadúra no es buéna

This binding is not good

No está bién cosído éste líbro

This book is not well sewed

Ahí tiéne vm. ótro en su lugár

There is another in its stead

Cuánto píde vm. por éste líbro?

How much do you ask for this book?

Le costará á vm. dos pésos

It will cost you two dollars

Ésto es demasiádo

This is too much

Es el précio último	It is the lowest price
Le daré á vm. véinte reáles	I will give you twenty rials
Me sále á mas de lo que vmd me ofréce por él	It turns out to me more than you offer me for it
Es múy cáro	It is very dear
Le aseguro á vm. que me cuésta péso y médio sin la encuadernadúra	I assure you it costs me one dollar and a half without the binding
No querrá vm. que piérda en mis líbros	You will not wish me to lose by my books
Múy al contrário, quiéro que gáne álgo	Quite to the contrary, I wish you to gain something
Es precíso pués que me dé véinte y cuátro reáles	You must then give me four-and-twenty rials
Ahí los tiéne vm., no repáro en úna cortedád	There you have them, I do not mind a trifle
No necesíta vm. ótros líbros?	Do you not want other books?
Por ahóra no	Not at present
Péro he menestér de papél, plúmas, tínta, arenílla, lácre y obléas	But I have occasion for paper, pens, ink, sand, sealing-wax and wafers
No véndo náda de éso	I sell nothing of that
Péro lo hallará vm. tódo en la tiénda próxima que es de un Papeléro	But you will find it all at the next shop which is a Stationer's
Á Diós, Señór	Farewell, Sir
Múy humílde servidór de vm., caballéro	Sir, your most humble servant
Hágame vm. el favór de acordárse de mí pára ótra vez	Do me the favour to remember me again
Siémpre esperimentará múy buén tráto	You will always experience good treatment
Lo espéro	I hope so

Diál. IX. *Del alquilár un alojamiénto.*	Dial. IX. Of hiring a lodging.
Señór, quiére vm. hacérme un favór?	Sir, will you do me a favour?
De múy buéna gána, que me mánda vm.?	Very willingly, what do you command me?
Que vénga vmd. conmígo, para alquilár un alojamiénto	That you would come with me to hire a lodging

Le acompañaré á dónde quisiére	I shall wait on you wherever you please
Vámos á la cálle de Santiágo	Let us go into St. James' street
Le vóy siguiéndo	I follow you
Aqui háy úna cédula á ésta puérta que díce cuártos de alquilár	Here is a. bill at this door which says rooms to let
Lláme vm. á la puérta	Knock at the door
Quién es?	Who is there?
Génte de paz	A friend, peaceable people
Con quién quiére vm. hublár?	Whom do you wish to speak with?
Con el ámo ó áma de cása	With the master or mistress of the house
Aquí está mi Señóra	Here is my Lady
Señóra tiéne vm. cuártos de alquilár?	Madam, have you any rooms to let?
Sí, Señór, quiére vm. vérlos?	Yes, Sir, do you wish to see them?
Víne con ésa intención	I came for that purpose
Cuántos aposéntos necesíta vm.?	How many apartments do you want?
Quiéro un comedór ó sála, úna alcóba, un gabinéte pára mʼ ʃ un desván pára mi criado	I want a dining room or parlour, a bed-chamber, a closet for myself, and a garret for my man-servant
Han de ser sus cuártos alhajádos ó no?	Must your rooms be furnished or not?
Han de ser alhajádos	They must be furnished
Hágame el favór de esperár un ráto en ésta sála bája, miéntras vóy por las lláves	Be so kind as to wait a moment in this lower parlour, while I go for the keys
Múy bién, Señóra, aguardaré	Very well, Madam, I'll wait
Quiére vm. tomárse el trabájo de subír?	Will you take the trouble to go up?
Seguirémos á vm., Señóra	We will follow you, Madam
Ésta es la viviénda del primér álto	This is the apartment on the first floor
Ahí tiéne vm. úna cáma múy buéna y límpia	There you have a very good and clean bed
Bién ve vm. que háy tódo lo precíso en un cuárto alhajádo	You see that there is every thing necessary in a furnished room

Cómo mésa, espéjo, síllas, alfómbras, alacénas, escaparátes, &c.	*As table, looking-glass, chairs, carpets, closets, presses, &c.*
Péro dónde está el gabinéte?	*But where is the closet?*
Aquí está, y es bastánte cápáz	*Here it is, and is large enough*
Me cuádra múy bién éste alojamiénto	*These apartments suit me very well*
Me alégro múcho	*I am very glad of it*
Cuánto píde vm. por semána?	*How much do you ask a week?*
Núnca alquílo mis cuártos sinó por mes ó por áño	*I never let my apartments but by the month or year*
Bién, los tomaré por mes; cuánto es el précio de éllos?	*Well, I shall take them by the month; what is the price of them?*
Jamás túve ménos de diéz guinéas al mes por éstos dos cuártos	*I never had less than ten guineas a month for these two rooms*
Son demasiádo cáros	*They are too dear*
Ha de considerár vm. que éste es el mas hermóso bárrio de la ciudád	*You ought to consider that this is the finest ward of the city*
Y que está vm. á un páso de la córte	*And that you are within a step of the court*
Pára que véa vm. que no sóy amígo de regateár, le daré ócho guinéas por éllos	*That you may see that I do not like cheapening, I will give you eight guineas for them*
Es damasiádo póco, no sábe vm. la rénta que págo por ésta cása	*It is too little, you do not know the rent I pay for this house*
Náda me impórta sabérlo	*It is no concern of mine to know it*
Péro en úna palábra, partirémos la diferéncia	*But in a word, we will divide the difference*
Yó le asegúro que piérdo	*I assure you that I lose*
Péro siénto que vm. se váya	*But I am sorry to have you go away*
Y por el desván de mi criádo, cuánto he de pagár por mes?	*And for my man's garret, how much must I pay a month?*
Me dará vm. dos guinéas	*You will give me two guineas*
No daré mas de guinéa y média	*I shall give only one guinea and a half*

30

No es bastánte, péro lo haré por vm., séa así | It is not enough, but I will do it for you, let it be so

No vále la péna de parárse en semejánte cortedád | It is not worth while to dwell on so small a matter

Péro dígame vm., no puédo yó comér aquí con vm.? | But tell me, may I not board here with you?

Sí, Señór, bién puéde vm. | Yes, Sir, you may

Cuánto tóma por semána de cáda huésped? | How much do you take from each boarder a-week?

Á razón de ócho guinéas al mes | At the rate of eight guineas a month

Y cuánto tóma vm. por cuárto y comída júntos? | And how much do you take for board and lodging together?

Cínco líbras por semána | Five pounds a-week

Pués, empezaré mañána | Well, I shall begin to-morrow

Cuándo gustáre | When you please

Buénas nóches, Señóra | Good night, Madam

Buénas se las dé Diós, Señór | Sir, I wish you the same

Diál. X. *Del informárse de algúno.* | **Dial. X.** Of inquiring after one.

Quién es ése caballéro? | Who is that gentleman?

Es un Inglés | He is an Englishman

Le túve por un Francés | I took him for a Frenchman

Se ha engañádo vm. pués | Then you have mistaken

Sábe vm. dónde víve? | Do you know where he lives?

Víve en el bárrio de la córte | He lives in the ward of the court

Tiéne cása? | Does he keep house?

No, Señór, víve en cuártos alhajádos | No, Sir, he lives in furnished lodgings

En cása de quién alója? | At whose house does he lodge?

Víve en cása de fuláno, en la cálle de —— | He lives at Mr. such a one, in the street of ——

Que edád tiéne? | How old is he?

Créo que tiéne véinte y cínco áños de edád | I believe he is five and twenty years of age

No me paréce tan viéjo | He does not appear to me so old

No puéde ser mas mózo | He cannot be younger

Es casádo? | Is he married?

No, Señór, es soltéro | No, Sir, he is a bachelor

Están sus pádres vívos? | Are his parents living?

Su mádre aún víve, péro su pádre murió dos áños ha
His mother is still alive, but his father died two years ago

Tiéne hermános y hermánas?
Has he any brothers and sisters?

Dos hermános y úna hermána tiéne
He has two brothers and a sister

Está su hermána casáda?
Is his sister married?

Sí, Señór
Yes, Sir

Con quién?
To whom?

Con el Cónde de——
To the Earl of——

Éra pués partído ríco
She was a rich match then

Túvo sesénta mil pésos de dóte
She had sixty thousand dollars for her portion

Es hermósa?
Is she handsome?

No es féa
She is not ugly

Es bastánte boníta
She is pretty enough

Está álgo picáda de viruélas
She is a little pitted with the small pox

Péro tiéne múcho entendimiénto
But she has a great deal of understanding

Es múy ingeniósa
She is very ingenious

Hábla éste caballéro la léngua Españóla?
Does this gentleman speak the Spanish language?

Aunqué es Inglés, hábla tanbién Español, que los Españóles le créen Español
Although he is an Englishman, he speaks Spanish so well, that the Spaniards think him a Spaniard

Hábla Italiáno cómo los Italiános mísmos
He speaks Italian like the Italians themselves

Éntre los Alemánes pása por Alemán
He passes for a German among the Germans

Cómo puéde saber tántas lénguas diferéntes?
How can he know so many different languages?

Góza de úna memória felíz y ha viajádo múcho
He enjoys a happy memory and has travelled a great deal

Ha estádo dos áños en París, séis méses en Madríd, año y médio en Itália, y un áño en Alemánia
He has been two years at Paris, six months at Madrid, a year and a half in Italy, and a year in Germany

Ha vísto tódas las córtes principáles de la Európa
He has seen all the principal courts of Europe

Cuánto tiémpo ha que le conóce vm.? — How long is it since you know him

Al rededór de tres áños ha que téngo el honór de conocérle — It is about three years since I have the honor of being acquainted with him

Dónde hízo vm. conocimiénto con él? — Where did you make acquaintance with him?

En Róma le conocí — I got acquainted with him at Rome

Es de bélla estatúra — He is of a fine stature

Ni demasiádo álto, ni demasiádo chíco — He is neither too tall, nor too short

Se puéde decír que es hómbre garbóso — One may say he is' an elegant man

Siémpre ánda múy aseádo y bién compuésto — He is always very neat and very fine

Se víste múy bién — He dresses very well

Es bién parecído, tiéne buén áire — He is very genteel, he has a good air

Tiéne bélla preséncia, y el aspécto nóble — He has a fine presence, and a noble look

Náda disgústa en sus módos — Nothing is disagreeable in his manners

Es cortés, afáble, urbáno con cualquiéra — He is civil, courteous, complaisant to every body

Tiéne múcho entendimiénto, y es muy festívo en conversación — He is very sensible, and is very sprightly in conversation

Dánza béllaménte, esgríme y mónta múy bién — He dances beautifully, fences and rides very well

Tóca la fláuta, el cláve, la guitárra, el piáno y ótros múchos instruméntos — He plays upon the flute, the harpsichord, the guitar, the piano and many other instruments

En úna palábra, es un caballéro cumplído y perfécto — In a word, he is an accomplished and perfect gentleman

Por el retráto que vm. háce de él, me da gána de conocérle — By the picture you make of him, you give me a desire to know him

Le procuraré su conocimiénto — I will procure you his acquaintance

Se lo agradeceré á vm. múcho	I shall be much obliged to you for it
Cuándo quiére vm. que váyamos á visitárle júntos?	When will you have us go and wait upon him together?
Cuándo á vm. le gustáre	When you please
Á que hóra se puéde vórle en su cása?	At what o'clock may one see him at home?
Á cualquiéra hóra puédo vérle, pués es múy amígo mío	I can see him at any time, for he is a great friend of mine
Vámos pués á vérle mañána por la mañána	Let us go then and see him to-morrow morning
Séa en hóra buéna	I will; well and good
De tódo mí corazón	With all my heart
Cuándo le conviniére	When it suits you
Á Diós, Cabállero	Farewell, Sir
Servidór de vm.	Your servant
Sóy múy súyo	I am truly yours
Ténga vm. buénas nóches	I wish you a good night
Múy buénas se las dé Diós	I wish you the same

Diál. XI. *Del partír.* — Dial. XI. Of departing.

Señór, véngo á despedírme de vm.	Sir, I come to take leave of you
Porqué quiére vm. írse?	Why will you go away?
Se acérca la hóra de comér	Dinner time draws near
No puéde vm. comér con nosótros?	Can't you dine with us?
Se lo estímo múcho, no me es posíble hóy	I thank you for it, it is not in my power to-day
Porqué? que negócios tiéne vm.?	Why? what business have you?
No téngo múcho que hacér, péro he de ir á comér á cása	I have not much to do, but I must go and dine at home
Ha convidádo vm. á algúno á comér á su cása?	Have you invited any body to dine at your house?
No, péro he promctído á un cabállero Inglés, que no sábe el Español, de ir con él á comprár algúnas menudéncias	No, but I have promised an English gentleman, who does not know Spanish, to go with him to buy some trifles
Á que hóra le espéra vm.?	At what hour do you expect him?

Le aguárdo á las dos	*I expect him at two o'clock*
Está vm. segúro de que vénga?	*Are you sure he will come?*
No lo sé de ciérto; péro habiéndoselo prometído, es precíso que esté en cása	*I do not know it for certain; but having promised it to him, it is necessary I should be at home*
Tiéne vm. razón	*You are in the right*
No le quiéro pués detenér	*I will not detain you then*
Váya vm. con Diós, servidór súyo	*Farewell, go with God, your servant*
Quéde vm. con Diós	*Good by, remain with God*
Muchácho, ábre la puérta al Señór	*Boy, open the door for the gentleman*
Múy bién la abriré yó	*I will open it myself*
Péro no tiéne vm. la lláve	*But you have not the key*
Que! écha vm. la lláve á la puérta?	*How! do you lock your door?*
Así lo acostumbrámos	*So is our custom*
Suplícole me pónga á los piés de mi Señóra su hermúna	*I beg you would present my best respects to your sister*
No faltaré á éllo, Señór	*Sir, I will not fail to do it*
Cuándo nos volverémos á ver?	*When shall we see one another again?*
Manáña, si Diós quiére	*To-morrow, if it please God*
Vendré á visitárle	*I will come to visit you*
Hágame éste favór	*Do me this favour*

Diál. XII. *De notícias*	*Dial.* XII. Of news.
Que se díce de buéno?	*What is said good?*
Que notícias tenémos?	*What news have we*
No sé ningúna	*I know none*
Que se díce de nuévo?	*What do people say new?*
Sábe vm. algúna novedád?	*Do you know any news?*
Que notícias córren	*What news are spread?*
No háy ningúna	*There is none*
No he sabído náda de nuévo	*I have heard nothing new*
Ha leído vmd. los papéles?	*Have you read the papers?*
He vísto el *Patrióta*, la *Crónica*, el *Diário Avisadór*	*I have seen the Patriot, the Chronicle, the Daily Advertiser*
Que se díce en la ciudád?	*What do they say in the city*
No se húbla de náda	*They talk of nothing*

He oído decír, he sabído que	I heard, I have known that
Ésta es buéna notícia	This is a good piece of news
No ha oído vm. hablár de la guérra?	Have you not heard speak of the war?
No se díce náda de élla	Nothing is said of it
Se hábla de un sítio	They talk of a siege
Se díce que —— está sitiáda	They say that —— is besieged
Se ha levantádo el sítio	They have raised the siege
Péro han vuélto á ponérle	But they have laid it again
Ha habído algún combáte naval?	Has there been any sea-fight?
Se decía, péro salió fálso	They said so, but it proved false
Al contrário, háblan de úna batálla	On the contrary, they talk of a battle
Ésta novedád requiére confirmación	This news requires confirmation
Quién se la comunicó?	Who communicated it to you?
De buéna párte me viéne	It comes to me from good authority
El Señór N . . . . me la díjo	Mr. N . . . . told it me
Crée vm. que tengámos páces?	Do you think we shall have a peace?
Háy múcda apariéncia	There is a great probability
Pára conmígo, créo que no	For my part, I believe not
En que se funda vm.?	What do you ground yourself upon?
En que véo que los ánimos de entrámbas pártes están múy póco inclinádos á la paz	Because I see the minds of both parties are very little inclined to peace
Sin embárgo, tódos necesítan de la paz	Every body wants peace, however
Sóbre tódo los comerciántes y mercadéres	Especially merchants and traders
La guérra háce múcho dáño al comercio	War does a great injury to trade
Sin dúda, la paz es mas ventajósa al comércio	Without question, peace is more advantageous to commerce
Que se díce en la córte?	What do they say at court?
Se hábla de armár úna flóta de véinte búques de guérra	They talk of fitting out a fleet of twenty men of war
Háblan de úna espedición	They talk of an expedition

Cuándo se crée que la escuádra saldrá?

When do they think the fleet
will sail?

No se díce, no se sábe

It is not said, it is not known

Á dónde irá la Princésa?

Where will the Princess go

Únos dícen á Windsór; ótros
á Kew

Some say· to Windsor, others
to Kew

Que díce la Gacéta?

What says the Gazette?

No la he leído

I have not read it

Hablándole sínceraménte, los
designios de la córte son
tan secrétos que nádie
puéde sabérlos

To speak freely, the designs
of the court are so se-
cret, that nobody can know
them

Póco se me da de los negócios de estádo

I care little about state affairs

No me méto jamás en arre-
glár el estádo

I never meddle with settling
the nation

Hablémos de notícias particuláres

Let us ˙talk of private intelligence

Cómo está el Señór D . . . .?

How is Mr. D . . . .?

Cuándo le ha vísto vm.?

When have you seen him?

Ayér le ví

I saw him yesterday

Es verdád lo que dícen de él?

Is what is said of him true?

Que se díce de él?

What do they say of him

Dícen que riñó al juégo

They say that he quarrelled
at the game

Con quién?

With whom?

Con un caballéro Francés

With a French gentleman

Han peleádo?

Have they fought?

Sí, Señór, peleáron

Yes, Sir, they fought

Está herído?

Is he wounded?

Dícen que salió herído mortalménte

They say he came out mor-
tally wounded

Lo siénto, es hómbre de bién

I regret it, he is an honest
man

Sóbre que riñéron?

About what did they quarrel?

Lo ignóro entéraménte

I am quite ignorant of it

Se díce que lo desmintió

They say he gave him the lie

No lo puédo creér

I cannot believe it

Ni yó tampóco

Nor I neither

Séa lo que fuére, prónto se
sabrá

Be what it may, it will soon
be known

En su cása lo preguntaré

I will inquire about it at his
house

Diál XIII. *Éntre dos ami-gos,*	*Dial.* XIII. Between two friends.
Que! es vm.?	*What! is it you?*
De dónde viéne que no me míra vmd.?	*How comes it that you do not look at me?*
Ciérto que no reparába en vm.	*Indeed I did not take notice of you*
No le veía	*I did not see you*
Pása vm. cérca de mí, me tóca con el códo, y no me ve?	*You pass close by me, touch me with your elbow, and do not see me?*
Iba cavilándo en álgo	*I was cogitating about something*
Pensába vm. quizás en su querída	*Perhaps you were thinking of your love*
Ótros negócios téngo en mi cabéza	*I have other business in my head*
Que negócios?	*What business?*
Hallándome escáso de diné-ro, vóy á ver á un sugéto que me débe	*Being in want of money, I am going to see a person who owes me*
É iba pensándo sóbre si le mandaría arrestár en cáso de no pagárme	*And I was thinking whether I should cause him to be arrested in case he does not pay me*
Víve léjos de aquí?	*Does he live far from here?*
Á cuátro pásos de aquí	*Four steps from here*
Está vm. ciérto de hallárle en cása?	*Are you sure to find him at home?*
Créo que le hallaré á éstas hóras	*I believe I shall find him at this time*
Se estará vm. múcho tiémpo?	*Shall you stay long?*
Ni un cuárto de hóra	*Not a quarter of an hour*
Despáche vm. pués, que le vóy á esperár en éste café	*Make haste then, I go and wait for you in this coffee-house*
Estaré con vm. luégo	*I shall be with you presently*
Yá de vuélta?	*Back already?*
Cómo lo ve vm	*As you see*
Le halló vm.?	*Did you find him?*
Sí, Señór	*Yes, Sir*
Le pagó á vm.?	*Did he pay you?*

Grácias á Diós	*Thank God*
Lo celébro múcho	*I am very glad of it*
Péro si no le hubiéra pagádo, yó le hubiéra prestádo dinéro	*But if he had not paid you, I would have lent you money*
No le hubiéra faltádo dinéro	*You should not have wanted money*
Mi bólsa estába á su servício	*My purse was at your service*
Se lo estímo múcho	*I am much obliged to you*
Nos quedámos aquí?	*Shall we stay here?*
No, vámos á bebér úna botélla, pára pasár média hóra júntos	*No, let us go and drink a bottle, to pass half an hour together*
En hóra buéna, péro quiéro regalárle y pagárla yó	*With all my heart, but I will treat you and pay for it*
Cuándo se háya bebído hablarémos de éso	*We will talk of it when we have drank it*
Vámonos	*Let us go away*
Le vóy siguiéndo	*I am following you*
Diál. XIV. *Del escribír úna cárta.*	Dial. XIV. *Of writing a letter.*
No es hóy día de corréo?	*Is not this a post-day?*
Porqué?	*Why?*
Porqué he de escribír úna cárta	*Because I have a letter to write*
Á quién escríbe vm.?	*Whom do you write to?*
Á mi hermáno	*To my brother*
No está en la ciudád?	*Is he not in town?*
No, Señór, está en el cámpo	*No, Sir, he is in the country*
En que cámpo?	*In what part of the country?*
En las águas de Tunbrídge	*He is at Tunbridge-wells*
Cuánto tiémpo háce?	*How long since?*
Quínce días	*A fortnight*
Déme vmd. úna hója de papél dorádo, úna plúma y tínta	*Give me a sheet of gilt paper, a pen and ink*
Éntre vm. en mí gabinéte, y hallará sóbre la mésa recádo de escribír	*Step in my closet, and you will find upon the table what is necessary to write*
No háy plúmas	*There are no pens*
Ahí están en el tintéro	*There they are in the inkstand*
Náda válen	*They are good for nothing*

Allí háy ótras	*There are some others*
No están cortádas éstas plúmas	*These pens are not made*
A dónde está su córta-plúmas?	*Where is your pen-knife?*
Sábe vm cortár plúmas?	*Can you make pens?*
Las córto á mi módo	*I make them after my fashion*
Ésta no es mála	*This is not bad*
Es bastánteménte buéna	*It is good enough*
Miéntras acábo ésta cárta, hágame vmd. el favór de hacér un pliégo de éstos papéles	*While I finish this letter, be so kind as to make a packet of these papers*
Que séllo quiére vm. que le pónga?	*What seal will you have me put to it?*
Séllela vm. con mis úrmas ó con mi cífra	*Seal it with my coat of arms or with my cypher*
Que lácre le he de ponér?	*What wax shall I put to it?*
Pónga vm. rójo ó négro, no impórta	*Put either red or black, no matter*
No bastarán obléas?	*Will not wafers suffice?*
Es lo mísmo	*It is all one*
Ha puésto vm. la fécha?	*Have you put the date?*
Créo que sí, péro no he firmádo	*I believe I have, but I have not signed*
Que día del mes tenémos?	*What day of the month is this?*
El diéz, el véinte, &c.	*The tenth, the twentieth, &c.*
Pliégue vm. ésta cárta	*Fold up this letter*
Póngale el sobrescríto	*Put the superscription to it*
Ciérrela vm. y séllela	*Close it and seal it*
Dónde está la arenílla?	*Where is the sand?*
En la salvadéra	*In the sand-box*
Deséque su escritúra con teléta	*Dry your writing with blotting-paper*
Cómo envía vm. sus cártas?	*How do you send your letters?*
Las remíto por el harriéro, ó por el corréo	*I send them by the waggoner or by the mail*
Mi criádo las llevará al corréo, si vm. gustáre confiárselas	*My man will carry them to the post office, if you will trust them to him*
Lléva las cártas del señór al corréo, y no te se olvíde el franqueárlas	*Carry the gentleman's letters to the post office, and do not forget to free them*
No téngo dinéro	*I have no money*

Ahí lo tiénes, vé présto y vuélve luégo	There is some, go quick and come back immediately
Estaré de vuélta en ménos de médio cuárto de hóra	I will be back in less than half a quarter of an hour
Ha llegúdo el corréo?	Has the mail come?
Ahóra acába de llegár	It is just arrived this minute
Háy cártas pára mí?	Are there letters for me?
Créo que sí	I believe so
Porqué no las has traído?	Why did you not bring them?
Aún no se entregában	They were not delivered yet

Diál. XV. *Del trocár.* — Dial. XV. Of exchanging.

Quiére vm. trocár su relój?	Will you barter your watch?
Con que?	For what?
Con mi espáda ó espadín	For my sword or small sword
En hóra buéna, péro cuánto me dará vm. de vuélta?	With all my heart, but how much will you give me in return
Cuánto me píde vm.?	How much do you ask me?
Me dará vm. dóce pésos	You will give me twelve dollars
En cuánto aprécia vm. su relój?	What do you value your watch at?
En tréinta y séis pésos	At thirty-six dollars
No vále tánto	It is not worth so much
Es viéjo	It is old
Lo confiéso, péro ánda bién	I own it, but it goes well
No le volveré yó náda	I will return you nothing
Mi espáda vále tánto cómo su relój	My sword is worth as much as your watch
Ciértaménte se búrla vm.	You joke surely
No, Señór	No, Sir
Que espáda es ésta?	What sword is this?
Acábo de comprárla en la espadería	I have just bought it at the sword cutler's
Es la guarnición de cóbre dorádo?	Is the hilt of gilt copper?
Bélla pregúnta! no ve vm. que es de pláta sobredoráda?	A fine question! do not you see it is silver gilt?
Es el púño de pláta?	Is the hilt of silver?
Sin dúda que lo es	Without doubt it is so

Cuánto le costó á vm. éste espadín?

How much did this small sword cost you?

Á cómo le sále?

What does it come to you at?

Me cuésta tréinta pésos

It costs me thirty dollars

Me ha de dar vm. pués séis pésos de vuélta

You must give me six dollars to boot then

No lo haré por ciérto

I will not do it certainly

Bién, dégese de éllo

Well, leave it off, let it alone

Véa vm. si quiére trocár iguál?

See whether you will change even?

Buéna está ésta!

This is a good one!

No es tan fácil engañárme cómo le paréce

It is not so easy to take me in as you think

Pués, váya sin náda de vuélta

Well, let us change even

Hécho, en hóra buéna

Done, with all my heart

Diál. XVI. *De los juégos en generál; y priméro de él de los dádos.*

Dial. XVI. Of gaming in general; and first of that of dice.

Juéga vm. algúnas véces?

Do you play sometimes?

Sí, Señór, péro jamás juégo sinó pára divertírme

Yes, Sir, but I never play only to divert myself

Mas, me paréce, que el juégo es úna diversión múy peligrósa

But, methinks, gaming is a very dangerous diversion

Sí, cuándo se juéga múcho dinéro

Yes, when one plays deep, high, or for much money

Péro siémpre juégo póco dinéro

But I always play for a small matter, or little money

Con que la pérdida ó ganáncia es úna cortedád

And so the loss or gain is a trifle, inconsiderable

Juéga vm. á los juégos de suérte, ó de habilidád?

Do you play at games of chance, or of skill?

Que entiénde vm. por juégos de suérte?

What do you mean by games of chance?

Juégos de náipes, dádos, &c

Games at cards, dice, &c.

Y por los de habilidád?

And by those of skill?

El ajédrez, las dámas, los bólos, el trúco, &c.

Chess, draughts, bowls, billiards, &c.

Juéga vm. múcho á los dádos?

Do you play a great deal at dice?

Múy rára vez

Very seldom

31

Porqué?	Why?
Porqué háy múchos trampósos múy astútos	Because there are many very dexterous sharpers
Se córre múcho riésgo con ésos ratéros, pués parécen hómbres de fórma	One runs a great danger with those cheats, because they appear like gentlemen
Tiénen dádos fálsos	They have loaded dice
Váya, á que juégo jugarémos?	Well, what game shall we play at?
Á él que vm. quisiére	Which you please
Jugarémos á los náipes?	Shall we play at cards?
Cómo le gustáre	As you please
Juguémos al hómbre, á los ciéntos	Let us play at ombre, at piquet
Váyan los ciéntos	Let us play at piquet
Es un juégo múy de móda	It is a game much in fashion
Dénos dos barájas y únos tántos	Give us two packs and some counters
Que jugarémos á cáda juégo?	What shall we play each game?
Juguémos un péso pára pasár el tiémpo	Let us play one dollar to pass away time
Jugámos partída dóble?	Do we play lurches?
Cómo quisiére	As you please
Cuántos tántos me da vm.?	What odds do you give me?
Me píde vm. tántos y juéga también cómo yó!	You ask me odds and you play as well as I!
Está cabál ésta barája?	Is this pack whole?
No, le fálta un náipe	No, a card is wanting in it
Quíte vmd. los náipes bájos	Throw out the low cards
Veámos quién da	Let us see who deals
Sóy máno	I have the hand
Vm. da el náipe	You deal the cards
Baráge vm. las cártas	Shuffle the cards
Tódas las figúras están júntas	All the court-cards are together
Dé vm. los náipes	Deal the cards
Á mí me fálta una cárta	I want a card
Vuélva vm. á dar	Deal again
Levánte vm.	Cut, raise
Tiéne vm. sus cártas?	Have you your cards?
Créo que están cabúles	I believe they are complete
Ha descartádo vm.?	Have you discarded?
Cuántas tóma vm.?	How many do you take in?

Tómolas tódas	*I take them all*
No, déjo úna	*No, I leave one*
Téngo mal juégo	*I have bad cards, a bad game*
Ha de tenér vm. béllo juégo, pués yó náda téngo	*You must have a fine game, since I have nothing*
Mi juégo me apúra	*My cards puzzle me*
Díga vm. su juégo	*Call your game*
Cuánto de púnto?	*How much is your point?*
Cincuénta, sesénta, &c.	*Fifty, sixty, &c.*
Buéno, buén púnto	*Good, it is a good point*
No sírven	*They are not good, avail not*
He descartádo la partída	*I have laid out the game*
Sésta mayór, quínta al Réy, ó cuárta de cabállo, tercéra á la sóta ó de diéz	*A sixieme major, a quint to the king, or quart to the queen, a tierce to the knave or ten*
Ótro tánto téngo, igúal	*I have just as much, it is equal*
Tres áses, tres réyes, &c. son buénos?	*Are three aces, three kings, &c. good?*
No, téngo un catórce	*No, I have fourteen*
Téngo catórce de cabállos	*I am fourteen by queens*
Váya jugándo	*Play on*
Juégo cópa, espáda, óro, básto	*I play a heart, spade, diamond, club*
El as, el réy, el cabállo, la sóta, el diéz, el nuéve, el ócho, el siéte	*The ace, the king, the queen, the knave, the ten, the nine, the eight, the seven*
Hágo un píque, repíque, capóte	*I make a pique, a repique, a capot*
Gáno los náipes	*I win the cards*
Téngo siéte bázas	*I have seven tricks*
He perdído	*I have lost*
Ha ganádo vm.	*You have won*
Me débe vm. un péso	*You owe me a dollar*
Me lo debía vm.	*You owed it to me*
Estámos pués en paz	*We are then even, quits*
Váya ótra partída	*Let us play another game*
En hóra buéna, con múcho gústo	*With all my heart, with great pleasure*

Diál. XVII. *Del jugár al ajédrez.*	Dial. XVII. Of playing at chess.
En que emplearémos la tárde?	*How shall we spend the afternoon?*

Juguémos al ajédrez	Let us play at chess
Juguémos, en hóra buéna	Let us play, I am willing
Péro juéga vm. mejór que yó	But you play better than I
Es vm. mas fuérte que yó	You are an over-match for me
No lo créa vm.	Do not think it
Me ha ganádo vm. siémpre	You always have beat me
No jugaré mas con vm., si no me diére algúna ventája	I will play no more with you, unless you give me some odds
Es precíso que me dé un alfíl y la máno	You must give me a bishop and the move
En verdád que no puédo, juéga vm. tan bién cómo yó	Indeed I cannot, you play as well as I do
Véa vm. si quiére jugár á la par	See if you have a mind to play even
Múy bién, lo haré úna vez	Well, I will do it for once
Cuánto jugarémos?	What shall we play for?
Siémpre juégo póco dinéro	I always play for little money
Váya médio péso cáda juégo	Let us play for half a dollar a game
Juégo priméro	I have the move, I play first
Tómo éste peón	I take this pawn
Me alégro, pués vóy á tomár éste alfíl y dárle jáque	I am glad of it, for I am going to take this bishop and check you, give you check
Róque me llámo	I castle, I call myself rook
Náda gána vm. en éso; pués á su róque ó tórre me llévo con mi cabállo	You get nothing by that; for I take your rook or castle with my knight
Péro cómo resguardará vm. á su réina?	But how will you save your queen?
Dándole jáque y máte con mi alfíl y mi róque	By checkmating you with my bishop and rook
He perdído el juégo, yá no puédo movér el réy	I have lost the game, I can no longer move the king
Me débe vm. pués médio péso	You owe me half a dollar then
Así es	It is so
Péro vm. me lo debía ántes	But you owed it me before
Bién, estámos en paz	Then, we are quits or even
Dénos vm. un tabléro	Give us a draughts-board
Juégue vm. priméro	I give you the move, play first
Sóplo éste peón	I huff this man
Hága dáma éste peón	King that man

Cuántas dámas tiéne vm.? — *How many kings have you?*

Téngo dos — *I have two*

Cóma vm. éste, que luégo comeré tres — *Take this, then I shall take three*

Piérdo el juégo — *I lose the game*

Diál. XVIII. *Del jugár á la pelóta.* — Dial. XVIII. *Of playing at tennis.*

Véa vm. que béllo día háce — *See what a fine day it is*

Aprovechémonos de éste día tan hermóso — *Let us improve this so fair a day*

Que harémos hóy? — *What shall we do to-day?*

El buén tiémpo nos convída á jugár ó á paseár — *The fine weather invites us to play or to walk*

En que juégo hémos de entretenérnos? — *What play shall we amuse ourselves in?*

Él de pelóta es el mejór pára el egercício — *That of tennis is the best for exercise*

Péro es juégo mas de inviérno que de veráno — *But it is a play fitter for winter than summer*

Sudarémos ménos, si jugámos con raquétas — *We shall perspire less, if we play with rackets*

Vámos al juégo de pelóta — *Let us go to the tennis-court*

Jugarémos con pálas — *We will play with battledoors*

Hagámos la partída — *Let us make the match*

Está vm. conmígo — *You are with me*

No impórta cómo estámos — *It is no matter how we are*

Éste está con nosótros — *He is on our side*

Es vm. mejór jugadór que yó — *You are a better player than I*

Estése cáda úno en su lugár — *Let every one stand at his place*

Manténgase detrás de mí, y cója la pelóta — *Stand behind me, and catch the ball*

Pasó por encíma de mí — *It flew over me*

La cogí en el áire — *I caught it in the air*

Recháce la pelóta — *Strike the ball back*

Es vm. mal compañéro — *You are a bad second*

No ha ganádo vm. aún — *You have not beat yet*

Aún puéde vm. perdér — *You may lose yet*

Tenémos la superioridád — *We have the best of it*

Perdió vm., ganámos — *You have lost, we have won*

Cuánto jugámos? — *What did we play for?*

31*

Dos pésos	Two dollars
Ha puésto vm. en el juégo?	Have you staked?
No, péro ahí está mi dinéro	No, but there is my money
Es lo mísmo	It is all one
Mañána jugarémos ótra vez	To-morrow we will play again
Cuándo vmd. quisiére	When you please

Dial. XIX. *De las diver-siónes del cámpo, particu-larménte de la caza y de la pésca*	Dial. XIX. Of country sports, especially of hunting and fishing.
Señór, me alégro de ver á vm.; dónde ha estádo tan lárgo tiémpo?	Sir, I am overjoyed to see you; where have you been so long a while?
Á dónde se méte vm.?	Where do you keep yourself?
Dos méses ha que estámos en úna cása de cámpo	We have been these two months at a country house
Ha venído vm. á la ciudád pára quedárse?	Are you come to town to stay?
No, Señór, vuélvo mañána por la mañána	No, Sir, I go back to-morrow morning
Cómo pása vm. su tiémpo en el cámpo?	How do you pass your time in the country?
Párte de él empléo en estudiár	I bestow a part of it on books
Péro cuáles son sus diver-siónes, después de sus ne-gócios sérios?	But which are your diver-sions, after your serious business?
Vóy tal vez á cazár	I go sometimes a hunting
Á que cáza?	What do you hunt?
Á véces á la cáza del venádo, á véces de la liébre	We sometimes hunt a stag, sometimes a hare
Tiéne vm. buénos pérros?	Have you good dogs?
Tenémos múchos pérros de muéstra	We have a number of point-ers
Dos gálgos, dos gálgas, cuá-tro jatéos ó zorréros, y tres perdiguéros	Two grey-hound dogs, two grey-hound bitches, four fox-hounds and three set-ting-dogs
No cáza vm. áves?	Do you not go a fowling?
Cáza vm. á véces con la es-copéta?	Do you go a shooting some-times?
Sí, Señór, múy á menúdo	Yes, Sir, very often
Sóbre que tíra vm.?	What do you shoot at?

Sóbre tódo género de cáza cómo perdíces, faisánes, gallinétas, conéjos, &c. | *At all manner of game, as partridges, pheasants, sandpipers, rabbits, &c.*

Tíra vm. al vuélo la piéza ó corriéndo? | *Do you shoot at the game flying or running?*

De ámbas manéras | *Both ways*

Cómo cóge vm. los conéjos? | *How do you catch rabbits?*

Á véces con rédes, y á véces á escopetázos | *Sometimes with nets, and sometimes with a gun*

Y las codorníces? | *And the quails?*

Solémos tomárlas con úna red y un pérro perdiguéro | *We catch them commonly with a net and a setting-dog*

Es vm. amígo de pescár? | *Are you fond of fishing?*

Muchísimo | *Extremely*

Pésca vm. á menúdo con red? | *Do you fish often with a net?*

Múy ráras véces | *Very seldom*

Mas quiéro pescár con la cáña y anzuélo | *I prefer fishing with a line and hook*

La pésca y la cáza son diversiónes múy nóbles | *Fishing and hunting are very noble diversions*

El Réy mas río y mas póbre de Európa no se diviérte en ótra cósa | *The richest and poorest king of Europe does not divert himself in anything else*

Un día quizá pensarán sus minístros que sus vasállos están anualménte dándo á sus vecínos millónes por pescádo saládo y hedióndo | *One day perhaps their ministers will think of their subjects giving yearly to their neighbours millions for stinking salt-fish*

Tiénen no obstánte múy buénos péces en sus cóstas | *They have notwithstanding very good fish on their coast*

Péro no tóman el trabájo de curárlos | *But they do not take the trouble to cure it*

Ésto sucéde por fálta de animár la pésca | *This arises from want of encouraging the fisheries*

Y de ótros múchos motívos | *And from many other causes*

Cóge vm. múchos péces en su estánque? | *Do you catch much fish in your pond?*

Que háce vm. cuándo no cáza ó pésca? | *What do you do when you neither hunt nor fish?*

Jugámos á la bóla, al trúco, ó á los bólos | *We play at bowls, at billiards, or nine-pins*

Según ésto, no puéde vm. estár cansádo del cámpo | *According to this, you cannot be tired with the country*

Así le paréce á vm., y es lo contrário	So it seems to you, and it is otherwise
Yá empiézo á anhelár por la ciudád, y espéro présto pasárme á élla	I already begin to long for the city, and I hope shortly to proceed to it

Diál. XX. *Del ir á la comédia.*	Dial. XX. Of going to the play.
Se díce que hóy represéntan úna piéza nuéva	They say there is a new play acted to day
Es comédia, tragédia, ópera, ó entremés?	Is it a comedy, a tragedy, an opera, or a farce?
Es úna tragédia	It is a tragedy
Cómo la lláman?	How do they call it?
La ——	The ——
Quién es su autór?	Who is its author?
El Señór ——	Mr. ——
Es ésta la priméra representación?	Is this the first representation?
No, Señór, yá se ha representádo tres véces	No, Sir, it has been already acted three times
Éste es el día del autór	This is the author's night
Cómo se recibió en las priméras representaciónes?	How was it received on the first representations?
Con universál apláuso	With universal applause
El autór éra yá célebre	The author was already famous
Y ésta última tragédia ha aumentádo múcho su fáma	And this last tragedy has much increased his fame
Irémos á vérla?	Shall we go and see it?
De múy buéna gána	Very willingly
Vóy á mandár al cochéro que aprónte el cóche	I am going to bid the coachman to get the coach ready
Irémos á un aposénto?	Shall we go to a box?
En hóra buéna, péro mas quisiéra ir al pátio	As you please, but I had rather go to the pit
Porqué?	Why?
Porqué podémos ver y oír mejór allá que en los pálcos	Because we can see and hear better there than in the boxes
Que tal le paréce la sinfonía?	How do you like the overture?
Múy buéna me paréce	I think it is very fine
Los corredóres están yá llénos	The galleries are full already

Y cómo vm. lo ve, estámos múy apretádos en el pátio	And as you see, we are very much crowded in the pit
No cáben las dámas en los aposéntos	The ladies cannot be contained in the boxes
Núnca ví la cása tan lléna	I never saw the house so full
Éstas Señóras están múy bién vestídas	These ladies are very well dressed
Repára vm. aquélla señóra en el aposénto del Réy?	Do you observe that lady in the king's box?
Jamás he vísto róstro tan hermóso en mi vída	I never have in my life seen so beautiful a face
Quién es?	Who is she?
La Duquésa de ——	The Duchess of ——
Y quién es la Señóra jóven que está con élla?	And who is the young lady who is with her?
Su hermána, la Señóra de—	Her sister, Lady —
Péro yá se levánta la cortína, escuchémos	But the curtain rises already, let us attend
Tendrémos ántes el Prólogo	We shall first have the Prologue
El segúndo ácto está acabádo	The second act is over
Las escénas están muy béllas	The scenes are very fine
Don — es múy buén actór	Mr.·—— is a very good actor
Éste es el último ácto	This is the last act
Acabóse la piéza—cómo le gústa á vmd.?	The piece is over—how do you like it?
Muchísimo, me paréce escelénte tragédia y múy bién representáda	Very much; I think it an excellent tragedy and very well performed
Túvo gránde apláuso	It received great applause
Ahóra tendrémos el Epílogo	Now for the Epilogue
Quién lo díce?	Who speaks it?
La Señóra ——	Mrs. ——
Lo díce con múcho ánimo	She speaks it with great spirit
Quiére vmd. quedárse pára ver la Pantomíma?	Will you stay to see the Pantomime?
No, yá la he vísto, y cómo es tárde, harémos mejór de írnos	No, I have seen it already, and as it is late, we had better go away
De tódo mi corazón	With all my heart
Irémos á la Ópera mañána	We will go to the opera tomorrow

Dial. XXI. *Del vestírse.*	**Dial. XXI.** Of dressing one-self.
Señór Maéstro, tráe vm. mi vestído entéro?	*Master, do you bring my full suit of clothes?*
Sí, Señór, aquí está	*Yes, Sir, here it is*
Le estába aguardándo; prué-bemelo	*I was waiting for you; try it on me*
Quiére vm. probár la casáca?	*Will you try the coat?*
Véamos si está bién hécha	*Let us see if it is well made*
Créo que le gustará á vm.	*I believe it will please you*
Me paréce múy lárga	*It seems to me very long*
Yá no se llévan tan córtas cóma ántes	*They do not wear them now so short as formerly*
Se úsan lárgas ahóra	*They wear them long now*
Abotóneme vm.	*Button me*
Me ajústa demasiádo	*It is too close*
Es precíso que ajúste bién	*It ought to be very close*
Éste vestído le cóge múy bién el tálle	*This suit fits your shape very well*
No son las mángas demasiádo lárgas y ánchas?	*Are not the sleeves too long and too wide?*
No Señór, van múy bién	*No, Sir, they fit very well*
Se llévan ahóra múy lárgas y ánchas	*They wear them now very long and wide*
Los pantalónes son demasiá-do angóstos y córtos	*The pantaloons are too narrow and short*
Los calzónes son múy estré-chos	*The small clothes are very strait, tight*
Es la móda	*It is the fashion*
Déme la chúpa	*Give me the waistcoat*
Le va muy bién éste vestído	*This suit becomes you very well*
Péro las médias no viénen con éste páño	*But the stockings do not match this cloth*
Que le paréce de mi sombréro?	*What do you say to my hat?*
Es un castór hermóso	*It is a beautiful beaver*
Que galón le pondrá vm.?	*What lace will you put to it?*
Un galón de óro con úna he-bílla de diamántes	*A gold lace with a diamond buckle*
Me compró vm. las lígas có-mo le díge?	*Did you buy me the garters as I told you?*
Sí Señór, ahí están	*Yes, Sir, there they are*

Son éstas médias de séda de París ó de Lóndres?	*Are these silk stockings from Paris or London?*
Son de Fráncia	*They are from France*
À cuánto las vénden?	*How much do they sell them for?*
Tres pésos el par	*Three dollars a pair*
Es bastánte baráto, siéndo tan fínas	*It is cheap enough, being so fine*
Muchácho, ha venído el zapatéro?	*Boy, is the shoemaker come?*
No, Señór, no ha venído	*No, Sir, he is not come*
Córre pués á su cása, y díle que me tráiga mis zapátos	*Run then to his house, and bid him bring me my shoes*
Señór, aquí está, le encontré en el camíno	*Sir, here he is, I met him on the way*
Son éstos mis zapátos?	*Are these my shoes?*
Sí, Señór	*Yes, Sir*
Póngamelos vm.	*Put them on me*
Están múy ajustádos	*They are very tight*
Me apriétan un póco	*They pinch me a little*
Póngalos en la hórma pára ensanchárlos	*Put them on the last to widen them*
Bastánteménte se ensancharán llevándolos	*They will widen enough by wearing them*
Ésta piél da de sí cómo un guánte	*This leather stretches like a glove*
Siénto múy bién que me lastimarán	*I feel very sure that they will hurt me*
Mis cállos lo padecerán	*My corns will suffer for it*
Me duélen múcho los piés	*My feet ache much*
El empéine de éste zapáto no vále náda	*The upper leather of this shoe is good for nothing*
El talón es demasiádo bájo	*The heel is too low*
Las suélas no son bastánte fuértes ni gruésas	*The soles are neither strong nor thick enough*
Hágame vm. ótro par	*Make me another pair*
Es vm., Señór, muy difícil de contentár	*You are, Sir, very hard to please*
Quiére vm. probár ótro par que tráje por acáso?	*Will you try another pair which I brought by chance?*
En hóra buéna	*I am willing*
Créo que le irán bién	*I believe they will fit you*
Mi pié está mas descansádo	*My foot is more at ease*

Cuánto válen éstos zapátos?	What are these shoes worth?
Á cómo los vénde vm.?	How much do you sell them at?
Dos pésos y médio	Two dollars and a half
Es demasiádo cáro	It is too dear
Es précio hécho	It is a fixed price
Es un zapáto bién hécho y y bién cosído	It is a shoe well made and well stitched
Hágame ótro par cómo éste	Make me another pair like this
Tóme mi medída	Take my measure
Ahí tiéne su dinéro	There is your money
Víva vm. múchos áños, Caballéro	May you live many years, Sir I thank you, Sir

Diál. XXII. *Del hablár á un mózo de cabállos.*	Dial. XXII. Of speaking to a groom.
Almoháza mi cabállo	Curry my horse
Estriéga y límpiale bién con un manójo de pája	Rub and clean him well with a wisp of straw
Mi cabállo está sin herradúras	My horse is unshod; is without shoes
Le fáltan dos herradúras	He wants two shoes
Llévale á cása del herradór	Take him to the farrier
Mándalo herrár	Get him shod
Llévalo después al río	Lead him afterwards to the river
Le has dádo de bebér	Have you watered him?
Sí, Señór	Yes, Sir
Dále su piénso de cebáda	Give him his allowance of barley
Paséale ésta tárde	Walk him this afternoon
Dále también salvádo	Give him also some bran
Ha comído su cebáda?	Has he eaten his barley?
Échale pája ahóra	Give him now some straw
Ensílla mi cabállo y tráemelo	Saddle my horse and bring him to me
Tómale por el fréno	Take him by the bridle
No le hágas corrér	Do not make him run
No le recaliéntes	Do not overheat him
Está cansúdo?	Is he tired?
Quítale el fréno	Unbridle him
Pónle en la caballcríza	Put him in the stable

Diál. XXIII. *De ir á un viáge.*

Véngo á despedírme de vm. y á recibír sus órdenes
Á dónde va vm., Señór?
Vóy á Madríd
Cuándo párte vm.?
En éste instánte
Va vm. á cabállo ó en cóche?

Á cabállo
Muchácho, tráeme mi cabállo
Aquí está, Señór
Está bién almohazádo?
Múy bién, Señór
Cuántas léguas háy de aquí á M———?
Diéz léguas
Son léguas lárgas?
No, Señór, son las mas córtas de España
Le paréce á vm. que podámos caminár tánto hóy?
Sin dúda, no es tan tárde
Darán présto las dóce
Tiéne vm. bastánte tiémpo pára llegár ántes de ponérse el sol
Háy buén camíno?
Múy hermóso
Ningún pantáno se encuéntra
Péro tiéne vm. bósques que atravesár y ríos que pasár
Háy pelígro en el camíno reál?
¿No se hábla de que háya ladrónes en los bósques?
No se díce náda de ésto
No háy que temér náda ni de día ni de nóche

Dial. XXIII. Of going on a journey.

I come to bid you farewell and take your commands
Where are you going, Sir?
I am going to Madrid
When do you set out?
Presently; this minute
Do you go on horseback or in a coach?

On horseback
Boy, bring me my horse
Here he is, Sir
Is he well curried?
Very well, Sir
How many leagues is it from here to M———?
Ten leagues
Are they long leagues?
No, Sir, they are the shortest in Spain
Do you think we can travel so far to day?
Without doubt, it is not so late
Twelve o'clock will soon strike
You have time enough to arrive before the sun sets

Is there a good road?
Very fine
You meet with no quagmire
But you have woods to go through and rivers to cross
Is there any danger upon the highway?
Do they not talk of there being highwaymen in the woods?
There is said nothing of this
There is nothing to fear either by day or night

32

Es un camíno en que ánda génte siémpre | It is a road where you always meet with people
Que camíno he de tomár? | Which way must I take?
Cuándo esté vm. cérca de la priméra aldéa, tomará á máno derécha | When you are near the first village, you will take to the right
He de subír el mónte? | Must I go up the mountain?
No, Señór, dégelo vm. á la izquiérda | No, Sir, leave it to the left
Es el camíno dificultóso en los bósques? | Is the way difficult through the woods?
No, Señór; váya vm. siémpre derécho, no se puéde estraviár | No, Sir; go always straight along, you cannot lose your way
Dónde encontrarémos el río? | Where shall we come to or find the river?
Á la salída del bósque | At the issue of the wood
Se puéde vadeár, es vadeáble? | Can one ford it, is it fordable?
No, Señór, se pása en un bárco | No, Sir, people pass it over in a ferry
Vámos, caballéros, montémos | Come, gentlemen, let us mount
Á Diós, Señóres | Farewell, gentlemen
Diós les dé buén viáge | God grant you a good journey
Les dóy múchas grácias | I give you many thanks
No quiére vm. echár un trágo? | Will you not take a draught?
Cómo vmd. gustáre | As you please
Váya, á su buén viáge | Come, to your good journey

Dial. XXIV. En úna posáda. | Dial. XXIV. In an Inn.

Dónde está la mejór posáda de la ciudád? | Where is the best inn in the city?
Á la señál del Cabállo Blánco | At the sign of the White Horse
En que paráge de la vílla está? | In what part of the town is it?
Cérca de la iglésia mayór | Near the principal church
Podrémos alojárnos aquí? | Can we lodge here?
Sí, Señór, tenémos béllos cuártos y buénas cámas | Yes, Sir, we have fine chambers and good beds
Apcémonos, Señóres | Let us alight, gentlemen

Dónde está el mózo de pája y cebáda, de cabállos?	Where is the hostler, the groom?
Aquí estóy, Señór	Here I am, Sir
Tóma nuéstros cabállos	Take our horses
Llévalos á la caballeríza	Lead them to the stable
Cúidalos bién	Take good care of them
Véamos, ahóra, que nos dará vm. de cenár?	Now, let us see, what will you give us for supper?
Véan vms., Señóres, lo que mas gustáren	See yourselves, gentlemen, what you like best
Dénos média docéna de pichónes, dos perdíces, séis codorníces, un buén capón y úna ensaláda	Give us half a dozen pigeons, a brace of partridges, six quails, a good capon and a salad
Tendré cuidádo de tódo; no se inquiéten vms.	I will take care of all; do not trouble yourselves
No quiéren vms. ótra cósa?	Will you have nothing else?
No, básta con ésto; péro dénos buén víno y frúta	No, that is sufficient; but give us good wine and fruit
Les aseguro, que les daré gústo	I shall please you, I warrant you
Quiéren vms. ir á ver sus aposéntos?	Will you go and see your chambers?
Sí, lláme á su camaréro	Yes, call your chamberlain
Alúmbra á éstos Señóres que súban arríba	Light these gentlemen that they may go up stairs
Háganos cenár cuánto ántes	Give us our supper as soon as possible
Ántes que se háyan quitádo las bótas, estará la céna prónta	Before your boots are pulled off, supper will be got ready
Dónde están nuéstros lacáyos?	Where are our lackeys?
Ahí súben con sus balíjas	There they are coming up with your portmanteaux
Han traído nuéstras pistólas?	Have they brought our pistols?
Sí, Señór, aquí están	Yes, Sir, here they are
Quíta mis bótas, botínes, y vé despúes á cuidár de nuéstros cabállos	Pull off my boots, half-boots, buskins, and then go and take care of our horses
Lláma pára cenár	Call for supper

Señóres, la céna está prónta, está en la mésa

Gentlemen, supper is ready, it is on the table

Vámos, Señóres, á cenár, pára podér acostárnos tempráno

Let us go to supper, gentlemen, that we may go to bed early .

Sentémonos á la mésa

Let us sit down at table

Vm. no cóme náda; que tiéne?

You eat nothing; what ails you?

No téngo gánas, estóy cansádo

I have no appetite, I am tired

Estóy molído

I am beaten down

Estaré mejór en la cáma que en la mésa

I shall be better in bed than at table

Tóme vmd. ánimo

Take courage

Si se siénte málo, váyase á acostár

If you feel unwell, go and lay down

Mánde calentár su cáma

Get your bed warmed

Que no les impída de cenár, vóy á descansár

That I may not hinder you from supping, I am going to rest

Ha menestér vm. álgo?

Do you want any thing?

Náda quiéro sinó descansár

I want nothing but rest

Téngan vms. buénas nóches

I wish you a good night

Tráe los póstres, y di á la patróna que vénga á hablárnos

Bring the dessert, and bid the landlady come and speak with us ▪

Aquí viéne

Here she is coming

Señóres, les gústa á vms. la céna?

Gentlemen, are you pleased with your supper?

Sí, Señóra, péro ahóra es menestér satisfacér á vm.

Yes, mistress, but now we must satisfy you

Cuánto hémos gastádo?

How much have we spent?

Que hémos de pagár?

What have we to pay?

El escóte no súbe múcho

The reckoning does not rise high

Véa vm. cuánto le debémos por nosótros, nuéstros criádos y cabállos

See how much we owe you for ourselves, our servants, and our horses

Por la céna, la cáma y el almuérzo

For the supper, bed and breakfast

Tódo impórta diéz pésos

All amounts to ten dollars

Me paréce que es demasiádo

I think it is too much

Al contrário, es múy baráto

On the contrary, it is very cheap

Haga vm. mismo la cuénta, y hallará que no les pído demasiádo	Reckon yourself, and you will find that I do not ask you too much
Pagarémosle mañána por la mañána después del almuérzo	We will pay you to-morrow morning after breakfast
Cómo vms. quisiéren	As you please
Dénos sábanas límpias	Give us clean sheets
Las sábanas que les envío son múy buénas	The sheets I send you are very good
Buénas nóches, Señóra	Good night, landlady
Buénas nóches les dé Diós á vms., caballéros; servidóra de vms.	I wish you the same, gentlemen; your servant
Necesítan vms. de álgo?	Do you want any thing?
Náda nos háce fálta	We are in want of nothing
Sólo que se haga buén fuégo	Only that a good fire be made
Las nóches son múy frías	The nights are very cold
Es menestér cuidárse en viáge	One must take care of oneself travelling
Diál. **XXV.** *Pára hablár con los empleádos en las aduánas.*	Dial. **XXV.** To speak with the officers in the custom-houses.
Tráen vms. álgo cóntra las órdenes de su magestád, del soberáno, del estádo, ó de la república?	Do you bring any thing contrary to the orders of his majesty, of the sovereign, the state, or republic?
No, yó no téngo géneros de contrabándo algúno	No, I have no contraband goods at all
Téngo sólaménte algúnos efectos que págan impuéstos, y vóy á declarárselos	I have only some goods that pay duty, and I am going to manifest them to you
Cuánto débo pagár por ésto?	How much must I pay for this?
Es menestér dárme sus lláves	You must give me your keys
Hélas aquí. Hágame vmd. la grácia de despachárme luégo, porqué téngo múcha prísa	Here they are. Be so kind as to expedite me directly, for I am in great haste
Se lo estimaré múcho	I shall be much obliged to you for it

32*

Ahí tiéne vmd. la lláve del candádo; he aquí la lláve de la cerradúra

Hágame vmd. la grácia de buscár con precaución, porqué háy múchas cósas que puéden quebrárse

Ha acabádo vmd.?

No emplomará vmd. ahóra el baúl y los cófres, pára que no me los regístren ótra vez?

No podría vm., en lugár de registrárme aquí en ésta puérta, venír á hacérlo en la fónda, ó en la cása á dónde vóy á posár?

Grácias, páselo vmd. bién. Diós guárde á vmd., S.ᵒʳ

Diál. XXVI. *Pára úna persóna estraviáda en úna ciudád.*

No me haría vmd. el favór de decírme, si estóy léjos del bárrio de San Francísco, ó de la cálle de San Páblo?

Háy múy léjos de aquí á — ?

Búsco la posáda del Señór —— ó de la Señóra ——

Por que ládo débo ir?

Despúes, ¿daré vuélta á la derécha ó á la izquiérda?

Es aquí que víve el Señór—?

Quisiéra vm. dárme su direccíon?

Podría vmd. señalárme el camíno que débo tomár, pára ir á cása del Señór ——?

There is the key to the padlock; here is the key to the lock

Do me the favour to search with care, for there are many things that may be broken

Have you done?

Will you not put a lead stamp now upon the trunk and chests, that they may not be searched again?

Could not you, instead of searching me here at this gate, come and do it at the inn, or house where I am going to lodge?

Thank you, farewell. Your servant, Sir

Dial. XXVI. For a person who has lost his way in a city.

Would you not oblige me so far as to tell me, whether I am a great way from the Ward of St. Francis, or Street of St. Paul?

Is it very far from here to—?

I am looking for the residence of Mr. ——, or Madam——

Which way must I go?

Shall I turn, afterwards, to the right or left?

Does Mr.—- live here?

Would you favour me with his address

Could you point out to me the way I must take, in order to go to the house of Mr —— ?

Quiére vmd. conducírme allá, le pagaré bién; le daré ——

Will you lead me there, I will pay you handsomely; I will give you ——

Páse vm. adelánte, yó le seguiré

Walk before, I will follow you

No ánde tan á prísa

Do not walk so fast

Condúzcame vm. por el camíno mas córto

Lead me the shortest way

Ésta cálle está embarazáda, tomémos ótro camino

This street is obstructed, let us take another way

Lláme vm, un cóche de alquilér

Call for a hackney-coach

Cochéro, queréis llevárme?

Coachman, will you drive me?

Móro én la cálle de ——

I reside in the street of ——

Diál. XXVII. *Un militár vencedór estableciéndose en úna cása de los vencídos, y hablándo á los duéños de la cása.*

Dial. XXVII. A military man victorious, quartering in a house of the conquered, and speaking to the masters of the house.

No tengáis miédo, sómos Ingléses, Alemánes, Rúsos, Francéses, &c. Nuéstro carácter nacionál puéde aseguráros de nuéstra generosidád, y la obediéncia que debémos á nuéstro soberáno es un segúndo fiadór. El enemígo vencído no es pára nosótros sinó un amígo desdichádo

Be not afraid, we are Englishmen, Germans, Russians, Frenchmen, &c. Our national character may assure you of our generosity, and the obedience we owe to our sovereign is a double security. A subdued enemy is considered by us only as an unfortunate friend

Entregáos con seguridád á vuéstras ocupaciónes ordinárias; os prometémos seguridád, atenciónes, sosiégo, protección y ayúda, si necesitáreis de élla

Give yourselves up with confidence to your customary business; we promise you safety, kindness, tranquillity, protection and assistance, if you should want any

Si mi génte os diére algún motívo de quéja, recurríd á mí con confiánza, yó no

If my people should give you any cause of complaint, apply openly to me, I will not

sufriré que se páse álgo que puéda dáros disgústo — *suffer that any thing should occur that may be unpleasant to you*

No tengáis miédo, un soldádo valeróso no es temíble sinó en el cámpo de batálla — *Be not afraid, a brave soldier is dreadful only on the field of battle*

Camarádas, comportémonos cómo hómbres de valór; respetémos la desdícha, y no ocasionémos aquí ni alboróto ni desórden — *Comrades, let us behave ourselves as brave men; let us respect misfortune, and let us cause here neither commotion nor disorder*

Diál. XXVIII. *Idiotísmos.* — ## Dial. XXVIII. Idiotisms.

Buscár á úno de zéca en méca — *To seek any one by sea or land*

Es tan cláro cómo el sol — *It is as clear as day*

Con su pan se lo cóma — *That is his concern*

No me está á cuénta — *That is not to my profit*

Cáda úno se entiénde — *Each one knows his own business*

Éso está colgádo de un hílo — *That hangs only by a thread*

Cáda ovéja con su paréja — *Birds of a feather flock together*

Cuánto va que ésto sucéde? — *What will you bet that that will happen?*

Cáesele la cára de vergüénza — *He blushes to his eyes*

No está pára fiéstas — *He is not good-humoured*

No háy fórma de vivír con ése hómbre — *One cannot live with such a man*

Mas vále buéna fáma que cáma doráda — *A good name is above wealth*

Tenér álgo en el píco de la léngua — *To have any thing on the tip of the tongue*

No tenér cása ni hogár — *To have neither house nor home*

Sacár fuérza de flaquéza — *To make virtue of necessity*

Sóbre gústo no háy dispúta — *There is no disputing about taste*

FÁBULAS.

N. B. In looking for words in the Dictionary, the student should bear in mind the observations made in pages 17, 18, 19 and 20, in regard to pronunciation and orthography.

Remember that the Spanish Academy considers *ch*, *ll*, and *ñ*, as distinct characters from *c*, *l* and *n*, and in its Dictionary, as in all others who follow this single legitimate standard of the Spanish tongue, you must look through all the words beginning with these simple characters, before you find those commencing with the aforesaid compound.

Fábula Priméra.

Los Animáles en conséjo júntos pára elegír un Réy.

HABIÉNDO muérto el león, tódas las áves y béstias se congregáron á su cuéva pára condolérse con la réina viuda, que hacia resonár sus laméntos y grítos en los móntes y bósques.

Despué́s de los acostumbrádos cumplimiéntos, procediéron tódos á la elección de un réy, la coróna del difúnto monárca fué colocáda en médio de la asambléa.

Su aparénte heredéro éra demasiádo jóven y endéble pára obtenér la dignidád reál, á la que tántos animáles mas fuértes que él pusiéron su demánda.

Dégenme crecér un póco, dijo su altéza, y entónces esperimentaréis que puédo llenár el tróno, y con el tiémpo hacér felíces á mis súbditos. Entretánto estudiaré las acciónes heróicas de mi pádre, con la esperánza de que algún día, podré sérle iguál en glória.

Por mi párte, díjo el leopárdo, insísto en mi derécho á la coróna, por la mayór semejánza que téngo al último réy éntre tódos los candidátos.

Yó, por ótro ládo, gritó el óso, sostendré que se me hízo injustícia cuándo su magestád anterió́r se me prefirió: sóy tan fuérte, intrépido, y sangriénto cómo éra; y ademá́s, sóy maéstro de un árte que él jamás púdo adquirír, cuál es, el trepár por los árboles

Yó apélo, díjo el elefánte, al juício de ésta augústa asambléa, si algúno de los preséntes puéde con algún colorído jactárse de ser tan álto, de tan nóble preséncia, tan robústo, ó tan circunspécto cómo yó.

Yó sóy la mas nóble, y la mas hermósa criatúra éntre tódos vosótros, díjo el cabállo.

É yó sóy la mas política, díjo la zórra. ·

É yó sóy el mas velóz en corrér, díjo el córzo.

En dónde encontraréis, díjo el míco, un réy mas agradáble, mas ingenióso, y mas divertído que yó? Yó divertiría contínuaménte á mis vasállos, y sóy además el mas semejánte al hómbre, que es el Señór del Univérso.

El papagáyo interrumpiéndole, hízo su arénga: supuésto que vm. se alába de su semejánza al hómbre, me paréce que puédo yó alabárme con múcha mas justícia. Tóda la semejánza de vm. consíste en su hocíco féo y algúnos géstos ridículos; péro yó puédo hablár cómo un hómbre, é imitár su lenguáge, señál indicatíva de su razón, y su mayór adórno.

Guardád vuéstra maldíta garúlla, replicó la móna: habláis, es ciérto, péro no cómo hómbre; repetís siémpre úna mísma cósa sin entendér úna sóla palábra de lo que decís. .

Tóda la asambléa se rió de éstos dos riváles imitadóres del género humáno, y confiriéron la coróna al elefánte, porqué éra fuérte y sábio; y no sólo éra exénto del bárbaro naturál de las béstias de rapíña, sinó también de la vanidád y amór própio de que múchos están tocádos, siémpre pareciéndoles ó fingiéndo ser lo que, en la realidád, no son.

Fábula Segúnda

El Dragón y las Dos Zórras

Un dragón guardába con ánsia un tesóro inménso en úna cuéva profúnda; núnca dormía de día ni de nóche, pára asegurárlo.

Dos zórras aduladóras, artificiósas, y pícaras de profesión, se introdugéron en su grácia con sus lisónjas fastidiósas. Ambas éran sus íntimas amígas.

Los que son mas cortéses y oficiósos no son siémpre los mas sínceros. Le rindiéron sus obséquios con la mayór sumisión: admiráron sus fantasías ociósas; conviniéron con él en sus idéas, y se burláron de su crédula tontería.

Finalménte, quedóse un día dormído éntre sus confidéntes: le ahogáron, y tomáron posesión de su tesóro.

Éra precíso repartír el pilláge; un púnto múy delicádo, y no éra fácil de ajustárse, porqué dos villános no conviénen sinó en la egecución de sus delítos.

Úna de éllas empezó á exhortár en éstos términos: de que nos servirá tódo éste dinéro? Un gazápo nos sería un botín, ó présa mas agradáble: no podémos hacér úna comída de éstos doblónes, son múy indigéstos. Los hómbres son múy lócos, en dejárse arrebatár de riquézas tan imaginárias. No seámos nosótras criatúras tan insensátas, cómo éllos lo son.

La ótra pretendió que éstas reflexiónes la habían hécho úna impresión fuérte, y la aseguró que en lo venidéro estaría conténta de continuár úna vída filosófica, y cómo Bías llevár su tesóro tódo consígo.

Al parecér, ámbas estában dispuéstas á abandonár su tesóro mal adquirído: péro ámbas se quedáron á la míra, hásta que se despedazáron.

Al espirár la úna díjo á la ótra, que estába tan mortalménte herída cómo élla: que querías hacér con tódo aquél óro? Lo mísmo que tú te proponías hacér con él, replicó la ótra.

Siéndo informádo un viajadór de su pendéncia, les díjo, que éran tóntas. Así lo es el mayór número del género humáno, replicó úna de las zórras. Tampóco á vosótros puéde servír de comída, y con tódo, os asesináis únos á ótros por el dinéro.

Nosótras, las zórras, hémos sído bastánte súbias, á lo ménos hásta aquí, pára mirár al dinéro cómo úna cósa inútil. Lo que habéis introducído éntre vosótros cómo úna conveniéncia, es vuéstra desgrácia. Dejáis un bién sustanciál, sólaménte por seguír un bién fantástico.

Fábula Tercéra.

Las Dos Zórras.

Úna nóche entráron dos zórras furtívaménte en un gallinéro: matáron el gállo, las gallínas, y los póllos: despúes de ésta matánza, empezáron á devorár su présa.

Úna que éra jóven y sin reflexión, propúso comérlos tódos de úna vez; la ótra viéja y codiciósa quería ahorrár pára ótro día.

Híja, díjo la viéja, la esperiéncia me hízo sábia; en mi tiémpo he vísto múcho múndo. No consumámos á la vez pródigaménte tódo nuéstro caudál; tuvímos buén sucéso, y debémos cuidár de no mal gastárlo.

Replicó la jóven, estóy resuélta á recreárme miéntras lo téngo por delánte, y saciár mi apetíto por tóda úna semána; por lo que tóca á venir aquí mañána, es cuénto: éso es esponérnos: mañána vendrá aquí el ámo, y por vengár la muérte de sus póllos, nos dará con úna tránca en la cabéza.

Despues de ésta réplica, cáda úna de éllas óbra cómo le paréce mas própio.

La jóven cóme hásta que reviénta, sin podér apénas arrastrárse á su cuéva ántes de morír. La viéja que le pareció múcho más prudénte gobernár su apetíto, y ser frugál, fué el día siguiénte al gallinéro, y la mató el labradór.

Así cáda edád tiéne su vício favoríto: los jóvenes son fogósos é insaciábles en sus placéres; y los viéjos incorregíbles en su avarícia.

———

Fábula Cuárta.

El lóbo y el Cordéro.

Había un rebáño de ovéjas, que pacían seguras de tódo mal en un cercádo; tódos los pérros dormían, y sus ámos tocában la gáita rurál con sus compañéros bájo de un álamo frondóso.

Un lóbo hambriénto víno al redíl á registrárlos por las rendíjas.

Un cordéro inespérto, y que núnca había estádo fuéra entró en conversación con él.

Y le díjo, que es lo que tú quiéres aquí, lóbo?

Un póco de ésta yérba frésca, le respondió el lóbo. Bién sábes que no háy cósa mas agradáble, que matár la hámbre en un prádo vérde esmaltádo con flóres, y apagár la sed en úna fuénte trasparénte. Aquí encuéntro cópia de úno y ótro, que puéde úno deseár mas? pór mi párte, yó ámo la filosofía que nos enséña á contentárnos con póco.

Es verdád pués, replicó el cordéro, que tú te abstiénes de la cárne de las béstias, y que un póco de yérba te satisfáce? Si es así, vivámos cómo hermános y pastémos júntos.

El cordéro, luégo, saltó del redíl al prádo en dónde el gráve filósofo le despedazó, y de úna vez le devoró.

Desconfíate siémpre de las lénguas lisongéras de los que se jáctan de su própia virtúd. Fórma tu juício según sus acciónes, y no según sus palábras.

EPÍTOME DE LA HISTÓRIA DE ESPAÑA.

(Sacádo de las Cártas Marruécas de Don JOSÉ CADÁLSO, Cárta III.)

"LA península, llamáda España, sólo está contígua al continénte de Europa por el ládo de Fráncia de la que la sepáran los móntes Pirinéos. Es abundánte en óro, pláta, azógue, hiérro, piédras, águas mineráles, ganádos de esceléntes calidádes, y péscas tan abundántes cómo deliciósas. Esta felíz situación la hízo objéto de la codícia de los fenícios y ótros puéblos. Los cartaginéses, párte por dólo, y párte por fuérza, se estableciéron en élla; y los romános quisiéron completár su podér y glória con la conquísta de España; péro encontráron úna resisténcia, que pareció tan estráña cómo terríble á los sobérbios duéños de lo restánte del múndo Numáncia, úna sóla ciudád, les costó catórce áños de sítio, la pérdida de tres egércitos, y el desdóro de los mas famósos Generáles, hásta que reducídos los numantínos á la precisión de capitulár ó morír, por la totál ruína de la pátria, córto número de vívos, y abundáncia de cadáveres en las cálles (sin contár los que habían servído de pásto á sus conciudadános despúes de concluídos tódos sus víveres) incendiáron sus cásas, arrojáron sus mugéres, niños y anciános en las llámas, y saliéron á morír en el cámpo ráso con las ármas en la máno. El gránde Escipión fué testígo de la ruína de Numáncia, pués no puéde llamárse própiamente conquistadór de la ciudád: siéndo de notár que Lúculo, encargádo de levantár un egército pára aquélla espedición, no halló en la juventúd romána reclútas que llevár, hásta que el mísmo Escipión se alistó pára animárla. Si los romános conociéron el valór de los españóles cómo enemígos, también esperimentáron su virtúd cómo aliádos. Sagúnto sufrió por éllos un sítio iguál al de Numáncia cóntra los cartaginéses; y désde entónces formáron los romános de los españóles el álto concépto que se vé en sus autóres, oradóres, historiadóres y poétas. Péro la fortúna de Róma, superiór al valór humáno, la hízo señóra de España, cómo de lo restánte del múndo, ménos algúnos móntes de Cantábria, cúya totál conquísta no cónsta de la his-

33

tória, de módo que no puéda dudárse. Lárgas revoluciónes inútiles de contárse en éste paráge tragéron del nórte enjámbres de naciónes feróces, codiciósas y guerréras, que se estableciéron en España: péro con las delícias de éste clíma tan diferénte dél que habían dejádo, cayéron en tal grádo de afeminación y flogedád, que á su tiémpo fuéron esclávos de ótros conquistadóres venídos del médio día. Huyéron los gódos españóles hásta los móntes de una província, hóy llamáda Astúrias: y apénas tuviéron tiémpo de desechár el sústo, llorár la pérdida de sus cásas y ruína de su réino, cuándo saliéron mandádos por Peláyo, úno de los mayóres hómbres que la naturaléza ha producído.

Désde aquí se ábre un teátro de guérras que duráron cérca de ócho síglos. Várias réinos se levantáron sóbre la ruína de la Monarquía Góda Españóla, destruyéndo él que querían edificár los móros en el mismo terréno, regádo con mas sángre españóla, romána, cartaginésa, góda y móra de cuánto se puéde ponderár con horrór de la plúma que lo escríba, y de los ójos que lo véan escríto Péro la población de ésta península éra tal, que despúes de tan lárgas guérras y tan sangriéntas, aún se contában véinte millónes de habitántes en élla. Incorporáronse tántas províncias, y tan diferéntes, en dos corónas, la de Castílla y la de Aragón; y ámbas en el matrimónio de Don Fernándo y Dóña Isabél, Príncipes que serán inmortáles éntre cuántos sépan lo que es gobiérno. La refórma de abúsos, auménto de ciéncias, humillación de los sobérbios, ampáro de la agricultúra y ótras operaciónes semejántes formáron ésta Monarquía: ayudóles la naturaléza con un número increíble de vasállos insígnes en létras y ármas; y se pudiéron habér lisongeádo de dejár á sus sucesóres un império mayór y mas duradéro, que él de Róma antígua (contándo las Américas nuévamente descubiértas,) si hubiéran lográdo dejár su coróna á un heredéro varón. Nególes el ciélo éste gózo á truéque de tántos cómo les había concedído; y su cétro pasó á la cása de Aústria, la cúal gastó los tesóros, taléntos y sángre de los Españóles en cósas agénas de España por las contínuas guérras, que así en Alemánia, cómo en Itália túvo que sostenér Cárlos I. de España; hásta que cansádo de sus mísmas prosperidádes ó tal vez conociéndo con prudéncia las vicisitúdes de las cósas humánas, no quíso esponérse á sus revéses, y dejó el tróno á su híjo Don Felípe II.

Éste Príncipe, acusádo por la emulación, por ambicióso y político cómo su pádre, péro ménos afortunádo, siguiéndo los proyéctos de Cárlos, no púdo hallár los mísmos sucésos aún á cósta de egércitos, de armádas y de caudáles. Murió dejándo á su puéblo estenuádo con las guérras, afeminádo con el óro y pláta de América, disminuído con la población de un múndo nuévo, disgustádo con tántas desgrácias, y deseóso de descánso. Pasó el cétro por las mános de tres Príncipes ménos actívos pára manejár tan gránde Monarquía, y en la muérte de Cárlos II. no éra España sinó el esquelé o de un gigánte."

CHÍSTES.

Uu hómbre discréto preguntándo á su híjo de dónde venía, pués éra tan tárde, le respondió: Pádre, yó véngo de ver á úno de mis amígos. De tus amígos, le respondió el pádre sorprendído; ¡Tú tiénes pués tántos amígos! Oh! cómo has hécho siéndo tan jóven pára alcanzár múchos; pues que yó en mas de sesénta áños no he podído encontrár úno.

El Cabálléro Tomás Móro, famóso Cancellér de Inglatérra, puésto en prisión por Enríque octávo, dejó crecér sus cabéllos y bárba, y viniéndo un barbéro pára cortárlos y afeitárle; amígo, le díjo: el Réy é yó pleitcámos sóbre mi cabéza; é yó no quiéro hacér el menór gásto en éste pléito, sin sabér ántes quién de los dos ha de disponér de élla.

Luís dóce, Réy de Fráncia, cuándo no éra sinó Dúque de Orleáns, había padecído múchos pesáres de dos persónas que habían sído favorítos en el reinádo precedénte. Úno de sus allegádos procurába inspirárle que les mostráse resentimiénto. No, respondió su Magestád, que indígno es de un Réy de Fráncia tomár párte en la vengánza del Dúque de Orleáns.

Conrádo tercéro, Emperadór, despúes de habér tomádo á Munick, determinó pasár los hómbres á fílo de la espáda, permitiéndo sólo á las mugéres salír de allí, pudiéndo llevár sóbre éllas sus muébles mas preciósos. Éstas mugéres aprovechándo la ocasión tomáron sóbre sus hómbros á sus marídos, asegurándo éran sus mas preciósos muébles. Esto agradó tánto al Emperadór, que no sólo perdonó á los habitántes, sinó también á su Príncipe que había destinádo á la muérte

La Réina Isabél observándo la bélla grácia de un nóble Español en un tornéo, le preguntó un día que le digése absolútaménte el nómbre de su Dáma. El Españól lo resistió algún tiémpo. En fin cediéndo á su curiosidád, prometió á su Magestád enviárle su retráto. El día siguiénte hízo presentár á su Magestád un paquetíllo, dónde la Réina no hallándo sinó un espejíto, quedó sonrojáda al púnto.

Los cortesános del Réy Filípo le aconsejában que se vengáse de un hómbre que había habládo mal de él. Antes es menestér sabér, si yó no le he dádo razón, díjo Filípo: y habiéndose averiguádo que el tal hómbre jamás había recibído cósa algúna, le envió rícos preséntes. Súpo el Réy póco después que el mísmo le llenába de alabánzas. Mirád pués, díjo á los cortesános, que yó sé mejór que vosótros apaciguár úna léngua mála.

Continuándo las dispútas éntre Francísco priméro, Réy de Fráncia, y Enríque octávo, Réy de Inglatérra, resolvió éste de enviár al priméro un Embajadór portadór de palábras fiéras, y amenázas; pára lo cuál hízo elección del Obíspo Bonnér en quién tenía gran confiánza. Este Obíspo le díjo que ponía su vída en gran pelígro, si dába táles recádos á un Réy tan altívo cómo Francísco priméro. No témas, le díjo el Réy que si el Réy de Fráncia hiciése tal, yó haría caér múchas cabézas de Francéses que están aquí. Páse por éllo, señór; péro cuál de ésas cabézas me vendría tan bién sóbre los hómbros cómo ésta, poniéndo el dédo á su sién.

Cuándo el Mariscál de la Ferté hízo su entráda en Metz, los judíos que allí éran tolerádos se presentáron al cumplimiénto con tódos los vecínos; y anunciándolos en la antecámara, no quiéro vérlos, díjo; porqué éllos hiciéron morír á nuéstro Señór. Que no éntren de ningún módo. Digéronles pués que no podían ver á su Esceléncia. A que replicáron sentídos; pués traían un presénte de cuátro mil doblónes. Lo que dícho inmediátaménte á su Esceléncia; oh bién! díles que éntren; que éstos póbres diáblos segúraménte no lo conocían cuándo lo crucificáron.

¡Oh hómbre, séas él que fuéres noble ó artesáno; ríco ó póbre; dócto ó ignoránte; eclesiástico ó seculár; religióso ó militár; soberáno ó súbdito; desciénde déntro de tí mísmo, y en un siléncio profúndo y no interrumpído, reflexióna sóbre los horróres de la náda que precediéron á tu concepción! ¿Cómo de la náda has pasádo á ser? cómo en un instánte has llegádo á ser espíritu y cuérpo, ésto es; conjúnto de dos sustáncias, cúya unión paréce incompatíble, y cúya acción es un prodígio continuádo?

Ni tu pádre, ni tu mádre tuviéron conocimiénto ni podér pára coordinár tus músculos, pára diluír ni liquidár tu sángre, ni pára endurecér tus huésos. Úna inteligéncia supréma, superiór á tódas las poténcias de la tiérra, y superiór á tódas tus idéas, quíso, y comenzó tu existéncia; quíso, y crecíste al estádo en que te hállas. ¡Ay de mí! ¿Y quién es ésta inteligéncia? ¡Ay! Quién puéde ser, sinó el motór universál, el princípio de tódo lo que vegéta y respíra, y el infiníto ser, al que llamámos *Diós!* Su máno omnipoténte te bosquejába, cuándo tú no podías conocérle, y te consérva y mantiéne en un síglo en el que se háce vanidád de ultrajárle. Péro si no éras ayér, y puéde ser déges de ser hóy; ¿posíble es que se te páse el día, que tan rápidaménte se húye, sin pensár en éste criádor y conservadór, sin dárle grácias, y sin adorárle?

EL MARQUÉS CARACCIÓLI.

La verdád es la que ríge los ciélos, alúmbra la tiérra, susténta la justícia, gobiérna las Repúblicas, confírma lo que es cláro, y aclára lo que es dudóso; con élla tódas las virtúdes tiénen su perfección. Élla es un homenáge que núnca cáe, un escúdo que no se pása, un tiémpo que no se túrba, úna flóta que no peréce, úna flor que no se marchíta, úna mar que no se altéra, y un puérto en dónde nádie peligra. La Verdád tiéne en sí tan gran fuérza, que sin élla la fortaléza es fláca, la prudéncia es malícia, la templánza es miséria, la justícia es sanguinolénta, la humildád es traidóra, la paciéncia fingida, la castidád vána, la riquéza perdída, y la piedád supérflua. La verdád es un céntro adónde tódas las cósas repósan, el nórte por dónde el múndo se ríge, el antídoto con que tódos se cúran: es la sómbra á dónde tódos descánsan, el terréro á dónde tódos tíran, péro el blánco á dónde pócos aciértan.   DON PÉDRO DE MEDÍNA.

El temór de la justícia divína es el princípio que hízo nacér en la imaginación de várias libertínos las horríbles idéas filosóficas, yá de negár á Diós la existéncia, yá de despojár de su inmortalidád al álma   Tóda la desdícha de éstos miserábles viéne de que, léjos de contemplár al Omnipoténte cómo á un pádre cariñóso, sólo se figúran en él un juéz sevéro; y pára sacudír de sí el temór que ésta calidád les inspíra, forcéjan á persuadírse, ó con la priméra de éstas dos quiméras, que no háy Diós que los castígue; ó con la segúnda, que sólo puéden temér de él un castígo léve y de córta duración, cómo lo es cualquiéra péna temporál. ¿Péro que lógran con ésto? Puntualménte lo que el réo, que huyéndo de su justícia, se arrója por un despeñadéro, y por evitár un suplício contingénte, abráza úna muérte indubitáble. Por el precipício mayór de tódos, que es él de la impiedád, procúran huír de la justícia divína. Y aún los que niégan á Diós la existéncia, no tánto aspíran á huír de la justícia divína, cómo que la justícia divína húya de éllos, pretendiéndo que el soberáno juéz se desaparézca de aquél augústo tróno, en que los ha de sentenciár.   FEIJÓO.

El aváro yá se sábe que es un mártir del demónio, ó un anacoréta, que con su abstinéncia y su retíro háce méritos pára ir al infiérno. El corazon, partído éntre los dos deséos de conservár y adquirír, padéce úna contínua fiébre, mezcláda con un mortál frío; pués, se abrása con la ánsia de conseguír lo agéno, y tiémbla con el sústo de perdér lo própio. Tiéne hámbre, y no cóme; tiéne sed, y no bébe: tiéne necesidád, y no repósa: jamás se ve líbre de sobresáltos. Ningún ratón se muéve en el siléncio de la nóche, que con el ruído no le dé espécie de ser un ladrón que le escála. Ningún viénto sópla que en su imaginación no amenáce naufrágio al navío que tiéne puésto en comércio: Ningúna guérra se suscíta, que no considére yá á los enemígos talándo sus tiérras

cualquiér rencílla de particuláres, déntro de su idéa viéne á
parár en populár tumúlto, que lléva á sáco el caudál. No
háy nubecílla que no imagíne tempestuósa pára sus víñas y
miéses; no háy intempérie, que no amágue corrupción á lo
que tiéne recogído en las trójes.   FEIJÓO.

———

El Ambicióso es un esclávo de tódo el múndo; del príncipe, por que concéda el empléo; del valído, por que intercéda;
de los demás, por que no estórben. Tiéne el álma y el
cuérpo en contínuo movimiénto, porqué es menestér no perdér instánte. Á tódos téme, porqué ningúno háy que con
úna acusación no puéda desvanecér tóda su solicitúd. ¡O
cuánto forcéja con su semblánte por que muéstre agrádo á los
mismos á quiénes proféza mortál ódio! ¡Cuánto trabájo le
cuésta reprimír tódas aquéllas inclinaciónes viciósas que puéden dificultár sus médras! De la pasión dominánte son vícti-
mas tódas las demás pasiónes; y el vício de la ambición, cómo tiráno duéño, sóbre atormentárle por sí mísmo, le prohíbe
tódos aquéllos gústos á que le lléva el deséo. Ve ál que va á
la comédia, ál que lógra el paséo honésto, ál que asíste al
banquéte, ál que góza el saráo; tódo lo ve y lo envídia; péro
los apetítos están en él, aunqué furiósos, aprisionádos cómo
los viéntos en la cárcel de Eólo.   FEIJÓO.

———

Cuánto mas abúlta el cuérpo de un hómbre, tánto mas tiéne
dónde le hiéra el enemígo: y cuánto mas es la amplitúd de
la fortúna, tánto mas háy dónde hiéra la adversidád. Son
las rícas tórres elevádas, y las póbres chózas humíldes; y el
ráyo mas véces descárga en la tórre su fúria, que en la chóza. Úno de los mayóres máles que háy en lo temporál, si no
el mayór de tódos, es la salúd quebráda; cómo el mayór
bién la salúd robústa. Y no tiéne dúda que, en igualdád de
temperaménto, múcho mas sáno es el póbre que el ríco; porqué éste con los escésos se estrága la salúd, y aquél se la
consérva con su sobriedád.
  Que bélla digresión háce Lucáno en el líbro quínto de la
guérra civíl, sóbre la felicidád del póbre barquéro Amíntas,
cuándo pínta á César en el siléncio de la nóche pulsándo la
puérta de su chóza, pára que le condúzca próntaménte á la

Calábria. Tódo el múndo está conmovído y temblándo con los movimiéntos de la guérra civíl; y déntro de la mísma Grécia, que es el teátro de la guérra, vecíno á los mísmos egércitos, duérme, sin temór algúno, un póbre barquéro sóbre enjútas óvas. Despiértanle los gólpes que da á su puérta el generóso Caudíllo, sin introducír en su pécho el menór sústo: pués, aunqué no ignóra que está tóda la campáña cubiérta de trópas, sábe también que no háy en su chóza cósa que puéda brindár los militáres insúltos. ¡O vída del póbre, esclámna el poéta, que tiénes la felicidád de estár exénta de las violéncias! ¡O pobréza, benefício gránde de los Dióses, aunqué no reconocída de los hómbres! Que múros ó que témplos gozarán el privilégio que tiénen Amíntas y su chóza de no temblár á los gólpes de la robústa máno de César!

FEIJÓO.

La modéstia es la prénda mas amáble de una doncélla, aún en cotéjo de la hermosúra. Ésta, no háy dúda, halága y solicíta múcho mas la pasión del hómbre, péro aquélla se grangéa su mayór estimación y aprécio. La pasión náce de los atractívos que le hácen amár aquéllo que la provóca: mas el aprécio y estimación que infúnde el decóro de la modéstia, procéden del respéto que adúra en la esteriór compostúra de un róstro la belléza interiór del álma, á quién aquélla retráta. Aquélla mísma es también segúro indício de la dulzúra de génio, y de la suavidád del carácter á quién sírve de álma, de la cuál espéra su mayór satisfacción y dícha en el casamiénto el hómbre que preténde poseérla. La hermosúra es don accidentál de la naturaléza, que éntre pócos la repárte; péro la hermosúra interiór del álma, la da la virtúd sóla, á cualquiéra que deséa conseguírla.

PÉDRO DE MONTENGÓN.

Én tódas aquéllas cósas, que esenciálménte compónen la felicidád temporál, conviéne á sabér; Vída, Salúd, Hónra y Haciénda, es múy mejorádo el virtuóso, respécto de él que no lo es. La Hónra nádie ignóra que es párto legítimo de la Virtúd. Por éso los Romános edificáron unídos los témplos de éstas dos díchas, que venerában cómo deidádes, de módo que sólo por el témplo de la Virtúd se podía entrár al témplo del Honór.   Los mísmos que húyen de la práctica de la Virtúd, la míran con estimación y reveréncia.   La Salúd y lárga vída es mas naturál y posíble en el hómbre virtuóso, por la templánza con que víve, al páso que el vicióso con sus escésos se estrága la salúd, y se acórta la vída.   La Haciénda tiéne úna gran maéstra de economía en la Virtúd, siéndo ciérto que se consérva evitándo tóda superfluidád.

La suavidád y dulzúra que al álma ocasióna la buéna conciéncia, colóca en múy eminénte grádo la fortúna de los jústos sóbre la de los pecadóres.   Es ésta úna felicidád de póco búlto, péro de múcha mónta; úna piédra preciósa, que en bréves dimensiónes enciérra grándes quilátes.   Es la conciéncia espéjo del álma, y sucéde al jústo y al pecadór, cuándo se míran en éste espéjo, lo que á la hermósa y á la féa al vérse en el cristál; aquélla se compláce, porqué ve perfecciónes; ésta se entristéce, porqué no regístra sinó lunáres.

FEIJÓO.

¡O Muérte, cuán amárga es tu memória!   Cuán présta tu venída!   Cuán secrétos tus camínos!   Cuán dudósa tu hóra! Cuán universál tu señorío! Los poderósos no te puéden huír; los sábios no te sáben evitár; los fuértes contígo piérden las fuérzas;   pára contígo ningúno háy ríco;   pués, ningúno puéde comprár la vída, ni aún por tesóros.   Tódo lo ándas, tódo lo cércas, y en tódo lugár te hállas.   Tú páces las yérbas; bébes los viéntos; corrómpes los áires; múdas los síglos; truécas el múndo, y no déjas de sorbér la mar.   Tódas las cósas tiénen sus creciéntes y menguántes; mas tú, siémpre permanéces en un mísmo ser.   Éres un martíllo que siémpre hiére; espáda que núnca se embóta; lázo en que tódos caén; cárcel en que tódos éntran; mar dónde tódos pelígran;   péna que tódos padécen; y tribúto que tódos págan—¡O muérte cruél! ¿Cómo no tiénes lástima de venír al mejór tiémpo é impedír los negócios encaminádos á bién?   Róbas en úna hóra, en un minúto, lo que se ganó en múchos áños; córtas la sucesión de los lináges; déjas los Réinos sin heredéros; hínches el múndo de orfandádes; córtas el hílo de los estúdios; háces malográdos los buénos ingénios; júntas el fin con el princípio, sin dar lugár á los médios.—¡O muérte, muérte!   O implacáble enemíga del género humáno!   ¿Porqué tuvíste entráda en el múndo?...

LUÍS de GRACIÁN.

—◆—

CÁRTA I.

De Gazél á Ben-Beléy.

Aún no me hállo capáz de obedecér á las nuévas instáncias que me háces sóbre que te remíta las observaciónes que vóy haciéndo en la capitál de ésta vásta monarquía. Sábes tú cuántas cósas se necesítan pára formár úna verdadéra idéa del país en que se viája? Bién es verdád, que habiéndo hécho vários viáges por Európa, me hállo mas capáz, ó por mejór decír. cón ménos obstáculos que ótros Africános; péro aún así he halládo tánta diferéncia éntre los Européos, que no básta el conocimiénto de úno de los países de ésta párte del múndo, pára juzgár de ótros estádos de la mísma. Los Européos no parécen vecínos, aunqué la esterioridád los háya uniformádo en mésas, teátros, paséos, egército, y lújo: no obstánte las léyes, vícios, virtúdes, y gobiérno son súmaménte divérsos, y por consiguiénte las costúmbres própias de cáda nación.

Aún déntro de la Española háy variedád increíble en el carácter de sus províncias. Un Andalúz en náda se paréce á un Vizcaíno; un Catalán es totalménte distínto de un Gallégo; y lo mísmo sucéde éntre un Valenciáno y un Montañés. Ésta Península, dividída tántos síglos en diferéntes réinos, ha tenído siémpre variedád de tráges, léyes, idiómas, y monédas.

Acábo de leér la História de España, y me paréce que de la relación se puéde inferír, lo. priméro; que ésta península no ha gozádo úna paz que puéda llamárse tal en cérca de dos mil áños; y que por consiguiénte es maravílla, que aún téngan yérbas los cámpos, y águas las fuéntes. Lo segúndo; que habiéndo sído la religión motívo de tántas guérras cóntra los descendiéntes de Taríf, no es múcho que séa objéto de tódas sus acciónes. Lo tercéro; que la continuación de estár con las ármas en la máno, les háya hécho mirár con desprécio el comércio é indústria mecánica. Lo cuárto; que de ésto mísmo názca lo mucho que cáda nóble en España se envanéce de su nobléza. Lo quínto; que los múchos caudáles adquirídos rápidaménte en Índias, distráen á múchos de cultivár las ártes mecánicas en la península y de aumentár su población.

Las demás consecuéncias moráles de éstos evéntos políticos las irás notándo en las cártas que te escribiré sóbre éstos asúntos.

CÁRTA II.

Del mismo, al mismo.

El atráso de las ciéncias en Espáña en éste síglo ¿ quién puéde dudár que procéde de la fálta de protección que hállan sus profesóres? Háy cochéros en Madríd, que gánan trescientos pésos dúros; péro no háy quién no sépa que se ha de morír de hámbre, cómo se entrégue á las ciéncias, esceptuádas las *de pane lucrando*, que son las únicas que dan de comér.

Los pócos que cultívan las ótras, son cómo los aventuréros voluntários de los egércitos .que no llévan pága y se espónen mas. ·Es un gústo oírlos hablár de matemáticas, física modérna, história naturál, derécho de géntes, antigüedádes, y létras humánas, á véces con mas recáto que si hiciéran monéda fálsa. Víven en la oscuridád y muéren cómo viviéron, tenídos por sábios superficiáles en el concépto de los que sáben ponér seténta y siéte silogísmos seguídos sóbre si los ciélos son fluídos ó sólidos.

Hablándo pócos días ha con un sábio escolástico de los mas condecorádos en su carréra, le oí ésta espresión con motívo de habérse nombrádo á un sugéto escelénte en matemáticas; *sí, en su país se aplican múcho á ésas cosíllas, cómo matemáticas, lénguas orientáles, física, derécho de géntes, y ótras semejántes.* Péro yó te asegúro, Ben-Beley, que si señalásen prémios pára los profesóres, prémios de honór ó de interés, ó de ámbos, ¡ que progrésos no harían! Si hubiése siquiéra quién los protegiése, se esmerarían sin mas estímulo positívo; péro no háy protectóres.

Tan persuadido está mi amígo Núño de ésta verdád, que hablándo de ésto, me díjo: en ótros tiémpos, allá cuándo me imagínaba, que éra útil y glorióso dejár fáma en el múndo, trabajé úna óbra sóbre várias pártes de la literatúra que ha-

bía cultiv́ado, aunqué con mas amór que buén sucéso. Quíse
que saliése bájo la sómbra de algún poderóso, cómo es naturál á tódo autór principiánte. Oí á un magnáte decír, que
tódos los autóres éran lócos: á ótro, que las dedicatórias
éran estáfas: á ótro, que renegába de él que inventó el papél;
ótro se burlába de los hómbres que se imaginában sabér álgo: ótro me insinuó, que la óbra que le sería mas acépta,
sería la létra de úna tonadílla: ótro me díjo, que me viéra
con un criádo súyo, pára tratár de ésta matéria; ótro ni me
quíso hablár; ótro ni me quíso respondér; ótro ni me quíso
escuchár; y de resúltas de tódo ésto, tomé la determinación
de dedicár el frúto de mis desvélos al mózo que traía el água
á cása.

_____

CÁRTA III.

Del mismo, al mismo.

Cuándo híce el primér viáge por Európa, te dí notícia de
un país que láman Fráncia, y está mas allá de los móntes
Pirinéos. Désde Inglatérra me fué múy fácil y córto el
tránsito. Registré sus províncias septentrionáles; llegué á
su capital, péro no púde examinárla á mi gústo, por ser córto el tiémpo que podía gastár entónces en éllo, y ser múcho
él que se necesíta pára egecutárlo con provécho.

Ahóra he vísto la párte meridionál de élla, saliéndo de
España por Cataluña, y entrándo por Guipúzcoa, internán-
dome hásta León por un ládo, y Burdéos por ótro.

Los Francéses están tan mal querídos en éste síglo, cómo
los Españóles lo éran en el anteriór; sin dúda, porqué úno y
ótro síglo han sído precedídos de las éras gloriósas respectí-
vas de cáda nación, que fué la de Cárlos V pára España, y
la de Luís XIV pára Fráncia. Éste último es mas reciénte;
con que también es mas fuérte su efécto; péro bién examiná-
da la cáusa, créo hallár múcha preocupación de párte de tódos los Européos cóntra los Francéses. Conózco, que el
desenfréno de su juventúd; la mála condúcta de algúnos que
viájan fuéra de su país, profesándo un súmo desprécio de tódo lo que no es Fráncia; el lújo que ha corrompído la Európa, y ótros motívos semejántes repúgnan á tódos sus vecínos mas sóbrios; á sabér, al Español religióso, al Italiáno
político, al Inglés sobérbio, al Holandés aváro, y al Alemán
áspero; péro la nación entéra no débe padecér la nóta por

cúlpa de algúnos indivíduos. En ámbas vuéltas, que he dádo por Fráncia, he halládo en sus províncias (que siémpre mantiénen las costúmbres mas púras que la capitál) un tráto humáno, cortés y afáble pára los estrangéros; no producído de la vanidád de que se les visíte y admíre, (cómo puéde sucedér en París,) sinó dimanádo verdadéraménte de un corazón fránco y sencíllo, que hálla gústo en procurárselo al desconocído. Ni aún déntro de su capitál, que algúnos píntan cómo el céntro de tódo desórden, confusión y lújo, fáltan hómbres verdadéraménte respetábles. Tódos los que llégan á ciérta edád, son sin dúda los mas sociábles del Univérso; porqué desvanecídas las tempestádes de su juventúd, les quéda el fóndo de úna índole sincera, prolíja educación (que en éste país es común,) y esteriór agradáble, sin la astúcia del Italiáno, la sobérbia del Inglés, la asperéza del Alemán, la avarícia del Holandés, y el despégo del Españól.

En llegándo á los cuarénta áños, se transfórma el Francés en ótro hómbre distínto de lo que éra á los véinte. El militár concúrre al tráto civíl con súma urbanidád; el magistrádo con sencilléz, y el particulár con sosiégo; tódos con ademánes de agasajár al estrangéro que se hálla mediánaménte introducído por su Embajadór, calidád, talénto ú ótro motívo. Se entiénde tódo ésto éntre la génte de fórma; que con la mediána y común, el mísmo hécho de ser estrangéro, es úna recomendación superiór á cuántas puéde llevár él que viája.

La mísma desenvoltúra de los jóvenes, insufríble á quién no los conóce, tiéne un no sé que, que los háce amábles. Por élla se descúbre tódo el hómbre interiór incapáz de rencóres, astúcias bájas, ni intención dañáda. Cómo procúro indagár precisaménte el carácter de las cósas verdadéro, y no graduárlas por las apariéncias, cási siémpre engañósas, no me paréce tan odióso aquél bullício y descompostúra, por lo que llévo dícho. Del mísmo dictámen es mi amígo Núño, no obstánte lo quejóso que está de que los Francéses no séan iguálménte imparciáles, cuándo háblan de los Españóles.

CÁRTA IV.

De Ben-Beléy á Gazél.

Acábo de leér el último líbro de los que me has enviádo en los vários viáges que has hécho por Európa; con el cuál llégan á algúnos centenáres las óbras Européas de distíntas

naciónes y tiémpos que he leído. Gazél! Gazél! sin dúda
tendrás por gránde lo que vóy á decírte: y si publícas éste
mi dictámen, no habrá Européo que no me lláme bárbaro
Africáno; péro la amistád que te proféso es múy gránde,
pára dejár de correspondér con mis observaciónes á las túyas;
mi sinceridád es tánta, que en náda puéde mi léngua hacér
traición á mi pécho. En éste supuésto, dígo, que de los líbros que he referído, he hécho la siguiénte separación. He
escogido cuátro de matemáticas, en los que admíro la esten-
sión y aciérto que tiéne el entendimiénto humáno, cuándo va
bién dirigído: ótros tántos de filosofía escolástica, en que me
asómbra la variedád de ocurréncias estraordinárias que tiéne
el hómbre, cuándo no procéde sóbre princípios ciértos y evidéntes: úno de medicína, al que fálta un tratádo compléto de
los símples, cúyo conocimiénto es diéz mil véces mayór en
África: ótro de anatomía, cúya lectúra fué sin dúda la que
dió motívo al cuénto del lóco, que se figurába tan quebradizo
cómo el vídrio: dos de los que refórman las costúmbres, en
las que adviérto lo mucho que aún tiénen que reformár;
cuátro del conocimiénto de la naturaléza, ciéncia que lláman
filosofía; en los que nóto lo mucho que ignoráron nuéstros
abuélos, y lo mucho mas que tendrán que aprendér nuéstros
niétos. Algúnos de poesía, delicióso delírio del álma, que
prúeba la ferocidád en el hómbre si la aborréce; puerilidád,
si la proféa tóda la vída; y suavidád, si la cultíva algún
tiémpo.

Tódas las demás óbras de las ciéncias humánas las he ar-
rojádo ó distribuído, por parecérme inútiles estráctos, com-
péndios defectuósos, y cópias imperféctas de lo yá dicho y
repetído úna y mil véces.

CÁRTAS FAMILIÁRES

Del Pádre JOSE FRANCÍSCO *de* ÍSLA, *escritas á vários sugétos.*

CÁRTA I.

El Pádre de Ísla á su hermána.

La Corúña, 24 de Setiémbre, de 1755.

Mi amáda María Francísca: discúrro que tus oraciónes, y
las de tu penitenciário me consiguiéron un tiémpo tan felíz

hásta úna légua ántes de llegár á la Corúña,en que me llovió un póco, sin dúda pára que conociése lo múcho que debía á las devótas álmas que me encomendában á Diós; y acáso será efécto de lo mísmo la descomposición de viéntre que me dúra tres días ha; pués cómo no prosíga adelánte, será mas benefício que indisposición, aunqué·sírva de moléstia miéntras persevére. Tu salúd me tiéne con mas cuidádo de él que manifiésto, siéndo razón que yó ocúlte mi dolór á quién por no aumentármelo me disimúla lo que padéce, porqué así lo píde la buéna correspondéncia. Núnca he pretendído sabér mas de lo que me quisiéren decír, ni que me quiéran mas de lo que me quisiéren querér; con que siéndo en éste púnto súmaménte fácil la conformidád, sólo aspiraré á manifestár en tódas ocasiónes que ningúno te áma ni puéde amárte mas que   *Tu amánte hermáno y padríno,*

JOSÉ FRANCÍSCO

CÁRTA II

Del mísmo, á su cuñádo.

Villagarcía, 2 de Enéro, de 1756.

Amádo hermáno y amígo: no es de estrañár que en corréo de páscuas (1) y en la mísma víspera de éllas hubiésen .ardádo tánto en dár cártas. Si el múndo amaneciéra un áño con juício, en ningún tiémpo se debiéra tardár ménos; péro dejémosle corrér su trén, pués no se puéde remediár. No obstánte yó he conseguído éste áño no habér recibído hásta ahóra mas que tres cártas de páscuas, y ésas de génte novícia en mi correspondéncia á escepción del Señór Taránco, á quién, por mas que he hécho, no he podído espelér del cuérpo éste espíritu malígno, siéndo las páscuas mas segúras en su cárta que en el calendário.

Diviértete en leér ésa nécia satisfacción que me da N... á la piéza que me jugó, suponiéndo que yó había de ir á Villár de Frádes á esperár el cóche pára dar las órdenes á los cochéros. Allá tiéne úna respuésta, cuál la meréce su bobería, con el nuévo cárgo de que su híjo pasáse á vísta de Villagarcía sin entrár en élla; y suponiéndo que él por sí no éra capáz de hacérla, si no mediáran las instrucciónes de su

---

(1) *Páscua*, en Españól, significa tódas las grándes fiéstas, especialménte las de Navidád.

pádre, le pregúnto que motívo le he dádo pára que le instru-
yése tan mal; él me ha dádo málos rátos, péro no los llevará
buénos con mis cártas, y estóy esperándo las de pádre é híjo
pára ver por dónde párten. Éste último es naturál que
truéque el viáge de Portugál por él de París, á dónde dicen
que irá el Cónde de Aránda por embajadór ordinário, después de habér evacuádo yá su embajáda estraordinária, que
paréce se redújo precísaménte á condoléncia por la destrucción de Lisbóa, y á socorrér á aquéllos Príncipes con caudáles
y con géneros.

Recibí úna cárta atrasadísima de D. Miguél de Medína, en
que me resúme lo que le escríbe Mascaréñas, *désde el cámpo
delánte de la que fué Lisbóa, á los diéz y ócho días de su totál
destrucción.* Dice que se salvó con tóda su família éntre úna
espésa llúvia de piédras y de cascájo por especiál protección
de la santísima vírgen, habiéndo vísto· priméro desplomárse
tóda su cása, y despúes ardér con tódos los muébles, alhájas
y papéles. Éstos últimos y los líbros son los que mas le duélen,
no habiéndose eximído mas que únos pócos que tenía en úna
quínta, y un cajón de éllos que le llegó de Madríd, el día
despúes de la fatalidád. Sólo píde á Medína mas y mas
líbros, especialménte de arquitectúra, porqué el réy de Portugál tráta de edificár úna nuéva córte de plánta, en paráge
distínto de la antígua, aúnque éste todavía no se ha determinádo. Á mí aún no me ha escríto, no obstánte tenér tres ó
cuátro cártas mías, péro ni lo estráño, ni me quéjo.

Llegáron los diéz y ócho barríles de escabéches y de dúlce,
buénos tódos, á escepción de úno de sardínas, que debía de
estár mal calafeteádo, y se abrió en el camino. Repíto grácias, y renuévo tódo lo que te supliqué en la pósta pasáda.

Díme, si has recibído ése cajoncíllo de cigárros de la Ha-
bána, porqué cáda día me confírmo mas en la sospécha de
algúna manióbra del mesonéro de Villár de Frádes, en cúyo
podér los púso el P. Manuél de Barachagurén, administradór
de ésta iglésia; y el pícaro del mesonéro no háy fórma de
decír cómo se llamába el maragáto á quién díce se· los en-
tregó, y que se obligó á llevárlos. Ántes de ayér víno de
allá Pinílla, que está encargádo de ésta averiguación, y sólo
me trájo razón de que el maragáto había vuélto á pasár á
Madríd, y que á su regréso á Santiágo le haría cárgo el mesonéro de dícho cajoncíllo. Yó hubiéra yá ído en persóna á
Villár de Frádes á liquidár éste embúste, y á escarmentár al

mesonéro, si el tiémpo lo hubiéra permitído; péro á resérva de dos días que por fuérza éran ocupádos en la iglésia, tódos los demás han sído intratábles.

Húbo cárta de Róma de 17 de noviémbre; péro náda díce de congregación, ni del P. Idiaquéz. Tampóco me ocúrre mas añadír, sinó rogár á Diós te me guárde cómo ha menestér,
Tu amánte hermáno y amígo, JOSÉ.

CÁRTA III.

Del mísmo, al mísmo.

Búrgos, 21 de Enéro, de 1757.

Amádo hermáno y amígo: salí de Villagarcía el día 15; en él se estancó dos véces la calésa sóbre el hiélo, y la segúnda vez estúvo encíma de él désde las cuátro de la tárde hásta las ónce del día siguiénte, y nosótros déntro de élla por espácio de tres hóras. Socorriéronnos caritativaménte de un lugár vecíno, enviándonos caballerías pára que subiésemos á él, y llegámos cómo puédes considerár. Allí tomámos ótras dos múlas pára que ayudásen á rompér el hiélo y niéve hásta Paléncia: péro aún así no quise entrár en la calésa, y fui á cabállo hásta la mísma ciudád. En élla me detúve día y médio: tomé ótra calésa, mejoró el tiémpo, y vóy caminándo, grácias á Diós, con felicidád, despúes de habér padecído múchas tentaciónes de volvérme á mi colégio.

No téngo tiémpo de escribír á María Francísca, ni á las demás persónas que me hácen mercéd, y sirva ésta pára tódas. Hóy llegué á Búrgos éntre mil trabájos y peligros. Mañána párto tomándo de aquí ótras dos múlas pára pasár los móntes de Óca, que son lo mas peligróso del camíno. La salúd buéna, á escepción del pécho, que se me cerró el día que estúve sóbre el hiélo. Á Diós,
Tu hermáno, JOSÉ.

CÁRTA IV.

Del mísmo, al mísmo.

Zaragóza, 18 de Márzo, de 1756.

Amádo hermáno y amígo; según lo que me díces en la túya de dos del corriénte, contémplo yá á mádre en la ótra vída, y á pádre múy cérca de élla: ¡cúmplase en tódo la voluntád del Señór! Yó vóy continuándo con felicidád mi car-

34*

réra, teniéndo yá andádo mas de la mitád de élla. Me han pedído vários sermónes pára imprimírlos, péro no lo conseguirán. La salúd se ha resentído un póco, porqué no sóy de alabústro; péro no me ha estorbádo, grácias á Diós, cumplír con mi ministério.

Un abrázo á María Francísca, y víve cómo necesíta

Tu amánte hermáno y amígo,

JOSÉ FRANCÍSCO.

CÁRTA V.

Del mísmo, al mísmo.

Zaragóza, 22 de Márzo, de 1757.

Amádo hermáno y amígo: cuándo esperába la notícia de la muérte de nuéstros dos enférmos, me hállo gustósaménte sorprendído con la que me das de su recóbro en la túya de 9 del corriénte. ¡Bendíto séa Diós por éste nuévo benefício! Sólo, sí, me da cuidádo la salúd de María Francísca, cúyos escésos de amór son incorregíbles. Yó estóy molído y médio reventádo despúes de véinte y ócho sermónes, faltándome todavía diéz y séis. El frúto es gránde, y éste es mi único consuélo. Á Diós, que te guárde cómo ha menestér

Tu amánte hermáno y amígo,

JOSÉ FRANCÍSCO.

CÁRTA VI.

Del mísmo, á su hermána.

Villagarcía, 17 de Júnio, de 1757.

Híja mía: tus cártas de priméro y ócho del corriénte que llegáron júntas, porqué así lo quiéren los señóres estafetéros, me déjan con la mísma alternatíva de aféctos que tú esperiméntas en tu salúd. De buéna gána partiría contígo mi robustéz, porqué aunqué no me sóbra múcha, ménos me bastaría pára mis taréas ordinárias y estraordinárias. Los báños cási fuéron las priméras medicínas que se conociéron en el múndo, y por múchos síglos las únicas; por éso téngo múcha fe con éllos. La dificultád está en atinár que espécie de báños son los que se opónen á tal espécie de enfermedádes, y cuáles acháques son los que no puéden resistír á táles báños. En tódo camínan á tiéntas los médicos; mas por lo mísmo puédo ser que aciérten, porqué tal vez háce la casualidád lo que no puéde hacér la elección y el discernimiénto. Yá estámos en el mejór tiémpo de tomárlos, que es el mes de júnio y cercanías de S. Juán, especialménte si por allá comiénzan á esplicárse los calóres, que por acá todavía están múy remísos. Mi parecér es que no piérdas día, pués si surtiésen buén efécto, tendrás lugár pára recobrár las fuérzas que son menestér pára repetirlos pára setiémbre. Yó no abandonaría el úso de los pólvos de Aix, habiéndolos esperimentádo tan propícios, sin estrañár que hásta ahóra no hubiésen desarraigádo la cáusa, porqué cuándo las raíces son profúndas, es menestér no dejár el azadón de la máno hásta arrancárlas, y éso no se háce en un día.

No puédo negár que cuánto mas lárgas son tus cártas, mas me gustan; péro tampóco me puéde gustar finéza túya que séa en detriménto de tu salúd; y así miéntras Diós no te la mejóre, me contentaré con úna fe de vída, pára lo cuál básta tu fírma, y me darás que sentír siémpre que tuviéres que padecér por consolárme. Las memórias acostumbrádas; y A Diós, híja,   *Tu amánte hermáno,*
                              JOSÉ FRANCISCO.

CÁRTA VII.

Del mismo, á la misma.

León, 4 de Máyo, de 1759.

Híja mía; hóy háce ócho días que llegué á ésta ciudád, habiéndo gastádo cuátro en el camíno, porqué me detúve dos en el monastério de Véga con mi príma. La mitád del viáge fué con gran calór, y la ótra mitád con escesívo frío, el que ha continuádo désde que llegué acompañádo de água, de viéntos fuértes, y también de álgo de niéve. Pagué la paténte en la priméra nóche con un fuérte dolór cólico, que me obligó á guardár cáma tódo el día siguiénte; péro cómo rompió por ámbas vías, quedé présto desahogádo. Lo mísmo sucedió al Generál de S. Beníto, que se hálla en ésta ciudád; sólo que á éste le acometió á la despedída, y á mí á la entráda; por cúya razón y por el mal tiémpo suspendió el viáge, que yá tenía echádo á Espinaréda. Visitóme al día siguiénte de mi arríbo: comí con su Reverendísima ótro día. Me ha visitádo tóda la ciudád, y cómo con el Intendénte los días que me déjan líbres ótros convítes. He celebrádo múcho ver la fábrica de télas, aunqué témo que se atráse por la

desunión de los que principalménte la manéjan. Luégo que
el tiémpo lo permíta, me restituiré á mi celdíta, cúya quietúd
se me háce mas apetecíble, siémpre que carézco de élla.

Vive tánto cómo tu amánte,
JOSÉ.

———

CÁRTA VIII.

Del mísmo al Sr. D. G. R.

Pontevédra, 25 de Máyo, de 1764.

Múy Señór mío y mi duéño: téngo la fortúna de que
V. S. me conózca múchos áños ha. Si no se le ha borrádo
de la memória mi carácter, tendrá múy presénte mi realidád
y mi enteréza. La cárne y sángre no me hácen fuérza, ni
las pasiónes humánas me han cegádo núnca la razón. Con-
cederésela á mi mayór enemígo, siémpre que la ténga; ne-
garéscla, y se la negué algúna vez á mí mísmo pádre, cuándo concebí que no la tenía.

Hermáno mío es Don José Joaquín de Ísla y Losáda. Si
en el injústo, voluntário y empeñádo pléito criminál que le
suscitáron sus contrários, no hubiéra sído testígo oculár de su
inocéncia, é yó hubiése de sentenciárle, el primér vóto que
tendría cóntra sí sería el mío, y no sería el mas benígno.
Sobrádas esperiéncias tiéne él mísmo de ésta mi enteréza en
los vários sucésos de su vída. En los mas me túvo cóntra sí,
péro en el presénte no puédo desamparárle, ni es razón que
niégue á un hermáno mío lo que en iguáles circunstáncias
concedería á quién hubiése quitádo violéntaménte la vída á
mi pádre y á mi mádre.

Pasáron á mi vísta tódos los lánces, porqué me hallába en
Santiágo en aquél turbádo día. No hallé que condenár en
éste mózo, y lo que mas es, ni tampóco lo halláron sus mísmos
contrários. Éllos formáron los priméros áutos, y por éstos
mísmos áutos le absolviéron los Señóres juéces del récto
tribunál de que V. S. es dígno miémbro. Me asegúran que
la segúnda probánza náda añáde á la priméra, sinó confirmár
mas y mas el empéño de acabár de arruinár á ése mózo, pára
cubrir úna inconsideración con la pérdida de un inocénte.

Alégan los contrários su honór y él de úna comunidád ver-
dadéraménte múy respetáble. Ésta le tendrá siémpre múy
resguardádo, y núnca podrá dependér de la precipitación de
algunos particuláres ménos detenídos. Péro supongámos que

depénda: y no se interesará también el honór del tribunál de V. S, en que sin nuévos, grándes y evidéntes documéntos no refórme lo que pronunció con tánto exámen y con tánta maduréz? Mas náda de ésto es del cáso. El dictámen de que conviéne que perézca un inocénte, pára que no perézcan múchos culpádos, yá sabémos tódos la bája cúna que túvo. Núnca le adoptáron por súyo los tribunáles cristiános. En éllos réina y reinará la máxima contrária: ménos málo es absolvér á múchos culpádos, que condenár á un inocénte.

Estálo sin dúda mi hermáno en el féo delíto que le impútan. Tódos los esfuérzos de sus contrários, siéndo tántos, tan poderósos y tan empeñádos, no pudiéron conseguir que dejáse de conocérlo y de definírlo así el rectísimo tribunál. Gránde es la fuérza de la inocéncia, cuándo no bástan á oprimírla las máquinas del podér. Mejór diré: siémpre es múy débil el podér cón los tribunáles dónde presíde la justícia. Éste es hóy tódo mi consuélo y tóda mi esperánza.

Náda mas téngo que esponér á V. S. Pedírle que hága grácia á mi hermáno, sería suponérle réo, pués en pléitos crimináles no cábe ótro que moderár el rigór de las léyes. Suplicárle ótra cósa, sería agraviár su integridád, que téngo múy conocída. Con que, en súma, ésta cárta sólo se redúce á dar testimónio de que mi profúndo siléncio no ha dependído de que ténga por culpádo á José Joaquín, cómo algúno ha querído soñár; sinó precisaménte de habér descansádo y decansár en la justícia de la cáusa, y en la equidád de los juéces. Tampóco he querído malográr ésta oportúna y cási necesária ocasión de renovár á V. S. tódo mi antíguo respéto. Nuéstro Señór gúarde á V. S. múchos áños, cómo puéde y le suplíco. B. L. M. de V. S.

Su mas alénto servidór y capellán,
JOSÉ FRANCÍSCO DE ÍSLA.

CÁRTA IX.

Del mismo, á su hermána.

Bolónia, 8 de Júnio, de 1780.

Amáda hija, hermána y Señóra mía: recíbo tu estimadísima cárta de 2 del pasádo, acompañáda con la gacéta de Madríd, su fécha 23 del mísmo, con que me regála siémpre nuéstro amantísimo sobríno. Según éstas dos féchas tu cárta se detúvo véinte y un días en Madríd ó en Párma, porqué si hubiéran caminádo júntas la gacéta y élla, no pudiéra la úna ganár á la ótra las enórmes ventájas que la ganó en el camíno. Él que las recíbe en Párma, no es capáz de detenérlas ni un sólo moménto, porqué deseosísimo de servírte á tí, y de complacérme á mí, é informádo también de que ní á tí, ni á mí nos ha quedádo ótro consuélo iguál á él de nuéstra inocénte conversación, tampóco él tiéne ótro mayór que él de cooperár á que lo logrémos con tóda la posíble puntualidád y prudénte frecuéncia. Résta pués, que dícha cárta se hubiése quedádo traspapeláda en tu escritório ó en el buró de él que nos háce el singulár favór de dirigírlas. Parecióme que debía advertírte ésto pára tu gobiérno.

He celebrádo múcho que háyas abandonádo la cása húmeda, fría y sín ventilación que habitábas, atribuyéndo á élla con sobráda razón, á lo ménos gran párte de lo que has padecído en el pasádo inviérno. Alegraréme infiníto de que te tráte mejór, cómo lo espéro, la cálle de Atócha, júnto á Loréto, dónde te has pasádo. Si no téngo trastornáda la memória, (cómo lo témo) paréceme que la cálle de Atócha háce párte del cuartél del oriénte de Madrid, reputádo por el mas sáno; lo que si fuére así, no contribuirá póco á tu recóbro. No me díces el número de la cása, ni el cuárto que en élla habítas, lo que dícen es necesário pára guía de los sobrescrít.

Al Señór Cónde de Aránda solaménte le escribí désde Cálvi sóbre los manuscrítos que me habían embargádo en España, suplicándole que si después de examinádos no se hálláse en éllos cósa que ofendiése á la religión ni al estádo, se sirviése su Esceléncia disponér que aquéllos inocéntes hijos viniésen á hacér compañía á su póbre y desterrádo pádre. Respondióme aquél Señór que éso yá no estába en su máno; péro que estuviése sin cuidádo porqué aquéllos hijos estában á cárgo de quién haría que fuésen tratádos cómo los trataría su mísmo pádre, sin permitír que ningúno se metiése con éllos. Ésto fué en súma la respuésta.

Correspóndo cordialísimaménte á la memória que hácen de mí los amígos Ramírez y Casáus. Deséo con las mayóres ánsias que el priméro triúnfe cuánto ántes, y no céso de rogár á Diós por el recóbro del segúndo.

Días ha que está concluída la versión de *Gil Blas*; péro ni mi cabéza ni mi púlso me han permitído emprendér todavía el prólogo y dedicatória. Los calóres son escesívos, y con éllos se háce mayór cáda día mi dejamiénto y ni súma debilidád.

Á Diós, híja mia: á Diós, y mánda á éste tu amánte hermáno,

Padríno y servidór,

JOSÉ FRANCÍSCO.

CÁRTA X

Del mismo á un amígo súyo.

Quién siéndo póco mas ríco que el Pádre de Ísla, péro habiéndo oído que éste estába múy necesitádo, le escribió ofreciéndole partír con él lo póco que le quedába.

Querído amígo: ¡que sobrehumána fuérza es ésta! !que álma ha jamás sído capáz de tan heróicas accciónes! Témes, te persuádes que estóy necesitádo, ¡y quiéres partír conmígo lo póco que te quéda! Meréces que te erijan estátuas: y si fuéra éste el tiémpo de la gentilidád, te adorarían cómo á Diós de la amistád. Yó no puédo esplicárte mi reconocimiénto á la piedád que úsas conmígo. Es cósa deploráble el vérse en estádo de necesitárla; péro, ¡cuán dúlce y consolánte es encontrár álmas tan tiérnas y tan grándes cómo la túya que lo compadézcan! Tódos mis infortúnios, tódos mis máles son náda en comparación de la satisfacción que me cáusa tu humanidád y afécto. ¡Y quiéres condenár mi gratitúd al siléncio! yá sé, amígo, sí, yá sé que tu corazón egercíta su beneficéncia no pára recibír el lisongéro tribúto del reconocimiénto, sinó pára satifacér su nóble inclinación. Péro, ¿cómo quiéres que dége de ser reconocído á tan singuláres benefícios cómo he recibído de tu generósa amistád? Éso no puéde ser, amígo: con que, permitirás que, obedeciéndo á la voz imperiósa de mi corazón, te díga que mi gratitúd será indeléble, y que mi afécto pára tí tendrá un siémpre por término de su duración.

Envíame sólo la mitád de lo que me ofréces, y sobrará pára hacér de múy póbre múy ríco á

Tu fino amígo, JOSÉ.

CORRESPONDÉNCIA MERCANTÍL.
COMMERCIAL CORRESPONDENCE.

Cártas de Comércio, y Modélos de úna Factúra, un Conocimiénto, úna Cuénta, Létras de Cámbio, Cárta Promisória y Cárta de Crédito, Protesta.

Commercial Letters, and Models of an Invoice, Bill of Lading, an Account, Bills of Exchange, Promissory Note and Letter of Credit, Protest.

Propuésta pára úna Correspondéncia.

A proposal for a Correspondence.

Mégico, 1 de Enéro, de 1825.

Mexico, January 1, 1825
Sir,

Múy Señór mío; cómo ésta es la priméra vez qué téngo el honór de dirigírme á vm., espéro que me perdonará la libertád que me he tomádo.

As this is the first time I have the honour of addressing you, you will, I hope excuse the liberty I have taken.

El ventajóso carácter que mi buén amígo el Señór Don N. me ha dádo de su persóna y cása de vm., me aníma á pensár en úna correspondéncia mercantíl que puéda ser ventajósa á vm., cómo á mí.

The honourable character my worthy friend Mr. N. has given me of your person and house, encourages me to think of a commercial correspondence which may be to our mutual advantage.

Péro ánte tódas cósas, necesíto me franquée vm. el favór de dárme úna relación de los pésos y medídas que comunménte se úsan en Inglatérra, porqué créo que se diferéncian múcho de los de éste país.

But before this, I must beg the favour of you to give me an account of the weights and measures which are commonly used in England, as I believe they differ materially from those in this country.

Yó estimaré ésta relación cómo un favór particulár, y vm. puéde confiár en mi sinceridád y prontitúd que le serviré en cuánto depénda de mis facultádes.

I shall esteem this as a particular obligation, and you may rely upon my sincerity and readiness to serve you in whatever may lie in my power.

Esperándo que vm me hónre con su favoráble respuésta, quédo rogándo á Diós me guárde su vída múchos áños.

B. L. M. de vm.

In the expectation of your honouring me with a favourable answer, I remain, Dear Sir,
    Your obedient and
        humble servant.

S^{or}. Don ——.

Bostón, Febréro, 1825.

Múy Señór mío; me es múy apreciáble el favór que he recibído de vm. en la del 1° del últ°, en la que me manifiésta los deséos que tiéne de entablár conmígo úna correspondéncia mercantíl; yó me tendré por dichóso si puédo correspondér á las esperánzas de vm., y á la idéa lisongéra que se ha servído tomár de mi cása y família.

Vm. no ignóra, que nosótros los comerciántes debémos vivír de nuéstra profesión, y promovér nuéstros interéses en cuánto séa compatíble con el honór y la equidád.

Yó admíto la proposición de vm., y en pruéba de mi reconocimiénto, remitiré á vm., por el primér búque que sálga de éste puérto pára ése, várias partídas fabricádas en éste país, y al précio mas bájo que se puéden dár; la nómina de éllas, júntaménte con los précios, irán insértas en las factúras.

Espéro serán del gústo de vm., y que servirán de motívo pára nuéstro mayór conocimiénto y tráto; y esté vm.

35

Mr. ——

Boston, February, 1825.

Sir,

I am most agreeably favoured by yours of the first ult°, wherein you show a desire to commence a commercial correspondence with me; I shall think myself happy if I can answer your expectations, and the flattering idea you have been pleased to form of my house and family.

You well know, that we merchants, must live by our profession, and promote our interest as far as is consistent with honour and equity.

I accept your proposal, and as a proof of my acknowledgement, I will send you, by the first vessel that sails from this port to your place, sundry parcels manufactured here, and at the lowest price that can be afforded; the particulars thereof, together with the prices, will be inserted in the invoices.

I hope they will prove to your satisfaction, and be the foundation of our farther acquaintance and dealing;

segúro de que cualquiéra cósa que confíe á mi cuidádo, será egecutáda y manejáda con el mayór candór y fidelidád: y si éstas mercaderías cómo las que puéde vm. necesitár en adelánte, al tiémpo de enfardelárlas ó de cualquiér ótro módo, sufriésen algúna avería, se hará la correspondiénte rebája, dándome vm. el avíso.

Inclúyo á vm. muéstras de ótras producciónes que puéden tenér despácho en ése mercádo: y en éste cáso, podré provéerle de tódo cuánto necesíte.

Si vm. puéde hacérme retórnos cómodos con sus vínos esquisítos, aguardiénte, y frútas; cómo tambien dos zurrónes de cochinílla, y 20 quintáles de barrílla, se le dará á vm. su comisión; el corretáge, almacenáge y tódos los demás gástos de puérto se pagarán á párte.

En consecuéncia de las órdenes de vm., le envío un estádo de las pésas y medídas de Inglatérra: y además la diferéncia de las monédas de España y las nuéstras. Tocánte á la subída y bája de los cámbios y fóndos, se informará vm. por nuéstros papéles públicos.

Quédo rogándo á Diós me guárde su vída múchos áños. B. L. M. de vm. Su aténto amígo.

and assure yourself that whatever you trust to my charge, shall be performed and managed with the greatest candour and fidelity imaginable; and if these goods or those you may want hereafter, should suffer any damage in the packing or otherwise, proper allowance will be made, upon your notice.

I herewith send you a sample of other staple commodities which may answer your market; in that case, you may be furnished with every article you may want.

If you can conveniently make returns in some of your exquisite wines, brandy, and fruits; as also two zeroons of cochineal, and of kelp 20 quintals, you shall have your commission; brokerage, storage and all other port-charges will be paid apart.*

Pursuant to your orders, I send you a statement of the weights and measures used in England; as also the difference of the value of coins between Spain and ours. As to the rise and fall of exchange and stocks, you may be informed by our public papers.

I remain your obedient humble servant, and respectful friend.

* *Kelp* se llúma también *barilla* en Inglés.

FACTÚRA.

Factúra de las Mercaderías embarcádas por el S^{or}. Don *Agustín S.* pára los Señóres *Cristóbal B. é hijos* de Cádiz, á bórdo del Navío nombrádo el *Cisne,* su Capitán *Martín D.*, destinádo pára dícho Cádiz, por órden y cuénta de los díchos Señóres, siéndo numerádas y marcádas cómo sígue,

Á sabér.

No. 1 á 2.) 2 Zurrónes de Cochinílla - - -
   1 á 75. ⟩ 75 Quintáles de Azafrán - - - '
  B.C.E.) 315 Cájas de Azúcar quebrádo

Súma, $
Deréchos y Gásto - -
Comisión á 5 por ciénto -

Súma totál, $

Sálvo Yérro y Omisión.

Bostón y Abríl 9, de 1825.   R. D. T.

Un Conocimiénto.

Lóndres, Febréro, 1825

Yó —— vecíno de ——
Maéstre que sóy del buén Navío (que Diós sálve) nombrádo N. N , que al presénte está súrto y ancládo en el río Támesis, puérto de Lóndres, pára con la buéna ventúra seguír éste presénte viáge al puérto de Cádiz; reconózco haber recibído, y téngo cargádo déntro del dícho mi Navío debájo de cubiérta, de vos N. N., séis fárdos de baquéta de Moscóvia, siéte díchos de páño Inglés, ócho de estófas,

A bill of Lading.

London, February 1825.

Shipped by the grace of God in good order and well conditioned, by Mr. (or Messrs.) N. N. in and upon the good ship called N. N. whereof is master under God, for this present voyage,——now riding at anchor in the river Thames, at London, and by God's aid bound for Cadiz: to wit; six bales of Russia leather, seven ditto of English cloths, eight ditto of stuffs, nine ditto of bays, ten ditto of says and serges, five

INVOICE.

Invoice of Merchandise shipped by Mr. AUGUSTIN S. *for* Messrs. CHRISTOPHER B. & SONS *of Cadiz, on board the Ship named* SWAN, *her master* MARTIN D., *bound to said Cadiz, per order and account of the said Gentlemen, being numbered and marked as follows,*

TO WIT:

No. 1 *a* 2. ⎫ 2 *Zeroons of Cochineal* - - -
   1 *a* 75. ⎬ 75 *Quintals of Saffron.* - - -
  C.B.E. ⎭ 315 *Boxes of Brown Sugar* -

Amount, $
Duties and Charges - -
Commission at 5 *per cent.*

Total, $

Errors and Omissions excepted.

Boston, 9*th April,* 1825.   R. D. T.

nuéve de bayétas, diéz de anascótes y sárgas, quiniéntas piézas de liénzo superfíno de la fábrica de Irlánda, seténta díchas de batístas, cincuénta táblas de mantéles adamascádos y cincuénta docénas de servillétas, un cajón de hója de láta, dos de latón ó azófar, tres de acéro, cuátro quintáles de cóbre, séis cájas de relójes de faltriquéra y díjes, séis cajónes de quinquillería ó buhonería, siéte de herramiéntas de córte, tódo enjúto y bién acondicionádo, numerádos y marcádos con la márca al márgen   Con lo cuál promé- *hundred pieces of superfine Irish linen, seventy ditto of cambric, fifty diaper table cloths, and fifty dozen of napkins, one chest of tin, two ditto of latten or brass, three ditto of steel, four quintals of copper, six boxes of watches and trinkets, six chests of hardware, seven ditto of edge tools, all in good order and condition, marked and numbered as in the margin; and are to be delivered in the like good order and condition (the dangers of the seas only excepted) in the aforesaid port unto Mr. N. N. or Messrs*

to, y me obligo, llevándome Diós en buén salvaménto con el dícho mi Navío al espresádo puérto, de acudír y entregár, por vos y en vuéstro nómbre, díchos géneros igualménte enjútos y bién acondicionádos (sálvo los pelígros del mar) á Don N. N. ó á los Señóres——ó á quién allí por él fuére párte: pagándome de fléte á razón de cuarénta chelínes esterlínos por cáda toneláda, con diéz por ciénto de cápa y avería. Y en fe de que así me obligo á cumplír, os dóy tres conocimiéntos de un tenór, firmádos de mi nómbre, por mí ó mi escribáno; el úno cumplído, los ótros no válgan. Fécho en Lóndres, á priméro de Febréro, de 1825.

——, or *his* or *(their) assigns; he* or *(they) paying freight at the rate of forty shillings per ton, with the usual primage and average. In witness whereof, the said Commander or his clerk has signed three bills of lading, all of this tenor and date; one of which being fulfilled, the other two to stand void. Dated in London, the 1st day of February, 1825.*

35*

CUÉNTA.

Débe Don F. D.			á	Don R. D. T			Ha de haber.
1825.				1825.			
Abril	Por 100 Cajas de Azúcar,	$2000		Abril	Por 200 Barríles de Harína.	$1000	
,,	100 Cajónes de Cigárros	1000		,,	100 idem Puérco saládo	2000	
	Total,	$3000			Total,	$3000	

Bostón y Abril 9, de 1825.   Sálvo Yérro y Omisión.   (Firmádo)   R. D. T.

ACCOUNT.

Debit Mr. F. D.			to	R. D. T.			Credit.
1825.				1825.			
April	To 100 Boxes Sugar,	$2000		April	By 200 Barrels Flour,	$1000	
,,	100 Boxes Cigars,	1000		,,	100 ditto Pork,	2000	
	Total,	$3000			Total,	$3000	

Boston, 9th April, 1825.   Errors and Omissions excepted.   (Signed)   R. D. T.

Létra de Cámbio.
La Priméra.
Lóndres, 1825.
Por £400 esterlínas.

Á dos úsos (*ó á úso y médio, ó á ócho dias vista*) se servirá vm. mandár pagár por ésta mi priméra de cámbio á Don ——, ó á su órden, cuátro ciéntas líbras estcrlínas, valór recibido de D. N. N., que sentará vm. cómo por avíso. M. N.

A' Don ——,
Comerciánte en Cádiz.

A Bill of Exchange.
The First.
London, 1825.
For £400 sterling.

At double usance (or at usance and a half, or at eight days sight) *pay by this my first bill of Exchange to Mr* ——, *or order, the sum of four hundred pounds sterling, value received of Mr. N. N., and place it to account as per advice.* M. N.

To Mr. ——,
Merchant in Cadiz.

Priméra.
Aviso de úna Létra de Cámbio.
Lóndres 1 *de Enéro de* 1825.

Múy Señór mio; Hóy mísmo he librádo cóntra vm. úna létra de cámbio, á úso y médio, á favór de Don ——, ó á su órden, por la cantidád de cuátro ciéntas líbras esterlinas, que me hará vm. la finéza de honrár, y cargár á mi cuénta.

Quédo rogándo á Diós me guárde su vida múchos áños.

B. L. M. de vm.
S. S. S.

Á Don ——,
Del comércio de Cádiz.

Prima.
Advice of a bill of Exchange.
London, January 1, 1825.
Sir;

I have this day drawn on you a bill of Exchange, at one and a half usance, in favor of Mr. ——, *or his order, for four hundred pounds sterling, which I beg you to honor, and place to my account.*

I have the honor to be,
Sir, respectfully,
your obedient servant.

To Mr. ——,
Merchant in Cadiz.

La Segúnda.
Lóndres, 1825.
Por £400 esterlínas.

Á dos úsos se servirá vm. pagár por ésta mi segúnda de cámbio (no habiéndolo hécho por la priméra) á Don N. N. ó á su órden, cuátro ciéntas líbras esterlínas, &c. El Endóso.

Páguese á Don N. N. ó á su órden, valór en cuénta con, (ó valór recibido de) dicho.

The Second.
London, 1825.
For £400 sterling.

At double usance pay this my second bill of Exchange (first not paid) to Mr. N. N., or order, the sum of four hundred pounds sterling, &c.

The Endorsement.

Pay to Mr. N. N., or his order, value in account with (or value received from) the said.

Cárta Promisória.

Lóndres, 1 *de Enéro*, 1825.

Á úso y médio contádo désde la presénte dáta, prométo pagár á Don ——, ó á su órden, la cantidád de ——, por valór recibido, en dinéro contádo, ó en géneros á mi satisfacción.

A. B.

Promissory Note.

London, January 1, 1825.

At one and a half usance after date, I promise to pay to Mr. ——, *or his order, the sum of* ——, *for value received, in ready money, or in goods to my satisfaction.*

A. B.

Cárta de Crédito.

Lóndres, 1 *de Enéro de* 1825.

Múy Señor mío. Vmd. recibirá ésta de la máno del Señór Don ——, (que pása á viajár por divérsas pártes de Európa) y me hará la finéza de proveérle de cártas de recomendación pára las principáles ciudádes de Espáña; su objéto es salir de aquí inmediatáménte pára ésa. Créo que tendrá vmd. múcho gústo en tratárle por ser un caballéro igualménte distinguído por su mérito personál y por su naciménto; por lo que espéro que vm. le franquée la mas generósa recepción, y duránte su estáda en ésa ciudád le sírva con tódo el acataménto que esté en su podér. Al mísmo tiémpo me hará vm. el favór de franqueárle sóbre dóble recíbo el dinéro que necesíte, hásta la suma de ——, que podrá vm. reembolsár cargándolo á mi cuénta, enviándome úno de sus recíbos. Espéro que vm. me desempeñará cómo amigo en ésto asúnto; y miéntras,

Quédo rogándo á Diós me guárde su vída múchos áños.

B. L. M. de vm.

S. S. S.

Á Don ——,
Banquéro de Cádiz.

Letter of Credit.

London, January 1, 1825.

Sir,

You will receive this by the hands of Mr. ——, (*who is upon his travels into divers parts of Europe*) *and I beg you will provide him with recommendatory letters to the principal cities in Spain: his design is to set out from hence for your city immediately. I think you will be pleased with his acquaintance, as he is a gentleman equally distinguished for his personal merit and birth; be so kind, therefore, to give him the best reception, and serve him as effectually as in your power during his abode in your city. You will also do me the favor to supply him on his double receipt with what money he may have occasion for, to the amount of* ——, *for which you may reimburse yourself by charging it to my account, and transmitting one of his receipts to me. I hope you will attend to my request as a friend, and in the mean time,*

I have the honor to be,

Respectfully,

Your obedient servant.

To Mr. ——,
Banker in Cadiz.

FORM OF A SPANISH PROTEST.

EN la Ciudad de Cádiz, á cuatro del mes de Abril, de mil ochocientos veinte y siete, Ante mí, Gil Perez, Escribano Público del Número de esta Ciudad, y los Testigos abajo nombrados, pareció Don Ambrosio Lamela, Vecino y Comerciante de dicha ciudad, á quien doy fe, conozco, y quien para efecto de protesto me exhibió una Letra de Cambio cuyo tenor es el siguiente : " *Londres, Febrero 1º, 1827, pᵣ. pˢ. 2300. á dos usos,* " *mandará vm. pagar por esta primera de Cambio á la órden* " *de Don Juan Sangredo, Dos mil y trecientos pesos, en oro ó* " *plata, al curso conocido aquí hoy, que sentará vm. en cuenta* " *como por aviso de Pedro Sedillo. Al Señor Don Manuel* " *Peña, en Cádiz.   Endoso, Páguese á la órden de Don* " *Ambrosio Lamela, Cádiz, 26 de Marzo, 1823, Juan San-* " *gredo." Y despues de copiada, me pidió la presentase original á Don Manuel Peña, á cuyo cargo está librada, requiriéndole, que mediante cumplirse su plazo en el dia de hoy, con los dias de cortesía que son de estilo, la pague luego al punto, y en su defecto, se la proteste con todos sus Cambios, Recambios, Intereses, Costos, y Gastos, para repetirlos y cobrarlos del susodicho Don Pedro Sedillo, como Librador, ó del dicho Don Juan Sangredo, como Endosador, y de quien mas haya lugar, y que todo se lo diese por testimonio.   En virtud de lo cual, yo, el referido Escribano Público, pasé á la casa, morada del mencionado Don Manuel Peña, y habiendo preguntado en ella por él, se me respondió, por un sugeto que manifestó llamarse Don Antonio Bolsones, y ser cajero de Don Manuel Peña, que este se hallaba ausente en la ciudad de Sevilla.   Y habiendo hecho á Don Antonio Bolsones el requerimiento, y protestas arriba esplicadas, y enterádole de sus efectos, para que lo noticiase al citado Don Manuel Peña, dijo que no se hallaba con órden ni providencia para hacer el pago de dicha letra.   Esto dió por respuesta, y mediante ella, yo el referido escribano, y á pedimento del men-*

cionado *Don Ambrosio Lamela, he protestado, como por el presente solemnemente protesto, una, dos, tres, y mas veces en derecho necesarias, tanto contra el Sacador y contra el Endosador de la susodicha Letra de Cambio, como contra todos los demás que convenga á mas de la cantidad principal de su importe, por todos los Cambios, Recambios, Costos, Gastos, Daños, Menoscabos, Perjuícios, é Intereses, que en cualquiera manera se hayan seguido, ó causado, y en adelante se siguieren, ó causaren, por falta del pagamento de la referida Letra de Cambio. Hecho y Protestado en Cádiz, á cuatro del mes de Abril, de mil ochocientos veinte y siete. Lo firmó Don Ambrosio Lamela, siendo Testigos Don Juan Manuel Romero, y Don Luis Gomez. Ante mí, Gil Perez. Concuerda con su original en mi Registro, á que me remito, y para entregar á Don Ambrosio Lamela, y á su pedimento, mandé sacar esta copia que signo y firmo en Cádiz, en el dia de su fecha.*

GIL PEREZ.

Los que abajo firmamos Escribanos Públicos de esta Ciudad, certificamos en cuanto podemos, que Gil Perez, de quien va dada, signada, y firmada, la precedente copia, como se titula, es Escribano Público, del Número de esta Ciudad, fiel, legal, y de entera confianza, y á sus semejantes siempre se ha dado, y da, entera fe y crédito en juicios y fuera de ellos, y para que conste damos la presente en esta dicha Ciudad de Cádiz, fecha ut supra, Andres Corzuelos, Fabricio Nuñez, Fernando Perez de la Fuente, Escribanos Públicos.

TRANSLATION OF THE PROTEST.

IN the City of Cadiz, on the fourth day of the month of April, One thousand eight hundred and twenty-seven, Befoi e me, Gil Perez, Notary Public, Member of the Corporation of Notaries of this City, and the undermentioned witnesses, appeared Don Ambrose Lamela, Resident and Merchant in this City, whom I certify I know, and who exhibited to me a Bill of Exchange in order to have the same protested, the tenour whereof is as follows : "London, 1st February, 1827. " For 2300 dollars, at two usances, you will be pleased to " pay this first of Exchange, to the order of Don John San- " gredo, Two thousand three hundred dollars, in gold or " silver, at the exchange known here this day, which you " will place to account as per advice of Peter Sedillo. To " Don Emanuel Peña, Cadiz. *Endorsement* — Pay to the " Order of Don Ambrose Lamela, Cadiz, 26th of March, " 1823, John Sangredo." And which being first copied, he requested me to present the original to Don Emanuel Peña, on whom the same is drawn, to require of him immediate payment thereof, its term as well as the customary days of grace being this day elapsed, and in default thereof, to protest the same against him for all its Exchanges, Re-exchanges, Interests, Costs, and Charges, in order to reclaim and recover the same from the aforesaid Don Peter Sedillo, as the Drawer, from Don John Sangredo as the Endorser, or from whomsoever else it might concern, and to deliver him a copy thereof, by virtue of which I, the aforesaid Notary Public, did repair to the dwelling-house of the aforementioned Don Emanuel Peña, and having there inquired for him, I was answered by a person, who represented himself to be Don Anthony Bolsones, and cash-keeper of Don Emanuel Peña, that the latter was absent in the city of Seville ; and having made the above-mentioned demand of, and signified the protest to Don Anthony Bolsones, and acquainted him fully with the consequences thereof, in order that he might communicate the same to the aforesaid Don Manuel Peña, he answered that he was without orders or provision to make the payment of the said Bill. This he gave for an answer ; and on account thereof, and at the request of the above-mentioned Don Ambrose Lamela, I the aforesaid Notary have protested, as by these Presents I do solemnly protest once, twice, thrice, and as often as by law is required, as well against the Drawer and Endorser of the said Bill of Exchange as against all others whom it may concern, in addition to the principal amount of its value, for all Exchanges, Re-exchanges, Costs, Charges, Damages, Deficiencies, Loss, and Interests, which in any manner whatsoever have accrued or been occasioned, or that may hereafter accrue or be occasioned, for want of payment of the aforesaid Bill of Exchange.   Done and Protested in Cadiz, on the Fourth day of April, One thousand eight hundred and twenty-seven.   This Don Ambrose Lamela signed, the witnesses being Don John Emanuel Romero and Don Lewis Gomez.   Before me, Gil Perez.   It is conformable to its original in my Register, to which I refer, and in order to deliver to Don Ambrose Lamela, and at his request, I caused this copy to be transcribed, which I mark and sign in Cadiz, on the day of the date thereof.

GIL PEREZ.

We, the undersigned Notaries Public of this City, do certify, as far as we are able, that Gil Perez, by whom the foregoing copy is granted, marked and signed, is, as he styles himself, a Notary Public, Member of the Corporation of Notaries of this City, faithful, legal, and of entire confidence, and that to all his similar acts, full faith and credit ever have been and are given, in and out of court.   In witness whereof, we have granted these Presents in this said City of Cadiz, dated *ut supra*.   Andrew Corzuelos, Fabrice Nuñez, Ferdinand Perez de la Fuente, Notaries Public.

TREATISE ON SPANISH VERSIFICATION.

Spanish versification is the art of making Spanish Verses according to certain rules.

These rules regard, 1st. the structure of the verses; 2d. the mixture of the verses with one another.

ARTICLE I.

Of the structure of verses.

SECTION I.

Of the different kinds of verses.

The Spanish verses are measured by the number of syllables   Variety in the number of syllables produces differe··t kinds of verses.

1st.   The verses of *eleven* syllables or *endecasílabo*, hendecasyllable.

> Sálga mi trabajáda voz y rómpa
> El son confúso y mísero laménto
> Con eficácia y fuérza, que interrómpa
> El celésto y terréstre movimiénto:
> La fáma con sonóra y clára trómpa,
> Dándo mas fúria á mi cansádo aliénto,
> Derráme en tódo el órbe de la tiérra
> Las ármas, el furór y nuéva guérra.
>
> ALONSO DE ERCILLA.

2d.   The verse of *ten* syllables or *decasilabo*, decasyllable

> Los que andáis empollándo óbras de ótros,
> Sacád, pués, á volár vuéstra cría.
> Yá dirá cáda autór: ésta es mía;
> Y verémos que os quéda á vosótros.
>
> T. DE YRIARTE.

3d. The verse of *nine* syllables.

> Si querér entendér de tódo
> Es ridícula presunción,
> Servír sólo pára úna cósa
> Suéle ser fálta no menór.   T. DE YRIARTE.

4th.   The verse of *eight* syllables or *de redondílla mayór*
(large roundelay.)

> Al infiérno el Trácio Orféo
> Su mugér bajó á buscár,
> Que no púdo á peór lugár
> Llevárle tan mal deséo.
>
> Cantó, y al mayór torménto
> Púso suspensión y espánto,
> Mas que lo dúlce del cánto,
> La novedád del inténto.
>
> El Diós adústo ofendído,
> Con un estráño rigór,
> La péna que halló mayór
> Fué volvérle á ser marído.
>
> Y aunqué su mugér le dió
> Por péna de su pecádo;
> Por prémio de lo cantádo,
> Perdérla facilitó.   F. de Quevedo.

5th.   The verse of *seven* syllables.

> ¿Quién es aquél que bája
> Por aquélla colína,
> La botélla en la máno,
> En el róstro la rísa;
> De pámpanos é yédra
> La cabéza ceñída;
> Cercádo de zagáles,
> Rodeádo de nínfas;
> Que al son de los pandéros
> Dan vóces de alegría,
> Celébran sus hazáñas,
> Apláuden su venída?
> Sin dúda será Báco,
> El pádre de las víñas;
> Pués no, que es el poéta,
> Autór de ésta letrílla,   J. Cadalso.

6th.   The verse of *six* syllables or *de redondílla menór*
(small roundelay.)

> De amóres me muéro,
> Mi mádre acudíd,

·Si no llegáis prónto
Veréisme morír;
Catórce áños téngo,
Ayér los cumplí,
Que fué el primér día
Del florído abríl;
Y chícos y chícas
Me suélen decír:
¿ Porqué no te cásan,
Mariquílla ? di.
De amóres me muéro, etc. J. Cadalso.

7th. The verse of *five* syllables.

Poderóso caballéro
Es don Dinéro,
Núnca ví álmas ingrátas
Á su gústo y afición,
Que á las cáras de un doblón,
Hácen sus cáras barátas;
Y pués las háce bravátas
Désde úna bólsa de cuéro,
Poderóso caballéro
Es don Dinéro. F. de Quevedo.

8th The verse of *four* syllables.

¿Quién los juéces con pasión,
Sin ser ungüénto, háce humános,
Pués untándoles las mános
Les ablánda el corazón ?
Quién gásta su opilación
Con óro y no con acéro ?
El dinéro.
Quién procúra que se aléje
Del suélo la glória vána ?
Quién siéndo tóda cristiána
Tiéne la cára de herége ?
Quién háce que al hómbre aquéje
El desprécio y la tristéza?
La pobréza. F. de Quevedo.

9th.   The verse of *three* syllables

> Dinéros son calidád,
> Verdád:
> Mas áma, quién mas suspíra,
> *Mentíra.*   L. DE GÓNGORA.

10th.   The verse of *two* syllables.

> Ingráta, hermósa Antándra,
> En cúyas centéllas
> *Béllas,*
> El álma es salamándra,
> Que respíra encendída,
> Dúlce ardór, blándo incéndio, ardiénte vída.

11th.   The verse of *fourteen* syllables, which is nothing more than the union of two verses of seven syllables.

> Yó leí, no sé dónde, que en la léngua herbolária,
> Saludándo á un tomíllo la yérba parietária
> Con socarronería le díjo de ésta suérte·
> Diós te guárde, Tomíllo: lástima me da vérte,
> Que aunqué mas oloróso que tódas éstas plántas,
> Apénas médio pálmo del suélo te levántas.
>   T. DE YRIARTE.

12th.   The verse of *thirteen* and *twelve* syllables, *á la francésa* (after the French fashion.)

> En ciérta catedrál úna campána había
> Que sólo se tocába algún solémne día.
> Con el mas récio son, con pausádo compás
> Cuátro gólpes ó tres solía dar no mas.
> Por ésto, y ser mayór de la ordinária márca,
> Celebráda fué siémpre en tóda la comárca.
>   T. DE YRIARTE.

13th.   The verse of *twelve* syllables or *de árte mayór* (of great art,) which is only the union of two verses of six syllables.

> ¿No hémos de reírnos siémpre que chochéa
> Con anciánas fráses un novél autór?
> Lo que es afectádo júzga que es primór;

Hábla púro á cósta de la claridád,
Y no hálla voz bája pára nuéstra edád,
Si fué nóble en tiémpo del Cid campeadór.

T. DE YRIARTE.

The verses of *fourteen, ten* and *nine* syllables, are not frequently used. Those *á la francésa* and *de árte mayór,* which were often used in the early times of Spanish poetry, are but seldom used at present.

The verses of *eight, six, five, four, three* and *two* syllables are known under the general denomination of *vérsos de redondílla* (roundelay verses,) and the verses of *eleven* and *seven* syllables under that of *vérsos italiános* (Italian verses.)

The Spaniards call *vérsos entéros* (entire verses) the verses of *eleven, eight* and *six* syllables, and *vérsos de pié quebrádo* (verses of broken measure) or simply *vérsos quebrádos* (broken verses) the verses of *seven, five, four, three* and *two* syllables.

SECTION II.

Of the Accent.

In every Spanish word there is a long syllable, that is, upon which more stress is laid than upon the others. This syllable is said to bear the accent, and though this accent is not always marked, it is, however, not the less sensible for it. The word *accent* is then synonymous with *long.*

We call *agúda* (acute) the syllable that bears the accent.

All the syllables which precede or follow the long syllable are brief.

The monosyllables are naturally long, but they are brief when they are placed next to another word, or when they precede a word with which they have an immediate relation.

The accent generally falls upon the antepenultima, penultima or last syllable of words, but most commonly upon the penultima.

The words which have the accent upon the antepenultima syllable are called *esdrújulos* (gliding) and those which have it upon the last syllable *agúdos* (acute.)

The Spaniards call *vérsos llános* (plain verses) the verses terminated with a word which has the accent upon the penultima syllable; *vérsos esdrújulos* (gliding verses) the verses

36*

terminated with a word *esdrújulo*, and *vérsos agúdos* (acute verses) the verses terminated with a word *agúdo*.

In the verses *llános* the number of syllables is equal to that determined by the kind to which they belong; thus a verse *lláno* of eleven syllables has eleven syllables, a verse *lláno* of eight syllables has eight syllables, &c &c.

```
1   2  3   4   5  6  7   8 9  10  11
Sál|ga|mi|tra|ba|já|da|voz|y|róm|pa...
1   2  3  4   5   6   7   8
La|no|ve|dád|del|in|tén|to...
1   2   3   4   5   6   7
El|pá|dre|de|las|ví|ñas...
```

The verses *esdrújulos* have one syllable more than the kind to which they belong indicates; thus a verse *esdrújulo* of eleven syllables has twelve, a verse *esdrújulo* of eight syllables has nine, &c. &c.

```
1   2   3  4   5   6   7  8  9  10 11 12
Un|gá|to|pe|dan|tí|si|mo|re|tó|ri|co...
1   2  3   4  5  6  7  8  9
Ál|tó|dos|los|a|ca|dé|mi|cos...
```

The verses *agúdos* have a syllable less than the kind to which they belong indicates; thus a verse *agúdo* of eleven syllables has only ten, and a verse *agúdo* of eight syllables has only seven, &c. &c.

```
1   2   3   4   5   6   7
Con|un|es|trá|ño|ri|gór...
1   2   3   4   5
Ve|réis|me|mo|rír...
```

The verses which are formed of the union of two smaller verses may have more or less syllables, according as these verses are either *llános* or *agúdos*; thus a verse of *árte mayór*, which is formed of the union of two verses of six syllables, will have twelve syllables if these two verses are *llános*; it will have only eleven if one is *agúdo* and the other *lláno*, and it will have only ten if both are *agúdos*.

```
1   2   3   4  5  6   7   8   9  10 11 12
Di|chó|sos|vos|ó|tros—á|quién|los|cui|dá|dos
1   2   3   4  5   6   7   8  9 10 11 12
Del|mún|do|no|túr|ban—el|dúl|ce|re|pó|so...
```

```
 1   2   3   4   5  6    7   8  9 10 11
```
El|rós|tro|cu|biér|to—con|tris|te|pe|sár
```
 1  2   3   4  5  6    7  8   9 10 11.
```
De|nó|ta|la|pe|na—del|grá|ve|do|lór...
```
 1   2   3   4  5   6  7  8  9 10
```
No|quié|ro|vi|vír—ví|da|con|do|lór...

The verses *llános* are those of general use in Spanish poetry. The verses *agúdos* are only used mixed with the
verses *llános* and solely in light poetry, for they are avoided
in elevated poetry. The verses *esdrújulos* are seldom used
alone, they are most often mingled with verses *llános*, and
this mixture is not common.

The Spanish verses, of whatsoever kind they may be, being most always *llános*, it may be said that they require an
accent upon the penultimate syllable.

Independently of this final accent, the hendecasyllable
verses, or of eleven syllables, require also an accent upon
their fourth or sixth syllable.

As to the number of accents which may also enter into the
hendecasyllable verses, and the place which they should occupy, it is impossible to determine it by fixed rules, nothing
but the harmony of the verse can serve as a guide. Be it sufficient to observe 1st. that, the more accents are introduced
in a verse, the more its harmony is slow and sustained; 2d.
that there may be introduced in a hendecasyllable verse, besides the final accent and that of the 4th. or 5th. syllable
which are indispensable, one, two, and even three accents;
3rd. that they are placed nearly at an equal distance from
each other and not unfrequently upon the syllables which are
paired.

Di|chó|so|quién|en|vér|so|ge|ne|ró|so
Ce|lé|bra|las|ha|zú|ñas|in|mor|tá|les,
Y el|vi|gór|y el|es|fuér|zo|va|le|ró|so.

In the verses which are not hendecasyllable, the final accent is the only one indispensable; one or many other accents may be in truth introduced in them, as the measure
permits or harmony requires, but the place which they should
occupy is not fixed, and the ear alone should be consulted.

The verses of *árte mayór* require, besides the final accent,
an accent upon the second and upon the eighth syllable.

Of the elision.

When a word ends in a verse with a vowel and the following word begins with a vowel or an *h*, there is an elision of
the final vowel, that is, it is not counted as anything.

O|bé|lla in|grá|ta *á*|quién|el|úl|ma *a*|dó|ra !

If there should be a monosyllable consisting of a single
vowel between two words, one of which ends and the other
begins with a vowel, the three syllables shall be blended so as
to make only one syllable.

En|ví|dia *á a*|qué|llos|prá|dos|la *h*er'mo|sú|ra...
Fal|tán|do *á Es*|pá|ña|su|ma|yór|te|só|ro...

The initial *y* being a consonant cannot occasion an elision,
it is not so with the final *y* and the conjunction *y*.

Di'chó|so|*yó*|que|ví|ne *á*|tan|buén|puér|to...
De|lán|te|de *és*|ta'pé|ña|tós|ca *y*|dú'ra...

The elision may be omitted, 1st. when the first word consists of a single vowel or is terminated with an accented vowel, 2d. when the second word begins with an *h*, 3d. when
there is a natural pause or the conjunction *y* stands between
the two words.

Di|chó|so|*h*óm|bre|que|ví|ves..
O|*á*l|ma|des|ven|tu|ra|da!...

Un|pé|rro|*y* un|bo|rrí|co|ca|mi|ná|ban,
Sir|vién|do *á* un|mís|mo|dué|ño.

Of the vowels which form or do not form diphthongs.

When several vowels are in succession in the same word,
sometimes they form a single syllable and at others two.
The vowels AA, AE, AI, when the accent bears upon the
I, and AO, form two syllables; AI when the accent does not
bear upon the I, AU and AY form but one.   Ex. *Sa-avédra,
a-érco, sará-o, distra-ído, estáis, auróra, háy.*

The vowels EA, EE, and EO form two syllables, but when EA and EO are final and the accent bears upon the preceding syllable, they form but one; EI, EU and EY form but one syllable. Ex. *Océ-ano, pose-ér, trofé-o, línea, etéreo, momentáneo, deidád, déuda, réy.*

The vowels IA, IE, IO, IU form but one syllable, but when the accent bears upon the I, they form two. Ex. *Gló ria, siémpre, contrário, triúnfo, alegrí-a, temí-a.*

The vowels OA, OE, OI, when the accent bears upon the I, and OO, form two syllables; OI when the accent does not bear upon the I, OU and OY form but one. Ex. *Bo-áto, po-éta, o-ido, bo-ótes, cóime, Toucán, estóy.* In *héroe* OE forms but one syllable.

The vowels UA, UE, UI, UO, UY, UIE, UEY, form but one syllable; but when the accent bears upon the U, they form two. Ex. *Iguál, fuégo, guirnálda, mónstruo, múy, quién, quietúd, buéy, ganzú-a.*

The preceding rules are general, and liable to few exceptions: nevertheless the poets do not always strictly confine themselves to them, and sometimes unite vowels to form but one syllable which ought to form two, while at others they separate vowels in order to form two syllables which ought not to form but one. In this manner we find *poéta* forming two syllables instead of three, *reál* forming one syllable instead of two, *diálogo* forming four syllables instead of three, *triúnfo* forming three syllables instead of two, &c. &c.

Of Rhyme.

The Spaniards have two kinds of rhymes, the rhyme *consonant* and the rhyme *assonant*.

The rhyme *consonant* (consonáncia) is the perfect agreement of two sounds which terminate two verses.

The rhyme *consonant* always begins at the vowel upon which the accent bears; thus in the verses *esdrújulos* it will begin at the vowel of the antepenultima, in the verses *llános* at the vowel of the penultima and in the verses *agúdos* at the vowel of the last syllable.

The rhyme *consonant* being only made for the ear, regard should be had to the pronunciation rather than the orthography of the final syllables; thus *hijo* will rhyme well with *fixo,*(now *fijo,*) *iniquo* (now *inicuo*) with *chico,* &c.

The rhyme *assonant* (asonáncia) consists in the resemblance of the vowels found in the final syllables of two words the consonants of which are different.

The rhyme *assonant* always begins in the same manner as the rhyme *consonant* at the vowel upon which the accent bears; thus *ligéra, cubiérta, mésa, auménta, péna, lléva, trégua,* which have the accent upon the penultimate syllable, may rhyme by *assonance,* and the same will happen with *caracól, dolór, corazón, Diós, vóz, amó, nació,* which have the accent upon the last syllable, which shows, 1st, that no regard is had for the rhyme *assonant* but to the resemblance of the vowels, and that in diphthongs, nothing is regarded but the last vowel; 2d. that the consonants must be different, and that when there are two consonants in succession, it is sufficient that one of the two should not be found in the other word.

In the words *esdrújulos,* one may be content for the rhyme *assonant* with the resemblance of the vowels of the antepenultima and of the last syllable of the two words, thus, *oráculo* and *tártago* will form a good rhyme *assonant,* though the vowel of the penultima of the one be not similar to that of the penultima of the other.

The use of the rhyme *consonant* is much more common than that of the rhyme *assonant,* therefore whenever in speaking of rhyme the kind shall not be designated, the rhyn . *consonant* will be the one meant.

Rhyme is not indispensable in the Spanish verses as it is in the French, and the Spaniards have verses not rhymed or blank verses which are called *vérsos suéltos* (free verses) in which it is necessary carefully to avoid the least final *consonance.*

SECTION VI.

Of the ENJAMBEMENT, *or running of one verse into another to complete the sense.*

In Spanish the *enjambement* of verses is permitted even in elevated poetry, that is, that the sense may remain in suspense at the end of a verse, and end only at the beginning of the following verse; which happens principally whenever the beginning of a verse is the regimen or necessary dependence of what is found at the end of the preceding verse.

Volvéd las ármas y ánimo furióso
Á los péchos de aquéllos que os han puésto
En dúra sujeción, con afrentóso
Partído á tódo el múndo manifiésto.

ALÓNSO DE ERCÍLLA

Even sometimes the Spanish poets transport the syllable *mente* of an adverb to the following verse or make en elision of the final vowel of the word that terminates the verse with the vowel of the word which begins the other verse, but these *enjambemens*, which can only take place between an entire verse and a broken one, are so uncommon, that they should be considered as poetical licenses.

Y miéntras miseráble—
Ménte se están los ótros abrasándo
Con sed insaciáble
Del peligróso mándo,
Tendído yó á la sómbra esté cantándo.

FRAY LUÍS DE LEÓN.

SECTION VII.

Of poetical licenses, and what should be avoided in verses.

Though the language of Spanish poetry be not different from that of prose, and the same expressions be commonly used in it, nevertheless it is permitted to make in the construction of the phrase certain transpositions which prose would not admit of, and which contribute in a high degree to the harmony and nobleness of verses. It is always necessary to make these transpositions with intelligence and taste, so as they may not occasion any harshness or obscurity.

Harmony also requires us generally to avoid in all kinds of verses, words too long and of a difficult pronunciation, or which may have too great a conformity of sound with words already used; those having the guttural letters should be employed sparingly; the too frequent meeting of vowels, and that of rough or hissing consonants, such as the *s* or *r*, &c. should not often recur.

In short, no use should be made in poetry, particularly in high poetry, of low and prosaic words; but taste and discernment, supported by deliberate reading, will teach, better than all the rules that can be given, the choice of words that should be made; for, often, an able poet uses happily a word which seemed proscribed from poetry.

Of the mixture of verses with one another.

The mixture of verses, either as to measure or rhyme,
being generally arbitrary in Spanish poetry, it evidently must
be extremely various; we shall therefore limit ourselves to
make known the combinations used by the best poets, and
give examples of those which particularly deserve to be known.

SECTION I.

Of successive rhymes.

Paréjas or *pareádos* are called the verses of which the
rhymes are successive, that is, the 1st of which rhymes with
the 2d, the 2d with the 4th, and so on, taking care to vary
the rhyme every two verses.

The successive rhymes are used in the verses imitated from
the French, which are called for this reason *vérsos á la francésa;* and in order to supply the want of masculine and feminine rhymes, the verses *llános* are caused alternately to be
followed by two verses *agúdos*, as may be seen in the example of which we have before cited when speaking of this kind
of verse, which is now seldom used.

Entire pieces of verses *de redondilla*, and even of Italian
verses may be composed in successive rhyme, by intermixing
arbitrarily with hendecasyllables small verses of seven syllables which rhyme with the following hendecasyllable; but
these compositions are rare, unless it be to set them to music,
and the successive rhymes are but seldom used except for
proverbs, distichs and epitaphs.

SECTION II.

Of rhymes crossed and intermixed.

The Spaniards give the generick name of *cóplas* to all
kinds of assemblages or combination of verses, but this denomination is particularly appropriate to what we call *stánzas.*

The Spanish *stánzas* are not strictly bound to any pause,
and may run into one another; however, when they consist
of more than four verses, one or more pauses are introduced,
according as harmony requires it; and generally the *enjambement* or running of one *stánza* into another is carefully avoided.

Of stanzas of three verses or Tercets.

The *tercets* are stanzas commonly composed of three verses either hendecasyllables or of *redondilla mayór*, the arrangement of which may take place in several manners. 1st. The first verse may be free, *suélto*, and the 2d. rhyme with the 3d. 2d. The first verse may rhyme with the 3d. and the 2d. be free. These two kinds of mixture are used in the *villancícos*. 3d. Sometimes the 1st verse rhymes with the 2d. and the third is free. 4th. Finally in the pieces of verses composed of *tercétos*, the 1st. and 3d. verses rhyme together, the first verse of the second *tercéto* rhymes with the 2d. verse of the preceding tercet, and so on to the last *tercéto* which consists of four verses to complete the rhyme.

Should there be but one or two successive *tercétos* of Italian verses, there might be admitted among the hendecasyllables a small verse, *vérso quebrádo* of seven syllables, which would be the 1st. or 2d.

The satires, epistles and elegies are composed in hendecasyllable *tercétos;* they are also sometimes used in descriptive poems, eclogues and idyls.

Hendecasyllable Tercétos.

En aquél prádo allí nos reclinámos,
Y del Céfiro frésco recogiéndo
El agradáble espírtu (1) respirámos.

Las flóres á los ójos ofreciéndo
Diversidád estráña de pintúra,
Diversaménte así estában oliéndo;

Y en médio aquésta fuénte clára y púra,
Que cómo de cristál resplandecía
Mostrándo abiertaménte su hondúra;

El aréna (2) que de óro parecía
De bláncas pedrezuélas variáda,
Por do (3) manába el água se bullía.

---

(1) *Espírtu* for *espíritu*, (poet. lic.)
(2) *El aréna* for *la aréna.*
(3) *Do* for *dónde.*

En derrededór ni sóla úna pisáda
De fiéra, ó de pastór, ó de ganádo
Á la sazón estába señaláda.

Después que con el água resfriádo
Hubímos el calór y juntaménte
La sed de tódo púnto mitigádo;

Élla, que con cuidádo diligénte
Á conocér mi mal tenía el inténto,
Y á escudriñár el ánimo doliénte;

Con nuévo ruégo y fírme juraménto
Me conjuró y rogó que le contáse
La cáusa de mi gráve pensamiénto...

GARCILÁSO DE LA VÉGA, égloga, 2^ᵃ.

2.   *Of stanzas of four verses, or quatrains.*

The *quatrains* are stanzas of four verses, the 1st of which rhymes with the 4th. and the 2d with the 3d., or the 1st of which rhymes with the 3d. and the 2d. with the 4th.

The verses that enter into the composition of *quatrains* are commonly verses of *redondílla mayór*, verses of *redondílla menór* or *hendecasyllables*.

The *quatrains* in verses of *redondílla* are called *cuartíllas* or *cuartélas* and those in hendecasyllable verses *cuartétes*.

In the *quatrains* in verses of *redondílla menór*, the 1st. and 3d. verses may be free (*suéllos*.)

Though all kinds of stanzas may be composed in verses of *redondílla menór*, nevertheless they are seldom used except in the *quatrains*, and it is for this reason that sometimes the name of *redondílla menór* is given to the *quatrains* composed with this kind of verse.

Cuartíllas de redondílla mayór.

Deseáis, señór Sarmiénto,
Sabér en éstos mis áños
Sujétos á tántos dáños,
Cómo me pórto y susténto.

Yó os lo diré en brevedád,
Porqué la história es bién bréve,
Y el dáros gústo se os débe
Con tóda puntualidád.

Salído el sol por oriénte
De ráyos acompañádo,
Me dan un huévo pasádo
Por água, blándo y caliénte;

Con dos trágos dél (1) que suélo
Llamár yó néctar divíno,
Y á quién ótros lláman víno,
Porqué nos víno del ciélo.

Cuándo el luminóso váso
Tóca en la meridionál,
Distándo por un iguál
Del oriénte y del ocáso;

Me dan asáda y cocída
De úna gruésa y gentíl áve,
Con tres véces del suáve
Licór que alégra la vída.

Después que cayéndo viéne
Á dar en el mar Hespério,
Desamparándo el império
Que en éste horizónte tiéne;

Me suélen dar á comér
Tostádas en víno múlso,
Que el enflaquecído púlso
Restitúyen á su ser.

Luégo me ciérran la puérta,
Yó me entrégo al dúlce suéño;
Dormído sóy de ótro duéño,
No sé de mí nuéva ciérta.

Hásta que habiéndo sol nuévo,
Me cuéntan cómo he dormído,
Y así de nuévo les pído,
Que me den néctar y huévo

Ser viéja la cása es ésto,
Véo que se va cayéndo,
Vóyle puntáles poniéndo,
Porqué no cáiga tan présto.

---

(1) *Dél* for *de él,* (poet. lic.)

Mas tódo es váno artificio,
Présto me dícen mis máles,
Que han de faltár los puntáles,
Y allanárse el edificio.

BALTASÁR DE ALCÁZAR.

3. *Of the stanzas of five verses.*

The stanzas of five verses, called *cóplas redondíllas* or *quintíllas*, are commonly composed in verses of *redondílla mayór*, they also might however be composed in hendeca-syllable verses. In these stanzas, the verses are intermixed in all manners, provided they should all be upon two rhymes, and that there may never be more than two successively upon the same rhyme.

4. *Of stanzas of six verses, or sixains.*

The stanzas of six verses, called *redondíllas de séis vérsos* are commonly composed in verses of *redondílla mayór;* they might also be composed in hendecasyllable verses. In these stanzas, the verses are intermixed in all manners, provided they should all be upon two rhymes, and that there may never be more than two successively upon the same rhyme.

5. *Of the stanzas of seven verses*

The stanzas of seven verses, *redondíllas de siéte vérsos*, are little used; they are composed of verses of *redondílla mayór,* the 1st. of which rhymes with the 4th. and the 5th.; the 2d with the 3d.; and the 6th. with the 7th. Stanzas of seven hendecasyllable verses might also be composed.

6th. *Of the stanzas of eight verses, or octaves.*

The stanzas of eight verses are commonly composed in hendecasyllable verses, or in verses of *redondílla mayór,* the rhymes of which are intermixed in different manners.

1st. The 1st. verse may rhyme with the 4th. 5th. and 8th.; the 2d. with the 3d., and the 6th. with the 7th.

2d. The first verse may rhyme with the 3d., the 2d. with the 4th. 6th. and 8th., the 5th. with the 7th.

3d. The rhymes may be crossed.

4th Finally the rhymes of the six first verses may be crossed, and the two last rhyme together, which commonly happens in the stanzas of eight hendecasyllable verses.

We call *octávas* the stanzas of eight hendecasyllable verses, and *redondíllas de ócho vérsos* the stanzas of eight verses of *redondílla*.

The octaves serve principally in epic and didactic poems, they are also used in descriptive poems, eclogues and idyls.

Octávas.

¿ Porqué con tánta sáña procurámos
Ir nuéstra sángre y fuérzas apocándo,
Y envuéltos en civíles ármas dámos
Fuérza y derécho al enemígo bándo?
¿ Porqué con tal furór despedazámos
Ésta unión invencíble, condenándo
Nuéstra cáusa aprobáda y ármas jústas
Justificándo en tódo las injústas?

¿ Que rábia ó que furór desatinádo
Habéis cóntra vosótros concebído,
Que así queréis que el Araucáno estádo
Vénga á ser por sus mános destruído,
Y en su virtúd y fuérzas ahogádo
Quéde con nómbre infáme sometído
Á las estráñas léyes y gobiérno
Y en dúra servidúmbre é yúgo etérno?

Volvéd sóbre vosótros, que sin tiénto
Corréis á tóda prísa á despeñáros,
Refrenád ésa fúria y movimiénto
Que es la que puéde en ésto mas dañáros:
¿ Sufrís al enemígo en vuéstro asiénto
Que quiére cómo á brútos conquistáros,
Y no podéis sufrír aquí impaciéntes
Los conséjos y avísos conveniéntes?...

ALÓNSO DE ERCÍLLA.

The *cópla de árte mayór*, thus called because it was composed in verses of twelve syllables or of *árte mayór*, was a stanza of eight verses, the 1st. of which commonly rhymed with the 4th. 5th. and 8th., the 2d. with the 3d., and the 6th. with the 7th. This stanza is no more used at present. *Paréjas, tercétos, cuartétes*, &c. might be made in verses of *árte mayór* as also in hendecasyllable.

37 *

7. *Of stanzas of nine verses.*

The stanzas of nine verses bear the name in Spanish of *redondíllas místas*, because they are composed of the reunion of a stanza of four verses and of a stanza of five verses of *redondílla mayór*. Stanzas of nine verses might also be composed of a stanza of four verses and of a stanza of five hendecasyllable verses.

8. *Of the stanzas of ten verses, or dizains.*

The *décimas* are stanzas of ten verses, commonly of *redondílla mayór*, the 1st. of which rhymes with the 4th. and 5th.; the 2d. with the 3d., the 6th. with the 7th. and 10th., and the 8th. with the 9th.

The *décima* may also be composed of the union of two stanzas of five verses *quintíllas*, in each of which the mixture of the rhymes may be uniform, but it is better that it should be different. This kind of *décima* is called *cópla reál*.

Cópla reál.

Aquí la envídia y mentíra
Me tuviéron encerrádo.
¡Dichóso el humílde estádo
Del sábio que se retíra
De aquéste múndo malvádo,
Y, con póbre mésa y cása,
En el cámpo deleitóso,
Con sólo Diós se compása;
Y á sólas su vída pása,
Ni envidiádo, ni envidióso !

FRÁY LUÍS DE LEÓN.

Remark. The stanzas of more than ten verses are not composed of entire verses only, but of entire verses, *vérsos entéros*, mixed with broken verses, *vérsos quebrádos.*

SECTION III.

Of the mixture of entire with broken verses.

Commonly the hendecasyllable verses are mixed with the verses of seven syllables, those of eight syllables with those of four, and those of six syllables with those of three. Sometimes also entire verses of different measure are mixed with broken verses of different measure.

There is nothing determined however in such cases, as to the number of verses of each kind that may be mixed together. The verses thus mixed sometimes form stanzas, and at others do not form any. When they form stanzas of less than ten verses, the mixture of rhymes is the same as in the stanzas composed only of entire verses. But when they form stanzas of more than ten verses, and when they are not disposed in stanzas, the mixture of rhymes is absolutely arbitrary; even unrhymed verses may be admitted among the verses rhymed. It is however proper to remark 1st. that in mixed verses, whether they form stanzas or not, the corresponding rhymes must never be too distant from one another; 2d. that in the stanzas in mixed verses as in the stanzas in entire verses, the mixture adopted for the rhymes in the 1st. stanza must generally be followed in all the other stanzas of the same piece, and that it is the same with the mixture of the verses of different measure; 3d. that the stanzas in mixed verses do not contain commonly more than twenty verses.

The following examples will give an idea of the great variety of the mixture of the entire and broken verses which is commonly used in odes, light poetry, and pieces destined to be set to music.

> Íba cogiéndo flóres
> Y guardándo en la fálda
> Mi nínfa pára hacér úna guirnálda;
> Mas priméro las tóca
> Á los rosádos lábios de su bóca,
> Y les da de su aliénto los olóres.
> Y estába (por su bién) éntre úna **rósa**
> Úna abéja escondída,
> Su dúlce humór hurtándo;
> Y cómo en la hermósa
> Flor de los lábios se halló, atrevída
> La picó, sacó miél, fuése volándo.   L. MARTÍN.

Profecía del Tájo.

> Folgába (1) el réy Rodrígo
> Con la hermósa Cába en la ribéra

----

(1) *Folgába* for *Holgába*, (obsolete.)

De Tájo sin testígo;
El pécho sacó fuéra
El río, y le habló de ésta manéra:

En mal púnto te góces,
Injústo forzadór, que yá el sonído
Óyo (1) yá, y las vóces,
Las ármas y el bramído
De Márte, de furór y ardór ceñído.

¡ Áy! ésa tu alegría
¡ Que lllántos acarréa! y ésa hermósa
Que vió el sol en mal día,
Á España ¡ Áy! cuán llorósa,
Y al cétro de los Gódos cuán costósa!

Llámas, dolóres, guérras,
Muértes, asolamientos, fiéros máles
Éntre tus brázos cierras,
Trabájos inmortáles
Á tí y á tus vasállos naturáles.

Á los que en Constantína
Rómpen el fértil suélo, á los que báña
El Ébro, á la vecína
Sansuéña, á Lusitáña,
Á tóda la espaciósa y tríste España.

Yá dénde (2) Cádiz lláma
El injuriádo Cónde, á la vengánza
Aténto, y no á la fáma,
La bárbara pujánza,
En quién pára tu dáño háy tardánza.

Óye, que al ciélo tóca
Con temeróso son la trómpa fiéra,
Que en África convóca
El Móro á la bandéra,
Que al áire desplegáda va ligéra.

La lánza yá blandéa
El Árabe cruél, é hiére el viénto
Llamándo á la peléa,
Innumeráble cuénto
De escuádras júntas véo en un moménto.

(1) *Óyo* for *Óigo*, (obsolete.)
(2) *Dénde* for *désde*, (idem.)

Cúbre la génte el suélo,
Debájo de las vélas desparéce (1)
La mar, la voz al ciélo
Confúsa y vária créce,
El pólvo róba el día y le oscuréce.

¡Ay! que yá presurósos
Súben las lárgas náves; ¡Ay! que tiénden
Los brázos vigorósos
Á los rémos, y enciénden
Las máres espumósas por do hiénden.

El Éolo derécho   .
Hínche la véla en pópa, y lárga entráda
Por el Hercúleo estrécho
Con la púnta aceráda
El gran pádre Neptúno da á la armáda.

!Áy trísto!   ¿Y aún te tiéne
El mal dúlce regázo?   ¿Ni llamádo
Al mal que sobreviéne
No acórres? ¿ocupádo
No ves yá el puérto á Hércules sagrádo?

Acúde, córre, vuéla,
Traspása el álta siérra, ocúpa el lláno,
No perdónes la espuéla,
No des paz á la máno,
Menéa fulminándo el hiérro insáno.

¡Áy cuánto de fatíga!
¡Áy cuánto de dolór está presénte
Á él que víste loríga,
Al infánte valiénte,
Á hómbres y cabállos juntaménte!

Y tú, Bétis divíno,
De sángre agéna y túya amancilládo,
Darás al mar vecíno,
¡Cuánto yélmo quebrádo!
¡Cuánto cuérpo de nóbles destrozádo!

_____

(1) *Desparéce* for *desaparéce*, (obsolete.)

El furibúndo Márte
Cínco lúces las háces desordénu
Iguál á cáda párte;
La sésta ¡Ay! te condéna
O cára pátria, á bárbara cadéna.

FRAY LUÍS DE LEÓN, óda.

Fonséca, yá las hóras
Del inviérno aterído,
Aunqué tárde se fuéron,
Y su vez agradáble permitiéron
Al Céfiro florído.
Yá el veráno
Nos descúbre su frénte,
De rósas y de púrpura ceñído:
Remíte el aíre el desabrído céño,
Y el sol líbra sus ráyos
De las núbes oscúras;
Y con lúces mas vívas y mas púras,
Regalándo las niéves,
Al blándo pié de los parádos ríos
Las prisiónes de yélo alégre quíta,
Y su antíguo corrér les solicíta...   F. DE RIÓJA.

¡Cuán présto se va el placér,
Cómo después de acordádo,
Da dolór!
Cómo á nuéstro parecér
Cualquiéra tiémpo pasádo,
Fué mejór!   JÓRGE MANRÍQUE.

SECTION IV.

Of blank verses.

We have just seen that blank verses, *suéltos,* that is, which are not subject to rhyme, are mixed with the rhymed verses; they are likewise mixed with the *assonant* verses, as will be seen hereafter; but they may also be used alone without mixture of any other kind of verse.

Conciseness in thought, force of expression, and above all elegance and harmony in versification resulting from the symmetrical disposition of long and brief syllables; this is, what constitutes the beauty of blank verses and gives them a great analogy with the Greek and Latin verses; thus the Spaniards without rigorously observing, however, the rhythm of the ancients, have imitated it in blank verses with considerable success.

The hendecasyllable is the verse most used in works in blank verse; it is called *heroic*, not because it is used in preference in the heroic poem and other works of a serious kind; for, these are composed commonly in octaves or *tercétos* of rhymed verses, but because it imitates best the harmony of the great Greek and Latin verses, and seems therefore more proper to be used in the translations of the master works of antiquity.

In mixing hendecasyllables with broken verses of different measures, almost all the lyrick combinations of the ancients may be imitated. In the following ode, the *cuartétos* of which are composed of three hendecasyllable verses and a broken verse of five syllables, the harmony of the Sapphick strophe may be easily discovered, which is one of the most beautiful of these combinations.

Al Céfiro.

Dúlce vecino de la vérde sélva,
Huésped etérno del abríl florído,
Vitál aliénto de la mádre Vénus,
  Céfiro blándo,

Si de mis ánsias el amór supíste,
Tú, que las quéjas de mi voz lleváste,
Óye, no témas, y á mi nínfa díle,
  Díle que muéro.

Fílis un tiémpo mi dolór sabía,
Fílis un tiémpo mi dolór llorába,
Quísome un tiémpo; mas ahóra témo,
  Témo sus íras.

Así los Dióses con amór patérno,
Así los ciélos con amór benígno
Niéguen al tiempo que felíz voláres,
  Niéve á la tiérra.

Jamás el péso de la núbe párda,
Cuándo amanéce en la eleváda cúmbre,
Tóque tus hómbros, ni su mal granízo
  Hiéra tus álas.   ESTÉBAN DE VILLÉGAS.

Of works in verse.

The principal works in verse are; epic poems, didactic and descriptive; theatrical pieces, odes, epistles, elegies, eclogues, idyls and fables. As these different kinds of works are common to the Spanish literature and that of other nations, we shall not consider them. It is true that the Spaniards deviating sometimes in their composition, and particularly in that of theatrical pieces, from the precepts dictated by good taste, would seem to require some details; but these details are foreign to a treatise on versification and would exceed its limits. It will be sufficient to remark that the Spanish theatrical pieces are sometimes in prose, and at others in rhymed or unrhymed verses, and that all kinds of stanzas, sonnets, romances, &c. are introduced in the plays; in short, that all the other works in verse are generally composed of stanzas. As to the kind of stanzas which is proper for every class of works, we have indicated it as far as possible when speaking of the different kinds of stanzas; the choice of them however being often left to the fancy of the poets, it is the works of those who have excelled in each class that ought to be taken as models. We shall only treat here of the small works in verse which are in some manner peculiar to the Spanish language, or which at least are subject in that language to some particular rules, and we shall pass over those, such as the sonnets in echos, *saládos*, labyrinths, cubic poems, &c. the whole merit of which consisted in a ridiculous difficulty, and which good taste has proscribed long ago

1. *Sonétos.*

The sonnet, *sonéto*, occupies yet in Spanish poetry the rank which it formerly occupied in French poetry.

The Spaniards have several kinds of sonnets which are, the simple sonnet, the double sonnet, the crossed sonnet, the sonnet with a tail, and the continued sonnet.

The simple sonnet, *sonéto simple*, is composed of fourteen hendecasyllable verses, the first eight of which named *piés* are divided in two *quatrains*, and the last six form two *tercels* which are called *ruéltas*. The two quatrains are made upon the same rhymes, and in each of them the first verso rhymes with the fourth, and the two intermediate ones together. The verses of the two tercets rhyme together upon two or three rhymes, which must not resemble those used in the two quatrains.

The double sonnet, *sonéto dobládo*, is subject to the same rules as the simple sonnet; the only difference there is between the two consists in this, that, in the double sonnet, broken verses of seven syllables are interposed among hendecasyllables, namely: one or several in each quatrain and one alone in each tercet. Every one of these broken verses having the same rhyme as the entire verse which precedes it, this rhyme is double, and is the reason why this sonnet is named a double sonnet.

The crossed sonnet, *sonéto terciádo*, is thus called, because the rhymes of the two quatrains are crossed; in other respects it is like the simple sonnet.

The sonnet with a tail, *sonéto con cóla*, differs from the simple sonnet because there is interposed after the second and fourth verses of each quatrain, and after each tercet, a broken verse called *cóla*. The broken verses thus interposed are of four or five syllables; those of the quatrains rhyme with each other, and their rhyme must be different from the rhymes of the quatrains; those of the tercets rhyme also with each other, and their rhymes must be different from the rhymes of the quatrains and tercets.

The continued sonnet, *sonéto continuo*, is similar as to the quatrains to the simple sonnet or to the crossed sonnet, but the rhymes of the tercets are crossed and the same as those of the quatrains.

The simple sonnet is more used than the others, we shall give two of them, the French imitations of which are well known.

> Un sonéto me mánda hacér Violánte,
> Que en mi vída me he vísto en tal apriéto,
> Catórce vérsos dícen que es sonéto,
> Búrla burlándo van los tres delánte.
>
> Yó pensé que no hallára consonánte.
> Y estóy á la mitád de ótro cuartéto,
> Mas si me véo en el primér tercéto
> No háy cósa en los cuartétos que me espánte.
>
> Por el primér tercéto voy entrándo,
> Y aún paréce que entré con pié derécho,
> Pués fin con éste vérso le vóy dándo.

Yá estóy en el segúndo, y aún sospécho
Que estóy los tréce vérsos acabándo:
Contád si son catórce, y está hécho.

Lópe de Véga

Sobérbias tórres, áltos edifícios,
Que yá cubrístes (1) siéte escélsos móntes,
Y ahóra en descubiértos horizóntes
Apénas de habér sído dáis indícios:
Griégos licéos, célebres hospícios
De Plutárcos, Platónes, Genofóntes,
Teátro que lidió Rinoceróntes,
Olímpias, lústros, báños, sacrifícios;
¿Que fuérzas deshiciéron peregrínas
La mayór pómpa de la glória humána,
Impérios, triúnfos, ármas y doctrínas?
¡O gran consuélo á mi esperánza vána,
Que el tiémpo que os volvió bréves ruínas,
No es múcho que acabáse mi sotána!

Lópe de Véga.

2. Silvas.

The Spaniards give the name of *silva* to a piece of hendecasyllable verses mixed at pleasure with broken verses of
seven syllables, in which no order is observed for the distri-
bution of the rhymes, and in which some blank verses may
even be introduced. There are also *silvas* in verses of seven
syllables. The *silva* is a composition after the manner of
the ode, which is proper for all sorts of subjects.

Á la Riquéza.

¡O mal segúro bién!   ¡O cuidadósa
Riquéza, y cómo á sómbra de alegría,
Y de sosiégo engáñas!
Él que véla en tu alcánce, y se desvía
Del póbre estádo, y la quietúd dichósa,
Ócio y seguridád preténde en váno.
Pués tras el luéngo (2) errár de água y montáñas
Cuándo el metál precióso cója á máno,
No ha de ver sin cuidádo abrír el día.

---

(1) *Cubristes* for *cubristeis* (obsolete.)
(2) *Luéngo* for *lárgo* (idem.)

No sin cáusa los dióses te escondiéron
En las entráñas de la tiérra dúra:
¿Mas que halló difícil y encubiérto
La sediénta codícia?
Turbó la paz segúra,
Con que en la antígua sélva floreciéron
El abéto y el píno,
Y trájolos al puérto
Y por cámpos de mar les dió camíno.
Abrióse el mar, y abrióse
Altaménte la tiérra,
Y salíste del céntro al áire cláro,
Híja de la avarícia,
Á hacér á los hómbres crúda guérra.
Salíste tú, y perdióse
La piedád que no habíta en pécho aváro.

. . . .
¡Á cuántos armó el óro de cruéza! (1)
¡Y á cuántos ha dejádo
En el último tránce! ¡o dúra suérte!
Piérde su flor la virginál puréza
Por tí, y vése manchádo
Con adultério el lécho no esperádo.
Al ménos animóso
Pára que te poséa,
Das riquéza, ardimiénto licencióso,
Ningúno háy que se véa
Por tí tan abastádo y poderóso,
Que carézca de miédo.
¿Que cósa habrá de máles tan cercáda,
Pués óra pretendída, óra alcanzáda,
Y aún estándo en deséos,
Péna ocúltan tus ciégos devanéos?
Pero cánsome en váno, decír puédo,
Que si sómbras de bién en tí se viéran,
Los inmortáles Dióses te tuviéran.   F. DE RIÓJA.

3. *Románces.*

They call *románce* a piece of verse destined to be set to music, composed of a series of quatrains, the 1st. and 3d. verses of which are blank, whilst the 2d. and 4th. rhyme by assonance. Assonance is the greatest difficulty of romances,

---

(1) *Cruéza*, obs. : now *crueldád.*

because it must be the same in all the quatrains. Romances are commonly in verses of *redondilla mayór* or *menór*, and sometimes in hendecasyllable verses, for which reason they are then called *románces heróicos*. They are also in verses of seven syllables, and one of the verses of each quatrain may be hendecasyllable, this is commonly the fourth; one or two broken verses of any kind, particularly of five or four syllables may likewise be mixed with the verses of *redondilla;* in short, romances may be composed in quatrains of verses *esdrújulos* and even of *árte mayór*, pure or mixed; in a word, nothing is more varied than the versification of romances, but it is necessary that the mixture adopted in the first quatrain be followed in all the others. The romances commonly have no ritornello, *burden*, there are however, some romances in which the last or the two last verses of the first quatrain are repeated after the second, and so one after each quatrain, or every other quatrain. The *burden* sometimes begins only in the middle of the romance and does not always continue till the end, neither is it necessary that it should be composed of the last or of the two last verses of the 1st quatrain, it may be formed of one or two verses which are added.

The *románce* is the favourite kind of poetry of the Spaniards, it is really their national lyric poetry, it equally accommodates itself to the accents of joy and to those of sorrow. They sing in them alternately the exploits of warriors, love, adventures, &c. They call *jácara* a romance sang to a popular air bearing that name.

> De las Africánas pláyas
> Alejádo de sus huértas,
> Míra el forzádo horteláno
> De España las áltas tiérras.
> Míra las golósas cábras
> En las peládas ladéras,
> Que apénas se determína
> Si son cábras ó son péñas:
> Tiénde la envidiósa vísta
> Por las abundósas (1) végas
> Y comarcánas cabáñas,
> Que cási á la par huméan.
> Mirába por Gibraltár
> Las heládas rócas yértas,
> Azotádas de las óndas,

---

(1) *Abundóso* synonymous of *abundánte*

Y arrancádas de la aréna.
Míra el estrécho cubiérto,
Y las hirviéntes arénas,
Que le paréce que bráman,
Y por mil pártes resuénan.
O sagrádo mar, le díce,
Haz con mis suspíros tréguas;
Perdóna si éllos ó el viénto
Son cáusa de tu torménta.
Pásame en esótra pláya;
Que si en élla me preséntas,
Te ofreceré un blánco tóro
El mejór de mis dehésas.
No quiéro que mis deséos
Váyan á tiérras agénas;
Da vída á un nuévo Leándro,
Que en tus mános se encomiénda.
Ésto diciéndo el forzádo,
En las blándas óndas se écha
Con los brázos á remár;
Hiénde, rómpe, rásga y huélla.
Mas allá á la média nóche,
Cuándo los miémbros le aquéjan,
Temeróso de su dáño
Habló así á las óndas;
Queridas y amádas ólas,
Pués determináis que muéra,
Dejádme salír amígas,
Que yó os pagaré ésta déuda.
Fuéle el viénto favoráble,
Oyó fortúna sus quéjas,
Y al nacér el rúbio sol,
Hízo pié sóbre la aréna.
Dió grácias al mar piadóso,
Al viénto, nórte y estréllas,
Y con ceremónia humílde
Besó y adoró la tiérra.   Romancero general.

The verses of seven syllables disposed in *cuartétos* of blank and assonant verses as in the *románces*, and which for this reason are often called *vérsos de románce* are those generally used in Anacreóntic odes.

No con mi blánda líra
Serán en áyes trístes
Llorádas las fortúnas
De réyes infelíces;
Ni el gríto del soldádo
Feróz en crúdas lídes,
O el truéno con que arrója
La bála el brónce horríble.
Yó tiémblo, y me estremézco;
Que el númen no permíte
A el (1) lábio temeróso
Canciónes tan sublímes.
Muchácho sóy, y quiéro
Decír mas apacíbles
Queréllas, y gozárme
Con dánzas y convítes.
En éllos coronádo
De rósas y alelíes,
Éntre rísas y vérsos
Menudéo los bríndis.
En córos las mucháchas
Se júntan por oírme,
Y al púnto mis cantáres
Con nuévo ardór repíten;
Pués Báco y él de Vénus
Me diéron, que felíce
Celébre en dúlces hímnos
Sus glórias y festínes.   J. Meléndez Valdés.

Quiéro cantár de Cádmo,
Quiéro cantár de Atrídas,
¡Mas, áy! que de amór sólo,
Sólo cánta mi líra.
Renuévo el instruménto,
Las cuérdas mudo á prísa,
Péro si yó de Alcídes,
Élla de amór suspíra.
Pués, héroes valiéntes,
Quedáos désde éste día;
Porqué yá de amór sólo,
Sólo cánta mi líra.
        E. de Villégas, *Imitación de Anacreónte.*

---

(1) *A el* for *al*, article, definite, often used by writers, as they also use *al* improperly for *á él*, pronoun.

Vuélve, mi dúlce líra,
Vuélve á tu estílo humílde
Y déja á los Homéros,
Cantár á los Aquíles.
Cánta tú la cabáña
Con tónos pastoríles,
Y los épicos métros
Á Virgílio no envídies.
No espéres en la córte
Gozár días felíces,
Y vuélvete á la aldéa,
Que tu preséncia píde.
Yá te aguárdan zagáles
Que con flóres se vísten,
Y adórnan sus cabézas,
Y cuéllos juveníles.
Yá te espéran pastóres
Que deseósos víven
De escuchár tus canciónes
Que con gústo repíten.
Y pára que sus vóces
Á los écos admíren,
Y repítan tus vérsos
Los melodiósos císnes;
Vuélve, mi dúlce líra,
Vuélve á tu tóno humílde;
Y déja á los Homéros
Cantár á los Aquíles.   J. CADÁLSO.

4. Endéchas.

The *endéchas* are elegies or funeral songs in praise of the dead, they are a kind of *románce* commonly in verses of seven syllables. The *endéchas*, in which the last verse of each *quatrain* is a hendecasyllable, are called *endéchas reáles;* they are also rhymed *endéchas.*

5. Seguidíllas.

The *seguidílla* is composed of a series of *quatrains* in crossed verses of seven and five syllables. The *seguidílla* has a great resemblance with the *románce;* the only difference existing, is that the couplets of the *seguidílla* being commonly detached, the assonance may change at every-couplet.

There is a kind of *seguidilla* called *chambérga*, from the name of the air upon which it is sung, each *quatrain* of which is followed by six verses alternately of three and seven syllables, rhyming by assonance two by two, that is, every verse of three syllables rhymes with the verse of seven which immediately follows it.

6. *Letríllas.*

The *letrílla* is a kind of lyric poetry of a simple and graceful style. It is commonly composed of a series of *quatrains* in verses of six or eight syllables. The *letrílla* has a great resemblance with the *románce;* but it is shorter. The 1st. and the 3d. verse of each *quatrain* are blank or rhymed, the 2d. and the 4th. are assonants; all the verses may nevertheless be also rhymed. It is requisite, as in *románces*, that the assonance be the same ·in all the *quatrains*. There are some *letríllas* which have a ritornello, *burden*, others have none, sometimes the *burden* forms a part of the quatrain, sometimes it is added.

No álma primavéra
Bélla y apacíble,
O el dúlce Favónio
Que ámbares respíro;
No rosáda Auróra
Tras la nóche tríste,
Ni el pincél que en flóres
Béllo se matíce;
No núbe que Fébo
Su pabellón pínte,
O álamo que abráce
Dos émulas vídes;
No fuénte que pérlas
Á cién cáños fíe,
Ni lírio éntre rósas,
Clavél entre jazmínes;
Al rompér el día
Son tan apacíbles
Cómo el pastorcíllo
Que en mi pécho vivo.   YGLÉSIAS.

De éste módo ponderába
Un inocénte pastór
Á la nínfa á quién amába
La eficácia de su amór.

¿Ves cuántas flóres al prádo
La primavéra prestó?
Pués míra, duéño adorádo,
Mas véces te quiéro yó.

¿Ves cuánta aréna doráda
Tájo en sus águas llevó?
Pués míra Filis amáda,
Mas véces te quiéro yó.

¿Ves al salír de la auróra
Cuánta avecílla cantó?
Pués míra hermósa pastóra,
Mas véces te quiéro yó.

¿Ves la niéve derretída
Cuánto arroyuélo formó?
Pués míra bién de mi vída,
Mas véces te quiéro yó.

¿Ves cuánta abéja industriósa
De ésa colména salió?
Pués míra, ingráta y hermósa,
Mas véces te quiéro yó.

¿Ves cuántas grácias la máno
De las deidádes te dió?
Pués míra, duéño tiráno,
Mas véces te quiéro yó.   J. CADÁLSO.

7. Líras.

The *líra* is a small piece of hendecasyllable verses mixed with broken verses, composed to be sung with the accompaniment of a guitar or lyre. The *líras* are composed of five or six verses. In the *líras* of five verses, the four first are broken verses of seven syllables and the fifth is a hendecasyllable; the 1st. verse rhymes with the 3d., the 2d. 4th. and 5th. rhyme together. In the *líras* of six verses, the odd verses are broken verses of seven syllables, and the others are hendecasyllables; the rhymes of the four first verses are crossed, and the two last verses rhyme together. There are also *líras* of six verses the 1st. 2d. 4th, and 5th. of which are broken verses of seven syllables, the 3d. a broken verse of two syllables and the 6th. a hendecasyllable, then the 1st. verse rhymes with the 4th., the 2d. with the 3d. and the 5th. with the 6th.

8. *Canciónes.*

The *canción* is a kind of lyric poetry, which is composed of several *estánzas* or *estáncias*, in hendecasyllable verses mixed with broken verses of seven syllables. The *canción* has not commonly more than from ten to twelve stanzas, and is often terminated by a shorter stanza called *remáte* or *represa*. The mixture of rhymes as well as that of entire and broken verses is arbitrary, it varies even sometimes from one stanza to the other, but in general the mixture adopted in the 1st. stanza is followed in all the others. The mixture of the verses and rhymes is not the same in the *remáte* as in the other stanzas, it is likewise arbitrary.

¡O libertád preciósa,
No comparáda al óro,
Ni al bién mayór de la espaciósa tiérra!
Mas ríca y mas gozósa
Que el precióso tesóro
Que el mar del Sur éntre su nácar ciérra;
Con ármas, sángre y guérra,
Con las vidas y fámas,
Conquistádo en el múndo!
Paz dálce, amór profúndo,
Que el mal apártas y á tu bién nos llámas;
En tí sólo se anída
Óro, tesóro, paz, bién, glória y vída.
      Cuándo de las humánas
Tiniéblas ví del ciélo
La luz, princípio de mis dúlces días;
Aquéllas tres hermánas,
Que nuéstro humáno vélo
Tegiéndo llévan por inciértas vías;
Las dúras pénas mías
Trocáron en la glória,
Que en libertád poséo
Con siémpre iguál deséo;
Dónde verá por mi dichósa história,

Quién mas leyére en élla,
Que es dúlce libertád lo ménos délla. (1)
   Yó pués, señór exénto
De ésta montáña y prádo,
Gózo la glória y libertád que téngo;
Sobérbio pensamiénto
Jamás ha derribádo
La vída humílde y póbre que entreténgo;
Cuándo á las mános véngo
Con el muchácho ciégo,
Haciéndo róstro embísto;
Vénzo, triúnfo y resísto
La flécha, el árco, la ponzóña, el fuégo;
Y con líbre albedrío
Llóro el agéno mal, y espánto el mío.
Cuándo la auróra báña
Con heládo rocío,
De aljófar celestiál el mónte y prádo;
Sálgo de mi cabáña
Ribéras déste (2) río
Á dar el nuévo pásto á mi ganádo.
Y cuándo el sol dorádo
Muéstra sus fuérzas gráves
Al suéño el pécho inclíno
Debájo de un sáuce ó píno,
Oyéndo el son de las parléras áves,
O yá gozándo el áura,
Dónde el perdído aliénto se restáura.
   Cuándo la nóche oscúra
Con su estrelládo mánto
El cláro día en su tiniébla enciérra,
Y suéna en la espesúra
El tenebróso cánto
De los noctúrnos híjos de la tiérra;
Al pié de aquésta siérra
Con rústicas palábras
Mi ganadíllo cuénto,
Y el corazón conténto
Del gobiérno de ovéjas y de cábras,
La temerósa cuénta
Del cuidadóso réy me represénta.

---

(1) *Délla* for *de élla*, (poet. lic.)
(3) *Déste* for *de éste*, (poet. lic.)

Aquí la vérde péra
Con la manzána hermósa
De guálda y rója sángre matizáda,
Y de colór de céra,
La cerméïa olorósa
Téngo, y la endrína de colór moráda;
Aquí de la enramáda
Párra que el ólmo enláza,
Melósas úbas cójo;
Y en cantidád recójo,
Al tiémpo que las rámas desenláza
El caluróso estío,
Membríllos que corónan éste río.
No me da desconténto
El hábito costóso
Que de lascívo el pécho nóble infáma:
Es mi dúlce susténto
Del cámpo generóso
Éstas silvéstres frútas que derráma;
Mi regaláda cáma
De blándas piéles y hójas,
Que algún réy la envidiára;
Y de tí, fuénte clára,
Que bulliéndo el aréna y água arrójas,
Éstos cristáles púros,
Susténtos póbres, péro bién segúros.
Estése el cortesáno
Procuríndo á su gústo
La blánda cáma y el mejór susténto;
Bése la ingráta máno
Del poderóso injústo,
Formándo tórres de esperánza al viénto;
Víva y muéra sediénto
Por el honróso ofício,
Y góce yó del suélo,
Al áire, al sol, al hiélo,
Ocupádo en mi rústico egercício;
Que mas vúle pobréza
En paz, que en guérra mísera riquéza.
Ni témo al poderóso,
Ni al ríco lisongéo,
Ni sóy camaleón dél que gobiérna;
Ni me tiéne envidióso

La ambición y deséo
De agéna glória, ni de fáma etérna:
Cárne sabrósa y tiérna,
Víno aromatizádo,
Pan blánco de aquél día
En prádo, en fuénte fría,
Hálla un pastór con hámbre fatigádo,
Que el gránde y el pequéño
Sómos iguáles lo que dúra el suéño. LÓPE DE VÉGA.

9. *Baláta.*

The ballad, *baláta,* is a small piece of verse which is now
but little in use, its name comes from this, that it was originally sung while dancing. The ballad is composed in pure
hendecasyllable verses, or mixed with broken verses of seven
syllables, and is divided into four parts, the 1st. of which is
called *represa,* (repetition,) because it is wholly or partly
repeated at the end of the ballad; the 2d. *priméra mudánza*
(1st. change,) the 3d. *segúnda mudánza* (2d. change,) because the tone of the *represa* is changed in it, and the 4th.
vuélta (return,) because they return to the 1st. tone. The
represa and *vuélta* are commonly composed of three or four
verses, and each *mudánza* almost always has one verse less.

Représa. { Tras su manáda Elísio lamentándo
Mil véces éste vérso repetía
¡Ay! quién se viéra cuál se vió algún día!

1 *a. Mu-* { Víme yó tan señór de mi fortúna,
dánza. Tan líbre de dolór, tan prosperádo,

2 *a. Mu-* { Que no temí jamás mudánza algúna
dánza. De aquél priméro y venturóso estádo:

Vuélta. { Yá tóda mi ventúra se ha trocádo;
No sóy ni yá seré quién ser solía:
¡Ay! quién se viéra cuál se vió algún día!

10. *Villancícos.*

The *villancíco,* (country lay) has a great relation to the
ballad, and is likewise made for singing. It begins with a
cabéza, which is repeated as the *burden* of the ballad. The
cabéza is a kind of introduction containing a sentence of two,
three or four verses. It is followed by a stanza of six verses

39

called *piés*, which is its comment. The two first *piés* form
the 1st. *mudánza*, the two following the 2d. *mudánza*, and the
two last the *vuélta*, after which the last or the two last of the
cabéza are repeated. The *villancícos* are composed in verses of pure *redondilla mayór* or *menór*, or mixed with broken
verses. The two following *villancícos* will serve as examples for the mixture of the verses and rhymes.

Cabéza.	En lo próspero y advérso Lo que sólo satisfáce, Es pensár que Diós lo háce.
1 *a. Mudánza.*	Que me súba ó báje el múndo, O que me pónga fortúna
2 *a. Mudánza.*	Sóbre el cuérno de la lúna, O me húnda hásta el profúndo;
Vuélta.	La razón en que me fúndo Pára que tódo lo abráce,
Repelición.	Es sabér que Diós lo háce.

———

Cabéza.	Cuándo el corazón se abrása, Echa luégo Por las ventánas de cása Vívo fuégo.
1 *a. Mudánza.*	No se puéde reprimír El amór
2 *a. Mudánza.*	Aunqué mas quiéra encubrír Su fervór,
Vuélta.	Que cómo es níño y ciégo, Da sin túsa
Repelición.	Por las ventánas de cása Vívo fuégo.
1 *a. Mudánza.*	Suspíros y ánsias estráñas Van saliéndo,
2 *a. Mudánza.*	Cuándo se están las estráñas Derritiéndo,
Vuélta.	Que el álma hécha úna brása Envía luégo
Repelición.	Por las ventánas de cása Vívo fuégo.

APPENDIX.

BY McHENRY.

On the verbs SER and ESTÁR.*

AMONG the difficulties which Englishmen encounter in the study of the Spanish Language, there is, perhaps, none greater than the one attending the proper choice of these verbs. A Spaniard, no doubt, perceives a very striking difference between them; yet he finds it almost impossible to make an Englishman sensible of their different meanings   SER and ESTÁR equally signify in English *to be;* but SER denotes absolute, and ESTÁR a relative existence; might I be allowed the definition, I would say that SER expresses the kind, and ESTÁR the manner of being, and therefore we find that ESTÁR is employed when the existence is connected with, and as if it were modified by, some circumstances either of time or of place. If I say " *éste hómbre* ES *valiénte,*" this man is valiant; I mean that this man possesses that certain portion of natural courage requisite to form what is meant by a valiant man; but if ESTÁR be substituted, " *éste hómbre* ESTÁ *valiénte,*" will then mean that the man is at that time inspired with valour by some existing circumstance.

In the same manner, *ésta naránja* ES *ágria,* this orange is sour; denotes that the orange belongs to a species, of which the acid taste is a characteristic: change the verb into ESTÁR, and *ésta naránja* ESTÁ *ágria* will then convey the idea that the orange might have been sweet had it not been gathered too soon, or some other circumstance prevented its reaching the necessary degree of maturity.

From the foregoing remarks may be drawn the following general rule: viz. that when the attribute is inherent in, or essential to the subject, we express it by SER, and when it is only accidental or contingent we make use of ESTÁR: thus, if we saw a man with a wooden leg, we should say, *éste hómbre* ES *cójo,* this man is lame; but if a man walking with crutches only, it might be expressed by *éste hómbre* ES or ESTÁ *cójo:* with ES we should denote that his lameness was

---

* See also Josse's Grammar, page 95.

deemed permanent, and with ESTÁ that we considered it as temporary only. This, however, will be more clearly shown in the following rules.

RULE I. General truths on the qualities of the mind are expressed with SER, and emotions with ESTÁR; Ex.

La muérte *es* terríble,	*Death is terrible.*
Sóy humílde,	*I am humble.*
Eres sobérbio,	*Thou art proud.*
Es infeliz,	*He is unhappy.*
Estóy enfadádo,	*I am angry.*
Estás tríste,	*Thou art sorrowful.*
Está conténto,	*He is pleased.*

II. The natural beauties of the body, and its defects when deemed permanent, are denoted by SER; as

La muchácha *es* boníta,	*The girl is pretty.*
El híjo *éra* féo,	*The son was ugly.*
La mádre *es* cója,	*The mother is lame.*
El pádre *es* ciégo,	*The father is blind.*

III. The physical changes in the animal body are expressed with ESTÁR, as

El níño *está* frío,	*The child is cold, (to the touch.)*
Yó *estába* ciégo,	*I was blind.*
Estúve cójo la semána pasáda,	*I was lame last week.*

IV. The natural qualities of substances are expressed by SER; as

El yélo *es* frío,	*Ice is cold.*
La miél *es* dúlce,	*Honey is sweet.*
La léche *es* blánca,	*Milk is white.*
El plómo *es* pesádo,	*Lead is heavy.*

V. The chemical and mechanical changes in substances are expressed with ESTÁR; as

La léche *está* ágria,	*The milk is sour.*
El plómo *está* derretído,	*The lead is melted.*
El água *está* caliénte,	*The water is warm.*
La cárne *estába* asáda,	*The meat was roasted.*

VI. When *to be* connects two nouns, two pronouns, two infinitives, or one of each, it is translated SER: as

El amór de Diós *es* el princípio de la sabiduría,	*The love of God is the beginning of wisdom.*
Perdonár las injúrias *es* obrár cómo Cristiános,	*To forgive injuries is to act like Christians.*
¿ Quién *sóy* yó?	*Who am I?*
Acuérdate hómbre que tú *éres* pólvo,	*Remember man that thou art dust.*

VII. The materials of which bodies are formed are denoted by SER; as

El vestído *es* de páño,	*The suit is of cloth.*
Las médias *éran* de séda,	*The stockings were of silk.*
Los candeléros *son* de pláta,	*The candlesticks are of silver.*
La mésa *es* de caóba,	*The table is of mahogany.*

VIII. *To be,* forming the passive voice, or used impersonally, is generally translated SER; as

El hómbre *fué* criádo,	*Man was created.*
Los pecádos *serán* castigádos	*Sins will be punished.*
¿No *es* de maravillárse que la virtúd *séa* tan á menúdo despreciáda?	*Is it not to be wondered at that virtue should be so often despised?*

IX. Possession and destination are expressed with SER; as

La coróna *es* del Réy,	*The crown is the King's.*
El cabállo *éra* mío,	*The horse was mine.*
Este vino *es* de España,	*This wine is from Spain.*
Éstas ruédas *son* pára un cóche,	*These wheels are for a coach.*
La flor *es* pára élla,	*The flower is for her.*
La cárta *éra* pára España,	*The letter was for Spain.*
Ésta máquina *es* pára copiár cártas,	*This machine is to copy letters.*

X. Locality is denoted by ESTÁR; as

Él *estába* en la cálle,	*He was in the street.*
Yó *estaré* á la puérta,	*I shall be at the door.* [*diers.*
El desertór *estába* éntre dos soldádos,	*The deserter was between two soldiers.*
El réo *está* delánte del juéz,	*The culprit is before the judge.*
Tú *estábas* con tu amígo,	*Thou wast with thy friend.*

XI. ESTÁR is employed always to conjugate a verb in the gerund; as

Estóy escribiéndo,	*I am writing.*
Élla *estába* leyéndo,	*She was reading.*
Él *estará* predicándo,	*He will be preaching.*
Hémos *estádo* arguyéndo,	*We have been arguing.*

XII. Before adverbs or adverbial expressions denoting manner, we generally use ESTÁR; as

Está de móda,	*He is in the fashion.*
Estába de rodíllas,	*He was on his knees.*
Estóy de prisa,	*I am in haste.*
Estóy del mísmo parecér,	*I am of the same opinion.*

NOTE. The last of these sentences is often found with *ser;* but the observation already made on the different meaning of the two verbs is equally applicable in this instance, and if we examine the expression, we shall find that *ser* denotes my way of thinking in a more general, and *estár* in a more limited point of view; and that *sóy de éste parecér* means, this is the way I always thought; and *estóy de éste parecér,* this is my present opinion.

XIII. Ser requires the same case before, as after it; as
Si yó *fuéra* tú, *If I were thou.* Si tú *fuéras* élla, *If thou wert she.*

NOTE. The objective case of the neuter pronoun *éllo,* (*lo*) is frequently used with *ser* and then is generally translated *so,* as,

Vmd. dice que *es* viéjo, péro ni vm. ni yó lo *sómos,*	*You say that you are old, but neither you nor I are so.*
Vm. piénsa que élla *es* ríca, péro no lo *es,*	*You think that she is rich, but she is not so.*
Crée que *estóy* enojádo, y á la verdád lo *estóy,*	*He thinks that I am angry, and so indeed I am.*

Sometimes it may be omitted; as

Vmd. *es* rico, péro yó no, *or* yó no lo *sóy,*	*You are rich, but I am not,* or *no*

NOTE II. Although the verbs *ser* and *estár*, as has been observed, may be used sometimes with the same adjective; yet this cannot always be done, there being some adjectives which vary their meaning according as they are coupled with *ser* or *estár;* as

Ser buéno,	To be good.	Ser cansádo,	To be tiresome.
Estár buéno,	To be well.	Estár cansádo,	To be tired.
Ser málo,	To be wicked.	Ser vívo,	To be lively.
Estár málo,	To be ill.	Estár vívo,	To be alive, or living

OBSERVATION. The verb *estár* is often followed by infinitives, which are preceded by the preposition *pára* or *por*: with *pára* it denotes that the action or energy of the verb, which is in the infinitive, is about to take place; as, Estába *el brázo pára descargár el gólpe;* the arm was ready, *or*, about to, to strike the blow: with *por* it describes the action, &c. as not having taken place, or expresses an inclination on the part of the agent to execute it; as, *La cása* está *por acabár:* the house is to be finished, or is not yet finished. Estóy *por ir á vérle,* I have a mind to go and see him.

TENÉR and HABÉR, *to have.**

Both of the above imply possession; but the employment of the latter is now limited to that of an auxiliary, in order to form the compound tenses of other verbs.

RULE I. *To have,* used as an active verb, is translated TENÉR, and as an auxiliary HABÉR, as

Tenér amígos,	*To have friends.*	*Habér* dícho,	*To have said.*
Téngo pariéntes	*I have relations.*	*Habémos* habládo,	*We have spoken.*

NOTE. The verb *tenér* is sometimes found used apparently as an auxiliary.

OBSERVATION. When in English the verb *to be* precedes the adjectives *hungry, thirsty, afraid, ashamed,* it is changed into the Spanish verb *tenér,* and the adjective into a corresponding substantive: as

Are you hungry?	¿ *Tiéne* vm. gána ó hámbre ?	i. e.	*Have you hunger?*
We were thirsty,	*Teníamos* sed,	i. e.	*We had thirst.*
He was not ashamed,	*No túvo* vergüenza,	i. e.	*He had no shame.*
Art thou afraid?	¿ *Tiénes* miédo ?	i. e.	*Hast thou fear?*

The adjective *old,* when equivalent to *of age* in English, is also changed into a substantive; as, he was éighty years old when he died; tenía *ochénta áños de edád cuándo murió.* It may also be omitted in Spanish; as, Hark ye ! Gil Blas, you are seventeen years old ; *¡Holá! Gil Blas,* tiénes *diéz y siéte áños.* The adjectives *hot* and *cold* admit also the same construction, provided they are applied to a sentient being; as, we shall be hot; tendrémos *calór.* He was so cold that he could not move himself; tenía *tánto frío que no podia movérse.* But if the being be supposed insensible, we use *estár* instead of *tenér;* as, He was so cold (to the touch) that I thought he was dead; estába *tan frío que pensé que habia muérto.*

RULE II. When the auxiliaries *to have* and *to be,* followed by an infinitive, denote some future action, the former is translated *tenér que,* and the latter *haber de;* as

Teníamos que escribír, *We had to write. Habia* de venír, *He was to come.*

NOTE. The verb *habér,* when used impersonally, requires also *que* before the following infinitive; as, No *háy que* temér, there is nothing to fear.

---

* See also Josse's Grammar, pages 86 and 156.

A

TABLE OF CONTENTS.

SPANISH EXERCISES.

Upon the Rules of the Grammar and their application,
with remarks and observations.

VOCABULARY. VOCABULÁRIO.

FAMILIAR PHRASES.   FRÁSES FAMILIÁRES.

FAMILIAR DIALOGUES.   DIÁLOGOS FAMILIÁRES.

FINIS.

O

www.ingramcontent.com/pod-product-compliance
Lightning Source LLC
Chambersburg PA
CBHW022009110726
47901CB00006B/1456